185

R40. 30

AUTOCOURSE

Nigel Snowdon

Publisher: Richard Poulter
Editor: Maurice Hamilton
Executive Publisher: Liz Wagstaff
Production Editor: Hilary Foakes
Publishing Assistant: Jane Chapman
Secretary: Nicky Harrop
Art Editor: Jim Bamber
Results and Statistics: John Taylor
Lap Charts: Angela Poulter
French Editor: José Rosinski
United States Editor: Gordon Kirby
Chief Photographer: Nigel Snowdon

UK distribution by

Osprey Publishing Limited

12-14 Long Acre
London WC2E 9LP

United States distribution by

Motorbooks International
Publishers & Wholesalers Inc
Osceola, Wisconsin 54020, USA

AUTOCOURSE is published by Hazleton Publishing
3 Richmond Hill, Richmond, Surrey TW10 6RE
Printed in Holland by drukkerij de Lange/van Leer b.v., Deventer
Typesetting by C. Leggett & Son Ltd, Mitcham, Surrey, England.

The photograph on the dust jacket is by Paul Henri Cahier and depicts the 1984 World Champion, Niki Lauda, in his Marlboro McLaren MP4/2 on his way to winning the Italian Grand Prix at Monza.

Contents

Photo: Paul Henri Cahier

Photographs in *Autocourse* 1984-85 have been contributed by:
Bernard Asset/Agence Vandystadt, Jeff Bloxham, Malcolm Bryan, Peter Burn, Diana Burnett, Paul Henri Cahier, Mark Clifford, John Colley, Maurice Hamilton, Robert Harmeyer, Michael Hewitt, Jeff Hutchinson/International Press Agency, David Hutson, Jaguar Cars Ltd, Michael Keppel, Charles Knight/Zooom, Mike Levasheff, Duncan Raban, Jad Sherif/International Press Agency, Nigel Snowdon, Keith Sutton, Steve Swope, John Townsend

ACKNOWLEDGEMENTS

The Editor of *Autocourse* wishes to thank the following for their assistance in compiling the 1984-85 edition:
Canada: Canadian Automobile Sports Club. France: Automobiles Ligier, Renault Sport, Jean Sage. Germany: BMW GmbH, Dieter Stappert. Great Britain: Arrows Racing Team, ATS Engineering, John Barnard, Cosworth Engineering, Bernard Ecclestone, Barry Griffin, Brian Hart, Patrick Head, Tony Jardine, Alan Jenkins, Edgar Jessop, Brian Lisles, McLaren International, Motor Racing Developments, RAM Automotive, Spirit Racing, Team Lotus, Toleman Motorsport, Tyrrell Racing Organisation, Dave Wass, Williams Grand Prix Engineering. Italy: Pierluigi Corbari, Euroracing, Ferrari Spa SEFAC, Giorgio Piola, Brenda Vernor. Switzerland: Kaspar Arnet, Olivetti/Longines. United States of America: Championship Auto Racing Teams, Daytona International Speedway, International Motor Sports Association, NASCAR News Bureau, Sports Car Club of America, United States Auto Club.

Lucas

1

MINUTE

FROM THE START
OF ANOTHER SUCCESS

Over the years Lucas equipped cars have been driven to more championship victories, simply because they have performed with total reliability throughout the season.

This illustrious record has been achieved by our technical support, monitoring and constant development of Lucas competition equipment which has attained a level of reliability unsurpassed in motor sport today. To pass this support on to the competitive motorist there is a nationwide network of dealers known as the "Lucas Special Section". To find your nearest dealer phone: 021-236 5050, Lucas Electrical Limited, Rallysport, Great Hampton Street, Birmingham B18 6AU.

Lucas Electrical

"For those destined to go further"

TEAM BARCLAY ARROWS

Marc Surer

Thierry Boutsen

BMW Turbo-Powered.
Valvoline Protected.

Fast cars, great drivers and a superior motor oil — In his challenge for the 1984 World Championship, Team Barclay Arrows manager, Jackie Oliver, chose drivers Marc Surer and Thierry Boutsen for his new turbocharged BMW-powered cars. To protect his expensive, high-horsepower engines, Oliver chose Valvoline® Racing Motor Oil. The engine oil he knew would survive the severe heat build-up of Grand Prix competition, — on or off the track. Change to Valvoline for proven protection.

Valvoline Motor Oil
SYMBOL OF QUALITY SINCE 1866.

Foreword

by Niki Lauda

Since I last wrote the foreword to AUTOCOURSE, when I won my second championship in 1977, there have been a couple of years during which I never thought I would drive a racing car again. Indeed, I had taken a conscious decision to leave the sport and, at the time, that decision was irrevocable.

It therefore seems slightly strange to be writing the introduction again in 1984, although my third championship has given me enormous satisfaction and sense of achievement. That's not surprising, perhaps, when you consider the brilliant quality of opposition I have been facing from my own team-mate Alain Prost at Marlboro McLaren International! I would like to thank all the people within the team who have worked so hard on my behalf to make 1984 such a memorable season.

When I returned to Formula 1, it was good to see that AUTOCOURSE had not lowered the excellent standards set in the past. I am sure this year's book will continue to provide the usual detailed and accurate memoir of what, for me, has been an incredible year.

What do Denis Law and Alain Prost have in common? Both men enjoy a game of football, that's true. But there's more. Both have suffered excruciating disappointment while, at the same time, achieving the almost impossible.

In January 1961, Denis Law played for Manchester City in an F.A. Cup tie against Luton. He scored six goals. This remarkable double hat trick ensured an easy passage for Manchester into the next round; Luton managing a measly goal or two in reply to such brilliance. Then, with 10 minutes remaining, the match was abandoned because of bad weather.

There was a replay. Law scored again. But City lost 3-1. Seven goals – and nothing to show for it.

If the former Scottish International was watching the Portuguese Grand Prix on television last October, he must surely have known how Alain Prost felt. Seven wins – and nothing to show. Niki Lauda, the man standing on the lower level of the rostrum, was World Champion.

It seems absurd that Prost should become the first driver to equal Jim Clark's record and yet not carry off the title in the same way the Lotus driver dominated the 1963 season. Nevertheless, the fact that he did not says a lot about the dramatic season which unfolds throughout the pages of this book.

We have become accustomed to eleventh-hour finishes during recent years yet this was a different story entirely since the contenders came from within the same team. It was a fair fight in every respect; same car; same engine; same tyre choice; same rigorously impartial treatment from a first class team; same division of luck, good and bad. The result was a splendid battle, settled by half a point.

It may have been tedious to watch Marlboro McLaren International win 12 races but the in-house competition and the drivers' reaction to it was fascinating. Prost was the quicker of the two but Lauda got there in the end and his achievement is made richer by defeating such a worthy opponent.

In world-wide terms, it has been good for the sport. Niki Lauda is News. His third title has added another chapter to an already remarkable story in which the public outside motor racing are well-versed. We salute 'The Rat' for such outstanding personal achievement and congratulate McLaren, Porsche and Michelin for such exceptional consistency.

Niki's championship goes hand in hand with Alain's dominant performances and it seemed appropriate, therefore, to ask Nigel Roebuck to examine such a unique partnership on the pages normally devoted to a profile of the new World Champion.

While two distinguished campaigners were slogging it out at the front, a further highlight of the year has been the progress of a superb influx of new talent – Alliot, Bellof, Brundle, Hesnault, Palmer and Senna. All six started the season with high hopes and their fortunes have been related to the quality of their equipment. None the less, each driver acquitted himself in a professional manner and such an explosive store of talent promises an exciting future for Formula 1.

The destiny of Grand Prix racing in recent years has been shaped, almost single-handed, by one man: Bernard Ecclestone. We have been critical of some of Bernie's decisions in the past and it seemed right and proper that he should have the opportunity to air his views. In a forthright and exceptionally revealing interview, Bernie shows the same uncluttered thinking which has helped guide Formula 1 to the forefront of the international sporting arena. You may not agree with everything he says – but he does grab your attention! We are grateful to Bernie for setting aside much of his valuable time to answer Alan Henry's questions.

When we asked Brian Hart whether he would be interested in writing about engine development in what has been an important year in that department, we weren't sure what the response might be. He accepted with alacrity and his pursuit of perfection in putting together his shrewd observations made it clear just why Hart engines have become such incredibly strong little fishes in a pond dominated by industrial leviathans.

Jumping in at the deep end of Grand Prix journalism, Russell Bulgin, complete with pink sunglasses and matching socks, became a colourful addition to the pit lane as he went about his business for *Motor*. His seasonal review (page 22) is complimented nicely by Doug Nye's usual meticulous attention to detail as he unearths some remarkably frank statements and hitherto unknown facts while delving into the nuts and bolts of 1984.

The surveys, written with the corrective powers of hindsight, give further depth to Grand Prix reports, compiled two weeks after the event by either myself or Alan Henry and illustrated by what we consider to be the best work from a frequently stunning selection contributed by the world's leading motor sport photographers.

Autocourse would not be complete without the comprehensive reviews of American Racing (Gordon Kirby), Formula 2 (Ian Phillips), Endurance Racing (Quentin Spurring), Formula 3 (David Tremayne), and, for the second year, the European Touring Car Championship (Andrew Whyte). These specialist surveys are backed by John Taylor's immaculate results section, made possible with the help of the leading automobile clubs of the world.

Points and their effect on the World Championship are, at the time of writing, a major topic of discussion. In our opinion, the championship scoring structure should stay exactly as it is. We can see very little wrong with a system which, for the fourth year in succession, provided a championship which ran until the last lap of the last race and, in doing so, caught the imagination of the World at large.

Lauda and Prost knew the the rules and played by them accordingly. It was unfortunate that one of them had to lose. No doubt Denis Law would appreciate just why Alain Prost isn't exactly 'over la lune' after such a magnificent achievement. More a case of feeling 'malade comme un parrot'.

C'est la vie.

Maurice Hamilton
Ewhurst
Surrey
October 1984

Seven nothing

Alain Prosts of the future? The class of '84 on parade at Detroit.

John Townsend

Diana Burnett

Bernard Asset/Agence Vandystadt

Michelin ended their highly successful involvement with Grand Prix racing on a high note, the French tyre manufacturer winning the vast majority of Grands Prix in 1984 and scoring their fourth World Championship since introducing radial technology to Formula 1 in 1977.

Mark Clifford

The Editor's evaluation of the leading Grand Prix drivers in 1984

TOP TEN

Alain Prost

10

1 **Alain Prost**
2 **Nelson Piquet**
3 **Niki Lauda**
4 **Keke Rosberg**
5 **Elio de Angelis**
6 **Michele Alboreto**
7 **Derek Warwick**
8 **Ayrton Senna**
9 **Nigel Mansell**
10 **Patrick Tambay**

1 Alain Prost

The move to McLaren allowed Prost to show just how much natural talent had been squandered during previous seasons. His constant search for perfection was such that each race in 1984 seemed to highlight various facets of his ability: Kyalami and Hockenheim; the last-minute switch to the T-car said as much for McLaren's excellent preparation as it did for Prost's belief in himself and his team. Imola; the perfectly timed decision to stop for tyres after his spin. Monaco; a truly stunning pole position lap and a flawless performance in the wet. Dijon; unbelievable commitment after almost losing his left-front wheel at the most daunting of right-handers. And so it goes on, an impressive list punctuated by occasional mistakes – Dallas and the Österreichring. Then there was the spin during the warm-up at the Nürburgring. That was an error which might have phased a lesser driver in such a high-pressure situation. But Prost just carried on winning. A superb year.

2 Nelson Piquet

Arguably faster than Prost. Piquet's nine pole positions were earned with a blend of natural skill and unwaning enthusiasm backed up by prodigious amounts of BMW qualifying power. Appalling reliability prevented Piquet and Brabham from being the only serious standard for McLaren but, outwardly at least, Nelson did not allow the run of retirements to get him down. The maturity which developed in 1983 blossomed and his drive at Detroit, switching to the T-car in the aftermath of the hysteria surrounding the start-line shunt, was simply brilliant, even surpassing his perseverance at Montreal. A disinterested performance at Monaco and dismal starts were the weak points; the kerb-hopping moment at Monza, the spin at Estoril and the acceptance of another McLaren victory at the Österreichring when, in fact, he could have won; these were curious anomalies for a driver of such all-round ability.

3 Niki Lauda

Does not have the outright speed of either Piquet or Prost but still the shrewdest man around when it comes to racecraft. Rarely qualified well but his climb through the field at Dijon and Imola proved that the sharpness, hunger and aggression were still there. There is no doubt that the presence of Prost at the head of the field acted as the catalyst for vintage Lauda performances. Occasional misjudgements – Monaco, Dallas, the Nürburgring – interrupted a classic, fluent style but his determination could not be questioned. Monza exemplified just how much Lauda wanted to become World Champion again, his back trouble being a mere technicality which would have to be overcome.

Now that he has helped sort the McLaren-TAG turbo; now that he is Champion again, what next? Will assisting Prost to win the title provide enough motivation for one of the greatest drivers we have seen?

Nigel Snowdon

Keith Sutton

Members of the Marlboro World Championship team produced superb performances in 1984: Michele Alboreto winning in Belgium; Alain Prost and Niki Lauda helping Marlboro McLaren establish new records for the season; Keke Rosberg and René Arnoux, first and second in difficult conditions at Dallas.

4 Keke Rosberg

A year with the Williams-FW09 has shown just how good, how incurably resilient, Keke Rosberg is. To say that the car was not the best would understate the case just as it would be an oversimplification to say that Rosberg tried hard. He was simply superb. Take almost any race and you will find an example of his determination to carry the Williams-Honda single-handed. Zolder; the charge through the field. Montreal; the same. Detroit; likewise. And Hockenheim. But, as for his practice lap at Estoril . . . If that was the single most exciting lap of the year then his victory at Dallas, where car control and a clear head offset handling deficiencies was unquestionably the drive of the season.

5 Elio de Angelis

On paper, Elio de Angelis has had a good season. But, there is the feeling that he still could make more of his outstanding natural ability, a flair which is particularly evident during wet practice sessions. His third place in the Championship and the succession of finishes in the points were achieved by a new-found application to the job in hand rather than a burst of outright speed although, under the difficult circumstances of racing a Renault-powered car on Goodyears, this approach may have been the correct one. At Monaco, for example, he was completely overshadowed by Mansell. He took a long time to pass Ghinzani but, once ahead, he was lapping quickly. And he was there at the finish.

6 Michele Alboreto

A difficult year and, under the circumstances, a difficult man to judge. Michele Alboreto lacks total commitment when the car is as bad as the 126C4 has been and his team are in such apparent disarray. Alboreto is one of the smoothest and most stylish drivers around but he appears to be at his best only when the equipment is his equal – such as at Zolder. At Detroit, he was excellent but, two weeks later at Dallas, the appalling handling of the Ferrari appeared to blunt his enthusiasm. Then, at Brands Hatch, he drove superbly and during the latter part of the season, his canny, clean performances matched improvements by Goodyear and Ferrari.

His every move, of course, was under constant scrutiny and the fact that he did not succumb to the unenviable pressure exerted on an Italian at Maranello indicates that he is well-equipped to handle the success which will surely come his way – provided the package is right.

PUT YOURSELF IN POLE POSITION WITH THE Marlboro AUTOCOURSE DIARY AND CALENDAR

Marlboro WORLD CHAMPIONSHIP TEAM

Throughout 1985 (the 34th year of Autocourse) stay well ahead with all the latest information on Formula 1 Grand Prix Motor Racing with our famous pocket diary and wall calendar. Now with 96 pages (16 in fantastic colour) the Marlboro Autocourse Diary is bigger and better than ever – with a whole page for each week, but stays at the same price. It includes comprehensive profiles of the 24 leading Formula 1 drivers, a record of previous world champions since 1950, plus sections for recording race-by-race results and keeping an up-to-date list of the Drivers' World Championship positions.

Other features that keep this diary out in front are the detailed diagrams of all the major Grand Prix circuits, together with addresses and phone numbers of the Formula 1 teams – in fact, all the information the motor racing enthusiast needs at his fingertips. And to complement the diary, a superb, 13-leaf, large-format wall calendar featuring 14 sensational full-colour racing shots.

The Pocket Diary measures 172 x 81mm and costs £4.00. The Calendar measures 590 x 420mm and costs £6.50. Order your Calendar or Diary from the address given below – but order both together and take advantage of the special combined offer price of £9.50 – a saving of £1. (All prices include VAT, postage and packing.)

Send your order today, making cheque or postal order payable to HAZLETON PUBLISHING. Note that cheques on orders from outside the U.K. must be drawn on a London bank in £ Sterling, no Eurocheques. Calendars/Diaries will be despatched separately. Order now – they go fast!

Marlboro Autocourse Diary Offer

Hazleton Publishing
3 Richmond Hill, Richmond, Surrey TW10 6RE

7 Derek Warwick

It may seem a strange thing to say, but Derek Warwick has had a disappointing season. Yes, he did lead at Rio and he did reach the rostrum four times but those performances merely set standards which he found difficulty in emulating elsewhere. Part of the trouble was Renault's inability to supply equipment which was both durable and race-competitive. Detroit, perhaps, was his best drive of the season but that was soured by his fourth retirement in succession. As a racer, Derek Warwick has it all; fast, uncompromising, straightforward and honest – particularly with himself. It is because of these very qualities and such enormous potential that 1984 was not the resounding success it could have been. And as for lap 11 at Dallas . . .

8 Ayrton Senna

An unbelievable year. Ayrton Senna's ability to step from Formula 3 into turbocharged Formula 1 and drive with such authority and speed merely confirms his opinion that he will be World Champion one day. The surprise, if anything, is that he didn't actually win a Grand Prix! His overwhelming self-belief is backed up by that natural flair and delicacy of touch which are the hallmarks of brilliance.

However, there is a long way to go. He needs to learn that success may not come as quickly as he believes it should. The accident during practice at Detroit, where he dumped the Toleman into the wall in full view of the pits, came just in time to deflate an ego pumped up by the accolades showered on such a deft performance at Monaco. In fact, he was lucky to get away with a mistake at Monte Carlo but, in the event, he survived and went on to make the most of an excellent car and engine which did much for his flourishing reputation later in the year.

9 Nigel Mansell

Failing to win at Monaco, when he had the race in his pocket, had, perhaps, a more far-reaching effect than even Nigel Mansell cares to admit. His self-esteem and determination are unshakeable and such a public error of judgement merely added to the need to prove just how capable he is. It's a fair bet that, had he won at Monaco, he would have been more confident, more circumspect, at Detroit and Dallas. The need to win became tinged with a desperation which led to almost irrational actions during and after the races. However, he was not helped by a string of retirements (a mixture of driver error and mechanical problems) and the rather authoritarian way of doing things at Lotus. To run such a doughty race at Dijon in the face of personal grief; to pace himself beautifully at Hockenheim and Zandvoort; to take pole at Dallas; these superb achievements proved that the raw talent is there. It is up to Williams to hone those skills and put Mansell at ease in what will be a critical year for the Englishman.

10 Patrick Tambay

A superb start to the season and an excellent finish. Inbetween? There was the brilliance of Dijon – and precious little else. It was as though the fuel consumption problems at Rio and Kyalami sapped a motivation which disappeared altogether at Zolder where his performance was pathetic. At least he was honest enough to admit it – a rare commodity in a racing driver. He was back on form at Imola but the first lap collision at Monaco destroyed any flow of continuity, in spite of a brave performance at Detroit. Mechanical problems at Hockenheim aside, it was not until the Öster-reichring that we had the first indication of the return of pace and style which characterised his 1983 season. Monza was classic Tambay, the reason for his retirement, a classic example of how Renault failed to get the best out of a gifted but rather complex driver.

Of the rest (as they appeared on the entry list), Teo Fabi paid the price for attempting to mix CART with Formula 1. It was not until he abandoned his trans-Atlantic commitment that the Italian began to show the form he is capable of. Practice invariably suffered in comparison with Piquet and his 'spare' car but, Fabi's race performances, particularly at Kyalami and Monza, indicated what is possible – provided he is hungry enough. Corrado Fabi is potentially the faster of the two but his natural talent seemed to be overwhelmed by the Brabham team as the younger brother tackled just three races. By Dallas, he appeared to be getting to grips with the BMW power but a great talent may have been lost.

Tyrrell gambled by signing Martin Brundle and Stefan Bellof but their mature performances proved Ken had made a shrewd move. Brundle, serious, methodical and very neat, showed immense potential epitomised by a clean, crisp drive at Detroit in the wake of his horrendous shunt at Monaco. Brundle's accident at Dallas should have been 'one of those things' but, sadly, the consequences heavily outweighed the margin of error.

Bellof came to Formula 1 with a reputation for driving out of his skin. He *has* been fast but, with help from Tyrrell, he managed to keep his boyish enthusiasm under control. The ability to feel at home while flinging the Tyrrell around Monaco highlighted the supreme confidence of a driver who, with Brundle, will be a star of the future.

At the beginning of the season it seemed absurd that Stefan Johansson should be without a drive. The chance to stand in for Brundle was seized with the Swede's usual enthusiasm. With no power to help him on to the grid, he simply put the hammer down and continued in the same vein for each and every lap of the race. He was the obvious man for Toleman when a drive became available and his run from the back of the grid at Monza points towards a great future with an equally promising team.

At Kyalami, where he was heading for a well-deserved third place, Jacques Laffite seemed set for a competitive year before winding down to retirement. It was not to be (neither was that third place) and the desperate lack of competitiveness meant a decline of enthusiasm. At Zolder and Monaco, he was not interested although his vast experience was evident at Dallas where a finish, even after starting from the back of the grid, would earn points. He gathered momentum in the second half of the season, particularly at Hockenheim, but it was clear that after more than 145 Grands Prix, Jacques Laffite did not *need* to try that hard for a mid-field position.

Phillipe Alliot and Jonathan Palmer, on the other hand, required every ounce of determination in what was a most difficult season for the novices. With no budget for either testing or a spare car in the second half of the season, the RAM team had their backs to the wall while Palmer and Alliot tried to carve some sort of reputation. Both men never stopped trying with a cumbersome car and both came out of the season well, Palmer slightly ahead. Apart from not putting a mark on the 02 (his two shunts were due to mechanical or tyre failures) Palmer outqualified his team-mate and survived a character-building season for a driver who had been accustomed to running at the opposite end of the field. Alliot shunted on more than one occasion and his nil reaction to the Patrese incident at Brands Hatch caused concern as well as giving the hard-working little team even more work.

Excellent qualifying and a run in the top six at Zolder gave some inkling of Manfred Winkelhock's form in a potentially excellent car. Otherwise, his talent and incredible bravery were frittered away by the usual problems spawned by Gunter Schmid's autocratic behaviour and a host of niggling reliability problems. Gerhard Berger not only looks like a lean and quick racer but he also drives like one although his rather wild weekend at the Nürburgring, hopefully, is not typical of the

Austrian.

Marc Surer and Thierry Boutsen had a disjointed season due to the late arrival of the Arrows A7. And, when it appeared, it was something of a disappointment since there was little time for testing during the height of the season. Surer raced better than he practised (Austria and Monza) but, overall, he had to take second best to the Belgian. Worthy of consideration for the Top Ten, Boutsen continued to pace himself beautifully with a fast, consistent style. His drive at Hockenheim (passing several cars in the opening laps) and a run into fifth place (before retiring) at Detroit being two of his best performances.

Johnny Cecotto lived under the shadow of Senna and allowed himself to suffer – which was a pity since he could be competitive in the races even if he continued to treat practice as if it were for a motorcycle grid. Mauro Baldi did a good job for the under-financed Spirit team and Huub Rothengatter proved to be an excellent replacement midseason despite his long absence from single-seater racing.

The switch from Brabham to Alfa Romeo marked the end of what looks like being the only peak in Riccardo Patrese's Formula 1 career. His driving has been inconsistent and there can be no better example of that than his elementary mistake at Brands Hatch. Eddie Cheever, meanwhile, retained his infectious enthusiasm for driving racing cars despite the fact that many fine race performances were wiped out by the Alfa V8's appetite for fuel. On the other hand, it seemed that Eddie drove the only way he knows and had little consideration for the need to make his race an economy run. Whether he was right or wrong depends on your point of view . . .

The Alfa consumption problem applied to Osella, which was unfortunate since they had their best-ever chassis and an underrated driver in Piercarlo Ghinzani. He made an exceptionally brave comeback after Kyalami and his race performance at Monaco was matched by his practice lap at Dallas: in both cases, under circumstances where the driver's contribution counted for more than usual. Jo Gartner had a difficult start in Formula 1 with the V12 Osella. Once into the turbo-powered car, he gave the impression of driving beyond his capabilities although, in fairness, he didn't lose control as often as his rather ragged style suggested he might.

With no more than two seasons of French Formula 3 racing on his international record, François Hesnault appeared to have more money than talent when he joined Ligier as Number 2. He is, however, worthy of consideration with Brundle and Bellof. Accepting that the Ligier Number 2 is exactly that, Hesnault has never been far off de Cesaris's pace and, indeed, he destroyed the Italian in the wet at Dijon. Yet there were times when he looked ill at ease; Detroit and Dallas for example, although whether an all-round skill will come with time and a better chassis remains to be seen.

Whatever happened to the Andrea de Cesaris we saw in 1983? The speed remained but the composure vanished to make way for the irrational mistakes and bad-mannered driving which characterised his early days. It was as though he was attempting to make up for the deficiency between the Alfa Romeo 183T and the Ligier JS23 all on his own. Given the lack of direction within the French team, he probably was.

Zolder summed up René Arnoux. Disheartened after making a pit stop, he lost interest. Then it became apparent that points were at stake after all – and he flew. And then spun. His first half of the year was more consistent and culminated in a brilliant charge at Dallas under the most difficult circumstances of the season. In the second half, he was blown off by Alboreto and, at Zandvoort, he made a typically selfish move which could have killed Thierry Boutsen. The natural talent is there but the car must be right – and the 126C4 was usually far from that.

Does your for NC

Formula 1 by Ferrari. Performance by Goodyear.

Astra GL by Vauxhall. NCT tyres by Goodyear.

Goodyear and only Goodyear make the NCT.

Neutral Contour Technology was formulated by Goodyear mathematician Charles Purdey.

Put simply it plants more rubber more firmly on the road.

The tread and profile of the NCT were developed directly from our Formula 1 rain-racing tyre.

No surprise then that Porsche and Lotus specify NCT for their road-burning supercars.

But now we've extended the list of qualifiers for NCT performance.

Is your car among them?

car qualify T tyres?

911 3.3. Turbo by Porsche. NCT Performance tyres by Goodyear.

Freefone NCT.

Find out by asking the operator for freefone NCT.

Over the phone we can tell you which tyre fits which car. And, whether you need a change of wheels too.

Alternatively, contact any of our High Performance Centres listed overleaf.

It won't cost you a penny to find out.

Find out if your car qualifies for NCT tyres.

GOODYEAR

NCT

Performance Tyre Centre

A

ABERDEEN.
Kenway Tyres, Broadfold Road, Bridge of Don.
Tyreservices Great Britain, Willow Bank Road.
ADDINGTON, Surrey.
PTA Tyre & Exhaust Centre, Selsdon Park Road.
ALTRINCHAM, Cheshire.
Q.H. Standard Motorists Centres, 282 Manchester Rd.
ASHTEAD, Surrey.
U.C.S. Barwell, Craddocks Parade.
AYLESBURY, Bucks.
Stapletons Tyre Service Ltd., Park Road.
AYR.
Smiley, Peebles Street.
McConechy Tyre Service, 37/45 Peebles Street.

B

BANBURY, Oxon.
Tyreservices Great Britain, Gatteridge Street.
BARROW-IN-FURNESS, Cumbria.
Tyreservices Great Britain, 20 Roose Road.
BASILDON, Essex.
Tyreservices Great Britain, Sava Centre, Eastgate.
BECKENHAM, Kent.
Q.H. Standard Motorists Centres, 81-83 High Street.
BENTHAM, N. Yorks.
Tatham Tyres, Mill Lane Garage, Mill Lane.
BERWICK-ON-TWEED, Northumbria.
Tyreservices Great Britain, Tweedside Trading Est.
BEXLEYHEATH, Kent.
Tyreservices Great Britain, 296 The Broadway.
BIRKENHEAD, Cheshire.
Frank Bather & Son Ltd., Chester New Road.
BIRMINGHAM.
D. & W. Tyre Service Ltd., 427-429 Bordesley Green.
Tyre Sales (Birmingham) Ltd., High Street, Digbeth, 5.
Tyreservices Great Britain, Kingsbury Road, Erdington.
BOGNOR REGIS.
Milestones Tyre & Battery Service, 96-98 Felpham Rd.
BOLTON, Lancs.
Lythgoe Motors, Sharples Service Station, Sharple.
BOOKHAM, Surrey.
U.C.S. (Kingston) Ltd., New Parade, Leatherhead Road.
BOSTON, Lincs.
B.A. Bush & Son Ltd., Norfolk Street.
BOURNEMOUTH, Dorset.
Tyreservices Great Britain, 905 Ringwood Road, West Howe.
BRADFORD, Yorks.
Troy Tyre & Auto Centre Ltd., Thornbury Garage, Leeds Road.
Tyreservices Great Britain, Ingleby Road.
BRAINTREE, Essex.
Dangate Motors Ltd., 38 Broomhills Industrial Estate.
BRIDGEND, Glam.
Celtic Tyre Services, Princess Way, Industrial Estate.
BRIDGEWATER, Somerset.
Tyreservices Great Britain, 130-140 Bristol Road.
BRISTOL.
Manor Tyres, Duckmoor Road.
Manor Tyres, Speedwell Road.
Mike Knight Tyres, 234 Southmead Road.
Q.H. Standard Motorists Centres, Bath Rd, Brislington.
Tyreservices Great Britain, 52 Whiteladies Rd, Clifton.
BROMLEY, Kent.
Tyreservices Great Britain, 16 London Road.
BROMSGROVE, Worcs.
Droitwich Tyre & Exhaust, 18 Sugarbrook Road, Astonfield Industrial Estate.
BUCKLEY, Clwyd.
Buckley Tyres, Lane End.
BURTON-ON-TRENT, Staffs.
Kenning Tyre Services, Park Street.
BURY-ST-EDMUNDS.
Cecil and Larter, 8 Out Risbeygate.
Q.H. Standard Motorists Centres, Tayfen Road.
Suffolk Tyres, Woolpit Road, Norton.
Tyreservices Great Britain, Out Northgate, Old Maltings.

C

CAERPHILLY.
Watts Tyre & Rubber Co. Ltd., Western Industrial Estate, Lon-y-Llyn.
CAMBERLEY, Surrey.
Q.H. Standard Motorists Centres, London Road, Blackwater.
CAMBRIDGE.
Tyre Service Company, Histon Road.
Tyreservices Great Britain, 56 Newmarket Road.
CANTERBURY, Kent.
Tyreservices Great Britain, 80 Wincheap Industrial Estate.
CARDIFF, Glam.
Celtic Tyre Services, Brindley Road, off Penarth Road.
Tyreservices Great Britain, 51 Penarth Road.
CARLISLE, Cumbria.
Tyreservices Great Britain, Durranhill Industrial Est.
CHELMSFORD, Essex.
Tyreservices Great Britain, Unit 4, Grafton Place, Dukes Park Industrial Estate.
CHELTENHAM, Glos.
Tyreservices Great Britain, 249 Gloucester Road, Lansdown Industrial Estate.
CHESHAM, Bucks.
Q.H. Standard Motorists Centres, Amersham Road.
CHESSINGTON, Surrey.
U.C.S. Ltd., 314 Hook Road.
CHESTER.
Q.H. Standard Motorists Centres, Sealand Road.
CHESTERFIELD, Derbys.
Q.H. Standard Motorists Centres, Sheffield Road.
CHICHESTER, Sussex.
Cedo Company Ltd., 104/106 The Hornet.
CIRENCESTER, Glos.
Ebley Tyre Services, Love Lane Industrial Estate.
COLCHESTER, Essex.
Kenning Tyre Services, Whitehall Industrial Estate.
Williams Tyres Ltd., 193 Magdalen Street.
CONSETT, Co. Durham.
Tyreservices Great Britain, Sherburn Terrace.
CROYDON, Surrey.
Q.H. Standard Motorists Centres, 145-149 London Rd.

D

DARLINGTON, Co. Durham.
Tyreservices Great Britain, 27 Coniscliffe Road.
DERBY.
Tyreways, 1042 London Road, Alveston.
DEWSBURY, West Yorks.
Tyreservices Great Britain, 499 Huddersfield Road.
DONCASTER, Yorks.
Tyreservices Great Britain, Derby Road.
DUDLEY, West Midlands.
Tyreservices Great Britain, New Mill Street.
DUMFRIES, Dumfriesshire.
Tyreservices Great Britain, 46 Academy Street.
DUNDEE.
Tyres & Accessories, 27 Arbroath Road.
DUNFERMLINE.
Central Tyres, 3 Halbeath Road.
Smiley, St. Leonards Place.
Tyres & Accessories, 43 Hospital Hill.

E

EASTBOURNE.
Sir Speedy Silencers Ltd., Lottbridge Drove.
Tyreservices Great Britain, Lottbridge Drove.
EAST DEREHAM.
Holburn Tyres, Station Yard, Norwich Road.
EAST KILBRIDE
Derntop Ltd., Strathcoma Place.
Smiley, West Mains Road.
EDGWARE, Middx.
Q.H. Standard Motorists Centres, Imperial Works, High Street.
EDINBURGH.
JB Wheels, 128 Dalry Road.
Lowland Tyres, Dundee Street.
Smiley, Milton Road West.
Smiley, Stevenson Road.
ELGIN.
Northern Oils, Kindsmill Yard.
EVESHAM, Worcs.
Evesham Auto Brake Co. Ltd., Unit 1, Briar Close.

F

FALKIRK.
McConechy Tyre Services Ltd., Daldere Avenue.
Smiley, Union Road, Camelon.
FELSTEAD, Essex.
Red Star, The White House, Dunmow Road.
FLEET, Hants.
North Hants Tyre & Remoulding Co. Ltd., Fleet Road.

G

GATESHEAD, Tyne & Wear.
Tyreservices Great Britain, Hawks Road.
GLASGOW.
Central Tyres, Hunter Street.
McConechy Tyre Services Ltd., 569 Ballater Street.
Smiley, Alexandra Parade.
Smiley, Battle Place, Langside.
Smiley, Campsie Road, Kirkintilloch.
Smiley, Edinburgh Road.
Smiley, Rosevale Street, Partick.
Smiley, St. Georges Road.
Strathmore Silencers, Kilbirnie Street.
Tyres & Accessories, 94 Ballieston Road.
Tyres & Accessories, Cambuslang Road, Cambuslang, Nr. Glasgow.
GLOUCESTER.
Ebley Tyre Service Ltd., Eastern Ave.
Q.H. Standard Motorists Centres, 114 Eastgate Street.
Tyreservices Great Britain, 80 Bristol Road.
Tyreservices Great Britain, 1 Woodrow Way, Bristol Road.
Watts Tyre & Rubber Co. Ltd., Mercia Road.
GRANTHAM, Lincs.
Tanvic Tyres, Wharf Road.
GREAT YARMOUTH.
Holburn Tyres, Bridewell Lane, Acle.
GREENOCK.
Smiley, Dalrymple Street.
GRIMSBY, Lincs.
Kenning Tyre Services, Albion Street.
GWESPYR, Clwyd.
Lobitos Tyre Depot, Gwespyr, Nr. Holywell.

H

HALIFAX, West Yorks.
Tyreservices Great Britain, 70 Horton Street.
HAMILTON.
Smiley, Blackswell Lane.
HANWORTH, Middx.
Moraston Limited, 24 Cross Road.
HARROGATE, Yorks.
Moss Tyres, 6 Strawberry Dale.
HEMEL HEMPSTEAD.
Tyreservices Great Britain, 909 Paradise Estate.
HEXHAM, Northumberland.
Tyreservices Great Britain, Tyne Mills Estate.
HIGH WYCOMBE, Bucks.
Q.H. Standard Motorists Centres, 511 London Road.
HINCKLEY, Leics.
Tyreservices Great Britain, 8/22 New Street.
HITCHIN, Herts.
Stapletons Ltd., Paynes Park.
HORSFORTH, Nr. Leeds.
Charlie Browns Supermarkets Ltd., Ring Road, Low Lane.
HORSHAM, Sussex.
Elite Garages S & M Tyres, Brighton Road, Mannings Heath.
HOUNSLOW, Middx.
General Tyres, Staines Road.
HUDDERSFIELD.
Kenning Tyre Service, New North Road.
HULL, Yorks.
Savoy Tyres, Willerby Road.
HYDE.
Steward Wilson Tyres Ltd., Market Street.

I

INVERNESS.
Macrae & Dick Ltd., Strothers Lane.
IPSWICH.
K.T.S. Fore Hamlet.
Mann Egerton, Woodbridge Road.
Q.H. Standard Motorists Centres, 445-449 Norwich Road.
Tyreservices Great Britain, 580 Woodbridge Road.

K

KEMPSTON, Beds.
Tyreservices Great Britain, Duncombe St.
KENDAL, Cumbria.
Tyreservices Great Britain, Mintsfeet Trading Est.
KETTERING, Northants.
Tyreservices Great Britain, Unit 1, Telford Way.
KIDDERMINSTER, Worcs.
Tyreservices Great Britain, Worcester Road.
KILMARNOCK.
Smiley, Grange Street.
KINGS LYNN.
Q.H. Standard Motorists Centres, 20-28 Blackfriars St.
KINGSTON-ON-THAMES.
Tyreservices Great Britain, 198 Cambridge Road.
KIRKCALDY.
Smiley, Rosslyn Street.
Tyres & Accessories, 3 Kinghorn Road.
Tyreservices Great Britain, The Esplanade.

L

LANCASTER.
Tyreservices Great Britain, Queen Street.
LEEDS, Yorks.
Central Tyres, Sheepscar Street South.
Charlie Browns Supermarkets Ltd., Crossgates.
Charlie Browns Supermarkets Ltd., Kirkstall Road.
Kenning Tyre Services, Otley Road.
Q.H. Standard Motorists Centres, 205 Dewsbury Road.
Tyreservices Great Britain, Whitehall Road.
LEICESTER.
E.T.C., Blackbird Avenue.
Walkers Tyre Service, Melton Road.
Walkers Tyre Service, Narborough Road.
Tyreservices Great Britain, Catherine Street.
LETCHWORTH.
Tyre Battery and Exhaust Centre, Works Road.
LINCOLN.
Tanvic Tyre Ltd., 61 Carholme Road.
Kenning Tyre Services, Monks Way, Monks Road.
Tyreservices Great Britain, 292/294 Wragby Road.
LIVERPOOL.
Smart Tyres, Anfield Road.
LIVINGSTON, West Lothian.
Tyres & Accessories, Carmondean Centre.
LLANELLI, Dyfed
Tyreservices Great Britain, Sandy Bridge, Pembrey Road.

LONDON AREA

Brew Brothers Ltd., 133 Old Brompton Road, SW7.
Charlton Tyre & Battery Co. Ltd., 31 Penhall Road, Charlton, SE7.
Grays Tyre Services Ltd., 400 Westhorne Ave., Eltham SE9.
Red Star Tyres, Unit B, Eastway Ind. Est., The Eastway, E9.
Southfields Tyre & Battery, 406 Merton Road, SW18.
Q.H. Standard Motorists Centres, Eastmans Trading Estate, The Vale, Acton.
Q.H. Standard Motorists Centres, 912-920 High Road, North Finchley.
Q.H. Standard Motorists Centres, North Circular Road, Walthamstow, E17.
Tynedale Trading Company, 39 East Dulwich Rd., SE22.
Tyreservices Great Britain, 238/240 Bethnal Green Road.
Tyreservices Great Britain, 76/80 Chatham Road, Battersea.
Tyreservices Great Britain, 1/3 Flower Lane, Mill Hill.
Tyreservices Great Britain, 311 Upper Richmond Road, East Sheen SW14.
Tyreservices Great Britain, 151 High Street, Enfield, Ponders End.
LOUGHBOROUGH.
Tyreservices Great Britain, 45/46 Leicester Street.
LOWESTOFT.
Holburn Tyres, 11 Clapham Road.
LUDLOW.
Tyreservices Great Britain, Corve Bridge Works.

M

MAIDENHEAD, Berks.
Stapletons Ltd., Moorbridge Road.
MAIDSTONE, Kent.
Tyreservices Great Britain, 95/97 Upper Stone Street.
MALTON, N. Yorks.
T. Elsey (Tyres Malton) Ltd., Showfield Lane Ind. Estate.
MALVERN, Worcs.
Tyreservices Great Britain, 315/317 Worcester Road.
MANCHESTER, Lancs.
Q.H. Standard Motorists Centres, Wilmslow Road.
MARKET HARBOROUGH.
Tyreservices Great Britain, 57/59 St. Mary's Road.
MELBOURN, Herts.
Mohawk Tyres, Whiting Way, Melbourn, Nr. Royston.
MICHELDEVER.
Micheldever Tyres, Coxford Down, Micheldever, Nr. Winchester.
MIDDLESBROUGH.
Central Tyres, 14 Cannon Park Road.
Tyreservices Great Britain, Longlands Road.
MORETON, Wirral.
Q.H. Standard Motorists Centres, 157 Hoylake Road.

N

NEWARK, Notts.
Tanvic Tyre Ltd., 96 Appleton Gate.
NEWCASTLE-UPON-TYNE.
Tyreservices Great Britain, Rothbury Terrace.
NEWMARKET.
Newmarket Tyre Service, 2 Exeter Road.
NEWPORT, Gwent
Tyreservices Great Britain, Leeway, Newport Ind. Estate.
NEWPORT PAGNELL.
Fred The Tread, 1 Chicheley Street.
NORTHALLERTON, N. Yorks.
Tyreservices Great Britain, Boroughbridge Road.
NORTHAMPTON.
Super Save Silencers, Towcester Road, Far Cotton.
Tyreservices Great Britain, Campbell Street.
NORTHFLEET, Kent.
Watling Tyre Service Ltd., 69 High Street.
NORTHWICH, Cheshire.
Tyreservices Great Britain, Manchester Road.
NORWICH.
Central Tyre Co. Ltd., 98 City Road.
Holburn Tyres, Old Palace Road.
Mann Egerton, Rose Lane.
Q.H. Standard Motorists Centres, Salhouse Road.
Tyreservices Great Britain, Sprowston Road.
NOTTINGHAM.
Central Tyre Co., Unit 1, Lenton Lane.
Q.H. Standard Motorists Centres, 68 Castle Boulevard.
Tyreservices Great Britain, 76/78 Castle Boulevard.
NUNEATON.
Heart of England Tyres, Abbey Green.

O

OAKENGATES, Shropshire
Tyreservices Great Britain, Holyhead Road.
OAKERTHORPE, Derbys.
Off the Road Tyres Ltd., Four Gates, Oakerthorpe, Nr. Alfreton.
ORPINGTON, Kent.
Petrocell Ltd., Sevenoaks Road.
OXFORD.
Tyreservices Great Britain, Old LMS Station, Park End Street.

P

PAISLEY.
McConechy Tyre Services Ltd., 39 Well Street.
Smiley, 10 Incle Street.
PETERBOROUGH.
Central Tyres, Royce Road, Carr Road Ind. Estate.
City Tyre Services, Welland Road.
Tyreservices Great Britain, High Street, Fletton.
PLYMOUTH, Devon.
Sav-On Tyres, Richmond Walk.
PONTEFRACT, W. Yorks.
Tyreservices Great Britain, Stuart Road.
PORTSMOUTH.
Tyreservices Great Britain, London Road, Hilsea.
PRESTON, Lancs.
J. Ainsworth Tyre & Exhaust Ltd., Fylde Road.
PUDSEY, W. Yorks.
Tyreservices Great Britain, 83 Bradford Road.

R

RAINHAM, Kent.
Man-on-Wheels, 192/196 High Street.
READING, Berks.
Q.H. Standard Motorists Centres, 716 Oxford Road.
REDDITCH, Worcs.
Tyre Sales (Birmingham) Ltd., Oxleasow Road.
REDHILL, Surrey.
Tyreservices Great Britain, 23/25 Brighton Road.
RUGBY.
Tyreservices Great Britain, Abbey Street.
RUGELEY, Staffs.
Tyreways, Mill Lane.

S

SALE, Cheshire.
Tyreservices Great Britain, 197/201 Cross St.
SALFORD, Lancs.
Tyreservices Great Britain, 225 Trafford Road.
SCARBOROUGH.
Moss Tyres, Westwood Road.
SCAYNES HILL, Sussex.
Fields Tyre & Exhaust Centre, Lewes Road.
SCUNTHORPE.
Kenning Tyre Services, Glebe Road.
SELBY, N. Yorks.
Moss Tyres, Union Lane, Bawtry Road.
SHAFTESBURY, Dorset.
M.C. Tyres, New Road.
SHEFFIELD, Yorks.
Charlie Brown Supermarkets, Barmouth Road/Abbeydale Road.
Dexel Tyre Company, Staniforth Road.
Kenning Tyre Services, Townhead Street.
SHIPLEY, N. Yorks.
Shipley Tyres, Midland Works, John Street, Saltaire.
SHREWSBURY.
Tyreservices Great Britain, Abbey Foregate.
SLOUGH, Berks.
City 1st Ltd., 1A Furnival Street.
Tredrite Tyres, 414 Farnham Road.
SOLIHULL.
Tyre Sales (Birmingham) Ltd., Lode Lane Industrial Estate, Boulton Road.
SOUTH HARROW, Middx.
Tithe Farm Tyres Ltd., Alexandra Avenue.
STAINES, Middx.
Q.H. Standard Motorists Centres, 273 London Road.
STAMFORD, Lincs.
Kingsway Tyres (Stamford) Ltd., 30-31 Scotgate.
ST IVES.
Cromwell Tyres & Exhausts, New Road.
STIRLING.
Smiley, Wallace Street.
Stuart, McIntyre & Stuart Ltd., Back o'Hill.
STOCKPORT.
Central Tyre Co., Wellington Grove.
STOKE-ON-TRENT.
Alpha Tyres, Montrose Street, Fenton.
Tyreservices Great Britain, Federation Road, Burslem.
ST. AUSTELL, Cornwall
Tyreservices Great Britain, 'Trevarrick' Truro Road.
ST HELENS
J. Ainsworth Tyres and Exhausts, Knowsley Road.
ST PETER PORT, Guernsey.
Target Tyres, Pitronnerie Road.
STROUD, Glos.
Ebley Tyre Services, Westward Road, Ebley.
SUDBURY, Suffolk.
Trade Tyres, Egremont Street, Glemsford.
SUNBURY-ON-THAMES.
Sunbury Tyre Care, 195/197 Staines Road West.
SUNDERLAND, Tyne & Wear.
Tyreservices Great Britain, Inkerman Street.
SUTTON, Surrey.
Tyreservices Great Britain, 312 High Street.
SUTTON-IN-ASHFIELD.
Tyreservices Great Britain, Alfreton Road.
SWANSEA, Glamorgan
Tyreservices Great Britain, Beaufort Road, Morriston.
SWINDON.
Mike Knight Tyres, Boundary Works, Shrivenham Rd.

T

TAMWORTH,
Tame Tyre & Exhaust Ltd., Unit 7G, Claymore, Tame Valley Industrial Estate.
TAUNTON, Somerset.
County Tyres, Priory Bridge Road.
THRUPP.
Thrupp Tyres Co. Ltd., 13/15 Griffin Mill Estate, London Road.
TIPTON. West Midlands.
JBW Superstores, Burnt Tree, Dudley Port.
Tyreservices Great Britain, High Street.
TONBRIDGE, Kent.
Baffles Exhaust & Tyre Centre, 75 Vale Road.
TRURO, Cornwall.
Tyreservices Great Britain, St. Austell Street.

U

UDDINGSTON.
Smiley, Old Edinburgh Road, Birkenshaw.
UTTOXETER, Staffs.
Tyreways, Church Street.

W

WAKEFIELD, W. Yorks
Charlie Browns Supermarkets Ltd., Northgate.
WALSALL, West Mids.
D & W Tyre Service Ltd., 71 Park Road, Bloxwich.
WARWICK. Q.H. Standard Motorists Centres, 79 Emscote Road.
WATFORD.
Stapletons Ltd., 223/229 High Street.
WATH ON DEARNE.
Charlie Browns Supermarkets Ltd., Doncaster Road, Manvers, Nr. Rotherham.
WEDNESBURY, West Mids.
Ideal Motorist Centre, Holyhead Road.
WEST BROMWICH, West Mids.
Guest Motors Ltd., Old Meeting Street.
WHITCHURCH, Shropshire
Tyreservices Great Britain, Station Road.
WHYTELEAFE, Surrey.
Wrayesbury Tyres, Godstone Road.
WIMBORNE, Dorset.
M.C. Tyre & Battery Service, Leigh Road.
WINSFORD, Cheshire.
Tyreservices Great Britain, Delamere Street.
WISBECH.
Concorde Tyres & Exhausts, Elm High Road.
WISHAW.
Cooper Bros., Overtown Road, Newmains.
WOLVERHAMPTON.
Ideal Motoring Centre, 2 Willenhall Road.
Thompsons Tyre Service Ltd., Ettingshall Road.
Tyreservices Great Britain, Chapel Ash.
WORCESTER.
Auto Tyre & Battery Co., 2 Lowesmoor Place.
Tyreservices Great Britain, Droitwich Road.
WORKINGTON, Cumbria.
Tyreservices Great Britain, Clay Flatts Estate.
WORKSOP.
Dock Tyre Co., East Street.
WORTHING, Sussex.
Discount Tyre & Battery Service, Winton Place.
Kendad Tyre Services Ltd., 27-33 Lyndhurst Road.

Y

YORK.
Gladstone Tyre & Battery Co. Ltd., 110 Layerthorpe.
Moss Tyres, The Tyre Station, Foss Islands Road.
Moss Tyres, North York Trading Estate, Clifton.
Q.H. Standard Motorists Centres, 41-47 Lawrence Street.

Colour by numbers

by Russell Bulgin, Sports Editor, *Motor*

The colour: dayglo orange. The numbers: from McLaren, car MP4/2; from Michelin, race tyre compounds 05 and 010; from Porsche, TAG turbo engine TTE-PO1. The result: 12 Grands Prix wins and a World Championship for Niki Lauda.

And yet.

And yet there were times that Marlboro McLaren teetered and looked as vulnerable, as merely mortal as other teams. At Kyalami, Alain Prost started from the pit lane in the spare car. He was beaten only by team-mate Niki Lauda. Monaco was weather-wrecked and Prost was prepared to let a closing Ayrton Senna through to win. But the race was aborted with Prost ahead. Loosening left-front brake disc locating pegs gave Alain Prost wheel-wobble, two pit-stops and seventh place in France. Both MP4/2 chassis were in brake trouble at Montreal: Prost finished second, Lauda third. In Detroit, Prost's left-rear tyre softened and he made a late-race pit stop to replace it. At the flag he picked up two points for fifth place. Coming through the field at Hockenheim, Lauda took the edge off his rear tyres, losing a smidgen of grip. That was enough to make the difference: he finished second to Prost. Fourth gear exploded in Lauda's car at the Österreichring. He won. Picking soft-compound right-side Michelins was a mistake which cost Niki Lauda one place at Zandvoort. He finished second.

Somewhere deep within the Alain Prost-Niki Lauda-Marlboro-McLaren-TAG-Michelin agglomeration there was more than just a mix of man and machine, people and hardware. Call it racing luck, or success breeding success, but the most pronounced effect of this almost intangible catalyst was in the way McLaren integrated all the components necessary to produce super-success. The TAG-engine was Porsche-built — but to a detailed specification rigidly laid down by car designer John Barnard. That much-plagiarised Perrier-bottle planform became a McLaren trademark. But Barnard and his aerodyanmic team had spent hours of windtunnel time refining the low drag/high downforce shaping so that they could understand not only its performance in numerous conditions of pitch, yaw and car speed, but also fully comprehend how the wasp-waisted and steeply angled rear deck interacted with the rest of the car. It's brilliantly stiff carbon fibre-composites monocoque and gorgeously fabricated suspension, or the TAG V6's cooling demands judged in relation to the total aerodynamic demands of — what McLaren termed — the package.

If the McLaren was evolutionary in concept — externally resembling, as it did, the preceding Ford-engined MP4/1C and TAG-motored MP4/1E — it was revolutionary in effect. On a race-by-race basis what McLaren did was to recognise the realities of living with turbopower quicker than any other racing team. On one level, that might have been expected, given Porsche's ingrained turbocharging heritage: but it took Arrows over half a season to come to terms with running the 1983 World Championship-winning BMW power-unit. Then add in Alain Prost and Niki Lauda, the best-balanced driving team in Formula 1. While being so interchangable they could often test for each other, they each raced brilliantly: the drivers epitomised the hunger for success that pervaded down through a team of Ray-Banned mechanics.

If Prost was the better qualifier of the two, then Lauda responded with that mythic aura which imbues respect in those working with him. McLaren International Commercial Director Ron Dennis had assembled a 1984 line-up which could conceal no excuses: he had acquired everything — drivers, chassis, engine and sponsors — the team needed to do the job. That McLaren were successful was almost inevitable: what staggered the pit lane was the breadth of the success. A McLaren was quick everywhere from Monaco to the Österreichring: the team could never be discounted. There were worrying threads sewn into the fabric of the season: Bosch Motronic truculence ruining practice sessions which led to

the phrase 'engine mapping' becoming a staple in the McLaren pit lexicon, or gearbox reliability looking ever more marginal particularly in two-start races at Brands Hatch and the Österreichring.

Carbon fibre brakes were fundamental to the car: and occasionally untrustworthy in cold or wet conditions. But John Barnard was working on a heavy-duty gearbox alternative before the British Grand Prix. And Barnard was perhaps the single most important aspect — drivers aside — of McLaren's 12 wins. Because he carried the can. "As soon as you start making committee decisions in this business, you're history," he said: Barnard looked, listened to the race engineers, the tyre people, the drivers, assimilated, rationalised, and took responsibility for what ensued. Which was a year when McLaren rewrote the definitions of Grand Prix success, and were as dominant as no other team in contemporary Formula 1 history. If there is a parallel, it is in the Mario Andretti-Ronnie Peterson JPS Lotus 79 pacesetting of 1978.

But within the Lotus 79's sidepods was the secret of it's then-uncanny grip: ground-effect venturis. McLaren had no such quantum leap to stun the opposition with, but Formula 1 was playing to new rules this year. Cars could carry no more than 220 litres of fuel to complete the 200 mile maximum Grand Prix distance without a refuelling stop. And with Tyrrell the only team to use conventionally aspirated Ford-Cosworth power, so the equation to be solved was fuel-consumption-versus-race speed at the turn of the turbo-screw. There was the Heath Robinsonesque sight of frost forming on the outside of car fuel tanks at an icy Nürburgring in October: the colder the fuel the greater the quantity crammed into rubber bag-tanks. Or the hard plastic balls that teams stuffed into the fuel cell to guarantee that its volume was always below the permitted maximum.

In 1983, fuel consumption had been a virtual irrelevance: a mid-race fuel stop meant that a car could consume more fuel than it could physically contain in a single filling. And, in a turbo-world, more fuel means more power. Freezing the fuel led to Renault fitting heaters to warm up the Elf before it reached the metering unit: McLaren, typically, had an electronic engine management system sophisticated enough to cope with varying temperatures of petrol. Even the startline rules were changed to prevent on-grid topping up after the 5 minute board: there were suspicions that the aborted starts of the Brazilian and South African Grands Prix were due to pieces of 102 octane gamesmanship by certain heavy-drinking teams.

At the European Grand Prix on the new Nürburgring, the penultimate race of a 16-event series, second and third places were disputed on the home straight as both Michele Alboreto and Nelson Piquet ran out of fuel and spluttered towards the flag. Virtually on the line they swopped positions, Ferrari ahead of Brabham. Patrick Tambay ran out of gas in the first two races of the season: Renault's Gérard Larrousse threatened — in the season's lamest proclamation — that he would consider withdrawing temporarily if the team's engineers hadn't solved the problem by July's British Grand Prix. Having to slow Derek Warwick down to save petrol at San Marino — restricted to 95000rpm, Warwick was impotent as he fell from second to fourth — was not real racing, according to Larrousse. Maybe not: but the rules were the same for each team. What Larrousse was doing was tacitly admitting that Renault were unable to solve 1984's toughest task.

Renault began the year with two new drivers and a fresh car: Patrick Tambay, Derek Warwick and Michel Tétu-designed RE50. As Niki Lauda passed Derek Warwick in Brazil, the two cars touched: Warwick later held a 35-second lead over Prost and a front suspension upright, damaged in the coming together, broke. Which seemed to take the heart out of Renault: Warwick would later admit that the team did not begin to truly gel until the Canadian Grand Prix in June. By which time Renault had been through the awful embarrassment of having two cars collide and badly break-up at parking-lot speeds in the first corner Monaco

continued on page 26

Keke Rosberg at Dallas: 'a superbly skilful race of reflex and reactions.'
Photo: Mike Levasheff.

Not even a last-minute switch to the spare Unipart
McLaren at Hockenheim would prevent Alain Prost
from scoring yet another victory.
Photo: Nigel Snowdon

Niki Lauda used the impressive carbon fibre
chassis of the Unipart McLaren to increase his
standing in the table of Grand Prix victories.
Photo: John Townsend

incident. As in Warwick's previous accident at Dijon and subsequent practice shunt in Detroit, the front suspension penetrated the footbox: Patrick Tambay suffered a fracture of the lower left leg and a lingering lack of confidence that persisted until the British Grand Prix.

Yes, Michel Têtu produced a strengthened chassis: but the incidents provided damning evidence that the anti-carbon fibre chassis lobby were seeking. Besides which, Renault were in engine trouble. At the Austrian Grand Prix, five of the six Renault-powered cars blew up: François Hesnault's Ligier escaped – but that car was woefully down on boost pressure. Renault were also swopping between the new 1984 EF4 engine and the older '83 specification. The low compression 1983 engine would sustain higher boost pressures but not meet race fuel consumption criteria: often Renault teams used last year's engines to qualify with and the newer motors for the race.

If consumption looked good for the Grand Prix, then an '83 engine would be used: Patrick Tambay used an older engine to lead at Monza and had he not retired – with a broken throttle cable – Renault claim he had fuel enough to finish the race. But Renault this year were a changed team: ironically in view of his pidgin-French, Derek Warwick became the perfect Renault driver. He was attacking, sensible and as consistent as the car would allow. After final qualifying at the European Grand Prix a decision had to be made as to whether Warwick would run a normal Renault engine for the race or risk the new experimental electronically controlled unit. Larrousse, Têtu, technical chief Bernard Dudot and seven other team members discussed it in an arm-waving group. That gathering was the personification of everything John Barnard refused to succumb to at McLaren.

But, more than ever in 1984, Renault looked to lack in nothing but a cohesiveness: a unifying desire. Brabham had the need, the urge to build on their stunning late-season *blitzkrieg* which saw Nelson Piquet take the 1983 Championship at the final round in South Africa. But Brabham had six successive turbo failures in the opening races to balance against Nelson Piquet's 9 pole positions: that the BT53 mysteriously bogged on the line in Rio and Kyalami was rendered irrelevant. Piquet's victories in Montreal and Detroit, were as good an exhibition of perfection as could be produced by,

Proof that there *was* a gap at Detroit but, almost inevitably, one which would disappear as Piquet and Prost made their eyes-down sprint off the line.
Photo: Steve Swope.

say, Alain Prost: Detroit, using the spare car after the startline riot, was Piquet at his finest. Yet there were hints that Brabham had lost a little direction. Designer Gordon Murray introduced two modifications to the car for Friday practice sessions: the gaping-grin front oil-cooler duct for Dallas and a suspension and aerodynamic revamp at Brands Hatch: neither were retained for day two of practice. Then, in Austria, came the perfect metaphor for Brabham: Lauda passed Piquet – and Nelson backed off to save his tyres. He didn't know that Lauda was without fourth gear – Bernie Ecclestone, monitoring the pit wall television failed to spot Lauda throw his arm skyward when he thought his race was run – and Piquet was too far back to attack when the McLaren's lap-times tailed off. But Nelson led in Holland and Italy where running over a kerb and breaking a water radiator cost him the race. At the Nürburgring, he was out-run by the Prost-McLaren combination running a more conservative tyre choice than his Brabham. Qualifying showed Piquet's class – at Imola he made the pole on a damp track after passing three cars – and the phlegmatic way he accepted the destruction of a season by BMW's quality control problems emphasised his innate maturity.

Lotus were a team with almost everything: a superb Gérard Ducarouge designed chassis, Renault V6 engines and Goodyear tyres, plus drivers Elio de Angelis and Nigel Mansell. If a Renault engine was not as strong as a TAG, nor Goodyear as consistent as Michelin in the American Company's first year of radial development, that was enough to delineate Lotus from McLaren: the tiny differences between winning and just picking up points. Elio de Angelis was going to quit four laps into the Brazilian Grand Prix: the Renault engine had grumpy throttle response and was difficult to drive: he hung in and finished third. Which showed Elio the way in a year of economy crises and grids being wasted by turbo-trauma come Sunday. He finished the first ten races, scoring points in nine: then, in Germany he led. And the Renault broke.

Within Lotus, there was a sense of discord, de

Angelis and Mansell had huge dices in Montreal and Dallas – where Mansell led from pole – and inter-team relations became strained. Call it a clash of personalities: but it is doubtful whether it would have been allowed to fester so long at McLaren. De Angelis had four front-row starts, Mansell two: but it was the Englishman who spun off when in the lead at Monaco, got involved with – and fined for – the startline pile-up in Detroit and then angered Keke Rosberg by weaving while leading from pole in Dallas. In Texas, Mansell was trying to win a race that might have been shortened, at Motor City he was sandwiched between Piquet and Prost's eyes-down sprint off the line, in Monte Carlo a white line on a wet afternoon flicked him out. The car was good and the new Goodyears the most easily blamable part of the race-day equipment.

For Goodyear, going radial was a big operation. Unlike Michelin, which came in with Renault in 1977 and could thus learn in tandem with the fledgling team, the American company had to develop a whole new technology while supplying teams who had anticipated winning races before they had deduced just how tough the McLarens were to beat. On the scorecard, it looks a bad year for Goodyear: but, given the Michelin-shod McLaren dominance, 1984 could be judged the best season for Goodyear to make the switch. Come the Nürburgring in October, and Alboreto-Ferrari-Goodyear could share fastest race lap of the Nürburgring – to three places of decimals – with Piquet-Brabham-Michelin. That indicates the huge progress Goodyear made. What remains the year's least expected decision is that of Michelin to quit after Estoril: at the time of the September shock news, Michelin had won 12 of the year's 14 Grands Prix.

Those two Goodyear wins were Michele Alboreto's Zolder victory and Keke Rosberg's epic drive in Dallas. McLaren had practice niggles at Zolder: the source was either belligerent electronics or incorrectly blended fuel. In the race, engine and engine-electronics failures put both cars out. An all-scarlet front row turned into Michele Alboreto's first Ferrari victory, despite a brief off-track excursion: never again would Ferrari, tyres and track be so well matched. Ferrari's season-long development to turn the 126C4 into a consistent front runner was marked by the emergence – in Austria – of a long-wheelbase derivative and – in Italy – the adoption of McLaresque sidepods. Along the way technical director Mauro Forghieri, a Ferrari race regular since the early sixties, was seconded to base in a dramatic reshuffle: *Ingenere Tomaini* took over race weekend duties with Harvey Postlethwaite heading the chassis design team at Fiorano. René Arnoux put in a brilliant drive at Dallas to finish second after starting from the back of the grid: but he made a driving error of staggering ineptitude at Zandvoort to wipe out Thierry Boutsen's Arrows against the barriers, Arnoux taking a late decision to head for the pits. Not all Ferrari's virtues disappeared: the cars were often reliable and strong, with Alboreto coming seemingly from nowhere to take second during the last laps at Monza as the rest of the world fell by the wayside.

Track conditions were so bad at Dallas – the track broke up during practice and was still being bonded into a semblance of sanity on race morning – that no car had a grip advantage. Which was what Keke Rosberg needed to win the most spectacular Grand Prix of the year in the unloved, ungainly, and understeering Williams FW09. At a track with just a one-car wide racing line amid the marbles, Rosberg turned the race into a dust-up. Alain Prost – yet again – was 7.5s ahead when he clipped a piece of metal jutting out from between two of the concrete blocks encircling the track: the same effectively invisible impediment also claimed Lauda, Alboreto and Senna. Keke missed the metal in a sliding, superbly skilful race of reflex and reactions. Williams had windtunnel tested a model mock-up of the McLaren rear end back in the Ford-Cosworth days and found it no better than the then FW08 contender's boxy flanks: they re-evaluated it this year and – along with a longer wheelbase – applied the B-spec treatment to the pug-nosed FW09 which had finished fifth on its '83 Kyalami debut and second in Rio. Then there were the stiffened chassis and the revised front suspension pick-ups to compare, the new Williams gearbox casing to investigate: Williams tried hard in 1984. But Honda turbos had phases of destructiveness: and the car always understeered. FW09 had been created in a year when Chief Designer Patrick Head was also working on the four-wheel-drive MG Metro 6R4 rally prototype for Austin Rover: whatever sum ARG paid Williams for the comprehensive development work carried out, the low frontal grip of the FW09 cost the Williams Grand Prix team dear.

And Dallas, too, was the most eccentric Grand Prix of the year: racing in a stockyard in 103°F heat on a track that dissolved into gravel come race-day. That a Grand Prix happened at all was down to Texan entrepreneurship and image-association from the eponymous television soap opera. With all the grey-tinged sterility of a motorway service area, the new Nürburgring hosted the European Grand Prix: it was – predictably – as bitterly cold and dank in October as Dallas was scorched in July. At least the track was safe: safe enough with football-pitch sized run-off areas to stage an off-the-grid shunt at a first chicane too close to the start. No-one was hurt in the multi-car ballet over damp grass.

There were also accidents in 1984: none, thankfully, fatal. Opening lap destruction derbies marred Detroit, Brands Hatch and the Nürburgring, without casualties. Piercarlo Ghinzani suffered a huge pre-race warm-up accident at Kyalami, but his Osella stood up to the impact well, carbon fibre survival cell intact. He was burned about the face and hands. During his first ever race car lap at Brands Hatch, Johnny Cecotto tried to go too fast, too soon on cold tyres. Once cut free from his Toleman he was found to have suffered two badly smashed legs: his recovery time was impressively short. Martin Brundle escaped a Tyrrell final qualifying roll along the waterfront at Monaco as he battled to keep inside the fastest twenty who would start the race: two months later in Dallas he broke a leg and an ankle against an unyielding wall.

Brundle was one of the positive aspects of 1984: along with Ayrton Senna, Stefan Bellof, Philippe

Alliot, Jonathan Palmer and François Hesnault he began a Grand Prix career in Rio – and scored points on his debut. He and Ayrton Senna had spent 1983 disputing the British Formula 3 series: their quality was such that their abilities belied their relative inexperience. Senna was as natural in Formula 1, as poised a driver, as he had been in Formula Ford. He should have won Monaco, scored a good third in Britain and frequently qualified well: that Toleman immediately instituted legal action against him when he signed for Lotus for 1985 is as much a reminder of how the team rated him as a driver as well to castigate his abrupt career decision. Stefan Bellof, brilliantly quick in the early part of the season, was out-run by Brundle stand-in Stefan Johansson in mid-year – and then saw his drive collapse beneath him.

In the afterglow of 1984's chase-the-McLaren story, the FISA-versus-Tyrrell affair still rankles as being as distasteful as it was ill-considered. Whether or not Tyrrell was plying his 012 cars with lead ballast during a late-race pit stop or – and this is more far-fetched – mixing additive into the water injected into the engine to ward off piston and valvegear failures has become a moot case. What is more relevant is not only the way that FISA conducted his trial – for example, introducing fresh evidence at an appeal hearing and barring Tyrrell from approaching expert witnesses who had analysed water samples for FISA – but also the severity of the fine. If Andrea de Cesaris and Niki Lauda have their practice times discounted on the days at Dijon and Dallas where the Ligier was found to be running with an empty fire extinguisher bottle and the McLaren declared to have a rear wing 2mm too wide, then excluding Tyrrell from the World Championship for infringements committed during Martin Brundle's gutsy drive to second in Detroit ranks as a kneejerk reaction of an inappropriate magnitude.

But the decision was final, costing Tyrrell his FOCA membership and $1,000,000 in concessionary travel arrangements to transcontinental races. Underlying the season had been the backstage arguments over the proposed 195-litre fuel capacity maximum intended for 1985: to stick at the current 220-litre allowance required team unanimity – and Ken Tyrrell was the only dissenting voice. Naturally after he was barred from the Championship, so 220 litres became a fixed part of the '85 technical regulations, neatly, tidily and with no outward fuss.

Even with the Tyrrell controversy tainting the year, 1984 was – superficially at least – a positive year for Grand Prix racing. John Macdonald's RAM team had no astounding results: that the compact organisation could bounce back from two write-offs at Dallas to make the next race at Brands Hatch before turning up at Hockenheim, ready to race once more, was a marvellous achievement. Spirit ran 16 races with a 12 man team and a budget that was positively petty cash: when the German metal-workers strike left a consignment of Hart engine blocks stranded, Spirit hired a Ford-Cosworth DFV and rejigged a car to take the V8 for Detroit: it was a world away from

McLaren using TAG boss Mansour Ojjeh's private jet to ship in a batch of race tyres from Michelin's Clermont-Ferrand headquarters to Zolder. That gave Alain Prost a slightly harder left-rear race tyre and left the motorhome park dumbfounded.

Alfa Romeo illustrated the turbo conundrum perfectly. A race weekend for the Euroracing team often consisted of suffering an economy shortfall in the race after blowing up in high-boost qualifying. Getting out on your second set of qualifying tyres before the Alfas attempted to do likewise was one of the keys to getting a fast racing grid lap this year: otherwise an oil-smeared racing line rendered the rest of the session meaningless.

For one corollary to turbocharging was an increasing number of stratas of complexity. Teams used special qualifying cars, qualifying engines, qualifying water or gas sprays to cool intercoolers air qualifying fuel brews and qualifying gear-ratios in a bewildering array of permutations in their quest for the perfect lap. Cars grew longer – Ferrari, Williams, Arrows, Osella – and suspension components stiffer, the better to cope with the torque. Perhaps the perfect example of a 1984 retirement was the departure of Marc Surer's Arrows-BMW on the first lap of the German Grand Prix. A sensor detached itself from inside the plenum chamber of the engine, and thus sent an inaccurate signal down to the Bosch brainbox. According to the sensor, the engine was receiving too-little air: so the computer cut the supply of petrol to the engine and Surer faced a walk back to the pits.

As ever there were memories to marvel over. Stefan Bellof passing René Arnoux – Tyrrell against Ferrari – on the pavement at Monaco's Mirabeau corner. Derek Warwick looking to be home and dry in Rio. The fantastic job performed by Toleman from June to August which erased memories of the ugly divorce from Pirelli which soured the Imola paddock. Martin Brundle's grin, part incredulity, part fatigue after finishing second in Detroit. Keke Rosberg's up-and-at-'em qualifying laps at Kyalami and Estoril, wheels in the dirt and foot hard on the floor. Nelson Piquet on the grid awaiting for the restart at Detroit: impassive, serene, as the Brabham mechanics worked miracles around him on the spare car. Enzo Osella's jump-for-joy as Piercarlo Ghinzani finished fifth in Dallas . . .

And yet.

And yet what remains is the year of McLaren, in so many ways the ultimate season. Thierry Boutsen's graphic description of Alain Prost lapping him at Imola, only to spin through 360° as the carbon fibre brakes cried wolf. "It was a big spin, I tell you: a big, big spin. And he held it, too." That Prost could then go on to win the race was the microcosm of McLaren in 1984: when disaster loomed, more often than not McLaren could ride through the storm. Not only just to survive, but to be in a position to win. In the end it came down to Lauda-versus-Prost, names that began to sound like commands in McLaren's computer-code of success. The two McLaren drivers. In a class of their own. Where they had been all year long.

Balestre is good for you – particularly if you are a prospective French World Champion . . .
Photo: Nigel Snowdon

THE BMW 635CSi. FOR EVERYDAY USE,

The racing version of the BMW 635CSi can top 160 mph at the drop of a flag.

That's some 20 mph faster than its road-going stable-mate. But what little the road version lacks in speed,

WCRS

WE RECOMMEND THE 140 MPH VERSION.

it more than makes up for in luxury.
There's another not insignificant advantage: you

can actually buy one. The going rate is about £178
for every mile an hour. **THE ULTIMATE DRIVING MACHINE**

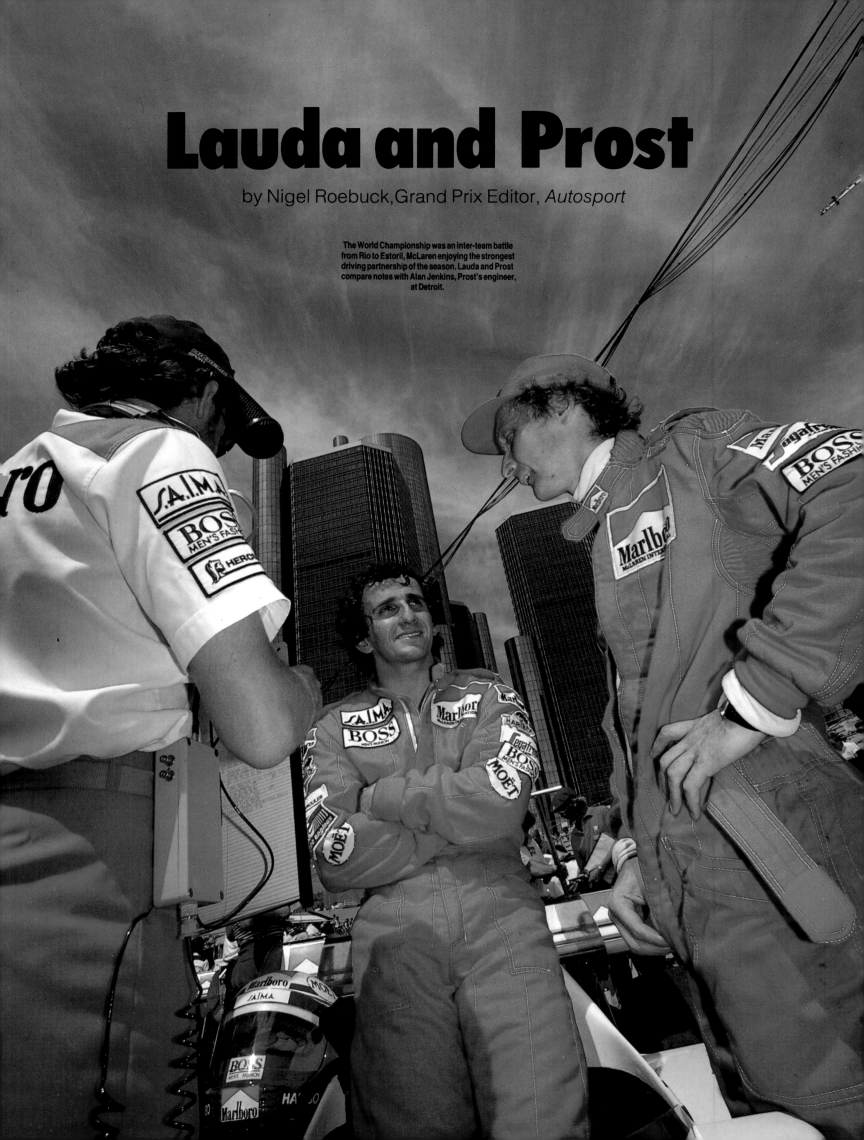

Lauda and Prost

by Nigel Roebuck, Grand Prix Editor, *Autosport*

The World Championship was an inter-team battle from Rio to Estoril, McLaren enjoying the strongest driving partnership of the season. Lauda and Prost compare notes with Alan Jenkins, Prost's engineer, at Detroit.

There were no team orders at McLaren in 1984, and that, more than anything else, tells you about the drivers. No need for Ron Dennis to tell them to watch it, not be silly, not take each other off. Lauda and Prost, indeed, would have taken it amiss if he had tried.

As season's end approached it became clear that the World Championship would be decided by car reliability, probably by a single bad break for Alain or Niki. Such was the quality of McLaren preparation, the inherent dependability of the cars, the similarity of the drivers' talents.

Who would have believed, in the modern era, that one team could win three-quarters of a season's races? Or that one driver could take seven of them, yet still lose the World Championship? These, however, are the bare bones of 1984.

Renault's contribution to the McLaren domination cannot be underestimated. A couple of days after losing the Championship in '83 the Régie sacked Prost, a matter of the management asserting itself, perhaps trying to show that this was *their* team, not his. Whatever their motive, they were dispensing with a man who had won nine races for them in three years.

For Marlboro and McLaren, signing the Frenchman was the work of a moment. You rarely find diamonds out on the street. Hence, Ron Dennis got himself a bargain, Prost a team in which his ability could truly thrive.

"In my karting days," Alain said, "Niki was my idol. I used to model myself on him, dream of achieving success like him. And now I was in the same team, with the same equipment, same chances. It was something fantastic. And I was free of all that responsibility I'd had at Renault."

Lauda, typically, was more circumspect about the new partnership. "It's not my team – I'm just a driver," he shrugged. "So now comes Mr Prost to McLaren. Sure, I work with him. Of course. He seems to be a sensible guy . . ."

Niki, however, insisted that the team give him priority in testing. Indeed, a clause to that effect was in his contract, and over the winter he exercised it absolutely. While the Austrian pounded round Paul Ricard his new team-mate spent many a lonely day in the pits, hanging about.

"It was a bit difficult, because we only had one test car at that time . . ." Alain would go no further than that, despite suggestions in the press that he seemed very much the number two in this team. "I was not too concerned because from the start the team treated me fairly, gave me the same tyres and everything – and I was nearly always quicker than Niki . . ."

John Barnard's MP4/2 was not ready for the Rio tests in January, and work with the original hybrid TAG-powered car did not go well in Brazil. Particularly worrying was the continued temperament of the Bosch Motronic engine management system, which had proved so quirky during the car's early races.

Days, however, before everyone returned to Rio for the opening Grand Prix, the new car ran at Ricard, and both drivers were ecstatic about it, setting off for South America with high hopes.

Everything seemed to come right at the same time. Porsche and Bosch had come to terms with the urgency of Formula 1, so that the TAG V6, as well as being absolutely competitive on horsepower, was – almost alone – untroubled by the new 220-litre fuel limit. Only in throttle response, said the drivers, could the engine be faulted.

A minor problem with the Bosch system kept Lauda from victory in that first race, but Prost took over and won. As he crossed the line the little man had both arms in the air and was waving wildly, as is always the case when he considers a victory of crucial importance. It was an expression of spontaneous joy.

"You can't imagine the importance of that win. Some of the French press, you know, gave me a very hard time when I left Renault, and if Warwick had won and I had not finished, it would have been very bad for me. But the problem disappeared after Brazil."

Niki was now in no doubt about his new team-mate. In the past any team with Lauda in it had effectively become Lauda's team, such is the force of the man's personality. John Watson, his team-mate at both Brabham and McLaren, put it

this way: "The thing about having Niki in a team is that it doesn't matter what's written on a contract, nor how a team is basically run. Niki will assume what he wants to assume. He will take his position. There's nobody like him . . ."

Very early in the season, though, the Austrian had to face the fact that, for the first time in his career, he had a team-mate undeniably quicker than himself. And, pragmatic as ever, he did not delude himself. He would not beat Prost on sheer speed, so it was a matter of thinking of other ways to do it.

True enough, Lauda was sometimes shaken by Prost's pace – particularly during qualifying. "How does he do it?" he asked John Barnard, on seeing Alain's pole time at Monaco, more than a second faster than his own.

Their styles are remarkably similar, smooth and devoid of flamboyance, and one of the reasons for the team's success this year has been the fact that their tastes in set-up are virtually identical. Minor cockpit differences apart, therefore, the spare MP4/2 has always been instantly available to either man, a decided advantage in the urgency of a final qualifying session or warm-up problem on race day.

Lauda and Prost share a preference for slight understeer (whereas Watson liked his cars a little looser). McLaren test sessions in 1984, therefore, have been of benefit to both drivers even when conducted by only one of them. There, and at the races, Niki and Alain have scrupulously pooled information, a matter of mature common sense to men such as these.

Ironically, of course, this has meant that each has contributed to the success of the other – ideal from the point of view of winning the Constructors' title for McLaren, less so in terms of their own rivalry for the World Championship . . .

Prost was much the stronger when it came to qualifying, first or second on 11 of the 16 grids, whereas Lauda's best start position was third. Only once, at Dallas, did Niki qualify better. In the races, too, Alain was the McLaren hotshoe, leading 352 of the season's laps, to his team-mate's 152. On wins he was ahead seven to five. Yet, in the face of all these statistics, it was Lauda who won the points battle.

Perhaps, in a sense, Niki's comparatively poor qualifying record worked for him. In race day set-up, the McLarens truly came into their own. No matter how far back he might have been on the grid, Lauda's name was always well to the fore in the warm-up times. Time after time he picked his way through the field with exquisite precision.

By this stage one of two things would have happened to Prost. Either he would be in front, untouchable, or he would be striving to find a way past Nelson Piquet's Brabham-BMW, the inevitable pole-sitter, inferior in chassis to the McLaren but with more sheer horsepower than anything else.

This was a most curious aspect of the 1984 World Championship. Two men fighting it out, driving for the same team, yet their actual races very rarely touched. On four occasions they finished 1-2, but never did we see an out-and-out battle between them. It was as if two point totals brought them mysteriously together in Portugal. Only in the freak conditions of Dallas did they spend most of a race together – and both finished up in the wall . . .

Mistakes by either were few. Prost spun on de Angelis's oil in Austria, and Lauda pirouetted out of the Monaco Grand Prix. A snatching brake spun Alain at Imola, and Niki revolved at the Nürburgring, both drivers keeping the engine alive and continuing to the finish. Another mark of quality.

At the beginning of the year there looked to be all sorts of possibilities. Alboreto's Ferrari led the opening laps at Rio, and Warwick's Renault later gave the McLarens a fight. At Zolder Prost and Lauda were off the pace in qualifying, retired early in the race, giving their rivals cause for hope. Apart from Dallas, though, this was the only race of the year in which a McLaren did not finish in the points. The three-race American tour brought no victories for Niki and Alain, but thereafter they were unstoppable, the challenge from rival teams depressingly weak.

When Prost lasted, he won, with Lauda

somewhere behind. But when Niki won, Alain was usually watching from the pits. It was that simple. The Austrian finished – and scored – in each of the last seven races, while his team-mate won four of them, retired in three. At Monza both needed engine changes after the morning warm-up. Who got which was decided by the flip of a coin. Prost's blew up after three laps, Lauda's lasted for an eventual victory.

In the end, though, it came down to Portugal, to the closing laps. Alain led, with Niki third and powerless to take the second place he needed. Upon the flimsy thread of Lotus-Renault reliability hung the World Championship, for Mansell separated the two McLarens. Less than 50 miles from the flag the Englishman retired, and the title changed hands.

It is fair to say, whether they would admit it or not, that a majority of McLaren people would have preferred to see Prost take the title. For one thing, the Frenchman has been absolutely central to every race this year, fast or slow, wet or dry. For another, the legend of Niki Lauda is such that a World Championship for him would be seen across the world as exactly that: a World Championship for *him*, with the name of McLaren somewhat in the background. A Prost title would have brought more publicity for the team.

The Frenchman, too, was always going to stay with McLaren for 1985, whereas Lauda, as ever seeking new challenges, re-signed only after talks with Renault had fallen apart. "This team," Alain enthused, "is something incredible. In Germany I had to take the spare car at the last second and I won without problem. Psychologically, something like that makes a big difference to a driver. They are doing their best for you, and so you feel always you must do the same.

"I am glad Niki is staying next year. OK, he is World Champion, and I am not. I can live with that – after all, I lost the title at the last race in '83 also! I will win it next year. What is important is the trust between us. A little example: at Brands Hatch, before the race was stopped, we both blistered our left rear tyres. Before the restart we agreed that if we had a problem with Piquet – our only rival – the guy who passed him first would *not* make a break for it, perhaps forcing the other to screw his tyres in attempting to pass Nelson. Only when we were both past would we go for it. We thought always as a team. At Montreal my car broke in qualifying, and Niki was in the spare. He did not hesitate to let me use his race car.

"I did not know Niki very well when I came to McLaren – it's not easy to know him well. But I believed he was completely honest, the most important thing, and now I know it for sure."

Many people believe that Prost's presence in the team has spurred Lauda to his World Championship. "Niki," commented Keke Rosberg, "has driven harder this year than I have ever seen before. He's had Prost so big in his eyes. I've been with him in a few corners, and I've been given a very clear picture: either I move, or something's going to happen. Absolutely clean – but also absolutely uncompromising."

Niki does not deny it. "Alain is *extremely* quick. Having him as a team-mate has stimulated me, for sure, but it has also haunted me. There is no break in the pressure. He is always right there, always on form. In qualifying he is unbelievable.

"It is true that I was never in this position with a team-mate before. Sometimes one of them would beat me, but I always felt it would be me in front next time. With Prost it's different. I have had to drive faster and faster, better and better all the time. This has been the most satisfying season I have known . . ."

The highlights of the McLaren season have been many: Prost's brilliant drive to second at Kyalami, after starting from pit lane in the spare car; Lauda, 10th on the first lap at Dijon, coming through to win majestically; the breathtaking pole position lap by Alain at Monaco; Niki in Austria, coping with his late-race gear problem . . .

Was it significant, we wondered, that at the Nürburgring Lauda appeared the tenser of the two? Was the pressure getting to him? On the grid at Estoril, it was Niki who told Alain to relax. The man would make a hell of a poker player . . .

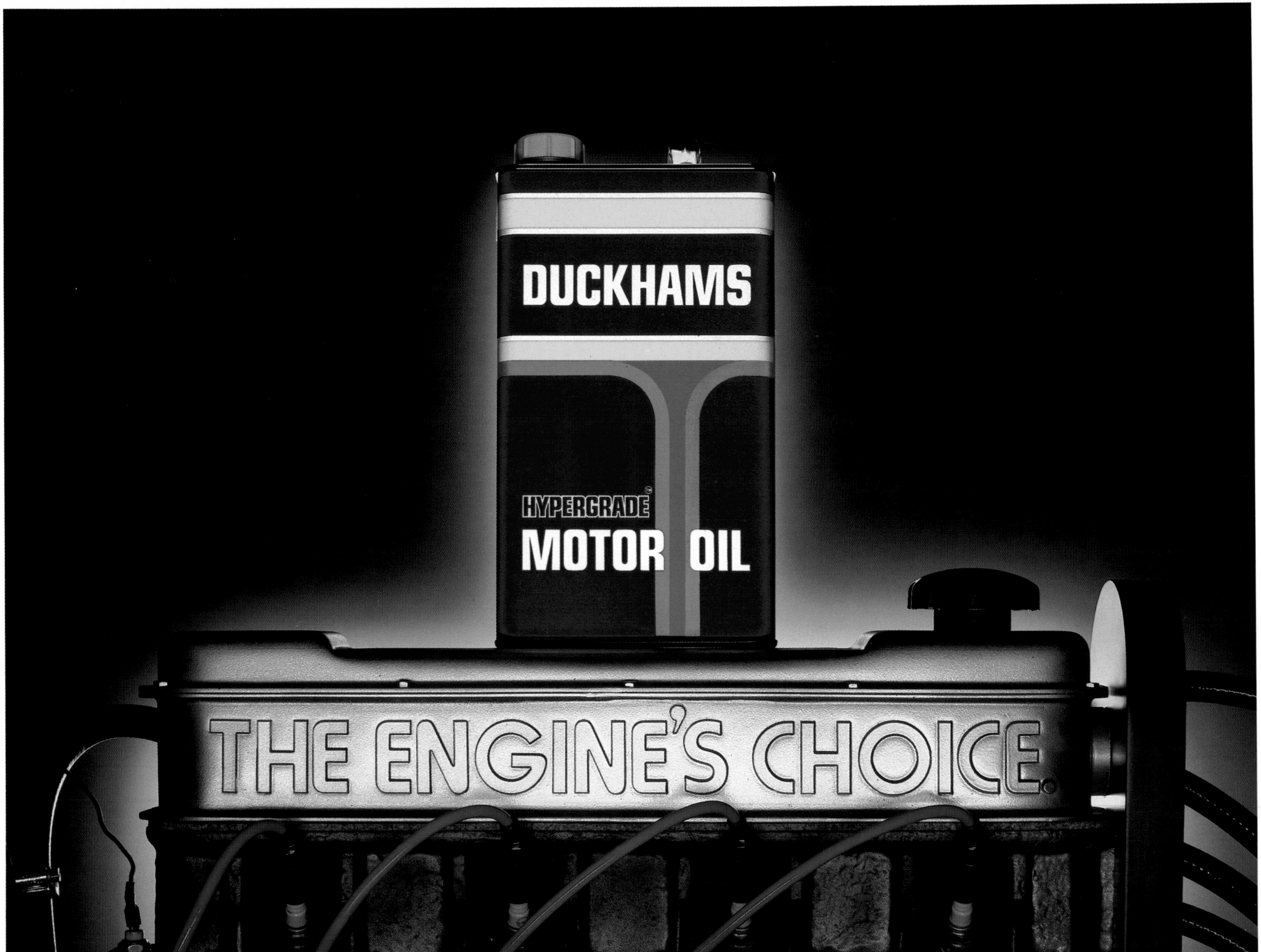
DUCKHAMS
HYPERGRADE™
MOTOR OIL
THE ENGINE'S CHOICE.

1984 Formula 1 car specifications

McLaren International rewrote the record books in every department, not least, in the Constructors' Championship where they established a stunning total of 143½ points. Lauda and Prost scored points 20 times from 32 starts. In 1983, Tambay and Arnoux gave the Constructors' Cup to Ferrari by taking points 17 times from 30 starts. The difference is that the McLaren drivers finished either first or second 17 times!

The battle for second place swung wildly in the early stages, then settled into a three-way fight between Lotus, Ferrari and Renault before the French team fell away mid-season. Lotus came close to challenging Ferrari but Alboreto's consistency in the final three races settled the issue. To put that in perspective, however, Ferrari were 86 points behind McLaren – a figure which is three points short of Ferrari's championship-winning score in 1983!

The engines

1984 saw the final rout of the Ford-Cosworth after 16 years as the backbone of Grand Prix racing. Turbocharged engines won every race, the TAG-Porsche pulverising its rivals. After making its debut four races from the end of the previous season, the TAG-Porsche won the opening Grand Prix of 1984 and went on to take 11 more victories. BMW won two, Ferrari took one and Honda scored a victory in their first full season with the V6 turbo.

BMW supplied their M12/13 to Arrows, in addition to Brabham and ATS. Ligier joined Lotus as a customer for Renault engines while Hart provided power for Spirit (now without Honda) and RAM as well as continuing their association with Toleman. The Alfa Romeo turbo was made available to Osella, who also used the normally-aspirated 1260 on one occasion.

Tyrrell set out with the intention of using the Ford-Cosworth DFY engine for the full season while Arrows continued with the DFV as they waited for the BMW-powered A7. The exclusion of Tyrrell from the final three races notwithstanding, the Austrian Grand Prix became the first race in the World Championship to be run without an unsupercharged engine on the grid.

BMW took nine pole positions and set three fastest laps; TAG-Porsche claimed three poles and eight fastest laps; Lotus, two pole positions; Ferrari, one pole and three fastest laps (one shared with BMW) while Renault took just one pole and two fastest laps compared with four of each in 1983.

	Alfa Romeo 1260	Alfa Romeo 183T	BMW M12/13 Turbo	Ferrari 126C Turbo	Ford Cosworth DFV	Ford Cosworth DFY
No. of cylinders	V12	V8	4-in line	V6	V8 (90°)	V8 (90°)
Bore and stroke	78·5 mm × 51·5 mm	74 mm × 43·5 mm	89·2 mm × 60 mm	81 mm × 48·4 mm	90·0 mm × 58·8 mm	90 mm × 58·8 mm
Capacity	2995 cc	1496 cc	1500 cc	1496 cc	2994 cc	2994 cc
Compression ratio	11·5:1	7:1	6·7:1	7·5:1	12·2:1	12·3:1
Maximum power	540 bhp	670 bhp	850 bhp	680 bhp	510 bhp	510 bhp
Maximum rpm	12,300	11,800	11,000	11,500	11,000	11,000
Valve sizes	30 mm × 2	—	35·8 mm - Inlet	—	36·06 mm - Inlet	—
	25 mm × 2		30·3 mm - Exhaust		31·75 mm - Exhaust	
Valve lift	9 mm	—	—	—	11·00 mm - Inlet	—
					10·41 mm - Exhaust	
Valve timing	50-70/70-50	—	—	—	102°	102°
Block material	Aluminium	Aluminium	Cast iron	Aluminium alloy	LM 25 Aluminium alloy	LM 25 Aluminium alloy
Pistons and rings	Mahle	Mahle	Mahle/Goetze	Mahle/Goetze	Cosworth/Goetze	Cosworth/Goetze
Bearings	Clevite	Clevite	Glyco	Vandervell/Clevite	Vandervell	Vandervell
Fuel injection	Lucas	Spica	Bosch	Lucas/Ferrari-Weber/Marelli	Lucas	Lucas
Ignition system	Marelli Dinoplex	Marelli	Bosch	Marelli	Lucas/contactless	Lucas/Contactless
Turbocharger(s)	—	Avio/KKK	KKK	2 × KKK	—	—
Weight (less intercooler)	—	160 kg	160 kg	148 kg	320 lb/145 kg	300 lb/136 kg

	Hart 415T Turbo	Honda RA163-E Turbo	Renault EF1	TAG PO1 (TTE PO1) Turbo
No. of cylinders	4-in line	V6	V6	V6
Bore and stroke	88 m × 61·5 mm	—	86 mm × 42·8 mm	82 mm × 47 mm
Capacity	1496 cc	1500 cc	1492 cc	—
Compression ratio	6·7:1	—	7:1	7·5:1
Maximum power	600bhp at 2·1 bar boost (race)	—	750 bhp	750 bhp (race boost)
Maximum rpm	10,750	12,000	11,500	11,500
Valve sizes	35·0 mm - Inlet	—	29·8 mm - Inlet	—
	30·0 mm - Exhaust		26·1 mm - Exhaust	
Valve lift	10·5 mm	—	10·5 mm	—
Valve timing	—	—	318°	—
Block material	Aluminium	Cast iron	Aluminium	Aluminium alloy
Pistons and rings	Mahle/Goetze	Honda	Mahle/Goetze	Mahle/Goetze
Bearings	Vandervell	—	Glyco	Glyco
Fuel injection	Hart/BRA	Honda	Electronic Renix	Bosch Motronic MS3
Ignition system	Marelli	Honda	Marelli	Bosch Motronic MS3
Turbocharger(s)	Holset	2 × IHI	Garret	2 × KKK
Weight (less intercooler)	290 lb	—	—	145 kg

Formula 1 car specifications

	Alfa Romeo 184T	Arrows A6-Cosworth	Arrows A7-BMW
Sponsor(s)	Bennetton	Barclay/Nordica	Barclay/Nordica
Designer(s)	M Tollentino/B Zava	Dave Wass/Jim Filmer	Dave Wass/Dave Nielson
Team Manager(s)	G P Pavanello/	Alan Rees/	Alan Rees/
	G C Casoli	Geoff Chamberlain	Geoff Chamberlain
Chief Mechanic(s)	–	Dave Luckett	Dave Luckett
No of chassis built	5	5	4
ENGINE			
Type	Alfa Romeo 890T	Ford-Cosworth DFV	BMW
Fuel and oil	Agip	Valvoline	BMW/Valvoline
Sparking plugs	Champion	Champion	Champion
TRANSMISSION			
Gearbox/speeds	Euroracing/Alfa Romeo	Arrows/Hewland (5)	Arrows
Drive-shafts	Euroracing/Alfa Romeo	Arrows	Arrows
Clutch	Borg & Beck	Borg & Beck	AP
CHASSIS			
Front suspension	Push rods	Double wishbones,	Top & bottom wishbones,
		pull rods,	pull rods,
		inboard springs	inboard springs
Rear suspension	Pull rods	Top rocker arms,	Top rocker arms,
		lower wishbones,	lower wishbones,
		inboard springs	inboard springs
Suspension dampers	Koni	Koni	Koni
Wheel diameter	13 in front	13 in front	13 in front
	13 in rear	13 in rear	13 in rear
Wheel rim widths	12 in front	11 in front	11·5 in front
	16·5 in rear	16 in rear	16 in rear
Tyres	Goodyear	Goodyear	Goodyear
Brakes	Brembo	Lockheed	AP
Brake pads	Ferodo	Ferodo	Ferodo
Steering	Euroracing/Alfa Romeo	Knight/Arrows	Arrows
Radiator(s)	IPRA	Serck/Sofica	Behr
Fuel tank	ATL	Aerotech	ATL
Battery	Marelli	YUASA	YUASA
Instruments	Borletti	VDO	VDO
DIMENSIONS			
Wheelbase	107 in/2720 mm	106 in/2692 mm	104 in/2642 mm
Track	70 in/1780 mm front	72 in/1829 mm front	68 in/1727 mm front
	68·1 in/1680 mm rear	62 in/1575 mm rear	63 in/1600 mm rear
Gearbox weight	110 lb/50 kg	95 lb/43 kg	100 lb/45·5 kg
Chassis weight (tub)	60 lb/27 kg	75 lb/34 kg	80 lb/36 kg
Formula weight	1201 lb/545 kg	1191 lb/540 kg	1191 lb/540 kg
Fuel capacity	48·4 gall/220 litres	42 gall/191 litres	48·3 gall/220 litres
Fuel consumption	–	5·0-5·8 mpg/49-57 litres/100 km	4·3 mpg/65 litres/100 km

Alfa Romeo 184T

Arrows A6

Arrows A7

	ATS D6	ATS D7	Brabham BT53-BMW
Sponsor(s)	ATS Wheels	ATS Wheels	Parmalat
Designer(s)	Gustav Brunner	–	Gordon Murray/David North
Team Manager(s)	Gunter Schmid	Gunter Schmid	Bernard Ecclestone/
			Herbie Blash
Chief Mechanic(s)	–	–	Charlie Whiting
No of chassis built	3	2	6
ENGINE			
Type	BMW M12/13	BMW M12/13	BMW M12/13 Turbo
Fuel and oil	Shell	Shell	-/Castrol
Sparking plugs	Bosch	Bosch	Bosch
TRANSMISSION			
Gearbox/speeds	ATS/Hewland (5)	ATS/Hewland (5)	Hewland/Brabham/Weismann/Getrag (5/6)
Drive-shafts	ATS/Löbro	ATS/Löbro	Brabham
Clutch	Borg & Beck	Borg & Beck	Borg & Beck
CHASSIS			
Front suspension	Double wishbones,	Double wishbones,	Double wishbones,
	pull rods,	pull rod	pushrods,
	inboard springs		
Rear suspension	Double wishbones,	Double wishbones,	Double wishbones,
	pull rods,	pull rod	pushrods,
	inboard springs		
Suspension dampers	Koni	Koni	Koni
Wheel diameter	13 in front	13 in front	13 in front
	15 in rear	13 in rear	13 in rear
Wheel rim widths	11 in front	11 in front	12 in front
	16 in rear	17 in rear	16·5 in rear
Tyres	Goodyear	Pirelli	Michelin
Brakes	Lockheed	Lockheed	Hitco/Brabham/Girling/AP
Brake pads	Ferodo	Ferodo	Hitco/Ferodo
Steering	ATS/Knight	ATS/Knight	Brabham rack and pinion
Radiator(s)	Behr	Behr	Behr
Fuel tank	Marstons/ATL	ATL	ATL
Battery	YUASA	YUASA	YUASA
Instruments	VDO/Smiths	VDO	Bosch
DIMENSIONS			
Wheelbase	104 in/2642 mm	108 in/2743·2 mm	115 in/2921 mm
Track	69 in/1753 mm front	–	69 in/1753 mm front
	64 in/1626 mm rear	–	65 in/1651 mm rear
Gearbox weight	110 lb/50 kg	110 lb/50 kg	105 lb/48 kg
Chassis weight (tub)	60 lb/27 kg	70·5 lb/32 kg	94 lb/42·7 kg
Formula weight	1191 lb/540 kg	1191 lb/540 kg	1208 lb/548 kg
Fuel capacity	50 gall/227 litres	48·3 gall/220 litres	47·96 gall/218 litres
Fuel consumption	4 mpg/68 litres/100 km	–	3·5-4·5 mpg/63-80 litres/100 km

ATS D7

Brabham BT53

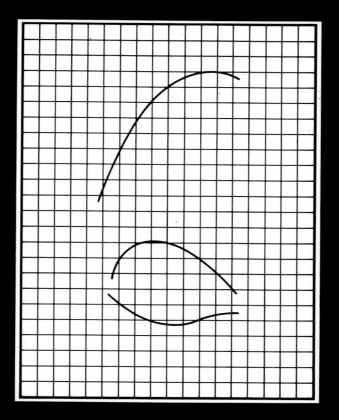

COSWORTH ENGINEERING

**The success of Cosworth engines in international
motor racing is legendary.
We're making legends too in -:
High performance engine designs and
specialist projects for Automotive, Marine
and Aero applications.
Prototype, pre production and series engine build.
High integrity precision Aluminium castings.**

COSWORTH ENGINEERING LTD.

ST. JAMES MILL ROAD, NORTAMPTON, NN5 5JJ U.K.
TEL: NORTHAMPTON (0604) 52444
TELEGRAMS: COSWORTH, NORTHAMPTON
TELEX: 31454

Formula 1 car specifications

	Ferrari 126C4	Ligier JS23-Renault	Lotus 95T-Renault
Sponsor(s)	Fiat/Agip/Goodyear	Loto/Gitanes/Antar/Europcar	John Player & Sons
Designer(s)	Ferrari: Ufficio Tecnico	M Beaujon/C Galopin	Gerard Ducarouge/Martin Ogilvie
Team Manager(s)	Enzo Ferrari	Guy Ligier	Peter Warr
Chief Mechanic(s)	Bellentani/Scaramelli	C Galopin/D Vizier	Bob Dance
No of chassis built	7	5	4
ENGINE			
Type	126/C4	Renault EF1	Renault EF1
Fuel and oil	Agip	Elf	Elf
Sparking plugs	Champion	Champion	Champion
TRANSMISSION			
Gearbox/speeds	Ferrari (5)	Ligier/Hewland	Lotus/Hewland (5)
Drive-shafts	Löbro/Ferrari	Lobro	Löbro
Clutch	Borg & Beck	Borg & Beck	AP
CHASSIS			
Front suspension	Double wishbones, pull rods,	Upper and lower wishbones, push rods	Double wishbones, pull rods, inboard springs
Rear suspension	Double wishbones, pull rods,	Upper and lower wishbones, push rods	Double wishbones, pull rods, inboard springs
Suspension dampers	Koni	Koni	Koni
Wheel diameter	13 in front	13 in front	13 in front
	13 in rear	13 in rear	13 in rear
Wheel rim widths	11 in/12·5 in front	12 in front	11 in front
	16 in rear	16·5 in rear	16·5 in rear
Tyres	Goodyear	Michelin	Goodyear
Brakes	Brembo/SEP	Brembo	Lotus/Brembo/SEP
Brake pads	Ferodo/SEP	Ferodo	Ferodo/SEP
Steering	Ferrari rack and pinion	Ligier	Lotus/Knight
Radiator(s)	Behr/Valeo/IPRA	IPRA	IPRA/Secan
Fuel tank	Pirelli	ATL	ATL
Battery	Varley/YUASA	YUASA	YUASA
Instruments	Borletti	Contactless	Contactless/Poinsot
DIMENSIONS			
Wheelbase	102·4 in/2600 mm	111 in/2810 mm	107 in/2720 mm
Track	70·5 in/1790 mm front	70·9 in/1800 mm front	70·9 in/1800 mm front
	64·7 in/1644 mm rear	67·3 in/1710 mm rear	63 in/1600 mm rear
Gearbox weight	97 lb/44 kg	137 lb/62 kg	95 lb/43 kg
Chassis weight (tub)	88 lb/40 kg	75 lb/34 kg	81·57 lb/37 kg
Formula weight	1190 lb/540 kg	1201 lb/545 kg	1191 lb/540 kg
Fuel capacity	48 gall/218 litres	48·3 gall/220 litres	48·4 gall/220 litres
Fuel consumption	–	4·1 mpg/68 litres/100 km	4·3 mpg/65 litres/100 km

Ferrari 126C4

Ligier JS23

Lotus 95T

	McLaren MP4/2-TAG	Osella FA1E-Alfa Romeo	Osella FA1F-Alfa Romeo
Sponsor(s)	Marlboro/Saima/Unipart/Michelin/Boss/Hercules	Kelemata	Kelemata
Designer(s)	John Barnard	Tony Southgate	Osella
Team Manager(s)	Ron Dennis	Enzo Osella	Enzo Osella
Chief Mechanic(s)	Dave Ryan	–	–
No of chassis built	5	2	3
ENGINE			
Type	TAG Turbo PO1 V6	Alfa Romeo 1260	Alfa Romeo 890T
Fuel and oil	Shell	Agip	Agip
Sparking plugs	Unipart	Champion	Champion
TRANSMISSION			
Gearbox/speeds	McLaren/Hewland (5)	Alfa Romeo	Alfa Romeo
Drive-shafts	McLaren	Alfa Romeo	Alfa Romeo
Clutch	AP/Borg & Beck	AP	AP
CHASSIS			
Front suspension	Push rod operating inboard auxiliary rockers, lower wishbones, inboard springs	Double wishbones, push rods, inboard springs	Double wishbones, pull rods, inboard springs
Rear suspension	Top rocker arms, lower wishbones, inboard springs	Top rocker arms, lower wishbones, inboard springs	Double wishbones, push rods, inboard springs
Suspension dampers	Bilstein	Sachs (front), Koni (rear)	Koni
Wheel diameter	13 in front	13 in front	13 in front
	13 in rear	13 in rear	13 in rear
Wheel rim widths	11·75 in front	11·5 in front	11·5 in front
	16·25 in rear	16 in rear	16 in rear
Tyres	Michelin	Pirelli	Pirelli
Brakes	McLaren/SEP Discs	Brembo (front), Lockheed (rear)	Brembo
Brake pads	SEP	Ferodo	Ferodo
Steering	McLaren	Osella/Knight	Osella/Knight
Radiator(s)	McLaren/Unipart and Behr Cores	IPRA	IPRA
Fuel tank	ATL	Pirelli	Pirelli
Battery	YUASA	Magneti/Marelli	Magneti/Marelli
Instruments	Contactless/VDO/Motometer	–	VDO
DIMENSIONS			
Wheelbase	110 in/2794 mm	109 in/2769 mm	107 in/2720 mm
Track	71·5 in/1816 mm front	70 in/1778 mm front	–
	66·0 in/1676 mm rear	65 in/1651 mm rear	–
Gearbox weight	125 lb/57 kg	–	–
Chassis weight (tub)	78 lbs/35 kg	85 lbs/38·6 kg	–
Formula weight	1191 lb/540 kg	1201 lb/545 kg	1228 lb/557 kg
Fuel capacity	48·4 gall/220 litres	48 gall/218 litres	48·3 gall/220 litres
Fuel consumption	4 mpg/68 litres/100 km	–	–

McLaren MP4/2

Osella FA1F

The winner of the 1981
Le Mans 24-hour
used Dunlop tyres.

(Look out for
this ad next year.)

Formula 1 car specifications

	RAM 02-Hart	Renault RE50	Spirit 101-Hart
Sponsor(s)	Skoal Bandit	Elf	Honda/Various
Designer(s)	Dave Kelly	Renault Sport/Michel Tetu	Gordon Coppuck
Team Manager(s)	Mick Ralph	Gerard Larrousse/Jean Sage	John Wickham
Chief Mechanic(s)	Ray Boulter	Daniel Champion	–
No of chassis built	3	9	2
ENGINE			
Type	Hart 415T	Renault EF1	Hart 415T
Fuel and oil	Shell Racing 40	Elf	Elf/Shell
Sparking plugs	Champion	Champion	Champion
TRANSMISSION			
Gearbox/speeds	Hewland/RAM (6)	Renault/Hewland (5)	Hewland (5/6)
Drive-shafts	RAM Automotive	Renault Glaenzer	Spirit
Clutch	AP	Borg & Beck	Borg & Beck
CHASSIS			
Front suspension	Upper and lower wishbones, pull rods, inboard springs	Double wishbones, pull rods	Top rocker arms, lower wishbones, inboard springs
Rear suspension	Upper and lower wishbones, pull rods, inboard springs	Double wishbones, pull rods	Top rocker arms, lower wishbones, inboard springs
Suspension dampers	Koni	De Carbon	Koni
Wheel diameter	13 in front / 13 in rear	13 in front / 13 in rear	13 in front / 13 in rear
Wheel rim widths	11 in front / 16 in rear	11·5 in front / 16·25 in rear	11·5 in front / 17 in rear
Tyres	Pirelli	Michelin	Pirelli
Brakes	AP	Brembo	Lockheed
Brake pads	Ferodo	Valeo	Ferodo
Steering	RAM Automotive/Knight	Renault	Spirit
Radiator(s)	RAM Automotive/Behr	Secan	Serck
Fuel tank	Premier/Marston	Supple Norms (FT3)	Marston/Premier
Battery	Saft	Marelli	–
Instruments	VDO	Renault Poinsot	Smiths
DIMENSIONS			
Wheelbase	110 in/2794 mm	105·6 in/2680 mm	107 in/2718 mm
Track	69-70·5 in/1753 - 1791 mm front / 63·25 in/1607 mm rear	71·6 in/1820 mm front / 65·6 in/1667 mm rear	73 in/1854 mm front / 65 in/1651 mm rear
Gearbox weight	–	–	110 lb/50 kg
Chassis weight (tub)	77 lb/169·8 kg	–	76 lb/34·5 kg
Formula weight	1191 lb/540 kg	1191 lb/540 kg	1232 lb/559 kg
Fuel capacity	48 gall/218·5 litres	48·4 gall/220 litres	48·4 gall/220 litres
Fuel consumption	4·5 mpg/63 litres/100 km	–	4·2 - 4·5 mpg/63 - 67 litres/100 km

RAM 02

Renault RE50

Spirit 101

	Toleman TG183B-Hart	Toleman TG184-Hart	Tyrrell 012-Cosworth
Sponsor(s)	Magirus/Segafredo	Magirus/Segafredo/Candy	Systime
Designer(s)	Rory Byrne/John Gentry	Rory Byrne/John Gentry	Maurice Phillippe/Brian Lisles
Team Manager(s)	Peter Gethin	Peter Gethin	Ken Tyrrell
Chief Mechanic(s)	John Mardle	John Mardle	Roger Hill
No of chassis built	5	5	6
ENGINE			
Type	Hart 415T	Hart 415T	Ford-Cosworth DFY
Fuel and oil	AGIP	AGIP	Various
Sparking plugs	Champion	Champion	Champion
TRANSMISSION			
Gearbox/speeds	Toleman/Hewland (5)	Toleman/Hewland	Tyrrell/Hewland (5/6)
Drive-shafts	Toleman	Toleman	Tyrrell
Clutch	Borg & Beck	Borg & Beck	Borg & Beck
CHASSIS			
Front suspension	Upper and lower wishbones, tension link operated inboard springs	Upper and lower wishbones, tension link operated inboard springs	Pull rod, upper and lower wishbones
Rear suspension	Upper and lower wishbones, tension link operated inboard springs	Upper and lower wishbones, compression link/bellcrank operated inboard springs	Pull rod, upper and lower wishbones,
Suspension dampers	Koni	Koni	Koni
Wheel diameter	13 in front / 13 in rear	13 in front / 13 in rear	13 in front / 13 in rear
Wheel rim widths	11·5 in front / 17 in rear	11·8 in front / 16·25 in rear	11·5 in front / 16·5 in rear
Tyres	Pirelli	Michelin	Goodyear
Brakes	Lockheed	Brembo	Lockheed
Brake pads	Ferodo	Ferodo	Ferodo
Steering	Toleman/Knight	Toleman/Knight	Tyrrell
Radiator(s)	Behr	Behr	Serck/Setrab
Fuel tank	Marston	Marston	ATL
Battery	Saft	Saft	Radio Spares
Instruments	Smiths	Smiths	Smiths/Contactless
DIMENSIONS			
Wheelbase	106 in/2692 mm	106 in/2692 mm	104 in/2642 mm
Track	72·25 in/1835 mm front / 66·25 mm/1683 mm rear	71·50 in/1816 mm front / 66·25 in/1683 mm rear	65 in/1651 mm front / 58 in/1473 mm rear
Gearbox weight	110 lbs/50 kg	110 lbs/50 kg	112 lb/51 kg
Chassis weight (tub)	74 lbs/33·6 kg	65 lbs/29·5 kg	65 lb/29·5 kg
Formula weight	1190 lbs/540 kg	1190 lbs/540 kg	1191 lb/540 kg
Fuel capacity	48·3 gall/220 litres	48·3 gall/220 litres	39 gall/177 litres
Fuel consumption	3·8-4·2 mpg/67-74 litres/100 km	3·8-4·2 mpg/67-74 litres/100 km	5-6 mpg/47·57 litres/100 km

Toleman TG183B

Toleman TG184

Tyrrell 012

ENGINEERED
FOR
SUCCESS

Withstanding the formidable stress and strain generated by Grand Prix racing engines is a challenge that Vandervell bearings have met, and won, race upon race, year upon year.

With vastly superior fatigue and corrosion resistance, and excellent lubricity in all conditions, they perform in a way no other bearing can match.

Quite simply, they're engineered for success.

Vandervell

At the heart of every good engine

Available from:

  Advance Motor Supplies **Replacement Services** **GKN Autoparts**

Formula 1 car specifications

**Williams FW09-
Honda**

Sponsor(s)	ICI/Mobil/Goodyear/Saudia
Designer(s)	Patrick Head
Team Manager(s)	Frank Williams/Peter Collins
	Alan Challis
Chief Mechanic(s)	
No of chassis built	–
ENGINE	
Type	Honda RA163-E
Fuel and oil	Mobil
Sparking plugs	NGK
TRANSMISSION	
Gearbox/speeds	Williams/Hewland (6)
Drive-shafts	Williams
Clutch	AP
CHASSIS	
Front suspension	Upper & lower wishbones,
	pull rods,
	inboard spring/dampers
Rear suspension	Top rocker arms,
	lower wishbones,
	inboard spring/dampers
Suspension dampers	Koni
Wheel diameter	13 in front
	13 in rear
Wheel rim widths	11·75 in front
	16·5 in rear
Tyres	Goodyear
Brakes	AP/SEP
Brake pads	Ferodo/SEP
Steering	Rack & pinion
Radiator(s)	Behr
Fuel tank	ATL
Battery	Panasonic
Instruments	–
DIMENSIONS	
Wheelbase	105 in/2667 mm (FW09)
	110 in/2794 mm (FW09B)
Track	71 in/1803 mm front
	66 in/1676 mm rear
Gearbox weight	–
Chassis weight (tub)	–
Formula weight	1191 lb/540 kg
Fuel capacity	48·3 gall/220 litres
Fuel consumption	–

Williams FW09B

40

One day you
with a roof o

ll settle down
er your head.

Golf GTi.

Efficiency and chips

Technical Review by Doug Nye

Ending this section last year I asked which of the 1500cc turbo engines might become King, now that the old King Cosworth was dead? During 1983 the 3-litre Formula 1 engine had won only two of the year's 15 World Championship GPs, and by the end of the season it was obviously outgunned, out-moded and obsolete. Only the Tyrrell team was unable to find a replacement turbo engine for '84 and so they became the last refuge of the legendary 'Cossy', until they were so controversially bundled-out of Formula 1 and the 3-litre atmospherically-aspirated Formula 1 engine went with them . . .

Before their ejection, Tyrrell failed to qualify for only one race, the Austrian GP at Österreichring on August 19, and so it became the first *Grand Épreuve* to be run without 'unsupercharged' participation since the Italian GP, at Monza, on September 11 . . . 1938!

Forty-five years and 363 days later, on September 9, 1984, the Italian GP was again run at Monza as an all-supercharged race – and this time there wasn't even a single unblown engine running round in practice.

It was the end of an era.

McLaren utterly dominated the season's results with their Porsche-produced TAG Turbo V6 engine, but Brabham-BMW ran them hard. Ferrari won a race, as did Williams-Honda, but both had awful problems for much of the year. Lotus made better use of the Renault engine than Renault themselves, but neither managed to win a race. Toleman used their Hart engines to great effect once they put their cars on sensible tyres and a classical rising-star driver in the cockpit.

Now that annual rule changes are the norm in Formula 1, each year poses new problems. During 1983 engineers had struggled to make the most of flat-bottom legislation banning ground-effect aerodynamic devices within the wheelbase. Through that year the 250-litre, 55-Imperial gallon, race fuel allowance had posed no great problem and standard strategy included mid-race refuelling stops to change soft and sticky quick-lap tyres.

But for 1984, as pre-arranged, race fuel allowance fell to only 220 litres, 48.4 Imperial gallons, and then at short notice in-race refuelling was banned on safety grounds.

This was a relief, as the teams considered themselves lucky to have got away without a major pit fire. But now many of them encountered major problems in combining competitive race power with race-distance fuel economy. Everyone packed as much liquid energy as possible into their 220 litres fuel volume by deep-chilling the fuel before filling the car. Petrol contracts by around one per cent for every 10 degrees C reduction in temperature. This means a gain of an extra 2.2 litres in 220 litres. By chilling the fuel 60 degs from around 10C right down to minus-50C, a gain of some six per cent is achieved, around 13.2 extra litres, or three more precious gallons . . . all contracted within that regulation 220-litre volume.

This was well worth the trouble, but of course it began to heat up and expand the instant it entered the car. Early in a race it became a toss-up between how rapidly the fuel expanded and how quickly the engine consumed it before those precious extra litres would gurgle away through the breather.

Occasionally a change in fuel wrought havoc amongst some of the high-stressed turbocharged engines, notably at Zolder where several TAG Turbos and 10 of Brabham's BMWs burned pistons and blew apart. Because of the fuel economy consideration there was pressure to run very lean mixtures to conserve fuel yet produce competitive power so it was vital to run a fuel closely matched to the management system electronic 'chip'. It's irrelevant how potent or poor that fuel might be as long as the chip is properly set-up for it and the same fuel is always used with that particular chip. If the fuel in the system isn't that for which the chip is chosen there's usually an expensive BANG! To be competitive everything must run to such fine margins.

Early in the season it still paid dividends to run a pit stop race, purely to change tyres. But as the season progressed so engine power increased and

the chassis developed and began to work their tyres harder. The soft pit stop rubber began to 'go off' in fewer laps than before. Drivers had to back-off to stabilise their tyres before being able to lean on it once more. Overall it was soon obvious that the pit stop strategy offered negligible advantage over a non-stop run on harder tyres. As one Chief Engineer put it "a scheduled pit stop is always a potential cock-up" and therefore the brief pit stop period in modern Formula 1 finally died away.

So it was a year in which engine management systems assumed great importance in promoting fuel-efficient performance. It was a year in which Michelin's well-developed radial race tyres proved generally superior to Goodyear's newly-adopted radials, though Goodyear offered good qualifiers on occasion. And in effect it was the year in which McLaren alone got everything just about right.

Their Porsche-built engine combined competitive power with reliability and fuel-efficiency, thanks largely to its super-expensive McLaren financed Bosch all-electronic management system. This capricious piece of chippery caused untold grief early on, but generously misbehaved more in test and practice sessions than in the races themselves. The latest McLaren MP4/2 carbon-fibre chassis housed its custom-built TAG Turbo engine in the best-integrated package in Formula 1, and it was brilliantly operated by the McLaren International team. Not only did they have the outstanding engine of the year in the best (if not an unmatched) chassis; they also had the services of the strongest driver pairing in the business, and it showed.

Then there was Luck. Any top-notch team on the crest of a wave will make its own luck and then is able to ride whatever good fortune comes along. McLaren certainly did that in Rio, Monaco and Österreichring, while elsewhere they won from supreme strength. Let's see how they and the other leading teams shaped-up in '84 . . .

McLaren

With a record number of wins in a Championship season and his first Formula 1 Constructors' World Championship title under his belt, McLaren Chief Engineer John Barnard faced the following winter rather glum; "There is a big feeling of 'How do I follow that?' ". Almost three years had passed since Ron Dennis made the first tentative approach to Porsche, and asked the right question.

Several other teams had asked them "Are you going to build a Formula 1 turbo engine which we could buy?" and the answer had always been "*Nein!*". Now Ron asked them "If I find the money to pay for it, could I commission you to build us a Formula 1 turbo engine?", and the answer to that was "*Jawohl!* It would be a pleasure, step right this way . . ." Mansour Ojjeh's TAG concern combined with McLaren International to form TAG Turbo Engines which paid for every Porsche pencil lead, and TTE-PO1 V6 nut, bolt and washer. The engine was designed and built to John Barnard's broad specification by Hans Mezger's compact engine group at Porsche's Weissach R&D centre. John is a *hard* taskmaster and he was a demanding customer for Porsche, and for Bosch whom they called in to produce the necessary management system. It seems initially to have been a rather prickly relationship but it was productive, with all concerned setting out to show the others just what they could do. It set out to be the ultimate no-compromise engine for ground-effects Formula 1, but the arbitrary ban flat-bottom ruling of November '82 shattered that vision. So this third-generation F1 turbo in fact emerged with some compromises built-in, but they detracted little from its effectiveness.

Since McLaren commissioned the engine for their exclusive use it is idle to speculate how well another team might have performed with it. Yet McLaren's detractors dismiss their MP4/2 chassis and team capability and credit their superb season totally to Porsche's engine. Equally, the few Porsche detractors give all credit to McLaren. Of course the truth lies somewhere in between and I am certain that neither one could have shone so brilliantly without the other. Anyone daft enough to dismiss the part played by McLaren's chassis

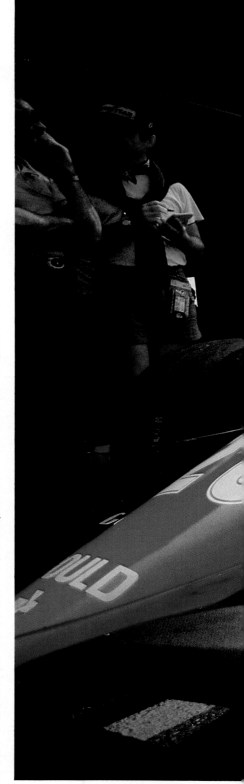

Ferrari's dominant performance in Belgium flattered to deceive, the team's search for traction and grip exacerbated by Goodyear's first season racing with radials.

44

Bernard Asset/Agence Vandystadt.

should study their last four races with Cosworth power in '83. That's right, they won the 'Cosworth class' every time, and their MP4/1 chassis was the class of the field.

The late Bruce McLaren built his cars well, built them early, and tested the bugs out of them long before their first race. Barnard works differently at McLaren International today. He likes to think through a new design and research it extensively, before building as late as possible to extend that thinking time. Because the basic thinking has been right his cars have so far worked "straight out of the box". This throws immense pressure on the workforce to build the cars late, quick and right, but it has paid off. Gordon Murray and Brabham often work in the same way. Five MP4/2 tubs were built during the year, the fifth being held in reserve, and MI's biggest problem all season was getting parts made on time.

The MP4/2 like its predecessors changed hardly

at all during a hard season's racing. They had a problem with heat from the exhaust exit under the upswept underbody diffuser behind the rear tyre line. "We ended-up running a metal-sided gearbox shroud which I hated," John admits, "before a proper heat-resistant carbon fibre shroud replaced it with the exhaust playing on to its outer surface. Otherwise the only bodywork change was in Austria when we introduced a complete new front-wing package . . ."

In itself that was the product of lengthy research in the wind tunnel and to tool-up the carbon fibre wing itself. "We looked at it every way to improve sensitivity and the ground-effect of the front wing and couldn't find any great improvement. I've got to be sure of improvement, not just make changes for effect, and the further you go the harder it gets to find real advance. The fall in lap times really is slowing down . . ."

The MP4/2 introduced a new rear suspension

package and John also took some of the MP4/1E interim turbo car compromises out of the chassis and put them into the engine. In the '1Es the twin KKK turbochargers were set at a shallow angle to the centreline to permit a smooth feed-in by the exhaust manifolds. In the '2 the rear body sides waisted-in more acutely at that point and to allow this he turned the turbos round at a sharper angle with the manifolds performing quite a sharp turn into them. On the '1E former-Cosworth chassis there had not been room for the TAG Turbo's bulky intercooler pipes to pass beneath the strap plates which link engine and monocoque, as specified in John's original requirement. On the '2 adequate space was drawn-in so the pipes tucked low within the required silhouette.

MI required around 15-20 complete race engines with some five-10 extra sets of parts available at any given time. The production engine spec was settled to replace the 10 or so development units of 1983. These production V6s were usefully lighter with titanium crankcase studs and cast magnesium inlet manifolds replacing the original bolt-together machined-block type used to study different shapes on the prototype units. The new race cars tested at Ricard for only three days prior to the Rio trip. Their electronics behaved and throttle response was better, if not ideal. Prost remembered Renault throttle response affectionately all season . . .

The hard-pressed, basically Cosworth-car transmission took a savage beating from turbo power and its oiling system was completely revised for '84. McLaren played with differentials, introducing "some cleverness" at Monaco and using it thereafter. They commissioned KKK to make some lightweight turbo casings with tighter internal clearances which made their debut at Monaco. On a good day they could see a small improvement. New front uprights and other mods were tested but showed no conclusive advantage. Over the bumps at Dallas both cars broke their front anti-roll bars so John had to re-stress the design, running interim arms while the lightweight titanium replacements were delayed in manufacture. Big change in Holland was "the new big hole" for the turbo inlet in the cars' hips, while brake cooling occupied their thoughts all season. Since '83 their experience in operating carbon fibre brakes had grown rapidly and throughout '84 they ran their own carefully-cooled SEP type exclusively both in practice and the race, despite problems notably at Imola where Prost spun and at Monaco where he *just* managed not to.

In Austria where the little Frenchman spun off and reported he had been holding-in fourth gear, gearbox-strip down suggested that only fifth had been held-in with any force. His inability to restart his undamaged car there was agonising. The McLarens are unusual in still carrying onboard starters with ring-gear teeth on the engine flywheel – the detail starter motor installation being elegant in the extreme, designed into a crankcase tunnel in the engine. But a hot turbo needs more of a churn to restart it than a hot Cosworth and the old aluminium air-bottle has insufficient capacity, while an aluminium one big enough to restart the TAG Turbo would be very heavy, so Hercules who mould the McLaren tubs spun-up some double-capacity half-weight pressure vessels in carbon fibre. They were on Barnard's desk as Prost abandoned his silent car on the Österreichring verge. They hadn't been fitted, because they leaked air . . .

Through the season the team suffered considerable engine problems but they were normally confined to testing or practice periods. The TTE-PO1 was dogged by mysterious water loss, Bosch's electrickery was eventually brought under control, while most engine breakages were traced to apparent burn-down failures, torching down the side of a piston after initial valve-gear problems in the late '83 GPs. It was sad to see Porsche's house magazine pretending there had never been an F1 mechanical failure. This was worse than untrue, it was utterly unworthy.

But winning is the name of the game, and Hans Mezger's men at Porsche did a superb job in this respect, as did Barnard and his race engineers Steve Nichols and Alan Jenkins and the rest of the team. The one major chassis problem seems to have been Prost's front wheel working loose at Dijon . . . otherwise by Formula 1 standards McLaren International must earn ten-plus for an historic season. The question their opposition must ask now is "Where do they go from here . . .?" – and after a year of such effort the easiest way is down. McLaren know that . . .

BRABHAM

"Well, 1984 has been a disaster for Brabham results, worse really than when we were using Alfa Romeo engines, but on the other hand though exasperating it's been quite satisfying from the performance point of view. It's always satisfying to see your car on pole and leading races against such serious opposition . . ."

Gordon Murray takes a philosophical view of the season for Brabham-BMW, in which Nelson Piquet's BT53 was quicker than the McLarens more often than they were quicker than it. In effect Brabham-BMW and McLaren-TAG Turbo Porsche formed the A-team of '84, with everyone else in Class B and Team Lotus normally heading them home as Renault, Ferrari and Williams suffered such troubles.

It was the pattern of their own failures which so frustrated Brabham and BMW. "Normally, if you start a new year with a problem," Gordon considers, ". . . you must write-off two races before you sort it out. But as we've sorted-out one problem something else has gone wrong and there's been incredible inconsistency in our problems . . ."

According to BMW, main work for '84 involved Paul Rosche's department in optimising fuel efficiency while maintaining or improving power output for Brabham's 25-engine pool. Brabham are their development partner and take latest-specification engines but run the risk of their failure. Arrows and ATS paid a fixed sum for their engines – 16 and eight respectively – and had to accept a settled, less potent "and safer" standard. BMW came to see Arrows as "a very professional partner" and were very happy with the team's efforts, but ATS proved bitterly disappointing and their deal was terminated at the end of the year.

BMW use Bosch/BMW electro-mechanical management developed in conjunction with a different Bosch department from that involved with Porsche and TAG Turbo. The TAG V6 ran around 750bhp in race-tune, and BMW claimed that their M12/13 4-cylinder was racing with around 650 bhp at the end of '83, rising to 770 bhp at the end of '84, with 850 in qualifying. Brabham generally pay more attention than other teams to qualifying specials as their record shows. Great attention was paid to quality control but they still had that early spate of turbocharger failures. These abated for the mid-season North American trip when the BT53's weight distribution changed with

continued on page 48

A perfect blend. Niki Lauda made the most of Hans Mezger's excellent work with the TAG-Porsche engine.

SAMSON. GUARANTEED TO FLATTEN OTHER BATTERIES.

UNIPART

No topping up
Kein Nachsüllen
Pas de re-remplissage

SAMSON

Unlimited
Guarantee
For as long as you own your car

Samson is made to the toughest possible specifications.

So tough we guarantee it for as long as you own your car – no matter how long you own it.

So if you keep your car for 3, 5, 10 or even 20 years, you'll never have to buy another battery.

And if you think that's amazing, here's something to really knock out the competition: Samson costs no more than other premium batteries:

Where else, but out in front.

the relocation of 'hot elements' which put the oil cooler in a nose duct. Back at Brands Hatch, another turbo failure. Gordon: "We barely repeated the same failure twice, this was the frustrating thing, we had bearings go, seals go, bad welding, wrong fuel, timing problems, an overheating turbo . . . At Zolder that fuel batch blew ten engines, pistons would collapse, detonation problems . . . BMW developed a lot on power and tried hard on reliability with different compressors and turbines, waste-gates too, while Nelson was just superb. This was his best year yet but we couldn't give him a worthy car. Austria looks like his only mistake, when he rolled-off six secs a lap when he could have caught Niki easily if he'd kept trying. He had just about the same rear rubber left as Niki, but we'd missed seeing Niki was in trouble on the TV due to lap-charting, so we couldn't help Nelson by telling him . . . we didn't know."

Six new 220-litre tanked Brabham BT53 tubs were built, little-changed except in detail from the successful pit stop tanked BT52, still essentially aluminium with rather more carbon fibre insert. They carried new-style side pods and underwings and through the early season a series of changes were made to improve cooling, BMW attributing some of their turbo troubles to running them too hot in the new car layout. In mid-season Gordon's modified BT53B for Brands Hatch promised much in the wind tunnel "but was a disaster at Brands because although it handled well we couldn't get any tyre temperature". Although the B-spec car overall was shelved its underwing and rear suspension mods were retained.

Non-engine failures included the pinion-bearing collapse which sidelined Piquet at Hockenheim and an oil union coming undone at Zandvoort. At Monza a radiator punctured, possibly when Piquet ran over a kerb early on.

Generally the BT52-originated Brabham turbo-car gearbox proved man enough for the job, having been strengthened further in some areas, using mainly Brabham parts, very few Hewland components and a few from Weissmann. Brabham have used carbon fibre brakes (by Hitco) longer than any other team. Winter developments were made to cool them better, but at Detroit and Zolder they ran iron brakes to be absolutely safe when the carbon fibre type looked marginal. Like McLaren, Brabham found their Michelin tyres very good and consistent, with excellent quality control. Goodyear's decision to go radial put them instantly 'in a catch-up situation' and whereas in previous years Goodyear's qualifiers had normally been well ahead of Michelin's, in '84 this was true on only a few occasions, but the French company's development slowed towards the end of the year and their abrupt withdrawal from Formula 1 was not totally unexpected, although their teams received little prior notice. Still Brabham signed with Pirelli for '85 after the Italian GP and before Michelin's announcement; it pays to keep one's ear to the ground . . .

The pattern of BMW engine reliability with one problem being corrected and another instantly taking its place lends credence to suspicion that the in-line 4-cylinder is near the end of its development. BMW and Brabham disagree, admitting some areas might be in trouble and near the end of their development life, "but not overall". Essentially a stock block engine will always be a compromise, but what a fine compromise Bee-Emm have produced regardless of its future.

WILLIAMS

The Williams deal with Honda was made initially in the winter of 1982-83 for a development car but it fell apart as Honda waited to see how the Spirit F1 venture would evolve. In mid-summer '83 Williams got the go ahead and Patrick Head initiated design of the FW09-Honda car to be tested at Donington prior to the Italian GP. There was at that time no intention to race it in '83, but at Monza Patrick remarked to Frank Williams that if they were to challenge seriously for the Championship in '84 they ought to throw themselves in at the deep end with one car, maybe two, for South Africa at the end of the current season. They rang home base at Didcot and sent a telex immediately to Honda asking if they could sanction the entry and supply engines. Mr Kawamoto, Chief Executive Honda R&D Wako, said yes, but typically it took a little time. Meanwhile Williams Grand Prix Engineering had taken a flyer and begun work on the cars. First time out with '09 both Rosberg and Laffite remarked how well the car handled, how much better than the Cosworth-engined '08s. But initially there was insufficient intercooling capacity on the car so in South Africa they could not run as much boost as they would have liked.

In November WGPE moved into their stunning new factory picturesquely situated under the cooling towers of Didcot power station. The FW08 was a well-understood quantity and Patrick's engineers set about making certain areas of '09 stiffer still. They did a complete new gearbox design with pullrod rear suspension in search of reliability, lighter weight and better traction. In initial testing the car looked quite good but back in South Africa, though quick, the car displayed the dominant understeer which would dog its season. In Rio this understeer caused steam to issue from Rosberg's ears and WGPE didn't have the option to revert to the old set-up because bits were not available. So the pullrod car ran unhappily up to Dijon. The new gearbox gave trouble due to a cutting problem with the crownwheel-and-pinion and Patrick now wanted to adopt a waisted-in planform *à la* McLaren which offered a useful download advantage without additional drag. This layout demanded a rocker-arm rear suspension which the new gearbox could not accept. Therefore the tailor-made FW09 'box was shelved and replaced by the old FW08, basically-Hewland FGB, transaxle with rocker-arm rear end and the cars ran in this form from Monaco.

An FW09B test car was run with the new bobbed-in tail at Brands Hatch prior to the mid-season North American trip. One such car ran in Canada but it suffered an engine problem related to the revised exhaust system, so was hastily converted back to original form. There wasn't enough room to squeeze everything in. The definitive FW09B emerged thereafter with a 5-inch longer wheelbase, long rear adaptor, new exhaust system, altered body and side panels, FGB gearbox and FW08-like wider track rocker arm rear suspension. The cars ran essentially in this form for the rest of the year, while a new FW10 went on to the drawing boards for '85.

The dreaded understeer was present in varying degree all season. Some appeared to be in the Goodyear tyres, other teams suffering to a lesser extent on the same rubber. But the normal method of killing understeer is to increase rear roll-stiffness, decrease it at the front and, if on fast corners, to increase front download relative to the rear. But whereas Williams cars and most others used to be sensitive to spring and bar changes, on the new-generation radial-ply Goodyears these changes had little effect. On fast circuits where the car's behaviour can be dominated by aerodynamic loading the FW09s' understeer could be diminished in this way, but it was accompanied by "a diabolical effect on the traction which goes all to pot!"

This grievous situation was made worse by the Honda engine's vicious power characteristics in which the power came in with a stupendous BANG at a certain point in the rev range. The drivers complained continually of wrestling the car in an understeering but stable slide until the engine suddenly burst into life, and in a split-second the rear wheels would be spinning, tail out and the steering wheel a blurr to catch it all . . .

The Honda V6 engine is an untidy-looking unit compared to the similarly 80-degree V6 TAG Turbo and intensive further development is under way, not least I suspect to improve its behaviour as a structural part of the car. Some criticised WGPE for having a flexible chassis by modern standards, because it's silver, not black – ie. aluminium honeycomb, not carbon fibre. But like Gordon Murray, Patrick Head doesn't feel comfortable with carbon fibre's reaction to crash impact, the '09 tubs were very rigid and FW10 will be aluminium again, with carbon inserts . . . With Honda R&D also hard at work fortunes must improve.

FERRARI

This most charismatic of all Formula 1 teams has the people, the money and the equipment to win every motor race they enter. If they are narrowly beaten but finish regularly in the points, it's because they are doing something wrong technically. If they are lapped and slow and uncompetitive then something else is awfully wrong within the organisation, and 1984 looked like the year in which the late-season decline of '83 became endemic and called for radical change.

The new year's 126C4 cars were effectively revised 1983 'C3s. The bottom of the 'C4 carbon-fibre tub was identical to the 'C3, the upper section slightly different, they went together in a different way and were a little stiffer. Ferrari claimed to have trimmed 10 per cent off the engine weight, eight per cent off the gearbox, a redesign allowing a small reduction in centre of gravity height which is a fine old traditional route towards improved handling and traction, but which involves so much time and trouble that a modern aerodynamic package could easily do better, quicker. Nine 'C4s were built, the team taking four to most races, but only seven were used, the eighth being complete ready for build-up just prior to Nürburgring and the ninth was then fresh out of the tooling but not bonded together. The cars could not make best use of admittedly problematic Goodyear tyres for much of the year, though in one area – Brembo brakes – they excelled.

An early arrow-head shape was tried with the radiators upright and angled back but this contributed to early Marelli-Weber injection problems as they discharged hot air against the tub and boiled the fuel! Measures were then taken to cool the fuel before alternative aerodynamic solutions were adopted. Possibly the worst thing for Ferrari was their win at Zolder, where the 'C4s were as good as they could be, the drivers well charged-up, the Goodyear tyres were excellent on the hot, grippy surface and that rogue fuel batch decimated their opposition. The troublesome electronic ignition had been replaced by a Lucas-Ferrari mechanical system and the win made Ferrari's day, they were back on top again. And then they slipped into the abyss.

Their pre-season figures of 660bhp in race tune, compared to 625 in '83 make poor reading now against the German claims. If these figures are true, Ferrari were beaten before they started but I doubt if the figures represent actuality. Just pre-British GP crisis management prevailed at Maranello. At Brands two of their four 'C4s – '075' and '076' – were revised with differently-mounted radiators and intercoolers in reshaped top-vented sidepods. Pushrod suspension replaced pullrod as development progressed. In Austria these 126C4/M cars – M standing for *Modificato*, modified – tried a 13cm (5.1-inch) wheelbase stretch with altered underwing, but if run in anything other than high-download configuration just did not perform. At Monza, '075' had been testing a side-vented body. A similar 'K4' solution was tried at the Österreichring, but abandoned. At Monza the Ferraris were out-qualified by *green* Alfa Romeos which must have stung, but salvaged a fortuitous second place. Two McLaren-like waisted-in 'C4/M2s made their debut there on chassis '072' and '074', but '/M1s '076' and '077' raced. The 'M2s ran more effectively in the last two races.

Mauro Forghieri and Dr Harvey Postlethwaite seemed to work well together. Harvey had been splitting his time between Formula 1 and road car development but was back 100 per cent on Formula 1 by the year's end. Newcomer *Ing.* Ranzetti joined Tomaini's race team since, for the second time in his long career, Forghieri was seconded to the *Reparto URSA – Ufficio Ricerche Studi Avanzati* – to develop long-term projects.

This poor year was one for Ferrari to recoup, learn and plan for '85, but nothing would suit Ferrari better than a change in Formula, and talk of new 1200cc regulations makes brown eyes positively gleam . . . They will be back.

continued on page 52

1984 saw the total domination of Formula One racing by cars shod on Michelin. To such an extent that Marlboro McLaren won the World Constructors' Championships and Niki Lauda became World Champion driver. It's something very few would have predicted back in 1977. The year that Michelin Formula One radials made their debut on a lone, experimental Renault Turbo at the British Grand Prix.

But by 1979 the shape of things to come was made apparent when Jody Sheckter drove a Michelin equipped Ferrari and gained the World Championship.

Success then followed success to give us our world-beating performance of today.

However, to develop radial-tyre technology even further, we're going to concentrate on the international rally and motorcycle circuits. And if the results we've achieved so far are any indication, we already have the winning formula.

MICHELIN

Formula Won.

ALL YOU NEE
AND A LITTLE S

At times we've all felt the urge to drive faster than we should.

But the owner of a Manta GT/E needs to resist the temptation all the more.

The fuel injected cam-in-head engine can take you from 0-60 in just 8.9 seconds.

Then it can go on to reach a maximum of 120 miles per hour.

And as for handling, both the front and rear suspension are as finely tuned as the engine.

The GT/E boasts uprated front and rear springs controlled by gas filled shock absorbers.

And the 195/60HR ultra low profile tyres on 6Jx14 alloys give an iron grip on the road.

(Perfect for rallying you may think, and we'd have to agree. After all, the GT/E is derived from

D IS £7,000
ELF CONTROL.

the World Rally Championship Manta 400).

Distinctive styling makes the Manta look even meaner than the price.

Colour keyed front and rear spoilers match the flared door sills, which blend into the rear wheel arches.

And inside Recaro front seats hug your body to give greater support for faster cornering.

Manta prices start at a mere £6,260 for the GT, £7,061 for the Coupé you see above and £7,282 for the GT/E Hatchback. Tempting isn't it?

OPEL MANTA GT/E.
Better. By Design.

GOING TO PRESS, INCLUDE CAR TAX AND VAT. DELIVERY AND NUMBER PLATES ARE EXTRA.

RENAULT

Renault Sport chassis designer Michel Tetu's new RE50 carbon-Kevlar chassis was ready early for '84 and was thoroughly tested by Derek Warwick and Patrick Tambay pre-season. After reservations about KKK turbochargers in '83, Renault's engine division head Bernard Dudot adopted large American Garrett AiResearch turbos for the new year. The new tubs were moulded by the Hurel-Dubois aviation company at Vélizy, near Matra's premises, while plans were laid for a springtime split in Renault Sport's factories. This would leave Dudot's engine plant with its 100 employees occupying all the original building at Viry-Chatillon, while Jean Sage took his chassis, gearbox and race 'shop with his 70-odd staff down the road to new premises at Evry.

Dudot and his predecessor François Castaing – originator of the Renault EF1 turbo V6 – had modified the old engine considerably since its F1 debut in 1977. Most major structural change had been Dudot's new light-alloy block which replaced the original cast-iron type without great fanfare in '83. Initially these alloy blocks had some flexing problems but this was corrected though costs soared as alloy blocks are now changed at least twice a year whereas the old cast-iron type ran for ever. The latest EF4 engine added redesigned heads for '84.

Reviewing the '84 season popular Team Manager Jean Sage admitted to some despondency: "after a good start when Derek nearly won at Rio. But we 'ad a mixture of technical problems and bad luck. Main problem was fuel consumption, specially at Imola, but we did a lot of work with the management system" – which is Renault-made combining Marelli-Weber injection with Renix (Renault electronics) management "and by the end of the season we could run race distance without turning down the turbo pressure. Porsche simply had more experience in fuel-efficient racing than we did, through their Group C programme."

Early in the Rio race Warwick's RE50 had been struck by Lauda's McLaren and bent a wishbone. This broke near the end, wrecking his chances. Stronger wishbones were adopted after that experience but, at Dijon and in the first-corner collision at Monaco involving the two RE50s, they proved so strong that shock loads were transmitted direct into the carbon fibre tub and punched the pick-ups straight into the cockpit area, injuring Patrick Tambay's leg, which should not have happened . . . Thereafter the tub pick-ups were reinforced to match the strengthened wishbones, adding a little more weight and RE50/08 introduced a redesigned carbon tub without Kevlar composite from Brands Hatch.

As the revised engines gave competitive power so Renault, like McLaren and Lotus, found they were carrying eggs transmission-wise. Their Renault-cased transaxle contains a mixture of Hewland and Renault internals but, since it originated as a Hewland TL200 it was distinctly 'marginal' by the year's end.

Intensive SEP-Renault carbon fibre brake tests continued all season but they were not raced until Monza after management leaned on the drivers who had been wary of their lack of progressive feel and tendency to lock, but both quite liked them in the race. Revised high-compression engines proved strong there.

Overall the team felt that as an organisation they had not achieved their potential. Warwick started the year well but fell away a little, perhaps his heavy crash at Dijon not helping, while Tambay came to impress too late in the year.

Engines were supplied to Team Lotus and Ligier as client teams, Lotus shone while Ligier proved a sad disappointment, their JS23 car regularly running the engine 50-degrees C too hot so compromising its performance until a replacement car layout appeared at the Nürburgring. Sage enjoyed the Lotus link; "It really drove us on, we 'ad to make great effort to give them good engines and it was always great competition not to be behind the Lotus. I liked it. The engineers didn't. We were beaten by them often in qualifying, not so often in the races, but for too long we could not run competitive power and achieve the fuel economy to survive the race against McLaren and Brabham . . ."

Really the great French team is forced to fight its war with one hand tied behind its back, for French labour laws and social requirements force them to be very rigid with working hours, overtime and weekend working. Even with enthusiastic union support they can never enjoy the 24-hour a day, seven days a week workforce commitment and flexibility of the best British teams and it affects their speed of response and the pace at which much-needed mods can be made. Neither are there the myriad quick-reacting small specialist subcontractors in France which play such a major part in the British teams' success. Nothing is easy in Formula 1 but this factor is very significant – it's a lot harder for the French.

LOTUS

Wonderful to see the Ketteringham team back in contention. After his mid-season '83 expedient Lotus 94T based on existing carbon-composite tubs, Team Lotus' new French Chief Engineer Gerard Ducarouge produced the Type 95T-Renault for '84 and it proved arguably the best-handling Formula 1 chassis *per se* of the year, bar none. Colin Chapman and Team Manager Peter Warr had been impressed by Ducarouge's approach to running the technical side of a racing team back in the early '70s at Matra's Ricard HQ. Some Matra practises were adopted then by Lotus while Ducarouge went to Ligier, then Alfa Romeo. Shortly before his death, Colin tried to lure Ducarouge to Lotus but it was not until after Colin had died that Gerard joined them, post-Spa '83. He brought an intensely methodical and correct way of working to Team, quite different from Chapman's mercurial approach with its flashes of glittering inspiration, while Team gave Ducarouge an immense human resource free of political pressures and imbued with the Chapman tradition that Nothing but Nothing is impossible.

So the 95Ts appeared early for '84 and instantly worked well. Ducarouge set down the spec and Team did not mess with it. Four cars were built, only one was lightly damaged underneath by hitting a kerb. All carbon-composite Lotus tubs have been made by the same six-man team in the Ketteringham carbon 'shop. Apparently they have made 17 since 1981 and not one has been destroyed. With the 95Ts there was a slow-speed aerodynamic package and a high-speed aerodynamic package and they were effectively the only changes made all year. The philosophy was "put it together and set it up the way it should be, and it will deliver", and it did. Unfortunately the car made more of its drivers than they made of it.

Goodyear gave Team terrific commitment in tyre development as Ferrari and Williams lost time, but their race tyres could never provide the consistent race grip of Michelin, so the Lotuses could not compete, due partly to tyres and partly to Renault's fuel-efficiency handicap. They completed more than a week's intensive testing pre-season and, even by the time of the British GP, had totalled some 26 days running at race meetings, and no less than 41 days testing. Renault service was outstanding, Peter Warr reports ". . . we never lacked a nut, bolt, hose or jubilee clip" and resident Renault engineer Bruno Mauduit had a super time with his cars out-performing Renault Sport's! As early as Rio '83 some of Team's engines had used alloy blocks, and they have had 7-10 engines available at any time. Team Lotus, Ligier and Renault Sport all drew on the same engine pool, so one week's factory engine could appear in a Lotus the following week and in a Ligier the week after that. While latest mods would be proven on one works car it was agreed that they should become available to the clients as soon as they went on to the second works RE50.

Team did not achieve the results they really deserved: "Elio could have won Rio but had a misfire due to the electronics, Nigel could have won Monaco but made an error, at Detroit we had a gearbox failure when Elio was catching up at a second a lap, at Dallas we had more gearbox trouble and another driver error and then at Hockenheim Elio was just uncatchable before it broke. Elio enjoyed a very good relationship with Gerard and proved himself very mature, he didn't press on hard when it threatened to destroy his tyres and his finishing record was excellent because of that . . ."

After Dallas a crash programme began to build a new gearbox, while interim stronger gears were obtained from Italy in time for Brands. The new gearbox casing, new selection system and DGB instead of FGB-type internals were running in September tests at Nürburgring, while Renault had initiated a new gearbox programme of their own simultaneously after Dallas and their new 'box would not be seen until the new season; clear evidence of the "Nothing's impossible" syndrome, Lotus' advantage.

Lotus tested carbon fibre brakes all year, Mansell raced a set at Rio but fell off due more to brain-fade, and they were tried again right at the end of the year. Team did a superb job for Renault and signed with them for another three years, this commitment prompting Régie President Bernard Hanon to unlock the door to R&D in recognition.

Life may be hard in Formula 1, but even if you don't win, quality is recognised. The big problem now is how to make essentially a first-generation turbo engine competitive with a third-generation one . . .

THE AUTOCOURSE SERIES OF MARQUE HISTORIES

AUTOCOURSE has commissioned the foremost writers in the motorsport field to produce a series of detailed histories of the most famous and successful Formula 1 marques. The first two volumes of this exclusive collection are now available.

McLAREN: The Grand Prix, Can-Am and Indy Cars by Doug Nye

This is the full story of McLaren Cars from 1963 to 1980 and of the subsequent McLaren International team carrying on the old traditions: the cars, the races, the men behind the scenes, with comprehensive appendices covering race results and chassis numbers.
AVAILABLE NOW
20 colour photographs and over 90 black and white photographs
270 pages 240mm x 170mm Hardback
Price: £12.95

FERRARI: The Grand Prix Cars by Alan Henry

This volume takes the story of the most famous Italian racing marque of them all from its first hesitant steps onto the Grand Prix stage in the early post-war years, through to its World Constructors' Championship winning status in the highly specialised and complicated world of turbocharged Grand Prix engines in the 1980's.
AVAILABLE NOW
35 colour photographs and over 100 black and white photographs
320 pages 240mm x 170mm Hardback
Price: £14.95

**Third in the series and due for publication in Spring 1985,
BRABHAM: The Grand Prix cars by Alan Henry.**

Worldwide Distribution:

USA
Motorbooks International
PO Box 2
729 Prospect Avenue
Osceola
Wisconsin 54020
Tel: 715 294 3345
Tlx: 499 6285

NEW ZEALAND
David Bateman Ltd
PO Box 65062 Mairangi Bay
Auckland 10
Tel: 444-4680
Tlx: NZ 60824

AUSTRALIA
Technical Book & Magazine Co
289-299 Swanston Street
Melbourne
Victoria 3000
Tel: 663 3951
Tlx: AA 151120

UK & OTHER MARKETS
Osprey Publishing Ltd
12/14 Long Acre
London WC2E 9LP
Tel: 01-836 7863
Tlx: 21667

Winning combination: Johnny Dumfries and the Team BP Ralt-VW dominated the Marlboro British Formula 3 Championship and carried BP colours successfully into Europe.
Photo: Diana Burnett

During 1984, 35 drivers from 14 countries participated in the season's 16 Formula 1 races (there were no non-championship events). They were seen in 15 different makes of car powered by eight makes of engine. Twelve drivers took part in all 16 races. Elio de Angelis scored points 11 times, Niki Lauda and Alain Prost 10, René Arnoux nine and Michele Alboreto seven. Nelson Piquet won nine pole positions but scored points just five times. Lauda set the fastest lap on five occasions, Prost and Piquet on three (Piquet sharing one with Alboreto) and Arnoux recorded fastest lap twice.

1984 Formula 1 Drivers' Statistics

Driver	Nat	Date of Birth	Car	Rio de Janeiro	Kyalami	Zolder	Imola	Dijon	Monte Carlo	Montreal	Detroit	Dallas	Brands Hatch	Hockenheim	Österreichring	Zandvoort	Monza	Nürburgring	Estoril	World Championship Points	No. of Grands Prix started	1st	2nd	3rd	No. of Grand Prix pole positions
Michele Alboreto	I	23/12/56	Ferrari	R	11*	1	R	R	6	R	R	R	5	R	3	R	2	2	4	30½	57	3	2	2	1
Philippe Alliot	F	24/7/54	RAM-Hart	R	R	NQ	R	R	NQ	10	R	DNS	R	R	11	11	R	R	R	0	13	–	–	–	–
Elio de Angelis	I	26/3/58	Lotus-Renault	3	7	5	3*	5	5	4	2	3	4	R	R	4	R	R	5	34	88	1	2	3	2
René Arnoux	F	4/7/48	Ferrari	R	R	3	2	4	3	5	R	2	6	6	7	12*	R	5	9	27	95	7	9	6	18
Mauro Baldi	I	31/1/54	Spirit-Hart	R	8	R	8	R	NQ	–	–	–	–	–	–	–	8	15		0	33	–	–	–	–
Stefan Bellof**	D	20/11/57	Tyrrell-Cosworth	R	R	6	5	R	3	R	R	R	11	–	NQ	9	–	–	–	(5)	11	–	–	–	–
Gerhard Berger	A	27/8/59	ATS-BMW	–	–	–	–	–	–	–	–	–	–	–	12*	–	6	R	13	0	4	–	–	–	4
Thierry Boutsen	B	13/7/57	Arrows-Cosworth / Arrows-BMW	6	12	R	5		11	NQ	R	R	R	R	R	5	R	10	9	5	25	–	–	–	–
Martin Brundle**	GB	1/6/59	Tyrrell-Cosworth	5	11	R	11*	12	NQ	10	2	NQ	–	–	–	–	–	–	–	(8)	7	–	–	–	–
Johnny Cecotto	YV	25/1/56	Toleman-Hart	R	R	R	R	R	R	9	R	R	NQ	–	–	–	–	–	–	0	18	–	–	–	–
Andrea de Cesaris	I	31/5/59	Ligier-Renault	R	5	R	6*	10	R	R	R	R	10	7	R	R	R	7	12	3	62	–	2	1	1
Eddie Cheever	USA	10/1/58	Alfa Romeo	4	R	R	7*	R	NQ	11*	R	R	R	R	R	14*	9*	R	17	3	69	–	2	5	–
Corrado Fabi	I	12/4/61	Brabham-BMW	–	–	–	–	–	R	R	–	7	–	–	–	–	–	–	–	0	12	–	–	–	–
Teo Fabi	I	9/3/55	Brabham-BMW	R	R	R	R	9	–	–	3	–	R	R	4	5	R	R	–	9	19	–	–	1	–
Jo Gartner	A	24/1/53	Osella-Alfa Romeo	–	–	–	R	–	–	–	–	–	R	R	R	13	5	R	16*	0	8	–	–	–	–
Piercarlo Ghinzani	I	16/1/52	Osella-Alfa Romeo	R	DNS	R	NQ	12	7	R	R	5	9	R	R	R	7*	R	R	2	22	–	–	–	–
François Hesnault	F	30/12/56	Ligier-Renault	R	10	R	R	DNS	R	R	R	R	R	8	8	7	R	10	R	0	15	–	–	–	–
Stefan Johansson	S	8/9/56	Tyrrell-Cosworth** / Toleman-Hart	–	–	–	–	–	–	–	–	–	R	9	NQ	8	4	R	11	3	12	–	–	–	–
Jacques Laffite	F	21/11/43	Williams-Honda	R	R	R	R	8	8	R	5	4	R	R	R	R	R	R	14	5	152	6	8	13	7
Niki Lauda	A	22/2/49	McLaren-TAG	R	1	R	R	1	R	2	R	R	1	2	1	2	1	4	2	72	157	24	20	9	24
Nigel Mansell	GB	8/8/54	Lotus-Renault	R	R	R	R	3	R	6	R	6	R	4	R	3	R	R	R	13	59	–	–	5	1
Pierluigi Martini	I	23/4/61	Toleman-Hart	–	–	–	–	–	–	–	–	–	–	–	–	–	NQ	–	–	0	0	–	–	–	–
Jonathan Palmer	GB	7/11/56	RAM-Hart	8	R	10	9	13	NQ	–	R	DNS	R	R	9	10	R	R	R	0	15	–	–	–	–
Riccardo Patrese	I	17/4/54	Alfa Romeo	R	4	R	R	R	R	R	R	R	12*	R	10*	R	3	6	8	8	112	2	4	4	2
Nelson Piquet	BR	17/8/52	Brabham-BMW	R	R	9*	R	R	R	1	1·	R	7	R	2	R	R	3	R	29	94	12	8	7	17
Alain Prost	F	24/2/55	McLaren-TAG	1	2	R	1	7	1	3	4	R	R	1	R	1	R	1	1	71½	73	16	7	3	13
Keke Rosberg	SF	6/12/48	Williams-Honda	2	R	4*	R	6	4	R	R	1	R	R	R	9*	R	R	R	20½	81	3	5	3	2
Huub Rothengatter	NL	8/10/56	Spirit-Hart / Spirit-Cosworth	–	–	–	–	–	–	NC	NQ	R	NC	10	NC	R	8	–	–	0	7	–	–	–	–
Ayrton Senna	BR	21/3/60	Toleman-Hart	R	6	6	NQ	R	2	7	R	R	3	R	R	–	R	R	3	13	14	–	1	2	–
Philippe Streiff	F	26/6/55	Renault	–	–	–	–	–	–	–	–	–	–	–	–	–	–	–	R	0	1	–	–	–	–
Marc Surer	CH	18/9/51	Arrows-Cosworth / Arrows-BMW	7	9	8	R	R	NQ	R	R	R	11	R	6	R	R	R	R	1	65	–	–	–	–
Patrick Tambay	F	25/6/49	Renault	5*	R	7	R	2	R	W	R	R	8*	5	R	6	R	R	7	11	85	2	4	3	5
Mike Thackwell	NZ	30/3/61	RAM-Hart / Tyrrell-Cosworth**	–	–	–	–	–	–	R	–	–	–	NQ	–	–	–	–	–	0	2	–	–	–	–
Derek Warwick	GB	27/8/54	Renault	R	3	2	4	R	R	R	R	R	2	3	R	R	R	11*	R	23	43	–	2	2	–
Manfred Winkelhock	D	6/10/51	ATS-BMW / Brabham-BMW	DNS	R	R	R	R	R	8	R	8	R	R	DNS	R	DNS	–	10	0	39	–	–	–	–

* Retired but classified as a finisher.
DNS = Qualified, did not start.
NC = Running at finish, not classified.
NQ = Did not qualify.
R = Retired.
W = Entry withdrawn.
** Disqualified and points removed from championship table. Finishing positions of other drivers adjusted accordingly in races in question.

Grand Prix Super Grid

by John Taylor

By adding together the length of all 16 circuits used in this year's Grand Prix World Championship, we arrive at a circuit with a length of 45·838 miles/73·769 kms. If we then add together the best official practice times of each of the 18 drivers who achieved a qualifying time in each event, we arrive at a hypothetical grid for the season.

With 9 pole positions to his credit one would have expected Nelson Piquet to gain pole position with ease on the Super Grid. What we in fact find is that Alain Prost comes out on top. A quick glance over the practice times will show that although Piquet beat Prost on 11 occasions during practice, such was the gap when positions were reversed, that Prost achieves pole by 1·98s. Prost actually made second fastest time on 8 of the occasions that Piquet took the pole.

Nelson Piquet (Brabham BT53)
22m 19·382s, 123·203 mph/198·276 km/h

Alain Prost (McLaren MP4/2)
22m 17·402s, 123·386 mph/198·570 km/h

Derek Warwick (Renault RE50)
22m 30·614s, 122·179 mph/196·628 km/h

Elio de Angelis (Lotus 95T)
22m 29·463s, 122·283 mph/196·795 km/h

Niki Lauda (McLaren MP4/2)
22m 37·747s, 121·537 mph/195·594 km/h

Michele Alboreto (Ferrari 126 C4)
22m 36·881s, 121·614 mph/195·718 km/h

Keke Rosberg (Williams FW09/FW09B)
22m 41·108s, 121·237 mph/195·112 km/h

Nigel Mansell (Lotus 95T)
22m 38·074s, 121·508 mph/195·548 km/h

Eddie Cheever (Alfa Romeo 184T)
23m 01·487s, 119·448 mph/192·232 km/h

René Arnoux (Ferrari 126 C4)
22m 48·421s, 120·589 mph/194·069 km/h

Jacques Laffite (Williams FW09/FW09B)
23m 06·774s, 118·993 mph/191·500 km/h

Andrea de Cesaris (Ligier JS23/JS23B)
23m 01·798s, 119·422 mph/192·191 km/h

Thierry Boutsen (Arrows A6/A7)
23m 21·603s, 117·734 mph/189·474 km/h

Riccardo Patrese (Alfa Romeo 184T)
23m 06·953s, 118·978 mph/191·426 km/h

Marc Surer (Arrows A6/A7)
23m 32·732s, 116·807 mph/182·982 km/h

François Hesnault (Ligier JS23)
23m 24·405s, 117·499 mph/189·096 km/h

Philippe Alliot (RAM 01/02)
24m 12·750s, 113·589 mph/182·803 km/h

Piercarlo Ghinzani (Osella FA 1E/FA 1F)
23m 53·652s, 115·102 mph/185·238 km/h

Practice positions Prost/Piquet

Race	BR	ZA	B	SM	F	MC	CDN	DET	DAL	GB	D	A	NL	I	E	P
Prost	4	5	8	2	5	P	2	2	2	2	P	2	P	2	2	2
Piquet	7	P	9	P	3	P	9	P	P	12	P	5	P	P	P	P

Points per start average (Career)

Position	Name	Nationality	Starts	Points	1st	2nd	3rd	4th	5th	6th	Pole	F. Lap	Points Average
1	Alain Prost	F	73	210·5	16	7	3	3	2	4	13	10	2·884
2	Niki Lauda	A	157	406·5	24	20	9	6	6	5	24	23	2·589
3	Nelson Piquet	BR	94	215	12	8	7	7	4	2	17	13	2·287
4	René Arnoux	F	95	161	7	9	6	3	5	3	18	12	1·695
5	Jaques Laffite	F	152	198	6	8	13	7	8	6	7	5	1·303
6	Keke Rosberg	SF	82	97·5	3	5	3	5	7	1	2	–	1·189
7	Michele Alboreto	I	57	66·5	3	2	2	4	2	3	1	3	1·149
8	Patrick Tambay	F	85	90	2	4	3	6	6	6	5	2	1·059
9	Elio de Angelis	I	87	89	1	2	3	10	11	5	5	2	1·023
10	Ayrton Senna	BR	14	13	–	1	2	–	–	2	–	1	0·929
11	Derek Warwick	GB	43	32	–	2	2	3	1	1	–	1	0·744
12	Eddie Cheever	USA	69	50	–	2	5	3	3	3	–	–	0·725
13	Riccardo Patrese	I	110	73	2	4	4	2	2	5	2	4	0·664
14	Nigel Mansell	GB	59	38	–	–	5	4	–	5	1	1	0·644
15	Teo Fabi	I	19	9	–	–	1	1	1	–	–	–	0·474
16	Andrea de Cesaris	I	62	24	–	2	1	1	1	3	1	1	0·387
17=	Jo Gartner	A	8	2	–	–	–	–	1	–	–	–	0·250
17=	Gerhard Berger	A	4	1	–	–	–	–	–	1	–	–	0·250
17=	Stefan Johansson	S	12	3	–	–	–	1	–	–	–	–	0·250
20	Thierry Boutsen	B	25	5	–	–	–	–	2	1	–	–	0·200
21	Marc Surer	CH	64	12	–	–	–	1	2	5	–	1	0·188
22	Mauro Baldi	I	33	5	–	–	–	–	1	3	–	–	0·152
23	Piercarlo Ghinzani	I	22	2	–	–	–	–	–	1	–	–	0·091
24	Johnny Cecotto	YV	18	1	–	–	–	–	–	1	–	–	0·056

Points per start average (Season)

Position	Name	Nationality	Starts	Points	1st	2nd	3rd	4th	5th	6th	Pole	F. Lap	Points Average
1	Niki Lauda	A	16	72	5	4	–	1	–	–	–	5	4·500
2	Alain Prost	F	16	71·5	7	1	1	1	–	–	3	3	4·469
3	Elio de Angelis	I	16	34	–	1	3	3	4	–	1	1	2·125
4	Michele Alboreto	I	16	30·5	1	2	1	1	1	1	1	2	1·906
5	Nelson Piquet	BR	16	29	2	1	1	–	–	1	9	3	1·813
6	René Arnoux	F	16	27	–	2	2	1	2	2	–	1	1·688
7	Derek Warwick	GB	16	23	–	2	2	1	–	–	–	1	1·438
8	Keke Rosberg	SF	16	20·5	1	1	–	2	–	1	–	–	1·281
9	Ayrton Senna	BR	14	13	–	1	2	–	–	2	–	1	0·929
10	Nigel Mansell	GB	16	13	–	–	2	1	–	1	–	–	0·813
11	Teo Fabi	I	12	9	–	–	1	1	1	–	–	–	0·750
12	Patrick Tambay	F	15	11	–	1	–	1	–	2	1	1	0·734
13=	Riccardo Patrese	I	16	8	–	–	1	1	–	1	–	–	0·500
13=	Stefan Johansson	S	6	3	–	–	–	1	–	–	–	–	0·500
15	Thierry Boutsen	B	15	5	–	–	–	–	2	1	–	–	0·334
16	Jacques Laffite	F	16	5	–	–	–	–	1	1	–	–	0·313
17=	Jo Gartner	A	8	2	–	–	–	–	1	–	–	–	0·250
17=	Gerhard Berger	A	4	1	–	–	–	–	–	1	–	–	0·250
19	Eddie Cheever	USA	15	3	–	–	–	1	–	–	–	–	0·200
20	Andrea de Cesaris	I	16	3	–	–	–	–	1	1	–	–	0·188
21	Piercarlo Ghinzani	I	14	2	–	–	–	–	–	1	–	–	0·143
22	Marc Surer	CH	14	1	–	–	–	–	–	1	–	–	0·071

Laps led (Drivers)

Driver	Laps led	Miles (to nearest mile)	Kms (to nearest km)
Alain Prost	345 (34·47%)	978	1573
Nelson Piquet	241 (24·08%)	714	1149
Niki Lauda	168 (16·78%)	463	745
Michele Alboreto	81 (8·09%)	220	354
Patrick Tambay	74 (7·39%)	208	335
Nigel Mansell	40 (4·00%)	95	153
Keke Rosberg	33 (3·30%)	82	132
Derek Warwick	12 (1·20%)	38	60
Elio de Angelis	7 (0·70%)	30	48

Laps led (Manufacturers)

Manufacturer	Laps led	Miles (to nearest mile)	Kms (to nearest km)
McLaren	513 (51·25%)	1440	2317
Brabham	241 (24·08%)	714	1149
Renault	86 (8·59%)	246	396
Ferrari	81 (8·09%)	220	354
Lotus	47 (4·70%)	125	201
Williams	33 (3·30%)	82	132

Total laps/miles/kms in season 1001 laps/2826 miles/4548 kms

OUR HEAD START.

In the 1950s, NGK pioneered the copper core spark plug for production cars. And we've never made any other kind of plug.

NGK have also sparked the winners in Formula I and II, so it's hardly surprising that we have perfected the art of producing a plug that operates efficiently across all engine temperatures.

Conventional plugs, on the other hand, are classified into types that run at their best under either 'cold' or 'hot' temperatures and are more prone to fouling or overheating. Today, other manufacturers, at last realising the advantages of copper core plugs, are introducing them as premium 'specials'. But what is 'special' to them has been our 'standard' for 25 years. At today's motoring costs, can you afford to accept anything less than NGK's standards?

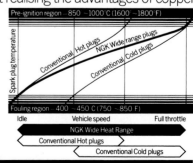

 **Copper Core Excellence.**

NGK Spark Plugs (UK) Ltd., 7/8 Garrick Industrial Centre, Hendon, London NW9 6AQ. Tel: 01-202 2151/4

A reflection of the supreme performance by McLaren in 1984 can be measured by the economy of their chassis production programme. Three cars were built at the beginning of the season and the same three were used throughout the year. A further chassis, intended originally for race work, was completed and used for test purposes while a fifth tub remained incomplete.

The MP4/2 McLaren was designed around lessons learned at the end of 1983. Most of the leading teams adopted similar principles at a time when the only major change required by the regulations was the inclusion of a fuel tank which conformed with the 220-litre capacity limit.

Listed below is the chassis record for 1984. As ever, we are indebted to the various team managers and mechanics who helped keep our records straight.

Alfa Romeo

Started the season with two new 184Ts and a 1983 183T.

183T
03 Spare car at Rio and Kyalami.

184T
01 New for Cheever at Rio. For Cheever at Kyalami. Spare car at Zolder, Imola, Dijon, Monaco and Montreal (raced by Patrese). For Patrese at Detroit and Dallas. Spare car at Brands Hatch.

02 New for Patrese at Rio. For Patrese at Kyalami, Zolder, Imola, Dijon, Monaco and Montreal (crashed during practice). Spare car at Detroit and Dallas. For Patrese at Brands Hatch, Hockenheim, Österreichring and Zandvoort. Spare car at Monza, Nürburgring and Estoril.

03 New for Cheever at Zolder. For Cheever at Imola, Dijon, Monaco, Montreal, Detroit, Dallas, Brands Hatch, Hockenheim, Österreichring, Zandvoort, Monza, Nürburgring and Estoril.

04 New; spare car at Hockenheim. Spare car at Österreichring and Zandvoort. For Patrese at Monza, Nürburgring and Estoril.

Arrows

Relied on modified A6 Cosworth cars while waiting for supply of BMW engines for A7.

A6
2 Spare car at Rio, Kyalami and Zolder. For Surer at Monaco, Montreal and Detroit (damaged in start-line accident. Written off).

4 For Surer at Rio, Kyalami and Zolder. For Boutsen at Imola and Dijon. Not seen again.

5 For Boutsen at Rio and Kyalami. Not seen again.

A7
1 Test car then spare car at Zolder. For Surer at Imola. Spare car at Dijon, Monaco, Montreal and Detroit. For Surer at Dallas, Brands Hatch, Hockenheim, Österreichring, Zandvoort, Monza and Nürburgring.

2 New for Boutsen at Zolder. Spare car at Imola. For Boutsen at Dijon, Monaco, Montreal, Detroit, Dallas, Brands Hatch, Hockenheim, Österreichring and Zandvoort (damaged during race).

3 At Brands Hatch, but not complete. Spare car at Hockenheim, Österreichring (raced by Surer), Zandvoort (raced by Surer), Monza, Nürburgring and Estoril.

4 New for Boutsen at Monza. For Boutsen at Nürburgring and Estoril.

ATS

Began the season with a new D7 and a 1983 D6.

D6
03 Spare car at Rio, Kyalami, Zolder, Imola, Dijon and Monaco (written off by Winkelhock during practice).

D7
01 New for Winkelhock at Rio. For Winkelhock at Kyalami, Zolder, Imola, Dijon, Monaco, Montreal, Detroit, Dallas, Brands Hatch. Spare car at Hockenheim. For Winkelhock at Österreichring, Zandvoort and Monza. For Berger at Nürburgring. Spare care at Estoril.

02 New; spare car at Brands Hatch. For Winkelhock at Hockenheim. For Berger at Österreichring. Spare car at Zandvoort. For Berger at Monza. Spare car at Nürburgring (damaged during practice). For Berger at Estoril.

Brabham

Tested extensively during winter with a new chassis, designated BT52C and then modified to BT52D. Became basis of 1984 BT53, was finally known as BT53 (1) and became test car. Had five BT53 tubs ready for the start of the season.

BT53
2 New for Teo Fabi at Rio. For Fabi at Kyalami, Zolder, Imola and Dijon. For Corrado Fabi at Monaco, Montreal and Dallas. For Teo at Detroit, Brands Hatch and Hockenheim.

3 New; spare car at Rio, Kyalami, Zolder, Imola, Dijon, Monaco, Montreal, Detroit (raced by Piquet), Dallas, Brands Hatch, Hockenheim, Österreichring, Zandvoort and Monza.

4 First seen at Dallas for Piquet. For Piquet at Brands Hatch, Hockenheim, Österreichring, Zandvoort and Monza. Spare car at Nürburgring and Estoril.

5 New for Piquet at Rio. For Piquet at Kyalami, Zolder, Imola, Dijon, Monaco, Montreal and Detroit. For Teo Fabi at Österreichring, Zandvoort, Monza and Nürburgring. For Winkelhock at Estoril.

6 New for Piquet at Nürburgring. For Piquet at Estoril.

Ferrari

Introduced the 126 C4 in February as a development of the 1983 C3.

070 Development car used during winter testing.

126 C4
071 new; spare car at Rio and Kyalami. Spare car for Arnoux at Imola, Dijon and Monaco.

072 New for Alboreto at Rio. For Alboreto at Kyalami. Spare car at Zolder. Spare car for Alboreto at Imola, Dijon and Monaco. For Alboreto at Hockenheim. For Alboreto at Monza (modified and known as 126 C4/M2). Spare car at Nürburgring and Estoril.

073 New for Arnoux at Rio. For Arnoux at Kyalami, Zolder, Imola and Dijon. Spare car for Alboreto at Brands Hatch, Hockenheim, Österreichring (used for race) and Zandvoort.

074 New for Alboreto at Zolder. For Alboreto at Imola and Dijon. For Arnoux at Monaco. Spare car at Montreal, Detroit and Dallas. Spare car for Arnoux at Brands Hatch, Hockenheim and Österreichring. For Arnoux at Monza (modified and known as 126 C4/M2). For Alboreto at Nürburgring and Estoril.

075 New for Alboreto at Monaco. For Arnoux at Montreal, Detroit, Dallas, Brands Hatch, Hockenheim and Zandvoort.

076 New for Alboreto at Montreal. For Alboreto at Detroit, Dallas, Brands Hatch, Österreichring and Zandvoort. Spare car at Monza (raced by Alboreto).

077 New for Arnoux at Österreichring. Spare car for Arnoux at Zandvoort and Monza (raced by Arnoux). For Arnoux at Nürburgring (modified and known as 126 C4/M2) and Estoril.

Ligier

Switched from Cosworth to Renault turbo engines and constructed three new cars for the start of the season.

JS23
01 New; spare car at Rio (raced by de Cesaris). Spare car at Kyalami, Zolder, Imola, Brands Hatch, Hockenheim, Österreichring, Zandvoort (raced by de Cesaris). For de Cesaris at Monza. Spare car at Nürburgring and Estoril.

02 New for Hesnault at Rio. For Hesnault at Kyalami, Zolder, Imola, Dijon, Monaco, Montreal, Detroit, Dallas, Brands Hatch, Hockenheim, Österreichring, Zandvoort, Monza. Nürburgring and Estoril.

03 New for de Cesaris at Rio. For de Cesaris at Kyalami. Spare car at Dijon, Monaco, Montreal, Detroit, Dallas. Converted to **JS23B** spec. Present at Monza but not taken from transporter. For de Cesaris at Nürburgring and Estoril.

04 New for de Cesaris at Zolder. For de Cesaris at Imola, Dijon, Monaco, Montreal, Detroit, Dallas, Brands Hatch, Hockenheim, Österreichring and Zandvoort. Spare car at Monza.

Lotus

95T unveiled in December 1983. Took one 1983 94T to South America.

94T
1 Spare car at Rio.

95T
1 Used for testing. Spare car at Rio, Kyalami, Zolder and Imola (raced by Mansell). Spare car for Mansell at Monaco.

2 New for Mansell at Rio. For Mansell at Kyalami, Zolder, Imola, Dijon, Monaco, Montreal, Detroit, Dallas, Brands Hatch, Hockenheim, Österreichring, Zandvoort, Monza. Nürburgring and Estoril.

3 New for de Angelis at Rio. For de Angelis at Kyalami, Zolder, Imola, Dijon, Monaco, Montreal, Detroit, Dallas, Brands Hatch, Hockenheim, Österreichring, Zandvoort, Monza, Nürburgring and Estoril.

4 New; spare car at Dijon. Spare car for de Angelis at Monaco. Spare car at Montreal (raced by de Angelis), Detroit (raced by de Angelis), Dallas, Brands Hatch, Hockenheim, Österreichring, Zandvoort, Monza, Nürburgring and Estoril (raced by de Angelis).

McLaren

Lessons learned from 1983 MP4/1E incorporated in new design for 1984, the MP4/2.

MP4/2
1 New for Lauda at Rio. For Lauda at Kyalami, Zolder, Imola, Dijon, Monaco, Montreal, Detroit, Dallas, Brands Hatch, Hockenheim, Österreichring, Zandvoort, Monza, Nürburgring and Estoril.

2 New for Prost at Rio. For Prost at Kyalami, Zolder, Imola, Dijon, Monaco, Montreal, Detroit, Dallas, Brands Hatch, Hockenheim, Österreichring, Zandvoort, Monza, Nürburgring and Estoril.

3 In the paddock at Rio but not complete. Spare car at Kyalami (raced by Prost), Zolder, Imola (raced by Prost), Dijon, Monaco, Montreal, Detroit, Dallas, Brands Hatch, Hockenheim (raced by Prost), Österreichring, Zandvoort, Monza (raced by Prost), Nürburgring and Estoril. Used for testing before completion of chassis 4.

4 Completed mid-season and used for testing.

Osella

Referred to their latest car as FA1F although the chassis used in Brazil and South Africa was not new but built around an Alfa Romeo 183T tub. The first FA1F proper did not appear until Zolder. Used Alfa Romeo V8 turbos all season except for the brief appearance of 1983 FA1E with Alfa Romeo V12.

FA1E
02 For Gartner at Imola.

FA1F
01 For Ghinzani at Rio and Kyalami (written off during warm-up on race morning).

02 New for Ghinzani at Zolder. For Ghinzani at Imola, Dijon, Monaco, Montreal, Detroit, Dallas, Brands Hatch and Hockenheim. Spare car at Österreichring and Zandvoort (raced by Ghinzani). For Ghinzani at Monza. For Ghinzani at Nürburgring and Estoril.

03 New; spare car at Monaco. Spare car at Montreal, Detroit, Dallas, Brands Hatch and Hockenheim. For Ghinzani at Österreichring and Zandvoort. Spare car at Monza. For Ghinzani at Nürburgring and Estoril.

04 New for Gartner at Brands Hatch. For Gartner at Hockenheim, Österreichring, Zandvoort, Monza, Nürburgring and Estoril.

RAM

Converted 1983 01 chassis to accept Hart engine while building new 02 models following switch from Cosworth engines.

01
03 For Palmer in Rio and Kyalami.

02
01 New for Alliot at Rio. For Alliot at Kyalami, Zolder, Imola, Dijon, Monaco, Montreal, Detroit and

RAM refused to be beaten by a soul-destroying series of accidents, John Macdonald's team bouncing back with immaculate cars prepared on a minimal budget.

Dallas (crashed during practice).
02 New for Palmer at Zolder. For Palmer at Imola, Dijon and Monaco. For Thackwell at Montreal, For Palmer at Detroit, Dallas, Brands Hatch (crashed during race, repaired), Hockenheim, Österreichring, Zandvoort, Monza, Nürburgring and Estoril.
03 New for Alliot at Brands Hatch (crashed during race, repaired). For Alliot at Hockenheim (crashed during race, written off).
04 Built around 02 (01) for Alliot at Österreichring. For Alliot at Zandvoort, Monza. Nürburgring and Estoril.

Renault

1984 RE50 models ready for start of season.
RE50
01 Used for testing then became show car.
02 New; spare car at Rio. Spare car at Kyalami, Dallas, Brands Hatch, Hockenheim, Österreichring (raced by Tambay) and Zandvoort (raced by Tambay). For Tambay at Monza, Nürburgring and Estoril.
03 New for Tambay at Rio. For Tambay at Kyalami. Spare car at Zolder, Imola, Dijon, Monaco, Montreal and Detroit (raced by Warwick). For Tambay at Dallas.
04 New for Warwick at Rio. For Warwick at Kyalami, Zolder, Imola, Dijon (crashed during race,

repaired), Montreal and Detroit (crashed during practice).
05 New for Tambay at Zolder. For Tambay at Imola, Dijon and Monaco (crashed during race).
06 New for Warwick at Monaco (crashed during race).
07 New for Tambay at Montreal (not raced; used during practice by Warwick). For Tambay at Detroit. For Warwick at Dallas. For Tambay at Brands Hatch. For Streiff at Estoril.
08 New for Warwick at Brands Hatch. For Warwick at Hockenheim, Österreichring, Zandvoort, Monza, Nürburgring and Estoril.
09 New for Tambay at Hockenheim. For Tambay at Österreichring and Zandvoort. Spare car at Monza (raced by Warwick), Nürburgring (raced by Warwick) and Estoril.

Spirit

Modified 101 chassis, seen at the end of 1983 with Honda engine, and changed to Hart 415T. Had to adapt this car to accept Cosworth DFV at Detroit due to shortage of Hart units. Built second chassis during season.
101
1B Tested by Fittipaldi. For Baldi at Rio, Kyalami, Zolder, Imola and Dijon. Spare car at Monaco. For Rothengatter at Detroit. Spare car at Brands Hatch, Hockenheim (raced by Rothengatter), Öster-

reichring, Zandvoort (raced by Rothengatter), Monza, Nürburgring and Estoril.
2B New; spare car at Zolder. Spare car at Imola and Dijon. For Baldi at Monaco. For Rothengatter at Montreal, Dallas, Brands Hatch, Hockenheim, Österreichring, Zandvoort and Monza. For Baldi at Nürburgring and Estoril.

Toleman

Continued with 1983 TG183B while waiting for completion of TG184.
TG183B
02 Spare car at Zolder and Imola.
03 Spare car at Rio and Kyalami (raced by Cecotto). For Cecotto at Zolder and Imola.
04 For Cecotto at Rio and Kyalami (written off during practice).
05 New for Senna at Rio. For Senna at Kyalami, Zolder and Imola.
TG184
01 New; spare car at Dijon. Spare car Monaco, Montreal, Detroit (raced by Senna) and Dallas.
02 New for Senna at Dijon. For Senna at Monaco, Montreal, Detroit, Dallas and Brands Hatch. Spare car at Hockenheim, Österreichring, Zandvoort and Monza (raced by Johansson). For Johansson at Nürburgring and Estoril.
03 New for Cecotto at Dijon. For Cecotto at Monaco, Montreal, Detroit and Dallas. Spare car at

Brands Hatch. For Martini at Monza. Spare car at Nürburgring (raced by Johansson) and Estoril.
04 New for Cecotto at Brands Hatch (written off during practice).
05 New for Senna at Hockenheim. For Senna at Österreichring and Zandvoort. For Johansson at Monza. For Senna at Nürburgring and Estoril.

Tyrrell

Continued development with 012, first seen at the Österreichring in 1983.
012
1 Spare car at Rio. For Brundle at Kyalami, Zolder and Imola. Spare car at Montreal, Detroit (raced by Bellof), Dallas, Brands Hatch, Hockenheim and Österreichring. For Bellof at Zandvoort.
2 For Bellof at Rio. Spare car at Kyalami, Zolder, Imola, Dijon and Monaco. For Brundle at Montreal, Detroit and Dallas (crashed during practice).
3 New for Brundle at Rio. For Brundle at Kyalami, Zolder, Imola, Dijon and Monaco (crashed during practice, written off).
4 New for Bellof at Dijon. For Bellof at Monaco, Montreal, Detroit (crashed during practice, repaired). For Johansson at Brands Hatch, Hockenheim, Österreichring and Zandvoort.
5 Built in Dallas for Bellof. For Bellof at Brands Hatch. For Thackwell at Hockenheim. For Bellof at Österreichring. Spare car at Zandvoort.

Williams

Used FW09, introduced at end of 1983, modifying to 'B' spec by mid-season.
FW09
1 Spare car at Zolder, Imola (raced by Rosberg), Dallas, Brands Hatch ('B' spec; raced by Rosberg), Hockenheim and Österreichring. For Rosberg at Zandvoort. Spare car at Monza (raced by Laffite).
2 Crashed by Laffite during 1983 South African Grand Prix. Became test car.
3 New for Laffite at Rio. For Laffite at Kyalami, Zolder, Imola, Dijon, Monaco, Montreal, Detroit, Dallas, Brands Hatch ('B' spec), Hockenheim, Österreichring, Zandvoort and Monza.
4 New for Rosberg at Rio. For Rosberg at Kyalami, Zolder and Imola. Spare car at Dijon and Monaco. For Rosberg at Brands Hatch ('B' spec).
5 New, spare car at Rio. Spare car at Kyalami and Zolder. For Rosberg at Dijon, Monaco, Montreal, Detroit and Dallas.
6 New for testing at Brands Hatch in 'B' spec. Back to old configuration after one day of practice as spare car at Montreal (raced by Rosberg). Spare car at Detroit (raced by Rosberg).
7 New at Hockenheim ('B' spec) for Rosberg. Spare car at Nürburgring and Estoril.
8 New at Österreichring ('B' spec) for Rosberg. Spare car at Zandvoort. For Rosberg at Monza, Nürburgring and Estoril.
9 New ('B' spec) at Nürburgring for Laffite. For Laffite at Estoril.

HART O

Engine development accelerated strongly in 1984 with the emergence of TAG-Porsche and Honda to join established manufacturers, such as Ferrari and BMW, as race winners. For the first time since the inception of the 3-litre formula, a starting grid was filled entirely by turbocharged engines. Among them, the British-built Hart 415T which has grown in power and stature along with an accumulation of championship points. *Brian Hart*, in an exclusive feature for *Autocourse*, examines the important features of engine development in 1984.

It may seem a curious logic, but to sum up engine development in 1984 you need look no further than Kyalami and the final race of the previous season. Here we had the strategy of planned pit stops for fuel and tyres polished to perfection by Brabham. Nelson Piquet, you may remember, used the tactic to build up a comfortable cushion and, once he had made his stop, he more or less cruised home. The BMW was only on full song for about 20 laps or so and that, in the light of the 220-litre limit which came into force this year, was highly significant.

And the South African Grand Prix, of course, was also notable for another pointer towards form in 1984; the emergence of the McLaren TAG-Porsche package as a truly competitive combination.

As we watched Piquet stroll towards his second World Championship, I honestly don't think we realised the *full* implication of the 220-litre fuel capacity limit and the ban on refuelling which was due to come into effect in 1984.

It hadn't *really* struck me just how much of a caning the engines would have to take. In 1983, a driver could do his 20 to 25 lap charge before stopping for fuel and tyres and, by that time, if everything had gone according to plan, he would have the psychological and physical advantage of a cushion of so many seconds in the lead. From then on, he would monitor his race accordingly.

Now the drivers are racing at full chat for 60 to 70 per cent of the race and, quite often, more than that and the stresses and strains on the engine increased dramatically. That leads me to an even more important point.

In 1983, we raced with an unlimited fuel quantity. Nobody knew how much fuel a driver started off with; nobody outside the team knew how much fuel was added during the fuel stop. As a result, fuel could be used to cool the turbos and reduce the engine's thermodynamic loads.

The cooling, in simple terms, was done by running rich and this could bring about a drop of between 80 and 100 degrees centigrade in turbine entry temperatures. All that went by the board with the introduction of the fuel capacity restriction and, into the bargain, the engines were running harder for longer. Now you can begin to understand the problem . . .

Fuel management became a primary area of development and it was a difficult problem to cope with no matter what form of control one used, be it electronic, electro-mechanical or pure mechanical. We have to assume that Porsche set the standards here because they could run faster than anyone else and still have fuel left at the end of the race.

Undoubtedly they had an advantage thanks to being able to backtrack on development with the Porsche 956 when they went from mechanical to Bosch Motronic; this must have saved considerable development time. And, doubtless they must have been more aware of the overall effect the new fuel regulations would have on engine design.

There is no question that the rule change affected the design parameters of the basic 1.5-litre turbocharged engine because frictional losses and mechanical efficiency have become very important. It is used to be the case where an engine designer's

Paul-Henri-Cahier

priorities lay in three areas; the induction management system, the engine and the turbocharger ancillaries. In 1984, the emphasis switched to the engine; the 7:1 compression ratio 'lump' which previously had been no problem. Now it needed a lot of work just to make it survive!

Apart from mechanical efficiency, the drag on the car, when related to the downforce that could be applied, in turn affected fuel consumption. And this directly affected how much power you had available.

Put another way, let us suppose you have two cars with equal downforce but, in order to obtain that, one car has a 20 per cent higher drag coefficient than the other. That means more fuel will be required to provide the same horsepower to drive that car at the same speed. And that brings us to the McLaren MP4/2: a clean, tidy aerodynamic package with great attention to detail and, as we have said, a good control system on the engine.

McLaren have gone to great lengths to cool their fuel for the race and this raises an interesting point. Apart from the obvious effect of increasing the tank capacity, the cold fuel is denser which means it is possible to run leaner mixtures at these lower temperatures. Therefore, not only do you put a higher volume into the tank, you can actually use less by the process of fuel mapping.

'In 1984, the emphasis switched to the engine, which previously had been no problem. Now it needed a lot of work just to make it survive!'

However, it is relevant that the management system used by BMW is electro-mechanical and they do not need to cool their fuel. They have, I think, probably the most potent engine and yet they do not appear to have a consumption problem; all of which indicates a particularly efficient combination. On the other hand, they have suffered a considerable number of turbocharger problems. Considering the run of reliability enjoyed by BMW at the end of 1983, their subsequent problems highlight another crucial factor in 1984; that of building a turbocharger which was capable of withstanding the increased loads and temperatures.

Renault, by switching at not inconsiderable cost from KKK to Garrett, provided a classic example. Renault quietly tested the Garretts at Rio and slowly introduced them throughout the early part of the season. They were very special in terms of castings and materials and the fact that they were ready in January indicates that Renault had anticipated the problems in the middle of 1983.

Turbocharger technology, with regard to Formula 1, is not highly developed and there are indications that we shall see radical advances made in this area. The time has come for engine builders to have an on-going R&D programme with a turbocharger manufacturer; you can no longer say 'here's a four-cylinder engine, bolt a turbo on there, please . . .'

A link with a turbocharger manufacturer is absolutely vital whether it be Renault, with their

Paul Henri-Cahier

clout and finance, dealing with Garrett or, in our case, an association with Holset which is based largely on the old fashioned engineering tradition where Holset are motivated by enthusiasm and sheer mechanical interest.

When you think about it, the turbocharger *is* the engine. So much depends on its efficiency which is why you need to go into great detail with the turbocharger manufacturer. He will need to know how hot it has got to run; what the airflow rate in lb/min should be; what the expected horsepower figures are; what the engine's rev range will be. They would look at the actual turbine revs in the turbocharger; the larger ones running at around 115,000 rpm while the smaller units on Vee engines would run at around 180,000 rpm, perhaps more. It goes without saying that the compressor should be developed and run at its highest possible efficiency.

Brian Hart

Diana Burnett

This then defines the size of the aftercooler you would need and this leads me into another important area of development which came to light in 1984.

As mentioned previously, we no longer had the luxury of fuel to cool the engine and this switched the emphasis on to more efficient aftercoolers and radiators. It was an area which many teams did not seem to appreciate fully – with disastrous results. Brabham and Ferrari, busily revising radiators mid-season are prime examples.

It is important to run a turbocharged engine as near as one can to optimum operating temperatures because, apart from increasing reliability, it saves horsepower. This meant a compromise with chassis installation, a requirement which, in the opinion of Rory Byrne and myself, was very important. Toleman spent a great deal of time achieving as much cooling, and its control, as possible. It's all very well having a huge radiator but if the air isn't being drawn through, you may as well not have it. As a result, during the early part of 1984, we saw teams make dramatic efforts to increase engine cooling to both obtain reliability and save horsepower. The one notable exception was McLaren

'... We thought 640 bhp minimum would be a good starting point.'

who had incorporated enormous radiators and good airflow from the start.

The importance of an optimum package cannot be understated. It is no use having a powerful engine if you do not have the correct tyres, good engineers, an intelligent, capable driver and a good chassis. The days are gone when you could win by horsepower and boost; when you could see the Cosworths stacked up behind a turbo which was

Nigel Snowdon

BMW engine, Brabham

very fast on the straight. In 1985, it is likely that you will be able to race with slightly less power if you have very good tyres and aerodynamics allied to fuel consumption which will match the race distance.

Indeed, of the points mentioned, tyres must contribute the largest percentage to a competitive package. If a designer can then make his chassis extract an extra seven-tenths of a second from a tyre which is from the same manufacturer but of a slightly softer construction to that used by a rival, then the seven-tenths performance gain is incredible. To gain that sort of advantage from the engine alone would be a massive power increase – regardless of the talk about horsepower figures achieved in 1984.

When discussing power outputs, it is necessary to establish the difference between figures seen while the engine is on the dynomometer and the flywheel horsepower once the unit is installed in the car. In most instances, I think the figures quoted have been from the dynomometer where the test conditions are fairly clinical and the engine runs at optimum temperatures. Assuming a relatively good car, there is likely to be a five to six per cent loss on installation alone.

My good friend Paul Rosche and I spent many hours in the winter of 1983/84 discussing this very point. We thought 640 bhp minimum would be a good starting point without going mad on fuel economy. It is likely that figure crept up very quickly

continued on page 68

There's no stopping us.

The new Surefire copper core spark plug from Unipart is exactly what you are looking for. It means outstanding reliability, even in the worst conditions.

That's because the copper core greatly reduces carbon fouling and resultant misfiring.

So it fires time after time after time. So you will remain happy start after start after start.

SUREFIRE
The copper-core spark plug.

from **UNIPART**

Where else, but out in front.

Williams — Honda

POWERED by HONDA

Ralt — Honda

Nigel Snowdon

to 700 and was in excess of 700 for a proportion of the race – bearing in mind that the majority of drivers are intelligent enough to handle boost controls. I don't think there is any way the magic 1000 bhp – or anything like it – has ever been seen in a car, even during qualifying.

No, from our knowledge and the performance of the Toleman TG184, it does seem reasonable to say that people are racing, at least to start with, in excess of 700 bhp. And, what's most important from an engine development point of view, is the fact that they have improved fuel economy from the first couple of races. Yet, having said that, I think it's interesting that top teams ran out of fuel despite the technology that is available in Formula 1 . . .

Why did it happen? I think some drivers possibly chose to ignore the fact that they would run out. Of course, it was very difficult for a driver, if he knew he had to back off while in the middle of a dice when there were three laps to go. That was probably the weakness in the 220-litre rule but it was only a matter of time before most people got used to it.

In fact, the fuel consumption problem did highlight the ability of certain teams to respond more quickly than others. The size of the budget or the fact that the team was linked to a manufacturer had little bearing on the speed of finding the solution. It seemed to be a matter of a key person within the team channelling the energy of the right people in the right direction. However, I don't want to create the wrong impression here; overall, the effect of a proper budget is more important than ever – but only if the people controlling it realise which areas should receive attention. It is very easy to spend money and not see a positive result. At the end of the day it was obvious that, despite a few cars running out of fuel, development by technicians at various factories would quickly improve fuel consumption – albeit with some loss of reliability. But, overall, teams were able to produce faster lap times than 1983 and yet finish races within the limits of 220 litres.

Discussion about finance naturally leads to the business of manufacturer participation. Whether one likes it or not; whether the argument that a

manufacturer can race for a few years and then withdraw is a valid one, we *have* reached a level of manufacturer participation which has created tremendous interest. My feeling is that it has stimulated development between rival manufacturers to the stage where we have Ferrari, Alfa Romeo, Honda, BMW, Porsche and Renault in Grand Prix racing – with Ford about to join the confrontation. It boils down to the necessity of manufacturer clout if a team wants to run a programme with continuity.

Paul Rosche

Take the business of engine configuration as an example. Going back to fundamental principles, the 1.5-litre eight cylinder is at a consumption disadvantage when compared with the simpler sixes or even the four cylinder. Now it could be that we might discover other restrictions which would lead

to a switch to four cylinder engines because of their higher mechanical efficiency. But, equally, there is a point where the mechanical loadings of the four-cylinder become a bit of a problem. This is where manufacturer-might comes in. They could run a research programme on an engine which is totally different to the one being raced and this illustrates the possible depth of involvement. Manufacturers are committed to the foreseeable future.

There has been talk of an engine for qualifying and an engine of a different specification of the same make for the race. That would mean more or less running two teams within one and I can't see that happening. The sort of team which could afford to do it is probably one which does not *need* to do it in the first place. They are competitive enough without having to contemplate the additional problems two engines would bring.

Ferrari always spring to mind when such matters are discussed and, of course, we know they built a four-cylinder engine in 1984. But, as the regulations stand at the moment, I feel that a wide-angled V6 is the best package since it can be made very efficient. The four-cylinder is perhaps better off than it was

continued on page 72

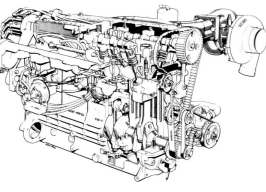

Hart 415T

Protection above all.

No conventional oil can meet the demands of hard driving quite like Gemini. Above all, Gemini, the latest and most advanced formula from Shell, sets new standards in protection. Through high revs and fierce temperatures Gemini stays in grade. Mile after mile, day after day, protection beyond the capabilities of conventional oils.

Technology you can trust

THE RENAULT 11 TURBO. THIS IS

AND THIS IS HOW IT GOES.

HOW IT COMES.

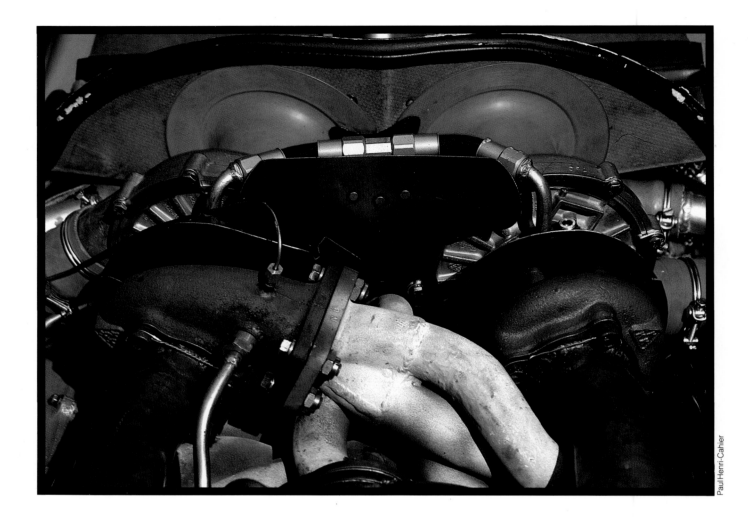

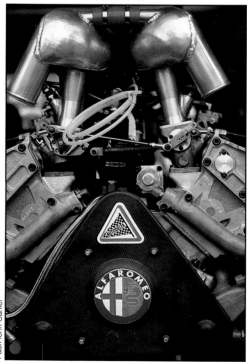

Alfa Romeo

thanks to fewer bearings and piston rings, meaning lower frictional losses which mean less fuel being used.

While one cannot fail to be impressed by the TAG-Porsche V6, the BMW four-cylinder has been just as competitive. When it was running well, the BMW was usually ahead of the TAG, an indication, perhaps, of the high specific power levels achieved by Paul Rosche. Honda have done the same although, for whatever reason, the Japanese V6 did not seem to be either as competitive or reliable as the BMW or TAG-Porsche. It may have had enough peak horsepower to give equal terminal speeds occasionally but its power curve characteristics did not seem as good.

It is also significant that Ferrari, who were once a match for BMW in qualifying, should have heavily revised their cylinder heads. They have been running various porting and turbine layouts in an effort to broaden their power curve and that has been borne out by the fact that, even during qualifying, Ferrari were not reaching the same terminal speeds compared to 1983 on certain circuits. They have obviously been trying to make the car more driveable and improve the response – or 'throttle lag' to use the popular terminology.

In fact, we are talking about boost response. Say a team races at 2.2 bar, then there will be certain corners where, due to the characteristics of the engine and, possibly, the chassis, the driver will not

'We are at the bottom of a very steep learning curve . . .'

be getting full boost. This is what he means when he says he has "terrible throttle lag". There have been lots of subtle ways of improving this. Electronic injection has been one. Turbocharger development and design is another and this is an area where we are improving all the time. We are at the bottom of a very steep learning curve and the progress made in 1984 has accelerated the need to respond to the demands of this new technology.

That progress can be allied to the arrival of other major manufacturers to challenge Ferrari, BMW and Renault. In 1983, Renault and BMW improved dramatically under the circumstances in which they were racing but, in 1984, suddenly we had other manufacturers making rapid strides in development. The biggest improvement of all came from the McLaren TAG-Porsche; it was there for all to see at Kyalami in 1983. And that's where we came in . . .

AP PARTS. FIT TO WIN.

"PEOPLE WHO BUY JAGUARS EXPECT A LOT THEY CERTAINLY DEMAND A VERY GOOD RIDE. WE BELIEVE OUR FORTE LIES IN COMBINING THAT RIDE REFINEMENT WITH EXCEPTIONAL HANDLING."

JIM RANDLE, DIRECTOR OF PRODUCT ENGINEERING, JAGUAR CARS.

"Automotive design always responds to good scientific logic. It isn't so much brilliance; it's more careful attention to detail.

In essence, it's getting the basic idea right from the start, applying good engineering practice and then, through dedication, turning that idea into something special.

Which is something Jaguar do well and is why Jaguar engineering tends to be evolutionary rather than revolutionary.

Take the Jaguar XK engine for instance.

It's a twin-cam straight-six that has benefited from 35 years of continuous production, and the only changes we've made have been to improve its power output and enhance emission control and efficiency.

The fact that it is the engine we use today in our XJ-6 saloon is a tribute to its fundamental correctness.

Styling is very much an integral part of

JAGUAR 3.4 £14,495! JAGUAR 4.2 £16,595. JAGUAR SOVEREIGN £18,995. JAGUAR SOVEREIGN H.E. £21,995. PRICES, BASED UPON MANUFACTURER

Jaguar Series III on high speed test track.

Jaguar engineering and it too evolves, as is so elegantly displayed by the body line of our current Series Three saloons.

When the XJ-6 was first launched, it stood out above all else for its refinement. It still does.

The interior has become synonymous with luxury. It means fine leather, walnut veneer and deep-pile carpeting. It is a classically English ambience that is in demand the world over.

Our philosophy is quite simple. We just try to better our own standards and always make the cars better than they were before.

That's why people love Jaguar cars. Whether building them or driving them, it's a state of mind. It's demanding further improvements; even beyond what many may already regard as the best.

We know that people who buy Jaguars are very demanding. They expect a lot. They certainly demand a very good ride.

We believe our forte lies in combining ride refinement with exceptional handling. It results from a careful blending of suspension geometry, damping and tyre characteristics. It demands a subtle understanding from our engineers, understanding that has grown from years of experience.

With a Jaguar, you can take for granted what other manufacturers offer as an extra or an option.

To our way of thinking, a desirable and functional feature is not something to shout about but rather what every car, certainly what every Jaguar, should have.

We were amongst the first to have such features as disc brakes, electronic fuel-injection and anti-dive suspension geometry as standard on our production cars.

Take, for instance, the silence of a Jaguar—it is uniquely Jaguar and is achieved, not by accident but by engineering design. Largely it's a question of siting the inevitable resonant systems at the right position in the frequency range so that you don't have too much interference, and by using the major masses in the system as attenuators.

If you've got to carry heavy things around, like axles and engines, then you should use them to benefit ride, handling and noise.

Again, it's all a question of detail.

Even the way the door opens is important: it's got to sound and feel as if it's been thoroughly engineered and has the right level of quality and craftsmanship.

That kind of attention to detail is an important part of our cars.

And to some extent explains, and underlines, what it is that makes a Jaguar so uniquely a Jaguar."

JAGUAR The legend grows
JAGUAR CARS, COVENTRY, ENGLAND.

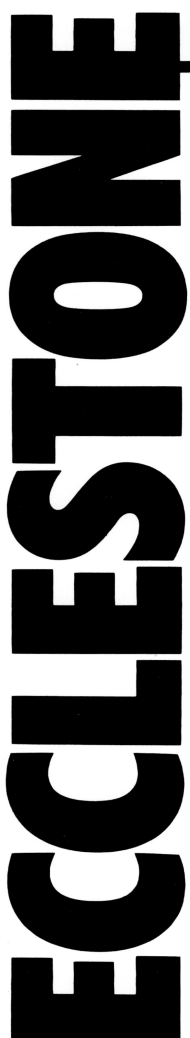

BERNARD ECCLESTONE

In discussion with Alan Henry, Grand Prix correspondent, Motoring News.

If you measure power in terms of wide-ranging influence, then Bernard Charles Ecclestone can honestly be described as the most powerful man in contemporary international motor racing. Admired by many, loathed by some and treated with more than a passing degree of respect and caution by most, Ecclestone's rise to fame and prominence is one of the many unsung achievements of post-War European motor sport, yet his contribution to its most prestigious front line, Formula 1, probably transcends that of any other single individual.

He is a man who, in the formal circumstances of a quiet interview, tends to play down the amount of influence he wields in Grand Prix circles: yet, out in the noise and bustle of a crowded pit lane, if Bernie so much as snaps his fingers, a considerable number of people jump. And some of them are rival FOCA team principals!

The "new wealth" which Ecclestone's agile business mind has channelled into the Formula 1 business over the past decade has made many others rich beyond their wildest ambitions. For Bernie, of course, the rewards that accrued to him were the makings of a second – or maybe even a third – fortune in the wake of his successful property dealings in the early 1960s. Many will argue strenuously that the raw materials of F1's current world-wide success were there, staring everybody in the face, long before Bernie arrived on the scene. But it was Ecclestone who sized up the sport's potential with the same prompt mathematical guile that his old motor trade rivals recall him using to value a showroom full of cars, accurately, almost at a glance. From the middle of 1971, Ecclestone forged ahead, consolidating his position not only as the new owner of the Brabham team (which he bought from Ron Tauranac in 1971) but also as President of the Formula One Constructors' Association, his influential and strong power base to this day.

Ecclestone is every bit as much a competitor as the drivers he employs. He is astute, imbued with an amusing self-deprecatory sense of humour, which he often employs to get off the hook when he is faced with awkward, perhaps unduly embarrassing, questions. When on the defensive, he will argue his corner resolutely, seldom giving ground and often advancing, perhaps dogmatically, if he wants to convince you on a rather questionable point. Time spent in his company is frequently an entertaining, absorbing hotchpotch of debate – but it is laced with icily serious undertones. You can have a lively, knockabout chat with Bernie – but that only goes so far. He never lets you quite forget that he is a deadly serious and highly competitive businessman.

You don't get a discreet fawn-liveried Lear Jet and a penthouse apartment on the South Bank, opposite the Houses of Parliament, by being a softy . . .

Today's Formula 1 success is largely based round the tremendously well-oiled world-wide television coverage which Ecclestone and his FOCA colleagues have promoted, unceasingly, for the past decade. As an appropriate starting point for this interview, I asked Bernie whether he was thinking in terms of television coverage when he first got involved as an F1 team owner in 1971.

"No, definitely not," he smiles, "I wasn't thinking in those terms at all when I bought the Brabham team. It was only when I began to get fully involved in the whole scene that I realised just how fragmented the coverage had been – some people did some races, others just a handful and some none at all. I thought that we ought to get the whole business grouped together in an effort to get some decent overall coverage . . ."

What did Bernie's fellow Constructors feel about the way in which the Brabham chief did the TV

deals on their behalf, leaving them simply to sit back and collect their half-yearly payouts from the FOCA "kitty"?

He grinned knowingly. "I'm lucky enough, as you know, that these people have been happy enough to follow what I do – at least they have up to now. I sort of went on with it and explained to them what had happened afterwards . . . I think that, when you start to pursue any particular course, people say 'let's see what happens'. If it works, they let you carry on until it doesn't work any more – then they throw you out."

Brushing aside the somewhat unlikely scenario of FOCA's members "ganging up" to throw Bernie out of the Presidency, I asked him just how much untapped interest he found when he went out to market F1 amongst the television companies.

"Yes, obviously, there was an enormous amount of interest. We'd been on and on at various countries round the world, telling them that they ought to be watching Formula 1, and it paid off. We produce now for, I think, 17 countries: we actually put a show together completely and supply it to those countries. All they've got to do is to put it on the air as if they were buying episodes of 'Dallas'!

"We have our own studio facilities now where we get all the material together, mix it all up, find the best bits and make a tape . . . in fact, it's often better than the live broadcasts. Who does it? Well, we don't have *owners* of anything, really . . ." He broke out into a laconic smile; "It's all FOCA, everything is FOCA. Status? My status? Well . . . I work there. It depends what people want to call me really . . . it's not necessary to put individual hats on people, is it?"

The question of on-board cameras fitted to competing Grand Prix cars was the next item he covered – "we haven't found a package light enough. We're working on something which is going to weigh around a kilo, perhaps a kilo and a half, but we're only a hair's breadth away from achieving that now" – before we moved on to potentially far more sensitive ground. It was suggested to him that, in its haste to accommodate television companies, the Formula 1 business has neglected the paying spectators. What about the fences behind the F1 paddock at Silverstone: or the restrictions on paddock access at Brands Hatch?

Bernie began to get firm. "There are two things here. Firstly, if it wasn't for the television, there wouldn't be the currently large number of spectators. The interest is generated by the other races in the series – and now the show has come to their home town and they want to see it.

"Secondly, I don't think you can tell me of any single sport where the spectators have the access to players as they do in Formula 1. Also the same applies to the press, who seem to complain about certain things . . . I mean, if I wanted to go to an ice hockey match as a member of the press, I couldn't sit behind the goals. In Formula 1 they seem to want to be on the edge of the track. Now, I've absolutely no problem with that, but what I *am* saying is that the press which reports on Formula 1 has better access than in any other sport."

Well, I replied, there are people who say that is just not the case.

"Well, they are probably the people who are lazy and don't try," replied Ecclestone firmly, ". . . or who don't know and just want to complain. You, here at Brands Hatch, can wander in and out of the paddock, you have access to everybody you want to talk to. You can go and speak to the President of the FISA, to the competing teams, to all the drivers, with no problems at all. You can't go and talk to McEnroe or Connors when they change ends at Wimbledon, but here you can go and speak to Nelson Piquet before he goes out on his pole position lap . . . and he'll answer you if you have a decent question!"

But what about the *spectators?*

"It's not practical to go and interview 11 footballers on the field," he continued, warming to

continued on page 82

"As far as I'm concerned, the fewer people who read this ad, the better."

Frank Williams. Williams Racing Team.

Frank Williams is a man who might be said to have more than a passing interest in motor oil.

After all, when what you know about something can mean the difference between success and failure in your chosen field (and in motor racing the difference is calculated in mega money), that something is likely to be high on your list of specialist subjects.

So when he approached us, back in 1980, to develop a new oil for his Formula One team, we knew he wasn't talking about anything less than a technological breakthrough.

What Frank was looking for was an oil which would give him something no other oil could give.

A competitive edge.

As you might have guessed, the oil we developed was Mobil 1 Rally Formula.

The oil that combines more power with more protection.

Obviously, any oil intended for use in Formula One racing has to be able to satisfy the stiffest demands as regards engine protection.

But Mobil 1 Rally Formula was also formulated to give extra brake horsepower.

And it was this extra brake horsepower that was crucial to Frank Williams.

So much so that he insisted on exclusive use of the oil.

The rest is history.

In 1981, the Williams team won the World Formula One Constructors' Championship.

In 1982, Keke Rosberg became World Champion driver in a Williams' car.

Then, late in 1983, despite Mr William's distinct lack of enthusiasm, we took the brave step (Mr Williams is no softy) of deciding to launch Mobil 1 Rally Formula to a wider audience.

Now, finally, comes the opportunity for those of you knowledgeable enough, or mad enough to pay around £12.00* for four litres of oil, to buy Mobil 1 Rally Formula.

It might be good enough for Frank Williams, but is it good enough for you?

A good question.

After all, the demands of Formula One racing are very different to the demands of everyday driving.

Yet the benefits of this oil are by no means limited to the race track.

Basically, Mobil 1 Rally Formula isn't formulated like an ordinary oil. It's a synthetic lubricant, built up molecule by molecule, by our technical experts to out-perform conventional oils.

Its grading for instance, is SAE 5W/50. A viscosity no ordinary oil can match.

The 5W figure means cold starting with Mobil 1 Rally Formula is a lot easier than with conventional mineral oils, especially in extreme cold conditions.

Trial by turbo.

Mobil 1 Rally Formula is the oil that's turbo-proven. So when things get hot, as they do in the galleries of a turbo charger, or even in an average car's spin down the motorway when piston rings can reach 550F, this oil really shows its class.

At those kinds of temperatures, a conventional oil soon begins to fall apart.

It breaks down chemically, thickens up, and cokes up just when it's needed most.

Scientists call this thermal degradation. It's something that happens to Mobil 1 Rally Formula, too, but in comparison it happens at a rate which is remarkably unhurried.

(In a laboratory test, waiting for it to occur, you'd be well advised not to hold your breath.)

Considering the price of a new engine, the price of our oil suddenly begins to look like good value.

More so when you realise it's been tested to give protection for up to 25,000 miles or 1 year between oil changes.** Most oils are changed every 6,000 miles.

But because our oil doesn't break down so quickly, it resists for that much longer the acids and impurities which form and then find their way into your sump.

This means less clogged valves and smoother running pistons for many more miles.

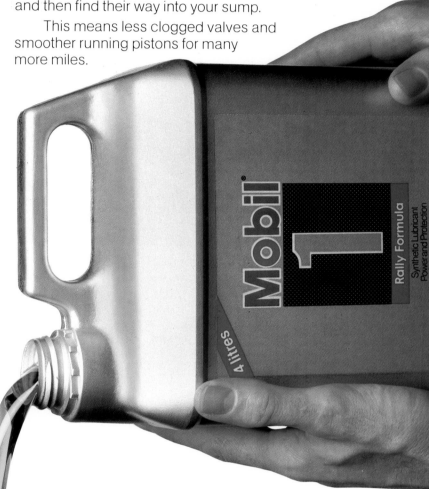

You've never bought an oil like this before.

Let's face it, to most motorists, oil is oil.

They simply aren't interested enough in their car's engine, or its performance, to pay any extra.

Even for an oil which, like Mobil 1 Rally Formula, can claim to be the most advanced oil in the world.

That's why you won't find this oil in many shops. (Quite frankly, it wouldn't sell enough to justify taking up the shelf space).

No, to get your hands on it, you'll have to track down one of the Mobil garages which do stock it, but don't worry if you can't find one, just write to the address below and we'll send you the address ourselves.

Mobil 1 Rally Formula.
The world's most advanced motor oil.
Retail Department Mobil Oil Company Limited, Mobil House, 54-60 Victoria Street, London SW1E 6QB.

*PRICE CORRECT AT TIME OF GOING TO PRESS. **SUBJECT TO MANUFACTURERS' RECOMMENDATION.

THE NEW 123 BHP C

Under the bonnet of the new Corolla GT Coupé lurks a truly awesome lump of power.

It's a rally bred 1587cc, 4-cylinder, twin overhead cam, 16-valve engine with electronic fuel injection.

And it's the main reason why the GT Coupé out-performs every other car in its class.

But there are other reasons. With a Cd factor of 0.35, it's aerodynamically better than

a Porsche 911 Carrera.

Its 5-speed box is so expertly set that every ounce of torque speaks its weight and you don't get any flat spots.

And positive steering, plus anti-

OROLLA GT COUPÉ.

roll bars front and rear, keeps everything on the straight and narrow and totally under your control.

Especially as you have dual circuit, servo-assisted brakes, with ventilated discs up front, to cool

the pace down if it gets too hot.

The GT Coupé is a car that generates 123.8bhp, does 0-60 in 8.3 seconds and has a top speed of 122mph.

Which is a superb engineering

achievement. But not a surprising one.

Because it's another thoroughbred from the Corolla stable.

And the Toyota Corolla is the car the world made perfect.

THE 16-VALVE, TWIN-CAM COROLLA GT COUPÉ.

PERSONAL EXPORT, THE QUADRANGLE, STATION ROAD, REDHILL, SURREY RH1 1PX. TELEPHONE: REDHILL (0737) 68585.

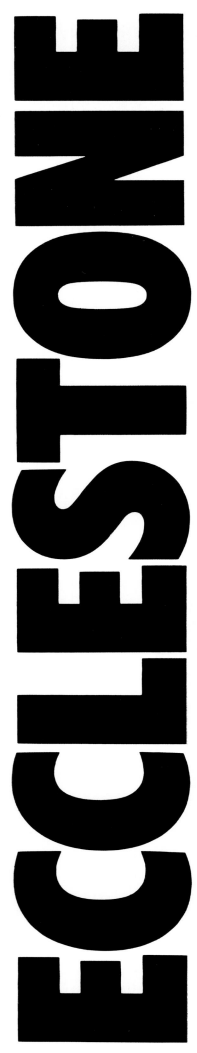

ECCLESTONE

continued from page 76

his theme, "and after the game has finished they seem to go off through that tunnel and nobody sees them again. Here, we are at Brands Hatch for three days, very accessible. But 150,000 people are coming to this race, so it isn't practical that they should all come in here to the Formula 1 paddock. But if they want to, they can buy tickets quite cheaply and have the pleasure of walking down the pit lane, looking at the cars and talking to the people."

Whether one agrees with Ecclestone or not on this particular point, one area where Formula 1 has certainly enjoyed a lot of popularity in the last ten years is the USA. Long Beach came and went, but Detroit is a firm fixture on the calendar, and Dallas, a cosmopolitan Texan city, opted for the international Formula 1 *milieu* rather than stage a race for the domestic CART category. The American Champcar series is seen by many of its enthusiastic supporters as one of Grand Prix racing's biggest rivals for the pot of gold which is the American viewing market. Bernie takes up, with obvious pleasure, the fact that Dallas opted for Formula 1 and expands his thoughts on his CART rivals.

"That's right. We had more people in Dallas for Friday practice than, maybe, at two or three CART races. I believe that Formula 1 has more to offer than CART because, ultimately, their spectator appeal is restricted – same cars, same engines, same tyres. In F1 now we have six or seven large manufacturers using Grand Prix racing as their flagship and this is keeping the interest going.

"In the past I talked to the CART people about promoting a World-wide Championship which would have seen us all running under some sort of compromise technical regulations. I wanted to run 25 races of which 16 would count and 11 would be mandatory. I thought this would give us a good cross-section and we would get a lot of American interest: I mean, America is a *very* important country in promotional terms. They have the same number of television viewers as we do in the whole of Europe!

"I talked to Roger Penske about all this and he said 'look, my team costs just over 2 million dollars to run and I can easily raise sponsorship to cover this – your team costs you 10 million dollars a year to run and you can only raise 8 million dollars in sponsorship. What do we want to get involved in that sort of racing for?' I told him that there was no answer to that, but it all depended on what you were trying to do.

"The trouble is, we are light years apart in terms of what we are trying to do. We're not knocking CART all the time – it is one of the best domestic formulae in the USA, perhaps second to NASCAR stock cars. That's how it should be. They don't *want* to be anything else . . . although every now and again they get delusions of grandeur, but eventually, when they get down to it, they understand why Formula 1 costs us so much."

Bernie went on to make the surprising prediction that CART's popularity would eventually wane, not, it has to be said, a point of view shared by many American enthusiasts who have supported Indy-style racing for half a century. However, the FOCA supremo does not back away from his opinion.

"I think that CART is running on a big up at the moment – and part of that stems from the publicity rub-off we gave them when we were thinking of getting together. I mean, there are so many domestic formulae in the USA that there are relatively few places that can really support an event. Michigan can, because it's Penske's, and Indy, of course . . . but then that is a big occasion. You and I could ride bicycles round Indy and they would still draw a capacity crowd . . ."

Talking of the North American scene, many of the recent Formula 1 street races have been beset by organisational and other problems on the occasion of their first event. But Long Beach, back in '75 was obliged to run a "warm up" Formula 5000 event prior to staging its first Championship race the following Spring. Montreal's *Ile Notre Dame* track staged an F/Atlantic event prior to its first Grand Prix in 1978 – but Dallas and Detroit

did not have to. This year's inaugural Dallas event was fraught with difficulties: did Ecclestone feel that it would be a wise thing to reintroduce these "warm up" races?

His response was surprisingly trenchant. "No, the idea is completely absurd. If there had been a preliminary race meeting at Dallas, nothing would have happened. They would have run Formula Super Vees, or something like that, round the circuit and nothing would have happened. Dallas was a simple problem of the circuit being surfaced with incorrect asphalt. That was compounded by the fact that, when it broke up, instead of immediately trying to rectify the situation after Formula 1 practice, they ran a Can-Am race for two hours which immediately destroyed everything – heavier cars, putting more power down . . .

"Sure, it was a difficult decision for the organisers to take, but then it depended whether they wanted to sacrifice the Grand Prix for the Can-Am. We had control of the whole programme and we originally let them have their Can-Am race because of Don Walker, the promoter, and his involvement with the series. But it was a difficult situation.

"You've got to remember, as well, that the reason we originally had this concept of a warm-up race was never to test things like the track surface. It was to see whether, on a new circuit, with new people running things, the marshals knew which way the cars were going. That's all. That was why we had the two hour session at Dallas on the Thursday – by the end of it we could decide 'it's no use putting a marshal here, we should put him there'. Otherwise, what you're saying is that when a doctor operates on a patient, he should do a warm-up operation on another patient beforehand. If these people are not professional enough to be able to come in cold and run a race, like the drivers, then they shouldn't be doing it."

Of course, Ecclestone is not only at the "sharp end" of the organisational department of Formula 1, he also represents his fellow Constructors' interests when it comes to formulating the technical regulations. How does he see technical regulations progressing over the next few years – or how would he *like* to see them progressing?

"I would like to see the engine regulations remain stable for five years," he replied positively, "but all other technical regulations could be changeable with one year's notice. That way we don't have to make silly, makeshift changes in the chassis regulations on the basis of safety . . . whatever you've done wrong in terms of formulating the rules, you've only got to live with them for a single season. But engine manufacturers need stability, so I think that five years is about right."

On a personal note, I then taxed Bernie on the subject of his personal enthusiasm for the business which has held his attention, on and off, since he first went motorcycle scrambling at the Brands Hatch grass track in the early post-War years. Did he feel that that his high-pressure commitment to the business of Grand Prix racing was still a pleasure – and how long did he feel it could hold his interest?

Again, his response was typically to the point. "I wouldn't do it if it wasn't a pleasure. I enjoy what I do. The wonderful thing about running a racing team is that you are running a business in which you get instant results. The Managing Director of BMW, for instance, doesn't *really* know how he is doing until the end of the year when he sees the bottom line . . . whereas we know on Sunday, at four o'clock in the afternoon, whether we've done it right or wrong. Then it's all history and we move on to the next race.

"From the FOCA point of view I enjoy the races, I enjoy finding new venues, creating new races . . . and afterwards, I enjoy watching them come on, I mean, it's a bit like having a family. I've started so many races now all round the world that it's nice to see them all healthy, surviving, do well and everybody happy . . ." Anticipating, perhaps, my mock horror at this unexpected display of paternal concern, Ecclestone grinned almost sheepishly after making that last remark . . . "I'm *not* a workaholic, you know," he continued when I challenged him with this suggestion. "You are," I

said firmly. "No, that's not the case," he repeated, pausingly briefly to add, "But there's always something to hold your attention in this business . . . you wake up in the morning and there's always something new to tackle."

Few people in the media get close to Bernie on a personal level and perhaps this, as much as for any other reason, is why he has been on the receiving end of adverse criticism over the years. Clearly it isn't something that bothers him. Is it true that he does not really care what the press or his critics say about him?

He thought quietly for a few moments. "Yes, that's about true I suppose. Mostly your critics don't bother to find the truth about things – they write what they want to write. Nobody wants to read about nice people or good news . . . and if you are good news, they write nasty things about you anyway.

"Look at the things that are written about John McEnroe. He can't be that bad! I mean, I've never met him, but I'm sure he must be quite a likeable person. Lots of things I read about people I know well are bad things, and I *know* they are nice people . . . so what do you do?"

On the subject of contemporary drivers, Bernie Ecclestone is known to sustain only limited amounts of enthusiasm. On many occasions he has expressed the opinion, directly and obliquely, that they are over-paid and spoilt – although that doesn't stop him from paying highly competitive market rates for his number one, currently possibly the best man in the business!

Did he feel they complained too much?

"Let's say that the drivers like to be heard and they very rarely have anything constructive to say, so as soon as they have anything to bring up they come right out and say it . . ." But, of course, Bernie's relationship with drivers has not always been cast in that sort of mould. He had a close personal friendship with Stuart Lewis-Evans, for whom he entered an ex-works Connaught in the 1957/58 Tasman series, and later went on to look after the business interests of both Jochen Rindt and Pedro Rodriguez. More recently even than that, Brazilian star Carlos Pace, his employee in the Brabham team, was a highly-regarded colleague.

"You can really bracket all the drivers together," suggested Bernie, almost reflectively, "because they are a bunch of very different people all trying hard to do the same job – all attacking the problem in different ways, their own individual personalities coming out in the way they approach the task. I mean, for example, Jochen was very laid back . . . he didn't make much of an effort to be honest with you. He was sick most of the time, almost always having a cold or some other ailment, but he just hopped into a car and zapped it onto pole with no effort. Other people needed to work at it . . .

"Some people are oozing with natural talent and get the job done easily. Others, like Graham Hill, who I don't believe ever had the talent of Jochen, got the job done a different way by working at it.

"Stuart Lewis-Evans? He was a magic driver, but he never had the best equipment. Never very healthy, he had an ulcer and wasn't very strong. But he got the job done.

"Things have changed, of course, it's as simple as that. Now I find myself remote from my drivers on a personal level. Not by choice, probably by circumstance. In the past, perhaps, people have lived much closer together, but now they are are living all over the place, flying round the world, testing and racing . . ." He paused with a wry grin, and adding, "and I'm stuck in the office, trying to make an honest living."

"Carlos Pace – we were very close. He, Stuart, Pedro, Jochen . . . their loss cut me up a lot. That's the bad thing about getting too close to people who work in this dangerous business, but Carlos was something a little bit special. He was my sort of guy, he was something . . . well, I like Brazilian people anyway. He had all the nice things I like about people. He was a lovely guy . . . and very, very good.

"I'd like to have a team with all those guys working for me. Niki? Two good years with him . . .

perfect. I never had one cross word with him. No arguments, never any trouble. The perfect professional to work with . . ."

What about Niki's sudden decision to quit the Brabham team for early (and, as it transpired, temporary) retirement mid-way through first practice for the '79 Canadian Grand Prix? Did Bernie think that Niki wanted to be seduced into staying?

Bernie replied firmly. "No. I think he wanted to be seduced into going . . . for somebody to confirm that he was doing the right thing. I think he was bored with it, he'd got a new and very quick team-mate in Nelson and I think he just thought, 'well, it's about time I hung up my hat'. I wasn't going to persuade him to stay. Think how awful I would have felt if I'd persuaded him to think about it and he'd gone out and had an accident. He wanted to go, so I said 'OK, go' ".

A practical reaction from a practical individual who has always made snap decisions and lived on his wits. Focussing a personal spotlight on Bernie's life, I asked him to expand a little about his early days, his "wheeler-dealing" days which started when he was at school. Was it true he sold pens to his classmates. Did he really black out half of South London when he was working at a power station in his early days?

Bernie, who incidentally trained as a chemist before he realised that his skills as a businessman might take him further, answered precisely. "Yes, I sold pens to my classmates at school . . . I bought them from the others first, though! I've always been well, an entrepreneur – I think that's the current word for it."

As far as the power station tale is concerned, as recounted by Max Mosley, Ecclestone smiled. "Max tells some good stories, but I'm not sure where that one came from. I think what happened was that I failed to do a check properly on a filter plant at a gas company I worked for . . . the pipes got a little clogged and they lost some pressure. But I don't think it was that serious. The eggs maybe took a little longer to boil . . ."

Unquestionably Bernie Ecclestone has come a long way since his teenage exploits at the gas company. Now in his mid-fifties (he is always reluctant to be specific about his precise age) he radiates as much energy and drive as many people half his age. If you stand and watch close by the Brabham pit, as like as not you will see Ecclestone spending ten minutes ensuring that a sponsor's decal is 'just so' on the side plate of a Brabham rear wing. Such attention to detail may well drive the Brabham team members round the bend under some circumstances, and Bernie freely admits that this attention to detail "is both my strongest and my weakest point.

"What you've got to remember, of course, is that if you're not prepared to attend to every detail throughout, then when are you going to say that you should be doing it or you shouldn't? It's in a person's character, this sort of thing. It's not something you can change. You can't say that you will attend to detail here, but you won't there . . . or you'll do it on Sundays and Tuesdays but not at any other time. I remember I used to complain when my mother put the nappies on – she put them on the wrong way! And you know what they say about delegation. It's the willingness to accept second best."

Master of the clever one-liner, Bernie Ecclestone has certainly never been one to accept second best. That is why, love him or loathe him, he occupies that position of strength and influence within professional motor racing. In closing, I asked him whether he recalled another phrase which he used to describe the creed of the Grand Prix driver some ten years ago when he had just taken over at Brabhams.

"First you get on, then you get rich, then you get honest," he repeated with glee. Would he describe that as his *own* personal creed, I suggested?

Bernie just smiled and shook his head . . . when you've got on as well as he has, I suppose you really don't *have* to answer questions when they are *that* searching!

WE·WERE·IN AT·THE·START

OUR ADVANCED TECHNOLOGY HAS HELPED US GAIN SOME VERY IMPRESSIVE RESULTS. IN FACT, DURING THE PAST DECADE CHAMPION HAVE WON CONSIDERABLY MORE FORMULA ONE WORLD CHAMPIONSHIP RACES THAN ANY OTHER MAKE OF PLUG. THAT RACING EXPERIENCE IS BUILT INTO THE CHAMPION + PLUGS. MADE FOR YOUR CAR. PLUGS WITH WIDER BASED, LONGER NOSED INSULATORS AND NEW COPPER CORES.

SO WHEN YOU FIT A SET OF CHAMPIONS, YOU CAN BE CERTAIN OF ONE THING. YOU'LL START AS YOU MEAN TO GO ON. **YOU·CAN'T·BEAT·A·CHAMPION**

GRANDS PRIX 1984

Photo: Diana Burnett

Same helmets, same overalls, same personal
sponsors. New tyres, new team. Patrick Tambay's
unceremonious departure from Ferrari at the end of
1983 meant a switch to Renault-Elf and Michelin.

europcar

RENAULT

P. TAMBAY

FASA

Keith Sutton

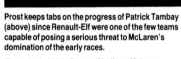

Prost keeps tabs on the progress of Patrick Tambay (above) since Renault-Elf were one of the few teams capable of posing a serious threat to McLaren's domination of the early races.

The arrival of Alain Prost at Marlboro McLaren galvanised Niki Lauda into producing some of the best performances of his distinguished career.

Michele Alboreto destroyed the opposition in Belgium but the Italian driver's performance at Zolder was not a true indication of the Ferrari team's faltering progress.

René Arnoux cocks a wheel (right) during one of the aggressive and spectacular performances needed to urge the Ferrari 126C4 into the points.

Derek Warwick responded immediately to the stimulus of driving for Renault-Elf by leading the Brazilian Grand Prix until the suspension on the RE50 failed.

RENAULT

ULTelf

RGIO
CCHINI

D. WARWICK

elf

europcar

RENAULT

FERODO

North American contrast. The Grand Prix scene moved from the fast, water-side curves on the Ile Notre Dame to the tight confines and glass towers of Detroit followed, two weeks later, by the concrete and wire-mesh of Fair Park, Dallas.

Alain Prost gave McLaren and Unipart maximum
exposure at Zandvoort by taking a superbly
controlled win in the Dutch Grand Prix.
Photo: Nigel Snowdon

Grande Prêmio do Brasil

"People are always saying that I look smug. I don't think it's fair. That's how I look and I can't do anything about it. But I'll tell you one thing. Tomorrow all the speculation stops and we'll see what sort of progress people have *really* been making over the winter. Our cars? Well, I'd be guessing, but if everybody has really been telling the truth about their performance during winter testing, then I'd say we were going to be in good shape."

The scene was the wide, sunlit pit lane of the Autodromo Riocentro. The time, late in the afternoon the day prior to first practice for the 1984 Brazilian Grand Prix. The speaker, McLaren International director Ron Dennis, one of the handful of key personalities within the Grand Prix world who had perhaps come under microscopic examination, even more so than his colleagues.

The race morning warm-up session told the true story. Lauda and Prost, who had qualified sixth and fourth respectively, headed the official list of times by a convincing margin. Nowhere near as worried about the 220-litre maximum fuel capacity limit as many of their rivals, both drivers seriously considered running the race non-stop on a "marginal" Michelin soft race tyre. The onus was firmly on Niki and Alain to make their minds up if they needed a stop.

At the start of the race Niki made a classic getaway, bursting through into fifth place behind Michele Alboreto's Ferrari 126C4, Derek Warwick's Renault RE50 and the Lotus 95Ts of Nigel Mansell and Elio de Angelis as the field streamed off down the back straight. At the end of the opening lap he had nipped through into fourth place, then third. Alboreto seemed secure at the head of the queue, but it didn't take long before the former World Champion, driving with all the precision and zest which earned him his magical reputation during the mid-1970s, eased up on to Warwick's tail to challenge for second.

Running down the long back straight on the tenth lap, Lauda was close, but perhaps not close enough. Yet that didn't stop him going for the gap on the inside of the Renault. Warwick, by his own admission, was slightly startled. Lauda had started his run from a long way back. This wasn't Niki's recently-developed style. None of the cool, calculated, unemotional rubbish here! The red and white Marlboro McLaren ducked by almost before Derek had realised it was coming through, its right rear wheel administering a hefty blow to the Renault's left front.

When Alboreto's Ferrari spun wildly with a brake caliper malfunction at the end of his 12th lap, Lauda was presented with the lead on a plate. Moreover, Alain Prost's **McLaren MP4/2** was also scything its way through the field with remorseless regularity and, when Warwick made a routine stop for fresh Michelins at the end of lap 29, he left the two McLarens touring round in splendid 1-2 formation.

Then, on lap 38, Prost came into the pit road for a routine stop and, as the mechanics fell on his car, they noticed to their horror that Niki was following him in. Alain resumed, now in second place behind Warwick, but Lauda undid his belts and climbed from the cockpit almost before he had stopped rolling. A trifling electrical fault . . .

Still, second place for Prost wasn't too bad. Bearing in mind the caution needed on the fuel consumption front in the closing stages of a Grand Prix, second to Warwick's Renault was a better way to start your McLaren career than coasting to a halt on the circuit with a dry fuel tank.

Then, with ten laps to go, Warwick's left front upper suspension wishbone broke, probably the long-term result of his earlier contact with Lauda. He spun gently at the hairpin and, as he limped away down the back straight towards the pits, and retirement, Prost's McLaren sped imperiously, almost symbolically, past into the lead.

A debt had been repaid. Alain Prost had wiped the Renault team in the eye, getting even with its management for bundling him out on to the driver market hardly before the '83 season had ended. In the pit lane, Ron Dennis's customary smug expression vainly tried to suppress a beaming grin . . .

ENTRY AND PRACTICE

Seldom had an off-season seen so much in the way of testing – and seldom had it all meant so little. That was the general consensus as the teams prepared for the opening race of the season at Rio de Janeiro, on the demanding *Autodromo Riocentro* round which many of them had thrashed for a week earlier in the year. There had also been tests at Kyalami, not to mention several at Paul Ricard, Clermont Ferrand (for the Michelin-shod Renaults), Fiorano (endlessly, for Ferrari!) plus the usual forays to Silverstone, Brands Hatch and even Goodwood (Cecotto made a brief appearance at the abandoned Sussex circuit in his Toleman TG183B!). At the end of the day, of course, it meant next to nothing in terms of predicting race performance. With only 220 precious litres of fuel to see competitors through the 180/200 mile Grand Prix battles, it was even more impossible to judge who had worked out a good *race* set-up as opposed to a successful configuration for a *banzai* pole position lap.

Renault had been impressively quick during the Rio tests but, as the scribes all pointed out, there hadn't been any Brabham-BMWs present. Nelson Piquet's sensational debut victory in the superb BT52 at last year's Rio meeting had set a standard which made all his rivals wary about any variation on that theme that the highly respected Gordon Murray might come up with. Would it be too much to expect a repeat performance?

One factor which had to be taken into account was Goodyear's progress with its radial tyre development. Over the winter Akron had thrown all the resources of its racing department behind its plan to match Michelin in this particular sphere and, from the outset of qualifying, it was clear that Lotus, at least, had evolved a chassis which worked particularly well with the American radial qualifying tyres.

At the wheels of their Ducarouge-designed Lotus

Thumb's up for the new season. Ferrari made an impressive start with the 126C4 when Michele Alboreto led the Brazilian GP but, apart from a dominant victory in Belgium, the Italian team's fortune slumped in the early **races.** Photo: John Townsend

Driving for show. Alain Prost celebrated his move from Renault to McLaren by taking an unexpected win with a car which had hardly turned a wheel before the start of official practice at Rio.

94Ts, both Nigel Mansell and Elio de Angelis started the new season brim-full of confidence and competition between the two men within their own team quickly rose to the level normally reserved for inter-team rivalry. After experiencing a few minor teething troubles during the Friday morning untimed session, including a minor electrical short-circuit which caused a brief conflagration beneath his cockpit seat, Mansell really got his head down in the opening qualifying session. Closely matching every move from Goodyear-shod Michele Alboreto's Ferrari C4, the Englishman emerged with a fastest lap of 1m 29.364s, achieved despite a spectacular fifth gear slide as he ran round the outside of Piercarlo Ghinzani's Osella-Alfa turbo. "I think I might have been a little quicker, but for that," he mused afterwards, "but there was nothing for me to do but keep my foot hard in it!"

De Angelis's 95T had started its qualifying runs using Garrett turbochargers on its Renault EF4 engine, as opposed to the KKK units employed on Mansell's machine. But the Italian driver noticed his temperatures were running a little on the high side and his car was changed back to its original aerodynamic trim (from the slightly revised form that had been evolved following some wind tunnel tests at St. Cyr) and the following morning Elio was happy to report that the gauges were all reading slightly lower. In the afternoon qualifying session de Angelis managed to find a clear lap on his second set of qualifiers and scorched round in a stunning 1m 28.392s, hurling pole position well out of reach. Mansell, trying hard to respond, found

himself on the receiving end of a rather questionable move on the part of Alain Prost, although whether the Frenchman pulled this stunt by accident or was repaying Mansell for holding up his McLaren earlier in the session, isn't quite clear. On Mansell's quickest lap, he came up behind the new McLaren driver who, in turn, was overhauling the Ligier JS23 of Andrea de Cesaris. Instead of keeping on the outside line, Prost moved across in front of the Lotus as if he was trying to overtake the Ligier and Nigel had little choice but to jam on the brakes and spin. Prost later reckoned he would have managed pole position if it hadn't been for the earlier intervention of Mansell. By the same token, Nigel reckoned he could have improved on his eventual fifth quickest 1m 29.364s, having been unable to improve on his Friday best. . .

From the point of view of traction and handling, Alboreto was absolutely delighted with his new mount, the Ferrari 126C4 looking smooth, undramatic and steady out on the circuit while at the same time recording very respectable times. Michele's race car, equipped with the latest version of the Marelli/Weber electronic injection/ management system, ran reliably throughout qualifying and the Italian was very content at starting his Ferrari Grand Prix career from the outside of the front row. By contrast, poor René Arnoux's 126C4 (equipped with Lucas injection) had a whole host of minor problems which sent Mauro Forghieri back to the paddock garage with a joyless scowl on his face. Once Friday's problem, a sticking valve in the fuel system, had been rectified, Arnoux found his second qualifying

"Car, tyres, no problem . . . only problem is Prost. He's bloody quick!"

NIKI LAUDA

session spoilt when he was badly baulked on his two quick runs and rounded off the afternoon with a turbocharger failure. The best he could manage was 1m 30.695s for tenth place on the grid.

Confident and optimistic after plenty of pre-season experience behind the wheel of his new Renault RE50, Derek Warwick proved his quality from the moment qualifying started. Once he had worked out a good race set-up on full tanks, the Hampshire driver opted for one hard set and one soft set of Michelin rubber for the first hour-long qualifying session only to have de Cesaris's Ligier JS23 move over on him going through a fast right-hander. At the end of the day neither Derek nor Rio testing pacemaker Patrick Tambay seemed as confident as they might have been.

After Saturday's untimed session the two Renault drivers agreed that it might be worth back-tracking slightly towards the higher down-force set-up they had employed during January testing and this immediately proved to be the right decision once the final qualifying session began. Having rectified a problem with a faulty warning light in the water injection system, Derek briefly held pole position with a fine 1m 29.025s although he wound up third after de Angelis and Alboreto went quicker. "It wasn't a perfect lap, either," confessed Derek, "because I went a little too deep into the first right-hander after the pits and came out a little wide . . ."

Tambay could only record a 1m 30.554s to secure eighth place on the grid, a great disappointment for the amiable French driver who freely admitted that the problem must be his rather than the car's.

By the customary frenzied pit lane standards, the McLaren International garage was an oasis of tranquillity throughout the two days of qualifying. Despite the fact that the latest John Barnard-designed MP4/2 had only undergone a brief test session at Paul Ricard, it was obvious that the amount of time and attention he had expended on the car was now paying dividends in terms of reliability.

Prost's return to McLaren was celebrated with a 1m 29.330s to take fourth place on the grid while Lauda, working hard to keep in touch, turned a 1m 29.854s to suggest that he can still demonstrate his old flair when he has a car worthy of his reputation. Typically terse, Niki acknowledged bluntly, "Car, tyres, no problem . . . only problem is Prost. He's bloody quick!" And that was about as near to a compliment as anybody was going to get from 'the Rat'!

What of Bernie Ecclestone's Brabhams? Well, on the face of it qualifying in Brazil seemed to pose nothing but trouble for World Champion Nelson Piquet and his diminutive team-mate Teo Fabi.

By his own admission Nelson ran wide on a corner during his best Friday lap and the following day his "favourite" qualifying car, the team spare, suffered an early engine failure which meant that he had to attempt his timed runs in his race chassis. Under the circumstances a 1m 30.149s for seventh place on the grid wasn't too bad. Fabi was hampered by throttle linkage problems on Friday as well as losing time while a broken gear was changed: on Saturday he spun into the catch

fencing at the end of the back straight on his first set of Michelins, lightly damaging the car. His best was a 1m 33.277s for 15th place in the line up.

Appearing at Rio for the first time behind the wheel of a turbocharged Formula 1 car, Keke Rosberg wasn't having an easy time with the Williams-Honda. The problem was that the new pull-rod rear suspension arrangement, which replaced the FW08-derived rocker arm system seen at Kyalami last October, simply gave too much grip when compared with the front end. Result? Understeer; the one thing that Rosberg hates with a passion. Throughout qualifying it was simply a case of juggling round the settings to arrive at the best possible compromise: the fundamental chassis characteristic seemed to stay there to stay. Keke man-handled it round to record 1m 30.611s, but that was only good enough for ninth place. "Still, the one thing we don't have to worry about is fuel consumption," grinned the Williams's team leader. Jacques Laffite, who spent much of practice in the team spare since his race chassis was bugged by a misfire, wound up 13th on 1m 31·548s.

After being dropped by Brabham and Renault respectively, Riccardo Patrese and Eddie Cheever were both out to re-establish their reputations quickly, but the attractive new Alfa Romeo 184T obviously needed a good deal more development before it could begin to look like a front-running proposition. Both men agreed that the chassis felt really good on its Goodyear qualifying tyres, but the Alfa V8 earned the unenviable distinction of being the first engine to suffer a major mechanical failure in the 1984 season, the first untimed practice session being barely 20 minutes old before Patrese coasted into the pit lane.

Patrese briefly took over the 183T spare, only to suffer a turbo failure, and with Cheever's new machine evening the score with its first similar breakage during first qualifying, it was quite clear that the Italian team hadn't shaken off its engine reliability problems, a perennial handicap. Patrese found his hopes of improving on his Friday best of 1m 30.973s dashed when he suffered another turbo failure in final qualifying while Cheever wound up on 1m 31.282s.

The new carbon fibre composite Ligier JS23 didn't attract much in the way of favourable comment, particularly from those who bothered to look closely at its somewhat precarious "bodged up" rear suspension pick-up points, but Andrea de Cesaris insisted that it "felt nice" although if it looked like that when he was happy, one was bound to ask what he would be like when upset! On Michelin rubber the Italian managed a 1m 32.895s which was only fractionally quicker than the best-placed Pirelli runner, Manfred Winkelhock's ATS D6. De Cesaris's team-mate, the pleasant 1983 French Formula 3 Championship runner-up François Hesnault, did a smooth and competent job to qualify for his first Grand Prix in undramatic 19th position.

Unfortunately Winkelhock's ATS was excluded from the proceedings on Saturday afternoon after the race stewards decided on a particularly harsh interpretation of the Formula 1 regulations. Manfred's car coasted to a halt, apparently out of fuel, in the pit lane approach road and when his

mechanics arrived to push the car back to its pit, they were told that such an action would be deemed a breach of Art. 10 of the World Championship Standing Regulations (a section of which forbids pushing a car on the circuit – and the circuit, technically, includes the pit lane). Team owner Gunter Schmid was subsequently summoned to the race control office where a debate over the whole matter quickly got out of hand. If it had been the organisers' intention to let Schmid off with a rap over the knuckles, their sense of generosity soon evaporated and the ATS found itself excluded from the meeting.

Winkelhock's exclusion meant that the best-placed Pirelli runner on the grid was brilliant new boy Ayrton Senna, the Marlboro British Formula 3 champion showing tremendous form at the wheel of his Toleman TG183B. Confident, cocky, yet somehow imbued with tremendous star quality, Senna instilled enthusiasm in the Toleman team and by the end of the weekend it was quite obvious that this talented newcomer had filled the breach caused by Derek Warwick's departure.

A dud batch of Pirelli rubber spoilt both Toleman drivers' qualifying efforts. No fewer than 12 sets, all allocated to the Toleman team, were showing signs of delaminating even before they had been fitted to the cars, but as they had been officially marked there was no way in which they could be changed. Senna wrestled his way round to a fine 1m 33.525s, the best part of two seconds quicker than Cecotto's sister car. The young Brazilian also suffered the first Hart engine failure of the season on Friday morning, a failure prompted by an extreme application of revs on the part of the driver and not any inherent problem with the unit itself!

In the normally aspirated ranks, Martin Brundle showed himself to be notably smooth and unflustered behind the wheel of Ken Tyrrell's DFY-engined 012 – which looked remarkably small and compact in amongst this sea of turbocharged contenders. Martin qualified respectably on 1m 36.312s, slightly faster than his more experienced team-mate Stefan Bellof.

Hesnault's Ligier and Thierry Boutsen's reliable Arrows A6 were next up while Piercarlo Ghinzani's Osella, based round an '83 Alfa Romeo carbon fibre composite monocoque, just pipped Bellof with a 1m 39.434s. On the inside of the penultimate row was former Alfa man Mauro Baldi, turning a respectable 1m 38.816s in the Hart-engined Spirit, a revamped version of the Honda-engined 101 which appeared in the paddock at Monza last year but was never raced, while Marc Surer's Arrows was 24th on 1m 37.204s. The Swiss driver was actually competing at the wheel of his own car, having purchased this chassis from his employers for show purposes at the end of the '83 season. "When it became clear that the new A7 wasn't going to be ready for the start of the year, Alan Rees asked me if the team could borrow it back."

Right at the back, on the 13th row, came the two Hart-engined RAM cars of Philippe Alliot and Jonathan Palmer, both of which suffered continuous fuel vaporization trouble which was only partially rectified when the engine covers were left off on the second day of practice.

RACE

Concern centred round the new Formula 1 regulations. How many cars would go the distance without running out of fuel? How many would stop for tyres and/or ballast? And who would provide the surprises? As the starting time for the 62-lap World Championship opener approached the cars were pushed out on to the dummy grid where many of them stood with their fuel tanks shrouded with reflective drapes intended to prevent the sun's rays from heating up the pre-cooled fuel to a point where it would begin to vaporize and start to be lost from the tank breathers. Finally, after all those months of preparation, it was time for the action to begin.

Unfortunately the first start was an anti-climax as de Cesaris couldn't select a gear in his Ligier JS23, the "start delayed" sign was held aloft and everybody switched off their engines. That provided something of a bonus for Cecotto as well, because his Toleman was late away from the grid prior to the parade lap and he had just taken up station at the back of the grid when the whole procedure was halted. This allowed the Venezuelan to regain his original allotted grid position for the second start, but de Cesaris by then was back in the pit lane waiting to chase after the pack in his spare Ligier.

To take into account the extra parade lap, the race distance was automatically reduced to 61 laps. As the starting light blinked green it was Alboreto's Ferrari C4 which bounded into the lead as they piled into the first right-hander, Warwick right in his wheel tracks, but from the crowd little could be heard but an enormous sigh. Further back down the grid Nelson Piquet had started his World Championship defence on the lowest possible note by stalling his Brabham BT53 and there were quite a few "close calls" as the pack scrambled in all directions to avoid him. Cecotto's luck was much the same as before and the Toleman was left on the line for the second time that afternoon!

At the end of the opening lap Alboreto was several lengths clear in the lead and although Warwick hung on a second or so behind for the first five laps, his Michelin-shod Renault began to drop back slightly thereafter. It wasn't difficult to envisage the Ferrari C4 leading the entire distance and one could easily understand Enzo Ferrari's wisdom in selecting Alboreto to be a member of his team: the cool, precise manner in which he had handled his Tyrrell in 1983 was now transposed into the cockpit of a fully competitive car and was reaping the appropriate benefits.

Just as we were getting used to the sight of an Italian in an Italian car comfortably holding the lead, it was all over. Coming into the 180-degree right-hander before the pits at the end of his 12th lap, Michele's C4 suddenly spun like a top as he touched the brakes. Warwick and Lauda slipped through before he could gather himself up, but although the C4 actually crossed the timing line in third place, it immediately spun again, just as violently, on the right-hander *after* the pits. Clearly this was a little more than driver trouble and the Italian limped back to the pits. The car was closely examined and, after another cautious lap, retired.

The front right brake caliper had broken, letting out all the fluid, so there was no way the fault could be quickly repaired.

This little drama permitted Lauda, who had lunged past Warwick at the end of the tenth lap, to cruise into a comfortable lead. Of the incident with the English Renault driver, Niki remarked, "I suppose that I didn't expect him to stay out on the wide line so long. I know my car jumped a little over the bump on the entrance to the corner, but I honestly thought I was clear of Derek by then and that he'd have moved in behind me to get the best line for himself through the corner. The fact that my right rear hit his left front indicated I was well past him when he began to turn in . . ."

The impact was noticeable, but not unusually so, and Warwick settled down to run a regular second as the good-handling McLaren-TAG gradually eased off into the distance. Mansell was now running a strong third, but his 95T's advantage was being gobbled up by Prost's slow-starting McLaren, while Arnoux and Tambay were fifth and sixth with de Angelis, whose Renault engine had refused to rev. properly from the word go, dropping away slightly in seventh spot.

Sadly for the Brazilian crowd, Ayrton Senna's Toleman had been the very first retirement, his Hart engine suffering loss of turbocharger boost pressure which was later attributed to a batch of faulty, cracked turbine blades produced by a third party component supplier to Holset. Prior to the race Ayrton and his old British Formula 3 rival Martin Brundle had made a deal that, should one prove dramatically quicker than the other in the opening stages, they wouldn't hold each other up. "Needless to say, that was soon forgotten," grinned Brundle at the end of the day, "Ayrton was all over the place trying to keep me behind him . . . and he had me on the grass as we went down to the first corner!"

Bellof's Tyrrell was briefly ahead of both these young tyros, but a broken throttle cable put paid to his chances, while Baldi's Spirit soon dropped out with a broken rotor arm in the distributor of its Hart engine and Laffite pulled in soon after Alboreto's demise, his Honda engine having cut out on one bank owing to electrical trouble and suffering loss of turbo boost pressure as a result.

Nelson Piquet, meanwhile, was getting his head down and hauling his way back through the field in the Brabham, but his progress began to get a bit slower once he caught Eddie Cheever's Alfa 184T for tenth place as the next on his list were team-mate Teo Fabi and Keke Rosberg's Williams. Keke and Patrick Head had decided to try to compensate for the FW09's inherent understeer by screwing on as much front wing as the Finn could live with: to some extent it worked, minimising the understeer to a great degree, but now the Williams-Honda pivoted dramatically round its front end as the Finn flicked it into the corners. Still, it was a long slog and Rosberg was hanging on in eighth place, waiting to take advantage of the misfortune of others.

He didn't have to wait very long. Coming up to complete his 31st lap, Arnoux's Ferrari began belching flame and stuttering violently, due to a battery malfunction, and it rolled to a silent halt on

the side of the circuit shortly before the start of the pit entrance lane.

Just around the 30-lap mark many of the leading cars began making scheduled stops for fresh rubber. Tambay stopped early on lap 26, Warwick and Mansell were both in on lap 29, and when Derek got back into the race still in third place it seemed that he was in with a good chance of a win. Neither McLaren had made a stop yet, and Prost knew that his chances of going non-stop were looking less and less likely: early on he had picked up a lot of dirt on his Michelins and they were beginning to lose their grip. What he would need was a very quick stop, as late as he dared, so that he would be in good shape to deal with Derek in the closing stages. Lauda, meanwhile, looked as though he had the race in the bag.

Finally, Prost came in at the end of lap 38. The pit was ready for him, but, to the crew's horror, Alain came into view down the pit lane first! They just had sufficient time to register that Lauda *hadn't* gone past on the circuit when they caught sight of McLaren number eight trailing in behind its stablemate. Quickly, but not quickly enough, they hurried through Prost's tyre change; a jammed rear wheel nut meant it took over 20 seconds. But by the time they fell on Lauda's car the Austrian was almost out of the cockpit. Electrical trouble; all over. Close examination revealed that the plug supplying current from the battery to the wiring loom was faulty and the Bosch "electronic brain" had switched off as a result.

So, from the position of running 1-2, Prost now resumed as McLaren's sole survivor in a distant second place. The Brabham challenge had come to an end on lap 33 when Piquet's BT53, up with Rosberg, had lost an oil pipe to its turbocharger, resulting in KKK seizure, whilst Fabi's BT53 had simply overheated thanks to a turbo intake blocked with a mass of paper debris, probably thrown up by the madly enthusiastic crowd. Amongst the tail-enders, Alliot's RAM was out after its battery fell off and de Cesaris's spare Ligier succumbed to precisely the same gear selector breakage that had afflicted his originally nominated race car.

Nigel Mansell's opening race of the year came to an end at the end of the back straight on lap 36, the Englishman getting off-line as he fought too hard to protect his fourth place from Tambay's advances (did he think it was Warwick?) and his Lotus 95T slid spectacularly into the catch-fencing. It was to have been a vain effort, for Patrick's RE50 was destined to grind to a halt with only two laps left to run, a leaking fuel cell and cracked intercooler causing the French V6 to use up its allotted 220-litres some six miles short of the flag.

However, Tambay's retirement wasn't going to be Renault's only disappointment. With about 15 laps left to run, and nursing a healthy advantage, Warwick noticed a vibration building up in the front end of his Renault. Soon afterwards, he noticed the left-front wheel wobbling slightly under hard acceleration and hard braking. But with just over 10 laps to go to his first Grand Prix victory, he wasn't about to come into the pits to complain. Braking for the hairpin which leads on to the back straight on lap 52, it happened. The Renault's left-front upper wishbone broke, the RE50 spun

gently and Derek knew his race was over.

It was a present for Prost. Alain could now take it easy all the way to the chequered flag, cutting his TAG engine's limit by 1000rpm and making sure that it lasted. Four laps from the finish, Rosberg stormed past a slowing Tambay, the Frenchman's cockpit fuel read-out emphasising the awful news that he wouldn't make it to the finish – and he didn't. Keke was delighted with his second place, remarking "we really didn't deserve something as good as this after starting from ninth – it's a real bonus". De Angelis echoed similar sentiments about his third place in the Lotus while eventual fourth man, Eddie Cheever, felt much the same way. "Fifteen laps from the end I was pulling up on Keke, but I just had to say 'right, that's the end of my race . . . economy run now all the way to the end'. It's just so bloody frustrating . . ."

In Ken Tyrrell's words, fifth-placed Brundle had done "everything and more" that had been expected of him to take two points on his debut outing, but Tyrrell's day was slightly soured by an incomprehensible protest from Jack Oliver to the effect that the car had been *refuelled* when it stopped for tyres and water ballast in the middle of the race. Predictably, the protest was rejected when the Tyrrell tank was found to be in order, leaving Jack's two slow Arrows A6s to come home seventh and eighth after undramatic non-stop runs, the two Cosworth cars finishing behind Tambay's stationary Renault which was classified sixth. The only other running at the finish was Jonathan Palmer's RAM-Hart, the English doctor easing down the boost pressure in the closing stages to make sure he kept his 100 per cent Formula 1 finishing record intact. Two races, two finishes!

But at the end of the day, the Grand Prix left a few quizzical expressions on faces in the paddock. How had McLaren got it so obviously right after so little testing? As Ron Dennis ambled in his distinctive, bouncy fashion towards the car park, that silly grin was still there, wider than ever.

Perhaps all the other teams *had* been telling the truth, after all!   AH

Anxious looks from the McLaren pit as the fuel runs low and Prost enters the last lap of his economy run *(top left)*.
A sweet victory for Alain Prost as he takes a somewhat fortunate win for McLaren at the expense of his old team, Renault *(top right)*.
Lotus set the pace during winter testing and the official practice at Rio. Nigel Mansell was fastest on Friday with Elio de Angelis taking pole the following day. Mansell spun out of the race and de Angelis, although hampered by turbo trouble, managed to take third place *(above)*.

Entries and practice times

No.	Driver	Nat	Car	Tyre	Engine	Entrant	Practice 1	Practice 2
1	Nelson Piquet	BR	Parmalat BRABHAM BT53	M	BMW M12/13	MRD International	1m 31·068s	**1m 30·149s**
2	Teo Fabi	I	Parmalat BRABHAM BT53	M	BMW M12/13	MRD International	1m 33·951s	**1m 33·227s**
3	Martin Brundle	GB	TYRRELL 012	G	Ford Cosworth DFV/DFY	Tyrrell Racing Organisation	**1m 36·081s**	1m 36·191s
4	Stefan Bellof	D	TYRRELL 012	G	Ford Cosworth DFV/DFY	Tyrrell Racing Organisation	1m 36·957s	**1m 36·609s**
5	Jacques Laffite	F	WILLIAMS FW09	G	Honda RA 163–E	Williams Grand Prix Engineering	1m 32·032s	**1m 31·548s**
6	Keke Rosberg	SF	WILLIAMS FW09	G	Honda RA 163–E	Williams Grand Prix Engineering	1m 31·778s	**1m 30·611s**
7	Alain Prost	F	Marlboro McLAREN MP4/2	M	TAG P01 (TTE P01)	McLaren International	1m 29·823s	**1m 29·330s**
8	Niki Lauda	A	Marlboro McLAREN MP4/2	M	TAG P01 (TTE P01)	McLaren International	1m 29·951s	**1m 29·854s**
9	Philippe Alliot	F	RAM 02	P	Hart 415T	Skoal Bandit Formula 1 Team	1m 38·124s	**1m 37·709s**
10	Jonathan Palmer	GB	RAM 01	P	Hart 415T	Skoal Bandit Formula 1 Team	1m 39·840s	**1m 37·919s**
11	Elio de Angelis	I	John Player Special LOTUS 95T	G	Renault EF4	John Player Team Lotus	1m 29·625s	**1m 28·392s**
12	Nigel Mansell	GB	John Player Special LOTUS 95T	G	Renault EF4	John Player Team Lotus	**1m 29·364s**	1m 30·182s
14	Manfred Winkelhock	D	ATS D7	P	BMW M12/13	Team ATS	1m 35·395s	**1m 32·997s**
15	Patrick Tambay	F	Elf RENAULT RE50	M	Renault EF4	Equipe Renault Elf	1m 30·719s	**1m 30·554s**
16	Derek Warwick	GB	Elf RENAULT RE50	M	Renault EF4	Equipe Renault Elf	1m 30·945s	**1m 29·025s**
17	Marc Surer	CH	ARROWS A6	G	Ford Cosworth DFV	Barclay Nordica Arrows BMW	**1m 37·204s**	1m 37·348s
18	Thierry Boutsen	B	ARROWS A6	G	Ford Cosworth DFV	Barclay Nordica Arrows BMW	1m 36·737s	**1m 36·312s**
19	Ayrton Senna	BR	TOLEMAN TG183B	P	Hart 415T	Toleman Group Motorsport	1m 36·867s	**1m 33·525s**
20	Johnny Cecotto	YV	TOLEMAN TG183B	P	Hart 415T	Toleman Group Motorsport	1m 35·988s	**1m 35·300s**
21	Mauro Baldi	I	SPIRIT 101	P	Hart 415T	Spirit Racing	**1m 36·816s**	1m 39·873s
22	Riccardo Patrese	I	Benetton ALFA ROMEO 184T	G	Alfa Romeo 183T	Benetton Team Alfa Romeo	**1m 30·973s**	1m 31·679s
23	Eddie Cheever	USA	Benetton ALFA ROMEO 184T	G	Alfa Romeo 183T	Benetton Team Alfa Romeo	1m 33·115s	**1m 31·282s**
24	Piercarlo Ghinzani	I	Kelemata OSELLA FA1E	P	Alfa Romeo 183T	Osella Squadra Corse	1m 40·431s	**1m 36·434s**
25	Francois Hesnault	F	LIGIER Loto JS23	M	Renault EF4	Ligier Loto	1m 36·257s	**1m 36·238s**
26	Andrea de Cesaris	I	LIGIER Loto JS23	M	Renault EF4	Ligier Loto	1m 34·622s	**1m 32·895s**
27	Michele Alboreto	I	Fiat FERRARI 126C4	G	Ferrari 126C	Scuderia Ferrari SpA SEFAC	1m 29·958s	**1m 28·898s**
28	René Arnoux	F	Fiat FERRARI 126C4	G	Ferrari 126C	Scuderia Ferrari SpA SEFAC	1m 30·832s	**1m 30·695s**

Friday morning and Saturday morning practice sessions not officially recorded.

Fri pm — Hot, dry
Sat pm — Hot, dry

G – Goodyear, M – Michelin, P – Pirelli.

Starting grid

27 ALBORETO (1m 28·898s) Ferrari
11 DE ANGELIS (1m 28·392s) Lotus

7 PROST (1m 29·330s) McLaren
16 WARWICK (1m 29·025s) Renault

8 LAUDA (1m 29·854s) McLaren
12 MANSELL (1m 29·364s) Lotus

15 TAMBAY (1m 30·554s) Renault
1 PIQUET (1m 30·149s) Brabham

28 ARNOUX (1m 30·695s) Ferrari
6 ROSBERG (1m 30·611s) Williams

23 CHEEVER (1m 31·282s) Alfa Romeo
22 PATRESE (1m 30·973s) Alfa Romeo

*26 DE CESARIS (1m 32·895s) Ligier
5 LAFFITE (1m 31·548s) Williams

19 SENNA (1m 33·525s) Toleman
2 FABI (1m 33·277s) Brabham

3 BRUNDLE (1m 36·081s) Tyrrell
20 CECOTTO (1m 35·300s) Toleman

18 BOUTSEN (1m 36·312s) Arrows
25 HESNAULT (1m 36·238s) Ligier

4 BELLOF (1m 36·609s) Tyrrell
24 GHINZANI (1m 36·434s) Osella

17 SURER (1m 37·204s) Arrows
21 BALDI (1m 36·816s) Spirit

10 PALMER (1m 37·919s) RAM
9 ALLIOT (1m 37·709s) RAM

*Started from pit lane in spare car
Did not start:
14 Winkelhock (ATS), 1m 32·997s, disqualified

Results and retirements

Place	Driver	Car	Laps	Time and Speed (mph/km/h)/Retirement	
1	Alain Prost	McLaren-TAG t/c V6	61	1h 42m 34·492s	111·543/179·511
2	Keke Rosberg	Williams-Honda t/c V6	61	1h 43m 15·006s	110·790/178·3
3	Elio de Angelis	Lotus-Renault t/c V6	61	1h 43m 33·620s	110·480/177·8
4	Eddie Cheever	Alfa Romeo t/c V8	60		
5	Martin Brundle	Tyrrell-Cosworth V8	60		
6	Patrick Tambay	Renault t/c V6	59	Out of fuel	
7	Thierry Boutsen	Arrows-Cosworth V8	59		
8	Marc Surer	Arrows-Cosworth V8	59		
9	Jonathan Palmer	RAM-Hart t/c 4	58		
10	Derek Warwick	Renault t/c V6	51	Collapsed front suspension	
11	Andrea de Cesaris	Ligier-Renault t/c V6	42	Gearbox	
12	Riccardo Patrese	Alfa Romeo t/c V8	41	Gearbox	
13	Niki Lauda	McLaren-TAG t/c V6	38	Electrical	
14	Nigel Mansell	Lotus-Renault t/c V6	35	Accident	
15	Nelson Piquet	Brabham-BMW t/c 4	32	Engine	
16	Teo Fabi	Brabham-BMW t/c 4	32	Turbo	
17	René Arnoux	Ferrari t/c V6	30	Battery	
18	Piercarlo Ghinzani	Osella-Alfa Romeo t/c V8	28	Gearbox	
19	Francois Hesnault	Ligier-Renault t/c V6	25	Engine overheating	
20	Philippe Alliot	RAM-Hart t/c 4	24	Battery mounting	
21	Johnny Cecotto	Toleman-Hart t/c 4	18	Turbo boost pressure	
22	Jacques Laffite	Williams-Honda t/c V6	15	Electrical	
23	Michele Alboreto	Ferrari t/c V6	14	Brake caliper	
24	Mauro Baldi	Spirit-Hart t/c 4	12	Distributor	
25	Stefan Bellof	Tyrrell-Cosworth V8	11	Throttle Cable	
26	Ayrton Senna	Toleman-Hart t/c 4	8	Turbo boost pressure	

Fastest lap: Prost, on lap 42, 1m 36·499s, 116·622mph/187·686km/h (record).
Previous lap record: Nelson Piquet (F1 Brabham BT49D-Cosworth DFV), 1m 36·582s, 116·523mph/187·525km/h (1982).

Past winners

Year	Driver	Nat	Car	Circuit	Distance miles/km	Speed mph/km/h
1972*	Carlos Reutemann	RA	3·0 Brabham BT34-Ford	Interlagos	183·01/294·53	112·89/181·68
1973	Emerson Fittipaldi	BR	3·0 JPS/Lotus 72-Ford	Interlagos	197·85/318·42	114·23/183·83
1974	Emerson Fittipaldi	BR	3·0 McLaren M23-Ford	Interlagos	158·28/254·73	112·23/180·62
1975	Carlos Pace	BR	3·0 Brabham BT44B-Ford	Interlagos	197·85/318·42	113·40/182·50
1976	Niki Lauda	A	3·0 Ferrari 312T/76	Interlagos	197·85/318·42	112·76/181·47
1977	Carlos Reutemann	RA	3·0 Ferrari 312T-2/77	Interlagos	197·85/318·42	112·92/181·73
1978	Carlos Reutemann	RA	3·0 Ferrari 312T-2/78	Rio de Janeiro	196·95/316·95	107·43/172·89
1979	Jacques Laffite	F	3·0 Ligier JS11-Ford	Interlagos	197·85/318·42	117·23/188·67
1980	René Arnoux	F	1·5 Renault RS t/c	Interlagos	195·70/314·95	117·40/188·93
1981	Carlos Reutemann	RA	3·0 Williams FWO7C-Ford	Rio de Janeiro	193·82/311·92	96·59/155·45
1982	Alain Prost	F	1·5 Renault RE t/c	Rio de Janeiro	196·95/316·95	112·97/181·80
1983	Nelson Piquet	BR	1·5 Brabham BT52-BMW t/c	Rio de Janeiro	196·95/316·95	108·93/175·30
1984	Alain Prost	F	1·5 McLaren MP4/2-TAG t/c	Rio de Janeiro	190·69/306·89	111·54/179·51

*Non-championship

Points

WORLD CHAMPIONSHIP OF DRIVERS

1	Alain Prost	9 pts
2	Keke Rosberg	6
3	Elio de Angelis	4
4	Eddie Cheever	3
5	Martin Brundle	2
6	Patrick Tambay	1

CONSTRUCTORS' CUP

1	McLaren	9 pts
2	Williams	6
3	Lotus	4
4	Alfa Romeo	3
5	Tyrrell	2
6	Renault	1

Circuit data

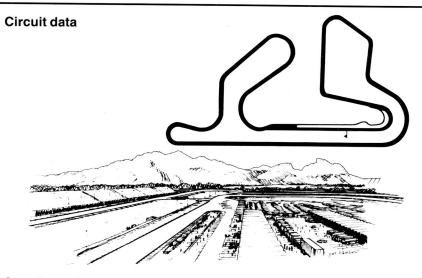

Autodromo Internacional do Rio de Janeiro, Baixada de Jacarepaguá

Circuit length: 3·126 miles/5·031 km
Race distance: 61 laps, 190·692 miles/306·889 km
Race weather: Hot, dry.

Lap chart

1st LAP ORDER		1	2	3	4	5	6	7	8	9	10	11	12	13	14	15	16	17	18	19	20	21	22	23	24	25	26	27	28	29	30	31	32	33	34	35	36	37
27	M. Alboreto	27	27	27	27	27	27	27	27	27	27	8	8	8	8	8	8	8	8	8	8	8	8	8	8	8	8	8	8	8	8	8	8	8	8	8	8	8
16	D. Warwick	16	16	16	16	16	16	16	16	8	8	16	16	16	16	16	16	16	16	16	16	16	16	7	7	7	7	7	7	7	7	7	7	7	7	7	7	7
12	N. Mansell	12	8	8	8	8	8	8	8	16	8	16	16	12	12	7	7	7	7	7	7	7	7	16	16	16	16	16	16	16	16	16	16	16	16	16	16	16
8	N. Lauda	8	12	12	12	12	12	12	12	12	12	12	12	7	7	12	12	12	12	12	12	12	12	12	12	12	12	28	11	11	12	12	12	15	15	15		
11	E. De Angelis	11	11	11	15	15	15	15	15	15	15	15	15	15	15	15	15	15	15	15	15	15	15	15	15	28	28	28	11	12	12	12	15	15	3	3		
15	P. Tambay	15	15	15	11	28	28	28	28	7	7	7	28	28	28	28	28	28	28	28	28	28	28	28	11	11	11	6	15	15	15	11	3	6	6			
28	R. Arnoux	28	28	28	28	7	7	7	7	28	28	28	11	11	11	11	11	11	11	11	11	11	11	11	11	6	6	6	1	1	3	3	6	11	11			
6	K. Rosberg	6	6	7	11	11	11	11	11	11	11	6	6	6	6	6	6	6	6	6	6	6	6	1	1	1	12	6	1	6	6	11	23	23				
23	E. Cheever	23	7	6	6	6	6	6	6	6	6	2	2	2	1	1	1	1	1	1	1	1	23	15	15	15	3	6	23	23	22	22						
7	A. Prost	7	23	2	2	2	2	2	2	2	2	23	23	1	1	2	2	23	23	23	23	23	15	23	23	2	2	22	22	22	18	26						
2	T. Fabi	2	2	23	23	23	23	23	23	23	23	1	1	23	23	23	23	2	22	22	22	22	22	22	3	3	23	18	18	18	26	18						
22	R. Patrese	22	22	22	22	22	22	22	22	22	1	5	5	22	22	22	22	3	3	3	3	3	3	3	2	18	22	26	26	26	17	17						
19	A. Senna	19	4	4	4	4	4	4	4	1	22	22	3	3	3	3	2	2	2	2	2	2	2	18	18	22	18	17	17	17	10	10						
4	S. Bellof	4	19	19	5	5	5	5	1	5	5	3	18	18	18	18	18	18	18	18	18	18	18	22	26	26	26	10	10									
3	M. Brundle	3	3	5	19	19	1	1	5	5	4	3	27	18	18	26	26	26	26	26	26	17	17	17	17	17	26	26	17	17								
5	J. Laffite	5	5	3	3	3	1	19	3	3	3	25	18	26	26	25	25	25	17	17	25	25	26	26	26	17	17	17	10	10								
25	F. Hesnault	25	25	25	25	1	3	3	25	25	25	18	25	25	20	20	17	17	25	26	26	25	25	10	10	10	10	10										
18	T. Boutsen	18	18	18	25	25	25	18	18	18	26	26	26	17	17	17	17	9	9	9	9	10	10	10	24	24	24											
24	P. Ghinzani	24	17	1	1	18	18	26	26	26	17	17	20	20	9	9	9	10	10	10	10	9	24	24														
17	M. Surer	17	24	17	17	17	26	17	17	17	17	20	9	9	10	10	10	24	24	24	24	24	9															
9	P. Alliot	9	1	24	26	26	17	17	20	20	20	9	9	10	10	24	24																					
21	M. Baldi	21	9	26	24	24	24	20	9	9	9	9	10	27	24																							
10	J. Palmer	10	26	9	9	20	20	24	10	10	10	10	21	24	24																							
1	N. Piquet	1	10	20	20	9	9	9	19	21	21	24																										
26	A. De Cesaris	26	20	10	10	10	10	21	24	24	24																											
20	J. Cecotto	20	21	21	21	21	21	21																														

38	39	40	41	42	43	44	45	46	47	48	49	50	51	52	53	54	55	56	57	58	59	60	61
7	16	16	16	16	16	16	16	16	16	16	16	16	7	7	7	7	7	7	7	7	7	7	7
8	7	7	7	7	7	7	7	7	7	7	7	7	16	15	15	15	15	15	6	6	6	6	6
16	15	15	15	15	15	15	15	15	15	15	15	15	6	6	6	6	6	6	15	15	15	11	11
15	6	6	6	6	6	6	6	6	6	6	6	6	11	11	11	11	11	11	11	11	11	23	
6	3	11	11	11	11	11	11	11	11	11	11	11	23	23	23	23	23	23	23	23	23	3	
3	11	3	3	3	23	23	23	23	23	23	23	23	3	3	3	3	3	3	3	3	3		
11	23	23	23	3	3	3	3	3	3	3	3	18	18	18	18	18	18	18	18	18			
23	22	22	22	26	18	18	18	18	18	18	18	17	17	17	17	17	17	17	17	17	17		
22	26	26	26	18	17	17	17	17	17	17	17	10	10	10	10	10	10	10	10	10	10		
26	18	18	18	17	10	10	10	10	10	10	10												
18	17	17	17	10																			
17	10	10	10																				
10																							

Fastest laps

Driver	Time	Lap
Alain Prost	1m 36·499s	42
Derek Warwick	1m 36·556s	47
Patrick Tambay	1m 37·211s	30
Elio de Angelis	1m 38·180s	36
Niki Lauda	1m 38·389s	7
Keke Rosberg	1m 38·506s	51
Michele Alboreto	1m 38·530s	3
Nigel Mansell	1m 38·796s	33
Eddie Cheever	1m 39·125s	39
Jonathan Palmer	1m 39·494s	9
Riccardo Patrese	1m 39·919s	35
Teo Fabi	1m 39·953s	25
Nelson Piquet	1m 40·003s	6
René Arnoux	1m 40·273s	6
Andrea de Cesaris	1m 40·673s	23
Martin Brundle	1m 40·804s	60
Jacques Laffite	1m 41·096s	5
Stefan Bellof	1m 41·676s	4
Ayrton Senna	1m 42·286s	6
Johnny Cecotto	1m 42·880s	11
Francois Hesnault	1m 42·998s	4
Thierry Boutsen	1m 43·247s	18
Piercrlo Ghinzani	1m 43·878s	20
Marc Surer	1m 43·960s	4
Philippe Alliot	1m 44·934s	14
Mauro Baldi	1m 46·380s	9

New for 1984

BRABHAM
Main interest through the winter surrounded the identity of driver to replace Patrese, who was unable to agree terms for 1984. Watson tipped until February when Teo Fabi was officially confirmed. He had signed in October 1983. Variations of BT52B tested. Final development and new chassis designated BT53.

TYRRELL
Alboreto signed by Ferrari. Benetton move support to Alfa Romeo leaving Tyrrell without a major sponsor once more. Brundle chosen on merit in the hope of attracting a British sponsor after promising test sessions in November and January. Sullivan nominated on a temporary basis for second car but Bellof takes the seat at the last minute thanks to financial help from a German consortium. Only team with plans to run Ford-Cosworth for full season.

WILLIAMS
Driver line-up unchanged. The winter spent consolidating lessons learned with the new FW09 Honda at the end of previous season.

McLAREN
Watson ousted by Prost at the end of 1983 season. New car, designed specifically for TAG turbo, announced just a few weeks before Brazilian GP.

RAM
Discarded Ford-Cosworth for Hart and secured sponsorship for one car from Alliot. Palmer signs in February with backing from various British sponsors. Team win support from Skoal a few days before Brazil.

LOTUS
Mansell's contract not renewed until negotiations with Watson terminated by the Ulsterman. Switched from Pirelli to Goodyear and unveiled their 95T in December. Set the pace during testing in Rio.

ATS
Pirelli tyres replace Goodyear. Designer Gustav Brunner leaves and Paul Owens stays briefly as Team Manager. Despite busy off-season discussion with various teams, Winkelhock and BMW stay.

RENAULT
A major restructuring in the immediate aftermath of 1983 season sees Prost being asked to leave. Tambay signed almost immediately. Cheever's contract not renewed and Warwick chosen in preference to de Cesaris. New car completed in December.

ARROWS
Win BMW engine deal against opposition from Toleman and Tyrrell but start season with Ford-Cosworth while awaiting completion of A7.

TOLEMAN
Lose Candy sponsorship. Recover from Warwick's departure to Renault by signing Senna. Cecotto, available after Theodore had switched to CART, replaces Giacomelli.

SPIRIT
Lost deal to run Honda turbo but secured Hart. Signed Baldi after testing with Emerson Fittipaldi in Rio. Deal to run Fulvio Ballabio in a Cosworth-powered car fell through when the Italian failed to gain Superlicence. Switched from Goodyear to Pirelli.

ALFA ROMEO
Marlboro and Michelin withdraw support. Patrese and Cheever signed while de Cesaris prevaricates. Goodyear supply tyres and Benetton provide sponsorship.

OSELLA
Gain access to Alfa turbo. Dropped by Michelin and change to Pirelli. Plan to enter second car later in season.

LIGIER
Run Renault V6 in preference to Ford Cosworth and keep Michelin. Additional sponsorship from Loto and Antar. Talked to Reutemann. Sign de Cesaris; Hesnault brings Superlicence and financial support.

FERRARI
Tambay sacked and replaced by Alboreto. C4 introduced in February.

National Panasonic Grand Prix of South Africa

After the race, they squeezed them, held them up to the light, poked them, sniffed them, shook them. There were about 40 in all; transparent plastic; about the size of tennis balls. And they came from the fuel tank of Niki Lauda's victorious Marlboro McLaren. Their volume equalled the amount by which the tank exceeded the 220-litre fuel capacity maximum; in other words, they made the MP4/2 legal – provided, of course, the balls were not found to have been carrying fuel, thereby circumventing the regulations.

But, on this or any other day, neither McLaren nor Lauda had need of such dubious tactics. The combination had simply devastated the opposition, Lauda reasserting himself after Prost had scored nine points at Rio. That had been a somewhat fortunate win for McLaren but there was nothing propitious about this victory at Kyalami, Prost underlining the point by finishing second after a brilliant drive from the back of the field in the team's spare car, the red and white phalanx lapping the entire field.

Mind you, during practice, it would have taken a brave man to wager on a result such as this. McLaren had been in trouble as their TAG engines refused to run cleanly at the 5,300ft altitude and it was left to Nelson Piquet's Parmalat Brabham-BMW to set the pace. Indeed, for the first ten laps or so, it seemed we would have a repeat of the Brabham domination in the South African Grand Prix six months previously as Piquet and Teo Fabi slaughtered everyone – bar a briskly determined Lauda.

Whereas, in 1983, Brabham had controlled the pace and treated their tyres with care, Lauda's attention played havoc with Brabham's Michelins and both blue and white cars were soon in the pits. By half distance, they would return for the duration, turbo trouble intervening, leaving Lauda to race towards a completely untroubled victory, his first in 18 months. Searching for his first Grand Prix win, Derek Warwick at least reached the victory rostrum for the first time when he finished third for Renault-Elf, thus making up for the disappointment of Rio. Ayrton Senna, Warwick's replacement at Toleman, reached a landmark in his promising career by scoring his first World Championship point. It was well earned. The Brazilian had struggled throughout with heavy steering, exacerbated by a damaged nose section, and Senna was removed to hospital suffering from exhaustion after finishing a lap down on the Benetton Alfa Romeo of Riccardo Patrese and Andrea de Cesaris's Loto Ligier, fourth and fifth respectively.

Ferrari produced the major change to form established in Rio when neither Michele Alboreto nor René Arnoux could make their cars handle well nor their engines run cleanly, both drivers stopping before the finish. Keke Rosberg, on the other hand, made the most of improvements to the Williams-Honda, the Finn taking a front row position and leading the first lap before being overhauled by the Brabhams. Rosberg's race was to end when a drive-shaft universal joint failed, but not before he had engaged in a brief but furious battle with Lauda as the Austrian re-established priorities within his team.

Two races down; a victory apiece for Lauda and Prost; McLaren leading the Constructor's Cup by 18 points. There was a long way to go, of course, but that sort of advantage was as impressive as the performances of both drivers – none of which would be denied by doubts over an armful of plastic balls.

ENTRY AND PRACTICE

During the winter there had been the usual doubts. The South African Grand Prix was on; it was off. There was no money; then, the emergence of a sponsor. But the modifications required by FISA would not be ready. Then, agreement. The pits could not be knocked down and rebuilt in time but a run-off at Crowthorne would be provided. The race was on; back in its usual slot at the beginning of the season and just six months after the championship finale of 1983 when an administrative quirk had moved the Kyalami date to the end of the season.

Kyalami, therefore, resumed its former importance as a testing venue and most teams had been present for a week in March. Keke Rosberg came away with the questionable honour of setting the fastest time in the Williams-Honda; questionable because most pundits were predicting things would be different in the heat of official practice. But, at the end of the first timed session on Thursday, Williams number six was at the top of the list and Rosberg was mildly surprised in the light of his handling problems at Rio.

Patrick Head had returned from Rio suffering from food poisoning but that did not prevent the Williams designer from thinking about a cure for the excessive understeer which afflicted his car. A modified differential, designed to provoke the rear of the car into a slide more readily, provided the answer to a degree as Rosberg claimed the overnight pole. The plan for Friday afternoon included running one set of race tyres and one set of qualifiers. Rosberg's car had been halted out on the circuit by a broken fuel pump drive-belt during the morning session and the team, conservative as ever, wanted to put more miles in, with the qualifiers standing by in case someone improved on Rosberg's time.

In the event, that someone turned out to be Nelson Piquet, the Brazilian taking over two tenths off Rosberg's time with a lap which contained all the fire and finesse we had come to expect from Nelson in full flight. It was a situation which Rosberg relished; nothing less than flat-out would redeem pole.

Rosberg's commitment to the job in hand was demonstrated to an exceptional degree when he came across a bunch of slower cars during that lap. He didn't lift his foot for a second as the Williams found space where none, apparently, existed. Then, turning into Club Corner, he ran wide and pole was lost there and then. None the less, he still managed to improve his time and keep Nigel Mansell off the front row; a superb performance.

Piquet, meanwhile, had been at pains to point out that the Brabham's relatively poor performance at Rio had little to do with a car which was not up to standard. They had not been testing there, he said, and he had stalled the car at the start. The Brabham was basically a sound car and the BMW was delivering the horsepower – a fact which the speed traps supported as Piquet and Fabi left the Hondas, Renaults and TAGs a poor second.

Nelson, of course, made full use of his 'qual-

"Take it away; I don't need any more trophies. Just give me the nine points." The South African organisers mislaid the trophy but Lauda wasn't bothered. Prost gave McLaren a clean sweep with a superb drive into second place while Derek Warwick reached the rostrum for the first time.

ifying' car which was fitted with a larger KKK turbo and Teo Fabi underlined the advantage of that particular chassis when he had need of it on Thursday. A broken turbo on the Italian's regular car meant he was allowed out in the spare chassis, recording a time good enough for the third row. The next day, back in his usual car, Fabi was over a second slower . . .

Brabham had experienced one or two problems during practice but, for Nigel Mansell, two days of near perfection put the Englishman in a contented frame of mind. Mind you, third place on the grid helped enormously. Mansell had completed various tests during a busy untimed session and, when it mattered, he was able to put together excellent laps on qualifying tyres. The JPS Lotus-Renaults had been fitted with bigger water radiators and it was Mansell who enjoyed the benefit of Garrett turbochargers from the start of practice. Elio de Angelis had to make do with the smaller KKKs on the first day but he improved on Friday after a fresh engine – with Garretts – had been fitted overnight.

Patrick Tambay, in contention throughout practice and fastest in both untimed sessions, slipped from third to fourth place on Friday afternoon. None the less, the Frenchman was optimistic since the Renault felt good in race trim and his fastest lap (in the spare car, fitted with larger Garrett turbos) had been spoiled by slower cars on Friday. Warwick had the larger turbos fitted to his car but the Englishman was surprised to find he had less boost than before. Then, on Friday, a slight hesitation in the engine while changing from third to fourth saw the Renault mechanics stripping the wiring in an attempt to trace the problem. As a result, Warwick had no rev-counter when he went out on his final set of qualifiers and, to compound his problems, he was baulked during that lap. Thursday's time, therefore, stood as his best; he would start from ninth place, behind the McLaren-TAG of Lauda.

Judging by their troublefree performance in Rio, it seemed that the Bosch technicians had sorted out their Motronic engine management system; the flat silver boxes had simply been bolted in place and they performed perfectly thereafter. At Kyalami, however, they were changed as frequently as the Grand Prix schedule. The engines would not pick up cleanly out of slow corners and a misfire between seven and eight thousand revs did not help either. The trouble, it was believed, lay with the fact that the micro-chips were not coping with the altitude; the effect, most certainly, was a reluctance for the turbos to accept qualifying boost.

The pick up problem had been improved slightly by Friday but, as frequently happens, the biggest breakthough came almost by accident. The spare car, no more than a chassis standing by in case of emergency in Rio, had been returned to England for completion and Prost used it briefly on Thursday morning. A problem with the gearlinkage stranded the Frenchman out on the circuit and a minor fire broke out when a heat shield caught alight. That extinguished, Prost used the car on Friday afternoon. Unlike the race cars, the spare

was fitted with smaller turbos and Prost found an improved throttle response – and 1.2 seconds; good enough for fifth place. Lauda would have smaller turbos fitted to his car for the race. . . .

At least McLaren were reasonably optimistic for the Grand Prix. The same could not be said for Ferrari, the Italian team, 10th and 15th, a picture of dejection after the promise shown at Rio. As a result of Michele Alboreto's retirement from the lead at Rio, Brembo had modified the brake caliper mountings but any thoughts of a repeat performance at Kyalami were quickly dispelled during practice. The red cars, clearly a handful on the fast corners, were struggling to match the pole position time set by Tambay's C3 in 1983. To improve the lack of grip, more wing was applied – which merely served to make the C4s painfully slow in a straight line. Blistered tyres told the story at the end of practice, Michele having turned in a white-knuckle lap for a place alongside Jacques Laffite.

If Rosberg preferred a car which oversteered, then Laffite was, if anything, happier with the original problem. Time had been lost on Thursday when an electrical problem with his race car meant Jacques had to use the spare and he just managed to beat Manfred Winkelhock's ATS with his very last lap of practice on Friday. Winkelhock, using the latest D7, was the fastest Pirelli runner, the German relying on his time from Thursday after spinning at Club Corner during the final session.

Manfred, as ever, had been brave and spectacular. Ayrton Senna, on the other hand, had about him the hallmark of a star in the making. His progress was smooth yet quick and, according to Brian Hart, executed with the minimum of revs. On Thursday, the Brazilian had lost most of the untimed session with low oil pressure. The afternoon proved to be just as frustrating when an electrical misfire cost a further 40 minutes of slow motoring. The following day he improved to 13th place, the Hart engine no longer suffering the boost pressure problems experienced in Rio after faulty components supplied to Holset had been tracked down. Johnny Cecotto, in 19th place, spent most of practice in the spare Toleman after a shunt at Barbecue on Thursday severely dented the monocoque on his regular car.

That sort of accident used to be the prerogative of Andrea de Cesaris but the Italian was continuing to show the more mature form seen at the end of 1983 as he urged the less than competitive Ligier-Renault into 14th place. François Hesnault, impressive considering his lack of both experience and Garrett turbos, was just half-a-second slower, the Frenchman trying a larger rear wing on Friday morning. The benefit marginally overcame the increased drag and both drivers took their turn at using it in the final session.

De Cesaris had been one of the star performers during the last visit to Kyalami but his old team, Alfa Romeo, looked unlikely to reproduce that form. Hamstrung by exceptionally heavy fuel consumption and small turbos (by 1984 qualifying standards), the green cars were just plain slow. In addition, the handling was a compromise, the Alfas either reasonably fast in a straight line and sliding in the corners or vice versa. Eddie Cheever took 16th spot while Riccardo Patrese, winner of the

1983 race for Brabham, was 18th after suffering from a misfire in the final session.

Osella had been one of the few teams to return to base after Rio in order to carry out windtunnel work. The result was larger nose wings and 20th fastest time for Piercarlo Ghinzani. Mauro Baldi was next, the Spirit-Hart continuing to suffer from a perplexing number of distributor rotor arm failures. But at least they were comfortably quicker than the RAM team of Jonathan Palmer and Philippe Alliot, neither driver having managed a single timed lap on Thursday.

The day had started badly for the Skoal sponsored team when Alliot was fined £2000 for failing to allow marshals to push his car when he kept his foot on the brake pedal after the RAM had stopped out on the circuit. Palmer, meanwhile, had suffered a broken crankshaft and, since there was no spare car, the plan was for the Englishman to share Alliot's car in the afternoon. All that took a dump when the Frenchman failed to complete one lap, a flap valve in the fuel system having jammed, stranding the car out on the circuit.

All was well on Friday, however, even though the drivers had found little time to complete any serious running, Palmer and Alliot qualifying ahead of Surer's Arrows-Cosworth and the Tyrrells and Bellof and Brundle. Tyrrell tried a larger rear wing but the loss of 300 revs was considered to be too expensive and, at the end of the day, Surer and Bellof achieved their times thanks to a tow from Winkelhock's ATS. Brundle, not aware of this tactic, just scraped in ahead of Thierry Boutsen, the only driver not to qualify. A glance at the speed trap times soon explained why; the Belgian driver's Arrows being the slowest at 158mph. Piquet, by comparison, had blasted through the radar beam at 190mph. The advantage of the turbo over the normally aspirated engine was considerable under normal circumstances; at 5,300ft, the Ford-Cosworth was from a bygone era.

RACE

Kyalami continued to retain a club atmosphere more akin to Snetterton or Laguna Seca but the 1984 Grand Prix was more low key than ever thanks to the race taking place during a holiday weekend. With the motorcycle Grand Prix having been held two weeks previously, it seemed the locals were more interested in a quiet weekend. And, with the additional attraction of the Rand Show at Pretoria, a mere 30,000 spectators made their way to Kyalami.

Those present to witness the morning warm-up got more than they bargained for when Piercarlo Ghinzani had a horrendous accident at the very fast Jukskei sweep. For reasons which were never quite clear, the Italian lost control as he turned into the left-hander at around 160mph, the Osella spinning to the right where a single layer of catch-fencing did little to prevent violent contact with the bank. The rear of the blue car took the initial impact, tearing the entire engine and gearbox away from the carbon fibre monocoque. Ghinzani, of course, had been running with a full load of fuel and the impact cut through the rear bulkhead as though it were made of wet cardboard. As a result, the rubber fuel cell was completely

exposed and at the mercy of a small fire which had broken out.

Fortunately, the cockpit section remained completely intact and the car did not turn over. Ghinzani, in a state of shock, removed his crash helmet and took off his left glove, the better to undo his safety harness. It was only the quick action of marshal Bert Fookes, as he pulled Ghinzani from the wreckage, which saved the driver from what could have been appalling injury as the whole area became an inferno just a few seconds later. Ghinzani was removed to hospital for treatment for burns to his hand, neck and forehead. The car was completely destroyed.

The warm-up had been brought to a halt and the short break favoured Niki Lauda. Anxious to try the smaller turbos for the first time, Lauda was perplexed to find his TAG engine suffering from a chronic misfire. Various components were changed while the track was cleared, thus giving Lauda time to complete a few laps – and set second fastest time!

Quickest of all had been Piquet although worries about overheating were manifesting themselves in the shape of ungainly ducting which had sprouted around the engine cover. Fabi was third fastest – followed by Prost: Brabham, McLaren, Brabham, McLaren; all four on Michelin.

Tyre choice then dominated the pre-race conversation. With refuelling a thing of the past, the latest game was to guess which teams might try to run non-stop. Warwick and Mansell gambled on running straight through while, of the Goodyear runners, Laffite took what looked like a clever option when he chose 'C' all round; if they lasted the distance, he would be in good shape. Rosberg and the Ferraris, for example, favoured the harder 'B' compound on the left-hand side with 'C' on the right. The Brabhams and the McLarens would run the softer '05s' and stop.

A more pressing problem for McLaren arose on the grid, however, when Prost's car refused to start in time for the final parade lap; the drive to the fuel pump having failed. Fortunately, in response to Lauda's problems during the morning, the spare car was fuelled and waiting, kitted out with the Austrian's seat and pedals. Prost vaulted the pit wall and the mechanics began to change as much as they could in the short space of time available.

Jacques Laffite's gamble on running non-stop
almost paid off with third place when a wheel nut
came loose on the Williams. Laffite receives
attention from Prost as the McLaren charges
through the field after starting from the pit lane. The
Frenchmen lap Alliot's RAM and challenge
Alboreto, the Ferrari driver having an altogether
unhappy weekend with handling and fuel-feed
problems *(left)*.
The remains of Ghinzani's Osella, delivered to
the paddock *(below)*.

Everything was replaced, with the exception of the brake pedal, and the pit lane, by now, was closed. Or, at least, it should have been.

A marshal, not well versed in the intricacies of the FIA Yellow Book, waved Prost on to the track and the Frenchman chased after the field, forming up at the back of the grid. A potential disqualification was avoided when two drivers stalled near the back of the grid and Derek Ongaro immediately ordered the start to be delayed. The McLaren management were on the ball immediately, calling Prost into the pit lane from where he would start in the prescribed manner.

Five minutes later and the field were back on the grid, this time taking the green light without further delay. No sooner had the race started than a potentially dangerous situation arose as Piquet almost stalled on pole position leaving Rosberg to make a clean and untroubled getaway. Mansell, right behind the Brabham, dodged to one side and a moment of glory in second place was short-lived as the Renault engine almost died. Suddenly, the black and gold car was engulfed by the pack and, ironically, Piquet was leading the charge, the Brabham driver having made a remarkable recovery to use the prodigious BMW power to the full as he reasserted himself in second place on the run down to Crowthorne.

Rosberg had the road to himself as he swept through the first corner but, by the time he had reached Leeukop, understeer and a general lack of grip told the Finn that it was merely a matter of time before the Brabham/Michelin combination would be on the attack. Sure enough, Piquet surged past the Williams at the start of lap two and, by the end of the lap, Fabi had also moved ahead to put the blue and white cars at the head of the field.

Behind the sliding Williams came Lauda, Warwick, Tambay, de Angelis, Alboreto and Laffite. Then a gap to Winkelhock and Patrese, who was about to come under pressure from an angry Mansell. The Lotus, in turn, was receiving attention from an equally hard-charging Arnoux, the Ferrari having passed de Cesaris. Senna was next and a threat from Cheever was to disappear at the end of lap four when the American became the first retirement, a balance weight having punched a hole in the Alfa Romeo's water radiator. So much for Cheever's belief that he had suffered just about every retirement reason in the book during the previous season. . . .

Cheever's departure helped clear a path for Prost, the Frenchman scything his way through after starting from the pit lane. He may have been in the spare car but it possessed the same qualities as its two sister cars; in other words, excellent balance and grip without abusing the Michelins.

Lauda was enjoying the same advantage, having managed to deal with Rosberg's Honda power on lap four and the Austrian immediately set about reducing the gap to Fabi. Two laps later and he was in touch with the Brabham, making Fabi work his tyres hard as he controlled the oversteering car. Lap 10 and Lauda was into second place, Fabi then making his way towards the pits for an unscheduled stop for tyres. As Lauda closed on Piquet, it would only be a matter of time before the same fate befell the World Champion.

The fuel consumption on the Renaults was measured by the digital read-out on the bottom left-hand corner of the dash panel. Ayrton Senna thoroughly deserved his first championship point, the Brazilian driver collapsing after struggling for most of the race with steering and handling made difficult by damage to the nose of his Toleman.

By lap 20, it was all over. Lauda had closed relentlessly, the pair sweeping on to the straight as one when Piquet raised his arm in warning that he, too, was making a stop for fresh Michelins. Now Lauda had a cushion of 20 seconds over Rosberg, the Williams leading an increasingly anxious queue of cars. Warwick led the attack but, while the Renault may have had the measure of the Williams in the corners, the French V6 could not cope with Japanese horsepower on the straight, thereby giving little opportunity for the Englishman to make the most of the favoured outbraking point into Crowthorne.

Fabi had rejoined in 15th place after a speedy stop but Piquet's tyre change took fractionally longer, the Brazilian rejoining as the Rosberg train rushed past the pits. Piquet then gave an impromptu demonstration of BMW power when he kept up with the gaggle of cars as they swept towards Crowthorne. In successive laps, Piquet picked off de Angelis, Tambay, Warwick and Rosberg to resume second place with a devastating display of the BT53's potential. Fabi, on the other hand, had retired with a broken turbo compressor and Piquet, although having little hope of catching Lauda, nevertheless ended a superb run with an identical problem on lap 29.

Lauda now had 40 seconds over Rosberg, the Williams continuing to keep four cars at bay. Among them was Prost, the McLaren driver working his way in front of Warwick, de Angelis and Tambay before stopping for tyres on lap 31. Now the pit stops began in earnest and it was time to examine the remainder of the field as the lap chart rearranged itself at the half-way stage.

The two RAM-Harts had retired after 25 laps, Palmer losing one gear after another and finally stopping with no electrics as he tried to make his way to the pits; Alliot stopping with a cooked engine after the Hart had lost most of its water. Cecotto suffered his second fright of the weekend when a tyre delaminated on the approach to Crowthorne, Johnny bringing the car safely to a halt in spite of a subsequent breakage to the suspension on the Toleman.

Senna was not without his problems even though the Brazilian was handily placed in the mid-field and planning to run non-stop. In the early stages, Ayrton had experienced a boost problem. In a bid to discover the cause, Senna was checking his temperature gauges when he hit an object lying on the track, just over the brow on the main straight. The impact took the top deck off the nose wings which, in turn, made the steering even heavier. To Aryton's surprise, however, the water radiators were not damaged and the engine, if anything, ran cooler after the impromptu modifications.

Warwick's plans to run non-stop were put to one side when he came in on lap 38 and, once the race had settled down, Lauda held a lead of around 30 seconds over Prost. Laffite was third (running non-stop and going superbly) ahead of Alboreto (no stop), Mansell (no stop) and Tambay. Rosberg, having almost stalled his Williams while trying to leave the pits, was eighth, ahead of Senna, Patrese, Bellof and Hesnault.

The order changed once more when Mansell's run came to an end, the inlet tract to the turbo

having collapsed giving the Renault engine no boost. Tambay, suffering an intermittent misfire from the start, made a second pit stop for tyres and, not long after, Rosberg slowed when the heat generated by the carbon fibre brakes caused a CV joint to seize. Almost unnoticed, Arnoux had stopped his Ferrari when a troublesome fuel injection system gave the impression of a fuel vapour lock. Alboreto was still going strongly, however, and the feature of the race became a fierce tussle for fourth place between the Ferrari and the Renault of Warwick. Sling-shotting from behind the Italian, Warwick drew alongside – slowly, very slowly – the two cars cresting the rise on the main straight at around 190mph and running side-by-side towards Crowthorne. Alboreto was not about to give up that easily but Warwick was not to be frightened as the Ferrari tried to edge the Renault towards the infield.

All this work was to be in vain, however when, five laps later, Warwick picked up a puncture in his right-rear tyre. It was at this point that radio contact came into play, Warwick preparing his crew for a rapid response which saw him return in sixth place behind his team-mate.

That soon became fifth when a very disconsolate Laffite walked back to the pits to inform his crew that a wheel nut had worked loose, thus depriving the Frenchman of his right-rear wheel and a well-deserved third place. Alboreto, now in trouble with his tyres and the electronic ignition, fell behind the two Renaults and, a few laps later, Warwick found himself in third place even though he had lost the use of his clutch. His good-fortune was at the expense of his team-mate, Tambay having parked by the track-side – with his tank empty. Just like Rio. The Frenchman was simmering with justifiable rage.

Half the field had retired now, Winkelhock stopping for good on lap 53 when the BMW engine cried enough. The cause was attributed to a poor battery which produced a misfire around half-distance. Not even Winkelhock could persuade the ATS to go much further once a valve had finally broken and dropped into the cylinder.

His fellow countryman, Bellof, made a more spectacular exit six laps later when a broken right-front hub caused brake failure as the Tyrrell reached Crowthorne. Bellof was thankful for the new run-off area as the black Tyrrell came to a dusty halt. Bellof had been running as strongly as his Cosworth would allow and Brundle had found the handicap too frustrating as he tried to get past the Ligier of Hesnault. Climbing all over the Frenchman in the corners, Brundle was helpless as the turbo pulled away on the straights. Bits of rubber flying past Brundle's helmet told of tyre trouble for the Ligier and Brundle tried to dive

inside Hesnault under braking for Leeukop. It didn't quite come off, the Tyrrell damaging its nose wings in the process, causing Brundle to make a quick pit stop, the English driver taking on ballast (or replenishing his water injection supply – depending on your point of view) at the same time.

On lap 62, Lauda set his fastest lap of the race, a feat which caused a little concern among his crew since the problems during practice meant there had been little time to closely examine fuel consumption. Despite exhortations to reduce his pace, Lauda kept reeling off reasonably fast laps since he wanted to make absolutely certain of this win. The team need not have worried since, at the post-race scrutineering, Lauda's car was found to have 13 litres remaining. Prost, having produced an altogether more hectic drive, cut his pace by over two seconds a lap, the McLaren never missing a beat as he gave the team maximum points.

Warwick, for all his problems, took a worthy third place and a consistent drive from Patrese meant three points for Alfa Romeo – just. There was half-a-litre of petrol remaining and had the race not been reduced by one lap in the event of the aborted start, Patrese would have been parked halfway round his final lap. De Cesaris, another steady if unspectacular drive, finished fifth to give Ligier their first points since 1982 while Senna crossed the line inches behind the French car. The Brazilian, not realising he was a lap behind, had been chasing fifth place – which, perhaps, was just as well since it took his mind off of growing fatigue. Indeed, once he had taken the flag, Ayrton relaxed and his hands fell from the steering wheel. It took all his effort to regain control and he had to be lifted from the car once he reached the pit lane.

Elio de Angelis, having lost time attending to a broken throttle linkage, took seventh place ahead of Mauro Baldi's Spirit, the Italian having a lonely run as he coped with a severe tyre vibration during the latter part of the race. The first Cosworth car home should have been the Arrows of Thierry Boutsen (allowed to start in the event of Ghinzani's accident) but, instead, that honour went to his team-mate Marc Surer. Thanks to a rare error by the Longines timing people, the Belgian driver was shown to have completed 70 instead of 71 laps. The omission was pointed out to the team but a protest was not lodged quickly enough and the results stood; Boutsen was classified 13th and last.

The organisers, meanwhile, were covering their embarrassment over an altogether more public affair; the silver trophy, a bowl valued at £14,000, could not be found and Lauda was presented instead with the Rand Grand Prix trophy. Not that Lauda cared. A cup was a cup as far as he was concerned. It didn't matter any more than the subsequent close scrutiny of about 40 plastic balls.

MH

THE pit lane at Kyalami was stunned by the news from the United States that the estate of Mark Donohue had been successful in a wrongful death suit brought against the Penske Corp. (entrants of the March 751 in which Donohue crashed during the Grand Prix warm-up at the Österreichring in 1975) and the Goodyear Tyre and Rubber Company (manufacturers of the tyre which was alleged to have contributed to the March leaving the track at the *Hella-Licht* curve).

Both companies were found negligent by the jury. After the verdict, the Judge ruled in favour of the cross-claim made by Penske against Goodyear, thus making the tyre company responsible for damages amounting to £19,584.00.

During practice at Kyalami, Trevor Hoskins, Director of Public Relations for the Goodyear International Corporation, issued the following statement:

"Despite the disappointing verdict by the jury in the Mark Donohue case, Goodyear will continue its existing programme of supplying auto racing tyres.

"We have been supplying tyres for auto racing for more than a quarter of a century, and we will continue to produce a reliable, dependable product to serve drivers in this demanding and sometimes dangerous sport.

"We are looking into further measures that can be taken to protect our interests in view of the apparent trend towards product liability litigation, even in an acknowledged high risk area such as motor sport.

"We have filed a notion for a new trial and, if unsuccessful, will appeal to the Rhode Island Supreme Court."

It was clear to everyone at Kyalami, and in motor sport in general, that the vagaries of the American legal system and the scope of the judgment had profound implications for the future of racing, particularly in the United States.

In such a specialised business, it had always been accepted that accidents caused by mechanical failure were part of the risk element and drivers were required to sign a waiver which said as much.

Donohue had signed such a disclaimer and, as a highly intelligent competitor and a competent engineer, he was more aware than most of the dangers involved in his chosen profession. Yet, by ignoring these facts and placing the blame directly at the door of Goodyear, the court in Providence, Rhode Island had given cause for a complete revision of thinking by manufacturers and team owners. If Goodyear failed in their appeal, the sport would be in jeopardy.

March:

Porsche decide to boycott Le Mans as a protest against the sudden announcement by FISA of rule changes scrapping the Group C fuel consumption formula in 1985.

Entries and practice times

No.	Driver	Nat	Car	Tyre	Engine	Entrant	Practice 1	Practice 2
1	Nelson Piquet	BR	Parmalat BRABHAM BT53	M	BMW M12/13	MRD International	1m 05·280s	**1m 04·871s**
2	Teo Fabi	I	Parmalat BRABHAM BT53	M	BMW M12/13	MRD International	**1m 05·923s**	1m 07·236s
3	Martin Brundle	GB	TYRRELL 012	G	Ford Cosworth DFY	Tyrrell Racing Organisation	1m 12·233s	1m 12·453s
4	Stefan Bellof	D	TYRRELL 012	G	Ford Cosworth DFY	Tyrrell Racing Organisation	1m 12·322s	**1m 12·022s**
5	Jacques Laffite	F	WILLIAMS FW09	G	Honda RA 163-E	Williams Grand Prix Engineering	1m 07·142s	**1m 06·762s**
6	Keke Rosberg	SF	WILLIAMS FW09	G	Honda RA 163-E	Williams Grand Prix Engineering	1m 05·127s	**1m 05·058s**
7	Alain Prost	F	Marlboro McLAREN MP4/2	M	TAG P01 (TTE P01)	Marlboro McLaren International	1m 06·576s	**1m 05·354s**
8	Niki Lauda	A	Marlboro McLAREN MP4/2	M	TAG P01 (TTE P01)	Marlboro McLaren International	1m 06·238s	**1m 06·043s**
9	Philippe Alliot	F	RAM 02	P	Hart 415T	Skoal Bandit Formula 1 Team	—	1m 10·619s
10	Jonathan Palmer	GB	RAM 01	P	Hart 415T	Skoal Bandit Formula 1 Team		1m 10·383s
11	Elio de Angelis	I	John Player Special LOTUS 95T	G	Renault EF4	John Player Team Lotus	1m 06·305s	**1m 05·953s**
12	Nigel Mansell	GB	John Player Special LOTUS 95T	G	Renault EF4	John Player Team Lotus	1m 05·792s	**1m 05·125s**
14	Manfred Winkelhock	D	ATS D7	P	BMW M12/13	Team ATS	**1m 06·974s**	1m 07·417s
15	Patrick Tambay	F	Elf RENAULT RE50	M	Renault EF4	Equipe Renault Elf	1m 05·588s	**1m 05·339s**
16	Derek Warwick	GB	Elf RENAULT RE50	M	Renault EF4	Equipe Renault Elf	**1m 06·056s**	1m 06·491s
17	Marc Surer	CH	ARROWS A6	G	Ford Cosworth DFV	Barclay Nordica Arrows BMW	1m 12·227s	**1m 11·808s**
18	Thierry Boutsen	B	ARROWS A6	G	Ford Cosworth DFV	Barclay Nordica Arrows BMW	1m 12·326s	**1m 12·274s**
19	Ayrton Senna	BR	TOLEMAN TG183B	P	Hart 415T	Toleman Group Motorsport	1m 07·657s	**1m 06·981s**
20	Johnny Cecotto	YV	TOLEMAN TG183B	P	Hart 415T	Toleman Group Motorsport	1m 09·829s	**1m 08·298s**
21	Mauro Baldi	I	SPIRIT 101	P	Hart 415T	Spirit Racing	1m 10·450s	1m 09·923s
22	Riccardo Patrese	I	Benetton ALFA ROMEO 184T	G	Alfa Romeo 183T	Benetton Team Alfa Romeo	1m 08·399s	**1m 08·042s**
23	Eddie Cheever	USA	Benetton ALFA ROMEO 184T	G	Alfa Romeo 183T	Benetton Team Alfa Romeo	**1m 07·704s**	1m 07·993s
24	Piercarlo Ghinzani	I	Kelemata OSELLA FA1F	P	Alfa Romeo 183T	Osella Squadra Corse	1m 10·829s	**1m 09·609s**
25	François Hesnault	F	LIGIER Loto JS23	M	Renault EF4	Ligier Loto	1m 09·909s	**1m 07·787s**
26	Andrea de Cesaris	I	LIGIER Loto JS23	M	Renault EF4	Ligier Loto	1m 09·132s	**1m 07·245s**
27	Michele Alboreto	I	Fiat FERRARI 126C4	G	Ferrari 126C	Scuderia Ferrari SpA	1m 07·404s	**1m 06·323s**
28	René Arnoux	F	Fiat FERRARI 126C4	G	Ferrari 126C	Scuderia Ferrari SpA	1m 07·514s	**1m 07·345s**

Thursday morning and Friday morning practice sessions not officially recorded.

G – Goodyear, M – Michelin, P – Pirelli.

Thur pm / Hot, dry
Fri pm / Hot, dry

Starting grid

1 PIQUET (1m 04·871s)
Brabham

6 ROSBERG (1m 05·058s)
Williams

12 MANSELL (1m 05·125s)
Lotus

15 TAMBAY (1m 05·339s)
Renault

*7 PROST (1m 05·354s)
McLaren

2 FABI (1m 05·923s)
Brabham

11 DE ANGELIS (1m 05·953s)
Lotus

8 LAUDA (1m 06·043s)
McLaren

16 WARWICK (1m 06·056s)
Renault

27 ALBORETO (1m 06·323s)
Ferrari

5 LAFFITE (1m 06·762s)
Williams

14 WINKELHOCK (1m 06·974s)
ATS

19 SENNA (1m 06·981s)
Toleman

26 DE CESARIS (1m 07·245s)
Ligier

28 ARNOUX (1m 07·345s)
Ferrari

23 CHEEVER (1m 07·704s)
Alfa Romeo

25 HESNAULT (1m 07·787s)
Ligier

22 PATRESE (1m 08·042s)
Alfa Romeo

20 CECOTTO (1m 08·298s)
Toleman

21 BALDI (1m 09·923s)
Spirit

10 PALMER (1m 10·383s)
RAM

9 ALLIOT (1m 10·619s)
RAM

17 SURER (1m 11·808s)
Arrows

4 BELLOF (1m 12·022s)
Tyrrell

3 BRUNDLE (1m 12·233s)
Tyrrell

18 BOUTSEN (1m 12·274s)
Arrows

*Started from pit lane
Did not start:
24 Ghinzani (Osella), 1m 12·274s, crashed during warm-up on race morning.

Results and retirements

Place	Driver	Car	Laps	Time and Speed (mph/km/h)/Retirement	
1	Niki Lauda	McLaren-TAG t/c V6	75	1h 29m 23·430s	128·367/206·587
2	Alain Prost	McLaren-TAG t/c V6	75	1h 30m 29·380s	126·822/204·1
3	Derek Warwick	Renault t/c V6	74		
4	Riccardo Patrese	Alfa Romeo t/c V8	73		
5	Andrea de Cesaris	Ligier-Renault t/c V6	73		
6	Ayrton Senna	Toleman-Hart t/c 4	72		
7	Elio de Angelis	Lotus-Renault t/c V6	71		
8	Mauro Baldi	Spirit-Hart t/c 4	71		
9	Marc Surer	Arrows-Cosworth V8	71		
10	François Hesnault	Ligier-Renault t/c V6	71		
11	Martin Brundle	Tyrrell-Cosworth V8	71		
12	Michele Alboreto	Ferrari t/c V6	70	Electronic ignition	
13	Thierry Boutsen	Arrows-Cosworth V8	70		
	Patrick Tambay	Renault t/c V6	66	Fuel metering unit	
	Jacques Laffite	Williams-Honda t/c V6	60	c/v joint	
	Stefan Bellof	Tyrrell-Cosworth V8	60	Broken hub	
	Manfred Winkelhock	ATS-BMW t/c 4	53	Battery/engine	
	Keke Rosberg	Williams-Honda t/c V6	51	Wheel nut/lost wheel	
	Nigel Mansell	Lotus-Renault t/c V6	51	Turbo inlet duct	
	René Arnoux	Ferrari t/c V6	40	Fuel injection	
	Nelson Piquet	Brabham-BMW t/c 4	29	Turbo compressor	
	Johnny Cecotto	Toleman-Hart t/c 4	26	Tyre failure	
	Philippe Alliot	RAM-Hart t/c 4	24	Water leak/engine	
	Jonathan Palmer	RAM-Hart t/c 4	22	Gearbox/electrics	
	Teo Fabi	Brabham-BMW t/c 4	18	Turbo compressor	
	Eddie Cheever	Alfa Romeo t/c V8	4	Damaged radiator	

Fastest lap: Tambay, on lap 65, 1m 08·877s, 133·279mph/214·492km/h.
Lap record: Alain Prost (F1 Renault RE30B t/c V6), 1m 08·278s, 134·455mph/216·385km/h (1982).

Past winners

Year	Driver	Nat	Car	Circuit	Distance miles/km	Speed mph/km/h
1934	Whitney Straight	GB	2·9 Maserati 8CM s/c	Prince George	91·20/146·77	95·68/153·98
1936	'Mario' Massacurati	I	2·0 Bugatti T35B s/c	Prince George	198·54/319·52	87·43/140·70
1937	Pat Fairfield	ZA	1·0 ERA A-type s/c	Prince George	198·54/319·52	89·17/143·50
1938	Buller Meyer	ZA	1·5 Riley	Prince George	198·54/319·52	86·53/139·26
1939	Luigi Villoresi	I	1·5 Maserati 4CM	Prince George	198·54/319·52	99·67/160·40
1960*	Paul Frère	B	1·5 Cooper T45-Climax	East London	145·80/234·64	84·88/136·60
1960*	Stirling Moss	GB	1·5 Porsche 718	East London	194·40/312·86	89·24/143·62
1961*	Jim Clark	GB	1·5 Lotus 21-Climax	East London	194·40/312·86	92·20/148·38
1962	Graham Hill	GB	1·5 BRM P57	East London	199·26/320·68	93·57/150·59
1963	Jim Clark	GB	1·5 Lotus 25-Climax	East London	206·55/332·41	95·10/153·05
1965	Jim Clark	GB	1·5 Lotus 25-Climax	East London	206·55/332·41	97·97/157·68
1966*	Mike Spence	GB	2·0 Lotus 33-Climax	East London	145·80/234·64	97·75/157·31
1967	Pedro Rodriguez	MEX	3·0 Cooper T81-Maserati	Kyalami	203·52/327·53	97·09/156·25
1968	Jim Clark	GB	3·0 Lotus 49-Ford	Kyalami	204·00/328·31	107·42/172·88
1969	Jackie Stewart	GB	3·0 Matra MS10-Ford	Kyalami	204·00/328·31	110·62/178·03
1970	Jack Brabham	AUS	3·0 Brabham BT33-Ford	Kyalami	204·00/328·31	111·70/179·76
1971	Mario Andretti	USA	3·0 Ferrari 312B-1/71	Kyalami	201·45/324·20	112·36/180·83
1972	Denny Hulme	NZ	3·0 McLaren M19A-Ford	Kyalami	201·41/324·20	114·23/183·83
1973	Jackie Stewart	GB	3·0 Tyrrell 006-Ford	Kyalami	201·45/324·20	117·14/188·52
1974	Carlos Reutemann	RA	3·0 Brabham BT44-Ford	Kyalami	198·90/320·10	116·22/187·04
1975	Jody Scheckter	ZA	3·0 Tyrrell 007-Ford	Kyalami	198·90/320·10	115·55/185·96
1976	Niki Lauda	A	3·0 Ferrari 312T/76	Kyalami	198·90/320·10	116·65/187·73
1977	Niki Lauda	A	3·0 Ferrari 312T-2/77	Kyalami	198·90/320·10	116·59/187·63
1978	Ronnie Peterson	S	3·0 JPS/Lotus 78-Ford	Kyalami	198·90/320·10	116·70/187·81
1979	Gilles Villeneuve	CDN	3·0 Ferrari 312T-4	Kyalami	198·90/320·10	117·19/188·60
1980	René Arnoux	F	1·5 Renault RE t/c	Kyalami	198·90/320·10	123·19/198·25
1981*	Carlos Reutemann	RA	3·0 Williams FWO7B-Ford	Kyalami	196·35/315·99	112·31/180·75
1982	Alain Prost	F	1·5 Renault RE 30B t/c	Kyalami	196·35/315·99	127·82/205·70
1983	Riccardo Patrese	I	1·5 Brabham-BMW BT52B t/c	Kyalami	196·35/315·99	126·10/202·94
1984	Niki Lauda	A	1·5 McLaren-TAG MP4/2 t/c	Kyalami	191·25/307·78	128·00/206·59

*Non-championship

Circuit data

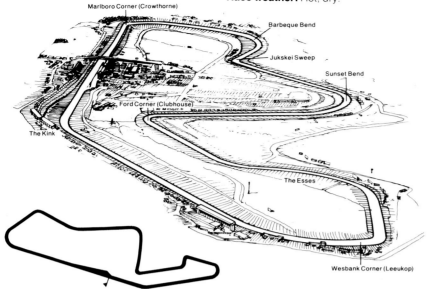

Kyalami Grand Prix Circuit, Johannesburg
Circuit length: 2·55 miles/4·104 km
Race distance: 75 laps, 191·247 miles/307·783 km
Race weather: Hot, dry.

Marlboro Corner (Crowthorne)
Barbeque Bend
Jukskei Sweep
Sunset Bend
Ford Corner (Clubhouse)
The Kink
The Esses
Wesbank Corner (Leeukop)

Fastest laps

Driver	Time	Lap
Patrick Tambay	1m 08·877s	65
Alain Prost	1m 08·961s	33
Derek Warwick	1m 09·526s	59
Niki Lauda	1m 09·666s	63
Nelson Piquet	1m 10·132s	6
Elio de Angelis	1m 10·150s	43
Teo Fabi	1m 10·345s	6
Keke Rosberg	1m 10·600s	39
Riccardo Patrese	1m 11·385s	44
René Arnoux	1m 11·421s	12
Jacques Laffite	1m 11·790s	6
Nigel Mansell	1m 11·825s	16
Michele Alboreto	1m 11·828s	4
Ayrton Senna	1m 12·124s	71
Stefan Bellof	1m 12·421s	2
Andrea de Cesaris	1m 12·510s	7
Johnny Cecotto	1m 12·523s	11
Manfred Winkelhock	1m 12·527s	5
François Hesnault	1m 13·054s	5
Mauro Baldi	1m 13·267s	69
Martin Brundle	1m 13·578s	30
Eddie Cheever	1m 14·046s	3
Marc Surer	1m 14·090s	67
Thierry Boutsen	1m 14·906s	57
Jonathan Palmer	1m 14·927s	14
Philippe Alliot	1m 14·943s	15

Points

WORLD CHAMPIONSHIP OF DRIVERS

1	Alain Prost	15 pts
2	Niki Lauda	9
3	Keke Rosberg	6
4=	Elio de Angelis	4
4=	Derek Warwick	4
6=	Eddie Cheever	3
6=	Riccardo Patrese	3
8=	Martin Brundle	2
8=	Andrea de Cesaris	2
10=	Patrick Tambay	1
10=	Ayrton Senna	1

CONSTRUCTORS' CUP

1	McLaren	24 pts
2=	Williams	6
2=	Alfa Romeo	6
4	Renault	5
5	Lotus	4
6=	Tyrrell	2
6=	Ligier	2
8	Toleman	1

Lap chart

1st LAP ORDER	1	2	3	4	5	6	7	8	9	10	11	12	13	14	15	16	17	18	19	20	21	22	23	24	25	26	27	28	29	30	31	32	33	34	35	36	37
6 K. Rosberg	6	1	1	1	1	1	1	1	1	1	1	1	1	1	1	1	1	1	1	1	1	8	8	8	8	8	8	8	8	8	8	8	8	8	8	8	8
1 N. Piquet	1	6	2	2	2	2	2	2	8	8	8	8	8	8	8	8	8	8	8	1	6	6	6	1	1	1	1	6	6	6	6	6	6	6	6	6	16
2 T. Fabi	2	2	6	8	8	8	8	8	2	2	6	6	6	6	6	6	6	6	6	6	6	16	16	1	6	6	6	16	7	16	16	16	16	16	16	16	11
8 N. Lauda	8	8	8	6	6	6	6	6	6	6	16	16	16	16	16	16	16	16	16	16	15	1	16	16	16	16	16	7	16	11	11	11	11	11	11	11	6
16 D. Warwick	16	16	16	16	16	16	16	16	16	16	16	15	15	15	15	15	15	15	15	15	1	15	15	15	15	7	7	7	11	11	7	27	27	27	27	5	5
15 P. Tambay	15	15	15	15	15	15	15	15	15	15	15	11	11	11	11	11	11	11	11	11	11	11	11	7	15	15	15	15	27	27	5	5	5	5	5	27	2
11 E. De Angelis	11	11	11	11	11	11	11	11	11	11	11	27	27	27	27	27	27	27	27	7	7	7	7	7	11	11	15	27	27	5	28	28	28	28	28	28	28
5 J. Laffite	5	27	27	27	27	27	27	27	27	27	27	5	5	5	5	5	5	5	7	27	27	27	27	27	27	27	27	5	5	28	12	12	12	12	12	12	12
27 M. Alboreto	27	5	5	5	5	5	5	5	5	5	5	28	28	28	28	7	7	7	5	5	5	5	5	5	5	5	5	28	28	15	7	7	7	7	7	7	7
22 R. Patrese	22	14	14	14	14	14	14	14	28	28	28	7	7	7	7	28	28	28	28	28	28	28	28	28	28	28	12	12	12	15	15	15	15	15	15	15	15
14 M. Winkelhock	14	22	22	22	12	12	12	28	14	12	12	12	12	12	12	12	12	12	12	12	12	12	12	12	12	12	26	26	26	26	26	22	22	22			
12 N. Mansell	12	12	12	12	28	28	28	12	12	7	7	14	14	14	14	14	14	14	14	14	14	14	14	26	26	14	26	26	22	22	22	22	22	19	19	19	
26 A. De Cesaris	26	26	26	28	22	22	22	26	7	14	14	26	26	26	26	26	26	26	26	26	26	14	14	26	22	22	19	19	19	19	19	26	25	25			
28 R Arnoux	28	28	28	26	26	26	6	7	26	26	26	2	22	22	22	22	22	22	2	22	22	22	22	22	19	25	25	25	25	25	5	4	4				
19 A. Senna	19	19	19	19	19	7	7	22	22	22	22	2	2	2	2	22	19	19	19	19	19	19	19	14	25	4	4	4	4	4	4	4	3	3			
23 E. Cheever	23	23	23	7	7	19	19	19	19	19	19	19	19	19	19	19	20	20	20	20	20	20	20	20	25	25	4	3	3	3	3	3	26	26			
21 M. Baldi	21	25	25	25	25	25	25	25	20	20	20	20	20	20	20	20	2	25	25	25	25	25	25	4	4	3	21	21	21	21	21	21	21				
4 S. Bellof	4	4	4	4	4	20	20	20	25	25	25	25	25	25	25	25	4	4	4	4	4	4	4	3	3	21	17	17	17	17	17	18	18				
7 A. Prost	7	21	7	23	20	4	4	4	4	4	4	4	4	4	4	4	3	3	3	3	3	3	3	21	21	17	18	18	18	18	18	17	17				
25 F. Hesnault	25	3	21	20	21	21	21	21	21	3	3	3	3	3	3	3	21	21	21	21	21	21	21	17	17	18	14	14	14	14	14	14	14				
3 M. Brundle	3	7	20	21	3	3	3	3	3	21	21	21	21	21	21	21	10	10	10	10	17	17	17	18	18	14											
10 J. Palmer	10	10	3	3	10	10	10	10	10	10	10	10	10	10	10	10	10	10	10	17	17	17	18	18	18												
20 J. Cecotto	20	20	10	17	17	17	17	17	17	17	17	17	17	17	17	17	17	17	17	18	18	18	9	9													
17 M. Surer			17	17	18	18	18	18	18	18	18	18	18	18	18	18	18	18	18	9	9	9															
18 T. Boutsen	18	18	18	18	9	9	9	9	9	9	9	9	9	9	9	9	9	9	9																		
9 P. Alliot	9	9	9	9																																	

38	39	40	41	42	43	44	45	46	47	48	49	50	51	52	53	54	55	56	57	58	59	60	61	62	63	64	65	66	67	68	69	70	71	72	73	74	75
8	8	8	8	8	8	8	8	8	8	8	8	8	8	8	8	8	8	8	8	8	8	8	8	8	8	8	8	8	8	8	8	8	8	8	8	8	8
11	11	11	5	5	7	7	7	7	7	7	7	7	7	7	7	7	7	7	7	7	7	7	7	7	7	7	7	7	7	7	7	7	7	7	7	7	7
16	5	5	27	7	5	5	5	5	5	5	5	5	5	5	5	5	5	5	5	5	5	27	15	15	15	15	15	16	16	16	16	16	16	16	16	16	16
5	27	27	7	27	27	27	27	27	27	27	27	27	16	16	16	16	16	27	27	27	27	15	27	27	16	16	16	27	27	27	27	22	22	22			
27	7	7	12	12	12	12	12	12	16	16	16	16	27	27	27	27	16	15	15	15	15	16	16	16	27	27	27	22	22	22	26	26	26				
28	28	28	15	15	15	16	16	16	12	12	12	6	19	19	15	15	15	16	16	16	22	22	22	22	22	26	26	26	26	19	19						
7	12	12	16	16	16	15	15	15	6	6	19	19	15	15	19	19	19	22	22	26	26	26	26	26	19	19	19	19	19	11							
12	15	15	6	6	6	6	6	6	15	22	22	22	22	26	26	26	19	19	19	19	19	19	19	11	11	11	11	21									
15	16	16	11	19	19	19	19	19	19	15	15	12	26	26	26	4	4	4	19	25	25	25	25	21	21	21	21	21									
6	6	6	19	22	22	22	22	22	22	22	4	4	4	4	19	19	17	21	21	21	21	21	11	25	25	17	25										
22	22	19	22	25	25	4	4	4	4	4	26	26	17	25	17	17	17	17	25	11	11	11	11	11	17	17	25	3									
19	19	22	25	4	4	25	25	26	26	26	4	4	25	25	25	25	21	3	3	3	3	17	17	3	3	3	3										
25	25	25	4	3	3	26	26	25	25	25	21	21	21	21	21	3	17	17	17	3	18	18	18	18													
4	4	4	3	26	26	26	3	3	3	21	21	3	3	3	3	11	18	18	18	18	18																
3	3	3	26	21	21	21	21	21	21	18	17	18	11	11	11	11	11	18																			
26	26	26	21	18	18	18	18	18	18	17	3	11	18	18	18	18																					
21	21	21	18	17	17	17	17	17	17	3	18	14	14																								
18	18	18	17	11	11	11	11	11	11	11	11																										
17	17	17	14	14	14	14	14	14	14	14																											
14	14	14																																			

115

Grand Prix of Belgium

Pole position, the first of Michele Alboreto's Grand Prix career, on Saturday; a totally dominant performance for 70 laps the day after.

That may have been the story of the Belgian Grand Prix but it would have taken a brave man to bet on such an outcome on Friday when the Ferrari driver could be found languishing in 10th place on the time sheet, with little hope of improvement.

Similarly, at the beginning of the week, it seemed Derek Warwick would have difficulty in completing the third round of the championship, never mind finishing second. Warwick had been relaxing in Spain with his daughters when he took a tumble from a go-kart and bruised his left knee. The swelling looked ominous but the Renault-Elf driver definitely felt no pain when he set fastest practice time on Friday.

Things were to change during the final session as improvements to the Ferraris put the red cars at the front, leaving Warwick to share the second row with the Williams-Honda of Keke Rosberg. A hesitant start by the Finn saw him drop to the back of the field but, for the next 90 minutes, we were treated to a truly remarkable drive as Rosberg, passing rivals as though they were stationary, worked his way into third place. Such a furious pace took its toll, however, the Williams running out of fuel on the last lap and allowing Arnoux to take the four points.

Rosberg was classified fourth ahead of Elio de Angelis, the JPS Lotus-Renault driver running non-stop on hard tyres and being made to work for his two points by Stefan Bellof as the Tyrrell driver made his mark with a forceful drive worthy of his first championship point.

Alboreto's first points of the season were never in doubt as he controlled the race from the front, Warwick settling for second place when he realised the Renault/Michelin combination was no match on the day for Ferrari and Goodyear. None the less, when the points were totted up at the end of a weekend which had been particularly frustrating for the favourites, Warwick had moved into second place in the championship.

Apart from a dramatic engine failure for Nelson Piquet while the Parmalat Brabham driver lay in a handy fourth place, the most talked about disasters befell the Marlboro McLaren team. Alain Prost and Niki Lauda were nowhere in practice and neither driver finished the race. After McLaren's successes in Brazil and South Africa, such a disastrous performance was as unexpected as Michele Alboreto dominating the Belgian Grand Prix in such a convincing fashion.

It was just as difficult to believe that Alboreto had become the first Italian driver to win for Ferrari since 1966. That seemed a long time ago. Michele was 10 years old then – and Derek Warwick was just beginning to play with go-karts.

"Who, me?" It was difficult to believe that Michele Alboreto had become the first Italian to win a Grand Prix for Ferrari since Ludivico Scarfiotti in 1966.

ENTRY AND PRACTICE

After much political manoeuvring, the Belgian Grand Prix was returned to Zolder; a move which was not well received, particularly after the delights of Spa Francorchamps the previous year. However, glorious weather from the start of practice helped dispel the gloom which seems to permanently hover over the place and teams began tackling the problems presented by the circuit rather than dwelling on Zolder's more unpleasant memories.

Derek Warwick had little time for emotion on Friday afternoon when he found his plans to run just one set of qualifying tyres spoiled by the inevitable traffic problems. Because he had not completed many laps during the unofficial session, Warwick had opted to run one set of race tyres during the timed session. Once he had the Renault to his liking, the qualifiers were bolted on but it was an angry Warwick who returned to the pits, his quickest lap blocked on at least one occasion. With the race rubber in place once more, Warwick took to the track and carried the RE50 by the scruff of the neck on to the overnight pole.

Apart from aerodynamic changes to suit Zolder, the Renaults were sporting bodywork which did not have the louvres designed to combat the heat of Rio and Kyalami. In addition, Warwick's car was running with SEP carbon fibre brakes but these were discarded when the car was found to be weaving alarmingly under braking. None the less, they did not prevent Warwick from earning his moment of glory, an achievement which was to be cancelled out the following day as the Englishman took over the T-car, his usual chassis having been carefully prepared with its race engine and then put to one side.

Warwick did manage to shave a few more tenths off his time but he could do nothing about the amazing turn around produced by Ferrari. In the days leading up to Zolder, Alboreto could be found testing the electronic engine management systems at Fiorano instead of simply bedding in the cars. It was a sure sign of Ferrari's desperation to make up for poor performances at Kyalami and both cars arrived at Zolder with the Lucas mechanical injection in place of the troublesome Marelli-Weber equipment. In addition, Michele had a revised exhaust system which turned out to be a successful bid to obtain more power at lower revs and reduce turbo lag even further.

Both drivers were slow on Friday thanks to uneven tyre temperatures front and rear. On Saturday, the weather was warmer still and the track perhaps worth another second per lap; whatever the circumstances, the Ferraris – with the aid of Harvey Postlethwaite, making a rare appearance – were in perfect shape to make the most of their Goodyears.

Early in the session, Arnoux recorded 1m 16.5s; just a few tenths short of Warwick's time from Friday. Alboreto equalled the Renault's time and it was Rosberg who then took pole with 15.4s. No sooner had the Williams returned to the pits than Arnoux was out once more to record 15.398s – but that wasn't the end of the drama. Screwing the boost control as high as they dared, the Ferrari team sent Alboreto out once more and he virtually cancelled practice for his rivals by taking the 126C4 round in 1m 14.846s; half a second faster than his team-mate. The rest were merely in the Second Division.

Rosberg, then, was third fastest and reasonably pleased to be there. Apart from continually chipping away at the understeer problem with the FW09, the Williams team were blighted by an abnormal number of engine failures (three on Friday alone). The problem was traced eventually to a lighter density but higher octane fuel for which insufficient compensation had been made on the fuel injection system. As a result, the mixture was too lean – and the Hondas finished their life with more oil outside than in. Bearing in mind the disruption to Frank Williams' carefully laid plans, Rosberg's time was most encouraging for the beleaguered team. Which was just as well since Laffite was down in 15th place, the Frenchman

being honest enough to admit a failure to make the most of his qualifying tyres.

Elio de Angelis (5th fastest) and Nigel Mansell (10th) were critical of slower drivers blocking the track as the Lotus-Renaults made their runs on qualifying tyres. The black and gold cars had reverted to older bodywork seen during winter testing in a bid to help cooling, while the reverse effect was intended when a small radiator was added between the fuel tank and pump in order to stop ice from the chilled fuel blocking the pump on race day.

ATS, to the surprise of many – including themselves, finished practice as the fastest BMW runner. While the Brabham team toiled through a chaotic two days, Manfred Winkelhock made the most of major developments to his D7. A spacer was inserted between the engine and gearbox as an aid to airflow to the rear wing and alterations to the

Derek Warwick was on top form all weekend in spite of bruising his knee while playing on a go-kart a few days earlier. The Renault/Michelin combination was no match for Ferrari and Goodyear but Warwick nevertheless took a fine second place.

suspension helped rid the yellow and black car of oversteer. A less scientific approach by Pirelli saw the tyre technicians shave the top layer off Winkelhock's used qualifiers, the German setting sixth fastest time when he discovered the tyres, in this modified form, offered more grip than before.

The ATS had been designed by Gustav Brunner before he left to join Euroracing at the beginning of the season and it was Riccardo Patrese who took seventh place on the grid; Eddie Cheever, three-tenths slower in 11th position. There was a spare 184T for the first time and both drivers were pleased with their cars in qualifying trim. Their main concern continued to be the Alfa V8's thirst for the limited amount of fuel during the race.

On the evidence of Friday's practice times, it seemed everything was in order within McLaren as Alain Prost sat in second place behind Warwick. Saturday afternoon, though, revealed the true extent of traumas affecting the championship leaders when Prost spun no less than three times! A malfunction with the Motronic management system meant the engine was cutting in and out and that was hardly conducive to Prost's smooth style. The Frenchman had to make do with Friday's time and slipped to eighth place – which was six better than his team-mate!

Lauda got off to a bad start when a fuel leak caused a sizeable fire and stranded his race car out on the circuit. Niki returned to collect the T-car but

had to wait for a new rear wing which was currently being used by Prost – Lauda's example being attached to the car parked out on the circuit. Once under way in the spare, Lauda found it was less than satisfactory and his hopes lay with an improvement on Saturday. That went wrong when a faulty coil cost 45 minutes in the morning. Then he had a pinion failure and the spare car was found to be suffering from a sticking fuel pressure relief valve. The winner of the South African Grand Prix finally emerged with 15 minutes of practice remaining and he could merely improve to a humble 14th place.

McLaren was in good company. Further along the pit lane, the scene in the Brabham garage was of seemingly endless stream of blue and white cars returning with their BMW engines trailing oil and water. Fresh supplies of fuel brought in from Germany on Friday night failed to cure the detonation problem, Piquet's engine on one occasion punching a rod through the block. This was the last thing the team needed since a busy test session at Snetterton had shown a heavily revised car to be of no benefit whatsoever and Gordon Murray had to quickly revert to older and, by now, rather tatty bodywork. Piquet's ninth place had been earned, fortunately, during one of the rare periods when the T-car was running well on Friday. On Saturday it destroyed another engine before he could get motoring and Fabi, meanwhile, stuttered into 18th place with a chronic misfire.

Not far from the Brabham garage, and right beside the Ferrari pit, the Zolder organisers had placed a memorial to Gilles Villeneuve, tragically killed at the circuit two years before. The sentiment was indeed merited but the rather gaudy nature of a memorial positioned at the entrance to the pit lane left a lot to be desired. By all means, let's remember a wonderful driver but let's not force drivers to recall that dark day as they go about their business.

Patrick Tambay, of course, was affected more than most by Gilles's death. The Frenchman did have problems with the gearchange on his new Renault but it was clear that Zolder and its environment held no pleasure whatsoever; practice being a chore, to be finished with as soon as possible. Tambay took 12th place on the grid.

There was also a new chassis available for Andrea de Cesaris but both he and François Hesnault seemed to be carrying most of the Renault engine problems of the weekend; the two Ligiers breaking turbos on Saturday afternoon. In addition, the Loto-sponsored team had to rebuild Hesnault's car after the Frenchman had crashed on Friday afternoon and torn off the right-hand suspension. De Cesaris was 13th quickest and Hesnault was 23rd although a time of 1m 19.710s from Friday morning gave a fairer indication of what the promising newcomer was capable of.

With their new car waiting in the wings, the Toleman team were making do with the now venerable TG183Bs, Johnny Cecotto setting the fastest time after Ayrton Senna had been parked out on the circuit on Friday with an electrical problem and slowed by an engine misfire the next day. Arrows, on the other hand, finally produced their BMW-engined A7 and it was Thierry Boutsen who was given the turbo since it was his home Grand Prix. There were in fact, two A7 chassis on hand but a shortage of the Heini Mader-tuned engines precluded its use and Marc Surer had to make do with the Cosworth A6. For a new car, the A7 performed well and the team were very satisfied with Boutsen's 17th place since they had not dared to run qualifying boost in view of the engine situation.

Following the massive accident at Kyalami, the Osella team had built a new FA1F and the surprise was that Piercarlo Ghinzani was there to drive it. With his left hand giving considerable discomfort, the Italian did well to qualify in 20th place. Stefan Bellof and Martin Brundle were not far behind, excellent handling with full tanks putting the Tyrrell drivers in good heart for the race even though the Cosworth cars were blown away by the turbos during qualifying. Well, most of the turbos.

Bringing up the rear were the Spirit of Mauro Baldi and Jonathan Palmer's RAM-Hart. Spirit had a spare car for the first time and they had need of it when Baldi had electrical trouble with his race car. The new car, painted white in deference to a sponsorship deal which didn't actually come off, was barely run in and it took Baldi time to work the combination into a reasonably competitive set-up. Palmer, meanwhile, was running a new 02 which hadn't turned a wheel before official practice. He lost valuable time with gearbox trouble and a blown turbo on Friday and, when he did get going, the handling of the Skoal-sponsored car was terrifying to watch. It was an altogether humbling experience for the man whose last visit to Zolder had seen him crowned European Formula 2 Champion. But, at least he had qualified. Philippe Alliot was the unlucky 27th when his RAM blew its engine on Saturday morning. The Frenchman waited to take over Palmer's car and, when he went out to set his time, the turbo failed.

RACE

Alain Prost arrived on race morning rubbing the back of his head. One of the spins the previous day had given him a pain in the neck in every sense of the expression but a course of treatment from Willi Dungl was keeping the discomfort to a minimum.

Indeed, there seemed little to trouble the McLarens during the warm-up and rivals noted with some disquiet that the red and white cars were

third and fourth. That, perhaps, was expected but the performance of Michele Alboreto, almost a second faster than the rest, showed that practice had not been a one-off deal. The Italian put in more laps than anyone else as he tried an engine with a revised exhaust system and declared himself happy with the benefit of more power at lower revs.

Ferrari's plans then appeared to take a dump when the bag tank on Michele's car required changing not long before the start. Alboreto watched dispassionately as his mechanics crammed the fuel tank into place in time for him to prepare for the start procedure.

There was no trouble as the drivers formed on the grid for the last time. Derek Ongaro gave the red light, followed by the green – and Rosberg moved a couple of inches before an electrical misfire flattened the engine at peak revs. Rosberg was unable to get the Williams moving as the rest of the pack surged forward and it seemed certain that someone at the back of the grid would fall foul of the green and white constriction in an already narrow pit straight.

Cars darted left and right, Piquet putting two wheels on the grass as he went by – but all was well. Warwick made the most of the situation, tucking in behind Alboreto and forcing Arnoux to take third place as they rushed towards the first corner. De Angelis had swerved to the right, almost collecting Winkelhock as he did so, but the ATS driver kept his foot hard on the power and took fourth place. Of the rest, Mansell was already in trouble with a slipping clutch while Cecotto had a more serious version of the same problem, the Toleman driver creeping round to the pits to post the first retirement. Rosberg, meanwhile, was finally under way. A dramatic performance was about to unfold.

APRIL:
FISA deny rumour suggesting ban on cooled fuel in Formula 1.
Jaguar make provisional entry for Le Mans.

As Alboreto put the hammer down and Warwick successfully fended off an early challenge from Arnoux, the most significant in what was to become a long list of retirements occurred during lap six when the leader of the World Championship slowed and stopped. A broken distributor rotor meant no points today for Alain Prost.

As the race began to settle down, Alboreto eased out a lead of six seconds over Warwick. After 10 laps, the Renault driver decided to see how much both he and Alboreto had in hand. Increasing his pace by a second a lap, and setting his fastest lap in the process, Warwick could make little impression and the Englishman realised that, barring mechanical misfortune, nothing would stop the smooth progress of Ferrari number 27. The Belgian Grand Prix was won there and then.

By now, Warwick had pulled eight seconds ahead of Arnoux with Winkelhock giving Pirelli an encouraging run by keeping in touch with the Ferrari. Piquet was making ground after his start from a lowly grid position, the Brabham closing on the ATS and taking fourth place on lap 23. De Angelis, running hard tyres with the intention of dispensing with a pit stop, was gradually dropping back into the clutches of Eddie Cheever while the pair of them were being caught by Rosberg, the Finn having worked his way into a remarkable eighth place.

Rosberg was the sole surviving Williams now that Jacques Laffite had retired from the back of the field. The Frenchman had been struggling for the start with an engine that kept cutting out, finally causing Jacques to spin and stall. Needless to say, the Honda started perfectly when returned to the garage after the race. . . .

Also out of the running were Patrese with ignition trouble; Mansell, who finally stopped after being acutely embarrassed by the non-turbo Tyrrells; Boutsen, who retired with a misfiring engine – caused by a loose plug on a wire to the alternator flattening the battery; Hesnault, with

overheating thanks to a radiator leak and, finally, Ghinzani with what was officially described as 'transmission' trouble. The Italian had cut through the field at an amazing rate and there was the suggestion that the Osella was running with a light load of fuel since Piercarlo's hand injury would prevent him from reaching the finish. Whatever, it was an impressive-looking drive while it lasted.

A few weeks before the Grand Prix, competitors in a Formula 3 race had complained bitterly about the Zolder track surface breaking up and the worst fears of the Grand Prix drivers began to be realised when the edge of the racing line became thick with treacherous 'marbles'. Passing became an even more difficult business than usual – but that scarcely seemed to bother either Nelson Piquet or Keke Rosberg.

The Brabham was showing signs of overheating but the reigning World Champion pressed on as though his race was going to finish any minute and he wanted to enjoy himself while the going was good. Having worked his way into fourth place behind Arnoux, Piquet took the Ferrari in a superbly incisive move through one of the very fast right-hand corners at the back of the circuit.

Arnoux wasn't too bothered since he was about to make his pit stop but the Frenchman was to lose further ground when his pit crew took 18.95 seconds and René, by now thoroughly disheartened, rejoined in 13th place to lap at almost a second off his previous pace. It would take several laps before Arnoux was to realise that his was not a lost cause and points were available.

Piquet, meanwhile, was continuing his impressive run and interest switched to Rosberg as the Williams, going quicker still, closed on the Brabham. However, there was to be no contest here; Nelson running wide at *Bolderbergbocht*, allowing Rosberg to quickly snap up third place on lap 32.

By now, the pit stops were under way and the true pattern of the race was emerging as we established just who was running non-stop. Warwick, of course, had planned originally to make his tyres last for 70 laps but that early spurt in pursuit of Alboreto had taken its toll on his Michelins. The Englishman came in on lap 33, the Renault crew sending him on his way in 11.5 seconds to rejoin in third place behind Rosberg. Winkelhock came in at the same time but the German's fifth place was about to disappear in a stop which took 27 seconds. Not that it was to make much difference since Winkelhock was already experiencing brake trouble and his eventual retirement would be caused by a broken exhaust pipe dislodging an electrical wire.

Lauda had already made his stop, the Austrian never having been in contention and he was to close a miserable weekend for McLaren when a water pump failure finally brought to an end a drive which had been hampered by a cracked intercooler and a loss of boost pressure. Lauda, of course, accepted the problem in his usual phlegmatic manner but Eddie Cheever was understandably frustrated when his Alfa Romeo, running strongly in fifth place, stopped with a piston failure.

and, at the start of lap 56, Keke produced one of the finest pieces of overtaking seen for some time.

Using his Honda power to the full, Rosberg out-accelerated the Tyrrell as they rushed down the pit straight. De Angelis, watching the move in his right-hand mirror, attempted to stall any further progress by Rosberg when they reached the braking area for the next corner – but Keke merely darted behind the Lotus and dived through on the left to take fifth place.

While all this had been going on, Brundle was walking back to the pits, his Tyrrell having rolled to a halt on three wheels. Martin had made his pit stop to take on ballast and tyres but, unfortunately, a thread on the left-front hub had seized before the wheel nut was properly in place. There was only about one-sixteenth of an inch in it, but it was enough for the wheel to part company with the car two corners later. Mauro Baldi, never having been in contention from the start, stopped at the same time with a broken damper-mounting on his Spirit.

The furious activity at the front of the field continued as Arnoux chased after Piquet, taking third place from the Brabham on lap 60. Not satisfied with that, René then set a new lap record as he gave serious thought to catching Warwick but those plans went awry when the Ferrari spun at *Kanaal Bocht* on lap 65. According to eye-witness reports from spectators, René received a push start as marshals helped him on his way to fifth place but the matter was not raised after the race.

Fifth became fourth as Piquet stopped with a massive engine failure which almost tore the Brabham apart. And fourth became third on the last lap when Rosberg rolled to a halt less than a mile from the finish, his fuel tank dry after a brilliant drive. Once back in the paddock, the Williams was weighed and found to be exactly on the limit. There was a certain amount of discussion within the team about how the car had run out of fuel when their driver had a gauge advising him of the car's consumption; figures which were backed up by advisory pit signals. To be sure, Rosberg had driven his car hard and the Honda had consumed more fuel than usual but, according to the team, the cockpit gauge told Rosberg so. The problem, it seemed, was that the driver thought he had 220 litres when, in fact, the tank held 217.5 litres. Either way, Williams were lucky to be classified fourth (on distance covered) on a day when McLaren had scored no points.

De Angelis thoroughly deserved his fifth place and Bellof, after stopping to take on ballast, scored his first championship point. Senna was seventh and Tambay was relieved to see the end of an unhappy weekend (which included a spin during the race) as he brought his Renault home in eighth place, two laps behind the leaders.

Alboreto had nothing but praise for his car. "Everything perfect. It ran like a watch," he said with a nonchalance which suggested it had been that way from the first lap of practice. Warwick, for his part, was delighted with second place. On reaching the paddock to be welcomed by his mechanics, the Englishman unclipped his belts and, on the way out of the cockpit, banged his knee. It was a sharp and painful reminder that nothing should be taken for granted in Grand Prix racing.

MH

Alboreto's Ferrari, meanwhile, continued to sound as though it could run all day but the Italian's smooth progress was suddenly and dramatically disrupted by a trip across the dirt at the exit of the first left-hander after the pits. Fortunately for Michele, no harm was done and this was ample warning that his rear Goodyears were past their best. Ferrari had perhaps cut a very fine edge with their calculations since Alboreto was due to stop at the end of that lap and this he did, getting away in 11.3 seconds without losing his comfortable lead over Rosberg.

The Williams, of course, had yet to stop and, since he held a mere six seconds over Warwick, it was clear that Rosberg would drop down the order after taking on tyres. Thus, on lap 43, the order was: Alboreto, 28 seconds clear of Warwick who was finding little improvement from his fresh set of Michelins; Piquet and de Angelis. The Lotus driver, battling gamely on his hard Goodyears, was being severely embarrassed by the Tyrrell of Stefan Bellof. Rosberg was sixth, Arnoux seventh and Brundle eighth, the Tyrrell running strongly with Fabi before the Brabham driver spun off while

trying to lap the RAM of Jonathan Palmer.

At the same point on the track, and just a few moments later, Andrea de Cesaris was to spin his Ligier into retirement and the question of whether the accident was caused by driver error or broken suspension was subject to different interpretations after the race. Whatever the reason, it was the end of a typically hard-charging drive from the Italian after working his way up the lap chart to briefly hold sixth place.

As Alboreto sailed serenely on, there was frantic activity at the bottom end of the top six. De Angelis had received respite from the attentions of Bellof when the German had been held up while attempting to lap the Arrows of Surer. Bellof eventually forced his way inside with a move which seemed to catch Surer by surprise, the Swiss almost losing control on the loose surface – right in front of Rosberg and Arnoux.

The Ferrari driver was awake and charging once more, the incentive of catching and eventually passing Rosberg spurring him into fourth place as he overtook Bellof and de Angelis on the same lap! Rosberg was keen to keep in touch with Arnoux

Entries and practice times

No.	Driver	Nat	Car	Tyre	Engine	Entrant	Practice 1	Practice 2
1	Nelson Piquet	BR	Parmalat BRABHAM BT53	M	BMW M12/13	MRD International	**1m 16·604s**	1m 24·286s
2	Teo Fabi	I	Parmalat BRABHAM BT53	M	BMW M12/13	MRD International	1m 20·193s	**1m 18·848s**
3	Martin Brúndle	GB	TYRRELL 012	G	Ford Cosworth DFY	Tyrrell Racing Organisation	1m 20·527s	**1m 20·123s**
4	Stefan Bellof	D	TYRRELL 012	G	Ford Cosworth DFY	Tyrrell Racing Organisation	1m 21·003s	**1m 19·811s**
5	Jacques Laffite	F	WILLIAMS FW09	G	Honda RA 163–E	Williams Grand Prix Engineering	1m 19·230s	**1m 18·125s**
6	Keke Rosberg	SF	WILLIAMS FW09	G	Honda RA 163–E	Williams Grand Prix Engineering	1m 18·617s	**1m 15·414s**
7	Alain Prost	F	Marlboro McLAREN MP4/2	M	TAG P01 (TTE P01)	Marlboro McLaren International	**1m 16·587s**	1m 16·595s
8	Niki Lauda	A	Marlboro McLAREN MP4/2	M	TAG P01 (TTE P01)	Marlboro McLaren International	1m 18·831s	**1m 18·071s**
9	Philippe Alliot	F	RAM 02	P	Hart 415T	Skoal Bandit Formula 1 Team	**1m 21·253s**	1m 44·990s
10	Jonathan Palmer	GB	RAM 02	P	Hart 415T	Skoal Bandit Formula 1 Team	1m 25·647s	**1m 20·793s**
11	Elio de Angelis	I	John Player Special LOTUS 95T	G	Renault EF4	John Player Team Lotus	1m 17·705s	**1m 15·979s**
12	Nigel Mansell	GB	John Player Special LOTUS 95T	G	Renault EF4	John Player Team Lotus	1m 18·048s	**1m 16·130s**
14	Manfred Winkelhock	D	ATS D7	P	BMW M12/13	Team ATS	1m 18·753s	**1m 17·171s**
15	Patrick Tambay	F	Elf RENAULT RE50	M	Renault EF4	Equipe Renault Elf	1m 18·753s	**1m 15·611s**
16	Derek Warwick	GB	Elf RENAULT RE50	M	Renault EF4	Equipe Renault Elf	1m 16·311s	**1m 15·611s**
17	Marc Surer	CH	ARROWS A6	G	Ford Cosworth DFV	Barclay Nordica Arrows BMW	**1m 20·615s**	1m 21·088s
18	Thierry Boutsen	B	ARROWS A7	G	BMW M12/13	Barclay Nordica Arrows BMW	1m 19·164s	**1m 18·351s**
19	Ayrton Senna	BR	TOLEMAN TG183B	P	Hart 415T	Toleman Group Motorsport	1m 18·914s	**1m 18·876s**
20	Johnny Cecotto	YV	TOLEMAN TG183B	P	Hart 415T	Toleman Group Motorsport	1m 19·537s	**1m 18·321s**
21	Mauro Baldi	I	SPIRIT 101	P	Hart 415T	Spirit Racing	1m 23·462s	**1m 20·644s**
22	Riccardo Patrese	I	Benetton ALFA ROMEO 184T	G	Alfa Romeo 183T	Benetton Team Alfa Romeo	1m 18·052s	**1m 16·431s**
23	Eddie Cheever	USA	Benetton ALFA ROMEO 184T	G	Alfa Romeo 183T	Benetton Team Alfa Romeo	1m 18·401s	**1m 16·746s**
24	Piercarlo Ghinzani	I	Kelemata OSELLA FA1F	P	Alfa Romeo 183T	Osella Squadra Corse	1m 21·432s	**1m 19·734s**
25	François Hesnault	F	LIGIER Loto JS23	M	Renault EF4	Ligier Loto	**1m 20·439s**	1m 21·493s
26	Andrea de Cesaris	I	LIGIER Loto JS23	M	Renault EF4	Ligier Loto	1m 18·239s	**1m 17·471s**
27	Michele Alboreto	I	Fiat FERRARI 126C4	G	Ferrari 126C	Scuderia Ferrari SpA	1m 18·369s	**1m 14·846s**
28	René Arnoux	F	Fiat FERRARI 126C4	G	Ferrari 126C	Scuderia Ferrari SpA	1m 18·017s	**1m 15·398s**

	Fri pm Warm, dry	Sat pm Warm, dry

Friday morning and Saturday morning practice sessions not officially recorded.

G – Goodyear, M – Michelin, P – Pirelli.

Starting grid

27 ALBORETO (1m 14·846s)
Ferrari

    28 ARNOUX (1m 15·398s)
    Ferrari

6 ROSBERG (1m 15·414s)
Williams

    16 WARWICK (1m 15·611s)
    Renault

11 DE ANGELIS (1m 15·979s)
Lotus

    14 WINKELHOCK (1m 16·130s)
    ATS

22 PATRESE (1m 16·431s)
Alfa Romeo

    7 PROST (1m 16·587s)
    McLaren

1 PIQUET (1m 16·604s)
Brabham

    12 MANSELL (1m 16·720s)
    Lotus

25 CHEEVER (1m 16·746s)
Alfa Romeo

    15 TAMBAY (1m 17·171s)
    Renault

26 DE CESARIS (1m 17·471s)
Ligier

    8 LAUDA (1m 18·071s)
    McLaren

5 LAFFITE (1m 18·125s)
Williams

    20 CECOTTO (1m 18·321s)
    Toleman

18 BOUTSEN (1m 18·351s)
Arrows

    2 FABI (1m 18·848s)
    Brabham

19 SENNA (1m 18·876s)
Toleman

    24 GHINZANI (1m 19·734s)
    Osella

4 BELLOF (1m 19·811s)
Tyrrell

    3 BRUNDLE (1m 20·123s)
    Tyrrell

25 HESNAULT (1m 20·439s)
Ligier

    17 SURER (1m 20·615s)
    Arrows

21 BALDI (1m 20·644s)
Spirit

    10 PALMER (1m 20·793s)
    RAM

Did not start:
9 Alliot (RAM), 1m 21·253s, did not qualify

Results and retirements

Place	Driver	Car	Laps	Time and Speed (mph/km/h)/Retirement	
1	Michele Alboreto	Ferrari t/c V6	70	1h 36m 32·048s	115·221/185·430
2	Derek Warwick	Renault t/c V6	70	1h 37m 14·434s	114·394/184·1
3	René Arnoux	Ferrari t/c V6	70	1h 37m 41·851s	113·835/183·2
4	Keke Rosberg	Williams-Honda t/c V6	69	Out of fuel	
5	Elio de Angelis	Lotus-Renault t/c V6	69		
6	Stefan Bellof	Tyrrell-Cosworth V8	69		
7	Ayrton Senna	Toleman-Hart t/c 4	68		
8	Patrick Tambay	Renault t/c V6	68		
9	Marc Surer	Arrows-Cosworth V8	68		
10	Nelson Piquet	Brabham-BMW t/c 4	66	Engine	
11	Jonathan Palmer	RAM-Hart t/c 4	64		
	Mauro Baldi	Spirit-Hart t/c 4	53	Suspension	
	Martin Brundle	Tyrrell-Cosworth V8	51	Lost wheel	
	Teo Fabi	Brabham-BMW t/c 4	42	Spun off	
	Andrea de Cesaris	Ligier-Renault t/c V6	42	Accident	
	Manfred Winkelhock	ATS-BMW t/c 4	39	Exhaust/electrics	
	Niki Lauda	McLaren-TAG t/c V6	35	Water pump	
	Eddie Cheever	Alfa Romeo t/c V8	28	Engine	
	Jacques Laffite	Williams-Honda t/c V6	15	Electrics	
	François Hesnault	Ligier-Renault t/c V6	15	Radiator leak	
	Thierry Boutsen	Arrows-BMW t/c 4	15	Loose wire/engine misfire	
	Piercarlo Ghinzani	Osella-Alfa Romeo t/c V8	14	Transmission	
	Nigel Mansell	Lotus-Renault t/c V6	14	Clutch	
	Alain Prost	McLaren-TAG t/c V6	5	Distributor	
	Riccardo Patrese	Alfa Romeo t/c V8	2	Ignition	
	Johnny Cecotto	Toleman-Hart t/c 4	1	Clutch	

Fastest lap: Arnoux, on lap 64, 1m 19·294s, 120·233mph/193·497km/h (record).
Previous lap record: John Watson (F1 McLaren MP4B-Cosworth DFV), 1m 20·214s, 118·854mph/191·278km/h (1982).

Past winners

Year	Driver	Nat	Car	Circuit	Distance miles/km	Speed mph/km/h
1950	Juan Manuel Fangio	RA	1·5 Alfa Romeo 158 s/c	Francorchamps	307·08/494·20	110·04/177·09
1951	Giuseppe Farina	I	1·5 Alfa Romeo 159 s/c	Francorchamps	315·85/508·31	114·32/183·99
1952	Alberto Ascari	I	2·0 Ferrari 500	Francorchamps	315·85/508·31	103·13/165·96
1953	Alberto Ascari	I	2·0 Ferrari 500	Francorchamps	315·85/508·31	112·47/181·00
1954	Juan Manuel Fangio	RA	2·5 Maserati 250F	Francorchamps	315·85/508·31	115·06/185·17
1955	Juan Manuel Fangio	RA	2·5 Mercedes-Benz W196	Francorchamps	315·85/508·31	118·83/191·24
1956	Peter Collins	GB	2·5 Lancia-Ferrari D50	Francorchamps	315·85/508·31	118·44/190·61
1958	Tony Brooks	GB	2·5 Vanwall	Francorchamps	210·27/338·40	129·92/209·09
1960	Jack Brabham	AUS	2·5 Cooper T53-Climax	Francorchamps	315·41/507·60	133·63/215·06
1961	Phil Hill	USA	1·5 Ferrari Dino 156	Francorchamps	262·84/423·00	128·15/206·24
1962	Jim Clark	GB	1·5 Lotus 25-Climax	Francorchamps	280·36/451·19	131·90/212·27
1963	Jim Clark	GB	1·5 Lotus 25-Climax	Francorchamps	280·36/451·19	114·10/183·63
1964	Jim Clark	GB	1·5 Lotus 25-Climax	Francorchamps	280·36/451·19	132·79/213·71
1965	Jim Clark	GB	1·5 Lotus 33-Climax	Francorchamps	280·36/451·19	117·16/188·55
1966	John Surtees	GB	3·0 Ferrari 312/66	Francorchamps	245·32/394·80	113·93/183·36
1967	Dan Gurney	USA	3·0 Eagle T1G-Gurney-Weslake	Francorchamps	245·32/394·80	145·99/234·95
1968	Bruce McLaren	NZ	3·0 McLaren M7A-Ford	Francorchamps	245·32/394·80	147·14/236·80
1970	Pedro Rodriguez	MEX	3·0 BRM P153	Francorchamps	245·32/394·80	149·97/241·36
1972	Emerson Fittipaldi	BR	3·0 JPS/Lotus 72-Ford	Nivelles-Baulers	196·69/316·54	113·35/182·42
1973	Jackie Stewart	GB	3·0 Tyrrell 006-Ford	Zolder	183·55/295·39	107·74/173·38
1974	Emerson Fittipaldi	BR	3·0 McLaren M23-Ford	Nivelles-Baulers	196·69/316·54	113·10/182·02
1975	Niki Lauda	A	3·0 Ferrari 312T/75	Zolder	185·38/298·34	107·05/172·28
1976	Niki Lauda	A	3·0 Ferrari 312T/76	Zolder	185·38/298·34	108·11/173·98
1977	Gunnar Nilsson	S	3·0 JPS/Lotus 78-Ford	Zolder	185·38/298·34	96·64/155·53
1978	Mario Andretti	USA	3·0 JPS/Lotus 79-Ford	Zolder	185·38/298·34	111·38/179·24
1979	Jody Scheckter	ZA	3·0 Ferrari 312T-4	Zolder	185·38/298·34	114·24/179·02
1980	Didier Pironi	F	3·0 Ligier JS11/15-Ford	Zolder	190·66/306·86	115·82/186·40
1981	Carlos Reutemann	RA	3·0 Williams FW07C-Ford	Zolder	143·01/230·15	112·12/180·44
1982	John Watson	GB	3·0 McLaren MP4B-Ford	Zolder	185·38/298·34	116·19/187·00
1983	Alain Prost	F	1·5 Renault RE40 t/c	Francorchamps	173·13/278·62	119·14/191·73
1984	Michele Alboreto	I	1·5 Ferrari 126C4 t/c	Zolder	185·38/298·34	115·22/185·43

Circuit data

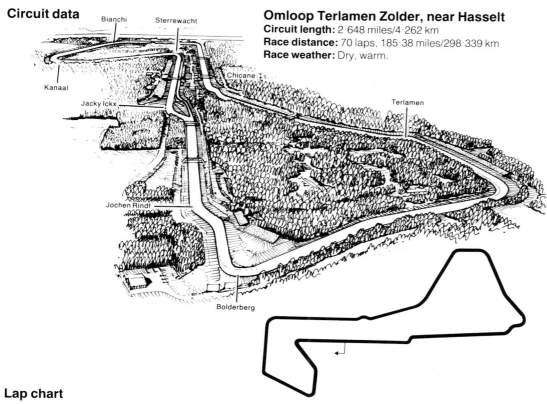

Bianchi · Sterrewacht · Chicane · Terlamen · Kanaal · Jacky Ickx · Jochen Rindt · Bolderberg

Omloop Terlamen Zolder, near Hasselt
Circuit length: 2·648 miles/4·262 km
Race distance: 70 laps, 185·38 miles/298·339 km
Race weather: Dry, warm.

Points

WORLD CHAMPIONSHIP OF DRIVERS

1	Alain Prost	15 pts
2	Derek Warwick	10
3=	Niki Lauda	9
3=	Michele Alboreto	9
3=	Keke Rosberg	9
6	Elio de Angelis	6
7	René Arnoux	4
8=	Eddie Cheever	3
8=	Riccardo Patrese	3
10=	Andrea de Cesaris	2
10=	Martin Brundle	2
12=	Ayrton Senna	1
12=	Patrick Tambay	1
12=	Stefan Bellof	1

CONSTRUCTORS' CUP

		Points
1	McLaren	24 pts
2	Ferrari	13
3	Renault	11
4	Williams	9
5=	Alfa Romeo	6
5=	Lotus	6
7	Tyrrell	3
8	Ligier	2
9	Toleman	1

Fastest laps

Driver	Time	Lap
René Arnoux	1m 19·294s	64
Keke Rosberg	1m 20·527s	62
Michele Alboreto	1m 20·727s	20
Derek Warwick	1m 21·245s	13
Nelson Piquet	1m 21·450s	12
Stefan Bellof	1m 21·650s	27
Eddie Cheever	1m 21·703s	28
Manfred Winkelhock	1m 21·754s	5
Teo Fabi	1m 21·812s	40
Niki Lauda	1m 21·853s	12
Elio de Angelis	1m 22·115s	11
Patrick Tambay	1m 22·298s	54
Martin Brundle	1m 22·324s	10
Andrea de Cesaris	1m 22·327s	28
Nigel Mansell	1m 22·374s	9
Thierry Boutsen	1m 22·560s	13
Ayrton Senna	1m 22·633s	58
Alain Prost	1m 22·879s	4
Piercarlo Ghinzani	1m 23·096s	10
Jacques Laffite	1m 23·164s	10
Marc Surer	1m 23·813s	15
François Hesnault	1m 23·945s	15
Riccardo Patrese	1m 24·430s	2
Mauro Baldi	1m 25·564s	11
Jonathan Palmer	1m 25·973s	9
Johnny Cecotto	1m 28·744s	1

Lap chart

1st LAP ORDER — laps 1–37

Driver	1	2	3	4	5	6	7	8	9	10	11	12	13	14	15	16	17	18	19	20	21	22	23	24	25	26	27	28	29	30	31	32	33	34	35	36	37
27 M. Alboreto	27	27	27	27	27	27	27	27	27	27	27	27	27	27	27	27	27	27	27	27	27	27	27	27	27	27	27	27	27	27	27	27	27	27	27	27	27
16 D. Warwick	16	16	16	16	16	16	16	16	16	16	16	16	16	16	16	16	16	16	16	16	16	16	16	16	16	16	16	16	16	16	16	16	16	6	6	6	6
28 R. Arnoux	28	28	28	28	28	28	28	28	28	28	28	28	28	28	28	28	28	28	28	28	28	28	1	1	1	1	1	1	1	6	6	16	16	16	16		
14 M. Winkelhock	14	14	14	14	14	14	14	14	14	14	14	14	14	14	14	14	14	14	14	14	14	1	1	14	6	6	6	6	6	6	1	1	1	1	1	1	1
11 E. De Angelis	11	11	11	11	7	11	11	11	1	1	1	1	1	1	1	1	1	1	1	1	1	1	1	1	14	14	6	14	23	23	14	14	14	14	11	11	11
22 R. Patrese	22	22	7	7	11	1	1	11	11	11	11	11	11	11	11	11	11	11	11	11	11	11	11	11	11	6	23	23	14	14	11	11	11	11	26	26	4
7 A. Prost	7	7	1	1	1	23	23	23	23	23	23	23	23	23	23	23	23	23	23	23	6	6	23	11	11	11	11	8	26	26	26	26	4	4	26	2	
23 E. Cheever	23	1	23	23	23	15	15	15	15	15	15	15	15	15	6	6	6	6	6	6	6	23	23	11	28	8	8	8	26	8	4	4	4	2	2	2	3
1 N. Piquet	1	23	15	15	15	26	26	8	8	8	8	8	8	6	15	8	8	8	8	8	8	8	8	8	2	26	26	4	4	2	2	2	3	3	3	28	
15 P. Tambay	15	15	26	26	26	8	8	26	26	6	6	6	6	8	8	15	15	2	2	2	2	2	2	2	26	4	4	3	3	3	3	3	28	28	28	14	
26 A. De Cesaris	26	26	8	8	8	18	2	2	6	26	2	2	2	2	2	2	2	15	15	26	26	26	26	26	26	4	2	3	2	2	28	28	28	8	14	14	26
8 N. Lauda	8	8	18	18	18	2	6	6	2	2	26	26	24	26	26	26	26	26	15	15	15	15	4	4	3	3	2	28	28	8	8	8	14	8	17	17	
18 T. Boutsen	18	18	2	2	2	24	24	24	24	24	24	24	26	4	4	4	4	4	4	3	3	3	4	3	3	28	28	28	19	19	19	19	19	19	17	15	15
2 T. Fabi	2	2	24	24	24	6	12	12	12	12	12	12	4	3	3	3	3	4	4	3	15	19	19	19	17	17	17	17	17	17	15	15	19	19			
24 P. Ghinzani	24	24	12	12	6	12	4	4	4	4	4	4	3	19	19	19	19	19	19	19	17	17	17	17	17	15	15	15	15	15	15	10	10				
12 N. Mansell	12	12	4	4	12	4	3	3	3	3	3	3	12	24	5	17	17	17	17	17	17	17	15	15	15	21	21	21	21	21	10	10	21	21			
3 M. Brundle	3	3	3	3	4	3	17	17	5	5	5	19	19	5	17	21	21	21	21	21	21	21	21	21	21	10	10	10	10	10	21	21					
4 S. Bellof	4	4	6	6	3	17	5	5	19	19	19	5	5	17	25	10	10	10	10	10	10	10	10	10	10	10	10	10									
17 M. Surer	17	17	17	17	17	5	19	19	17	17	17	17	17	25	21																						
6 K. Rosberg	6	6	5	5	5	19	25	25	25	25	25	25	25	21	10																						
5 J. Laffite	5	5	25	25	19	25	18	21	21	21	21	21	21	10	18																						
20 J. Cecotto	20	25	19	19	25	21	21	10	10	10	10	10	10	12																							
25 F. Hesnault	25	19	21	21	21	10	10	18	18	18	18	18	18	18																							
19 A. Senna	19	10	10	10	10																																
10 J. Palmer	10	21																																			
21 M. Baldi	21	20																																			

Laps 38–70

38	39	40	41	42	43	44	45	46	47	48	49	50	51	52	53	54	55	56	57	58	59	60	61	62	63	64	65	66	67	68	69	70
27	27	27	27	27	27	27	27	27	27	27	27	27	27	27	27	27	27	27	27	27	27	27	27	27	27	27	27	27	27	27	27	27
6	6	6	6	6	6	16	16	16	16	16	16	16	16	16	16	16	16	16	16	16	16	16	16	16	16	16	16	16	16	16	16	16
16	16	16	16	16	16	1	1	1	1	1	1	1	1	1	1	1	1	1	1	1	28	28	28	28	28	6	6	6	6	6	28	
1	1	1	1	1	1	11	11	11	11	11	11	11	11	11	11	28	28	28	28	1	1	1	1	6	1	1	28	28	28			
11	11	11	11	11	11	4	4	4	4	4	4	4	4	4	11	6	6	6	6	6	6	6	6	1	28	28	11	11	11			
4	4	4	4	4	4	4	6	6	6	6	6	6	6	6	11	11	11	11	11	11	11	11	11	11	11	4	4	4				
2	2	2	2	28	28	28	28	28	28	28	28	28	4	4	4	4	4	4	4	4	19	19	19									
3	3	3	3	3	3	3	3	3	3	3	3	3	15	15	15	15	15	19	19	19	19	19	19	19	19	15	15	15				
28	28	28	28	28	17	17	17	17	17	15	15	15	19	19	19	19	19	19	19	15	15	15	15	15	15	17	17	17				
14	14	26	17	17	17	15	15	15	15	15	17	17	21	21	10	10	10	10	10	10	10	10	10									
26	26	17	26	26	19	19	19	19	19	17	17	21	21	10	10	10	10	10	10	10	10	10	10									
17	17	15	15	15	21	21	21	21	21	21	21	21	10	10																		
15	15	19	19	19	10	10	10	10	10	10	10	10	10																			
19	19	21	21	21																												
21	21	10	10	10																												
10	10																															

Gran Premio di San Marino

It all seemed just a little too easy until he braked for the downhill left-hander at *Rivazza* on lap 23. Suddenly, under the eyes of television viewers, world-wide, the red and white Marlboro McLaren No. 7 pirouetted through 360-degrees, almost within its own length. It was a case of "blink, and you've missed it . . ." But Alain Prost kept the engine running and calmly accelerated back into the fray even before his Michelin tyres had stopped turning. The leader of the World Championship points table had been tripped into a momentary error of judgement thanks to a brake pedal which had developed an unusually long travel during the course of the race up to that point. That spin aside, Prost's performance during the 1984 San Marino Grand Prix was little short of perfection.

If you had glanced down the starting grid on race morning at Imola, you just *might* have come to the conclusion that the TAG-engined McLaren MP4/2 was going to have a strong fight on its hands. Prost had qualified second behind World Champion Nelson Piquet's Brabham-BMW BT53 and the second row contained Keke Rosberg's Williams-Honda FW09 and the Renault Elf RE50 of Derek Warwick, strong chargers both. But the challenge never materialised: Prost took the lead immediately once the starting lights flickered to green and never looked back, even through the spin, even through his routine pit stop for fresh rubber . . .

In reality, the only person who might have given him a run for his money was his own team-mate. Boxed in behind Rosberg's stalling Williams at the start, Niki Lauda completed the opening lap in tenth position. It was just the sort of challenge the Austrian relished. After a couple of laps getting into the swing of things, Lauda began to scythe his way into contention, steadily lapping seven-tenths of a second faster than his apparently dominant colleague, out on his own in the lead. This was not the old-style Lauda, reserved, methodical and "on rails" all the time: no, what we saw at Imola was a revitalised twice World Champion, revelling again in the knowledge that he can do *anything* now he is equipped with a fully competitive car. He dealt with both Ferrari C4s with contemptuous ease and was on the verge of dispatching Warwick's Renault for third place when a piston failed and McLaren No. 8 trickled to a halt at the side of circuit . . .

A fault with the BMW turbo wastegates knocked out both Brabhams and the Williams team was to have its worst race, in terms of results, since 1978, Rosberg and Laffite joining the long list of retirements early in the race. Arnoux was left as Maranello's sole survivor when Alboreto stopped with a broken exhaust, René chasing Prost's McLaren over the line in second place. The 126C4 was little more than 13s behind at the finish, but it might as well have been a lifetime. Alain Prost had been in total command at Imola; spin or no spin.

ENTRY AND PRACTICE

Those who came to Imola nurturing fond memories of cloudless skies, sweltering sunshine and the easy-going ambiance which one inevitably associates with Italy in the summer found their optimism rudely dashed when they arrived at the *Autodromo Dino Ferrari*. The sad fact of the matter is that just about anywhere on earth looks as depressing in the pouring rain as Cleethorpes in October. The clouds were dark and low in the sky, the rain torrential. What's more, this mournful scenario was sustained throughout much of the two days' practice and qualifying, the weather only perking up slightly for race day. Thus the two hour-long qualifying sessions were something of a lottery. On Friday the circuit started out wet and gradually dried throughout the session; on Saturday the circuit was damp, but dried out progressively although a few specks of rain from time to time towards the end of the session managed to keep all the participants on tenterhooks.

After Michele Alboreto's splendid victory in the Belgian Grand Prix at Zolder, much was expected from the Ferrari 126C4s on home soil. But by the end of Friday the team was almost ready to pack up and return to base in sheer despair; Michele's C4 ran out of fuel (would you believe!) on its first timed run, the bedraggled driver sprinting back to the pits in time to take over his spare car. Almost unbelievably, this then suffered injection pump failure out on the circuit which left the Italian 24th

fastest on 1m 47.919s. The following day Alboreto went some way towards retrieving the situation with a 1m 31.282s, but he frankly admitted that he had gone out for his quick run "at the wrong time and on the wrong tyres. I should have taken a couple of sets of qualifiers rather than one of each; race and qualifying tyres. If I could have got out on soft tyres during a lull in the traffic, well . . ." His voice trailed away. Michele had to resign himself to a 13th place start. René Arnoux, who had briefly held quickest time during Friday's qualifying session, wound up an eventual sixth on the grid after his C4's engine exploded in a cloud of oil, water and hot metal fragments right in front of Derek Warwick's Renault.

On Saturday afternoon several potential pole-winners were lured out on to the circuit a little too early and found their quickest runs wasted. Although the track surface was drying steadily during the final half-hour, the ominous clouds still swirled over the Imola area. It was a question of just whose nerve would last until the final moments of the session: in the end it was Piquet who gambled on waiting until a few minutes before the end of that crucial hour, sneaking pole position away from under Prost's nose with barely a couple of minutes left. The Brazilian went round in 1m 28.517s, running out of fuel on his slowing down lap.

While the majority of teams had driven straight from Zolder to Imola and prepared their cars in the spacious garages, McLaren had made a run for home, the better to sort out the problems which

had caused such a disastrous weekend in Belgium. It seemed a desperate measure since the transporter would have to be on road again by Tuesday night but Ron Dennis was convinced this was the best course of action. Prost's excellent front row starting position not withstanding, the team's problems during practice at Imola appeared to be proving the McLaren boss wrong.

Early on Friday morning Prost had switched to the team's spare car after his regular MP4/2-2 refused to run smoothly, so when Lauda's machine ground to a halt with a water leak (caused by bits of the broken water pump from Zolder remaining in the system), it left the Austrian with more than half an hour to wait before he could get his hands on the spare. The water pump was changed on Niki's race car in time for first qualifying, but Prost stayed with the spare throughout and eventually used it in the race as well.

Alain was quite happy with his machine, although he was somewhat hampered in the wet Friday session by having insufficient brake balance adjustment to wind as much bias on to the front wheels as he would have liked when the circuit began to dry. On Saturday, however, he had no such problems and was pretty satisfied with second on the grid. "This is the car I used at Kyalami, so I know that there's nothing much wrong with it!" Lauda, hampered by breaking fifth gear on Friday, found his MP4/2 understeering excessively the following day and had to make do with fifth place on the grid.

Over in the Williams camp Keke Rosberg was being quite frank about expressing his feelings on the subject of the FW09. "It still understeers and that's all there is to it," he grinned, "I suppose you might call it a bit of a basic conflict between the chassis and myself. The car wants to understeer, I want to oversteer . . . and we don't quite seem able to reach agreement on the subject!" In fact Keke's apparent light-heartedness over the whole affair concealed a growing level of concern within the Williams organisation that the FW09's understeer problem was not going to be an easy nut to crack.

The Honda engine unaccountably died for a few hundred yards when Rosberg was on his quickest run, eventually winding up with a 1m 29.418s which earned him third place on the grid – and was more a reflection on his determined driving than the quality of his machinery. Jacques Laffite clearly wasn't out to over-strain himself in a car which, he believes, offers him little chance of outright victory. He cruised on to the grid with a 15th quickest 1m 32.6s, some three seconds slower than his team-mate!

After his disappointing race outing at Zolder, Patrick Tambay underlined his sheer driving quality during Friday's untimed session by setting the quickest time, but things didn't really go smoothly when it came to the qualifying sessions. On Friday he was kicking himself for wasting two laps behind Marc Surer's Arrows A7-BMW, rather than dropping back and taking a run on a clear track, while Renault practice routine decreed

that he should spend Saturday in the spare car – which blew a turbo on its first set of tyres at the start of the final timed session. The result of all that trauma was a 1m 31.663s for 14th slot on the grid.

Derek Warwick wound up a fine fourth on 1m 29.682s, the Englishman very pleased with his RE50 although "on my quickest lap I caught up Alboreto when we were going into *Acque Minerale*, so that was my best time lost. I'm not too worried, though, because I reckon we might be potentially the fastest car of all in race trim."

Despite problems making his ATS D7's brakes last for more than a couple of laps, Manfred Winkelhock emerged as Pirelli's fastest runner with a 1m 30.723s to qualify on the inside of the fourth row ahead of Eddie Cheever, the lanky American very encouraged by the Alfa team's spare 184T with which he briefly held pole position during the final hour's qualifying. "We've been suffering turbo boost problems on my race car, so I used the spare for my fast runs this afternoon," explained Eddie, "and although I went slightly too soon on my final set, I'm trying to persuade them to let me have the spare for the race." The team originally didn't want him to, but Eddie's view eventually prevailed!

Cheever out-qualified team-mate Riccardo Patrese on the Italian's home ground, the former Brabham driver slotting in behind Teo Fabi's Brabham BT53 on row five, while row six saw two Italians with Renault power behind them, Elio de Angelis (Lotus 95T) and Andrea de Cesaris (Ligier

JS23). Elio had the advantage of the large "qualifying" Garrett turbochargers on his Renault engine, turning a 1m 31.173s best, while teammate Nigel Mansell had a miserable time with two heart-stopping moments during qualifying. On Friday he found himself ruthlessly " chopped" as he attempted to follow Nelson Piquet past Formula 1 debutant Jo Gartner's slow Osella-Alfa V12, the blue Italian car vaulting over the Lotus front wheel and smearing much of its distinctive livery down the JPS black and gold flanks. The following day Alliot's RAM moved over on him, inadvertently, as Mansell plunged down the hill to *Rivazza*, forcing the Lotus on to the grass where it spun like a top four or five times.

Arrows allotted one of its new BMW-engined machines to Marc Surer's custody on this occasion, shortage of freshly rebuilt engines being cited as the reason why Thierry Boutsen had to perform at the wheel of the Cosworth-engined A6, even though a spare A7 stood silently in the garage. Surer certainly enjoyed his first competitive experience of BMW turbo power, but he admitted that he was still adapting to the revised driving technique required by the car and couldn't improve on 1m 33.063s which put him 16th just behind Laffite's Williams and just in front of François Hesnault, the Frenchman continuing to progress smoothly and confidently at the wheel of his JS23.

As you can read elsewhere, the Toleman/Pirelli argy-bargy meant that the TG183Bs did not make an appearance on the circuit until Saturday morning. Eventually, and unfortunately, team leader Ayrton Senna failed to make the grid thanks to the intervention of a fuel pressure problem during final qualifying. What was thought to be a defective fuel pump was changed promptly, but the Toleman rolled to a silent halt out on the circuit shortly afterwards, consigning the unfortunate Brazilian to the list of non-qualifiers along, ironically, with Osella runner Piercarlo Ghinzani. Johnny Cecotto's TG183B therefore became the Witney team's sole representative on the starting grid, in 20th position.

Jo Gartner's behaviour during qualifying attracted unfavourable comment from his new colleagues, the Austrian not only tripping up Mansell, but also tottering across the bows of a horrified Martin Brundle who "just closed my eyes and waited for the impact". Ironically, it was only Gartner's presence at Imola which deprived Ghinzani, troubled by ignition problems, of a place in the race. Brundle was just out-qualified for 21st position by his team-mate Stefan Bellof, both Tyrrells equipped with small centre pillar rear wings for this very fast circuit, while the final two rows were made up by Alliot's RAM, Baldi's underfinanced Spirit-Hart 101B, Jonathan Palmer's RAM and the controversial Gartner.

THE RACE

As a change in the weather brought forth a typically enormous Imola crowd, there were obviously hopes that this climatic improvement would herald a corresponding upsurge in Maranello fortunes. However, the half-hour warm-up session gave a much more accurate prediction of what was to follow with Prost setting the fastest time and the Ferrari C4s struggling to stay in contention. Tambay's Renault engine had to be changed prior to the start and, since both similar units in the Lotus 95Ts also showed signs of overheating, Mansell was bundled into the spare car as a consequence. FISA safety man Derek Ongaro and FOCA medico Prof. Watkins took Gartner on one side for a quiet word about discipline, as a result of which the Austrian was to behave rather better during the race than he had in qualifying.

There was even more trouble in store for Keke Rosberg, his Williams FW09 coming in after the parade of leading Championship contenders spouting a major water leak. There was clearly nothing that could be done to deal with the problem, so the Finn was another to transfer to his spare car for the race. De Cesaris's Ligier wouldn't run properly, so after the warm-up lap he dived into the pit lane and by the time the problem had

MAY:
John Watson signed by Jaguar to drive Group 44 XJR-5 at Le Mans.

New 2.8-mile circuit at the Nürburgring opened officially. Ayrton Senna wins first race, an invitation event for celebrities in Mercedes 190E touring cars.

been rectified the pit exit had formally closed. Thus the fuming Italian lined up at the entrance to the circuit waiting to join in after the field had accelerated away.

When the starting light blinked green, Prost made a fabulous getaway to lead the pack away round *Tamburello* down towards *Tosa*, leaving Rosberg's Williams to stall on the starting grid while the pack scattered in all directions to avoid the stationary car. Under braking for *Tosa* Tambay aimed his Renault on to a patch of road down the inside – only to find Cheever's Alfa moving into it by the time he arrived there! The resultant contact between the Alfa's left rear wheel and the Renault's right front broke the suspension of the French car, leaving Patrick to slither to a halt on the grass, out of the contest. Cheever, his left-rear tyre punctured, trailed into the pits for a replacement

AYRTON SENNA had never driven at Imola before. He was keen to put in as many miles as possible during practice but those plans received a knock on the head from the moment he walked into the Toleman garage on Friday morning. All three TG183Bs were present but the engines were silent; the mechanics idle. For reasons which were not made clear, the team had been instructed by their headquarters in England not to take part in practice.

Mention was made of a financial discrepancy between the team and Pirelli, with whom Toleman had been associated in Formula 1 since 1981. There were also rumours that the team were switching to Michelin at the next race (speculation which turned out to be correct) and the temporary withdrawal was made to pre-empt any hostile reaction from Pirelli.

Either way, no official comment was available, save for a fatuous press release later in the day from Toleman to deny any financial dispute. Agreement was reached in time for practice on Saturday and Senna's plans received another set-back when his Hart engine developed a misfire. He failed to qualify and was clearly not amused. Neither, it seemed, were Segafredo, Toleman's Italian sponsor.

Meanwhile, the Italian press had launched a heavy attack on Toleman; criticisms which may, in part, have been unjustified but which were wholly predictable in the absence of key members of the Toleman team to put their point of view.

Two weeks later, at Dijon, Toleman produced a lengthy 'Statement of Facts' which did indeed highlight financial irregularities between the team and Pirelli. By then, of course, no one outside the dispute really cared and the damage caused by the distasteful airing of their grievances was not about to be patched up by another sad and inappropriate piece of public relations.

John Gentry, Brian Hart and the Toleman mechanics find time to catch up on the news while the dispute with Pirelli is resolved.

Goodyear to be fitted before resuming at the tail of the field.

At the end of the opening lap the order was Prost, Piquet, Warwick, Arnoux, Winkelhock, Alboreto, Patrese, de Angelis, Fabi and Lauda, the Austrian's prudence in avoiding Rosberg losing him five places in that early traffic jam. "I had my own problems at the start anyway", explained Niki, "I couldn't quite get my car into first gear, so I had to come off the clutch, depress it again, and stuff the lever in hard. By the time I got moving Keke was stopped in front of me and there were cars going in all directions. I thought I would hang on there and wait for things to calm down a bit!"

In addition to Tambay, François Hesnault's Ligier JS23 was also missing at the end of the opening lap, the new lad having been pushed briskly off the circuit by Jacques Laffite when he attempted to occupy a piece of track Laffite had already earmarked for himself! Rosberg staggered away after the tail-enders, but his entire weekend's efforts evaporated mid-way round the third lap as his Williams ground to a halt with electrical failure. At about the same time, Mansell's Lotus 95T shot off the circuit and embedded itself in one of the sand traps at the side of the track on the entrance to the *Acque Minerale* chicane. In the hurry to prepare the spare 95T after the problems of the untimed session, the mechanics had forgotten to replace the experimental front disc "bells" which had been tried in practice. Under hard braking one of these components, which attach the brake disc to the wheel hub, sheared off and pitched Nigel straight off the circuit . . .

By lap five Lauda was well into his stride and had moved up to seventh place behind Winkelhock's ATS. By this time the German driver was beginning to lose touch with the leading bunch as his car's brakes began to fade slightly, so Niki had no trouble picking off the BMW-engined machine. By the start of the 12th lap Lauda had towed up behind Alboreto's Ferrari C4 as the two cars set off past the pits through the fast *Tamburello* left-hander, but Niki's sheer *brio* and enthusiasm prompted him into making a most elementary Imola mistake. He nipped ahead of Michele as they went into the right-hander before *Tosa*, leaving the Ferrari on the inside line for the slow left-hander which meant that it could easily regain its position. You could almost feel the indignation shimmering from Niki's cockpit as the Ferrari outflanked him, so he counter-attacked with a brilliant overtaking move into the double left-hander at the top of the hill and forced his way through, the McLaren's right rear wheel almost brushing the C4's right front as he did so. That was Alboreto disposed of!

Arnoux was dealt with on lap 13 and then Niki began to close in on Warwick's Renault. The Englishman wasn't going to be intimidated by the presence of the most menacing pair of eyes in motor racing gazing at him through his RE50's mirrors. This was shaping up into what might have been the best battle of the afternoon. Might have been . . . On lap 16 it was all over: a puff of smoke from Lauda's exhaust as he braked for *Tosa* heralded a mighty piston failure. Niki pulled up and climbed out. Another nine points apparently in the bag for Prost and it was all going wrong for Lauda, again.

Ten laps into the race Piquet's clutch went solid and the World Champion spent the rest of his race changing gear without its use. Warwick was by that time getting a bit concerned about his Renault's potential fuel consumption because the digital read-out in his cockpit indicated that it was going to be marginal unless he eased back. "So I knocked it down to 10,250rpm and I still found myself catching Nelson quite easily," he admitted, "it was only later on in the race that the *real* problems started . . ." On lap 22 he surged ahead of the number one Brabham to take second place, but four laps later he dropped back behind Piquet as he dropped the Renault's revs. even more in an attempt to conserve his precious fuel load. At the end of lap 21 Alboreto pulled in to investigate fluctuating turbo boost pressure; the problem was a broken exhaust, so that was his race run.

On lap 23 Prost indulged in his quick spin, coming past the McLaren pit tapping the side of his

helmet in a gesture of self-admonishment. (He need not have been so self-critical. Tests carried out by Lauda at Dijon a few days later were to pin-point the problem – a faulty master cylinder which would jam without warning and clear itself just as quickly. The offending part was promptly thrown away. Lauda's piston failure, however, was to be a more serious portent of what was to come in France two weeks later.) Seven laps later Prost stopped for a routine change of Michelins as that earlier excursion ensured that the original set had no chance of lasting the entire race distance. Such was Alain's advantage at this point that he was able to accelerate back into the race without losing his lead. Everybody else that day was truly cast in a supporting role . . .

At the end of the "contest" it was to be René Arnoux who finished second, bringing the sole surviving Ferrari 126C4 to the chequered flag to collect six Championship points. But the former Renault ace only achieved that distinction after Piquet's BT53 retired with a turbocharger failure on lap 49 (as did Fabi's sister car, incidentally, at almost precisely the same time!) and a frustrated Warwick had been obliged to ease back to the point where his leisurely gear-changes had damaged the dog rings in the Renault gearbox, causing fourth initially to baulk and eventually to pack up altogether.

Warwick dropped to fourth place at the chequered flag behind Arnoux and Elio de Angelis's Lotus 95T which had performed very respectably only to run short of fuel on its very last lap. This was to prove a trifle unfortunate for Warwick, because he completed his final race lap on the tail of Prost's winning McLaren – not knowing that if he had only unlapped himself, he could have completed the last lap and passed de Angelis's Lotus which was stranded at the side of the circuit. Obviously there was no way Derek could realise this until after the race had finished – and his concern over his own car's marginal consumption led to his staying behind the McLaren to the flag, unwilling to run any further than absolutely necessary!

De Angelis wasn't the only one to run out of fuel: Andrea de Cesaris was on the receiving end of a similar reward after a brilliant drive from the tail of the field, the Italian climbing to third place with five laps left to run. Andrea stopped two laps from the finish and was classified seventh while Cheever, who had driven with similar flair and panache (and who hadn't bothered with a planned stop for tyres after his earlier delay!) was up to fifth at the same point when he, too, ran out of fuel. His reward was eighth place, the Alfa's rear tyres completely shot and virtually through to the carcass.

Behind Warwick, two Cosworth-engined cars completed the top six, the Tyrrell 012 of the superb Stefan Bellof and the Arrows A6 of Thierry Boutsen. Martin Brundle, after a truly sensational performance, failed to make it to the finish. His Tyrrell rolled to a silent halt out on the circuit with all the symptoms of fuel starvation five laps from the end of the race: it appeared, on subsequent examination, that the revised design of the fuel system left four gallons trapped in the collector tank and the engine was starved as a result. Martin had climbed to seventh place by half distance only to lose much of the advantage he had built up over de Angelis's Lotus when he came up to lap Jonathan Palmer's slow RAM for the second time. Palmer didn't feel it was his business to be unduly accommodating when it came to letting Martin through – and Brundle thought otherwise. After the race this incident led to a degree of tension between the two men, but the balance of opinion in the paddock agreed that Palmer was more wrong than right . . .

Earlier, almost unnoticed retirements had included Patrese's Alfa Romeo with electrical problems and Laffite's Williams with a piston failure. Winkelhock's ATS was parked when a membrane in the wastegate broke, causing the BMW's boost to go haywire, an identical fault having sidelined Marc Surer's Arrows as well as the Brabhams. Baldi's Spirit and Palmer's RAM were still running in ninth and 10th places but Alliot retired six laps from the end when his RAM-Hart suffered a loss of turbo boost pressure.

AH

Trouble from the word go. Piquet, Prost and Warwick make clean starts while the rest of the field scramble around Rosberg (6) and Lauda. Behind Alboreto (27), Laffite makes contact with Hesnault's left-front wheel, eliminating the Ligier on the spot. To the left, Cheever (23) gets away ahead of his team-mate, Patrese, the Alfa Romeos being caught by Tambay as the Renault storms through from the seventh row. Tambay (15) was to retire at the next corner after an incident with Cheever.
René Arnoux, sporting a new chic hairstyle and an English-registered Mercedes-Benz 500SEC, took a distant second place for Ferrari once Nelson Piquet had retired with yet another turbo failure.

Entries and practice times

No.	Driver	Nat	Car	Tyre	Engine	Entrant	Practice 1	Practice 2
1	Nelson Piquet	BR	Parmalat BRABHAM BT53	M	BMW M12/13	MRD International	1m 35·493s	**1m 28·517s**
2	Teo Fabi	I	Parmalat BRABHAM BT53	M	BMW M12/13	MRD International	1m 37·594s	**1m 30·950s**
3	Martin Brundle	GB	TYRRELL 012	G	Ford Cosworth DFY	Tyrrell Racing Organisation	1m 41·123s	**1m 36·531s**
4	Stefan Bellof	D	TYRRELL 012	G	Ford Cosworth DFY	Tyrrell Racing Organisation	1m 39·765s	**1m 36·059s**
5	Jacques Laffite	F	WILLIAMS FW09	G	Honda RA 163–E	Williams Grand Prix Engineering	1m 41·891s	**1m 32·600s**
6	Keke Rosberg	SF	WILLIAMS FW09	G	Honda RA 163–E	Williams Grand Prix Engineering	1m 37·024s	**1m 29·418s**
7	Alain Prost	F	Marlboro McLAREN MP4/2	M	TAG P01 (TTE P01)	Marlboro McLaren International	1m 35·687s	**1m 28·628s**
8	Niki Lauda	A	Marlboro McLAREN MP4/2	M	TAG P01 (TTE P01)	Marlboro McLaren International	1m 38·021s	**1m 30·325s**
9	Philippe Alliot	F	RAM 02	P	Hart 415T	Skoal Bandit Formula 1 Team	1m 43·132s	**1m 36·733s**
10	Jonathan Palmer	GB	RAM 02	P	Hart 415T	Skoal Bandit Formula 1 Team	1m 53·014s	**1m 37·262s**
11	Elio de Angelis	I	John Player Special LOTUS 95T	G	Renault EF4	John Player Team Lotus	1m 38·423s	**1m 31·173s**
12	Nigel Mansell	GB	John Player Special LOTUS 95T	G	Renault EF4	John Player Team Lotus	1m 38·363s	**1m 34·477s**
14	Manfred Winkelhock	D	ATS D7	P	BMW M12/13	Team ATS	1m 47·362s	**1m 30·723s**
15	Patrick Tambay	F	Elf RENAULT RE50	M	Renault EF4	Equipe Renault Elf	1m 36·250s	**1m 31·663s**
16	Derek Warwick	GB	Elf RENAULT RE50	M	Renault EF4	Equipe Renault Elf	1m 36·706s	**1m 29·682s**
17	Marc Surer	CH	ARROWS A7	G	BMW M12/13	Barclay Nordica Arrows BMW	1m 42·046s	**1m 33·063s**
18	Thierry Boutsen	B	ARROWS A6	G	Ford Cosworth DFV	Barclay Nordica Arrows BMW	1m 40·920s	**1m 36·018s**
19	Ayrton Senna	BR	TOLEMAN TG183B	P	Hart 415T	Toleman Group Motorsport	–	**1m 41·585s**
20	Johnny Cecotto	YV	TOLEMAN TG183B	P	Hart 415T	Toleman Group Motorsport	–	**1m 35·568s**
21	Mauro Baldi	I	SPIRIT 101	P	Hart 415T	Spirit Racing	1m 42·249s	**1m 36·916s**
22	Riccardo Patrese	I	Benetton ALFA ROMEO 184T	G	Alfa Romeo 183T	Benetton Team Alfa Romeo	1m 41·363s	**1m 31·163s**
23	Eddie Cheever	USA	Benetton ALFA ROMEO 184T	G	Alfa Romeo 183T	Benetton Team Alfa Romeo	1m 42·731s	**1m 30·843s**
24	Piercarlo Ghinzani	I	Kelemata OSELLA FA1F	P	Alfa Romeo 183T	Osella Squadra Corse	**1m 40·790s**	2m 05·421s
25	Francois Hesnault	F	LIGIER Loto JS23	M	Renault EF4	Ligier Loto	1m 40·356s	**1m 33·186s**
26	Andrea de Cesaris	I	LIGIER Loto JS23	M	Renault EF4	Ligier Loto	1m 36·613s	**1m 31·256s**
27	Michele Alboreto	I	Fiat FERRARI 126C4	G	Ferrari 126C	Scuderia Ferrari SpA	1m 47·919s	**1m 31·282s**
28	René Arnoux	F	Fiat FERRARI 126C4	G	Ferrari 126C	Scuderia Ferrari SpA	1m 38·389s	**1m 30·411s**
30	Jo Gartner	A	Kelemata OSELLA FA1E	P	Alfa Romeo 1260	Osella Squarda Corse	1m 50·979s	**1m 38·948s**

Friday morning and Saturday morning practice sessions not officially recorded.

G – Goodyear, M – Michelin, P – Pirelli.

Fri pm	Sat pm
Warm, damp	Warm, drying track

Starting grid

1 PIQUET (1m 28·517s)
Brabham

7 PROST (1m 28·628s)
McLaren

6 ROSBERG (1m 29·418s)
Williams

16 WARWICK (1m 29·682s)
Renault

8 LAUDA (1m 30·325s)
McLaren

28 ARNOUX (1m 30·411s)
Ferrari

14 WINKELHOCK (1m 30·723s)
ATS

23 CHEEVER (1m 30·843s)
Alfa Romeo

2 FABI (1m 30·950s)
Brabham

22 PATRESSE (1m 31·163s)
Alfa Romeo

11 DE ANGELIS (1m 31·173s)
Lotus

*26 DE CESARIS (1m 31·256s)
Ligier

27 ALBORETO (1m 31·282s)
Ferrari

15 TAMBAY (1m 31·663s)
Renault

5 LAFFITE (1m 32·600s)
Williams

17 SURER (1m 33·063s)
Arrows

25 HESNAULT (1m 33·186s)
Ligier

12 MANSELL (1m 34·477s)
Lotus

20 CECOTTO (1m 35·568s)
Toleman

18 BOUTSEN (1m 36·018s)
Arrows

4 BELLOF (1m 36·059s)
Tyrrell

3 BRUNDLE (1m 36·531s)
Tyrrell

9 ALLIOT (1m 36·733s)
RAM

21 BALDI (1m 36·916s)
Spirit

10 PALMER (1m 37·262s)
RAM

30 GARTNER (1m 38·948s)
Osella

*Started from pit lane
Did not start:
24 Ghinzani (Osella), 1m 40·790s, did not qualify
19 Senna (Toleman), 1m 41·585s, did not qualify

Results and retirements

Place	Driver	Car	Laps	Time and Speed (mph/km/h)/Retirement	
1	Alain Prost	McLaren-TAG t/c V6	60	1h 36m 53·679s	116·354/187·254
2	René Arnoux	Ferrari t/c V6	60	1h 37m 07·095s	116·072/186·8
3	Elio de Angelis	Lotus-Renault t/c V6	59	Out of fuel	
4	Derek Warwick	Renault t/c V6	59		
5	Stefan Bellof	Tyrrell-Cosworth V8	59		
6	Thierry Boutsen	Arrows-Cosworth V8	59		
7	Andrea de Cesaris	Ligier-Renault t/c V6	58	Out of fuel	
8	Eddie Cheever	Alfa Romeo t/c V8	58	Out of fuel	
9	Mauro Baldi	Spirit-Hart t/c 4	58		
10	Jonathan Palmer	RAM-Hart t/c 4	57		
11	Martin Brundle	Tyrrell-Cosworth V8	55	Fuel feed	
	Philippe Alliot	RAM-Hart t/c 4	53	Engine	
	Johnny Cecotto	Toleman-Hart t/c 4	52	Running, not classified	
	Nelson Piquet	Brabham-BMW t/c 4	48	Turbo	
	Teo Fabi	Brabham-BMW t/c 4	48	Turbo	
	Jo Gartner	Osella-Alfa Romeo V12	46	Engine	
	Marc Surer	Arrows-BMW t/c 4	40	Turbo	
	Manfred Winkelhock	ATS-BMW t/c 4	31	Turbo	
	Michele Alboreto	Ferrari t/c V6	23	Exhaust	
	Niki Lauda	McLaren-TAG t/c V6	15	Engine	
	Jacques Laffite	Williams-Honda t/c V6	11	Engine	
	Riccardo Patrese	Alfa Romeo t/c V8	6	Electrics	
	Nigel Mansell	Lotus-Renault t/c V6	2	Brakes; spun off	
	Keke Rosberg	Williams-Honda t/c V6	2	Electrical connection	
	Patrick Tambay	Renault t/c V6	0	Hit by Cheever	
	François Hesnault	Ligier-Renault t/c V6	0	Hit by Laffite	

Fastest lap: Piquet, on lap 48, 1m 33·275s, 120·869mph/194·521km/h (record).
Previous lap record: Riccardo Patrese (F1 Brabham BT52-BMW t/c 4), 1m 34·437s, 119·383mph/192·128km/h (1983).

Past winners

Year	Driver	Nat	Car	Circuit	Distance miles/km	Speed mph/km/h
1981	Nelson Piquet	BR	3·0 Brabham BT49C-Ford	Imola	187·90/302·40	101·20/162·87
1982	Didier Pironi	F	1·5 Ferrari 126C2 t/c V6	Imola	187·90/302·40	116·63/187·70
1983	Patrick Tambay	F	1·5 Ferrari 126C2/B t/c V6	Imola	187·90/302·40	115·25/185·48
1984	Alain Prost	F	1·5 McLaren MP4/2-TAG t/c	Imola	187·90/302·40	116·35/187·25

Circuit data

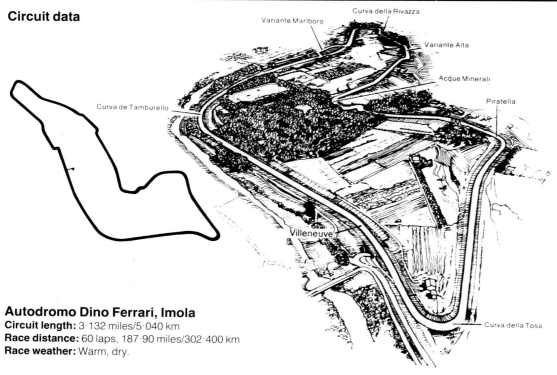

Curva della Rivazza
Variante Marlboro
Variante Alta
Acque Minerali
Piratella
Curva de Tamburello
Villeneuve
Curva della Tosa

Autodromo Dino Ferrari, Imola
Circuit length: 3·132 miles/5·040 km
Race distance: 60 laps, 187·90 miles/302·400 km
Race weather: Warm, dry.

Fastest laps

Driver	Time	Lap
Nelson Piquet	1m 33·275s	48
René Arnoux	1m 33·373s	44
Alain Prost	1m 33·580s	50
Andrea de Cesaris	1m 34·415s	55
Elio de Angelis	1m 34·525s	54
Niki Lauda	1m 34·686s	11
Teo Fabi	1m 35·534s	44
Eddie Cheever	1m 35·849s	27
Derek Warwick	1m 36·000s	12
Michele Alboreto	1m 36·053s	20
Stefan Bellof	1m 36·095s	43
Martin Brundle	1m 37·013s	38
Marc Surer	1m 37·089s	25
Manfred Winkelhock	1m 37·319s	11
Jonathan Palmer	1m 37·472s	44
Philippe Alliot	1m 38·199s	47
Johnny Cecotto	1m 38·208s	52
Thierry Boutsen	1m 38·430s	52
Jacques Laffite	1m 38·517s	11
Riccardo Patrese	1m 39·389s	3
Mauro Baldi	1m 39·404s	46
Keke Rosberg	1m 39·769s	2
Jo Gartner	1m 40·949s	41
Nigel Mansell	1m 41·622s	2

Points

WORLD CHAMPIONSHIP OF DRIVERS

1	Alain Prost	24 pts
2	Derek Warwick	13
3=	René Arnoux	10
3=	Elio de Angelis	10
5=	Michele Alboreto	9
5=	Niki Lauda	9
5=	Keke Rosberg	9
8=	Eddie Cheever	3
8=	Riccardo Patrese	3
8=	Stefan Bellof	3
11=	Andrea de Cesaris	2
11=	Martin Brundle	2
13=	Patrick Tambay	1
13=	Ayrton Senna	1
13=	Thierry Boutsen	1

CONSTRUCTORS' CUP

1	McLaren	33 pts
2	Ferrari	19
3	Renault	14
4	Lotus	10
5	Williams	9
6	Alfa Romeo	6
7	Tyrrell	5
8	Ligier	2
9=	Toleman	1
9=	Arrows	1

Lap chart

1st LAP ORDER	1	2	3	4	5	6	7	8	9	10	11	12	13	14	15	16	17	18	19	20	21	22	23	24	25	26	27	28	29	30	31	32	33	34	35	36	37
7 A. Prost	7	7	7	7	7	7	7	7	7	7	7	7	7	7	7	7	7	7	7	7	7	7	7	7	7	7	7	7	7	7	7	7	7	7	7	7	7
1 N. Piquet	1	1	1	1	1	1	1	1	1	1	1	1	1	1	1	1	1	1	1	1	1	16	16	16	16	16	1	1	1	1	1	1	1	1	1	1	1
16 D. Warwick	16	16	16	16	16	16	16	16	16	16	16	16	16	16	16	16	16	16	16	16	16	1	1	1	1	1	16	16	16	16	16	16	16	16	16	16	16
28 R. Arnoux	28	28	28	28	28	28	28	28	28	28	28	8	8	8	28	28	28	28	28	27	27	27	27	2	2	2	2	2	2	28	28	28	28	28	28	28	28
14 M. Winkelhock	14	14	27	27	27	27	27	27	27	27	27	8	28	28	28	27	27	27	27	28	2	2	2	28	28	28	28	28	2	2	2	2	2	2	2	2	2
27 M. Alboreto	27	27	14	14	14	14	14	8	8	8	8	27	27	27	27	2	2	2	2	2	2	28	28	28	11	11	11	26	26	26	26	26	26	26	26	26	26
22 R. Patrese	22	22	22	22	8	8	8	14	14	14	14	14	14	14	14	14	14	14	14	14	14	11	11	11	26	26	3	3	3	3	3	3	3	3	3	3	3
11 E. De Angelis	11	11	11	8	22	2	2	2	2	2	2	2	2	2	11	11	11	11	11	11	11	14	14	14	26	14	14	14	14	11	11	11	11	11	11	11	11
2 T. Fabi	2	2	8	11	2	22	11	11	11	11	11	11	11	11	3	26	26	26	26	26	26	26	26	3	3	3	3	11	23	23	23	23	23	23	23	23	23
8 N. Lauda	8	8	2	2	11	11	3	3	3	3	3	3	3	3	26	3	3	3	3	3	3	3	3	17	17	17	17	17	14	4	4	4	4	4	4	4	4
18 T. Boutsen	18	3	3	3	3	3	17	26	26	26	26	26	26	26	17	17	17	17	17	17	17	17	17	4	4	4	4	4	4	14	17	17	17	17	17	17	17
3 M. Brundle	3	18	18	17	17	17	26	17	17	17	17	17	17	17	4	4	4	4	4	4	4	4	4	23	23	23	23	23	17	17	18	18	18	18	18	18	18
17 M. Surer	17	17	17	18	4	26	4	4	4	4	4	4	4	4	18	18	23	23	23	23	23	23	23	18	18	18	18	18	18	20	20	20	21	21	21		
4 S. Bellof	4	4	4	26	26	4	18	18	5	5	5	18	18	18	18	20	23	18	18	18	18	18	18	20	20	20	20	20	20	21	21	21	20	20	20		
20 J. Cecotto	20	20	26	4	18	18	5	5	18	18	18	20	20	20	20	23	20	20	20	20	20	20	21	21	21	21	21	21	9	10	30	30	30	30			
12 N. Mansell	12	12	20	20	20	20	20	20	20	20	20	23	23	23	23	21	21	21	21	21	21	21	21	10	10	10	10	10	30	9	10	10	10	10			
26 A. De Cesaris	26	26	5	5	5	5	22	21	21	21	21	21	21	21	9	9	9	9	9	9	9	10	10	9	9	9	9	9	9	10	30	9	9	9	9		
21 M. Baldi	21	6	21	21	21	21	21	9	9	23	23	9	9	9	10	10	10	10	10	10	9	9	30	30	30	30	30	30	30								
6 K. Rosberg	6	21	9	9	9	9	23	23	9	9	5	30	10	10	30	30	30	30	30	30	30	30															
5 J. Laffite	5	5	30	30	30	30	30	30	30	30	30	10	30	30																							
9 P. Alliot	9	9	10	10	23	23	23	10	10	10	10	10	10																								
30 J. Gartner	30	30	23	23	10	10	10																														
10 J. Palmer	10	10																																			
23 E. Cheever	23	23																																			

38	39	40	41	42	43	44	45	46	47	48	49	50	51	52	53	54	55	56	57	58	59	60
7	7	7	7	7	7	7	7	7	7	7	7	7	7	7	7	7	7	7	7	7	7	7
1	1	1	1	1	1	1	1	1	1	1	28	28	28	28	28	28	28	28	28	28	28	28
16	16	28	28	28	28	28	28	28	28	28	1	16	26	26	26	26	26	26	26	11	11	
28	28	16	16	16	16	16	16	16	16	16	16	26	16	11	11	11	11	11	11	26	16	
2	2	2	2	2	2	2	2	2	2	2	26	11	11	16	16	16	16	16	16	16	4	
26	26	26	26	26	26	26	26	26	26	11	23	23	23	23	23	23	23	23	18			
3	11	11	11	11	11	11	11	11	11	11	23	4	4	4	4	4	4	4	4			
11	3	3	3	23	23	23	23	23	23	23	4	3	3	3	3	3	18	18	18			
23	23	23	23	3	3	3	3	3	4	4	2	18	18	18	18	18	21	21	21			
4	4	4	4	4	4	4	4	4	3	3	3	21	21	21	21	21	10	10				
17	17	17	18	18	18	18	18	18	18	18	18	20	20	20	10	10	10					
18	18	18	20	20	20	20	20	20	20	21	21	10	10	10	9	9						
21	21	21	21	21	21	21	21	21	21	20	20	9	9	9								
20	20	20	30	10	10	10	10	10	10	10	10											
30	30	30	10	30	30	30	30	30	9	9	9											
10	10	10	9	9	9	9	9	9	30													
9	9	9																				

127

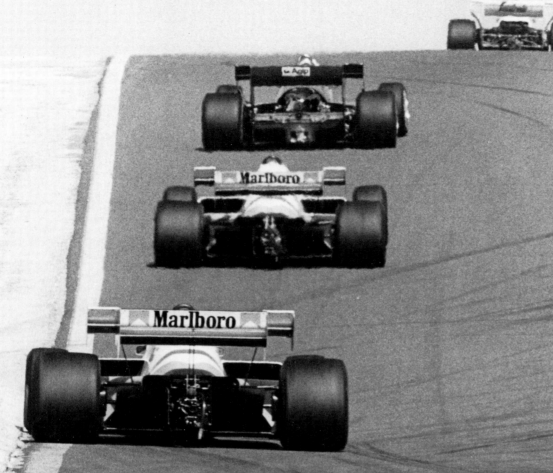

The McLarens were the class of the field on race day in spite of two days of practice punctuated by engine failures.

"For practice, I turn up the boost like this. For the race, I turn it down and wait to retire. And what makes it worse, you keep winning . . ." Lauda listens as Piquet *(right)* describes the seemingly unstoppable run of Brabham-BMW unreliability.

Watching from the almost flat-in-fourth *Courbe de Pouas*, Alain Prost was impressed. Niki Lauda was testing the Marlboro MP4/2 and his progress through the dauntingly fast downhill right-hander merely confirmed Prost's long-held view that the McLaren would be ideally suited to Dijon.

Prost, of course, knew the circuit well thanks to many hours spent pounding round the place for Renault. The MP4/2, he observed, adapted perfectly to the fast, sweeping corners and the race in a few days time would be the last opportunity to score maximum points before moving on to the tighter, less favourable circuits at Monte Carlo, Montreal and Detroit.

That, at least, was the theory.

McLaren did indeed take nine points home from Dijon but it was Lauda rather than Prost who did the winning. And the victory, while being as precise and commanding as any of the 20 which Lauda had scored before, came after two days of practice which saw the championship leaders blighted by a rash of engine failures.

Porsche reacted quickly by building two revised specification TAG turbos in time for the race and Lauda's V6 ran perfectly. Prost, meanwhile, was producing another of his superb comeback performances after two lengthy pit stops to cure damage caused, initially, by a front wheel working loose. The net result was fastest lap and seventh place – but no points. Just what Lauda wanted. Now they had scored two wins each and Prost's championship lead had been narrowed to six points.

McLaren were 20 points clear of Ferrari and 22 ahead of Renault-Elf in the Constructors' Championship and, appropriately enough, it was Patrick Tambay who had provided the main threat to McLaren in Renault's home Grand Prix.

Against a background of hollow-sounding threats of withdrawal if they failed to cure their fuel consumption problems, Renault took their first pole position in almost a year. The time sheet at the end of the first day's practice had dictated the grid thanks to rain on Saturday and Tambay made the most of his advantage during the race. However, a combination of brake and clutch problems meant he was no match for Lauda but, by finishing second, Tambay achieved the sort of result he had been threatening all season.

Much the same applied to Nigel Mansell although his third place was the result of a determined drive made even more difficult by personal grief, the JPS-Lotus driver producing perhaps his finest performance in the knowledge that he would leave France immediately after the race to attend his mother's funeral.

Dijon, as ever, lent itself to close racing and a promising duel between Mansell and Derek Warwick ended when the Renault driver locked his brakes and slid into Marc Surer as the Englishmen attempted to lap the Arrows driver. Warwick was fortunate to escape with no more than a heavily bruised leg but the incident cost him valuable points and second place in the championship. His only consolation was that Prost had failed to score even though his early prediction that the McLaren would be ideal for Dijon had been proved absolutely correct.

Grand Prix de France

ENTRY AND PRACTICE

Patrick Tambay was directing fire marshals to extinguish a small blaze at the back of his Renault, unaware that he had just won what would turn out to be pole position. A small oil leak had caused a fire to break out in his turbo just as the Renault crossed the timing line to beat the Lotus of Elio de Angelis. Tambay's performance on his second set of qualifiers went some way to take the heat out of a delicate public relations dilemma which had been of Renault's own making.

In the days preceding the Grand Prix, Gerard Larrousse had declared in an interview in *L'Equipe* that Renault would consider taking a break from racing if they had not solved their fuel consumption problems by the second half of the season. The news, of course, became distorted to the extent that the French team were thinking of quitting for good and both Larrousse and Jean Sage spent most of the weekend reassuring critics that this was not so.

An immediate step taken by Renault at Dijon had been the incorporation of a small auxiliary radiator designed to re-heat cold fuel before it reached the engine. The cold fuel, you may remember, was used on race day simply because more petrol could be squeezed into the 220-litre tank if the fuel was chilled. The disadvantage, however, was that the engine then consumed more cold fuel than it would have had the petrol been at the normal ambient temperature; hence the additional air-to-air intercooler.

But, for the moment, Renault were on overnight pole at the most important race of the season for the French team and rain on Saturday would ensure that a yellow and white car would have the prime starting position for the first time since Belgium 1983. This was something of a disappointment for de Angelis since the black and gold car was handling perfectly thanks, in part, to a new rear wing and the latest Goodyears. Elio had been fastest in the unofficial session and he went on to repeat the performance on Saturday morning. In the final session, he was equally impressive but had to give best to Nigel Mansell as the Englishman forced his way round the streaming circuit in a time which was nearly eight-tenths of a second faster. That helped make up for Mansell's disappointment at being sixth on the grid. Like his team-mate, Mansell felt the 95T was ideally suited to Dijon but a waste-gate problem while running his first set of qualifiers and a spin to avoid a slower car while using his second set was frustrating.

It was a feeling which the Parmalat Brabham team knew well. For four races now they had suffered all manner of niggling failures and come away with nothing to show for their endeavours. In a bid to help sort out the BMW maladies, the cars were unchanged and Piquet had put in a useful few days testing at Nogaro. Indeed, he held pole position briefly on Friday even though the BT53 had neither the power nor the grip of the McLaren. On Saturday, Nelson concentrated on running the T-car in the rain while the mechanics spent the day slowly preparing the race cars. That said much about their anxiety to break free of their bad patch.

The frustrating thing for Brabham and BMW had been the variety of failures. Williams, at least,

knew their problems lay with a poor chassis and the absence of Patrick Head indicated that major revisions were being worked out on the drawing boards at Didcot. In the meantime, it was hoped that a new front wing and lower pick-up points on the front suspension would cure the understeer but after the first day's practice, Rosberg said he could feel no improvement and asked for the car to be returned to the original specification. Fourth place on the grid was a tribute to Rosberg's determination and flair rather than the qualities of his car and the Finn put his mind to solving the mysterious habits of the Honda engine when he tried three full-blooded standing starts at the end of practice. The result was a spent clutch and no sign of the hesitation which had blighted his start at Zolder.

Third and fourth fastest times for the McLarens on Friday morning appeared to be the prelude to another walkover. At the end of the day, however, Prost was fifth and Lauda ninth. And the team were worried. Very worried. No less than three TAG engines had blown up with varying degrees of piston failures. Prost had lost an engine just as he was about to start a flier on his second set of qualifiers. Lauda, meanwhile, had completed his best lap with fluid trailing from the back of the car, the engine expiring completely just as he crossed the line. This was the T-car since Niki had already lost an engine in his race car during the morning and the Austrian was mildly frustrated at being unable to make the most of the handling round and stay on terms with Prost. There would be a lengthy meeting in the motorhome after Friday's practice and lines to Weissach were heavily patronised.

Derek Warwick was honest enough to ascribe seventh place to the driver's inability to come to terms with Dijon rather than lay any blame with his car. He did, in fact, suffer a turbo failure on

Friday afternoon, which meant setting his time in the T-car, but a lack of testing took its toll when it came to feeling comfortable with the RE50 in the fast right-hander leading on to the straight.

That same corner held no such fear for Manfred Winkelhock. In fact, *no* corner seemed to bother the German as he revelled in a much improved ATS, the team having taken off several kilos and discarded the large caliper brakes which had given trouble at Zolder and Imola. For a brief moment, Manfred was on pole at Dijon but then the BMW blew up. None the less, he was eighth, ahead of such luminaries as Lauda and Michele Alboreto.

The success of Zolder seemed a long way off as the red cars struggled with poor straight-line speed. This was due to the less suitable KKK turbos (Renault, for example, had switched completely to Garrett) and the fact that less rear wing meant the 126C4s destroyed their tyres in no time. Ferrari had four cars present, two of which had revised front and rear suspension. Alboreto's car also sported streamlining around the gearbox, a modification which was eventually fitted to René Arnoux's C4 but, at the end of the day, the Ferraris were a poor 10th and 11th.

An encouraging 13th, alongside the Williams of Jacques Laffite, sat the new Toleman-Hart 184 of Ayrton Senna, running on Michelins . . . The Brazilian was bubbling with enthusiasm for the new combination, particularly on race tyres. Being short on mileage, Senna used one set of race rubber on Friday afternoon and, the moment he chose to use his one set of qualifiers coincided with Lauda's oily engine failure. Johnny Cecotto was down in 19th place after experiencing fuel pressure problems on both his race car and the T-car in the morning and, as a result, the Venezuelan driver had little opportunity to learn about the latest product from the pen of Rory Byrne.

For François Hesnault, the French Grand Prix represented the most important race of the season on a circuit which he knew and liked. On Friday, he recorded 14th fastest time while his Ligier team-mate, Andrea de Cesaris, lapped in 1m 04.137s to set what would have been ninth fastest time. Would have been.

For the second French Grand Prix in succession, the Italian driver's car was found to have been running with an empty fire extinguisher bottle. This was discovered at post-practice scrutineering on Friday and all the pleading and claims that the liquid must have leaked away were to have no effect. The time set by de Cesaris was declared null and void in spite of an explosive outburst from Guy Ligier, indignant that he should be called a cheat.

The exclusion might have been all right had it not rained on Saturday. De Cesaris trashed round for 17 laps but his time was over ten seconds off the target, the 1m 11.625s set by 26th-placed man, Piercarlo Ghinzani on Friday. Then it was announced that Hesnault was stepping down, thus leaving a space at the back of the grid for de Cesaris. Hesnault put on a brave face and it must have been difficult to accept such a decision, particularly after he had just set a very impressive and competent third fastest time in the wet. He said he had not been put under any pressure to stand down. His expression suggested otherwise.

Thus, Thierry Boutsen moved from 15th to 14th spot on the grid, the Belgian driver making slow progress with the Arrows-BMW. Developments meant the A7 understeered rather than oversteered as Dave Wass tried to even tyre temperatures and stop the rears from blistering faster than the fronts. The shortage of BMW engines remained and Marc Surer, back in the Cosworth A6, took 20th place.

The long straight at Dijon played havoc with the Alfa Romeo turbos, both Eddie Cheever and Riccardo Patrese saying that their cars ran out of steam long before they had reached the pits. Adjustments to the rear wings merely made the handling more skittish although aerodynamic improvements had been attempted with the incorporation of longer side-pods which also accommodated bigger radiators. Cheever, who blew an engine while running his second set of qualifiers on Friday, was one tenth of a second slower than his team-mate.

Behind Cecotto and Fabi (forced to qualify in Piquet's car after losing a turbo) came the Cosworth cars of Surer and Stefan Bellof. Tyrrell had produced a new chassis for the German and he beat his team-mate by three places after Brundle lost a few tenths with a sideways moment. Martin made light contact with the catch fencing on Saturday but no harm was done whereas a spin for Philippe Alliot on Friday meant damaged suspension, the Frenchman being forced to share Jonathan Palmer's car during qualifying in the afternoon. Apart from revised plumbing to the intercoolers, the RAM-Harts were unchanged and John Macdonald decided there was nothing to be gained by letting his drivers venture out in the rain during the final session. The Skoal-sponsored cars split the Tyrrells and qualified ahead of Mauro Baldi, the Spirit team now operating on a race-to-race basis in terms of finance, and the Osella Alfa Romeo of Piercarlo Ghinzani. Bringing up the rear, of course, would be the Ligier of de Cesaris, the French team's only representative in their home Grand Prix. Guy's wrath, we were informed, rumbled long into the night . . .

RACE

As dawn broke, misty and cool, weary figures dressed in red and white made their way from the McLaren garage on race morning. Porsche had delivered the two revised TAG engines on Saturday evening and, by midnight, the V6s were plumbed in and running. Except that Prost's had a misfire which took over four hours to cure. And, at the end of it all, the team couldn't be sure that Porsche had solved the piston failure problem.

During the warm-up, McLaren were encouraged by third and fourth fastest times although Prost commented that the engine felt rough between eight and nine thousand revs. There was no question of changing to the T-car, of course, since that was fitted with an engine built to the troublesome specification.

In fact, McLaren were in much better shape than some. Lotus, for example, faced an engine change on Mansell's car during the lunchbreak while de Angelis prepared to take the spare chassis. Cheever blew an engine and the RAM team were busy installing a fresh Hart engine after Alliot said he had heard strange noises coming from behind his shoulders. Toleman, meanwhile, were making hurried changes to settings following their first experience with the 184 on full tanks!

The JPS mechanics changed the Renault V6 in 90 minutes while Mansell sat quietly by the pit wall, his mind wandering back to the tragedy which had overtaken his family. It would not be until after the race that he would reveal that his mother had died of cancer during the week.

The start, of course, diverted Mansell's thoughts, the Lotus driver getting off the line smartly to run down the outside and challenge Piquet into the braking area for the first corner. Already, there had been some frantic activity at the front caused, in part, by Tambay having clutch trouble on the line. The Renault began to creep on the red light and Piquet, watching Tambay rather than the light, rolled forward from row two. In fact, Nelson was so far out of place that he dabbed his brakes – and the lights turned green.

A seemingly inevitable shunt was avoided when Piquet simply floored the throttle, the BMW surging forward in company with de Angelis and Mansell. Tambay became trapped in the middle of this group but the pole position man soon reasserted himself and barged his way between Piquet and de Angelis, nudging the Brabham as he went. The Renault and Lotus were left to sit it out through the right-hander, Elio finally lifting off and slotting in behind.

As if that were not enough excitement, Rosberg's practice starts seemed to have paid off as the Williams challenged Mansell for third place. Mansell was in no mood to be trifled with and ran round the outside to take the place at the next left-hander. In all, it was an encouraging start for Williams as Laffite rocketed into sixth place but the Frenchman's momentum was lost when Wink-

elhock's BMW hesitated and Jacques was forced to take avoiding action.

At the end of the opening lap, the order read: Tambay, de Angelis, Mansell, Rosberg, Warwick, Piquet, Prost, Alboreto – and Lauda. Had it been known that Lauda was destined to win this race, we would have quickly surmised that the French Grand Prix was going to be an eventful one.

Tambay may have been pulling away but de Angelis, running stiffer springs than his team-mate, was learning the error of his ways as Mansell made one or two attempts to get by; attempts which were smartly cut off by the Italian.

Rosberg was working hard with the recalcitrant Williams but he was unable to prevent Warwick taking fourth place on lap three and Piquet, followed by the McLarens, moving ahead on the next lap. Alboreto and Warwick should have been next in line for a run at the Williams but Michele lost a couple of places when he indulged in a quick spin and Winkelhock made a pit stop before retiring not long after with a combination of brake and clutch trouble.

Prost, meanwhile, had moved ahead of Piquet and Warwick with an ease which suggested the McLaren had perfect balance through the long right-hander on to the straight. Lauda was soon closing on the Brabham and Renault but, by then, Prost had taken third place from Mansell.

Lauda's task was made easier when Piquet pulled into the pits on lap 12; what had been a small fire in the turbo erupting into a sizeable

conflagration as he posted yet another retirement for the reigning World Champions. Four laps later and Patrese's race was over with a blown engine, Bellof having joined the list not long before when he pulled off in the mistaken belief that his engine had failed. Tucked behind Laffite on the main straight, the Cosworth had bounced off the rev-limiter as the Tyrrell ran in the slip-stream of the Williams. Thinking the DFY was crying enough, Bellof switched off and rolled to a halt at the end of the straight. A simple but understandable error for a novice to make.

Tambay was making no mistakes in spite of increasing pressure from Prost as the McLaren moved past de Angelis on lap 18 to take second place. The gap of three seconds was quickly eroded but Prost seemed in no hurry to take the lead. On lap 23, however, it seemed he had been presented with the perfect opportunity as Cecotto's Toleman covered the track in front of the leaders with smoke as the Hart expired with a turbo failure.

Lauda, by now, was into third place and catching the leaders but events were to take an unexpected turn on lap 28. Prost was a few feet behind Tambay when the McLaren suddenly jumped to the left as they swept through *Pouas*. The left-front wheel had suddenly become loose and a nasty accident at the exit of a high-speed bend with minimal run-off area was prevented when the wheel somehow jammed itself against the brake caliper. Prost had the presence of mind to pull over to the right and head for the pits; another lap and the wheel most certainly would have come off.

The McLaren mechanics were not expecting this sudden visit since the plan had been to run as late as possible before making a tyre change; the better to take advantage of the race being stopped in the event of the thunderstorm which had been forecast. None the less, they leapt on the car, the man at the left-front finding it difficult to believe his eyes when he could find no nut to remove from the wheel . . . Indeed, it was to be a mystery to the entire team since the upright and hub assembly had been in use for some considerable time and subsequent tests failed to provide any answers.

After a lengthy stop, Prost returned in 11th place to begin another of his superb drives through the field. The more routine pit stops began when Mansell came in on lap 29 to make an 11-second stop and rejoin in seventh place. The Lotus driver had come in a lap later than expected since he had missed his pit signal first time round. Ironically, Martin Brundle, busily tucked under the wing of Michele Alboreto's Ferrari, had glimpsed the Union Jack on Mansell's board and thought the message was being hung out by the Tyrrell pit next door. Having seen Bellof's car parked by the side of the track, Brundle assumed the pit knew something he didn't and he duly stopped next time round – to find surprised Tyrrell mechanics running over to enquire what was wrong!

Alboreto ended a mediocre drive quietly by the side of the track when his engine failed on lap 34 while Senna, who had been lying in an encouraging ninth place with the new Toleman, stopped soon after with an identical turbo failure to the one suffered by his team-mate.

As the list of retirements grew, the leaders held station, Tambay coming under mounting pressure from Lauda. From the start, Patrick had been unhappy with his brakes and a slight sideways moment by the Renault at *Courbe des Gorgeolles* was all Lauda needed, the McLaren leading the field at the end of lap 41. Tambay made his pit stop three laps later, the Renault's advantage over Mansell enabling him to rejoin without losing his place.

Ten laps earlier, Warwick had made his stop to receive the softer 05 Michelins all round and the Englishman, enjoying excellent balance and grip, was soon past de Angelis and Rosberg and chasing after Mansell's third place. The two British drivers soon became locked in what promised to be a tough duel but all that changed on lap 54 when they came across Marc Surer, the Swiss running in a lonely 14th place. Seeing the Lotus and Renault approaching, Surer duly pulled over on the climb from the hairpin, Mansell diving for the inside at *Gorgeolles*. Warwick was close behind, perhaps too

Alain Prost remembers his fans. The Frenchman showed unbelievable commitment in the face of problems with the left-front wheel on his McLaren. At the end of the race, he had earned nothing more than fastest lap (left).
Nigel Mansell and Derek Warwick about to engage in a battle which ended when the Renault crashed as they tried to lap a back-marker. Mansell went on to take a fine third place (below).

MAY:
Renault threatens to consider temporary withdrawal to cure fuel consumption problems.

Toleman switches from Pirelli to Michelin.

Tom Sneva (March 84C-Cosworth DFX) takes Indy pole at 210.029mph.

Teddy Yip closes Theodore Racing Indycar team.

close because, when Mansell braked earlier than Warwick had anticipated, the Renault driver locked his brakes and promptly slid into, and then over the top of Surer, both the Arrows and Renault retiring on the spot.

The impact caused the right-front suspension to punch its way through the monocoque and badly bruise Warwick's leg, and the Englishman, momentarily concussed and unable to switch off the ignition, was trapped until marshals released him not long after.

While all this had been going on, Lauda was making his way into the pits where what should have been a routine stop changed a lead of 30 seconds into an 11-second deficit. Still, knowing how well the McLaren was handling, it would not take Lauda long to catch Tambay and he duly re-took the lead after a mere eight laps, the order then reading: Lauda, Tambay, Mansell, Arnoux, de Angelis, Rosberg and Laffite.

But what of Prost? The pit stop had secured the front wheel and Alain was soon scything his way through from 11th place, the McLaren inheriting fourth when Warwick had his incident with Surer. Somehow, though, the disc-housing on the front-left wheel had been damaged and vibrations warned Prost that the wheel was working its way loose once more. A lengthy stop saw the mechanics get down to a proper cure but Prost had lost a lap

on the leaders and he would rejoin in 10th place.

Now we had a chilling display of commitment. On a circuit where the left-front wheel is heavily loaded, Prost put any problems to the back of his mind and set the fastest lap of the race as he pursued at least one championship point. He took de Cesaris within two laps, passed Fabi on lap 69 and Laffite two laps later. Ahead lay Rosberg in sixth place, the Williams driver suffering from a failing turbo and poor handling. But, as ever, Keke was putting his heart and soul into keeping the FW09 on the track and, had the race been one lap longer, he may not even have had one point to show for his hard work.

So, Prost failed to score points on a day when Lauda was very pleased to have racked up nine and closed the gap on his team-mate at the head of the championship. We had the usual cheerful but clipped comments after the race; "car perfect, tyres perfect, engine perfect, thank you gentlemen and good afternoon." Tambay received a standing ovation from the crowd, fair reward for a difficult drive which had seen the Frenchman lead for 48 laps. The true spirit of Mansell's performance emerged at a time when he should have been celebrating an excellent third place and the Lotus team were rewarded with further points when de Angelis finished fifth after his second set of tyres had done little but promote time-consuming

oversteer. In between the black and gold came the brilliant red of Arnoux's Ferrari, René never having been a serious threat during what was a lonely and unspectacular race for the Frenchman.

Behind Rosberg, Prost, Laffite, Fabi and de Cesaris came Boutsen, the Arrows driver claiming 11th place just as his BMW blew up spectacularly as he crossed the line. Brundle was 12th, Ghinzani 13th with an exhausted Jonathan Palmer bringing up the rear after struggling with massive understeer on his RAM.

But at least he was pleased with the reliability of his car on a day when 12 drivers had fallen by the wayside, including Cheever when bits of the Alfa's rear wing flew off and the car finally came to rest a few laps later when he spun off.

Quite how Prost did not have a massive accident on at least one occasion remained one of the miracles of the weekend. That is not a reflection of his driving; quite the opposite. On this day, Alain Prost had demonstrated his skill and tenacity to a stunning degree. He had thrashed the TAG turbo during the closing stages and there had been not the slightest hint of a piston failure, nor had there been any worries over fuel consumption.

The car had been perfect and his prediction of a commanding performance had only been denied by an unusual mechanical problem – ironically at *Courbe de Pouas.* MH

Entries and practice times

No.	Driver	Nat	Car	Tyre	Engine	Entrant	Practice 1	Practice 2
1	Nelson Piquet	BR	Parmalat BRABHAM BT53	M	BMW M12/13	MRD International	**1m 02·806s**	1m 30·893s
2	Teo Fabi	I	Parmalat BRABHAM BT53	M	BMW M12/13	MRD International	**1m 06·370s**	—
3	Martin Brundle	GB	TYRRELL 012	G	Ford Cosworth DFY	Tyrrell Racing Organisation	**1m 09·554s**	1m 28·555s
4	Stefan Bellof	D	TYRRELL 012	G	Ford Cosworth DFY	Tyrrell Racing Organisation	**1m 08·608s**	1m 29·539s
5	Jacques Laffite	F	WILLIAMS FW09	G	Honda RA 163–E	Williams Grand Prix Engineering	**1m 05·410s**	1m 27·917s
6	Keke Rosberg	SF	WILLIAMS FW09	G	Honda RA 163–E	Williams Grand Prix Engineering	**1m 02·908s**	1m 30·872s
7	Alain Prost	F	Marlboro McLAREN MP4/2	M	TAG P01 (TTE P01)	Marlboro McLaren International	**1m 02·982s**	1m 25·397s
8	Niki Lauda	A	Marlboro McLAREN MP4/2	M	TAG P01 (TTE P01)	Marlboro McLaren International	**1m 04·419s**	1m 25·567s
9	Philippe Alliot	F	RAM 02	P	Hart 415T	Skoal Bandit Formula 1 Team	**1m 09·447s**	—
10	Jonathan Palmer	GB	RAM 02	P	Hart 415T	Skoal Bandit Formula 1 Team	**1m 09·047s**	—
11	Elio de Angelis	I	John Player Special LOTUS 95T	G	Renault EF4	John Player Team Lotus	**1m 02·336s**	1m 20·859s
12	Nigel Mansell	GB	John Player Special LOTUS 95T	G	Renault EF4	John Player Team Lotus	**1m 03·200s**	1m 20·061s
14	Manfred Winkelhock	D	ATS D7	P	BMW M12/13	Team ATS	**1m 03·865s**	1m 28·393s
15	Patrick Tambay	F	Elf RENAULT RE50	M	Renault EF4	Equipe Renault Elf	**1m 02·200s**	1m 24·855s
16	Derek Warwick	GB	Elf RENAULT RE50	M	Renault EF4	Equipe Renault Elf	**1m 03·540s**	1m·23·363s
17	Marc Surer	CH	ARROWS A6	G	Ford Cosworth DFV	Barclay Nordica Arrows BMW	**1m 08·457s**	1m 26·943s
18	Thierry Boutsen	B	ARROWS A7	G	BMW M12/13	Barclay Nordica Arrows BMW	**1m 05·972s**	1m 25·252s
19	Ayrton Senna	BR	TOLEMAN TG183B	M	Hart 415T	Toleman Group Motorsport	**1m 05·744s**	1m 28·225s
20	Johnny Cecotto	YV	TOLEMAN TG183B	M	Hart 415T	Toleman Group Motorsport	**1m 08·189s**	1m 31·359s
21	Mauro Baldi	I	SPIRIT 101	P	Hart 415T	Spirit Racing	**1m 09·629s**	1m 31·021s
22	Riccardo Patrese	I	Benetton ALFA ROMEO 184T	G	Alfa Romeo 183T	Benetton Team Alfa Romeo	**1m 06·172s**	1m 28·124s
23	Eddie Cheever	USA	Benetton ALFA ROMEO 184T	G	Alfa Romeo 183T	Benetton Team Alfa Romeo	**1m 06·281s**	1m 23·770s
24	Piercarlo Ghinzani	I	Kelemata OSELLA FA1F	P	Alfa Romeo 183T	Osella Squadra Corse	**1m 11·625s**	1m 32·541s
25	François Hesnault	F	LIGIER Loto JS23	M	Renault EF4	Ligier Loto	**1m 05·850s**	1m 22·272s
26	Andrea de Cesaris	I	LIGIER Loto JS23	M	Renault EF4	Ligier Loto	*1m 04·137s	**1m 22·388s**
27	Michele Alboreto	I	Fiat FERRARI 126C4	G	Ferrari 126C	Scuderia Ferrari SpA	**1m 04·459s**	1m 22·749s
28	René Arnoux	F	Fiat FERRARI 126C4	G	Ferrari 126C	Scuderia Ferrari SpA	**1m 04·917s**	1m 22·707s

* Time disallowed
Fri pm — Warm, dry
Sat pm — Cool, wet

Friday morning and Saturday morning practice sessions not officially recorded.

G – Goodyear, M – Michelin, P – Pirelli.

Starting grid

	15 TAMBAY (1m 02·200s) Renault
11 DE ANGELIS (1m 02·336s) Lotus	
	1 PIQUET (1m 02·806s) Brabham
6 ROSBERG (1m 02·908s) Williams	
	7 PROST (1m 02·982s) McLaren
12 MANSELL (1m 03·200s) Lotus	
	16 WARWICK (1m 03·540s) Renault
14 WINKELHOCK (1m 03·865s) ATS	
	8 LAUDA (1m 04·419s) McLaren
27 ALBORETO (1m 04·459s) Ferrari	
	28 ARNOUX (1m 04·917s) Ferrari
5 LAFFITE (1m 05·410s) Williams	
	19 SENNA (1m 05·744s) Toleman
18 BOUTSEN (1m 05·972s) Arrows	
	22 PATRESE (1m 06·172s) Alfa Romeo
23 CHEEVER (1m 06·281s) Alfa Romeo	
	2 FABI (1m 06·370s) Brabham
20 CECOTTO (1m 08·189s) Toleman	
	17 SURER (1m 08·457s) Arrows
4 BELLOF (1m 08·608s) Tyrrell	
	10 PALMER (1m 09·047s) RAM
9 ALLIOT (1m 09·447s) RAM	
	3 BRUNDLE (1m 09·554s) Tyrrell
21 BALDI (1m 09·629s) Spirit	
	24 GHINZANI (1m 11·625s) Osella
26 DE CESARIS (1m 22·388s) Ligier	

Did not start:
25 Hesnault (Ligier), 1m 05·850s, entry withdrawn to allow de Cesaris to start after his practice times from Friday had been disallowed

Results and retirements

Place	Driver	Car	Laps	Time and Speed (mph/km/h)/Retirement	
1	Niki Lauda	McLaren-TAG t/c V6	79	1h 31m 11·951s	125·531/202·023
2	Patrick Tambay	Renault t/c V6	79	1h 31m 19·105s	125·392/201·8
3	Nigel Mansell	Lotus-Renault t/c V6	79	1h 31m 35·920s	124·957/201·1
4	René Arnoux	Ferrari t/c V6	79	1h 31m 55·657s	124·572/200·4
5	Elio de Angelis	Lotus-Renault t/c V6	79	1h 32m 18·076s	124·025/199·6
6	Keke Rosberg	Williams-Honda t/c V6	78		
7	Alain Prost	McLaren-TAG t/c V6	78		
8	Jacques Laffite	Williams-Honda t/c V6	78		
9	Teo Fabi	Brabham-BMW t/c 4	78		
10	Andrea de Cesaris	Ligier-Renault t/c V6	77		
11	Thierry Boutsen	Arrows-BMW t/c 4	77		
12	Martin Brundle	Tyrrell-Cosworth V8	76		
13	Piercarlo Ghinzani	Osella-Alfa Romeo t/c V8	74		
14	Jonathan Palmer	RAM-Hart t/c 4	72		
	Mauro Baldi	Spirit-Hart t/c 4	61	Engine	
	Derek Warwick	Renault t/c V6	53	Accident with Surer	
	Marc Surer	Arrows-Cosworth V8	51	Accident with Warwick	
	Eddie Cheever	Alfa Romeo t/c V8	51	Engine	
	Ayrton Senna	Toleman-Hart t/c 4	35	Turbo	
	Michele Alboreto	Ferrari t/c V6	33	Engine	
	Johnny Cecotto	Toleman-Hart t/c 4	22	Turbo	
	Riccardo Patrese	Alfa Romeo t/c V8	15	Engine	
	Nelson Piquet	Brabham-BMW t/c 4	11	Turbo	
	Stefan Bellof	Tyrrell-Cosworth V8	11	Mistakenly thought engine had failed	
	Manfred Winkelhock	ATS-BMW t/c 4	5	Clutch	
	Philippe Alliott	RAM-Hart t/c 4	4	Electrical	

Fastest lap: Prost, on lap 59, 1m 05·257s, 133·242mph/214·432km/h (record).
Previous lap record: Alain Prost (F1 Renault RE t/c V6), 1m 07·477s, 125·973mph/202·735km/h (1982).

Past winners

Year	Driver	Nat	Car	Circuit	Distance miles/km	Speed mph/km/h
1950	Juan Manuel Fangio	RA	1·5 Alfa Romeo 158 s/c	Reims-Gueux	310·81/ 500·20	104·84/168·72
1951	Luigi Fagioli/	I				
	Juan Manuel Fangio	RA	1·5 Alfa Romeo 159 s/c	Reims-Gueux	373·94/ 601·80	110·97/178·59
1952	Alberto Ascari	I	2·0 Ferrari 500	Rouen-les-Essarts	240·39/ 386·88	80·13/128·96
1953	Mike Hawthorn	GB	2·0 Ferrari 500	Reims	314·56/ 506·23	113·64/182·89
1954	Juan Manuel Fangio	RA	2·5 Mercedes-Benz W196	Reims	314·64/ 506·36	115·97/186·64
1956	Peter Collins	GB	2·5 Lancia-Ferrari D50	Reims	314·64/ 506·36	122·29/196·80
1957	Juan Manuel Fangio	RA	2·5 Maserati 250F	Rouen-les-Essarts	313·01/ 503·74	100·02/160·96
1958	Mike Hawthorn	GB	2·4 Ferrari Dino 246	Reims	257·90/415·05	125·45/201·90
1959	Tony Brooks	GB	2·4 Ferrari Dino 246	Reims	257·90/ 415·05	127·43/205·08
1960	Jack Brabham	AUS	2·5 Cooper T53-Climax	Reims	257·90/ 415·05	131·80/212·11
1961	Giancarlo Baghetti	I	1·5 Ferrari Dino 156	Reims	268·22/ 431·66	119·85/192·87
1962	Dan Gurney	USA	1·5 Porsche 804	Rouen-les-Essarts	219·51/ 353·27	101·84/163·89
1963	Jim Clark	GB	1·5 Lotus 25-Climax	Reims	273·37/ 439·95	125·31/201·67
1964	Dan Gurney	USA	1·5 Brabham BT7-Climax	Rouen-les-Essarts	231·71/ 372·90	108·77/175·04
1965	Jim Clark	GB	1·5 Lotus 25-Climax	Clermont-Ferrand	200·21/ 322·21	89·22/143·58
1966	Jack Brabham	AUS	3·0 Brabham BT19-Repco	Reims	247·58/ 398·44	136·90/220·32
1967	Jack Brabham	AUS	3·0 Brabham BT24-Repco	Bugatti au Mans	219·82/ 353·77	98·90/159·16
1968	Jacky Ickx	B	3·0 Ferrari 312/66	Rouen-les-Essarts	243·90/ 392·52	100·45/161·66
1969	Jackie Stewart	GB	2·0 Matra MS80-Ford	Clermont-Ferrand	190·20/ 306·10	97·71/157·25
1970	Jochen Rindt	A	3·0 Lotus 72-Ford	Clermont-Ferrand	190·20/ 306·10	98·42/158·39
1971	Jackie Stewart	GB	3·0 Tyrrell 003-Ford	Paul Ricard	198·56/ 319·55	111·66/179·70
1972	Jackie Stewart	GB	3·0 Tyrrell 003-Ford	Clermont-Ferrand	190·20/ 306·10	101·56/163·44
1973	Ronnie Peterson	S	3·0 JPS/Lotus 72-Ford	Paul Ricard	194·95/ 313·74	115·12/185·26
1974	Ronnie Peterson	S	3·0 JPS/Lotus 72-Ford	Dijon-Prenois	163·49/ 263·11	119·75/192·72
1975	Niki Lauda	A	3·0 Ferrari 312T/75	Paul Ricard	194·95/ 313·74	116·60/187·65
1976	James Hunt	GB	3·0 McLaren M23-Ford	Paul Ricard	194·95/ 313·74	115·84/186·42
1977	Mario Andretti	USA	3·0 JPS/Lotus 78-Ford	Dijon-Prenois	188·90/ 304·00	113·72/183·01
1978	Mario Andretti	USA	3·0 JPS/Lotus 79-Ford	Paul Ricard	194·95/ 313·74	118·31/190·40
1979	Jean-Pierre Jabouille	F	1·5 Renault RS t/c	Dijon-Prenois	188·88/ 304·00	118·88/191·32
1980	Alan Jones	AUS	3·0 Williams FW07B-Ford	Paul Ricard	194·95/ 313·74	126·15/203·02
1981	Alain Prost	F	1·5 Renault RE t/c	Dijon-Prenois	188·88/ 304·00	118·30/190·39
1982	René Arnoux	F	1·5 Renault RE t/c	Paul Ricard	194·95/ 313·74	125·02/201·20
1983	Alain Prost	F	1·5 Renault RE t/c	Paul Ricard	194·95/ 313·74	124·19/199·87
1984	Niki Lauda	A	1·5 McLaren MP4/2-TAG t/c	Dijon-Prenois	186·53/ 300·20	125·53/202·02

Circuit data

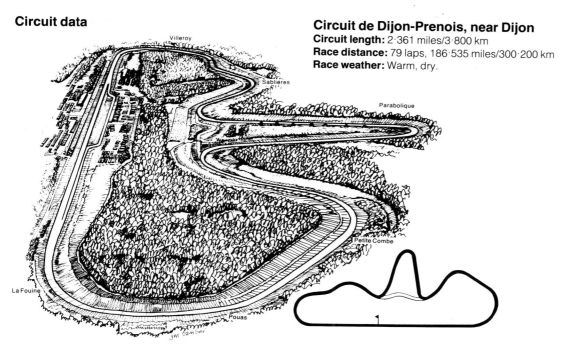

Villeroy
Sablières
Parabolique
Petite Combe
La Fouine
Pouas
jm camber

1

Circuit de Dijon-Prenois, near Dijon
Circuit length: 2·361 miles/3·800 km
Race distance: 79 laps, 186·535 miles/300·200 km
Race weather: Warm, dry.

Fastest laps

Driver	Time	Lap
Alain Prost	1m 05·257s	59
Niki Lauda	1m 06·100s	59
Patrick Tambay	1m 06·876s	54
René Arnoux	1m 07·286s	67
Derek Warwick	1m 07·293s	51
Nigel Mansell	1m 07·448s	77
Keke Rosberg	1m 07·490s	76
Teo Fabi	1m 07·839s	61
Jacques Laffite	1m 07·861s	64
Michele Alboreto	1m 08·400s	31
Elio de Angelis	1m 08·608s	70
Thierry Boutsen	1m 09·177s	73
Nelson Piquet	1m 09·186s	11
Andrea de Cesaris	1m 09·779s	77
Ayrton Senna	1m 10·100s	32
Eddie Cheever	1m 10·253s	42
Martin Brundle	1m 10·471s	36
Mauro Baldi	1m 10·692s	41
Johnny Cecotto	1m 10·999s	21
Riccardo Patrese	1m 11·047s	10
Stefan Bellof	1m 11·156s	10
Piercarlo Ghinzani	1m 11·179s	44
Manfred Winkelhock	1m 11·394s	5
Marc Surer	1m 11·783s	25
Philippe Alliot	1m 13·476s	4
Jonathan Palmer	1m 13·713s	31

Points

WORLD CHAMPIONSHIP OF DRIVERS

1	Alain Prost	24 pts
2	Niki Lauda	18
3=	René Arnoux	13
3=	Derek Warwick	13
5	Elio de Angelis	12
6	Keke Rosberg	10
7	Michele Alboreto	9
8	Patrick Tambay	7
9	Nigel Mansell	4
10=	Stefan Bellof	3
10=	Eddie Cheever	3
10=	Riccardo Patrese	3
13=	Andrea de Cesaris	2
13=	Martin Brundle	2
15=	Ayrton Senna	1
15=	Thierry Boutsen	1

CONSTRUCTORS' CUP

1	McLaren	42 pts
2	Ferrari	22
3	Renault	20
4	Lotus	16
5	Williams	10
6	Alfa Romeo	6
7	Tyrrell	5
8	Ligier	2
9=	Toleman	1
9=	Arrows	1

Lap chart

1st LAP ORDER	1	2	3	4	5	6	7	8	9	10	11	12	13	14	15	16	17	18	19	20	21	22	23	24	25	26	27	28	29	30	31	32	33	34	35	36	37
15 P. Tambay	15	15	15	15	15	15	15	15	15	15	15	15	15	15	15	15	15	15	15	15	15	15	15	15	15	15	15	15	15	15	15	15	15	15	15	15	15
11 E. De Angelis	11	11	11	11	11	11	11	11	11	11	11	11	11	11	11	11	11	7	7	7	7	7	7	7	7	7	7	8	8	8	8	8	8	8	8	8	8
12 N. Mansell	12	12	12	12	12	12	12	12	12	12	12	12	12	7	7	7	7	11	11	11	8	8	8	8	8	8	7	11	11	11	11	11	11	11	11	11	11
6 K. Rosberg	6	6	16	16	16	7	7	7	7	7	7	7	12	12	12	8	8	8	8	11	11	11	11	11	11	11	12	16	16	16	16	16	6	6	6		
1 N. Piquet	1	16	6	1	7	16	16	16	16	16	16	16	16	8	8	12	12	12	12	12	12	12	12	12	12	12	16	28	28	28	28	6	12	12	12		
16 D. Warwick	16	1	1	7	1	1	1	1	1	1	1	8	8	8	16	16	16	16	16	16	16	16	16	16	16	16	28	12	6	6	6	12	2	2	16		
7 A. Prost	7	7	7	8	8	8	8	8	8	8	8	28	28	28	28	28	28	28	28	28	28	28	28	28	28	28	6	6	12	12	12	2	16	16	2		
27 M. Alboreto	27	27	8	6	6	6	28	28	28	28	28	6	6	6	6	6	6	6	6	6	6	6	6	6	6	6	2	2	2	2	28	28	28	7		
14 M. Winkelhock	14	8	27	27	28	28	6	6	6	6	6	27	27	27	27	27	27	27	27	27	27	27	2	2	2	2	19	19	19	19	7	7	7	28		
8 N. Lauda	8	14	28	28	27	27	27	27	27	27	27	2	2	2	2	2	2	2	2	2	2	2	27	19	19	19	5	5	5	5	7	19	19	5	5		
19 A. Senna	19	19	19	19	19	19	2	2	2	2	19	19	19	19	19	19	19	19	19	19	19	19	19	5	5	5	7	7	7	5	5	5	18	18			
28 R. Arnoux	28	28	18	18	18	2	2	19	19	19	18	18	18	18	18	18	18	18	18	18	18	18	18	18	18	18	27	27	27	18	18	26	26				
18 T. Boutsen	18	18	2	2	2	18	18	18	18	18	22	22	22	23	23	23	23	23	23	23	23	5	23	26	26	26	27	18	18	18	26	26	23				
22 R. Patrese	22	2	22	22	22	22	22	22	22	22	23	23	23	26	26	26	26	26	26	26	5	23	26	23	23	23	26	26	26	26	23	23	17	17			
23 E. Cheever	23	22	23	23	23	23	23	23	23	26	26	26	26	22	3	5	5	5	5	5	26	3	3	27	27	23	23	23	23	17	17	24	24				
2 T. Fabi	2	23	5	5	5	5	5	5	5	5	5	3	3	3	5	3	3	3	3	3	27	3	3	17	17	17	17	17	24	24	21	21					
5 J. Laffite	5	5	4	4	4	4	4	4	4	4	3	5	5	5	20	20	20	20	20	17	17	17	17	24	24	24	24	21	21	3	3						
4 S. Bellof	4	4	3	3	26	26	26	26	26	26	20	20	20	17	17	17	17	17	24	24	24	24	24	21	21	21	21	3	3	19	10						
3 M. Brundle	3	3	20	26	3	3	3	3	3	3	1	17	17	22	24	24	24	24	21	21	21	21	21	3	3	3	3	10	10	10							
20 J. Cecotto	20	20	26	20	20	20	20	20	20	20	17	24	24	24	21	21	21	21	21	21	10	10	10	10	10	10	10	10									
26 A. De Cesaris	26	26	17	17	17	17	17	17	17	17	17	24	21	21	21	10	10	10	10	10	10																
17 M. Surer	17	17	24	24	24	24	24	24	24	24	10	10	10	10																							
24 P. Ghinzani	24	24	21	21	21	21	21	21	21	21	10																										
9 P. Alliot	9	9	9	9	10	10	10	10	10	10	10																										
21 M. Baldi	21	21	10	10	14	14																															
10 J. Palmer	10	10	14	14																																	

38	39	40	41	42	43	44	45	46	47	48	49	50	51	52	53	54	55	56	57	58	59	60	61	62	63	64	65	66	67	68	69	70	71	72	73	74	75	76	77	78	79
15	15	15	8	8	8	8	8	8	8	8	8	8	8	8	8	8	8	15	15	15	15	15	15	15	8	8	8	8	8	8	8	8	8	8	8	8	8	8	8	8	8
8	8	8	15	15	15	15	15	15	15	15	15	15	15	15	15	15	15	8	8	8	8	8	8	15	15	15	15	15	15	15	15	15	15	15	15	15	15	15	15	15	15
6	12	12	12	12	12	12	12	12	12	12	12	12	12	12	12	12	12	12	12	12	12	12	12	12	12	12	12	12	12	12	12	12	12	12	12	12	12	12	12	12	12
12	6	6	6	6	16	16	16	16	16	16	16	16	16	16	16	16	7	7	7	11	11	11	11	28	28	28	28	28	28	28	28	28	28	28	28	28	28	28	28	28	28
11	16	16	16	16	6	6	6	7	7	7	7	7	7	7	7	11	11	11	28	28	28	28	28	11	11	11	11	11	11	11	11	11	11	11	11	11	11	11	11	11	11
16	11	11	11	11	11	7	7	11	11	11	11	11	11	11	11	28	28	28	7	6	6	6	6	6	6	6	6	6	6	6	6	6	6	6	6	6	6	6	6	6	6
7	7	7	7	7	7	11	11	28	28	28	28	28	28	28	28	6	6	6	6	5	5	5	5	5	5	5	5	5	5	5	5	7	7	7	7	7	7	7	7	7	7
2	2	2	28	28	28	28	28	6	5	5	5	5	6	6	6	5	5	5	5	2	2	2	2	2	2	2	2	7	7	5	5	5	5	5	5	5	5				
28	28	28	2	2	2	2	2	5	6	6	6	6	5	5	5	2	2	2	2	26	26	7	7	7	7	7	7	2	2	2	2	2	2	2	2	2	2				
5	5	5	5	5	5	5	2	26	26	26	26	26	2	2	26	26	26	26	27	7	7	26	26	26	26	26	26	26	26	26	26	26	26	26	26	26	26				
18	18	26	18	26	26	26	26	23	2	23	23	2	26	26	18	18	18	18	18	18	18	18	18	18	18	18	18	18	18	18	18	18	18	18	18	18	18				
26	26	23	23	23	23	23	23	2	2	2	2	23	18	18	3	3	3	3	3	3	3	3	3	3	3	3	3	3	3	3	3	3	3	3	3	3	3				
23	23	18	18	18	18	18	18	18	18	18	18	18	3	3	24	24	21	21	21	21	21	21	21	24	24	24	24	24	24	24	24	24	24	24								
17	17	17	17	17	17	17	17	17	17	17	17	24	24	21	21	24	24	24	24	24	24	24	24	10	10	10	10	10	10	10	10	10	10									
24	24	3	3	3	3	3	3	24	24	24	24	4	21	24	10	10	10	10	10	10	10	10																				
3	21	21	21	21	21	21	21	21	21	21	21																															
10	10	10	10	10	10	10	10	10	10	10	10	10																														

Grand Prix de Monaco

The popular image of Monaco as the sun-kissed millionaire's playground, set on the edge of the brilliant blue Mediterranean, took something of a major dive for the spectators and participants during the 1984 Grand Prix. It may come as a surprise to some motor sporting enthusiasts, but the fact remains that when it rains on the *Cote d'Azur* it can rain every bit as hard as at Silverstone or Thruxton during a late October club meeting. Thus, it was in absolutely diabolical conditions of blinding rain, diminishing visibility and treacherous puddles that this motor racing classic was stopped prematurely after only 32 of the planned 77 laps had been completed. But the depressing, torrential conditions were as nothing compared with the floodgates of controversy which opened immediately after Clerk of the Course Jacky Ickx took the decision that the race should be stopped. FISA, at war with the Monaco organisers over such weighty matters as the assignment of television coverage rights, saw the organisers' misfortune as a golden opportunity to plunge in with a tidal wave of critical invective which would take many months to subside. It was a classic case of political advantage obscuring the immediate racing realities . . .

Fact number one: Alain Prost qualified his McLaren MP4/2 brilliantly on pole position and led almost all the way to the chequered flag, his super-sensitive approach keeping him on the circuit whilst many of his rivals plunged up escape roads or into guard rails. Fact number two: Britain's Nigel Mansell qualified on the front row of the starting grid for the first time at the wheel of his Lotus 95T and led a race for the first time before making an elementary error and clanging his way into retirement against the unyielding armco. Fact number three: Ayrton Senna drove quite brilliantly at the wheel of his Toleman TG184 and was gobbling up Prost's advantage when the race was stopped. Another couple of laps and he would have been through into the lead.

Undoubtedly the loneliest person in Monaco after the Grand Prix was Jacky Ickx, although he, more than anybody outside the current Formula 1 cockpits, knew from first-hand experience what the track conditions must have been like all round the circuit. His decision to stop the race was criticised by many people on the spur of the moment, but, on quiet reflection, it wasn't really the sort of outlandish, partisan course of action that it might have seemed. Ickx was accused of favouring the French (unlikely, when one considers that FISA and the ACM were at daggers drawn!) or, more absurdly, favouring a Porsche-built engine in the leading car bearing in mind his Rothmans Porsche connections (an absolutely outrageous slur on the Belgian's integrity). The hard facts of the matter were that Prost was the only driver not to make a mistake, either during practice or the race, and thoroughly deserved to win. Senna was brilliant, proving his natural ability behind the wheel of a Grand Prix car beyond all doubt. His day was sure to come, but *this* day deservedly belonged to Alain Prost.

ENTRY AND PRACTICE

Aside from the political debate over the future status of the Monaco Grand Prix in which FISA told the ACM that it would have to reapply for inclusion on the 1985 international calendar as if it was a totally new event (the penalty for not aligning its television coverage arrangements with the terms of the Concorde Agreement), there was a more immediate irritation once the cars appeared for practice round the sinuous 2.058-mile street circuit. The old habit of staging a pre-qualifying session prior to the start of official practice had been dispensed with, leaving no fewer than 27 competitors to thrash it out for 20 starting grid positions during the two hours' qualifying on Thursday and Saturday afternoons. This anomaly virtually guaranteed that the timed qualifying sessions would be more hazardous and crowded than the race itself – and begged the question that if 26 cars are allowed to start at places like Detroit, then why not at Monaco?

Before practice started the McLaren International team was regarding the whole affair with some caution, slightly worried that the continuing minor throttle lag problem on the TAG turbo engine might mean that Alain Prost and Niki Lauda could have a hard fight on their hands. However, Prost silenced those doubts in the most impressive fashion imaginable: during the final hour of qualifying he scorched his MP4/2 round in 1m 22.661s to throw pole position beyond the reach of all his rivals. Both Prost and team-mate Lauda enjoyed an untroubled two days of practice – "for a pleasant change," remarked the Austrian with an amused grin – and the Frenchman's pole time was no less than 2.2 seconds under his Renault RE40 pole time from the previous year. Lauda, badly baulked by Mauro Baldi's Spirit 101B on his second set of qualifiers during the final session, wound up a disappointed eighth on 1m 23.886s.

Although Prost flew the flag brilliantly for Michelin, Goodyear found itself in highly competitive shape on this road circuit with a new front construction cover which had originally been "discovered" by Patrese during Alfa Romeo tests at Imola. Fitted to the Lotus 95Ts it was clearly very effective indeed and Nigel Mansell, who loves Monaco, used it to good effect to qualify alongside

Alain Prost never put a foot wrong in the appalling conditions and went on to take a controversial win as officials brought the race to a premature halt.

the McLaren on the front row. In common with all other Goodyear users, Nigel "juggled" three qualifying tyres in conjunction with a harder 'C' compound left rear, a ruse initially tried on Alboreto's Ferrari C4 in an attempt to squeeze more than a single quick lap out of a set; an important factor on a circuit such as this with the ever-present possibility of being baulked by slower cars.

On Thursday Mansell didn't get a clear run and Saturday morning's untimed session saw him briefly collide with Arnoux's Ferrari and then glance the chicane with his two left-hand wheels. Then, apparently to cap everything, his spare car,

fitted with the hard left rear Goodyear, suffered engine failure early in the final qualifying session and stranded Mansell at the entrance to the tunnel. He sprinted back to the pits where his race car, equipped with a fresh engine for the Grand Prix, was waiting.

"I couldn't use qualifying boost and I only had a single set of soft qualifiers all round," Nigel reflected, "so I knew that I would only have one good crack at it . . ." What followed was Mansell at his brilliant best, the black and gold Lotus 95T virtually shaving the guard rails all round the Principality to complete its best lap in 1m 22.752s to snatch second place on the grid. By contrast, his team-mate Elio de Angelis never looked anywhere near as at home on the confined little circuit: the Italian spent much of his time complaining about unwanted oversteer and couldn't better an 11th fastest 1m 24.426.

With a quartet of 1265C4s at its disposal, including a brand new chassis (075) for Alboreto, the Ferrari team was in confident mood at the start of qualifying. More tests at Imola revealed that the Marelli-Weber electronic fuel injection system still wasn't ready for competitive use, so all four cars continued to use the Lucas mechanical system and C4 chassis designer Harvey Postlethwaite was on hand to assist Mauro Forghieri. Many people thought that Ferrari would produce special "Monaco spec." engines to provide extra torque for the tight circuit, but Postlethwaite insisted that the V6 units were exactly the same as those employed at Dijon two weeks earlier.

Alboreto and Arnoux had what might best be described as an acrobatic time during qualifying, Michele setting fastest time during Thursday's hour-long session before blotting his copybook on Saturday when he slid into the wall at *Ste. Devote*, knocking a front wheel askew. Arnoux somehow contrived to spin through the fast harbour-front chicane without hitting anything and eventually nipped in ahead of his team-mate to set third quickest time on 1m 22.35s, a scant fraction quicker than Alboreto.

Side by side on the third row of the grid were the two Renault Elf RE50s of Derek Warwick and Patrick Tambay, the Englishman just displacing his team-mate for fifth place in the final five minutes of the second session. The use of revised

smaller Garrett turbochargers endowed the French cars with an impressive degree of throttle response round Monaco and both men were generally satisfied with their machines, although a brush with Boutsen's Arrows on Thursday morning tweaked a front suspension pick-up point on Patrick's machine and obliged him to take the spare for the rest of the day. A broken third gear – "it made a terrible noise and I thought it was a turbo going!" – bugged Warwick's progress on Thursday and he also had a close shave when he came bounding over the rise out of Casino Square to find Manfred Winkelhock's ATS D6 (the German's spare car) shuddering to a halt as a pile of wreckage after bouncing off the guard rail!

Andrea de Cesaris kept his head well in the confined surroundings of the Monaco streets to record a 1m 23.578s, seventh fastest time. The usually explosive Italian survived a slight brush with his equally volatile compatriot Riccardo Patrese during the final session, but otherwise kept his nose clean in praiseworthy style. His teammate, François Hesnault, had got over his obvious disappointment at being "stood down" at Dijon

and manhandled his JS23 round to qualify in a reasonable 17th place on his first visit to the Principality at the wheel of a Grand Prix car.

Turbocharger boost control problems and only average handling left World Champion Nelson Piquet languishing down in ninth place at the wheel of his Brabham BT53, while Teo Fabi's absence (he was at the Milwaukee CART race) meant that his younger brother Corrado, 1982 European Formula 2 Champion, was at last given the chance to try his hand behind the wheel of one of these BMW-engined machines in front of a public audience. It was rather hard for the meek young Italian who had only a session at Nogaro under his belt when it came to *recent* Brabham testing and it has to be said that the whole philosophy of sharing the second BT53 entry between the two brothers was proving satisfactory to neither of them.

Persistent electrical problems which eventually stranded him out on the circuit meant that the rather bewildered Corrado went to sleep on Thursday night without qualifying, but he managed to squeeze in a respectable 1m 25.290s lap to

snatch 15th place during Saturday's qualifying session. When compared with Nelson's performance – in the team's spare "qualifying" car – young Fabi certainly had not disgraced himself.

Over in the Williams pit, hope was still flickering that the FW09 might, by some overnight technical miracle, be whipped into some sort of competitive shape. Keke Rosberg was trying as only Keke knew how . . . but even that sort of inspired effort seemed wasted on this lemon of a car which seemed to understeer, understeer, understeer no matter what combination of spring and rollbar settings was adopted by the team. The FW09s were almost blistering their front tyres in a single lap, such was the handling imbalance both drivers had to contend with, and the 1982 World Champion's most spectacular contribution to the final hour's qualifying was when he drove slowly back to the pits trailing a cloud of dense white smoke which heralded, unmistakably, a major turbocharger failure.

As the smokescreen cleared, Rosberg was strapped into the team's spare FW09 for another crack at qualifying which was soon thwarted by the

Honda V6 engine which cut out abruptly.
Fortunately for Keke, an unexpected break in the
proceedings followed Martin Brundle's violent
accident under braking for *Tabac* and the Williams
lads had sufficient breathing space in which to
replace the failed turbo on the race car. Rosberg
eventually made the grid in tenth place on 1m
24.151s with team-mate Jacques Laffite 16th on 1m
25.719s. Neither man was impressed with his
mount and each made his feelings clear to the team
– in his own charming manner!

The Toleman team's always-optimistic attitude
was heightened by the arrival on the scene of the
latest Hart 415T development engine, complete
with electronic "management system" and four
injectors per cylinder. Although a conservative
approach was taken to the amount of boost
pressure applied to it during its outing in
Saturday's untimed practice, Ayrton Senna
reported it was definitely more responsive than the

standard engines.

Following these initial tests in a competitive
environment, the new Hart engine in the spare car
was put on one side and the Brazilian continued to
qualify 12th on 1m 25.009s at the wheel of his
regular race car equipped with a regular specification 415T. Cecotto was, as had become customary,
significantly slower than his team-mate on 1m
25.872s – 18th fastest on the 20-car grid.

Prior to the Monaco race there had been
confidence amongst the handful of Cosworth
runners that their nimble machines might pose
realistic threats round this tight street circuit. It
proved not to be the case – this argument perhaps
forgetting the benefits reaped by sheer, unadulter-
ated turbo power on that long climb from *Ste. Devote*
to Casino Square. In the Arrows camp, the appeal
of Cosworth DFV power actually prompted Marc
Surer to opt for the older A6 chassis, but even more
was expected from the Tyrrell 012s of Stefan Bellof

and Martin Brundle.

The non-turbo brigade was in for a nasty shock.
Only Bellof managed to squeeze in, last out of the
20 qualifiers, and Brundle became involved in a
horrifying accident as he strained for those final few
tenths that would get him on to the grid. Up to the
point where he went on to the brakes for the *Tabac*
left-hander, his final qualifying lap was absolutely
stupendous. "I felt I'd got everything exactly
right," he later confessed ruefully, "I didn't put a
wheel wrong and I took the chicane appreciably
quicker than on any other lap. Then I went on to
the brakes and I think that I tagged the throttle
pedal with the edge of my boot . . ." From that
moment on, Brundle was out of control in a big
way: his Tyrrell charged the guard rail at a
worryingly acute angle and bounced back into the
middle of the circuit, shorn of its right-hand
wheels, almost upside down. Marshals ran out to
right the totally wrecked machine and Brundle,

The Renault-Elf team had a short race at Monaco,
Patrick Tambay and Derek Warwick crashing at the
first corner.
Photo: Bernard Asset/Agence Vandystadt

badly bruised and shaken, was quickly released
from the car. He couldn't remember running back
to the pits and preparing to take over the spare car.
"Only when I suddenly realised that I didn't know
which circuit I was at, did we decide that it
probably wasn't wise to go out again," smiled
Brundle. The Tyrrell carbon fibre composite/alloy
honeycomb monocoque protected the driver
encouragingly well during this dramatic impact.

Alongside Bellof's lone Cosworth-engined car on
the back row of the grid was Piercarlo Ghinzani's
Osella, leaving both Arrows entries, Cosworth and
BMW turbo-powered, in the ranks of non-
qualifiers. Eddie Cheever just couldn't get his
Alfa's V8 engine to perform remotely respectably,
so he got nowhere near team-mate Patrese's 1m
25.101s qualifying time, much to his unbridled
frustration. Less surprising non-qualifiers were the
slow RAM 02s of Palmer and Alliot along with
Baldi's Spirit.

RACE

As Sunday dawned, most of the drivers must have
wished they could have simply rolled over and gone
back to sleep for the rest of the day: the hitherto
sunny Monte Carlo scene had been transformed
into a bleak, wet, unpromising misery. It was one of
those days on which low cloud obscured the tops of
the towering cliffs behind the Principality: a day
when one just knew that it would rain unceasingly
for many, many hours.

Apart from the obvious fact that this sudden
change in the weather transformed the already
demanding street circuit into a skating rink,
another minor problem arose. The tunnel section
which runs beneath the fashionable Loews Hotel
had, during the untimed warm-up, "turned into a
good imitation of Park Lane after a summer storm
– absolutely like ice!" to quote one of the
competitors. In order to ensure that the entire

May:

*Fuengirola Grand Prix, scheduled for October 21,
cancelled.*

*Rick Mears (March-Cosworth 84C), wins Indy
500 from Roberto Guerrero and Al Unser Sr.; all 14
finishers use March chassis and Cosworth DFX
engines.*

*Ivan Capelli (Martini-Alfa Romeo Mk42) wins
Monaco Formula 3 race.*

circuit was "uniformly wet", a water tanker was called in to douse this enclosed section of the circuit, thereby delaying the start for 15 minutes or so. Of course, within a few laps, a dry line began to appear on this section and the initial problem was back again!

As Prost led the field round on the parade lap, huge rooster tails of spray thrown up by the Formula 1 cars' huge tyres, Clerk of the Course Jacky Ickx must have been thinking back to this very race 12 years earlier when he was Grand Prix racing's acknowledged wet weather exponent. On that famous afternoon his Ferrari 312B2 was obliged to give best to outsider Jean-Pierre Beltoise's BRM P160. Perhaps Monaco '84 would result in a similar upset to established form . . .

Smoothly and predictably, Prost eased his McLaren MP4/2 gently into the lead when the starting light turned green, Mansell following him tightly into the braking area for the *Ste. Devote* chicane. From his position on the third row of the grid Warwick had made a magnificent getaway and actually nosed into third spot as the pack scrambled into the corner; unfortunately he had the unyielding René Arnoux's Ferrari to his right and the Frenchman slid off the right-hand kerb, punting his Renault very firmly into the tyre barrier on the opposite side of the track. Tambay,

also looking for a way through, exited the corner on a slightly wider line and was faced with an inevitable path straight into his team-mate's car. Both RE50s were out of the race on the spot and Warwick wasn't particularly encouraged when he saw that the front of the carbon fibre monocoque on his machine had virtually snapped off in the impact. As for poor Patrick, a lower wishbone had entered the footwell during the accident (as it had two weeks earlier in Derek's French GP shunt) and broken his fibula, a small bone in the back of his lower left leg. As an incidental to all this, de Cesaris's Ligier was punted hard up the rear by team-mate Hesnault, resulting in Andrea's retirement at the end of the opening lap. Three Renault-engined contenders out of the running almost before the race had started . . .

At the end of that opening lap the order was Prost, Mansell, Arnoux, Alboreto, Lauda, Rosberg, Winkelhock, Laffite, Senna, Fabi, Bellof, Ghinzani, Piquet with de Angelis and Patrese quite a way back after being obliged to stop and back out of the Renault first corner débacle. Prost looked utterly in control, completely cool and confident, and as there really didn't look much chance that he would be challenged, most of the attention centred initially round Lauda's efforts to move past the Ferraris, a task he completed by lap seven after

dispatching Alboreto under braking for the Loews hairpin and Arnoux in a daring move up the hill out of *Ste. Devote*.

Once firmly ensconced in third place, Lauda settled down to run on his own, allowing attention to switch to new boys Senna and Bellof who were really getting into the swing of things in magnificent style, the torrential conditions making their relative lack of brake horsepower an irrelevant consideration. Both men were demonstrating a delightfully uninhibited brio, a magnificent blend of unrestrained car control and joyous enthusiasm: watching them both put one in mind of such revered names as Peterson, Villeneuve . . .

By the end of lap seven Senna was up into seventh place, and from that point onwards, he seemed to be picking off his rivals with all the ease of an established veteran. When Alboreto spun and briefly stalled his Ferrari he picked up another place and he picked off Keke Rosberg's misfiring Williams-Honda with great *élan* on lap 12 – despite having a lucky escape the previous time through the chicane when he got off line and launched his Toleman into a brief crazy flight over the apex kerbing. The impact tweaked the right front suspension, "stretching" the pull-rod. In retrospect, he was lucky to get away with it.

On lap 11, as Prost rounded *Portier* and

accelerated for the tunnel, he had just lapped Alboreto and came face-to-face with Corrado Fabi's Brabham BT53 which had spun and was now stationary in the middle of the track. More worryingly, as he squeezed through the narrow gap, Prost's McLaren side-swiped a marshal who was attempting to move the stricken Brabham. The marshal wasn't badly hurt, merely bruised and very frightened, but the whole muddle allowed Mansell to grasp the initiative and he poked his Lotus 95T through into the lead.

Prost was in no real position to respond, for his McLaren's carbon fibre brakes were snatching badly due to an uneven heat build-up in these diabolical conditions, so British enthusiasts sat back and revelled in the sight of Mansell leading the first Grand Prix of his career. Nigel's moment of glory lasted for only six laps . . .

Frankly, the Englishman was running too quickly when he didn't have to do so. He was pulling away from Prost at a quite unnecessary two seconds a lap when he went out of control on the slippery white painted road markings on the climb from *Ste. Devote* towards Casino Square and went clanging into the guard rails. In a hopeless effort to continue with his mortally damaged car, he staggered on as far as *Mirabeau* where he spun to a halt again, thanks to a deflated rear tyre and deranged aerofoil. Another 25 yards or so and he abandoned his Lotus, bitterly disappointed, but indignant that what he felt was such a minor error should have had such enormous consequences. The perils of motor racing!

As if to endorse just how slippery the Monaco surface really was, Niki Lauda spun out of what was now second place on lap 24 as he entered Casino Square. For a few laps previously, Niki had been grappling with a locking rear brake, but the Austrian veteran was big enough to shoulder all the blame for the incident. "McLaren no problem, all Lauda!" he snapped.

Meanwhile, if anything, the rain was getting heavier. But the heavier it became, the worse the visibility became, so Senna and Bellof seemed to drive faster and faster. Approaching the 30 lap mark the brilliant Toleman team leader was in second place and it didn't take a mathematical genius to calculate that he would easily catch Prost's leading McLaren before many more laps were run. What's more, the amazing Bellof was taking time off both of them, so it appeared that at about the time Senna caught the McLaren, so the Tyrrell would catch both of them!

Unfortunately the race was soon to end. Watching the track conditions all round the circuit on television monitors at the start/finish line, Jacky Ickx decided that the whole affair had run far enough. At the end of the 32nd lap he gave the instructions for the red flag to be shown at the start/finish line, just as Senna came roaring up on to Prost's tail. In fact, the Brazilian surged past the slowing McLaren virtually on the line, but as the results in these circumstances are taken at the end of the previous lap (i.e. the 31st), Senna's apparent success was academic. The Brazilian was classified second, the brilliant Bellof third. "I was having trouble with my brakes," confessed Prost later, "I would have let Senna go past me. The Championship is more important . . ."

As the remaining top six finishers struggled home in the order Arnoux, Rosberg and de Angelis, the recriminations predictably started. Some people over-reacted and saw it as a conspiracy by the French. The French? The Monegasque organisers were at war with the French in the form of the FISA, and when Jean-Marie Balestre pompously decreed that the ACM and Jacky Ickx were out of order over the manner in which they handled the premature stopping of the race, the Monaco club virtually told FISA to "stuff it". If the FISA stewards were so dissatisfied, said the ACM, then why did they approve the official results? Oh yes, and by the way M. Balestre, you approved Ickx's appointment as Clerk of the Course!

Good point! Within a few weeks much of this furore was forgotten. Prost had won the Monaco Grand Prix, truncated or not; the only driver not to make a single mistake all afternoon.   AH

THE subject of Monaco and the stopping of the Grand Prix continued to be a dinner table topic two weeks later at Montreal. Should the race have been stopped? If so, should it have been stopped at a point where Senna was poised to take the lead from Prost? Why did the organisers refuse to consider restarting the race? And if they believed it was too dangerous to continue, then why start the race in the first place?

It must be said that the rain did get considerably worse ten minutes before the red flag was shown. Conditions were appalling and, in our opinion, the correct decision was made even if the timing did cause offence. But that was bound to happen.

Had Jacky Ickx, the Clerk of the Course, waited until Senna had passed Prost, then not only would McLaren have been upset but Ken Tyrrell would have been bearing down on the Belgian to demand why he had not waited for Bellof, the fastest man on the track at the time, to catch and pass Senna. And so it would have gone on. As Ickx rightly said, better to stop the race a lap too soon than a lap too late. And there was no one better qualified to judge the situation than the man who had finished second at Monaco under similar conditions in 1972.

No, the fault lay with the organisers and their actions once the decision to stop the race had been taken. Ickx followed the correct procedure by showing the red flag; a signal which required each driver to stop on the track at a point alongside his pit. The officials should then have gone through a restart procedure and *then* decided whether it was safe to continue.

In the event, Michel Boeri took it upon himself to show the chequered flag, a meaningless act exacerbated by the fact that M. Boeri was not an official and had no right to be on the track issuing instructions. By the time Tyrrell and other team managers better versed in the regulations had reached Race Control to discover at what time the race would be restarting, Prost had been ushered to the Royal Box and the French National Anthem was being played. (It was suggested, in fact, that the entire affair was determined by television schedules as well as the wish not to keep Prince Rainier waiting unnecessarily.)

The FISA officials present were powerless to do anything since they had not been consulted in the first place and, by now, barriers had been dismantled and the track was being re-opened.

It is unlikely that the race would have been restarted given that the most dangerous point in a Grand Prix is the rush into the first corner. However, the general level of incompetence shown by the Automobile Club de Monaco left them wide open for criticism from FISA who were waiting to pounce in the light of earlier disagreements over television rights.

Whatever the rights and wrongs of the situation, it was the end of an enthralling race and it was difficult to judge who felt more uncomfortable; the drenched spectators or the hapless Jacky Ickx.

Grand Prix de Monaco, June 3/statistics

Entries and practice times

No.	Driver	Nat	Car	Tyre	Engine	Entrant	Practice 1	Practice 2
1	Nelson Piquet	BR	Parmalat BRABHAM BT53	M	BMW M12/13	MRD International	1m 24·139s	**1m 23·918s**
2	Corrado Fabi	I	Parmalat BRABHAM BT53	M	BMW M12/13	MRD International	1m 31·618s	**1m 25·290s**
3	Martin Brundle	GB	TYRRELL 012	G	Ford Cosworth DFY	Tyrrell Racing Organisation	1m 27·891s	**1m 26·373s**
4	Stefan Bellof	D	TYRRELL 012	G	Ford Cosworth DFY	Tyrrell Racing Organisation	1m 27·836s	**1m 26·117s**
5	Jacques Laffite	F	WILLIAMS FW09	G	Honda RA 163-E	Williams Grand Prix Engineering	1m 27·356s	**1m 25·719s**
6	Keke Rosberg	SF	WILLIAMS FW09	G	Honda RA 163-E	Williams Grand Prix Engineering	1m 26·017s	**1m 24·151s**
7	Alain Prost	F	Marlboro McLAREN MP4/2	M	TAG P01 (TTE P01)	Marlboro McLaren International	1m 23·944s	**1m 22·661s**
8	Niki Lauda	A	Marlboro McLAREN MP4/2	M	TAG P01 (TTE P01)	Marlboro McLaren International	1m 24·508s	**1m 23·886s**
9	Philippe Alliot	F	RAM 02	P	Hart 415T	Skoal Bandit Formula 1 Team	1m 29·637s	**1m 29·576s**
10	Jonathan Palmer	GB	RAM 02	P	Hart 415T	Skoal Bandit Formula 1 Team	1m 29·778s	**1m 27·458s**
11	Elio de Angelis	I	John Player Special LOTUS 95T	G	Renault EF4	John Player Team Lotus	1m 25·602s	**1m 24·426s**
12	Nigel Mansell	GB	John Player Special LOTUS 95T	G	Renault EF4	John Player Team Lotus	1m 24·927s	**1m 22·752s**
14	Manfred Winkelhock	D	ATS D7	P	BMW M12/13	Team ATS	1m 52·889s	**1m 24·473s**
15	Patrick Tambay	F	Elf RENAULT RE50	M	Renault EF4	Equipe Renault Elf	1m 24·828s	**1m 23·414s**
16	Derek Warwick	GB	Elf RENAULT RE50	M	Renault EF4	Equipe Renault Elf	1m 23·726s	**1m 23·237s**
17	Marc Surer	CH	ARROWS A6	G	Ford Cosworth DFV	Barclay Nordica Arrows BMW	1m 27·919s	**1m 26·273s**
18	Thierry Boutsen	B	ARROWS A7	G	BMW M12/13	Barclay Nordica Arrows BMW	1m 28·000s	**1m 26·514s**
19	Ayrton Senna	BR	TOLEMAN TG184	M	Hart 415T	Toleman Group Motorsport	1m 27·865s	**1m 25·009s**
20	Johnny Cecotto	YV	TOLEMAN TG184	M	Hart 415T	Toleman Group Motorsport	1m 28·241s	**1m 25·872s**
21	Mauro Baldi	I	SPIRIT 101	P	Hart 415T	Spirit Racing	**1m 28·360s**	1m 30·146s
22	Riccardo Patrese	I	Benetton ALFA ROMEO 184T	G	Alfa Romeo 183T	Benetton Team Alfa Romeo	1m 28·072s	**1m 25·101s**
23	Eddie Cheever	USA	Benetton ALFA ROMEO 184T	G	Alfa Romeo 183T	Benetton Team Alfa Romeo	1m 28·961s	**1m 26·471s**
24	Piercarlo Ghinzani	I	Kelemata OSELLA FA1F	P	Alfa Romeo 183T	Osella Squadra Corse	1m 27·723s	**1m 25·877s**
25	François Hesnault	F	LIGIER Loto JS23	M	Renault EF4	Ligier Loto	1m 27·678s	**1m 25·815s**
26	Andrea de Cesaris	I	LIGIER Loto JS23	M	Renault EF4	Ligier Loto	1m 25·939s	**1m 23·578s**
27	Michele Alboreto	I	Fiat FERRARI 126C4	G	Ferrari 126C	Scuderia Ferrari SpA	1m 23·581s	**1m 22·937s**
28	René Arnoux	F	Fiat FERRARI 126C4	G	Ferrari 126C	Scuderia Ferrari SpA	1m 24·661s	**1m 22·935s**

Thursday morning and Saturday morning practice sessions not officially recorded.

Thu pm Warm, dry
Sat pm Warm, dry

G – Goodyear, M – Michelin, P – Pirelli.

Starting grid

7 PROST (1m 22·661s) McLaren
12 MANSELL (1m 22·752s) Lotus

28 ARNOUX (1m 22·935s) Ferrari
27 ALBORETO (1m 22·937s) Ferrari

16 WARWICK (1m 23·237s) Renault
15 TAMBAY (1m 23·414s) Renault

26 DE CESARIS (1m 23·578s) Ligier
8 LAUDA (1m 23·886s) McLaren

1 PIQUET (1m 23·918s) Brabham
6 ROSBERG (1m 24·151s) Williams

11 DE ANGELIS (1m 24·426s) Lotus
14 WINKELHOCK (1m 24·473s) ATS

19 SENNA (1m 25·009s) Toleman
22 PATRESE (1m 25·101s) Alfa Romeo

2 FABI (1m 25·290s) Brabham
5 LAFFITE (1m 25·719s) Williams

25 HESNAULT (1m 25·815s) Ligier
20 CECOTTO (1m 25·872s) Toleman

24 GHINZANI (1m 25·877s) Osella
4 BELLOF (1m 26·117s) Tyrrell

Did not start:
17 Surer (Arrows), 1m 26·273s, did not qualify
3 Brundle (Tyrrell), 1m 26·373s, did not qualify
23 Cheever (Alfa Romeo), 1m 26·471s, did not qualify
18 Boutsen (Arrows), 1m 26·514s, did not qualify
10 Palmer (RAM), 1m 27·458s, did not qualify
21 Baldi (Spirit), 1m 28·360s, did not qualify
9 Alliott (RAM), 1m 29·576s, did not qualify

Results and retirements

Place	Driver	Car	Laps	Time and Speed (mph/km/h)/Retirement	
1	Alain Prost	McLaren-TAG t/c V6	31	1h 01m 07·740s	62·619/100·775
2	Ayrton Senna	Toleman-Hart t/c 4	31	1h 01m 15·186s	62·5/100·6
3	Stefan Bellof	Tyrrell-Cosworth V8	31	1h 01m 28·881s	62·3/100·2
4	René Arnoux	Ferrari t/c V6	31	1h 01m 36·817s	62·1/100·0
5	Keke Rosberg	Williams-Honda t/c V6	31	1h 01m 42·986s	62·0/99·8
6	Elio de Angelis	Lotus-Renault t/c V6	31	1h 01m 52·179s	61·9/99·6
7	Michele Alboreto	Ferrari t/c V6	30		
8	Piercarlo Ghinzani	Osella-Alfa Romeo t/c V8	30		
9	Jacques Laffite	Williams-Honda t/c V6	30		
	Riccardo Patrese	Alfa Romeo t/c V8	24	Steering	
	Niki Lauda	McLaren-TAG t/c V6	23	Spun off	
	Manfred Winkelhock	ATS-BMW t/c V6	22	Spun off	
	Nigel Mansell	Lotus-Renault t/c V6	15	Hit barrier	
	Nelson Piquet	Brabham-BMW t/c 4	14	Water in electrics	
	François Hesnault	Ligier-Renault t/c V6	12	Water in electrics	
	Corrado Fabi	Brabham-BMW t/c 4	9	Water in electrics/spun off	
	Johnny Cecotto	Toleman-Hart t/c 4	1	Spun off	
	Andrea de Cesaris	Ligier-Renault t/c V6	1	Accident damage	
	Derek Warwick	Renault t/c V6	0	Accident damage	
	Patrick Tambay	Renault t/c V6	0	Accident damage	

Fastest lap: Ayrton Senna, on lap 24, 1m 54·334s, 64·798mph/104·283km/h.
Lap record: Riccardo Patrese (F1 Arrows A3-Cosworth DFV), 1m 26·058s, 86·089mph/138·548km/h (1980).

Past winners

Year	Driver	Nat	Car	Circuit	Distance miles/km	Speed mph/km/h
1950	Juan Manuel Fangio	RA	1·5 Alfa Romeo 158 s/c	Monte Carlo	197·60/318·01	61·33/98·70
1952*	Vittorio Marzotto	I	2·7 Ferrari 225MM	Monte Carlo	195·42/314·50	58·20/93·66
1955	Maurice Trintignant	F	2·5 Ferrari 625	Monte Carlo	195·42/314·50	65·81/105·91
1956	Stirling Moss	GB	2·5 Maserati 250F	Monte Carlo	195·42/314·50	64·94/104·51
1957	Juan Manuel Fangio	RA	2·5 Maserati 250F	Monte Carlo	205·19/330·22	64·72/104·16
1958	Maurice Trintignant	F	2·0 Cooper T45-Climax	Monte Carlo	195·42/314·50	67·99/109·41
1959	Jack Brabham	AUS	2·5 Cooper T51-Climax	Monte Carlo	195·42/314·50	66·71/107·36
1960	Stirling Moss	GB	2·5 Lotus 18-Climax	Monte Carlo	195·42/314·50	67·48/108·60
1961	Stirling Moss	GB	1·5 Lotus 18-Climax	Monte Carlo	195·42/314·50	70·70/113·79
1962	Bruce McLaren	NZ	1·5 Cooper T60-Climax	Monte Carlo	195·42/314·50	70·46/113·40
1963	Graham Hill	GB	1·5 BRM P57	Monte Carlo	195·42/314·50	72·43/116·56
1964	Graham Hill	GB	1·5 BRM P261	Monte Carlo	195·42/314·50	72·64/116·91
1965	Graham Hill	GB	1·5 BRM P261	Monte Carlo	195·42/314·50	74·34/119·64
1966	Jackie Stewart	GB	1·9 BRM P261	Monte Carlo	195·42/314·50	76·51/123·14
1967	Denny Hulme	NZ	3·0 Brabham BT20-Repco	Monte Carlo	195·42/314·50	75·90/122·14
1968	Graham Hill	GB	3·0 Lotus 49B-Ford	Monte Carlo	156·34/251·60	77·82/125·24
1969	Graham Hill	GB	3·0 Lotus 49B-Ford	Monte Carlo	156·34/251·60	80·18/129·04
1970	Jochen Rindt	A	3·0 Lotus 49C-Ford	Monte Carlo	156·34/251·60	81·85/131·72
1971	Jackie Stewart	GB	3·0 Tyrrell 003-Ford	Monte Carlo	156·34/251·60	83·49/134·36
1972	Jean-Pierre Beltoise	F	3·0 BRM P160B	Monte Carlo	156·34/251·60	63·85/102·75
1973	Jackie Stewart	GB	3·0 Tyrrell 006-Ford	Monte Carlo	158·87/255·68	80·96/130·29
1974	Ronnie Peterson	S	3·0 JPS/Lotus 72-Ford	Monte Carlo	158·87/255·68	80·74/129·94
1975	Niki Lauda	A	3·0 Ferrari 312T/75	Monte Carlo	152·76/245·84	75·53/121·55
1976	Niki Lauda	A	3·0 Ferrari 312T-2/76	Monte Carlo	160·52/258·34	80·36/129·33
1977	Jody Scheckter	ZA	3·0 Wolf WR1-Ford	Monte Carlo	156·41/251·71	79·61/128·12
1978	Patrick Depailler	F	3·0 Tyrrell 008-Ford	Monte Carlo	154·35/248·40	80·36/129·33
1979	Jody Scheckter	ZA	3·0 Ferrari 312T-4	Monte Carlo	156·41/251·71	81·34/130·90
1980	Carlos Reutemann	RA	3·0 Williams FW07B-Ford	Monte Carlo	156·41/251·71	81·20/130·68
1981	Gilles Villeneuve	CDN	1·5 Ferrari 126CK	Monte Carlo	156·41/251·71	82·04/132·03
1982	Riccardo Patrese	I	3·0 Brabham BT49D-Ford	Monte Carlo	156·41/251·71	82·21/132·30
1983	Keke Rosberg	SF	3·0 Williams FW08C-Ford	Monte Carlo	156·41/251·71	80·52/129·59
1984	Alain Prost	F	1·5 McLaren MP4/2-TAG t/c	Monte Carlo	63·80/102·67	62·62/100·77

*Non-championship (sports cars)

144

Circuit data

Circuit de Monaco, Monte Carlo
Circuit length: 2·058 miles/3·312 km
Race distance: 31 laps, 63·797 miles/102·672 km
(Scheduled distance: 78 laps. Race stopped because of rain.)
Race weather: Cool, wet.

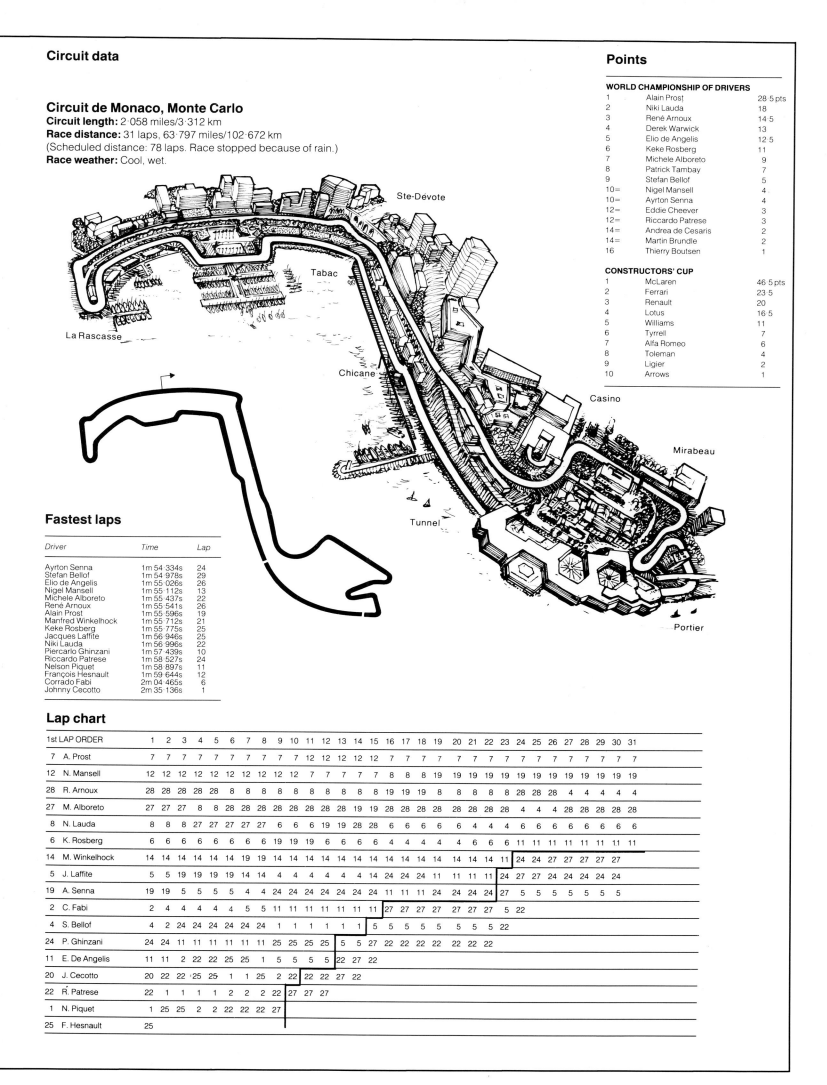

Ste-Dévote
Tabac
La Rascasse
Chicane
Casino
Mirabeau
Tunnel
Portier

Points

WORLD CHAMPIONSHIP OF DRIVERS

1	Alain Prost	28·5 pts
2	Niki Lauda	18
3	René Arnoux	14·5
4	Derek Warwick	13
5	Elio de Angelis	12·5
6	Keke Rosberg	11
7	Michele Alboreto	9
8	Patrick Tambay	7
9	Stefan Bellof	5
10=	Nigel Mansell	4
10=	Ayrton Senna	4
12=	Eddie Cheever	3
12=	Riccardo Patrese	3
14=	Andrea de Cesaris	2
14=	Martin Brundle	2
16	Thierry Boutsen	1

CONSTRUCTORS' CUP

1	McLaren	46·5 pts
2	Ferrari	23·5
3	Renault	20
4	Lotus	16·5
5	Williams	11
6	Tyrrell	7
7	Alfa Romeo	6
8	Toleman	4
9	Ligier	2
10	Arrows	1

Fastest laps

Driver	Time	Lap
Ayrton Senna	1m 54·334s	24
Stefan Bellof	1m 54·978s	29
Elio de Angelis	1m 55·026s	26
Nigel Mansell	1m 55·112s	13
Michele Alboreto	1m 55·437s	22
René Arnoux	1m 55·541s	26
Alain Prost	1m 55·596s	19
Manfred Winkelhock	1m 55·712s	21
Keke Rosberg	1m 55·775s	25
Jacques Laffite	1m 56·946s	25
Niki Lauda	1m 56·996s	22
Piercarlo Ghinzani	1m 57·439s	10
Riccardo Patrese	1m 58·527s	24
Nelson Piquet	1m 58·897s	11
François Hesnault	1m 59·644s	12
Corrado Fabi	2m 04·465s	6
Johnny Cecotto	2m 35·136s	1

Lap chart

1st LAP ORDER	1	2	3	4	5	6	7	8	9	10	11	12	13	14	15	16	17	18	19	20	21	22	23	24	25	26	27	28	29	30	31
7 A. Prost	7	7	7	7	7	7	7	7	7	7	12	12	12	12	12	7	7	7	7	7	7	7	7	7	7	7	7	7	7	7	7
12 N. Mansell	12	12	12	12	12	12	12	12	12	12	7	7	7	7	7	8	8	8	19	19	19	19	19	19	19	19	19	19	19	19	19
28 R. Arnoux	28	28	28	28	28	8	8	8	8	8	8	8	8	8	8	19	19	19	8	8	8	8	8	28	28	28	4	4	4	4	4
27 M. Alboreto	27	27	27	8	8	28	28	28	28	28	28	28	28	19	19	28	28	28	28	28	28	28	28	4	4	4	28	28	28	28	28
8 N. Lauda	8	8	8	27	27	27	27	27	6	6	6	19	19	28	28	6	6	6	6	6	4	4	4	6	6	6	6	6	6	6	6
6 K. Rosberg	6	6	6	6	6	6	6	6	19	19	19	6	6	6	6	4	4	4	4	4	6	6	6	11	11	11	11	11	11	11	11
14 M. Winkelhock	14	14	14	14	14	14	19	19	14	14	14	14	14	14	14	14	14	14	14	14	14	14	11	24	24	27	27	27	27	27	
5 J. Laffite	5	5	19	19	19	19	14	14	4	4	4	4	4	4	14	24	24	24	11	11	11	11	11	24	27	27	24	24	24	24	
19 A. Senna	19	19	5	5	5	5	4	4	24	24	24	24	24	24	24	11	11	11	24	24	24	24	24	27	5	5	5	5	5	5	
2 C. Fabi	2	4	4	4	4	4	5	5	11	11	11	11	11	11	11	27	27	27	27	27	27	27	27	5	22						
4 S. Bellof	4	2	24	24	24	24	24	24	1	1	1	1	1	1	1	5	5	5	5	5	5	5	5	22							
24 P. Ghinzani	24	24	11	11	11	11	11	11	25	25	25	25	5	5	27	22	22	22	22	22	22	22									
11 E. De Angelis	11	11	2	22	22	25	25	1	5	5	5	5	22	27	22																
20 J. Cecotto	20	22	22	25	25	1	1	25	2	22	22	22	27	22																	
22 R. Patrese	22	1	1	1	1	2	2	2	22	27	27	27																			
1 N. Piquet	1	25	25	2	2	22	22	22	27																						
25 F. Hesnault	25																														

145

Grand Prix Labatt du Canada

Nelson Piquet sat in his Brabham feeling distinctly unwell. His Chief Mechanic, Charlie Whiting, sat on the left-front wheel feeling distinctly alone. In a few minutes, the pit lane would be open but, in the meantime, photographers were jostling for position around the Marlboro McLaren pit.

Piquet may have been on pole but everyone knew he had started from the same position in Rio and Imola – and look what had happened. He had failed to finish each time just as he had failed to finish every race so far. Five of the races had been won by McLaren so it seemed a logical bet that either Alain Prost or Niki Lauda would finish first in Montreal. There was little future in taking photographs of Nelson Piquet today.

Piquet, as usual, didn't particularly care what they thought. He had arrived on the Ile Notre Dame with his stomach feeling as unsettled as the grey, churning waters of the nearby St. Lawrence. But, by the time the race was over, he would have a much more painful ailment to contend with and, ironically, the cause of the trouble would contribute towards the first win of the season for the Brabham-BMW.

In an effort to help control the rampant unreliability with the BMW and its component parts, Gordon Murray had introduced an additional oil cooler into the nose of the BT53. That the radiator did its job was evident by a trouble-free run; Nelson leading all but the first half lap. But, along the way, the heat had begun to penetrate the bulkhead in front of the driver's feet and, as Nelson kept the McLarens at bay, the sole of his driving boot began to wrinkle on the red-hot pedal. The pain was excruciating.

But it was worth it. Not only had Piquet scored his first points of the season, he had beaten McLaren. Prost had been in trouble with a down-on-power engine from the start and would finish third, leaving it to Lauda to move forward and challenge Piquet. Lauda set his fastest lap in pursuit of the Brabham – and Piquet responded by setting the fastest lap of the race. No contest. Lauda settled for second place.

Elio de Angelis brought his JPS Lotus-Renault into fourth place, a position which had been held by his team-mate, Nigel Mansell, before gearbox trouble forced the Englishman to drop back and collect just one championship point after René Arnoux took fifth place for Ferrari on the final lap.

Two years previously, Piquet had scored the very first victory for Brabham-BMW at Montreal and the win had been just as welcome; just as unexpected.

ENTRY AND PRACTICE

While Bernie Ecclestone talked percentages with the Montreal organisers as they haggled over terms for future races, his team got on with the business of finally securing a championship point or two in 1984. It was getting beyond a joke now; six races and nothing to show except ninth place for Teo Fabi at Dijon and a classification for Nelson in Zolder even though his car had been blown asunder by a massive engine failure.

Paul Rosche had lost a considerable amount of weight during the season. He said it was part of a diet although it seemed reasonable to suppose that the niggling reliability problems had also smoothed down the Bavarian's ample waistline. Whatever the reason for his emaciated appearance, the once jolly BMW engineer felt sure that quality control problems with the components accounted for most of the failures. As a result, extra care had been taken and Gordon Murray had played his part by introducing an extra oil cooler in the nose of his car and redesigning the rear bodywork.

Apart from a broken drive-shaft on Friday afternoon, Piquet had no problems and felt very happy with the car, both in qualifying and race trim. The broken shaft had disrupted his progress but, on Saturday, he took pole away from Alain Prost with a lap which looked the part, a fact which was confirmed by the speed trap clocking Nelson at 164 mph as he charged towards the dauntingly fast right-left-right swerves after the pits.

Not for an instant did the exhaust note on the BMW waver as the brave Brazilian earned his money in a most impressive manner. And, he felt, he could have gone quicker. The second set were duly fitted but, by failing to warm the qualifiers properly, he was unable to improve. Not that it mattered. No one could approach his time. Not even Prost who was in trouble on Saturday afternoon with a blown engine. And, ironically, that oily failure on the track would ensure Piquet was not disturbed at the top of the time sheet.

McLaren, of course, were smiling quietly while the rest of the pit lane continued to debate the rights and wrongs of Prost's victory at Monaco. It seemed nothing could stop the red and white onslaught and, when Alain set fastest lap on Friday afternoon, it was 'situation normal' – particularly when it was learned that the Frenchman was on an even faster lap when he spun at the last corner.

That mishap had been caused by the carbon fibre brakes running too hot (due to an excess of masking tape on the ducts) but Alain's engine failure on Saturday after just one quick lap was to be an altogether more serious affair. The Frenchman returned to the pits when his second set of qualifiers were bolted onto Lauda's car but there was nothing Prost could do about Piquet. Niki, meanwhile, was using the spare car and he spent the first part of Saturday's timed practice running race tyres. In the light of Prost's spray job, that turned out to be a mistake and Lauda had to be satisfied with eighth place behind Nigel Mansell.

The Lotus driver had started off confidently enough by slipping in the quickest lap of Friday morning right at the end of the session but, for the remainder of practice, there was to be nothing but frustration. Before he could take to the track in the afternoon, repairs to the pinion had to be carried out. Then, metering unit trouble meant the engine would not fire. And by the time the V6 was running cleanly, Nigel crossed the line after one quick lap to find that Andrea de Cesaris had just suffered a massive blow-up as he passed the pits. On Saturday morning, an engine failure meant remarkably fast work by the Lotus mechanics, Mansell taking to the track half-way through the final session; just in time for – yes, you've guessed – Prost's engine failure.

It was Elio de Angelis, then, who put Lotus near the front with an excellent third fastest time, recorded 'pre Prost' on Saturday. For a while, the Italian had been fastest during Friday's practice but de Cesaris's oil meant he was unable to respond to Prost's subsequent improvement.

There was a certain amount of mumbling by the Lotus drivers about insufficient spare cars to cater for the catalogue of problems. Derek Warwick had no such worries since he had no less than three chassis to choose from once Patrick Tambay had decided that he was not fit enough to take part. A new chassis had been brought out to Canada but a handful of laps on Friday morning was enough to convince Patrick that the buffeting from the chassis and the inability to brace his injured leg against the cockpit side would detract from his driving effort and perhaps delay his recovery.

Warwick had been given back his repaired chassis from Dijon but a down-on-power engine meant he was soon into Tambay's car. When the engine failed on that, Warwick stepped into the

Nelson Piquet shows Niki Lauda and Alain Prost how hard he had to drive to keep ahead of the McLarens. The Brabham driver scored his first points of the season and completely dominated the race.

T-car but all this chopping and changing meant there was no time for serious chassis tuning. And it showed. The RE50 was an appalling handful over the bumps, Warwick being very depressed with his performance on Friday. By Saturday he was feeling more cheerful, hard work in the morning having sorted the car. Preferring the feel of his team-mate's RE50, Warwick set off to establish a better grid slot and set what would be his best time on the first quick lap. The engine then suffered from pre-ignition on his second and potentially faster lap so he had the second set of qualifiers fitted to his own chassis. He got down to 1m 26.9s on his first lap – and then the turbo failed. But at least Warwick felt confident for the race.

Ferrari were not so sure. The fleet 126C4s continued to look the part while sitting in the pit lane but, out on the track, they remained a handful. Narrow front track suspension proved inconclusive and, by Saturday, the cars were back to their standard trim. They were also continuing to use the Lucas mechanical injection, the electronic system being too much of a gamble at a track which would claim the highest fuel consumption figures of the season. Apart from fuel pump bothers for Arnoux, there were few mechanical problems. Michele Alboreto, on the other hand, had a personal problem when a verbal disagreement with an Italian journalist over something he had written led to Michele receiving a punch!

On a high ever since his remarkable second place at Monaco, Ayrton Senna was raring to go, the Toleman driver being first out of the pit lane on Friday morning. Of course, the circuit was new to

him – not that you would have guessed if his subsequent lap times were anything to go by. Qualifying in the top ten for the first time, the Brazilian looked smooth and controlled in a car which clearly was working as well as the driver. Brian Hart had his electronic ignition (with two injectors per cylinder) on hand for Friday's practice but, since they had no consumption figures available, the unit was returned to England since it would be of no use in the race. As it was, the Hart personnel were kept busy by a faulty batch of valve gear components and Senna qualified in the spare car on Saturday. Indeed, if the team's stop-watches were to be believed, he was completing a phenomenally quick lap when he spun at the hairpin. To offset this brilliance, the team also had to contend with an increasingly unhappy Johnny Cecotto, the Venezuelan finding it difficult to cope with euphoria surrounding his team-mate and slipped to 20th place, four seconds slower.

Andrea de Cesaris completed the top ten with a Ligier-Renault showing few changes except for minor details to the aerodynamics and wings. Apart from the engine blow-up on Friday and a radiator failure the following day, there were few problems for the Loto-sponsored team. François Hesnault was less inclined to keep his right foot hard on the throttle going through the curves after the pits, which may have accounted for the Frenchman being over a second slower than his team-mate – even though it only meant a difference of three places on the grid.

There was an identical gap between the Benetton Alfa Romeos, Eddie Cheever coming off

best after Riccardo Patrese had crashed his car on Saturday morning and then found turbo problems with the spare chassis precluded any improvement over his time from Friday. The team were without Carlo Chiti, a management decision having caused the familiar, rotund figure to hang up his raincoat for good and take an office job while Giovanni Tonti, formerly with the Lancia WEC team, assumed technical control at the races.

Technical control at ATS came under the auspices of Gunter Schmid and the team appeared to be suffering as a result; retaining the wet settings from Monaco for the first day's practice at Montreal was hardly an encouraging start. Herr Schmid was of the opinion that the two circuits were roughly similar and not even Manfred Winkelhock could persuade him that the sweepers after the pits put Montreal into a different league. Not that it mattered much since Manfred was destined to complete just four laps before the transmission broke. On Saturday, it was the clutch and, each time, Winkelhock had to wait for either the car to be returned to the pits or repairs to be carried out since he no longer had a spare following the accident at Monaco. Twelfth place was not a bad effort in the light of these problems. . . .

For Williams, things seemed to go from bad to worse. On Friday, the spare car was in 'B' specification (a McLaren-type rear end which had been tested at Brands Hatch) in a bid to give more downforce at the rear and, indirectly, achieve greater straightline speed as a result of the smaller amount of wing required. It worked okay but the problem of understeer remained and, by Saturday, the car had been returned to normal specification. Whichever car he used, Keke Rosberg had to work hard as the chassis bottomed and bucked its way through the right-hander after the pits. A plan to run race tyres and then one set of qualifiers on Saturday was ultimately foiled by Prost's engine failure; Rosberg was 15th, Jacques Laffite not far behind in 17th place.

Splitting the Williams cars was Corrado Fabi, the Italian finding it difficult to come to terms with the BMW power. Major suspension alterations to the Barclays Arrows A7 were in hand but, in the meantime, a stiffer rear did not help cure a temperature imbalance front to rear when Thierry Boutsen ran qualifiers. It was the Belgian driver's turn to choose between turbo and Cosworth and he opted for the BMW (now running without an engine cover) while Marc Surer made do with the A6, a spin on Saturday helping keep the Swiss driver behind the Tyrrells.

Each time the maroon Yardley 012 went over a bump, Martin Brundle received a painful reminder of his Monaco shunt but, despite his heavy bruising, the Englishman returned the fastest time (albeit by a hundredth of a second) on a circuit which he was enjoying at first acquaintance. Stefan Bellof was as spectacular as ever as he tried to make up for a deficiency of 21mph in straight-line speed when compared to Piquet in qualifying trim but at least the Cosworths managed to beat the Hart-powered Spirit and the Skoal RAM team.

With Mauro Baldi and Jonathan Palmer busy at Le Mans, their respective replacements were Huub Rothengatter and Mike Thackwell. Considering the Dutchman had not raced a single-seater for two and a half years, he did a competent job, keeping out of everyone's way and overcoming a gearbox problem on Friday to beat Thackwell and Philippe Alliot. Thackwell, of course, was returning to the scene of his history-making Grand Prix debut four years earlier although this was to be his first experience of Formula 1 turbo power. He wasn't particularly impressed. When the power was on, the car felt reasonable but otherwise too much understeer. Alliot was slowest of all but, with Tambay's withdrawal from an entry of 27 cars, there was no question of anyone failing to qualify.

THE RACE

Perfect racing weather – sunny skies and a cool breeze – greeted the teams as they towed their cars alongside the Olympic rowing lake towards the pits. As designers plodded along the half-mile or so of walkway, you could be sure that the subject of fuel consumption was occupying their thoughts. René Arnoux confirmed it once the warm-up had been completed.

The Ferrari driver had been quickest yet he had doubts about his tank of Agip lasting the distance. Prost had been third fastest (behind Alboreto and ahead of Piquet) and it was clear that McLaren were taking no chances when Ron Dennis helped unload three massive barrels of chilled fuel in the McLaren pit. Elsewhere, the Lotus team were in engine trouble again, de Angelis being assigned the spare while Mansell's mechanics began yet another rapid engine change. Once again, they achieved the seemingly impossible by connecting the mass of wires and plumbing to the correct places, the V6 running with plenty of time to spare.

Sitting on the grid, Nelson Piquet thought back to 1980 when he started from the same spot, only to be eased into the wall at the first curve by Alan Jones. This time there was not so much at stake and Piquet let Prost take the lead on the green light. It was the only concession Nelson would make.

By the time the field had reached the bottom end of the circuit, Prost knew he was in trouble. The engine was not picking up cleanly and the McLaren driver was helpless as Piquet powered into the lead as they left the hairpin. De Angelis had made a good start but his third place was soon under pressure from Alboreto and Arnoux, the Ferraris justifying their warm-up performance and moving ahead by the end of the lap.

During the course of the next ten laps or so, it became clear that this would be a busy race, the field splitting into groups of drivers snapping at each other's heels. Piquet, once he had established a small gap, began to ease off, the better to conserve his rather marginal carbon fibre brakes under a full load of fuel. Prost, accordingly, closed the gap while the Ferraris seemed poised to threaten the McLaren at any minute. De Angelis could not keep pace when his engine began to inexplicably lose power and the Lotus was soon receiving attention from Warwick. Further back, Lauda had decided it was time to get after his team-mate and, by lap five, had taken Mansell, Warwick and de Angelis.

Into his stride now and lapping faster than anyone, Lauda began to claw back the gap to the Ferraris. His task was to be made easier six laps later when Alboreto pulled off with a blown engine. Four laps after Arnoux was in the pits, his choice of 'C' compound Goodyears unable to match his pace. Lauda was now third and some 15 seconds behind Prost who was keeping Piquet in sight.

Hesnault had retired with a broken turbo and Ghinzani was next to go when a drive-shaft broke. This was the sort of aggravation which Piquet had become accustomed to contending with in 1984 and he deliberately went as slow as he could afford to without letting Prost get too close. Would the BMW last? There was a long way to go. And Lauda was closing.

For a while, Warwick had been looking for a way past de Angelis and, on lap 13, resorted to running round the outside of the Lotus as they charged into the right-left-right complex after the pits, the Renault bouncing on the bumps. It was terrifying to watch but Warwick had the line for the left-hander; de Angelis was sixth.

Not far behind, Senna was beginning to flag slightly and the Toleman driver suddenly had his hands full as Arnoux rejoined in eighth place. It took him just two laps to find a way past and, by then, Senna was receiving attention from Rosberg, the Finn pushing the Williams into angles and places where it didn't really deserve to be. At the end of lap one, Keke had been in 14th place. At the end of lap 19, he had taken seventh place from Senna – and the recalcitrant FW09 was running on the hard 'A' compound Goodyears. It was a tingling performance by any standards.

And there was more of the same further down the field. Mansell, taking it easy with a full load of fuel, held ninth place behind Senna but, not far behind the Lotus, a furious battle was under way as de Cesaris and Cheever fought the bit out – with Stefan Bellof snapping at their heels. The Tyrrell was left behind on the straights but the enthusiastic German was climbing all over the turbos under braking and through the corners. Earlier, Bellof had dealt with Winkelhock (struggling without a clutch since lap six) and now the ATS was under attack from Laffite. Then a gap before an almighty battle between Boutsen, Patrese, Fabi, Cecotto and Brundle. The Tyrrell driver had made an excellent start but lost any advantage when he became squeezed out on the first lap. And now, like his team-mate, he was suffering the frustration of watching the turbos steam ahead on the straight. The group ahead of the Tyrrell constantly changed positions and a major reshuffle on lap 21 saw Patrese take up the rear-guard action against the Englishman. Brundle tried everything he knew but was rudely chopped off by the Alfa Romeo each time and the battle continued for 15 laps.

Then, at the end of lap 37, Brundle outfumbled Patrese, Cecotto and Boutsen going into and coming out of the hairpin. Patrese was not amused and immediately attacked the Tyrrell. Brundle simply gave the Italian some of his own medicine and, a few corners later, Patrese locked his brakes and crashed heavily.

A broken turbo had brought an end to a neat and consistent drive from Thackwell, the RAM driver having passed and edged away from Alliot and

"I tried to catch Nelson but couldn't, so I finished second." Those typically concise words from Niki Lauda summed up the Canadian Grand Prix. Not only had Nelson Piquet led every lap, he had *beaten* the championship leaders in the process, the Brabham driver being able to counter every move made by McLaren.

The lap times for Piquet and Lauda tell the story. Once he has established that Prost, struggling with a down-on-power engine, will be no problem, Piquet takes it comparatively easy during the first 15 laps or so, the better to conserve his marginal carbon fibre brakes while running with a full load of fuel. Lauda, meanwhile, is setting faster laps occasionally as he finds a clear track while working his way through the field.

The crucial point in the race occurs after lap 44 when Lauda passes Prost and sets after Piquet. Once the news has been relayed to Nelson, he increases his pace and Lauda matches it. The McLaren driver then sets his fastest lap but Piquet goes one better and records the fastest lap of the race. Lauda tries to respond. But it is not enough. Both drivers ease slightly and concentrate on finishing. The race belongs to Piquet and Brabham. Lauda accepts second place.

Lap	*Piquet*	*Lauda*
1	1m 38.290s	1m 43.619s
2	1m 32.218s	1m 35.101s
3	1m 30.859s	1m 33.067s
4	1m 30.755s	1m 32.180s
5	1m 31.518s	1m 33.647s
6	1m 31.748s	1m 32.599s
7	1m 31.495s	1m 31.521s
8	1m 31.082s	1m 30.979s
9	1m 31.873s	1m 31.027s
10	1m 31.470s	1m 30.597s
11	1m 31.584s	1m 31.326s
12	1m 31.796s	1m 31.330s
13	1m 32.637s	1m 31.283s
14	1m 32.957s	1m 33.997s
15	1m 31.760s	1m 31.676s
16	1m 31.065s	1m 31.565s
17	1m 30.185s	1m 30.632s
18	1m 30.897s	1m 31.119s
19	1m 30.558s	1m 31.083s
20	1m 32.679s	1m 30.740s
21	1m 31.660s	1m 30.677s
22	1m 32.401s	1m 32.422s
23	1m 31.296s	1m 30.914s
24	1m 30.837s	1m 30.745s
25	1m 31.320s	1m 30.741s
26	1m 33.120s	1m 30.420s
27	1m 30.902s	1m 31.163s
28	1m 30.849s	1m 32.930s
29	1m 29.754s	1m 31.375s
30	1m 30.102s	1m 29.673s
31	1m 30.292s	1m 30.106s
32	1m 30.228s	1m 29.601s
33	1m 32.376s	1m 30.801s
34	1m 30.313s	1m 29.515s
35	1m 31.467s	1m 29.529s
36	1m 30.619s	1m 30.361s
37	1m 29.950s	1m 29.642s
38	1m 30.169s	1m 29.171s
39	1m 30.485s	1m 31.074s
40	1m 30.121s	1m 29.238s
41	1m 31.243s	1m 30.056s
42	1m 30.711s	1m 31.722s
43	1m 30.008s	1m 30.741s
44	1m 31.132s	1m 31.334s
45	1m 29.717s	1m 32.939s
46	1m 29.970s	1m 29.511s
47	1m 29.364s	1m 29.638s
48	1m 29.314s	1m 29.099s
49	1m 30.076s	1m 29.907s
50	1m 29.340s	1m 29.092s
51	1m 29.635s	1m 29.300s
52	1m 30.190s	1m 29.973s
53	1m 30.710s	1m 29.516s
54	1m 29.200s	**1m 29.083s**
55	**1m 28.763s**	1m 30.436s
56	1m 29.645s	1m 29.957s
57	1m 29.962s	1m 29.617s
58	1m 29.211s	1m 29.638s
59	1m 29.908s	1m 30.576s
60	1m 30.793s	1m 30.799s
61	1m 31.135s	1m 31.432s
62	1m 30.605s	1m 32.059s
63	1m 30.713s	1m 31.885s
64	1m 31.283s	1m 32.638s
65	1m 32.161s	1m 33.897s
66	1m 33.403s	1m 32.981s
67	1m 33.282s	1m 32.722s
68	1m 33.815s	1m 33.262s
69	1m 35.213s	1m 32.667s
70	1m 37.559s	1m 30.697s

JUNE:

Brazilian AC complain to FISA regarding the stopping of Monaco Grand Prix.

FISA express dissatisfaction with Monaco organisation in official bulletin.

Henri Pescarolo/Klaus Ludwig (Porsche 956 B) win Le Mans 24 Hours.

There was little love lost between the Lotus drivers as Nigel Mansell tried to overtake Elio de Angelis. The Englishman found a way through but gearbox trouble meant he was forced to drop to sixth place while de Angelis went on to finish fourth (left).
The cause of Piquet's discomfort. In the interest of engine reliability, Brabham introduced an additional oil cooler in the nose of the BT53. The heat permeated the front bulkhead and blistered Nelson's right foot (below).
The drivers combined to play a team of journalists at football. Back row (left to right): Bellof, Patrese, Mansell, de Cesaris, Cecotto, Alboreto, Cheever and Winkelhock. Front row: de Angelis, Alliot, Warwick and Senna. The journalists lost comfortably (bottom).

no contest; no story for the columnists waiting, pens poised for the 'in-team confrontation situation scandal'. Lap 44 and Lauda was second.

Such sensible behaviour appeared to be lacking within the Lotus team as Mansell, his car handling nicely as the fuel load lightened, closed in on his team-mate in sixth place. Elio indulged in some excessive blocking and, on one occasion, Mansell nearly rammed his so-called team-mate. Eventually, he found a way by and, not long after, de Angelis was in trouble again. Arriving at the series of turns before the bottom hairpin, Elio got out of shape and opted to take a trip across the grass rather than spin the car. This coincided with the Lotus being lapped by Lauda, and de Angelis almost collected the McLaren as he regained the track. Lauda was forced to take to the dirt but soon regained his composure and set after Piquet.

Running between the McLarens and the Lotus were Arnoux and Warwick, the Ferrari driver having worked his way ahead of the Renault. Then the gap began to shrink as the Ferrari lost power due to a broken exhaust, Warwick regaining fourth place on lap 50. It was to be shortlived, the Renault's handling having deteriorated thanks to the underbody coming loose. At first Warwick thought he had a puncture and stopped for tyres, then he returned to the pits to have the suspension checked. Finding nothing amiss, the team sent him out again but he was soon to return for good, the car almost undriveable.

Mansell had passed Arnoux and was now fourth but the loss of second gear meant trouble. Having had the quick engine change before the start, Nigel half-expected problems with the V6 and he wound down the boost accordingly. The engine didn't miss a beat but, on one occasion, he could find no gears at all, and he slipped disconsolately down the field as first de Angelis, and then Eddie Cheever, moved ahead. The Alfa Romeo had been running beautifully but the American's worst fears over fuel consumption were to be realised a full seven laps from the end when he coasted into the pit lane with a dry tank. Mansell was back to fifth.

Back in the pit lane already were Bellof, his superb drive having ended with a broken driveshaft, and de Cesaris, out with brake trouble. Mansell and Arnoux persevered with their respective problems, Arnoux having the upper hand since he had at least a gearbox which worked well enough to allow him to out-accelerate the Lotus for fifth place on the very last lap. And then the Ferrari ran out of fuel as he coasted towards the scrutineering bay.

Piquet could not reach the parc fermé soon enough. Officials quickly sealed the area as Nelson wriggled from the Brabham and began tugging at the lace on his right boot. He was soon joined by his Chief Mechanic, delighted with a victory which the team desperately needed.

Piquet desperately needed to remove his boot and sock and Charlie Whiting was startled to discover an ugly blister on the sole of Nelson's foot.

Piquet would soon be carried off on the usual wave of whistle-blowing euphoria to the victory rostrum but, for a minute or more, they savoured a win which, quite clearly, had been painful work yet beautifully controlled. And, once again, driver and trusty mechanic were quite alone. The photographers, jostling for position around the victory podium, had had their chance.   MH

Rothengatter. Laffite had stopped with engine trouble at the end of lap 32 and the Williams pit was to become a very crowded place when, one lap later, Rosberg's superb drive was halted by a failure in the fuel system. Boutsen then stopped with an expensive engine failure and Fabi, having worked his way ahead of the Arrows, stopped with a broken turbo. Given BMW's track record, Piquet must surely join them any minute.

Fortunately for Nelson, he had little time to think about such things for he was heavily embroiled with lapping the battles at the back of the field. And, in addition, the sole of his right foot was becoming hot; very hot. In fact, the pain was

such that Nelson was tempted to pull into the pits every time he left the final hairpin. "Just another five laps, and then I'll stop," he kept telling himself. And, had there not been so much at stake in the light of such a miserable season for the World Champion, he probably would have stopped. In the meantime, he was busy maintaining the gap of between two and five seconds over Prost. And Lauda was inexorably catching them both.

This prompted the question of team tactics. Prost was in trouble; but would he let Lauda into second place? It was, after all, to be one of the few occasions when the McLaren drivers had actually raced wheel to wheel. In the event, there was to be

Entries and practice times

No.	Driver	Nat	Car	Tyre	Engine	Entrant	Practice 1	Practice 2
1	Nelson Piquet	BR	Parmalat BRABHAM BT53	M	BMW M12/13	MRD International	1m 27·154s	**1m 25·442s**
2	Corrado Fabi	I	Parmalat BRABHAM BT53	M	BMW M12/13	MRD International	1m 30·831s	**1m 29·764s**
3	Martin Brundle	GB	TYRRELL 012	G	Ford Cosworth DFY	Tyrrell Racing Organisation	1m 33·945s	**1m 31·785s**
4	Stefan Bellof	D	TYRRELL 012	G	Ford Cosworth DFY	Tyrrell Racing Organisation	1m 34·309s	**1m 31·797s**
5	Jacques Laffite	F	WILLIAMS FW09	G	Honda RA 163–E	Williams Grand Prix Engineering	1m 30·115s	**1m 29·915s**
6	Keke Rosberg	SF	WILLIAMS FW09	G	Honda RA 163–E	Williams Grand Prix Engineering	1m 29·423s	**1m 29·284s**
7	Alain Prost	F	Marlboro McLAREN MP4/2	M	TAG P01 (TTE P01)	Marlboro McLaren International	1m 26·477s	**1m 26·198s**
8	Niki Lauda	A	Marlboro McLAREN MP4/2	M	TAG P01 (TTE P01)	Marlboro McLaren International	1m 28·548s	**1m 27·392s**
9	Philippe Alliot	F	RAM 02	P	Hart 415T	Skoal Bandit Formula 1 Team	**1m 35·286s**	1m 36·900s
10	Mike Thackwell	NZ	RAM 02	P	Hart 415T	Skoal Bandit Formula 1 Team	1m 34·921s	**1m 33·750s**
11	Elio de Angelis	I	John Player Special LOTUS 95T	G	Renault EF4	John Player Team Lotus	1m 27·139s	**1m 26·306s**
12	Nigel Mansell	GB	John Player Special LOTUS 95T	G	Renault EF4	John Player Team Lotus	1m 28·277s	**1m 27·246s**
14	Manfred Winkelhock	D	ATS D7	P	BMW M12/13	Team ATS	1m 32·311s	**1m 28·909s**
15	Patrick Tambay	F	Elf RENAULT RE50	M	Renault EF4	Equipe Renault Elf	1m 29·682s	**1m 26·420s**
16	Derek Warwick	GB	Elf RENAULT RE50	M	Renault EF4	Equipe Renault Elf	—	**1m 26·420s**
17	Marc Surer	CH	ARROWS A6	G	Ford Cosworth DFV	Barclay Nordica Arrows BMW	1m 33·014s	**1m 32·756s**
18	Thierry Boutsen	B	ARROWS A7	G	BMW M12/13	Barclay Nordica Arrows BMW	1m 30·887s	**1m 30·073s**
19	Ayrton Senna	BR	TOLEMAN TG184	M	Hart 415T	Toleman Group Motorsport	1m 29·282s	**1m 27·448s**
20	Johnny Cecotto	YV	TOLEMAN TG184	M	Hart 415T	Toleman Group Motorsport	1m 34·731s	**1m 31·459s**
21	Huub Rothengatter	NL	SPIRIT 101	P	Hart 415T	Spirit Racing	1m 35·217s	**1m 32·920s**
22	Riccardo Patrese	I	Benetton ALFA ROMEO 184T	G	Alfa Romeo 183T	Benetton Team Alfa Romeo	**1m 29·205s**	1m 30·064s
23	Eddie Cheever	USA	Benetton ALFA ROMEO 184T	G	Alfa Romeo 183T	Benetton Team Alfa Romeo	1m 29·418s	**1m 28·032s**
24	Piercarlo Ghinzani	I	Kelemata OSELLA FA1F	P	Alfa Romeo 183T	Osella Squadra Corse	1m 32·189s	**1m 30·918s**
25	François Hesnault	F	LIGIER Loto JS23	M	Renault EF4	Ligier Loto	1m 31·146s	**1m 29·187s**
26	Andrea de Cesaris	I	LIGIER Loto JS23	M	Renault EF4	Ligier Loto	1m 29·618s	**1m 27·922s**
27	Michele Alboreto	I	Fiat FERRARI 126C4	G	Ferrari 126C	Scuderia Ferrari SpA	1m 28·604s	**1m 26·764s**
28	René Arnoux	F	Fiat FERRARI 126C4	G	Ferrari 126C	Scuderia Ferrari SpA	1m 27·917s	**1m 26·549s**

Friday morning and Saturday morning practice sessions not officially recorded.

Fri pm	Sat pm
Warm, dry	Hot, dry

G – Goodyear, M – Michelin, P – Pirelli.

Starting grid

	1 PIQUET (1m 25·442s) Brabham
7 PROST (1m 26·198s) McLaren	
	11 DE ANGELIS (1m 26·306s) Lotus
16 WARWICK (1m 26·420s) Renault	
	28 ARNOUX (1m 26·549s) Ferrari
27 ALBORETO (1m 26·764s) Ferrari	
	12 MANSELL (1m 27·246s) Lotus
8 LAUDA (1m 27·392s) McLaren	
	19 SENNA (1m 27·448s) Toleman
26 DE CESARIS (1m 27·922s) Ligier	
	23 CHEEVER (1m 28·032s) Alfa Romeo
14 WINKELHOCK (1m 28·909s) ATS	
	25 HESNAULT (1m 29·187s) Ligier
22 PATRESE (1m 29·205s) Alfa Romeo	
	6 ROSBERG (1m 29·284s) Williams
2 FABI (1m 29·764s) Brabham	
	5 LAFFITE (1m 29·915s) Williams
18 BOUTSEN (1m 30·073s) Arrows	
	24 GHINZANI (1m 30·918s) Osella
20 CECOTTO (1m 31·459s) Toleman	
	3 BRUNDLE (1m 31·785s) Tyrrell
4 BELLOF (1m 31·797s) Tyrrell	
	17 SURER (1m 32·756s) Arrows
21 ROTHENGATTER (1m 32·920s) Spirit	
	10 THACKWELL (1m 33·750s) RAM
9 ALLIOT (1m 35·286s) RAM	

Did not start:
15 Tambay (Renault), no time recorded, entry withdrawn due driver's leg injuries received during Monaco GP.

Results and retirements

Place	Driver	Car	Laps	Time and Speed (mph/km/h)/Retirement	
1	Nelson Piquet	Brabham-BMW t/c 4	70	1h 46m 23·748s	108·171/174·085
2	Niki Lauda	McLaren-TAG t/c V6	70	1h 46m 26·360s	108·118/174·0
3	Alain Prost	McLaren-TAG t/c V6	70	1h 47m 51·780s	106·689/171·7
4	Elio de Angelis	Lotus-Renault t/c V6	69		
5	René Arnoux	Ferrari t/c V6	68		
6	Nigel Mansell	Lotus-Renault t/c V6	68		
7	Ayrton Senna	Toleman-Hart t/c 4	68		
8	Manfred Winkelhock	ATS-BMW t/c 4	68		
9	Johnny Cecotto	Toleman-Hart t/c 4	68		
10	Martin Brundle	Tyrrell-Cosworth V8	68		
11	Philippe Alliot	RAM-Hart t/c 4	65		
12	Eddie Cheever	Alfa Romeo t/c V8	63	Out of fuel (but classified)	
	Marc Surer	Arrows-Cosworth V8	59	Engine	
	Derek Warwick	Renault t/c V6	57	Loose underbody	
	Huub Rothengatter	Spirit-Hart t/c 4	56	Running, but not classified	
	Stefan Bellof	Tyrrell-Cosworth V8	52	Driveshaft	
	Andrea de Cesaris	Ligier-Renault t/c V6	40	Brakes	
	Corrado Fabi	Brabham-BMW t/c 4	39	Lost boost	
	Thierry Boutsen	Arrows-BMW t/c 4	38	Engine	
	Riccardo Patrese	Alfa Romeo t/c V8	37	Accident	
	Keke Rosberg	Williams-Honda t/c V6	32	Fuel system	
	Jacques Laffite	Williams-Honda t/c V6	31	Lost boost	
	Mike Thackwell	RAM-Hart t/c 4	29	Broken wastegate	
	Piercarlo Ghinzani	Osella-Alfa Romeo t/c V8	11	Gearbox	
	Michele Alboreto	Ferrari t/c V6	10	Engine	
	François Hesnault	Ligier-Renault t/c V6	7	Turbo	

Fastest lap: Piquet, on lap 55, 1m 28·763s, 111·691mph/178·858km/h.
Lap record: Didier Pironi (F1 Ferrari 126C2 t/c V6), 1m 28·323s, 111·691mph/179·749km/h (1982).

Past winners

Year	Driver	Nat	Car	Circuit	Distance miles/km	Speed mph/km/h
1961*	Pete Ryan	CDN	2·5 Lotus 19-Climax	Mosport Park	245·90/395·74	88·38/142·23
1962*	Masten Gregory	USA	2·5 Lotus 19-Climax	Mosport Park	245·90/395·74	88·52/142·46
1963*	Pedro Rodriguez	MEX	3·0 Ferrari 250P	Mosport Park	245·90/395·74	91·55/147·34
1964*	Pedro Rodriguez	MEX	4·0 Ferrari 330P	Mosport Park	245·90/395·74	94·36/151·86
1965*	Jim Hall	USA	5·4 Chaparral 2B-Chevrolet	Mosport Park	245·90/395·74	93·78/150·92
1966*	Mark Donohue	USA	6·0 Lola T70 Mk 2-Chevrolet	Mosport Park	209·02/336·38	101·87/163·94
1967	Jack Brabham	AUS	3·0 Brabham BT24-Repco	Mosport Park	221·31/356·16	82·994/133·56
1968	Denny Hulme	NZ	3·0 McLaren M7A-Ford	St Jovite	238·50/383·83	97·22/156·47
1969	Jacky Ickx	B	3·0 Brabham BT26A-Ford	Mosport Park	221·31/356·16	111·19/179·93
1970	Jacky Ickx	B	3·0 Ferrari 312B/70	St Jovite	238·50/383·83	101·27/162·98
1971	Jackie Stewart	GB	3·0 Tyrrell 003-Ford	Mosport Park	157·38/253·27	81·96/131·90
1972	Jackie Stewart	GB	3·0 Tyrrell 005-Ford	Mosport Park	196·72/316·59	114·28/183·92
1973	Peter Revson	USA	3·0 McLaren M23-Ford	Mosport Park	196·72/316·59	99·13/159·53
1974	Emerson Fittipaldi	BR	3·0 McLaren M23-Ford	Mosport Park	196·72/316·59	117·52/189·13
1976	James Hunt	GB	3·0 McLaren M23-Ford	Mosport Park	196·72/316·59	117·84/189·65
1977	Jody Scheckter	ZA	3·0 Wolf WR1-Ford	Mosport Park	196·72/316·59	118·03/189·95
1978	Gilles Villeneuve	CDN	3·0 Ferrari 312T-3/78	Ile Notre-Dame	195·72/314·98	99·67/160·40
1979	Alan Jones	AUS	3·0 Williams FW07-Ford	Ile Notre-Dame	197·28/317·52	105·35/169·54
1980	Alan Jones	AUS	3·0 Williams FW07B-Ford	Ile Notre-Dame	191·82/308·70	110·00/177·03
1981	Jacques Laffite	F	3·0 Ligier JS17-Matra	Ile Notre-Dame	172·62/277·83	85·31/137·29
1982	Nelson Piquet	BR	1·5 Brabham BT50-BMW t/c	Ile Notre-Dame	191·82/308·70	107·93/173·70
1983	René Arnoux	F	1·5 Ferrari 126C2/B t/c	Ile Notre-Dame	191·82/308·70	106·04/170·66
1984	Nelson Piquet	BR	1·5 Brabham BT53-BMW t/c	Ile Notre-Dame	191·82/308·70	108·17/174·08

* *Non-championship (sports cars)*

Lap chart

1st LAP ORDER	1	2	3	4	5	6	7	8	9	10	11	12	13	14	15	16	17	18	19	20	21	22	23	24	25	26	27	28	29	30	31	32	33	34	35	36	37
1 N. Piquet	1	1	1	1	1	1	1	1	1	1	1	1	1	1	1	1	1	1	1	1	1	1	1	1	1	1	1	1	1	1	1	1	1	1	1	1	1
7 A. Prost	7	7	7	7	7	7	7	7	7	7	7	7	7	7	7	7	7	7	7	7	7	7	7	7	7	7	7	7	7	7	7	7	7	7	7	7	7
27 M. Alboreto	27	27	27	27	27	27	27	27	27	28	28	28	8	8	8	8	8	8	8	8	8	8	8	8	8	8	8	8	8	8	8	8	8	8	8	8	8
28 R. Arnoux	28	28	28	28	28	28	28	28	28	8	8	8	16	16	16	16	16	16	16	16	16	16	16	16	28	28	28	28	28	28	28	28	28	28	28	28	28
11 E. De Angelis	11	11	11	11	8	8	8	8	8	11	11	11	11	16	11	11	11	11	11	11	11	11	11	11	11	11	11	11	11	11	11	11	11	11	11	11	11
16 D. Warwick	16	16	16	8	11	11	11	11	11	16	16	16	28	19	19	19	19	28	28	28	28	11	11	11	11	11	11	11	11	11	11	11	11	11	11	11	11
12 N. Mansell	12	8	8	16	16	16	16	16	16	19	19	19	19	28	28	28	28	19	6	6	6	6	6	6	6	6	6	6	6	6	6	12	12	12	12	12	12
8 N. Lauda	8	19	19	19	19	19	19	26	26	12	12	6	6	6	6	6	19	19	19	19	19	19	12	12	12	12	12	12	19	19	19	19	19	19	19	19	19
19 A. Senna	19	12	26	26	26	26	26	26	26	26	12	12	6	12	12	12	12	12	12	12	12	12	19	19	19	19	19	19	23	23	23	23	23	23	23	23	23
26 A. De Cesaris	26	26	12	12	12	12	12	12	12	6	6	26	26	26	26	26	26	26	26	26	26	23	23	23	23	23	23	23	26	26	4	4	4	4	4		
23 E. Cheever	23	23	23	23	23	23	23	23	23	23	23	23	23	23	23	23	23	23	23	23	26	26	26	26	26	26	26	26	4	14	14	14	14				
14 M. Winkelhock	14	14	14	14	14	14	6	6	6	14	14	14	14	14	4	4	4	4	4	4	4	4	4	4	4	4	4	4	14	2	2	2	2				
22 R. Patrese	22	6	6	6	6	6	14	14	14	4	4	4	4	4	14	14	14	14	14	14	14	5	5	5	5	5	5	5	2	18	18	18	3				
6 K. Rosberg	6	22	22	22	22	4	4	4	4	22	22	5	5	5	5	5	5	5	5	5	5	14	14	14	14	14	2	18	20	20	20	22					
25 F. Hesnault	25	2	2	25	25	4	22	22	22	5	5	22	22	22	22	22	18	18	18	2	2	2	2	2	2	2	18	20	26	22	22	20					
2 T. Fabi	2	25	25	2	4	2	2	2	2	2	2	18	18	18	18	18	18	22	2	18	18	18	18	18	18	18	22	22	3	18							
4 S. Bellof	4	4	4	4	2	25	18	18	5	18	2	2	2	2	2	2	2	20	20	20	20	20	20	20	20	3	3	26	26	26							
18 T. Boutsen	18	18	18	18	18	5	5	18	18	20	20	20	20	20	20	20	20	22	22	22	3	22	22	22	3	17	17	17	17								
20 J. Cecotto	20	20	20	20	20	20	20	20	3	3	3	3	3	3	3	3	3	22	3	3	3	17	9	9	9	9											
17 M. Surer	17	17	17	17	17	5	17	17	3	24	17	17	17	17	17	17	17	17	17	17	17	9	21	21	21	21											
5 J. Laffite	5	5	5	5	5	17	3	3	3	24	17	10	10	10	10	10	10	10	10	10	10	10	10	10	9	9	21										
3 M. Brundle	3	3	3	3	3	24	24	24	17	10	21	21	21	9	9	9	9	9	9	9	9	9	9	9	21	21											
24 P. Ghinzani	24	24	24	24	24	25	21	21	10	21	9	9	9	21	21	21	21	21	21	21	21	21	21	21													
21 H. Rothengatter	21	21	21	21	21	21	10	10	10	21	9																										
9 P. Alliot	9	9	9	10	10	10	10	9	9	9																											
10 M. Thackwell	10	10	10	9	9	9	9																														

38	39	40	41	42	43	44	45	46	47	48	49	50	51	52	53	54	55	56	57	58	59	60	61	62	63	64	65	66	67	68	69	70
1	1	1	1	1	1	1	1	1	1	1	1	1	1	1	1	1	1	1	1	1	1	1	1	1	1	1	1	1	1	1	1	1
7	7	7	7	7	7	7	7	8	8	8	8	8	8	8	8	8	8	8	8	8	8	8	8	8	8	8	8	8	8	8	8	8
8	8	8	8	8	8	8	7	7	7	7	7	7	7	7	7	7	7	7	7	7	7	7	7	7	7	7	7	7	7	7	7	7
28	28	28	28	28	28	28	28	28	28	28	28	16	16	16	16	16	12	12	12	12	12	12	11	11	11	11	11	11	11	11	11	11
16	16	16	16	16	16	16	16	16	16	16	16	28	28	12	12	16	28	11	11	11	11	23	23	23	12	12	12	12	28			
11	11	11	11	12	12	12	12	12	12	12	12	12	28	28	28	11	23	23	23	23	12	12	28	28	28	28	12					
12	12	12	12	11	11	11	11	11	11	11	11	11	11	11	11	23	28	28	28	28	28	19	19	19	19	19						
19	19	19	23	23	23	23	23	23	23	23	23	23	23	16	16	19	19	19	19	19	14	14	14	14	14							
23	23	23	19	19	19	19	19	19	19	19	19	19	19	19	19	14	14	14	14	14	20	20	20	20	20							
4	4	4	4	4	4	4	4	4	4	4	4	14	14	14	14	3	3	3	20	20	20	3	3	3	3							
14	14	14	14	14	14	14	14	14	14	14	14	3	3	3	3	20	20	20	3	3	3	9										
3	3	3	3	3	3	3	3	3	3	3	3	20	20	20	20	17	9	9	9	9												
20	20	20	20	20	20	20	20	20	20	20	20	17	17	17	17	9	9															
18	26	26	17	17	17	17	17	17	17	17	17	9	9	9	9																	
26	17	17	9	9	9	9	9	9	9	9	9	21	21	21	21																	
17	2	9	21	21	21	21	21	21	21	21	21																					
2	9	21																														
9	21																															
21																																

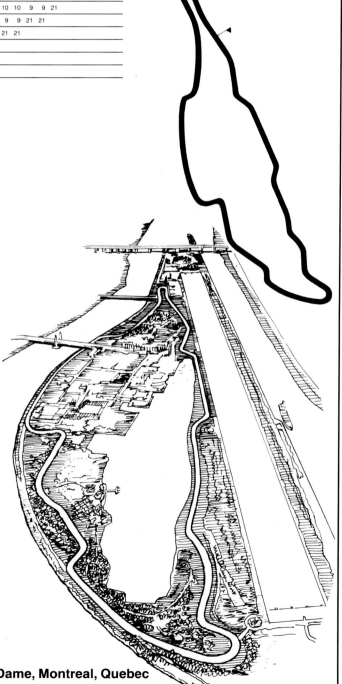

Fastest laps

Driver	Time	Lap
Nelson Piquet	1m 28·763s	55
Niki Lauda	1m 29·083s	54
Alain Prost	1m 29·433s	34
René Arnoux	1m 30·210s	36
Nigel Mansell	1m 30·503s	51
Derek Warwick	1m 30·560s	50
Eddie Cheever	1m 30·628s	56
Michele Alboreto	1m 30·990s	5
Manfred Winkelhock	1m 31·071s	66
Elio de Angelis	1m 31·305s	59
Keke Rosberg	1m 31·647s	31
Corrado Fabi	1m 31·767s	30
Ayrton Senna	1m 31·822s	67
Jacques Laffite	1m 32·124s	30
Martin Brundle	1m 32·385s	45
Stefan Bellof	1m 32·428s	36
Johnny Cecotto	1m 32·537s	59
Andrea de Cesaris	1m 32·591s	30
Riccardo Patrese	1m 32·716s	31
Thierry Boutsen	1m 33·069s	33
Marc Surer	1m 33·858s	33
Piercarlo Ghinzani	1m 34·664s	3
François Hesnault	1m 35·176s	5
Philippe Alliot	1m 35·498s	48
Mike Thackwell	1m 37·157s	14
Huub Rothengatter	1m 37·209s	3

Points

WORLD CHAMPIONSHIP OF DRIVERS

1	Alain Prost	32·5 pts
2	Niki Lauda	24
3	René Arnoux	16·5
4	Elio de Angelis	15·5
5	Derek Warwick	13
6	Keke Rosberg	11
7=	Michele Alboreto	9
7=	Nelson Piquet	9
9	Patrick Tambay	7
10=	Stefan Bellof	5
10=	Nigel Mansell	5
12=	Ayrton Senna	3
12=	Eddie Cheever	3
12=	Riccardo Patrese	3
15=	Andrea de Cesaris	2
15=	Martin Brundle	2
17	Thierry Boutsen	1

CONSTRUCTORS' CUP

1	McLaren	56·5 pts
2	Ferrari	25·5
3	Lotus	20·5
4	Renault	20
5	Williams	11
6	Brabham	9
7	Tyrrell	7
8	Alfa Romeo	6
9	Toleman	3
10	Ligier	2
11	Arrows	1

Circuit data

Circuit Gilles Villeneuve, Ile Notre Dame, Montreal, Quebec
Circuit length: 2·74 miles/4·41 km
Race distance: 70 laps, 191·82 miles/308·70 km
Race weather: Hot, dry

United States Grand Prix Detroit

A startline shunt, a stiff neck and a spare car failed to stem Nelson Piquet's winning ways when the Grand Prix community arrived in Detroit a week after the Brazilian's brilliant, dominant victory in the Canadian race at Montreal. In time-honoured Brabham team style, Nelson demolished his opposition with a searing pole position lap during the final hour-long qualifying session and started the 63 lap Detroit race in a confident frame of mind. But hardly had the starting lights blinked green than Piquet felt a bump from behind and, in a flash, his BT53 snapped sideways, plunging across the road to the right, T-boning Michele Alboreto's Ferrari C4 against the outside retaining wall before shuddering to a standstill minus its rear aerofoil and right-rear wheel. Scarcely had Piquet come to rest than Marc Surer's Arrows A6, deprived of any escape route, clouted the front-left wheel of the badly damaged Brabham, jarring Nelson's neck quite painfully. All that work down the pan . . .

But no! The red flag was already being waved as Piquet climbed from the wreckage: the Brazilian was to be given a second chance. As the cars trickled back to the starting grid once again, so the post mortem on F1's latest startline tangle got underway. Nigel Mansell's Lotus 95T had got away from its position on the inside of the second row impeccably, but the Englishman had aimed for a gap between front row men Piquet and Alain Prost which just wasn't big enough to accommodate his car. To make matter's slightly worse, the Lotus began to fishtail to the left as Mansell went for the gap, bouncing off Prost's McLaren and back into the pole position Brabham. Alright, so Nelson might have been *slightly* slow off the mark, but he hadn't really got a chance . . . there just wasn't sufficient room in which for Mansell to capitalise on his superb getaway.

The ripple effect of this multiple shunt went much further simply than the Brabham and Lotus team. Nelson, of course, had no choice but to take the restart at the wheel of his spare Brabham BT53, although Nigel's car escaped unscathed to compete again. But the wayward Brabham wheel had damaged Ayrton Senna's Toleman TG184 and he was faced with the prospect of trying again with his spare – without the new Brian Hart 415T development engine! Similarly handicapped was Alboreto, who transferred to his Lucas injected spare 126C4 in place of the Marelli/Weber equipped race car. And poor Surer, well, he just had to spend the rest of the afternoon on the sidelines . . .

At the second start Piquet made no mistakes, getting away quickly from any potential trouble in his wake to lead from start to finish in his customary, slightly disarming, yet crushingly dominant style. He led across the line on every lap, keeping pace with an initial challenge from Prost and a subsequent one from Nigel Mansell. But he wasn't going to be flustered into any sort of error, knowing full well that he was the man in complete control. In the closing stages he eased his pace significantly, allowing midfield survivor Martin Brundle to come at him with what looked like an alarming surge over the last few laps. For the Tyrrell new boy, it was a glittering opportunity to make his name, but Nelson was at the head of the column in MoTown – and that's the way it stayed!

ENTRY AND PRACTICE

Coming only a week after the Canadian Grand Prix at Montreal, there was obviously not much time available to the teams for technical changes, so most of the cars were exactly as raced at the *Circuit Gilles Villeneuve* the previous Sunday. After the relatively forgiving Montreal track, Detroit stopped some people (literally!) in their tracks as they tackled the tight 2.50-mile street course laid out through one of the less salubrious areas of this industrial city, the whole scene dominated by the plush, 70-storey Renaissance Centre with its virtually self-contained complex of hotel, shops and offices contrasting dramatically with its immediate surroundings. The circuit is bumpy, rutted and highly demanding with unyielding concrete barriers standing in wait for those careless souls who put a wheel so much as half a rim's width out of line. Montreal, by comparison, was positively forgiving with plenty of grassed run-off areas on which to escape, but there were no such concessions to indisciplined driving in MoTown.

Although the Formula 1 world has patronised the Detroit Grand Prix on two previous occasions, it seemed that many people were intent on learning about street circuits yet again in the most difficult

fashion possible. Endless excursions into the walls seemed to result in practice and qualifying being stopped quite regularly in order that some poor unfortunate's badly damaged car would be retrieved and returned to the pits. On most permanent circuits it would just be a case of "bad luck" to the unfortunate who had made the mistake, but crashed cars at Detroit inevitably result in a partially blocked track, so the programme ran very late on Friday and Saturday.

After being given a nasty fright by Nelson Piquet in Montreal, the McLaren International team had to face up to another dose of Brabham-BMW domination during qualifying at Detroit. The recipe was the well-tried, familiar one. Piquet wound himself up tight for a two flying lap qualifying run on Saturday afternoon, from which he emerged first with a 1m 41.290s – good enough for pole position anyway – and then a 1m 40.980s on his next lap. What's more, the Brabham BT53 lapsed onto three as Nelson hurtled into the Atwater tunnel on that second flying lap and Gordon Murray, listening and watching in the pits, was convinced the Brazilian had lost his best shot at fastest time.

"When he came into view before the last chicane, the engine sounded dreadful," reflected

the Brabham designer, "but he was still obviously running quickly as he came over the line, so I quickly checked his time . . ." Notwithstanding the broken valve, Piquet had thrown pole position beyond the capabilities of his TAG-engined rivals: a devastating indication of BMW power.

Over in the McLaren pit, Alain Prost began the weekend less than fully confident and, to be frank, just a little miffed at his team. "I told them that my race engine wouldn't rev. properly at Montreal," he complained, "so I get here and find it's still installed. Perhaps they don't believe what I'm telling them. The problem is also that it has too much throttle lag which is pushing the front end and causing it to understeer too much – that's exactly what I *don't* want round a circuit like this." By Saturday the engine had been fitted with fresh turbochargers, but Prost still didn't think much of the engine, so he transferred to the team spare for Saturday's qualifying and emerged much more content with his lot after turning a 1m 41.640s to join Piquet on the front row of the grid.

By contrast, Niki Lauda started off on an optimistic note, feeling very confident over the track performance of his McLaren MP4/2, but the Austrian's good humour took a knock when his time was disallowed at the end of Friday afternoon.

Trouble on the waterfront. Nigel Mansell makes a perfect start from the second row and aims for a gap between Alain Prost's McLaren and the Brabham of Nelson Piquet as the Brazilian makes a comparatively slow getaway from pole. The Brabham and Lotus make contact, Piquet slewing to his left before the rear of the BT53 swings right and collects the side of Michele Alboreto's Ferrari. Prost streaks into the lead while Mansell continues with no more than a dented left-rear wheel rim. Piquet eventually strikes a wall on the left of the picture, his right-rear wheel becoming detached and bouncing high in the air before crashing down on the front suspension of Ayrton Senna's Toleman.

The race was stopped after Marc Surer had hit the stationary Brabham and Alboreto had spun to a halt two corners later. Mansell claimed he had been squeezed out. Tyre marks show Prost scarcely veers from his expected course. The camera angle suggests that Piquet had started to move right to take his line for the first left-hander. Whatever the reason for the accident, the gap looks to have been very narrow from the outset. (Mansell was later fined $6,000 by FISA for dangerous driving.)

Close examination by the scrutineers revealed the rear aerofoil of his car to have infringed the maximum width limitation by 1 millimetre: the fact that the problem was almost certainly caused by heat distortion of a bond between the main aerofoil and its side plate, added to the anomaly that the aerofoil was actually fully legal when measured in another four places round the outer edge of the side plate, left most people feeling that this was taking pedantry beyond the limits of reason. Some optimistic cove mentioned that thunderstorms were forecast for Saturday afternoon, at just about the time the final qualifying hour was scheduled to take place. Nobody dared to think about Niki failing to qualify: in the end he did, of course, taking tenth place after a none-too-successful attempt at finding a break in the traffic.

Nigel Mansell had been fastest on Friday afternoon, the Lotus 95T driver making the most of the latest flatter-profile Goodyear radials available for the first time in 'B' and 'C' compounds. Exuding a heart-warming confidence, Mansell managed a 1m 45.130s on Friday, set the fastest time again in Saturday's unofficial session and then, disappointingly, dropped to third overall during that final, crucial hour. He did a 1m 42.172s on his first run, good enough for pole at the time, but he was close behind Stefan Bellof's Tyrrell when the ebullient German spun heavily into the wall while he was trying for his second time. "Waved flags everywhere, I dodged through and still did a 42.2s," mused Mansell, "otherwise, I reckon I'd have been quicker still . . ."

Although generally more consistent when it comes to actually finishing the races, Elio de Angelis failed to match his team-mate during qualifying and qualified fifth after glancing a wall and slightly damaging his 95T's suspension in the process on Saturday.

Ferrari appeared at Detroit with the two race cars for Alboreto and Arnoux equipped with the latest Marelli/Weber electronic fuel injection and the Italian did extremely well to post a 1m 42.246s fourth fastest time, joining Mansell on the second row. Arnoux, who never really got into the swing of Detroit, either in qualifying or the race, suffered an engine failure during Saturday's unofficial morning session and, after this was changed in time for final qualifying, he badly compromised his potential grid time by a spin on his first run while his second was hampered by Bellof's accident. On his first set of soft Goodyears, René pirouetted spectacularly as he exited the chicane before the pits, his C4 coming to rest, broadside across the track, adjacent to the Brabham pit. This prompted FOCA supremo Bernie Ecclestone to nip over the wall and attempt to push the Italian car back into the fray . . .

Over in the Renault camp, CART star Mario Andretti had been asked to stand by just in case Patrick Tambay had not recovered sufficiently to participate in the Detroit race. But Mario, although willing to take a serious crack at the race, wasn't prepared to go into the event "cold" after an 18 month absence from the Formula 1 scene, and, anyway, Tambay was able to face qualifying with more hope and optimism than he had been able to muster in Montreal.

"My leg is still a little on the weak side," he confessed, "but I've been training quite intensively with a health club and, although I'm expecting to be more tired than usual on Sunday evening, I don't think the race itself will be any great problem!"

Patrick was cautiously confident about his prospects at Detroit, but Derek Warwick rounded off the first unofficial session in a somewhat annoyed frame of mind. At the wheel of his regular RE50, the Englishman had asked for more wing to be wound on at the front in order to counter an initial touch of understeer on the tight circuit: unfortunately this contributed to his getting into a violent "fishtail" over one of the many bumps, spearing off the track into the wall as he did so. As a result, the front suspension broke and a front suspension member penetrated the footwell just as it had done on him at Dijon and on Tambay at Monaco. The message was becoming clear: *don't* have an impact against a solid object at the wheel of a Renault RE50.

This little drama meant that Derek spent the remainder of official practice at the wheel of the team's spare car, eventually working his way down to a commendable sixth quickest 1m 42.637s during the final session. On Friday afternoon he had almost been beside himself with frustration as his efforts were hampered by apparently endless turbo problems, but he emerged from Saturday's qualifying session in a noticeably more optimistic frame of mind. None the less, he did suffer another turbo failure, as well as falling foul of the oil deposited in the Bellof accident, so that sixth place was well earned. Tambay wound up ninth at the end of the day, frustrated by fourth gear braking on Friday and the fact that he felt rather more tired on the second day.

Ayrton Senna continued to hold everybody's attention, most notably on Friday afternoon when he got the chicane before the pits completely wrong, clipped the apex and slammed backwards into the wall separating the pit lane from the circuit. The rear end of the Toleman TG184 was virtually destroyed, the turbo briefly causing the car to catch fire as the wrecked machine slithered to rest. As if this was not enough, Johnny Cecotto managed to slam his TG184 into the wall quite heavily, leaving the Toleman lads with the task of rebuilding two cars in time for Saturday qualifying.

This demanding task involved replacing gearboxes, bellhousings, rear suspension units and the installation of fresh engines – in the case of Senna's car this was the electronically injected Hart 415T development unit which had been flown back to base for a rebuild during the week's break since Montreal. Ayrton used the unit to good effect in that final hour, squeezing in a 1m 42.651s to take seventh spot on the grid, but Cecotto was significantly slower. The Venezuelan former motorcycle ace seemed inhibited by the nature of tight, restrictive street circuits and his 1m 45.231s best at Detroit only amounted to 17th place.

Following his encouraging race performance at Montreal, Eddie Cheever faced Detroit with considerable optimism, a scheduled race distance of just under 160 miles hardly presenting the thirsty Italian V8 with its customary fuel consumption problems. Eddie did a 1m 43.065s to take eighth place on the grid, adding "if it hadn't been for a worryingly high water temperature reading, I reckon we could have used a touch more boost in final qualifying and gone even quicker." By contrast Riccardo Patrese's practice progress seemed fraught with problems: a serious misfire during the final hour heralded his 184T's demise with fuel pump failure. He immediately transferred to the team spare, but this also refused to run cleanly and the net result of all this aggravation was a 25th position on the grid – and a correspondingly sullen expression on the moody Italian's face!

Martin Brundle and Stefan Bellof both did splendid jobs at the wheel of their Tyrrells, qualifying 11th and 16th respectively, the German's efforts abruptly interrupted by his spectacular accident during final qualifying which damaged the monocoque of his race car and obliged him to use the spare for the race. Andrea de Cesaris managed to bounce a Ligier into one wall or another during the Friday morning, Saturday morning and Saturday afternoon sessions, this overtly energetic approach earning him 12th place on 1m 43.889s: his team-mate François Hesnault was slower, and more disciplined, ending up 18th.

In the Arrows camp designer Dave Wass arrived back from England with a four-inch spacer which was inserted in one of the A7's wheelbase ahead of the gearbox, improving the handling and feel of Thierry Boutsen's race car. The Belgian spent the two days hopping from one A7 to the other as he ran the gauntlet of a sticking throttle, a gearbox gremlin which resulted in the transmission selecting two ratios at once, a broken drive-shaft c/v joint, turbo problems and a fractured pipe between the engine and the intercooler. Bearing in mind all this, he did well to qualify 13th on 1m 44.063s while team-mate Surer, still contenting himself with a

Cosworth-engined A6, found himself turfed abruptly into the wall on his first qualifying lap when Teo Fabi's Brabham got out of control over a bump and sideswiped the Swiss.

The Arrows monocoque was ruined in the impact, but the A6 was successfully rebuilt round a new tub for Saturday, Marc managing a 1m 46.626s for 22nd on the grid. As far as Fabi was concerned, this accident put him right off his stroke and his Friday qualifying efforts were restricted to a few laps in the BT53 qualifying spare after Nelson had finished with it. Although he got back in his own repaired car the following day, he couldn't better 1m 47.335s for a lowly 23rd. "This business of trying to do CART and Formula 1 is a waste of time," Teo confessed, "I'm making lots of mistakes and doing neither properly . . ."

The Williams team, despite fitting revised FW08-based front uprights to its FW09s since Montreal, ended up in near-despair after qual-

Nigel Mansell, the centre of controversy, sits quietly by the Detroit River and waits for the restart.

ifying was over. "It's *slightly* better," admitted Keke Rosberg, his voice tinged with sarcasm, "but it's a bit difficult to make much progress when the wheels are hardly ever in contact with the ground over the bumps!" There was a blank look of disbelief on the Finn's face when it was found that he had not only qualified slower than the equally bewildered Jacques Laffite (who was 19th on 1m 46.225s), but also behind Philippe Alliot's Pirelli-shod RAM 02. In 21st place on 1m 46.495s, there was clearly no point in asking Keke why he was so slow – anymore than there was any point in asking the RAM team why Alliot was so quick . . .

Right at the back Palmer's RAM shared the penultimate row with Fabi's Brabham while Patrese and Piercarlo Ghinzani's Osella lined up on row 13, the last two qualifiers. The only driver not to make the race was Huub Rothengatter, his Spirit now revamped to accommodate a Cosworth DFV owing to a shortage of Hart 415T components: the 101C suffered from various teething troubles, including overheating, and the Dutchman never got into the swing of things.

THE RACE

After all the debris of the aforementioned startline shunt was eventually cleared up and the competitors reassembled, the second getaway proved much

more orderly with Piquet edging into a lead he was never to lose as the pack jostled into the first left-hander. Prost just squeezed into second place ahead of Mansell and this was the order at the end of the opening lap with Alboreto next up ahead of Cheever, Warwick, de Angelis, Lauda, Tambay, Senna, Brundle and the rest of the pack. The field had already been depleted by one as Winkelhock retired with engine failure mid-way round that first tour and, on lap three, Palmer's RAM hit the wall very hard when a rear tyre tread pulled off its sidewall. Hardly had the dust settled from this incident than Ghinzani and Hesnault knocked into each other, Osella and Ligier skating up an escape road. The Frenchman was out on the spot, but Ghinzani limped back to the pits to retire.

Although he was using the same Michelin soft '5' compound tyres which were eventually to prove such a problem to the McLaren MP4/2s on an abrasive track surface which had been washed clean by a torrential storm the previous evening, Piquet gradually began to edge away from Prost in the opening stages of the race. The World Championship leader was worried by an early deterioration in his McLaren's level of grip, so much so that Mansell's Goodyear-shod Lotus was able to slip through into second place on lap 10. By that time Warwick had carved his way through to fourth place ahead of Alboreto, the scintillating Cheever, then a long gap to Lauda, Tambay and a ferociously tight group of 'young lions' comprising Senna, Boutsen, Brundle and Bellof, all driving as if the lap they were on was their last . . .

On lap three Ferrari's efforts were badly compromised when Arnoux made a silly mistake, damaging his C4's front suspension in a gentle spin against a wall, the crestfallen Frenchman creeping in to retire, while, further back, Keke Rosberg had his head down and was charging through the slower cars with great determination, by lap 10 moving his way up on to the tail of the battling new boys' midfield bunch.

Although Mansell was keeping in touch with the leading Brabham, Piquet wasn't being flustered or hurried by the presence of the black and gold machine a few lengths behind his BT53 and one quickly got the impression that the reigning World Champion was dictating the pace of the contest. As the McLarens steadily dropped away, Cheever nipped ahead of Alboreto on lap 12 to take fourth place and this soon became third when Prost took a rather premature decision to stop for fresh rubber on lap 16, switching to the harder '10' compound when he did so.

By lap 14 Rosberg was well and truly embroiled with the "kids", the ferocity with which their battle was being waged impressing even this veteran of many close scraps – and, knowing Keke's form, that's certainly saying something! The Williams-Honda pilot scrambled his way to the front of this bunch on lap 22, by which time Senna's Toleman had departed the fray with a spectacular trip into the tyre barrier at the first corner. The initial suspicion was that the Brazilian had simply dropped it, but close examination of the damaged TG184 pointed firmly to a broken front wishbone.

On lap 15 Warwick also stopped for harder Michelin '10s' and resumed to stage an impressive comeback, climbing through the field from 16th after his pit stop to an eventual third on lap 36 (setting the race's fastest lap on lap 32) before fifth gear packed up. His progress through the field had been aided by Cheever's retirement on lap 22, his Alfa sidelined with a split turbo intercooler, but Derek wasn't destined to make the finish either. Eventually the Renault's gearbox began to break up completely and Derek had no choice but to stop. A similar malady also ended his team-mate's race, Tambay indulging in an early spin before making a predictable stop for fresh rubber: the atmosphere in the Renault camp at the end of the race was tense, to say the least.

Mansell's meticulous and assured performance in Piquet's wake was really most impressive and Nelson allowed the Englishman to close up on to his tail before the 20 lap mark had been reached. This lasted until lap 25 when Nigel suddenly lost second gear as he sped through the Atwater tunnel,

JUNE:
Lotus announce plans to build and run two cars in 1985 CART Championship and at Indianapolis.

Martin Brundle more than made up for the disappointment of Monaco. Qualifying in 11th place, the Tyrrell driver kept away from the walls which were to claim so many victims and he was perfectly poised to take second place. After the race, scrutineers would remove a sample from the water injection reservoir and spark off a major row which would not detract from the precision of Brundle's excellent drive.

dropping away from Piquet quite dramatically. In another three laps it was all over as the Englishman came slowly into the pits to retire, the Lotus's gearbox showing signs of failure.

From this point onwards, the race fell apart dramatically with retirements coming thick and fast. Brundle was soon left the only survivor of the earlier, frenzied midfield battle, dropping from fifth to seventh after a routine stop for ballast on lap 32. Despite the fact that his Tyrrell was suffering from a broken exhaust pipe, Martin was pressing on well, losing nothing as a result of this minor affliction. Boutsen's BMW engine blew its carbon fibre cam cover in half, Bellof's Tyrrell smote the pit wall with its left-rear wheel exiting the chicane on lap 33, demolishing the whole corner of the car, the German three-wheeling to a halt opposite Uncle Ken's intimidating gaze.

After his initial pit stop for fresh rubber, Prost successfully worked his way back on to the tail of the tussle between Rosberg and Brundle for fourth place, but by lap 39 a deflating rear Michelin had pitched the MP4/2 into a spin and he was obliged to make a second stop for fresh rubber. Lauda, meanwhile, had also been plugging away doggedly

after an earlier stop for new Michelins, but he arrived after 33 laps to report that the engine was running roughly. After a lengthy debate, and a plug change, Niki was sent out again to assess how bad the engine really was and whether or not it should be changed prior to first practice in Dallas. He returned after a lap: "I'll continue, if you like, but it's going to cost you a lot of money when that engine lets go," he said coolly. The McLaren was retired immediately!

Next of the survivors to quit the fray was Rosberg, his Williams having cracked an exhaust pipe which, in turn, had caused sufficient heat build-up to burn through an oil line to one of the turbos, which, starved of lubricant, then seized and caught the rear bodywork on fire. Marshals doused the car indiscriminately as Rosberg walked away with hardly a backward glance. "The thing that irritates me is that I'd done all the work, then the thing retired just as I was about to stroke it home to some points," he muttered. Other casualties by this stage included de Cesaris with suspension damage and Cecotto who thoughtlessly stopped to complain his clutch had gone solid and was then unable to restart!

In the closing stages of the contest the heat was taken off Piquet's Brabham by the fact that Alboreto's Ferrari blew up, the long-term legacy of a split intercooler, and de Angelis's second place Lotus 95T lost second gear, depriving the Italian of any vain chance of challenging for the lead. Thus Nelson was able to wind down the turbo boost, in response to signals from his pit crew who could see some debris blocking the turbo intercooler aperture. Brundle overtook de Angelis with little difficulty and came storming up on Nelson over the final few laps: but Martin was a realist, knowing full-well that Piquet was stroking it home. He didn't make any silly mistakes and, as a result, ended the day with a magnificent second place which looked a little closer than perhaps even Nelson had intended to judge it!

De Angelis's consistency was rewarded by third place while Prost still snatched two points for fifth place, sandwiched between the uninspiring Fabi and Laffite who drove gently round for the entire race and received rewards that must have been far above any hopes based on their grid positions. If only Prost hadn't made that initial stop, he might have been second, almost certainly third . . .

AH

Entries and practice times

No.	Driver	Nat	Car	Tyre	Engine	Entrant	Practice 1	Practice 2
1	Nelson Piquet	BR	Parmalat BRABHAM BT53	M	BMW M12/13	MRD International	1m 45·407s	**1m 40·980s**
2	Teo Fabi	I	Parmalat BRABHAM BT53	M	BMW M12/13	MRD International	1m 51·165s	**1m 47·335s**
3	Martin Brundle	GB	TYRRELL 012	G	Ford Cosworth DFY	Tyrrell Racing Organisation	1m 48·966s	**1m 43·754s**
4	Stefan Bellof	D	TYRRELL 012	G	Ford Cosworth DFY	Tyrrell Racing Organisation	1m 48·177s	**1m 44·940s**
5	Jacques Laffite	F	WILLIAMS FW09	G	Honda RA 163–E	Williams Grand Prix Engineering	1m 47·610s	**1m 46·225s**
6	Keke Rosberg	SF	WILLIAMS FW09	G	Honda RA 163–E	Williams Grand Prix Engineering	1m 47·919s	**1m 46·495s**
7	Alain Prost	F	Marlboro McLAREN MP4/2	M	TAG P01 (TTE P01)	Marlboro McLaren International	1m 45·717s	**1m 41·640s**
8	Niki Lauda	A	Marlboro McLAREN MP4/2	M	TAG P01 (TTE P01)	Marlboro McLaren International	*1m 45·238s	**1m 43·484s**
9	Philippe Alliot	F	RAM 02	P	Hart 415T	Skoal Bandit Formula 1 Team	1m 51·031s	**1m 46·333s**
10	Jonathan Palmer	GB	RAM 02	P	Hart 415T	Skoal Bandit Formula 1 Team	1m 51·493s	**1m 47·743s**
11	Elio de Angelis	I	John Player Special LOTUS 95T	G	Renault EF4	John Player Team Lotus	1m 47·316s	**1m 42·434s**
12	Nigel Mansell	GB	John Player Special LOTUS 95T	G	Renault EF4	John Player Team Lotus	1m 45·130s	**1m 42·172s**
14	Manfred Winkelhock	D	ATS D7	P	BMW M12/13	Team ATS	1m 47·303s	**1m 44·228s**
15	Patrick Tambay	F	Elf RENAULT RE50	M	Renault EF4	Equipe Renault Elf	1m 46·426s	**1m 43·289s**
16	Derek Warwick	GB	Elf RENAULT RE50	M	Renault Elf	Equipe Renault Elf	1m 42·866s	**1m 42·637s**
17	Marc Surer	CH	ARROWS A6	G	Ford Cosworth DFV	Barclay Nordica Arrows BMW	6m 22·502s	**1m 46·626s**
18	Thierry Boutsen	B	ARROWS A7	G	BMW M12/13	Barclay Nordica Arrows BMW	1m 47·866s	**1m 44·063s**
19	Ayrton Senna	BR	TOLEMAN TG184	M	Hart 415T	Toleman Group Motorsport	1m 47·188s	**1m 42·651s**
20	Johnny Cecotto	YV	TOLEMAN TG184	M	Hart 415T	Toleman Group Motorsport	1m 49·644s	**1m 45·231s**
21	Huub Rothengatter	NL	SPIRIT 101	P	Ford Cosworth DFV	Spirit Racing	1m 53·625s	**1m 49·955s**
22	Riccardo Patrese	I	Benetton ALFA ROMEO 184T	G	Alfa Romeo 183T	Benetton Team Alfa Romeo	**1m 47·974s**	1m 48·230s
23	Eddie Cheever	USA	Benetton ALFA ROMEO 184T	G	Alfa Romeo 183T	Benetton Team Alfa Romeo	1m 47·347s	**1m 43·065s**
24	Piercarlo Ghinzani	I	Kelemata OSELLA FA1F	P	Alfa Romeo 183T	Osella Squadra Corse	1m 49·141s	**1m 48·865s**
25	François Hesnault	F	LIGIER Loto JS23	M	Renault EF4	Ligier Loto	1m 49·697s	**1m 45·419s**
26	Andrea de Cesaris	I	LIGIER Loto JS23	M	Renault EF4	Ligier Loto	1m 46·834s	**1m 43·998s**
27	Michele Alboreto	I	Fiat FERRARI 126C4	G	Ferrari 126C	Scuderia Ferrari SpA	1m 47·719s	**1m 42·246s**
28	René Arnoux	F	Fiat FERRARI 126C4	G	Ferrari 126C	Scuderia Ferrari SpA	1m 46·805s	**1m 44·748s**

Friday morning and Saturday morning practice sessions not officially recorded.   *Time disallowed.*

Fri pm — Warm, dry   Sat pm — Hot, dry

G – Goodyear, M – Michelin, P – Pirelli.

Starting grid

1 PIQUET (1m 40·980s)
Brabham

7 PROST (1m 41·640s)
McLaren

12 MANSELL (1m 42·172s)
Lotus

27 ALBORETO (1m 42·246s)
Ferrari

11 DE ANGELIS (1m 42·434s)
Lotus

16 WARWICK (1m 42·637s)
Renault

19 SENNA (1m 42·651s)
Toleman

23 CHEEVER (1m 43·065s)
Alfa Romeo

15 TAMBAY (1m 43·289s)
Renault

8 LAUDA (1m 43·484s)
McLaren

3 BRUNDLE (1m 43·754s)
Tyrrell

26 DE CESARIS (1m 43·998s)
Ligier

18 BOUTSEN (1m 44·063s)
Arrows

14 WINKELHOCK (1m 44·228s)
ATS

28 ARNOUX (1m 44·748s)
Ferrari

4 BELLOF (1m 44·940s)
Tyrrell

20 CECOTTO (1m 45·231s)
Toleman

25 HESNAULT (1m 45·419s)
Ligier

5 LAFFITE (1m 46·225s)
Williams

9 ALLIOT (1m 46·333s)
RAM

6 ROSBERG (1m 46·495s)
Williams

*17 SURER (1m 46·626s)
Arrows

2 FABI (1m 47·335s)
Brabham

10 PALMER (1m 47·743s)
RAM

22 PATRESE (1m 47·974s)
Alfa Romeo

24 GHINZANI (1m 48·865s)
Osella

Did not start:
21 Rothengatter (Spirit), 1m 49·955s, did not qualify
* Surer eliminated in start-line accident. Could not take restart as no spare car available.

Results and retirements

Place	Driver	Car	Laps	Time and Speed (mph/km/h)/Retirement	
1	Nelson Piquet	Brabham-BMW t/c 4	63	1h 55m 41·842s	81·679/131·449
2	Martin Brundle	Tyrrell-Cosworth V8	63	1h 55m 42·679s	81·7/131·483
3	Elio de Angelis	Lotus-Renault t/c V6	63	1h 56m 14·480s	81·3/130·839
4	Teo Fabi	Brabham-BMW t/c 4	63	1h 57m 08·370s	80·7/129·874
5	Alain Prost	McLaren-TAG t/c V6	63	1h 57m 37·100s	80·3/129·23
6	Jacques Laffite	Williams-Honda t/c V6	62		
	Michele Alboreto	Ferrari t/c V6	49	Engine	
	Keke Rosberg	Williams-Honda t/c V6	47	Exhaust/turbo	
	Derek Warwick	Renault t/c V6	40	Gearbox	
	Stefan Bellof	Tyrrell-Cosworth V8	33	Accident	
	Patrick Tambay	Renault t/c V6	33	Transmission	
	Philippe Alliot	RAM-Hart t/c 4	33	Brakes/hit wall	
	Niki Lauda	McLaren-TAG t/c V6	33	Electronics	
	Nigel Mansell	Lotus-Renault t/c V6	27	Gearbox	
	Thierry Boutsen	Arrows-BMW t/c 4	27	Engine	
	Andrea de Cesaris	Ligier-Renault t/c V6	24	Overheating	
	Johnny Cecotto	Toleman-Hart t/c 4	23	Clutch mechanism	
	Eddie Cheever	Alfa Romeo t/c V8	21	Engine	
	Ayrton Senna	Toleman-Hart t/c 4	21	Accident	
	Riccardo Patrese	Alfa Romeo t/c V8	20	Spun, damaged suspension	
	François Hesnault	Ligier-Renault t/c V6	3	Accident with Ghinzani	
	Piercarlo Ghinzani	Osella-Alfa Romeo t/c V8	3	Accident with Hesnault	
	René Arnoux	Ferrari t/c V6	2	Accident	
	Jonathan Palmer	RAM-Hart t/c 4	2	Tyre failure/accident	
	Manfred Winkelhock	ATS-BMW t/c 4	0	Accident	
	Marc Surer	Arrows-Cosworth V8	0	Accident	

Fastest lap: Warwick, on lap 32, 1m 46·221s, 84·729mph/136·358km/h (record).
Previous lap record: John Watson (F1 McLaren MP4/1C-Cosworth V8), 1m 47·668s, 83·5902mph/134·525km/h (1982).

Past winners

Year	Driver	Nat	Car	Circuit	Distance miles/km	Speed mph/km/h
1982	John Watson	GB	3·0 McLaren MP4B-Ford	Detroit	154·57/248·75	78·20/128·85
1983	Michele Alboreto	I	3·0 Tyrrell 011-Ford	Detroit	150·00/241·40	81·16/130·61
1984	Nelson Piquet	BR	1·5 Brabham BT53-BMW t/c	Detroit	157·50/253·47	81·68/131·45

The Detroit circuit continued to raise adverse comments over its tight and rather tedious layout. Teo Fabi heads for his first championship points with the Brabham-BMW.

Circuit data

Detroit Grand Prix Circuit, Detroit, Michigan
Circuit length: 2·50 miles/4·0233 km
Race distance: 63 laps, 157·500 miles/253·471 km
Race weather: Hot, dry

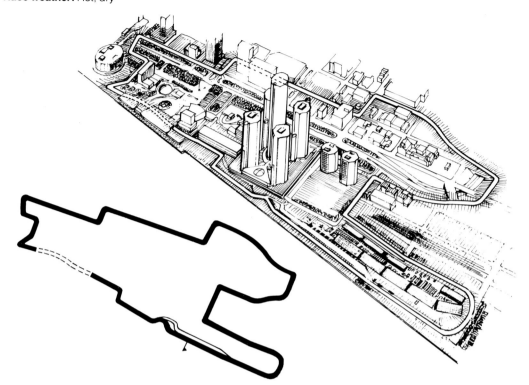

Points

Fastest laps

Driver	Time	Lap
Derek Warwick	1m 46·221s	32
Patrick Tambay	1m 46·739s	29
Stefan Bellof	1m 46·778s	21
Nigel Mansell	1m 46·921s	13
Martin Brundle	1m 47·037s	23
Nelson Piquet	1m 47·050s	30
Alain Prost	1m 47·074s	20
Niki Lauda	1m 47·192s	27
Keke Rosberg	1m 47·415s	26
Ayrton Senna	1m 47·444s	20
Thierry Boutsen	1m 47·561s	24
Michele Alboreto	1m 47·563s	31
Elio de Angelis	1m 47·662s	33
Andrea de Cesaris	1m 47·670s	17
Riccardo Patrese	1m 47·684s	19
Jacques La'fite	1m 48·146s	27
Teo Fabi	1m 48·232s	20
Eddie Cheever	1m 48·553s	20
Johnny Cecotto	1m 49·270s	10
Philippe Alliot	1m 51·147s	20
René Arnoux	1m 52·636s	2
Piercarlo Ghinzani	1m 53·489s	2
François Hesnault	1m 53·579s	2
Jonathan Palmer	1m 57·367s	2

Lap chart

1st LAP ORDER	1	2	3	4	5	6	7	8	9	10	11	12	13	14	15	16	17	18	19	20	21	22	23	24	25	26	27	28	29	30	31	32	33	34	35	36	37
1 N. Piquet	1	1	1	1	1	1	1	1	1	1	1	1	1	1	1	1	1	1	1	1	1	1	1	1	1	1	1	1	1	1	1	1	1	1	1	1	1
7 A. Prost	7	7	7	7	7	7	7	7	7	12	12	12	12	12	12	12	12	12	12	12	12	12	12	12	12	12	27	27	27	27	27	27	27	27	27	27	27
12 N. Mansell	12	12	12	12	12	12	12	12	12	7	7	7	7	7	7	23	23	23	23	23	27	27	27	27	27	27	11	11	11	11	11	11	11	16	16	11	
27 M. Alboreto	27	27	27	27	16	16	16	16	16	16	16	16	16	23	23	27	27	27	27	27	11	11	11	11	11	11	6	6	6	6	6	6	16	11	11	6	
23 E. Cheever	23	23	23	16	27	27	27	27	27	27	27	23	23	27	27	11	11	11	11	11	23	18	18	18	18	18	3	3	3	3	4	16	6	6	6	16	
16 D. Warwick	16	16	16	23	23	23	23	23	23	23	23	27	27	11	11	7	7	7	8	8	8	18	6	6	6	6	4	4	4	4	3	4	7	7	7	3	
11 E. De Angelis	11	11	11	8	8	8	8	8	11	11	11	11	11	16	8	8	8	18	18	18	6	3	3	3	3	3	16	16	16	16	16	7	3	3	7	7	
8 N. Lauda	8	8	8	11	11	11	11	11	11	8	8	8	8	15	18	18	18	19	19	19	19	3	4	4	4	4	7	7	7	7	7	3	2	2	2	2	
15 P. Tambay	15	15	15	15	15	15	15	15	15	15	15	15	18	15	19	19	6	6	6	4	16	16	16	16	16	2	2	2	2	2	2	5	5	5	5	5	
19 A. Senna	19	19	19	19	19	19	19	19	19	19	19	19	19	18	19	6	6	6	3	3	3	8	7	7	7	7	5	5	5	8	8	8	15				
3 M. Brundle	3	3	3	3	3	3	18	18	18	18	18	18	4	19	6	6	3	3	4	4	4	7	2	2	2	2	8	8	8	5	5	5	8				
18 T. Boutsen	18	18	18	18	18	18	3	4	4	4	4	4	18	6	3	3	4	4	2	2	7	16	5	5	5	5	15	15	15	15	15	15					
28 R. Arnoux	28	28	4	4	4	4	4	3	3	3	3	3	3	4	4	2	2	7	7	2	2	8	8	8	8	8	12	9	9	9	9	9					
4 S. Bellof	4	4	20	20	20	20	20	6	6	6	6	6	6	4	2	15	16	16	16	16	5	15	15	15	15	15	9										
25 F. Hesnault	25	20	6	6	6	6	6	20	20	20	22	22	20	20	16	20	5	5	5	15	20	20	9	9	9												
20 J. Cecotto	20	25	25	22	22	22	22	22	22	22	20	20	2	16	16	20	5	20	20	20	20	9	9	25													
6 K. Rosberg	6	6	24	2	2	2	2	2	2	2	2	2	22	5	5	15	15	15	15	9	26	26															
24 P. Ghinzani	24	24	2	5	5	5	5	5	5	5	5	5	5	9	9	9	9	9	9	9	26																
24 M. Winkelhock	14	2	22	9	9	9	9	9	9	9	9	9	9	9	22	22	22	22	22	22	22																
2 T. Fabi	2	5	5	24	26	26	26	26	26	26	26	26	26	26	26	26	26	26	26	26																	
5 J. Laffite	5	22	9	26																																	
22 R. Patrese	22	9	28																																		
9 P. Alliot	9	10	26																																		
10 J. Palmer	10	26																																			
26 A. De Cesaris	26																																				

38	39	40	41	42	43	44	45	46	47	48	49	50	51	52	53	54	55	56	57	58	59	60	61	62	63
1	1	1	1	1	1	1	1	1	1	1	1	1	1	1	1	1	1	1	1	1	1	1	1	1	1
27	27	27	27	27	27	27	27	27	27	27	27	11	11	11	11	11	11	3	3	3	3	3	3	3	3
11	11	11	11	11	11	11	11	11	11	11	11	3	3	3	3	3	11	11	11	11	11	11	11	11	11
6	6	6	6	6	6	6	3	3	3	3	3	2	2	2	2	2	2	2	2	2	2	2	2	2	2
16	16	16	3	3	3	3	6	6	6	6	2	7	7	7	7	7	7	7	7	7	7	7	7	7	7
3	3	3	7	2	2	2	2	2	2	2	7	7	5	5	5	5	5	5	5	5	5	5	5	5	5
7	7	7	2	7	7	7	5	5	5	5	5	5														
2	2	2	5	5	7	7	7	7	7																
5	5	5																							

LAS GRAN
ULY 6-8, 1984
ON CHA
GOODYEAR
1984 WINNER
Marlboro
Marlboro
Marlboro
NORMA
RECORD
RECORD

United States Grand Prix Dallas

About one hour before the scheduled starting time on race morning, the drivers were expressing concern over the quality of the track. As temperatures began to nudge a hundred degrees, occupants of the $25,000 suites were more concerned about the quality of the wine to accompany lunch. And Bernard Ecclestone was growing restive over what would become the final arbiter in the face of a threatened boycott; the intractable television schedule.

That said all you needed to know about the inaugural Dallas Grand Prix.

Doubtless the oil barons' wine could have been chilled a few degrees more but, at the end of the day, the VIPs and Bernard Ecclestone had their race. And, confounding all logic and a track surface which simply fell apart, the drivers produced an enthralling contest even though their initial fears had been proved correct.

The race ran for two hours. Concentration, lightning reflexes, stamina and fine judgement were paramount; the quality of the chassis counting for little. The conditions, then, were perfect for Keke Rosberg.

The Williams-Honda had been in contention throughout as four or five cars fought for the lead. By the end of the race, three of them, Alain Prost, Niki Lauda and Derek Warwick, were parked against the wall. A fourth, Nigel Mansell, had led from pole and resisted constant attacks for half of the race. After a pit stop for tyres, Mansell was eventually classified sixth as he lay on the track in a state of exhaustion after a fruitless attempt at pushing his broken car across the line.

In addition to Rosberg's classic performance, the crowd was treated to an electrifying drive from René Arnoux as the Ferrari driver stormed through to second place after starting from the back of the field. Elio de Angelis, always in contention, collected another four points for Lotus while Osella were delighted to simply open their championship score when Piercarlo Ghinzani finished fifth.

Jacques Laffite took fourth place. He had started from the back row of the grid and earned his points with a drive in keeping with his vast experience. Rosberg had earned his points with a performance which was in keeping with the television-nurtured romantic image of Dallas. He had been kept cool thanks to a skullcap through which chilled liquid circulated. The cap cost $2,500; a mere bagatelle when you consider the oil barons had parted with ten times that amount to handle their particular brand of chilled liquid and watch Rosberg at work.

ENTRY AND PRACTICE

When representatives of the Dallas Grand Prix organisation exuded pure American enthusiasm and optimism at a London press conference in January, there was the feeling that the good folks from Texas didn't really know what was about to hit them when the Formula 1 circus rolled into town.

That feeling persisted when, on the first day of unofficial practice on Thursday, the Fair Park circuit was cloaked in silence at a time when the towering facade of the Cotton Bowl should have been reverberating to the sound of engines. Someone, somewhere, was having a disagreement.

On this occasion, however, it was the organisers who were raising the objections. Flushed with that same enthusiasm, now tinged with a little power, the good folks of Texas wanted to control every aspect of pass distribution. The smoothly-run FOCA system of credentials for the teams was not acceptable. Bernard Ecclestone and the wife of organiser, Don Walker, had words. Lawyers were consulted. Bernie got his way. Unofficial practice started as soon as a minor problem with circuit security had been sorted out.

Meanwhile, there was trouble of a more serious

Keke Rosberg, a member of the ICI Record Sport Fibres team, turned the fortunes of the Williams team around by securing a superb win in the inaugural Dallas Grand Prix. Linda Gray (Sue-Ellen in television's 'Dallas') approves of Keke's style both on and off the track.
Photo: John Townsend

nature brewing. As each driver completed his initial inspection of the track, there would be a shaking of the head and mumbling about too many bumps, insufficient run-off areas, concrete walls which masked potential hazards. For sure, the circuit was fast and infinitely more interesting than the ninety-degree stop-and-go corners at Detroit but there was genuine concern over the clearing of wreckage after the seemingly inevitable brushes with the concrete.

The 60 minutes of practice did little to change the drivers' minds. A press conference afterwards was filled with gloom and despondency. While the complaints may have been genuine, the generally lethargic and brutish way in which the drivers presented themselves did not sit well with the locals. One newspaper summed up the scene succinctly – their reporter observed: 'It's not just the engines which whine in Grand Prix racing.'

But, the schedules were set. Official practice would start the next day as planned and, of course, the drivers to a man said the track was bound to be quicker with the addition of more rubber to the racing line. Sure enough, Derek Warwick's best time from the exploratory hour on Thursday was improved upon by Niki Lauda during the untimed session on Friday morning.

Lauda's time of 1m 36.317s was almost two seconds quicker than Warwick's efforts the previous day – and that was to stand as the fastest time of the entire weekend. Yes, the track was offering more grip but, by the time the final hour got under way, the track temperatures were measuring 150 degrees and the surface was beginning to break up. Things would only get worse.

Thus, with a time of 1m 37.041s on Friday afternoon, Nigel Mansell would establish pole position. The circuit would be at least one second slower on Saturday and the conditions were such that neither Mansell nor his team-mate, Elio de Angelis – second fastest on Friday – would bother to go out. A black and gold front row – the first since 1978 – was secure.

Mansell had been superb during practice, the Englishman attacking the circuit with all his customary enthusiasm and deftness. A more heavy-handed approach by Elio de Angelis not only underlined the Italian driver's dislike of the place but also kept the Lotus mechanics busy with suspension rebuilds on both days. Elio was also involved in his fair share of drama out of the cockpit as he made his feelings known on the subject of Mansell's performance in Detroit. Nigel clearly did not approve of his so-called team-mate's tactless behaviour any more than de Angelis favoured the Englishman's driving. The atmosphere was strained to say the least.

There were worried expressions within the ranks of the tyre companies. Without the benefit of testing, Michelin, Goodyear and Pirelli had produced tyres based on nothing more than guesswork and, without exception, they guessed wrong. As the surface changed continually, the balance swung wildly from one company to another during the course of a day's practice. On Friday morning, Michelin appeared to have the upper hand. By the end of the timed session, Goodyear filled the first three places. And, to complicate matters further, qualifying tyres were not capable of lasting longer than three or four

The absurd scene on the race track hours before the start. The Dallas organisers found there is more to staging a Grand Prix than erecting concrete walls and miles of fencing *(right)*.
Sporting improvised personal cooling to counteract the searing heat, Elio de Angelis raced into the points once more and took third place *(below)*.

corners of a fast lap.

Derek Warwick was disappointed to be in sixth place on Friday afternoon but the Renault driver, fastest on Saturday morning, felt there was room for improvement during the final session. Taking to the track as soon as the green flag was waved, Warwick reeled off a handful of laps, his fifth flying lap being 1.5 seconds faster than anyone else would record and good enough to elevate him to third place on the grid.

It was a brilliantly sharp lap by any standards and underlined the difference between Warwick and his team-mate as Patrick Tambay struggled to find top form after a lay-off in Hawaii to recuperate. His leg was not causing any trouble, not even during the merciless bumping and bucking dealt out by the track, but Tambay felt he could have improved on 10th place had he, say, been able to follow Warwick's example and complete a test session at Ricard inbetween races.

Renault were running a revised engine featuring different rocker arms and pistons and modified injection settings. Ferrari, meanwhile, were continuing to experiment with different injection and exhaust systems although, judging by the appalling handling of the 126C4 on the bumps, Mauro Forghieri would have been advised to concentrate on the chassis rather than the engine. It says much for René Arnoux's bravery that he qualified in fourth place, a full second faster than Michele Alboreto in ninth place.

Arnoux was not slow in condemning the circuit. He felt such tracks had no place in Grand Prix racing, a view shared by Alain Prost whose orderly way of doing things was upset by the completely unpredictable track conditions. And, if you needed an indication of just how difficult it was to master Fair Park, the sight of Niki Lauda walking back to the pits – twice – after hitting the wall, said it all. Lauda damaged the suspension on both his race car and the spare chassis, the second accident taking place at the fast right-hander after the pits; perhaps the most difficult corner on the track. For all that, the Austrian qualified in fifth place, half a second faster than Prost. That, in terms of the championship battle within the team, was more important than anything else although, to be fair, Prost suffered a deflating tyre during his first run on Friday and was later delayed by yellow flags.

Ayrton Senna was delayed by a problem of his own making on Friday. Forgetting to secure his helmet strap, the Brazilian was alarmed to find the helmet slip over his eyes as he braked heavily for the first corner. No harm was done and Ayrton went on to take an excellent sixth place. The question, however, was one of stamina. Each time Senna completed a run of ten laps or so, he climbed out of the car and required reviving with ice cubes and cold compresses. Lasting the race distance was clearly going to be a problem. Ensuring the Toleman suspension would stand the strain following the failure in Detroit, Rory Byrne had strengthened the wishbones and the team intended to race Brian Hart's experimental injection system after the electronic equipment had raced no more than a hundred yards in Detroit before Piquet's flying wheel interrupted progress. Johnny Cecotto was consigned to the spare car for the race after he

had caused irreparable damage to his race car when he hit the wall on Saturday morning. His Friday time was good enough for 15th place.

In the seemingly never-ending search for decent handling, the Williams team tried using FW07 uprights on the Honda-powered FW09. Rosberg said there was little improvement. But a small detail like that was hardly likely to stop the Finn from carrying the car into eighth place. Keke was second fastest on Saturday afternoon – but, at a price. He hit the wall and damaged his intended race car beyond immediate repair. Jacques Laffite, less keen to extend himself to the limit for a place in the middle of the grid, took a disappointing 25th. Still, the race would go to the man who had the stamina and good sense to keep his car in one piece. A finish would almost certainly be rewarded by championship points – even if you started from the back of the grid.

None the less, a place on the sixth row was not exactly what Nelson Piquet had in mind when it came to continuing his recent run of success. The Brabhams appeared with larger oil coolers in the nose but, by Saturday, the team had reverted to the

JULY:
Ferrari announce no change in driving team for 1985.

Watkins Glen reopened.

smaller and neater rads with an additional cooler mounted in the left-hand side pod. Apparently the additional weight at the front induced understeer. Also, the ugly appearance induced a less than favourable response from the immaculate Mr. Ecclestone. To add to their problems, Piquet crashed both his race and spare cars on Saturday and his poor starting position was underlined by an aggressive performance from Corrado Fabi, the young Italian qualifying half a second faster than the World Champion.

The ATS team, still running just one chassis, took a look at the concrete walls and hoped that Manfred Winkelhock's enthusiasm would not get the better of him. In the event, Manfred had one or two hairy moments but came away with 13th place

René Arnoux staged a magnificent comeback after starting from the back of the grid. The Ferrari driver, denied his place on the second row when the engine refused to fire for the parade lap, claimed second place with a car which handled badly on the bumpy circuit.

KEKE Rosberg may have won the race in superb style but, in the final analysis, the first Grand Prix of Dallas was dominated by the power of the dollar.

From the moment the temporary track surface began to break up during practice, the race had been in jeopardy and the sight of construction workers laying fresh concrete one hour before the scheduled starting time appeared to signal the end of another American dream.

The drivers requested 10 reconnaissance laps before the start in order to gauge the strength of the repairs but the request was turned down. Television schedules had to be kept and, appropriately enough, it was Larry Hagman (J. R. Ewing of television's 'Dallas') who mounted the rostrum in his lemon outfit and matching stetson to wave the cars off on their final parade lap. The Grand Prix started eleven minutes later than advertised.

It ended after two hours of racing which held the attention throughout of an estimated 90,000 spectators. The organisers claimed the inaugural Dallas Grand Prix had been a success. Based on the attendance figures and the relieved television executives, they were right. Based on the comments of drivers and those working in temperatures of a hundred degrees, the race bordered on a fiasco. And the irony is that FOCA and FISA had nobody to blame but themselves.

Dallas had merely asked to hold a Grand Prix. FISA had granted approval in 1983 even though the organisers would not have held a race of any description before the Grand Prix on the proposed track. (A CanAm race the day before was hardly the answer.) With the best will in the world, the promoters were bound to fall short of the required standard but, from FOCA's point of view, the financial package was right and that, in the light of the stumbling organisation, was all that appeared to matter.

There was a time when such inadequacies might have been avoided with the help of a rule which required the organisers at a new Grand Prix venue to hold an international event prior to the proposed Formula 1 race. That rule, of course, was quietly forgotten with the advent of the temporary track in the high-dollar climate of Las Vegas but the folly of such expediency was demonstrated all too clearly in Dallas in 1984.

The fact that there were no serious accidents was a tribute to the skills of Grand Prix drivers who got on with their jobs in a professional manner. In places, the track surface resembled a loose gravel road which was to cause havoc during a saloon car race for celebrities. It lasted a mere five laps but Steve Kanaly and Patrick Duffy (stars of 'Dallas') crashed into the walls within minutes. It was an appropriate end to a weekend which, paradoxically, had provided one of the best Grands Prix of the season under circumstances which would not have been out of place in a television script.

Against all predictions, the Dallas Grand Prix turned out to be a superb race. Nigel Mansell earned his first pole position and kept his place at the head of the queue in the early stages.
Photo: John Colley

and a car which remained intact. Eddie Cheever, next up in the Alfa Romeo, remained confident for the race since, for once, the relatively short mileage meant there would not be a fuel consumption problem for the V8. Cheever had his turn at brushing the wall and a broken engine on Saturday meant using the spare chassis in the afternoon.

Ligier were in a similar situation to ATS following the escapades of Andrea de Cesaris in Detroit. In an appropriately circumspect couple of days, Andrea did little other than damage a steering rack and it was left to François Hesnault to modify the suspension and bodywork of his JS23 against the scenery. Splitting the two Ligiers were Stefan Bellof and Piercarlo Ghinzani. Bellof had a new chassis at his disposal following his exuberant performances in Detroit and the team briefly tried a long Renault-type underbody fairing at the rear of the car.

Eighteenth place for Ghinzani was highly commendable, the Italian outqualifying Thierry Boutsen and Marc Surer, both Arrows drivers now enjoying BMW power. Indeed, there were no Cosworth cars left after the ravages of the previous race and it was clear that Dave Wass had yet to sort out the handling of the A7 despite the presence of spacers between engine and gearbox. In addition, both drivers were plagued by irritants such as misfire, broken turbos and locking brakes.

Spirit were back to two Hart-engined cars, Huub Rothengatter's impressive efforts gaining 23rd place and a brush with the wall on both days of practice. Philippe Alliot made contact with the concrete on a more permanent basis, the Frenchman damaging the RAM's revised suspension to such an extent on Friday that the bulkhead was seriously weakened. And this after the team had been flat-out rebuilding both cars after Detroit. But at least Jonathan Palmer returned each day with his car in one piece although he was troubled by an electrical fault in the final session. That didn't prevent him from qualifying, however, since Alliot was forced to withdraw and Martin Brundle finished Friday's practice in hospital.

The Tyrrell driver, boosted by his splendid success in Detroit, vowed to take it easy in Dallas. He had proved he could cope with street circuits and the plan was to play himself in gently on another circuit which would suit the agile Tyrrell-Cosworth. On his first flying lap on Friday afternoon, the Tyrrell suddenly twitched, as if the car had a puncture, and hit the wall. That, in turn, threw the Tyrrell across the track into the opposite wall and it was here that the damage was done. Compared to the Monaco shunt, this appeared to be a minor incident. But the front of the chassis was written off; Brundle sustaining injuries to both feet. He would be out of action for some time.

Few people registered surprise at the news. This was not a reflection on Brundle's driving, merely a comment on the perils of American temporary circuits. The surprise was that there had not been an accident of a more serious nature.

RACE

Jacques Laffite arrived for the race morning warm-up at seven o'clock dressed in pyjamas. It was the effervescent Frenchman's way of poking fun at the television schedules which dictated an eleven o'clock start for the race. It was also one of the few light-hearted moments in a morning which almost saw the race cancelled altogether.

A 50-lap CanAm race the previous day had caused havoc with the track surface. Undeterred, the organisers had carried out overnight repairs and, had the quick-setting concrete lived up to its name, we might have been spared the sight of contractors digging holes and laying cement 90 minutes before the race was due to start!

The warm-up had been postponed for two hours and then cancelled altogether. A few drivers returned to their hotels to watch the Wimbledon finals on television while those remaining at the circuit became increasingly dubious about the chances of running a race. There was talk of postponing the Grand Prix until Monday, stopping the race early, shortening the distance.

Niki Lauda completed a tour of inspection with Derek Ongaro and then reported to Race Control. Lauda wanted ten exploratory laps before making a decision. With eleven o'clock looming, that piece of news was not well-received by Bernie Ecclestone. No, the final arrangement would be three warm-up laps followed immediately by the count-down to the start. The race distance had already been reduced to 67 laps; hardly a major concession since it had been clear from the outset that the original distance of 78 laps would exceed the statutory two-hour limit. Besides, there was the unspoken feeling that the race would be stopped once the track began to break up – a situation so inevitable that one or two drivers did not bother to arrange their supply of on-board refreshments.

The warm-up was duly completed although three laps were barely sufficient to allow drivers to complete their usual tasks such as bedding-in brakes and selecting tyres. Once the green light came on, however, any talk of boycotts or protests was forgotten immediately as the field squirmed off the grid and rushed towards the blind approach to the first corner.

Mansell kept his advantage and took the line, followed by de Angelis and the Renault of Warwick. Before the start, Warwick had quietly expressed concern over the behaviour of Arnoux as the two cars left the second row of the grid. Any such problems were cancelled out when Arnoux, unable to start his engine promptly for the final parade lap, had been forced to catch the field and take a place at the back of the grid. By the exit of the first turn, he had passed three cars. There was more of the same to follow . . .

At the end of the first lap, Mansell had opened a small gap over de Angelis, with Warwick third, followed by Senna. It was an excellent opportunity for the Brazilian to make something of the handling of his car but he threw it all away by touching a wall and spinning. Senna crept into the pits where all four tyres were changed but, not long after, he made the same mistake at the same corner and dropped out of contention completely.

Any hopes de Angelis may have had of keeping pace with his team-mate were spoiled by an engine which appeared to be running on just five cylindsers and the Italian soon came under

pressure from Warwick, the Renault taking second place on lap four. The Englishman soon devoured the four second gap to Mansell and we had the prospect of a battle for the lead between two tough men anxious to prove a point about who was the leading British driver in Formula 1. It was Warwick who lost – in the biggest possible way.

Accelerating alongside Mansell at the exit of a tight left-hander, Warwick arrived at the braking area for the next corner to find that his pads, not properly bedded in, were pulling the car to the left. It was enough to put the Renault on the marbles and Warwick was helpless as he spun gently into the tyre barrier.

He was not the only driver to be approaching the pits on foot. Out already were Hesnault, after a first lap skirmish with Ghinzani, Cheever and Bellof, after separate meetings with the concrete walls on lap nine. Patrese would be next, followed by de Cesaris while Rothengatter, having avoided the walls, would make a speedy exit after his Spirit had stopped, most of the car's fuel finding its way into the cockpit rather than the engine. The Dutchman, his backside burning, was quickly in search of water, not necessarily to drink.

With Warwick out of the way, Lauda briefly inherited second place from de Angelis but the Italian, his engine running smoothly now, snatched the place back and soon caught up with Mansell. It became clear that de Angelis would like to lead but Mansell, perhaps remembering Montreal when the roles were reversed, proved difficult to overtake. This battle became a threesome when Rosberg, having passed Lauda, joined in and watched Lotus team spirit at work.

On lap 19, de Angelis tried a particularly desperate move which Mansell subsequently blocked and the upshot was second place for Rosberg while a furious de Angelis tried to compose himself in third spot. Mansell increased his pace, taking Rosberg with him, but increasing turbo temperatures told Rosberg it would be wise to drop back from the hot slipstream of the Lotus. A few laps later, however, and Rosberg was back on the attack, climbing all over the Lotus as

Mansell seemed to spend as much time looking in his mirrors as he did at the track. Lap 27, and a mistake by Mansell cost him three seconds and allowed not only Rosberg but also de Angelis and the McLaren of Prost to form a high-powered train. And not far behind them hovered the menacing Niki Lauda. Piquet, his helmet covered in silver foil, the better to deflect the angry rays of the sun, held sixth place although the Brabham was being caught rapidly by the remarkable Arnoux. Gone were Tambay, his right-rear wheel torn off as he tried to get on terms with Lauda, and Cecotto, the Toleman having brushed the wall.

As Rosberg tried everything he knew to get ahead of the wide Lotus, Prost slipped past de Angelis and, after one hour of racing, the McLaren was second. With the race likely to be stopped at any moment, it seemed the canny Frenchman was pacing himself beautifully. Then, on lap 35, he ran wide and Rosberg was second again!

Now Keke made a determined assault on Mansell and, as the Lotus driver brushed the wall, the Williams was alongside and into the lead. Almost immediately, Mansell responded, an attempt to regain the initiative being heavily blocked by a fist-shaking Rosberg. Now Keke put the hammer down and opened a five second lead in three laps. Mansell, his front tyres having lost their grip, appeared to lose heart as well and he fell to the back of the leading group before calling at his pit for fresh rubber on lap 39.

A few laps earlier, Piercarlo Ghinzani had lost an excellent ninth place (behind Laffite and Arnoux) when wheel vibrations (caused by the first lap incident with Hesnault) sent the exhausted Italian into the pits. The wheel change was not the slickest but the respite gave the team time to pour water over his dazed driver. Suitably revived, Piercarlo set off in 12th place.

Mansell rejoined in seventh place which would soon become sixth when Piquet, fighting all the way with a sticking throttle, was finally caught out and crashed into a tyre barrier. At the same time, Jonathan Palmer disappeared although not for what had become the customary retirement

reason. The Englishman's car was actually in one piece, the problem, apart from no second gear, being a loose wire to the spark box.

At the front of the field, Rosberg continued to lead but Prost was soon working his way through the gap of 4.8 seconds. By lap 47, he had caught the Williams. By lap 49, he was in the lead. Lauda was third but the Austrian was more concerned about Arnoux as the Ferrari caught the McLaren with no trouble at all. Nothing would stop Arnoux today and he continued to drive on the very limit as he streaked past Lauda on lap 51.

There was a 10 second gap to Rosberg and the pattern of the race seemed set; Prost was ready to take a beautifully judged nine points. Then the Frenchman made a mistake.

Clipping a wall with his right-front tyre, Prost crawled to a halt with a puncture at the same corner where the Arrows drivers had already parked their cars with various degrees of suspension damage. And soon they would be joined by Lauda, the Austrian clipping his right-rear wheel at a corner where the cars gingerly followed a narrow line marked by gravel and general debris.

Arnoux made one last attempt to catch Rosberg but the Williams driver was not about to be denied a superb win on a track which, if it had been in prime condition, would not have suited his car.

Accepting the congratulations of Dallas's 'Sue Ellen', Rosberg then proceeded to lambast Mansell over the public address system. It was an unfortunate way to end the race – not that Mansell cared since he was, by now, being carried off to the medical centre. A final touch against a wall somewhere had proved too much for his gearbox and the Englishman, gallant to the last, had tried to push his car to the line. It was a futile move which ended when Mansell, supposedly one of the toughest men in motor racing, collapsed dramatically by the side of his car.

The crowd loved it. As far as they were concerned, the race had been a success, packed with drama from start to finish. Doubtless another bottle of chilled white was cracked open in the suite above the pits.

MH

163

Entries and practice times

No.	Driver	Nat	Car	Tyre	Engine	Entrant	Practice 1	Practice 2
1	Nelson Piquet	BR	Parmalat BRABHAM BT53	M	BMW M12/13	MRD International	1m 39·439s	1m 39·630s
2	Corrado Fabi	I	Parmalat BRABHAM BT53	M	BMW M12/13	MRD International	1m 38·960s	1m 41·097s
3	Martin Brundle	GB	TYRRELL 012	G	Ford Cosworth DFY	Tyrrell Racing Organisation	2m 31·960s	1m 41·680s
4	Stefan Bellof	D	TYRRELL 012	G	Ford Cosworth DFY	Tyrrell Racing Organisation	1m 40·336s	1m 46·257s
5	Jacques Laffite	F	WILLIAMS FW09	G	Honda RA 163–E	Williams Grand Prix Engineering	1m 43·304s	1m 39·438s
6	Keke Rosberg	SF	WILLIAMS FW09	G	Honda RA 163–E	Williams Grand Prix Engineering	1m 38·767s	1m 41·344s
7	Alain Prost	F	Marlboro McLAREN MP4/2	M	TAG P01 (TTE P01)	Marlboro McLaren International	1m 38·544s	1m 41·835s
8	Niki Lauda	A	Marlboro McLAREN MP4/2	M	TAG P01 (TTE P01)	Marlboro McLaren International	1m 37·987s	—
9	Philippe Alliot	F	RAM 02	P	Hart 415T	Skoal Bandit Formula 1 Team	1m 43·222s	—
10	Jonathan Palmer	GB	RAM 02	P	Hart 415T	Skoal Bandit Formula 1 Team	1m 44·676s	1m 47·566s
11	Elio de Angelis	I	John Player Special LOTUS 95T	G	Renault EF4	John Player Team Lotus	1m 37·635s	—
12	Nigel Mansell	GB	John Player Special LOTUS 95T	G	Renault EF4	John Player Team Lotus	1m 37·041s	—
14	Manfred Winkelhock	D	ATS D7	P	BMW M12/13	Team ATS	1m 39·860s	1m 40·289s
15	Patrick Tambay	F	Elf RENAULT RE50	M	Renault EF4	Equipe Renault Elf	1m 38·907s	1m 40·790s
16	Derek Warwick	GB	Elf RENAULT RE50	M	Renault EF4	Equipe Renault Elf	1m 38·285s	1m 37·708s
17	Marc Surer	CH	ARROWS A7	G	BMW M12/13	Barclay Nordica Arrows BMW	1m 44·503s	1m 42·592s
18	Thierry Boutsen	B	ARROWS A7	G	BMW M12/13	Barclay Nordica Arrows BMW	1m 41·840s	1m 41·318s
19	Ayrton Senna	BR	TOLEMAN TG184	M	Hart 415T	Toleman Group Motorsport	1m 38·256s	—
20	Johnny Cecotto	YV	TOLEMAN TG184	M	Hart 415T	Toleman Group Motorsport	1m 40·027s	—
21	Huub Rothengatter	NL	SPIRIT 101	P	Hart 415T	Spirit Racing	1m 43·084s	1m 43·735s
22	Riccardo Patrese	I	Benetton ALFA ROMEO 184T	G	Alfa Romeo 183T	Benetton Team Alfa Romeo	1m 41·328s	1m 50·277s
23	Eddie Cheever	USA	Benetton ALFA ROMEO 184T	G	Alfa Romeo 183T	Benetton Team Alfa Romeo	1m 39·911s	1m 40·773s
24	Piercarlo Ghinzani	I	Kelemata OSELLA FA1F	P	Alfa Romeo 183T	Osella Squadra Corse	1m 41·176s	1m 42·439s
25	François Hesnault	F	LIGIER Loto JS23	M	Renault EF4	Ligier Loto	1m 41·303s	—
26	Andrea de Cesaris	I	LIGIER Loto JS23	M	Renault EF4	Ligier Loto	1m 40·095s	1m 41·464s
27	Michele Alboreto	I	Fiat FERRARI 126C4	G	Ferrari 126C	Scuderia Ferrari SpA	1m 38·793s	1m 42·005s
28	René Arnoux	F	Fiat FERRARI 126C4	G	Ferrari 126C	Scuderia Ferrari SpA	1m 37·785s	1m 39·633s

Friday morning and Saturday morning practice sessions not officially recorded.

G – Goodyear, M – Michelin, P – Pirelli.

Fri pm	Sat pm
Hot, dry	Hot, dry

Starting grid

	12 MANSELL (1m 37·041s) Lotus
11 DE ANGELIS (1m 37·635s) Lotus	
	16 WARWICK (1m 37·708s) Renault
*28 ARNOUX (1m 37·785s) Ferrari	
	8 LAUDA (1m 37·987s) McLaren
19 SENNA (1m 38·256s) Toleman	
	7 PROST (1m 38·544s) McLaren
6 ROSBERG (1m 38·767s) Williams	
	27 ALBORETO (1m 38·793s) Ferrari
15 TAMBAY (1m 38·907s) Renault	
	2 FABI (1m 38·960s) Brabham
1 PIQUET (1m 39·439s) Brabham	
	14 WINKELHOCK (1m 39·860s) ATS
23 CHEEVER (1m 39·911s) Alfa Romeo	
	20 CECOTTO (1m 40·027s) Toleman
26 DE CESARIS (1m 40·095s) Ligier	
	4 BELLOF (1m 40·336s) Tyrrell
24 GHINZANI (1m 41·176s) Osella	
	25 HESNAULT (1m 41·303s) Ligier
18 BOUTSEN (1m 41·318s) Arrows	
	22 PATRESE (1m 41·328s) Alfa Romeo
17 SURER (1m 42·592s) Arrows	
	21 ROTHENGATTER (1m 43·084s) Spirit
9 ALLIOT (1m 43·222s) RAM	
	5 LAFFITE (1m 43·304s) Williams
10 PALMER (1m 44·676s) RAM	

*Started from back of grid; engine refused to start immediately for final parade lap.

Did not start:
9 Alliot (RAM). Qualified, but car damaged beyond immediate repair during practice on Saturday.
3 Brundle (Tyrrell), 2m 31·960s, did not qualify; driver injured during practice

Results and retirements

Place	Driver	Car	Laps	Time and Speed (mph/km/h)/Retirement	
1	Keke Rosberg	Williams-Honda t/c V6	67	2h 01m 22·617s	80·283/129·203
2	René Arnoux	Ferrari t/c V6	67	2h 01m 45·081s	80·0/128·747
3	Elio de Angelis	Lotus-Renault t/c V6	66		
4	Jacques Laffite	Williams-Honda t/c V6	65		
5	Piercarlo Ghinzani	Osella-Alfa Romeo t/c V8	65		
6	Nigel Mansell	Lotus-Renault t/c V6	64	Gearbox (but classified)	
7	Corrado Fabi	Brabham-BMW t/c 4	64		
8	Manfred Winkelhock	ATS-BMW t/c 4	64		
	Niki Lauda	McLaren-TAG t/c V6	60	Hit wall	
	Alain Prost	McLaren-TAG t/c V6	56	Hit wall	
	Thierry Boutsen	Arrows-BMW t/c 4	55	Hit wall	
	Michele Alboreto	Ferrari t/c V6	54	Hit wall	
	Marc Surer	Arrows-BMW t/c 4	54	Hit wall	
	Ayrton Senna	Toleman-Hart t/c 4	47	Driveshaft	
	Jonathan Palmer	RAM-Hart t/c 4	46	Electrics	
	Nelson Piquet	Brabham-BMW t/c 4	45	Jammed throttle/hit wall	
	Patrick Tambay	Renault t/c V6	25	Hit wall	
	Johnny Cecotto	Toleman-Hart t/c 4	25	Hit wall	
	Andrea de Cesaris	Ligier-Renault t/c V6	15	Hit wall	
	Huub Rothengatter	Spirit-Hart t/c 4	15	Fuel leak in cockpit	
	Riccardo Patrese	Alfa Romeo t/c V8	12	Hit wall	
	Derek Warwick	Renault t/c V6	10	Spun off	
	Stefan Bellof	Tyrrell-Cosworth V8	9	Hit wall	
	Eddie Cheever	Alfa Romeo t/c V8	8	Hit wall	
	François Hesnault	Ligier-Renault t/c V6	0	Hit wall	

Fastest lap: Lauda, on lap 22, 1m 45·353s, 82·830mph/133·302km/h.
Lap record: Michael Roe (CanAm 5.0 VDS 002-Chevrolet V8), 1m 45·165s, 82·978mph/133·540km/h (1984).

Past winners

Year	Driver	Nat	Car	Circuit	Distance miles/km	Speed mph/km/h
1984	Keke Rosberg	SF	1·5 Williams FW09-Honda t/c	Fair Park	162·41/261·37	80·28/129·20

Circuit data

Fair Park Grand Prix Circuit, Dallas, Texas
Circuit length: 2·424 miles/3·901 km
Race distance: 67 laps, 162·408 miles/261·370 km
Race weather: Very hot, dry

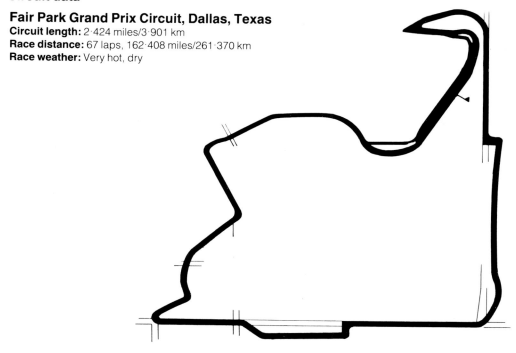

Fastest laps

Driver	Time	Lap
Niki Lauda	1m 45·353s	22
René Arnoux	1m 45·545s	38
Nigel Mansell	1m 45·593s	9
Derek Warwick	1m 45·648s	8
Alain Prost	1m 45·976s	23
Elio de Angelis	1m 46·042s	26
Keke Rosberg	1m 46·104s	9
Patrick Tambay	1m 46·373s	16
Ayrton Senna	1m 46·419s	39
Nelson Piquet	1m 46·502s	37
Michele Alboreto	1m 46·716s	34
Andrea de Cesaris	1m 47·341s	8
Johnny Cecotto	1m 47·827s	24
Thierry Boutsen	1m 48·229s	13
Corrado Fabi	1m 48·361s	10
Jacques Laffite	1m 48·532s	34
Piercarlo Ghinzani	1m 48·604s	22
Eddie Cheever	1m 49·010s	8
Stefan Bellof	1m 49·204s	7
Riccardo Patrese	1m 50·274s	8
Marc Surer	1m 50·374s	7
Manfred Winkelhock	1m 50·549s	32
Huub Rothengatter	1m 51·347s	9
Jonathan Palmer	1m 52·958s	7

Points

WORLD CHAMPIONSHIP OF DRIVERS

1	Alain Prost	34·5 pts
2	Niki Lauda	24
3	Elio de Angelis	23·5
4	René Arnoux	22·5
5	Keke Rosberg	20
6	Nelson Piquet	18
7	Derek Warwick	13
8	Michele Alboreto	9
9	Martin Brundle	8
10	Patrick Tambay	7
11	Nigel Mansell	6
12	Stefan Bellof	5
13=	Ayrton Senna	4
13=	Jacques Laffite	4
15=	Eddie Cheever	3
15=	Riccardo Patrese	3
15=	Teo Fabi	3
18=	Andrea de Cesaris	2
18=	Piercarlo Ghinzani	2
20	Thierry Boutsen	1

CONSTRUCTORS' CUP

1	McLaren	58·5 pts
2	Ferrari	31·5
3	Lotus	29·5
4	Williams	24
5	Brabham	21
6	Renault	20
7	Tyrrell	13
8	Alfa Romeo	6
9	Toleman	4
10=	Ligier	2
10=	Osella	2
12	Arrows	1

Lap chart

1st LAP ORDER	1	2	3	4	5	6	7	8	9	10	11	12	13	14	15	16	17	18	19	20	21	22	23	24	25	26	27	28	29	30	31	32	33	34	35	36	37
12 N. Mansell	12	12	12	12	12	12	12	12	12	12	12	12	12	12	12	12	12	12	12	12	12	12	12	12	12	12	12	12	12	12	12	12	12	12	12	6	6
11 E. De Angelis	11	11	11	16	16	16	16	16	16	16	16	8	11	11	11	11	11	11	11	6	6	6	6	6	6	6	6	6	6	6	6	6	6	7	7	6	7
16 D. Warwick	16	16	16	11	11	11	8	8	8	8	11	8	8	6	6	6	6	6	11	11	11	11	11	11	11	11	11	11	11	7	7	7	6	6	7	7	11
19 A. Senna	19	8	8	8	8	8	11	11	11	11	11	6	6	6	8	8	8	7	7	7	7	7	7	7	7	7	7	7	7	11	11	11	11	11	11	11	8
8 N. Lauda	8	6	6	6	6	6	6	6	6	6	7	7	7	7	7	7	8	8	8	8	8	8	8	8	8	8	8	8	8	8	8	8	8	8	8	8	12
6 K. Rosberg	6	7	7	7	7	7	7	7	7	7	15	15	15	15	15	15	15	15	15	15	15	15	15	15	1	1	1	1	1	1	1	1	1	1	1	1	1
7 A. Prost	7	27	27	27	15	15	15	15	15	15	1	1	1	1	1	1	1	1	1	1	1	1	1	1	28	28	28	28	28	28	28	28	28	28	28	28	28
27 M. Alboreto	27	15	15	15	27	27	1	1	1	1	26	26	26	26	26	28	28	28	28	28	28	28	28	28	5	5	5	5	5	5	5	5	5	5	5	5	5
15 P. Tambay	15	1	1	1	1	1	27	26	26	26	27	27	27	27	28	27	27	2	2	27	24	24	24	24	24	24	24	24	24	18	18	18	18	27	27	27	27
23 E. Cheever	23	23	23	26	26	26	26	27	27	27	2	2	2	27	27	27	24	5	5	5	5	5	5	18	18	18	18	24	2	27	18	18	18	18	18	18	18
1 N. Piquet	1	26	26	23	23	23	23	23	2	28	28	28	28	2	24	24	24	5	18	18	18	18	2	2	2	2	2	27	27	27	27	27	2	2	2	2	2
26 A. De Cesaris	26	2	2	2	2	2	2	4	28	24	24	24	24	24	18	18	18	5	18	27	2	2	2	2	27	27	27	27	27	24	24	24	24	24			
2 T. Fabi	2	4	4	4	4	4	4	28	24	18	18	18	18	18	5	5	5	18	2	2	27	27	27	17	17	17	17	17	17	17	17	17	17	17	17		
4 S. Bellof	4	24	24	24	24	24	24	24	18	5	5	5	5	5	17	17	17	17	17	17	14	14	14	14	14	14	14	14	14	14	14	14	14	14			
24 P. Ghinzani	24	18	18	18	18	18	18	18	18	5	22	22	17	17	17	14	14	14	14	14	20	20	14	10	10	10	10	10	10	10	10	10	10	10	10		
18 T. Boutsen	18	28	28	28	28	28	28	28	5	22	17	17	22	14	14	10	10	10	10	20	20	20	14	14	20	20	19	19	19	19	19	19	19	19	19	19	
22 R. Patrese	22	22	5	5	5	5	5	5	23	17	14	14	14	10	10	20	20	20	20	10	10	10	10	10	10	19											
28 R. Arnoux	28	5	22	22	22	22	22	22	22	14	10	10	10	20	20	19	19	19	19	19	19	19	19	19													
5 J. Laffite	5	17	17	17	17	17	17	17	10	20	20	20	20	21	21																						
17 M. Surer	17	14	14	14	14	14	14	14	14	21	21	21	21	19	19																						
14 M. Winkelhock	14	21	21	21	21	21	21	21	21	20	19	19	19																								
21 H. Rothengatter	21	10	10	10	10	10	10	10	10	19																											
10 J. Palmer	10	19	19	19	19	19	19	19	19																												
20 J. Cecotto	20	20	20	20	20	20	20	20	20																												

38	39	40	41	42	43	44	45	46	47	48	49	50	51	52	53	54	55	56	57	58	59	60	61	62	63	64	65	66	67
6	6	6	6	6	6	6	6	6	6	6	6	7	7	7	7	7	7	7	7	6	6	6	6	6	6	6	6	6	6
7	7	7	7	7	7	7	7	7	7	6	6	6	6	6	6	6	6	6	28	28	28	28	28	28	28	28	28	28	28
11	11	11	11	8	8	8	8	8	8	8	8	28	28	28	28	28	28	8	8	8	8	11	11	11	11	11	11	11	
8	8	8	8	11	11	11	11	28	28	28	28	28	8	8	8	8	8	8	11	11	11	11	5	5	5	5	5		
12	28	28	28	28	28	28	28	11	11	11	11	11	11	11	11	11	11	11	5	5	5	5	12	12	12	12	24		
1	1	1	1	1	1	1	1	12	12	12	27	27	27	27	27	5	5	12	12	12	12	24	24	24	24				
28	12	12	12	12	12	12	12	27	27	27	12	12	12	5	5	12	12	24	24	24	24	2	2	2	2				
5	5	5	5	5	5	5	27	5	5	5	5	5	12	12	12	18	24	2	2	2	2	14	14	14	14				
27	27	27	27	27	27	27	5	18	18	18	18	16	18	18	18	18	2	2	14	14	14	14							
18	18	18	18	18	18	18	18	2	2	2	2	2	2	2	2	24	14												
2	2	2	2	2	2	2	24	24	24	24	24	24	24	14															
24	24	24	24	24	24	24	24	17	17	17	17	17	17	17	17	17													
17	17	17	17	17	17	17	17	19	19	14	14	14	14	14	14														
14	14	14	14	14	14	14	14	14	14	19																			
19	19	19	19	19	19	19	19	10																					
10	10	10	10	10	10	10	10																						

Piercarlo Ghinzani scored his first championship points when he finished fifth. The fact that the Pirelli-shod Osella outlasted all the Michelin runners gives some indication of the curious nature of the race.

165

John Player Special British Grand Prix

Out on their own. Alain Prost and Niki Lauda
dominated the British Grand Prix. The McLaren
drivers abandon their cars on the starting grid after
the race had been stopped prematurely, Lauda
resuming to take his third victory of the season after
Prost had retired with pinion bearing failure.
Photo: Paul Henri Cahier

It was the result Niki Lauda dreamed of, and the one which Alain Prost feared most of all. The Austrian, mentally kicking himself with frustration over what he recognised as a stupid driver error at Dallas, came to Brands Hatch realising that "this could be my last shot for the Championship. I've just got to stop messing around like I was in North America. A win is what I need more than anything or it's probably goodbye to any chances of the title . . ."

One day, mused the pit lane observers, Lauda and Prost are going to start side-by-side on the front row of a Grand Prix starting grid and race between themselves for the entire distance. "Not if I've got anything to do with it," growled Brabham designer Gordon Murray in response. But the McLarens came nearer to that sort of confrontation than they had done at any time during the season so far: predictably, perhaps, Nelson Piquet's super competitive Brabham BT53 qualifying car nosed them out of a 1-2 domination of the front row, and once the John Player Special British Grand Prix got underway, the contest was a three-way fight between the two McLarens and Nelson's lone Brabham-BMW. But if it hadn't been for the race being red flagged after Jonathan Palmer's RAM crashed heavily on the outside of Clearways with 11 laps completed, we might well have seen Lauda and Prost battle it out all the way to the chequered flag.

As it was, we were presented with a second start, a second confrontation between the McLarens and that single Brabham and then Prost's surprise retirement with a gearbox failure. Perhaps if it hadn't been for the strain of that second start, Alain's transmission might not have wilted . . . Perhaps if it hadn't been for Nelson's Brabham losing boost pressure when a turbo vane broke, Lauda would have been pressed into a rare error . . . Perhaps – but then speculation doesn't really matter, does it?. At the end of the afternoon, the 1984 British Grand Prix belonged to one of the crowd's greatest favourites. The man who stumbled into the pits with his Ferrari B3 ten years earlier, a puncture and a blocked pit exit depriving him of his first British Grand Prix triumph, now racked up his third such success in typically meticulous, precise and fluid style. Possibly the best drive of Niki Lauda's McLaren career, it was also arguably the one from which he derived the most pleasure.

What's more, although it may not have been the world's most exciting Grand Prix, as the crowd cheered the first three finishers on the sun-kissed winner's rostrum, they were cheering possibly one of the most representative cross-sections of the Grand Prix community seen this year in the first three places. First; Lauda, the folk hero, the grizzled campaigner . . . Second; Warwick, the bright-eyed Brit whose time had surely arrived . . . Third; Senna, the brilliant new shooting star in the Formula 1 constellation. Look back with pleasure at Brands Hatch, 1984: the race might not have amounted to much, but the outcome certainly rewarded the worthy!

ENTRY AND PRACTICE

After the acrobatics of Detroit and Dallas, most drivers and teams breathed a sigh of relief as the Championship programme pointed everybody back to Europe for a resumption of the points' chase on a series of purpose-built circuits. And, for the drivers, where better could there be than Brands Hatch in the summer sunshine, the neatly manicured greensward on the infield contrasting so dramatically with the cement dust and catch-fencing which had predominated at the Stateside street tracks. After the "point, squirt, brake" syndrome of the confined artificial circuits, we were now back in an open, sweeping environment of fast curves, dramatic dips and plunges – in all, as Niki Lauda described it, "a circuit on which you can really work yourself up into an enjoyable rhythm. Very satisfying indeed and a place round which you need to be tidy and precise in order to gain a few tenths' advantage."

Off-stage, the Tyrrell team's technical dramas with FISA were monopolising attention, but on the track it looked as though we were going to be fed the familiar Brabham-versus-McLaren recipe with Lotus's splendid 95T playing a strong supporting role after Nigel Mansell had been fastest in pre-race tyre testing. Unfortunately the first 90-minute unofficial session was barely seven minutes old before a red flag appeared at the startline and the bubble of tension was prematurely pricked, all the cars on the circuit cruising slowly back into the pit lane.

The unfortunate cause of the interruption turned out to be a terrible accident which had befallen Toleman's Johnny Cecotto. The amiable Venezuelan had visited Brands Hatch in the past during his motorcycle racing days, but this was his first outing at the Kent circuit in a racing car. Running a little too quickly in the opening moments of the session, it seems that he failed to take into account the very dusty condition of the track surface. His team-mate Ayrton Senna later remarked "it was so slippery that you needed to run one gear down for the first few laps until a line began to develop."

On what was only his second flying lap, Cecotto lost control as he plunged out of Westfield and down into Dingle Dell, but as he slammed on opposite lock, the Toleman suddenly found all its grip, he slightly over-corrected and the TG184 hurled itself, head-on, at the guard rail on the left-hand side of the circuit. The impact was sufficient to demolish a considerable length of the guard rail and completely destroyed the front end of the Toleman, Cecotto sustaining severe leg and ankle injuries as a result. Practice was held up for well over an hour while the unfortunate driver was carefully extricated from his car and flown by helicopter to St. Mary's Hospital, Sidcup for emergency surgery, and track workers also took a long time to replace the guard rail so that the day's programme could continue.

Ayrton Senna certainly had not been unduly affected by his team-mate's accident as the Brazilian emerged from the first untimed session a splendid fastest overall, but it was the TAG-engined McLaren MP4/2s which dominated proceedings during the first hour of official qualifying.

Ten minutes from the end of the session Niki Lauda was sitting confidently on the pit wall, telling designer John Barnard "the car was absolutely perfect – it couldn't have been better!" after putting an impressive 1m 11.598s in the bag. The expression on Niki's face suggested this would be fastest of the day, but team-mate Prost came back at him with a 1m 11.494s to dislodge him from the top of the timing lists! Lauda turned away from the pit wall, his face a mixture of amusement and frustration . . .

The McLaren's tried and tested specification was significantly unchanged since Dallas, whereas the Brabham team had been hard at work with modifications to the BT53s in time for the Brands Hatch race. On Friday both Piquet and Teo Fabi emerged at the wheel of cars to the much-tested 'B' specification, changes to which not only included altered rear suspension geometry, but also the water radiator and intercooler repositioned at a much steeper angle which called for distinctively taller side-pods.

Unfortunately Friday afternoon wasn't a good time for the Brabham squad, Nelson's quickest lap of 1m 14.568s ending with loss of oil pressure as he came up to cross the finishing line, while both he and Fabi were unable to work their Michelins up to the correct operating temperature. Gordon Murray sat and thought for a while and then decreed that the BT53Bs should revert to their original specification in time for the Saturday morning session. Two of the team's three cars were thus modified, but Nelson's race car remained to the new 'B' specification until the World Champion had the benefit of a few laps in it for a final check. After some more debate it was decided that the 'B' spec. rear suspension geometry should be readopted, but with the *original* side-pod layout. This duly completed, Nelson strapped himself into his regular qualifying spare and hurled pole position out of sight with a magnificent 1m 10.869s.

Prost responded valiantly with a 1m 11.076s, but the outcome of that final hour's qualifying was in some way influenced by Andrea de Cesaris who not only managed to throw dirt all over the circuit with an early spin at Westfield (spoiling Lauda's first run), but then blew up his engine in a spectacular and expensive cloud of smoke with 15 minutes left to run, thoughtlessly dousing the circuit with lubricant as he attempted to make it back to the pits rather than abandoning the Ligier out on the circuit. As a result, there was nobody in a position to dislodge Piquet although Nelson went out on his second marked set of qualifiers shortly before the end, cruising round on the defensive – just in case!

Lauda worked his way down to 1m 11.344s to take third place on the inside of the second row, leaving Elio de Angelis to spearhead the Lotus-Renault-Goodyear challenge in fourth place on 1m 11.573s. Both de Angelis and team-mate Nigel Mansell had been hampered by a frustrating lack of grip on Friday as well as a worrying degree of understeer on full tanks. Elio managed to string things together successfully for a second row start during the Friday qualifying session, complaining only that he was slightly baulked by Piquet's "cruising" Brabham during the final few minutes, but Nigel Mansell was feeling very glum after a

disappointing practice for his home Grand Prix.

On Friday he was frustrated by an engine which was 1000rpm down, so this was changed overnight, only for his best qualifying run to be spoilt by gearbox failure. "To start with I lost third, then I suddenly found myself with a box full of neutrals, so that was the end of that," shrugged the Englishman as he faced up to the disappointing prospect of starting the race eighth on 1m 12.435s.

The Williams team turned up for the Brands Hatch race with a trio of the "definitive" FW09Bs, all significantly changed from the prototype 'B' spec. machine which made a fleeting appearance at Brands Hatch testing. The waisted rear bodywork was still present, but, in addition, a five-inch spacer had been inserted between the engine and gearbox in order to lengthen the wheelbase, while slightly revised rocker arm rear suspension was employed in conjunction with the Hewland FGB gearbox.

Fresh from optimistic tests at the Österreichring, Keke Rosberg couldn't honestly report that the FWO9B was anything special over the bumps and ripples at Brands Hatch, but was surprised to end Friday qualifying ninth overall "because it felt like a 15th or 20th place car!" Despite being hampered by a connecting pipe from the turbocharger to the intercooler becoming disconnected on two occasions during practice, Rosberg took the spare FW09B by the scruff of its neck and manhandled it round to a magnificent fifth quickest 1m 11.603s. By contrast, team-mate Jacques Laffite was almost in a black rage of frustration because his own car had an engine that just wouldn't run properly and, with Keke using the spare on Saturday afternoon, the Frenchman had to wait until Rosberg had finished his work before getting a crack at qualifying in the spare. He wound up 16th on 1m 14.568s, remarking, "Whenever Keke and I test with the same car at the same place, I'm as quick as him as you'll see from the Österreichring times . . ."

In the Renault camp Derek Warwick and Patrick Tambay faced a host of minor problems during qualifying, the Englishman's car being built round a brand new monocoque made solely out of carbon fibre composite with thicker side panels and bulkheads. Both cars suffered turbocharger failures on Friday while Derek not only had problems with a sticking throttle during both Friday and Saturday qualifying (something which left him *extremely* indignant), but he also yawed into the catch-fencing at Hawthorn during Saturday's untimed session when the RE50 got away from him on the climbing right-hander – possibly after bottoming out in the dip. The car suffered light damage to the steering arm and a front aerofoil, but it was ready to go at the start of the final session.

However, a combination of that sticking throttle "which gave me a huge moment on the grass coming out of Stirlings" and de Cesaris's oil all over the circuit, meant that Derek wound up only sixth on 1m 11.703s. Tambay was caught out with a quick spin at Druids on Friday when he was experimenting with carbon fibre brake discs and although these were changed for regular steel discs on both cars the following day, Patrick still reported the pedal going soft due to pad knock-off on several occasions. Feeling much sharper than he

did in North America as far as his completely recovered leg injury was concerned, Tambay emerged tenth quickest on 1m 13.138s: "Not bad, but I'm not getting through Hawthorn in fifth gear yet . . . which I ought to be!"

Despite his Toleman TG184 feeling pretty twitchy over the bumps, Ayrton Senna emerged fourth fastest on Friday and, after the chassis had been softened up slightly for the final session, found himself baulked by Arnoux's Ferrari on his first qualifying run and Lauda's McLaren on his second. He was thus obliged to rely on his Friday best as his quickest time, lining up seventh on the grid with 1m 11.890s to his credit.

Longitudinally mounted water radiators fitted beneath taller side-pods were the main modifications to be seen on the Ferrari C4s at Brands Hatch, both drivers opting to race their cars in this configuration although shortage of top speed and lack of grip bugged their progress for much of practice. Michele Alboreto managed a 1m 13.122s best for ninth place on the grid after suffering an engine failure on Friday. Arnoux, apparently at sea when it came to suggesting anything to Messrs. Forghieri and Postlethwaite that might improve the car's track manners, wound up a disappointing 13th on 1m 13.934s.

Although Manfred Winkelhock actually had a spare D7 (chassis No.2) at his disposal for the first time since he destroyed his old D6 T-car during practice at Monaco, the extrovert German concentrated his weekend's efforts on D7/1 since the new car had never turned a wheel prior to arriving at Brands Hatch and was being kept in reserve for use only in the most dire emergency. Manfred managed a 1m 13.374s, 11th best time to head the Pirelli runners, sharing the sixth row of the grid with a delighted Thierry Boutsen, the Belgian enthusing about his Arrows A7's handling with its revised rear suspension layout, despite the fact he suffered a couple of turbo failures on Friday caused by the team trying to run with excessive boost pressure. Surer's earlier-spec. A7, devoid of the new rear suspension, qualified 15th on 1m 14.336s.

Qualifying in close company down in 17th and 18th positions were the two frustrated Alfa 184T drivers, Eddie Cheever and Riccardo Patrese unable to run sufficient boost through their Italian V8 engines in order to qualify competitively, while both Ligier drivers were suffering over the bumps just as much as de Cesaris had been a month earlier during tyre testing at Brands. Andrea just pipped his unobtrusively improving team-mate to 20th spot on the grid.

Piercarlo Ghinzani did a respectable job to qualify 21st on 1m 16.466s, his best run in the Osella thwarted by de Cesaris's oil slick on Saturday afternoon, while Huub Rothengatter just managed to slip his Spirit 101B in ahead of the RAM 02s of Palmer and Alliot, both the Bicester-based cars sporting revised suspension geometry all-round in an effort to provide more camber change and consequently better tyre temperatures.

After the exclusion of the Tyrrell team from the Championship following that momentous FISA Executive Committee meeting in Paris the previous Wednesday, it came as no surprise that Ken Tyrrell immediately applied for a High Court injunction in order that his cars could compete at Brands Hatch. This was successfully done and FISA discreetly bowed to the authority of the British courts with the result that Stefan Johansson and Bellof qualified together on row 13, Brundle's Swedish stand-in just pipping his regular German team-mate. This decision apparently consigned Osella number two Jo Gartner, now armed with an FAIF turbo V8, to the role of non-qualifier, but the Stewards decreed that he be allowed to start as long as Osella could obtain the written agreement of every other team. This was duly done and the Austrian, who had his time for the first half of final qualifying disallowed when it was found that his car's rear wing was 1mm too high, took his place on the grid in 27th position.

RACE

Sunday morning brought with it boundless sunshine, enormous crowds and the customary Brands Hatch festival atmosphere with as many side shows, demonstrations and aerobatic displays as there were events on the circuit itself. The Kent circuit was packed to bursting like never before even by the time Prost and Lauda emerged to set fastest times in the half-hour warm-up session, while the Tyrrell team once more became the focal point of attention when both cars were re-submitted for scrutineering only to be told that they must plug a couple of small holes (drain holes or skid plate mountings?) in the underside of the monocoque before they could start the race. Tyrrell complied and everybody was in his correct grid position as Nelson Piquet led the pack round on its parade lap just before 14.45.

Despite the fact that Prost was up-camber from Nelson's Brabham, the World Champion's BT53 still got the jump on his arch-rival as the starting light blinked green, leading down Paddock Bend with de Angelis slotting into line behind the Frenchman and ahead of Lauda. Down the hill from Druids all the front runners negotiated the first few corners without any drama, but further back all hell broke loose as Patrese made an absurdly ambitious lunge down the inside of Laffite's car as they entered Graham Hill Bend.

Riccardo's Alfa snapped sideways as the Italian backed off suddenly, seeing that there just wasn't room to pull this stunt and, in a trice, there were cars going in all directions in his wake. Cheever stood on the brakes to avoid his team-mate, somehow Ghinzani slipped through unscathed, but Alliot's RAM went charging over the back of Johansson's slowing Tyrrell and landed on Cheever before spearing off to land, wrecked, on the grassy infield. Meanwhile Gartner was presented with no escape route whatsoever and went slamming into the tyre barriers on the outside of the corner, so that was four cars (Cheever, Gartner, Johansson and Alliot) out on the spot. Eddie was absolutely livid. "I asked Riccardo what the hell he thought he was doing, and he just told me to get lost," blurted the American.

Piquet was comfortably ahead at the end of the opening lap with Prost in his wheel tracks, while on the second tour both Lauda and Warwick nipped ahead of de Angelis, relegating the Italian to fifth place. Rosberg, Alboreto, Senna and Mansell were next in the convoy, Ayrton having moved ahead of Nigel's Lotus at Paddock as they swept into lap two, but Keke was soon in the pits with turbo problems after five laps, scuppering what looked like quite promising chances in this particular race.

Winkelhock's ATS spun off on bottom straight on the ninth lap, the German stalling his engine and retiring on the spot, while Teo Fabi's Brabham came crawling into the pits with electrical problems next time round. Meanwhile, Piquet was quickly discovering that his choice of Michelin rubber (05s on the right, 06s on the left) was going to be extremely marginal and his Brabham was oversteering more and more. After seven laps he was losing grip dramatically and at the end of lap 11 he decided to dive straight into the pits for fresh rubber, confident that there was sufficient time to haul back up into contention for the lead.

However, Piquet was going to receive an unexpected and rather controversial bonus: com-

Nelson Piquet was the only driver capable of
challenging the McLarens, the Brabham driver
leading both parts of the race.
Photo: Malcolm Bryan

ing into Clearways on lap 11, Palmer's RAM
suffered a steering breakage and plunged off the
road into the tyre barriers on the outside of the
corner. The Doc hopped out unhurt, but officials
decided that the car was standing in a very
vulnerable position and the red flag was produced
to stop the race just as the McLaren duo sailed into
Paddock Bend to start its 13th lap.

The fact that the red flag was displayed at the
end of the 12th lap, but when the leaders had
actually started their 13th, meant that a strict
application of the rule book dictated that the
re-start should be taken with the cars lined up in
the order they completed their 11th lap. Thus
Piquet was able to take the re-start on pole
position, not on the second row behind the
McLarens which would have been the case if the
red flag had gone out a lap later! This decision
caused some ill-considered mumbling and grumb-
ling in the pit lane, particularly from Alain Prost,
and the Frenchman wound up having to make a
public apology to FISA at Hockenheim for, in
effect, saying the whole affair was rigged in favour
of Piquet's Brabham.

Despite having struggled round another "inves-
tigative" lap after his pit-stop, Rosberg's Williams
was unable to take the re-start and Fabi's Brabham
was a permanent casualty as well. To take into
account all the slowing down laps and extra
warming up and parade lap, the balance of the race
was scheduled to take place over another 60 laps to
add to the 11 already run.

At the second start Prost jumped straight into
the lead from his position on the outside of the front
row, completing the opening lap ahead of Piquet
(now running harder Michelins on his left rims)
and Lauda, this trio already opening a gap back to
Warwick's Renault, Tambay, de Angelis,
Alboreto, Senna, Mansell, de Cesaris, Boutsen,
Arnoux and the rest.

Initally it looked as though the British Grand
Prix was going to settle down into a really boring,
routine procession, but when Lauda moved ahead
of Piquet into second place on lap 17 of the second

"heat", Prost really began to put his foot down
hard and onlookers at Surtees had the remarkable
sight of the super-smooth Frenchman cranking on
opposite lock and dropping his right rear wheel in
the dirt as he sought to counter Lauda's challenge.
By contrast, Niki never looked the slightest bit
flustered, keeping his Michelins well away from the
kerbs, and it looked as though we were going to be
treated to an eyeball-to-eyeball confrontation
between the McLaren International duo. Alas, it
was not to be. The luck was due to go Niki's way on
this occasion and the admittedly marginal
McLaren gearbox wilted under the strain of Prost's
efforts, the Frenchman suddenly slowing on lap 27
as he lost third . . . then fourth . . . then fifth. It was
all over thanks to a bearing failure, and Alain
cruised back to the pits to retire as Niki swept into
the lead he was never to lose.

Not that Piquet gave up by any stretch of the
imagination. Yard by yard, inch by inch, Nelson
clawed his way back on to the McLaren's tail to
such good effect that, by lap 45, it looked as though
Niki had got a fight on his hands. Unfortunately
Nelson bgan to suffer with fluctuating turbo boost
pressure and he gradually dropped out of contention in the closing stages of the race, staggering
round to finish an eventual seventh, his BT53
effectively powered by nothing more than a
four-cylinder normally aspirated 1½-litre engine
by the time he arrived at the chequered flag.

Piquet's misfortune allowed Derek Warwick to
drive smoothly home in a worthy second place, the
Englishman having a lonely race for much of the
afternoon, his RE50 not quick enough to challenge
the leading threesome but quite able to out-pace
any of the other opposition. Team-mate Patrick
Tambay dropped from his initial fifth place with a
stop for tyres at the end of lap 23, allowing de
Angelis to move his Lotus, by now troubled with
blistering Goodyears, up a place pursued by
Senna's splendid Toleman. Elio pulled every trick
in the book to shake the Brazilian newcomer from
his tail, but it was particularly noticeable that the
Toleman was quickly back with the Lotus each
time de Angelis managed to gain a little ground as
they weaved a path through the backmarkers.
Eventually, with five laps to go, Senna slammed
down the inside of de Angelis going into Paddock in
a move which brought the crowds to their feet – it
was the final factor which was to earn Ayrton a fine
third place behind Lauda and Warwick!

After his pit-stop Tambay settled down to run
smoothly in seventh place, which became sixth
when Prost retired and should have netted the
popular Frenchman fifth after Piquet's problems in
the closing stages of the race. Patrick hung in there
well, despite an engine that was cutting out badly
on right-handers, but a mammoth engine failure
two laps from the end set the RE50's whole engine
compartment ablaze and he rolled to a disappointed stop out on the circuit, eventually to be
classified eighth. Subsequent examination revealed that a portion of Piquet's failed turbocharger blade was embedded in one of Tambay's water
radiators . . . an absolutely amazing discovery!

An absurdly unruly battle between the obstructive Andrea de Cesaris and the pursuing Ferrari
C4s was eventually resolved with Alboreto and

Arnoux barging their way past the obstructive
Ligier. Michele pulled this move at Druids when
Andrea moved over to be lapped by Lauda, and
Arnoux duplicating this manoeuvre on lap 52, his
slightly less effective fashion seeing both cars
sliding, interlocked, to the outside of the corner
before René could resume his race. After it was all
over, both Ferrari drivers were about ready to put
one on de Cesaris, but the Italian, near to tears,
was unrepentant!

Thus Alboreto and Arnoux finished fifth and
sixth ahead of Piquet, Tambay, Piercarlo Ghinzani's Osella, de Cesaris (struggling round with a
deranged right-rear wheel after being mauled by
Arnoux), Bellof and Marc Surer. Laffite's Williams
was an early casualty with a broken water pump
and Nigel Mansell's disappointing home Grand
Prix ended with retirement when his gearbox broke
after his Lotus 95T had dropped away badly in the
early stages, still plagued by excessive understeer.
Boutsen's Arrows suffered an electrical failure, but
team-mate Surer was still running, four laps
behind the leaders, after a lengthy and unplanned
stop for fresh rubber, while Rothengatter's slow
Spirit was nine laps behind, running but not
classified, after a lengthy pit stop to replace his
car's nose section which had been damaged when
he ran into Hesnault's Ligier, the Frenchman
retiring on lap 44 with an engine breakage.

For Lauda, there were no such problems. The
MP4/2 had run perfectly all afternoon and the
Austrian was a happy man as he mounted the
rostrum to join an immaculate Ron Dennis. The
McLaren boss smiled and congratulated his driver;
Lauda patted Dennis playfully on the cheek. The
inference was clear. One-and-a-half points separated the McLaren drivers and, with six races to
go, there were no team orders. Niki Lauda had just
played himself back into contention. Dennis knew
it. And so, for that matter, did Alain Prost.   AH

JULY:

*FISA Executive Committee bans Tyrrell from 1984
World Championship following alleged
infringement of technical regulations resulting from
analysis of water taken from Martin Brundle's car
in Detroit. High Court injunction enables Tyrrell to
take part in British Grand Prix.*

*FISA fines Nigel Mansell $6000 for his
involvement in startline accident at Detroit and
defers suspension of his licence subject to Mansell's
future behaviour.*

*Jacky Ickx fined $6000 by FISA for stopping
Monaco Grand Prix without consulting Stewards.
Ickx's Clerk of the Course Licence suspended.*

*Organisers of Dallas Grand Prix censured by FISA
and instructed to deposit a $200,000 bond before the
final approval of the 1985 calendar to ensure
completion of work found necessary by FISA.*

Derek Warwick agrees to drive for Renault in 1985

*FISA ratify the axing of the European Formula 3
Championship and the introduction of Formula 3000
which will replace Formula 2 in 1985.*

Entries and practice times

No.	Driver	Nat	Car	Tyre	Engine	Entrant	Practice 1	Practice 2
1	Nelson Piquet	BR	Parmalat BRABHAM BT53	M	BMW M12/13	MRD International	1m 14·568s	**1m 10·869s**
2	Teo Fabi	I	Parmalat BRABHAM BT53	M	BMW M12/13	MRD International	1m 17·731s	**1m 14·040s**
3	Stefan Johansson	S	TYRRELL 012	G	Ford Cosworth DFY	Tyrrell Racing Organisation	1m 18·460s	**1m 17·777s**
4	Stefan Bellof	D	TYRRELL 012	G	Ford Cosworth DFY	Tyrrell Racing Organisation	**1m 17·893s**	1m 17·912s
5	Jacques Laffite	F	WILLIAMS FW09B	G	Honda RA 163–E	Williams Grand Prix Engineering	**1m 14·568s**	1m 26·939s
6	Keke Rosberg	SF	WILLIAMS FW09B	G	Honda RA 163–E	Williams Grand Prix Engineering	1m 13·740s	**1m 11·603s**
7	Alain Prost	F	Marlboro McLAREN MP4/2	M	TAG P01 (TTE P01)	Marlboro McLaren International	1m 11·494s	**1m 11·076s**
8	Niki Lauda	A	Marlboro McLAREN MP4/2	M	TAG P01 (TTE P01)	Marlboro McLaren International	1m 11·598s	**1m 11·344s**
9	Philippe Alliot	F	RAM 02	P	Hart 415T	Skoal Bandit Formula 1 Team	1m 24·043s	**1m 17·517s**
10	Jonathan Palmer	GB	RAM 02	P	Hart 415T	Skoal Bandit Formula 1 Team	1m 18·244s	**1m 17·265s**
11	Elio de Angelis	I	John Player Special LOTUS 95T	G	Renault EF4	John Player Team Lotus	1m 11·734s	**1m 11·573s**
12	Nigel Mansell	GB	John Player Special LOTUS 95T	G	Renault EF4	John Player Team Lotus	1m 13·184s	**1m 12·435s**
14	Manfred Winkelhock	D	ATS D7	P	BMW M12/13	Team ATS	1m 13·713s	**1m 13·374s**
15	Patrick Tambay	F	Elf RENAULT RE50	M	Renault EF4	Equipe Renault Elf	1m 14·106s	**1m 13·138s**
16	Derek Warwick	GB	Elf RENAULT RE50	M	Renault EF4	Equipe Renault Elf	1m 12·278s	**1m 11·703s**
17	Marc Surer	CH	ARROWS A7	G	BMW M12/13	Barclay Nordica Arrows BMW	1m 17·040s	**1m 14·336s**
18	Thierry Boutsen	B	ARROWS A7	G	BMW M12/13	Barclay Nordica Arrows BMW	1m 15·355s	**1m 13·528s**
19	Ayrton Senna	BR	TOLEMAN TG184	M	Hart 415T	Toleman Group Motorsport	**1m 11·890s**	1m 13·991s
20	Johnny Cecotto	YV	TOLEMAN TG184	M	Hart 415T	Toleman Group Motorsport		
21	Huub Rothengatter	NL	SPIRIT 101	P	Hart 415T	Spirit Racing	1m 17·665s	**1m 16·759s**
22	Riccardo Patrese	I	Benetton ALFA ROMEO 184T	G	Alfa Romeo 183T	Benetton Team Alfa Romeo	1m 14·871s	**1m 14·568s**
23	Eddie Cheever	USA	Benetton ALFA ROMEO 184T	G	Alfa Romeo 183T	Benetton Team Alfa Romeo	1m 15·113s	**1m 14·609s**
24	Piercarlo Ghinzani	I	Kelemata OSELLA FA1F	P	Alfa Romeo 183T	Osella Squadra Corse	**1m 16·466s**	1m 16·829s
25	François Hesnault	F	LIGIER Loto JS23	M	Renault EF4	Ligier Loto	1m 17·384s	**1m 15·837s**
26	Andrea de Cesaris	I	LIGIER Loto JS23	M	Renault EF4	Ligier Loto	1m 16·116s	**1m 15·112s**
27	Michele Alboreto	I	Fiat FERRARI 126C4	G	Ferrari 126C	Scuderia Ferrari SpA	1m 13·645s	**1m 13·122s**
28	René Arnoux	F	Fiat FERRARI 126C4	G	Ferrari 126C	Scuderia Ferrari SpA	1m 14·281s	**1m 13·934s**
30	Jo Gartner	A	Kelemata OSELLA FA1F	P	Alfa Romeo 183T	Osella Squadra Corse	1m 18·347s	**1m 18·121s**

Friday morning and Saturday morning practice sessions not officially recorded.

G – Goodyear, M – Michelin, P – Pirelli.

Fri pm Warm, dry — Sat pm Warm, dry

Starting grid

	1 PIQUET (1m 10·869s) Brabham
7 PROST (1m 11·076s) McLaren	
	8 LAUDA (1m 11·344s) McLaren
11 DE ANGELIS (1m 11·573s) Lotus	
	6 ROSBERG (1m 11·603s) Williams
16 WARWICK (1m 11·703s) Renault	
	19 SENNA (1m 11·890s) Toleman
12 MANSELL (1m 12·435s) Lotus	
	27 ALBORETO (1m 13·122s) Ferrari
15 TAMBAY (1m 13·138s) Renault	
	14 WINKELHOCK (1m 13·374s) ATS
18 BOUTSEN (1m 13·528s) Arrows	
	28 ARNOUX (1m 13·934s) Ferrari
2 FABI (1m 14·040s) Brabham	
	17 SURER (1m 14·336s) Arrows
5 LAFFITE (1m 14·568s) Williams	
	22 PATRESE (1m 14·568s) Alfa Romeo
23 CHEEVER (1m 14·609s) Alfa Romeo	
	26 DE CESARIS (1m 15·112s) Ligier
25 HESNAULT (1m 15·837s) Ligier	
	24 GHINZANI (1m 16·466s) Osella
21 ROTHENGATTER (1m 16·759s) Spirit	
	10 PALMER (1m 17·265s) RAM
9 ALLIOT (1m 17·517s) RAM	
	3 JOHANSSON (1m 17·777s) Tyrrell
4 BELLOF (1m 17·893s) Tyrrell	
	30 GARTNER (1m 18·121s) Osella

Did not start:
20 Cecotto (Toleman), did not qualify; crashed during practice.

Special dispensation given to 27th car (Gartner) due to doubts over eligibility of Tyrrells to score championship points.

Results and retirements

Place	Driver	Car	Laps	Time and Speed (mph/km/h)/Retirement	
1	Niki Lauda	McLaren-TAG t/c V6	71	1h 29m 28·532s	124·406/200·212
2	Derek Warwick	Renault t/c V6	71	1h 30m 10·655s	123·4/198·593
3	Ayrton Senna	Toleman-Hart t/c 4	71	1h 30m 31·860s	123·0/197·949
4	Elio de Angelis	Lotus-Renault t/c V6	70		
5	Michele Alboreto	Ferrari t/c V6	70		
6	René Arnoux	Ferrari t/c V6	70		
7	Nelson Piquet	Brabham-BMW t/c 4	70		
8	Patrick Tambay	Renault t/c V6	69	Turbo	
9	Piercarlo Ghinzani	Osella-Alfa Romeo t/c V8	68		
10	Andrea de Cesaris	Ligier-Renault t/c V6	68		
11	Stefan Bellof	Tyrrell-Cosworth V8	68		
12	Marc Surer	Arrows-BMW t/c 4	67		
13	Riccardo Patrese	Alfa Romeo t/c V8	66		
	Huub Rothengatter	Spirit-Hart t/c 4	62	Running, not classified	
	François Hesnault	Ligier-Renault t/c V6	43	Electrics	
	Alain Prost	McLaren-TAG t/c V6	37	Gearbox pinion bearing	
	Nigel Mansell	Lotus-Renault t/c V6	24	Gearbox	
	Thierry Boutsen	Arrows-BMW t/c 4	24	Electrical pick-up	
	Jacques Laffite	Williams-Honda t/c V6	14	Water pump	
	Jonathan Palmer	RAM-Hart t/c 4	10	Steering failure/accident	
	Teo Fabi	Brabham-BMW t/c 4	9	Electrical	
	Manfred Winkelhock	ATS-BMW t/c 4	8	Spun, could not restart	
	Keke Rosberg	Williams-Honda t/c V6	5	Intercooler hose/engine	
	Eddie Cheever	Alfa Romeo t/c V8	1	Accident damage	
	Stefan Johansson	Tyrrell-Cosworth V8	1	Accident damage	
	Philippe Alliot	RAM-Hart t/c 4	0	Accident	
	Jo Gartner	Osella-Alfa Romeo t/c V8	0	Accident	

Fastest lap: Lauda, on lap 57, 1m 13·191s, 128·523mph/206·837km/h.
Lap record: Didier Pironi (F1 Ligier JS11/15-Cosworth DFV), 1m 12·368s, 130·015mph/209·239km/h (1980).

Past winners

Year	Driver	Nat	Car	Circuit	Distance miles/km	Speed mph/km/h
1950	Giuseppe Farina	I	1·5 Alfa Romeo 158 s/c	Silverstone	202·20/325·41	90·96/146·38
1951	Froilán González	RA	4·5 Ferrari 375	Silverstone	259·97/418·38	96·11/154·67
1952	Alberto Ascari	I	2·0 Ferrari 500	Silverstone	248·80/400·40	90·92/146·32
1953	Alberto Ascari	I	2·0 Ferrari 500	Silverstone	263·43/423·95	92·97/149·62
1954	Froilán González	RA	2·5 Ferrari 625	Silverstone	263·43/423·95	89·69/144·34
1955	Stirling Moss	GB	2·5 Mercedes-Benz W196	Aintree	270·00/434·52	86·47/139·16
1956	Juan Manuel Fangio	RA	2·5 Lancia-Ferrari D50	Silverstone	295·63/475·77	98·65/158·76
1957	Tony Brooks/	GB				
	Stirling Moss	GB	2·5 Vanwall	Aintree	270·00/434·52	86·80/139·69
1958	Peter Collins	GB	2·4 Ferrari Dino 246	Silverstone	219·53/353·30	102·05/164·23
1959	Jack Brabham	AUS	2·5 Cooper T51-Climax	Aintree	225·00/362·10	98·88/159·13
1960	Jack Brabham	AUS	2·5 Cooper T53-Climax	Silverstone	225·00/362·10	108·69/174·92
1961	Wolfgang von Trips	D	1·5 Ferrari Dino 156	Aintree	225·00/362·10	83·91/135·04
1962	Jim Clark	GB	1·5 Lotus 25-Climax	Aintree	225·00/362·10	92·25/148·46
1963	Jim Clark	GB	1·5 Lotus 25-Climax	Silverstone	240·00/386·25	107·75/173·41
1964	Jim Clark	GB	1·5 Lotus 25-Climax	Brands Hatch	212·00/341·18	94·14/151·50
1965	Jim Clark	GB	1·5 Lotus 33-Climax	Silverstone	240·00/386·25	112·02/180·28
1966	Jack Brabham	AUS	3·0 Brabham BT19-Repco	Brands Hatch	212·00/341·18	95·48/153·66
1967	Jim Clark	GB	3·0 Lotus 49-Ford	Silverstone	240·00/386·25	117·64/189·32
1968	Jo Siffert	CH	3·0 Lotus 49B-Ford	Brands Hatch	212·00/341·18	104·83/168·71
1969	Jackie Stewart	GB	3·0 Matra MS80-Ford	Silverstone	245·87/395·69	127·25/204·79
1970	Jochen Rindt	A	3·0 Lotus 72-Ford	Brands Hatch	212·00/341·18	108·69/174·92
1971	Jackie Stewart	GB	3·0 Tyrrell 003-Ford	Silverstone	199·04/320·32	130·48/209·99
1972	Emerson Fittipaldi	BR	3·0 JPS/Lotus 72-Ford	Brands Hatch	201·40/324·12	112·06/180·34
1973	Peter Revson	USA	3·0 McLaren M23-Ford	Silverstone	196·11/315·61	131·75/212·03
1974	Jody Scheckter	ZA	3·0 Tyrrell 007-Ford	Brands Hatch	198·75/319·86	115·74/186·26
1975	Emerson Fittipaldi	BR	3·0 McLaren M23-Ford	Silverstone	164·19/264·24	120·02/193·15
1976	Niki Lauda	A	3·0 Ferrari 312T-2/76	Brands Hatch	198·63/319·67	114·24/183·85
1977	James Hunt	GB	3·0 McLaren M26-Ford	Silverstone	199·38/320·88	130·36/209·79
1978	Carlos Reutemann	RA	3·0 Ferrari 312T-3/78	Brands Hatch	198·63/319·67	116·61/187·66
1979	Clay Regazzoni	CH	3·0 Williams FW07-Ford	Silverstone	199·38/320·88	138·80/223·37
1980	Alan Jones	AUS	3·0 Williams FW07B-Ford	Brands Hatch	198·63/319·67	125·69/202·28
1981	John Watson	GB	3·0 McLaren MP4-Ford	Silverstone	199·38/320·88	137·64/221·51
1982	Niki Lauda	A	3·0 McLaren MP4B-Ford	Brands Hatch	198·63/319·67	124·70/200·68
1983	Alain Prost	F	1·5 Renault RE40 t/c	Silverstone	196·44/316·17	139·22/224·05
1984	Niki Lauda	A	1·5 McLaren MP4/2-TAG t/c	Brands Hatch	185·57/298·64	124·41/200·21

(Results are the aggregate of two parts after the race had been stopped and restarted after lap 11.)

Circuit data

Brands Hatch Grand Prix Circuit, Fawkham, Kent
Circuit length: 2·6136 miles/4·206 km
Race distance: 71 laps, 185·566 miles/298·638 km
Race weather: Hot, dry

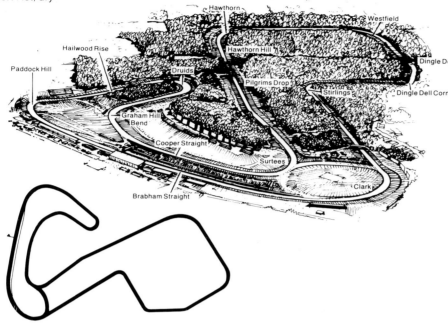

Lap chart

1st LAP ORDER		1	2	3	4	5	6	7	8	9	10	11		1st LAP ORDER RESTART		12	13	14	15	16	17	18	19	20	21	22	23	24	25	26	27	28	29	30
1	N. Piquet	1	1	1	1	1	1	1	1	1	1	7	7	7	A. Prost	7	7	7	7	7	7	7	7	7	7	7	7	7	7	7	7	7	7	7	7
7	A. Prost	7	7	7	7	7	7	7	7	7	7	8	8	1	N. Piquet	1	1	1	1	1	1	1	1	1	1	1	1	1	1	1	1	1	1	8	8
11	E. De Angelis	11	8	8	8	8	8	8	8	8	8	1	1	8	N. Lauda	8	8	8	8	8	8	8	8	8	8	8	8	8	8	8	8	8	8	1	1
8	N. Lauda	8	16	16	16	16	16	16	16	16	16	16	16	16	D. Warwick	16	16	16	16	16	16	16	16	16	16	16	16	16	16	16	16	16	16	16	16
16	D. Warwick	16	11	11	11	11	11	11	11	11	11	11	11	15	P. Tambay	15	15	15	15	15	15	15	15	15	15	15	15	15	15	15	15	15	15	15	15
6	K. Rosberg	6	6	6	6	19	19	19	19	19	19	19	19	11	E. De Angelis	11	11	11	11	11	11	11	11	11	11	11	11	11	11	11	11	11	11	11	11
27	M. Alboreto	27	27	27	19	27	27	27	27	27	27	27	27	27	M. Alboreto	27	19	19	19	19	19	19	19	19	19	19	19	19	19	19	19	19	19	19	19
12	N. Mansell	12	19	19	27	15	15	15	15	15	15	15	15	19	A. Senna	19	27	26	26	26	26	26	26	26	26	26	26	26	26	26	26	26	26	26	26
19	A. Senna	19	15	15	15	12	12	12	12	12	12	12	12	12	N. Mansell	12	26	27	27	27	27	27	27	27	27	27	28	28	28	28	28	28	28	28	28
15	P. Tambay	15	12	12	12	18	18	18	18	2	18	18	18	26	A. De Cesaris	26	18	18	18	28	28	28	28	28	28	27	27	27	27	27	27	27	27	27	27
18	T. Boutsen	18	18	18	18	14	14	2	2	18	26	26	26	13	T. Boutsen	18	28	28	28	18	18	18	18	18	18	12	12	24	24	24	24	24	24	24	24
14	M. Winkelhock	14	14	14	14	2	2	14	14	26	28	28	28	28	R. Arnoux	28	12	12	12	12	12	12	12	12	12	18	24	17	22	22	22	22	22	22	22
28	R. Arnoux	28	2	2	2	26	26	26	26	28	5	5	5	24	P. Ghinzani	24	24	24	24	24	24	24	24	24	24	24	17	22	25	25	25	25	25	25	25
2	T. Fabi	2	28	26	26	28	28	28	28	5	17	17	22	17	M. Surer	17	17	17	17	17	17	17	17	17	17	22	25	25	17	17	17	17	17	17	17
26	A. De Cesaris	26	26	28	28	17	17	17	5	17	2	22	17	5	J. Laffite	5	22	22	22	22	22	22	22	22	22	25	4	4	4	4	4	4			
17	M. Surer	17	17	17	17	5	5	5	17	22	22	22	4	22	R. Patrese	22	5	5	5	25	25	25	25	25	25	4	21	21	21	21	21	21			
5	J. Laffite	5	5	5	5	6	24	24	24	24	4	4	4	4	S. Bellof	4	4	4	25	4	4	4	4	4	4	18									
24	P. Ghinzani	24	24	24	24	24	10	22	22	10	10	25	25	25	F. Hesnault	25	25	25	5	21	21	21	21	21	21	21									
4	S. Bellof	4	10	10	10	10	22	10	10	4	4	21	21	21	H. Rothengatter	21	21	21	21																
10	J. Palmer	10	4	4	4	4	4	4	4	25	25																								
25	F. Hesnault	25	22	22	22	22	25	25	25	21	21																								
22	R. Patrese	22	25	25	25	25	21	21	21																										
21	H. Rothengatter	21	21	21	21	21																													
23	E. Cheever	23																																	

31	32	33	34	35	36	37	38	39	40	41	42	43	44	45	46	47	48	49	50	51	52	53	54	55	56	57	58	59	60	61	62	63	64	65	66	67	68	69	70	71
7	7	7	7	7	7	7	8	8	8	8	8	8	8	8	8	8	8	8	8	8	8	8	8	8	8	8	8	8	8	8	8	8	8	8	8	8	8	8	8	8
8	8	8	8	8	8	8	1	1	1	1	1	1	1	1	1	1	1	1	1	1	1	1	1	1	1	1	1	1	1	1	1	1	1	1	16	16	16	16	16	16
1	1	1	1	1	7	16	16	16	16	16	16	16	16	16	16	16	16	16	16	16	16	16	16	16	16	16	16	16	16	16	16	16	16	16	19	19	19	19	19	19
16	16	16	16	16	16	16	11	11	11	11	11	11	11	11	11	11	11	11	11	11	11	11	11	11	11	11	11	11	11	11	11	11	11	19	11	11	11	11		
15	15	15	15	11	11	11	11	19	19	19	19	19	19	19	19	19	19	19	19	19	19	19	19	19	19	19	19	19	19	19	19	19	11	1	15	27	27			
11	11	11	19	19	19	19	15	15	15	15	15	15	15	15	15	15	15	15	15	15	15	15	15	15	15	15	15	15	15	15	15	15	15	15	27	15	28			
19	19	19	15	15	15	15	15	26	26	26	26	26	26	27	27	27	27	27	27	27	27	27	27	27	27	27	27	27	27	27	27	27	27	1	28	1				
26	26	26	26	26	26	26	27	27	27	27	27	27	27	26	26	26	26	26	26	26	26	26	26	26	26	26	26	26	26	26	26	26	28	28	1					
28	28	28	28	28	28	28	28	28	28	28	28	28	28	28	28	28	28	28	28	28	28	28	28	28	28	28	28	28	28	28	28	28	24	24						
27	27	27	27	27	27	27	28	24	24	24	24	22	22	22	22	22	22	22	22	22	22	22	22	22	22	22	22	22	22	22	22	22	26	26						
24	24	24	24	24	24	24	24	22	22	22	22	24	24	24	24	24	24	24	24	24	24	24	24	24	24	24	24	24	24	24	24	4	4							
22	22	22	22	22	22	22	22	25	25	25	25	4	4	4	4	4	4	4	4	4	4	4	4	4	4	4	4	4	4	4	17									
25	25	25	25	25	25	25	25	4	4	4	4	17	17	17	17	17	17	17	17	17	17	17	17	17	17	17	17	17	17											
4	4	4	4	4	4	4	4	17	17	17	17	21	21	21	21	21	21	21	21	21	21	21	21	21	21	21	21													
17	17	17	17	17	17	17	17	21	21	21	21																													
21	21	21	21	21	21	21	21																																	

Fastest laps

Driver	Time	Lap
Niki Lauda	1m 13·191s	57
Nelson Piquet	1m 13·656s	52
Ayrton Senna	1m 13·951s	58
Alain Prost	1m 13·979s	24
Derek Warwick	1m 14·236s	43
Elio de Angelis	1m 14·389s	57
Patrick Tambay	1m 14·534s	38
Michele Alboreto	1m 15·131s	47
René Arnoux	1m 15·598s	62
Andrea de Cesaris	1m 16·062s	59
Huub Rothengatter	1m 17·091s	55
Piercarlo Ghinzani	1m 17·273s	37
Riccardo Patrese	1m 17·319s	44
Nigel Mansell	1m 17·326s	21
Thierry Boutsen	1m 17·750s	19
Stefan Bellof	1m 17·930s	45
Jacques Laffite	1m 18·006s	11
Marc Surer	1m 18·008s	22
François Hesnault	1m 18·126s	22
Teo Fabi	1m 18·364s	7
Manfred Winkelhock	1m 18·553s	6
Keke Rosberg	1m 19·336s	3
Jonathan Palmer	1m 20·114s	10

Points

WORLD CHAMPIONSHIP OF DRIVERS

1	Alain Prost	34·5 pts
2	Niki Lauda	33
3	Elio de Angelis	26·5
4	René Arnoux	23·5
5	Keke Rosberg	20
6	Derek Warwick	19
7	Nelson Piquet	18
8	Michele Alboreto	11
9	Ayrton Senna	8
10	Patrick Tambay	7
11	Nigel Mansell	6
12	Jacques Laffite	4
13=	Eddie Cheever	3
13=	Riccardo Patrese	3
13=	Teo Fabi	3
16=	Andrea de Cesaris	2
16=	Piercarlo Ghinzani	2
18	Thierry Boutsen	1
*	Martin Brundle	8
*	Stefan Bellof	5

CONSTRUCTORS' CUP

1	McLaren	67·5 pts
2	Ferrari	34·5
3	Lotus	32·5
4	Renault	26
5	Williams	24
6	Brabham	21
7	Toleman	8
8	Alfa Romeo	6
9=	Ligier	2
9=	Osella	2
11	Arrows	1
*	Tyrrell	13

* Points earned by Tyrrell removed by FISA Executive Committee

Grosser Preis von Deutschland

Forced to apologise for remarks made concerning the stopping of the British Grand Prix, Alain Prost extracts friendly revenge on Jean-Marie Balestre. Lauda and Warwick show little sympathy for the sodden FISA President . . .
Out on his own at Hockenheim. Not even a last minute switch to the spare McLaren would stop Alain Prost from scoring his fourth win of the season.

Before the race, they sat in the Marlboro trailer and found time to joke about their stranglehold on the championship. "I'm the oldest," said Lauda. "You should let me win this year and then I'll let you become champion next year." Prost said he wasn't prepared to wait that long. He was interested in 1984 and his immediate thoughts centred on the German Grand Prix.

"You won at Brands 'atch," he countered. "It's my turn to win today." Lauda nodded and grinned. He knew the little Frenchman was deadly serious. More important, perhaps, was the fact that the little Frenchman was on pole while the old Austrian was on the fourth row. Given Prost's ambitions and the current competitive state of the McLaren MP4/2, Lauda could ill-afford to allow his team-mate such an advantage.

In the event, he was proved correct. In spite of a last-minute switch to the spare car, Prost made the score four-three in his favour. Lauda finished second, his every move countered by Prost as the Austrian tried to close the gap. But, in the end, Prost had the final say, setting fastest lap of the race and stretching his championship lead to a meagre four and a half points. It was total domination by McLaren.

It was also a boring race. For the first 20 laps or so, Nelson Piquet provided serious competition for the McLarens, the Parmalat Brabham leading until its gearbox failed. Before that, we had another burst of race competitiveness from John Player Team Lotus as Elio de Angelis led for eight laps before his engine blew but, those two apart, the McLarens ran the race as they pleased.

Derek Warwick took a lonely third place for Renault-Elf, the Englishman having given best in the early stages to an inspired Keke Rosberg. As usual, the Finn had struggled with his Williams-Honda during practice but, in the race, the FW09B felt good and it took Rosberg just nine laps to work his way from 19th to fourth place. And then an electrical sensor on the engine failed.

However, it was questionable whether Rosberg's Goodyears would have withstood such a furious pace. Nigel Mansell, taking it easy during the opening stages, just made his left-hand tyres last the distance to take an intelligent fourth place. Patrick Tambay, struggling with a down-on-power engine, finished fifth for Renault and the final point went to René Arnoux, winner of the previous year's German Grand Prix.

That race had seen a fracturing of team spirit within Ferrari as Arnoux went back on his word and pushed Tambay aside. There were no such problems within McLaren in 1984 simply because there were no agreements, no team tactics. Prost and Lauda remained good friends in the paddock but, on the track, it was every man for himself. And, at Hockenheim, Alain Prost reasserted his authority – for the time being.

French highlight. The Ligier-Renaults of Andrea de Cesaris and François Hesnault provided one of the few battles in a boring race as they fought among themselves for seventh place. The Italian eventually finished ahead but not before Hesnault had made his mark.

ENTRY AND PRACTICE

For this race, national pride was at stake. The German Grand Prix would be the first confrontation on home soil between BMW and Porsche (alias TAG) and both companies were anxious to use a respectable result to help bolster recovery from a metal workers dispute which had savaged the German motor industry. Apart from that, BMW felt they were owed a victory or two and there could be fewer suitable locations than this. Porsche, for their part, said nothing. The V6, as the McLaren management kept reminding the more rebellious members of the press corps, was a TAG engine manufactured by Porsche.

On Friday afternoon, both camps received a jolt. Fastest, by over half a second, was the Renault-powered Lotus of Elio de Angelis. As ever, the elegant black and gold 95T showed excellent form – during practice at least – and Goodyear were showing signs of recovering from understeer problems which played havoc with their progress at Brands Hatch. Elio was helped in part by an engine failure on Tambay's Renault which subsequently covered the stadium section with oil but the Italian felt confident about defending his position the next day.

At first light on Saturday, it seemed pole position would stay with de Angelis since the Hockenheim area was cloaked in mist and fine rain. The unofficial session was run in damp conditions although, by the time the session had ended, the racing line was beginning to dry. With the exception of one or two patches at the chicanes, it had dried completely once the cars took to the track at one o'clock for the final session.

De Angelis remained in his pit for 45 minutes before wandering across to the Longines monitor. Alain Prost had just taken to the track for the first time. Agreed, Prost had not been in contention on Friday, the McLaren driver being forced to wait until a turbo was changed and, by then, Tambay's oil had ended any hope of responding to de Angelis. On his first set of qualifiers, Prost came within two-tenths of Elio's time and it was then that the Italian reached for his helmet. Sure enough, seven minutes later and Prost had taken pole with a lap which looked quick, precise and economical.

De Angelis used his second set of tyres to produce a time which showed an improvement of half-a-second over his Friday best, but it was not enough. And the Lotus driver was far from satisfied. Had he not been inadvertently blocked by Fabi at one of the chicanes, pole would have remained with Lotus. The car felt that good.

So, it was Philip Morris versus John Player on the front row but what of Lauda and Mansell? Niki had been fastest during the first unofficial session but he slipped to fourth place in the afternoon by taking off too much rear wing, sliding and overheating his rear tyres as a result. On Saturday, he committed a rare gaff and we had the unusual and almost unbelievable sight of McLaren number eight spinning onto the pit straight. Lauda put the incident down to overenthusiasm but his best efforts were to be thwarted by an engine which gradually lost power and allowed him to slip to seventh place. He was, however, confident of a competitive performance in the race although it had not escaped his attention that there was much work to be done before he could get on terms with his team-mate.

Mansell, languishing in 16th place, was worse off still. If de Angelis had enjoyed a relatively trouble-free practice, then the British driver was carrying the burden of the entire team. Gearbox components had been strengthened following the problems at Brands Hatch but within a few laps of practice, a bolt had come adrift. Then the car stopped out on the circuit with a blocked bleed hole in the fuel pump filter and, since de Angelis had blown the engine in the spare car, Mansell had no option but to lose valuable time on Friday.

Matters improved on Saturday and a quick lap in the final moments of practice was spoiled by an incident with de Cesaris at the *Sachs Kurve*. Anxious not to be delayed through the twisting section which followed, Mansell dived down the inside, only to completely misjudge his braking and slide wide. De Cesaris moved back in front and then proceeded to hold the Lotus up for the remainder of the lap. Mansell reckoned the move cost him about three seconds.

If that was the case, it also lost Nelson Piquet pole position since the Brabham driver was looking for a way past them both at the time! The Brazilian was livid since all he had to show was fifth place and he was convinced the Brabham was worth a place on the front row; anyone watching the lurid powerslides from the BT53 on full boost needed little convincing. This was the final straw since he had been caught behind Rothengatter as the Dutchman tried to urge his Spirit through its fastest lap on Friday.

JULY:
FISA lifts ban on Tyrrell team pending appeal. Mike Thackwell (Ralt-Honda RH6/84) wins European Formula 2 Championship.

AUGUST:
FISA discuss reduction in fuel octane rating as a means of reducing speeds in Formula 1.

THE German Grand Prix was essentially a battle between Alain Prost and Niki Lauda, the McLaren drivers using lap times as a means of discussion over the possible destiny of the World Championship.

Once Lauda had dispensed with Alboreto and the Renaults to take third place behind Prost on lap nine, he began closing the gap on his team-mate, setting fastest lap of the race so far on lap 18. Piquet dropped from contention on lap 22, leaving the McLarens to run the race as they pleased.

Prost improved on Lauda's time on lap 23, Lauda responding by setting his fastest lap of the race six laps later. The final word came from Prost on lap 31 as he shaved another two-tenths off Lauda's best, the gap between the two extending from 3.9 to 6.3 and then 7.1 seconds. Lauda has settled for second place; Prost wins the race in every sense.

Lap	Prost	Lauda
1	2m 01.570s	2m 06.476s
2	1m 55.483s	1m 56.382s
3	1m 55.230s	1m 56.566s
4	1m 54.996s	1m 56.621s
5	1m 54.709s	1m 57.902s
6	1m 54.967s	1m 54.527s
7	1m 54.837s	1m 54.909s
8	1m 56.060s	1m 56.083s
9	1m 56.488s	1m 55.700s
10	1m 58.494s	1m 57.368s
11	1m 56.869s	1m 56.051s
12	1m 55.504s	1m 55.939s
13	1m 55.042s	1m 55.064s
14	1m 55.618s	1m 56.139s
15	1m 55.880s	1m 55.251s
16	1m 55.586s	1m 55.464s
17	1m 55.606s	1m 54.641s
18	1m 55.191s	1m 54.257s
19	1m 55.823s	1m 54.580s
20	1m 54.719s	1m 54.372s
21	1m 54.576s	1m 53.983s
22	1m 54.507s	1m 54.097s
23	1m 53.821s	1m 53.870s
24	1m 53.916s	1m 53.848s
25	1m 54.248s	1m 53.965s
26	1m 54.189s	1m 54.163s
27	1m 55.153s	1m 54.855s
28	1m 53.933s	1m 54.105s
29	1m 53.843s	**1m 53.778s**
30	1m 54.519s	1m 56.061s
31	**1m 53.538s**	1m 54.273s
32	1m 53.748s	1m 54.431s
33	1m 54.374s	1m 54.753s
34	1m 54.163s	1m 55.304s
35	1m 54.767s	1m 55.242s
36	1m 55.380s	1m 55.714s
37	1m 55.619s	1m 55.406s
38	1m 55.831s	1m 55.411s
39	1m 55.803s	1m 55.365s
40	1m 55.125s	1m 55.777s
41	1m 55.369s	1m 56.431s
42	1m 56.759s	1m 55.961s
43	1m 59.161s	1m 57.674s
44	2m 02.196s	1m 56.600s

Brabham had retained the same bodywork and radiator layout which they had finally settled on at Brands Hatch and BMW, for their part, brought along revised specification engines on Saturday following detailed analysis of failures during a recent test session. Teo Fabi, now able to concentrate solely on Formula 1, showed the wisdom of his decision to quit CART racing by running competitively throughout practice, his only major problem being engine pick-up trouble on Friday morning. The Italian took eighth place, behind Lauda.

Renault occupied the second row, Derek Warwick beating his French team-mate by four hundredths of a second. Warwick had no major technical dramas to speak of and he even managed to find a clear lap on Friday. Unfortunately, that was before he turned the boost up for his second set of qualifiers and that lap was delayed fractionally by Winkelhock's ATS. On Saturday, he had eight cars to contend with on his quick lap, Warwick commenting that attempts to rid the car of slow turn-in had produced excellent handling overall.

Tambay was less fortunate. On Friday afternoon, a piston failed on his first lap, Patrick quickly switching to the spare car – which blew up as well. He then waited for Warwick to finish with his car before taking over and trying to qualify on a circuit coated with his own oil. Saturday was uneventful by comparison, Patrick setting fastest time in the wet session and a minor drop in revs preventing a completely satisfactory lap in the afternoon.

All was confusion within Ferrari. They not only turned up with four cars but there was a plethora of suspension variations; two having the regular pullrod activated rear spring damper units and two with revised pushrod arrangements and reprofiled underbodies. And neither driver could reach a firm conclusion. Michele Alboreto, finding the narrower, revised suspension nervous to drive, was forced to use that set-up on Saturday afternoon when his regular car developed an electrical problem. He eventually took sixth place while René Arnoux claimed 10th.

End of the Line. Elio de Angelis's excellent run of reliability ended when his engine failed after the Italian had led the first seven laps.

While Ferrari were in temporary decline, Toleman were buoyant after their third place at Brands Hatch and Ayrton Senna's stock had been raised by rumours linking his name with Lotus for 1985. Following Johnny Cecotto's unfortunate accident, the team entered just one car and built up a new chassis for the occasion. This featured Rory Byrne's latest thoughts on aerodynamics, the double rear wing making way for a more conventional single aerofoil and Senna declared himself very happy with the handling. The Brazilian used race tyres on his spare car while the track remained damp on Saturday afternoon but he soon switched to the race car for a run which was worth ninth place. This was achieved in spite of a slight engine misfire on the latest Hart which not only featured electronic ignition but also the larger Holset turbo first seen at Brands Hatch.

Judging by the rather tatty state of the Loto-Ligiers, development was standing still within the French team, Guy Ligier being notable by his absence once again. In spite of this and his troubles out on the track, de Cesaris took 11th place on his last lap of practice, François Hesnault being over one second slower. Jacques Laffite would start alongside de Cesaris, the Frenchman flinging the Williams FW09B through the stadium section in a gutsy, determined fashion. His efforts were to boost morale within the team following a dismal two days for Keke Rosberg.

While running his first set of qualifiers on Friday, Keke was baulked by Patrese and a second attempt on soft rubber was thwarted by a turbo failure. With no time to switch to the spare, the 1982 World Champion was bottom of the time sheet and praying that it would not rain. As a contingency measure, Frank Williams had gathered the approval of the pit lane to let Rosberg start in the same way that Gartner had been allowed to take a place on the grid at Brands Hatch but, in the event, that was to prove unnecessary. Rosberg did qualify – in 19th place, an engine failure ending his run on qualifiers after setting a time with race rubber at the start of the session. If nothing else, Rosberg had laid the groundwork for an exciting performance in the race.

ATS were generating their own excitement when yet another team manager, this time Colin Seeley of motorbike fame, held down the post for as much as a couple of days before learning about the idiosyncratic ways of Gunter Schmid. Seeley quit mid-way through practice on Saturday. The team had completed a second D7 (with a 7cm longer wheelbase) and Winkelhock, second fastest in the wet on Saturday, qualified in 13th place despite the loss of third gear during the final session.

The Barclays Arrows drivers proved evenly matched as they continued to run without the benefit of qualifying boost, Surer, the faster of the two, having a relatively trouble-free two days while Boutsen was slowed by a problem with the corner-weighting on his A7. The mood within the Benetton Alfa Romeo team remained tense following Patrese's unwillingness to recognise the fact that he had triggered off the accident at Brands Hatch which had cut Cheever's race short by about 70 laps! In addition, the Alfa V8s were delivering insufficient power, Cheever's frustration being

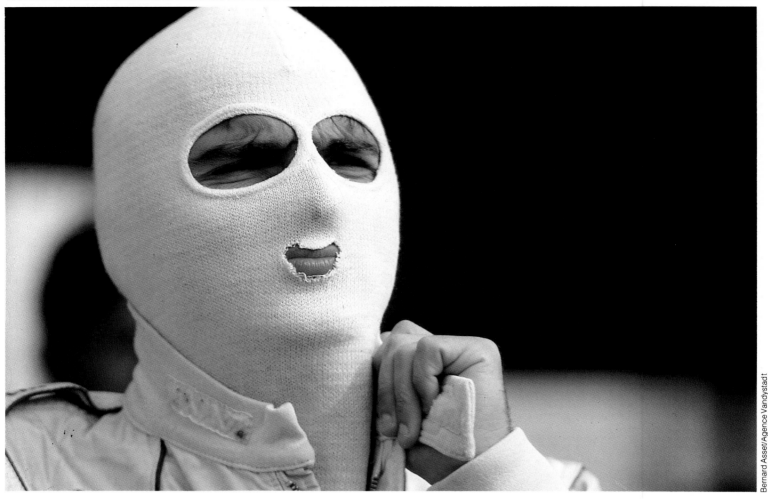

BMW Bandit. Once again, Nelson Piquet provided the only serious competition for McLaren, the Brabham
driver retiring with transmission trouble after leading in the early stages.

Bernard Asset/Agence Vandystadt

heightened by difficulty in dealing with the
Tyrrells on the straights.

The Kelemata Osella team had rebuilt Jo
Gartner's car following the Patrese-inspired shunt,
the Austrian qualifying comfortably in 23rd place
while his team-mate, Piercarlo Ghinzani, had a
couple of turbo failures to contend with on his
revamped car which now featured a longer
wheelbase. Ghinzani took 21st place and, splitting
the Osellas, Philippe Alliot proved to be the faster
of the RAM drivers after Jonathan Palmer had
been stranded out on the circuit with clutch trouble
on Saturday afternoon; poor reward for the
hard-working little team which had been stretched
to capacity following the ravages of the British
Grand Prix. Huub Rothengatter had to rely on his
Friday time to qualify the Spirit-Hart in 24th place
after completing just one lap in the final session
while Stefan Johansson put his Systime Tyrrell into
glorious power-slides only to be rewarded with the
last slot on the grid.

That left Mike Thackwell, standing in for Bellof
who was fulfilling a sportscar commitment at
Mosport, as non-qualifier even though the New
Zealander was just one-tenth of a second slower
than his team-mate. Ken Tyrrell, of course, tried to
follow the Williams example and he received the
agreement of every team manager – with the
exception of Marco Piccinini. Thackwell, therefore, was not allowed to join the grid for a race in
which a reliable Ford-Cosworth would reap the
benefits of the many anticipated turbo failures on
the long straights.

RACE

At six minutes past two, Alain Prost shot into the
pit lane, unbuckling his harness as he did so and
stabbing his finger in the direction of the McLaren
garage. His mechanics understood the message
immediately; the pole position man wanted to
swap to his spare car.

A change of fuel pump after the warm-up had
failed to cure a problem which now seemed to lie in
the drive to the pump and there was nothing for it
but to switch to the T-car, a chassis which had been
earmarked for Lauda this weekend and one in
which Prost had completed but one lap of
Hockenheim. McLaren, anticipating a last-minute
problem, had tailored the spare for Prost; it was
attention to details like that which had helped keep
them one step ahead of the competition . . .

There was no panic; just fast work as the
Frenchman was strapped in and sent on his way in
time to take his place on the grid. And, thanks to all
this drama, Prost failed to notice that officials had
set pole on the wrong side of the track. In fact, no
one appeared to notice the mirror image of the grid
and it was not until Derek Ongaro mounted the
rostrum that he spotted the error. But, since no one
was complaining, he let the countdown continue.

Any disadvantage, of course, would accrue to
Prost since he was on the outside and, into the
bargain, he was rushing towards the first corner
with brakes which were something of an unknown
quantity. It was not surprising, therefore, to find de
Angelis take the lead with Warwick doing his best
to tuck in behind the Lotus as they hit the brakes
for the right-hander. Prost would have none of it
and claimed the line, leaving Warwick to fend off a
strong attack from Piquet. By the time they
reached the far end, the Brabham was third.

Tambay held fifth place but the Renault driver,
fastest in the warm-up, was to be disappointed.
The engine which had felt sharp and powerful had
lost its edge for some unaccountable reason –
possibly due to the chilled fuel added for the race –
and the Frenchman was unable to offer any
resistance when Senna steamed by on lap two. By
lap four, Tambay was eighth, Lauda and Fabi
having passed the Renault under acceleration.

Senna's most promising race was to end on lap
five when the Toleman, flat in fifth gear, suddenly
spun and careered backwards into the barrier, the
impact ripping off the right-rear wheel. Senna

proved he was unhurt by climbing from the cockpit
and flinging the detachable steering wheel back
into the car. Subsequent examination would show
that the vibration from the Hart engine at 10,800
rpm had broken the bracket which held the bracing
wires to the new rear wing. The wing had suddenly
become detached to send the Toleman into its
high-speed orbit. (Tests at 10,500 rpm had proved
perfectly satisfactory).

By now, Prost had become confident enough
with his car to close the gap on de Angelis and pull
away slightly from Piquet. The momentary respite
had lulled Elio into a false sense of security, the
Italian turning down his boost before winding it up
once more as the McLaren crept closer. De
Angelis's worst fears were to be proved well-
founded on lap eight when the Renault suddenly
belched flame leaving the disconsolate driver to
make a rather pointless attempt at returning his
stricken car back to the pits. The 95T had been
handling perfectly but whether the Goodyear tyres
could have withstood the pace was to remain
unanswered.

Prior to his retirement, de Angelis had resorted
to weaving on the straight in a bid to keep Prost at
bay and the subsequent engine failure would cause
Alain to lift slightly and allow Piquet to close.
Maintaining this momentum, the Brabham driver
took the lead before reaching the stadium, the
order at the end of a busy lap eight being: Piquet,
Prost, Warwick, Lauda . . . and Rosberg!

The performance of the Williams was simply
astonishing. There had been warning during the
warm-up when Rosberg had been fourth fastest.
Any thoughts that he was running with a less than
full tank of fuel were quickly dispelled when the
Finn began his charge from 19th place on the grid
by overtaking Boutsen on the grass at the start. On
lap two, he passed four cars! The FW09B was
handling superbly – and the team were not entirely
sure why that should be but their man was
certainly making the most of this unexpected

With scarcely a backward glance, Keke Rosberg leaves his mechanics to push the unloved Williams-Honda away from the weighing area during official practice at Hockenheim. After a troubled two days, Rosberg stormed through from the back of the grid before retiring with an electrical failure.

turn-around.

Fabi was sixth, Tambay seventh followed by Laffite (also making excellent progress), Arnoux, Mansell and Boutsen, the Belgian soon to retire with no oil pressure. That was to make a short race for Arrows, Surer having crept into the pits at the end of lap one with his fuel metering unit having gone awry. Alliot then made an unsuccessful pit stop to cure an overheating problem, the RAM making it five retirements in eight laps.

The list, regrettably, was to grow longer on lap 10 when both Williams drivers retired, Laffite with a piston failure and Rosberg stopping when an electrical sensor on the engine failed to send out the necessary messages. It had been an enthralling drive but, once again, we were left to ponder just how much longer Rosberg's Goodyears could have withstood such energetic driving. As it was, the Akron company were having a difficult enough time with Michelin runners filling the first six places and another blow was dealt out when Alboreto stopped to investigate a misfire, the Ferrari eventually being pushed away.

With the field thinning rapidly, attention centred on the Brabham/McLaren tactical battle at the front. Nelson had begun to extend the gap from 2.7 to 3.3 and then 5.6 seconds while Prost was keeping an eye on the progress of Lauda in third place. By lap 20, all three had closed considerably and the reason became clear when Piquet came round in third place at the end of lap 22. The Brabham was in trouble.

A broken pinion bearing meant the loss of one gear after another and the Brazilian headed for the pit lane at the end of the next lap. The Brabham crew had gathered their man was in some sort of mechanical trouble and it was clear a change of tyres would not be necessary. But no! What's this? Nelson arrives at his pit, blipping the engine and pointing at each corner of the car. The startled mechanics threw themselves into action, jumping back and raising their arms in the air when the

fresh rubber had been fitted. Then, nothing . . . Piquet switched off the engine and applauded before climbing from the car, grinning broadly. The mechanics, seeing the joke, fell about.

Two years previously, Nelson Piquet had come to blows with Eliseo Salazar after losing the lead of the German Grand Prix. His relaxed attitude in 1984 said much about the mature Champion.

Over by the pit wall, however, the Brabham management were heartened by the performance of Fabi, the Italian now in fourth place and closing on Warwick. The Renault team kept their man advised of the danger and Derek increased his pace just enough to keep the Brabham at bay. By lap 23, it was all over, Fabi crawling into the pits with no boost and with the Italian's retirement went the final shred of interest at the front of the field. With Munich finally banished, Stuttgart were holding all the aces, the Porsche-engined McLarens now waging their private battle for the race and, more likely, the Championship.

As far as the German Grand Prix was concerned, Prost set the pace, successfully breaking a challenge from Lauda by setting the fastest lap of the race and extending the gap to around nine seconds. Lauda, ever the realist, decided that six points were to be his reward today. Had he been able to see the front of Prost's car, he might have thought otherwise.

With a dozen or so laps remaining, a large piece of polythene wedged itself into the gap between the left-front wing and the nose cone of McLaren number seven. If the airstream whisked it into the radiator inlet, Prost most certainly would be in trouble. In the event, the air flow merely served to wedge the wrapper more firmly and left Prost to worry about what might fail on the spare car.

The answer, of course, was nothing. MP4/2, chassis number 3, did not miss a beat. Neither for that matter did chassis number 1, Lauda maintaining the challenge until the end. Warwick would finish a lonely third, his only problem being a

last-minute change of ratio for second gear which proved to be too long. In the final stages, it seemed we might have a battle between two Englishmen as Nigel Mansell moved into fourth place but Warwick had the situation under control.

Mansell, for his part, had his own problems, the Lotus driver courageously nursing left-hand tyres which had long since passed their best. Mansell, seeing the blown engines around the circuit, had wisely taken it easy in the opening laps before moving though to engage in a difficult battle with Tambay. While the Renault may have been down on power on the straight, Tambay's tyres were in better shape and gave the Frenchman the crucial advantage in the corners. It would take Mansell 10 laps to find a way past.

Finishing sixth, René Arnoux, winner of the race in 1983. Never in the hunt from start, Arnoux had been forced to stop for tyres on lap 27, the Frenchman rejoining to take a lonely run to the flag. One of the few highlights of the German Grand Prix had been a battle between the Ligiers, François Hesnault overtaking Andrea de Cesaris on a number of occasions despite a broken brake balance adjuster which should have cured locking front brakes. The French cars finished seventh and eighth. But at least they were reliable. So, too, was the Tyrrell of Stefan Johansson, the Swede thoroughly enjoying himself as he kept ahead of Huub Rothengatter, the final finisher in tenth place and the only Hart representative.

For Porsche, it was a dream result. Pole position; fastest lap; first and second. What more could they ask? First and second fastest in practice perhaps. Certainly, Lauda would have preferred a front row start since it was apparent he could ill-afford to give his team-mate any advantage. Doubtless the senior member of the McLaren driving partnership mulled this over as he stood on the rostrum and watched Prost playfully spray champagne over Jean-Marie Balestre. Clearly, these young drivers had no respect for their elders . . .   MH

Entries and practice times

No.	Driver	Nat	Car	Tyre	Engine	Entrant	Practice 1	Practice 2
1	Nelson Piquet	BR	Parmalat BRABHAM BT53	M	BMW M12/13	MRD International	1m 48·698s	1m 48·584s
2	Teo Fabi	I	Parmalat BRABHAM BT53	M	BMW M12/13	MRD International	1m 51·693s	1m 49·302s
3	Stefan Johansson	S	TYRRELL 012	G	Ford Cosworth DFY	Tyrrell Racing Organisation	2m 00·268s	1m 59·461s
4	Mike Thackwell	NZ	TYRRELL 012	G	Ford Cosworth DFY	Tyrrell Racing Organisation	2m 01·320s	1m 59·516s
5	Jacques Laffite	F	WILLIAMS FW09B	G	Honda RA 163-E	Williams Grand Prix Engineering	1m 51·428s	1m 50·511s
6	Keke Rosberg	SF	WILLIAMS FW09B	G	Honda RA 163-E	Williams Grand Prix Engineering	2m 12·229s	1m 52·003s
7	Alain Prost	F	Marlboro McLAREN MP4/2	M	TAG P01 (TTE P01)	Marlboro McLaren International	1m 49·439s	1m 47·012s
8	Niki Lauda	A	Marlboro McLAREN MP4/2	M	TAG P01 (TTE P01)	Marlboro McLaren International	1m 48·912s	1m 49·004s
9	Philippe Alliot	F	RAM 02	P	Hart 415T	Skoal Bandit Formula 1 Team	1m 55·505s	1m 55·795s
10	Jonathan Palmer	GB	RAM 02	P	Hart 415T	Skoal Bandit Formula 1 Team	1m 56·797s	
11	Elio de Angelis	I	John Player Special LOTUS 95T	G	Renault EF4	John Player Team Lotus	1m 48·033s	1m 47·065s
12	Nigel Mansell	GB	John Player Special LOTUS 95T	G	Renault EF4	John Player Team Lotus	1m 52·958s	1m 51·715s
14	Manfred Winkelhock	D	ATS D7	P	BMW M12/13	Team ATS	1m 51·697s	1m 50·686s
15	Patrick Tambay	F	Elf RENAULT RE50	M	Renault EF4	Equipe Renault Elf	1m 51·414s	1m 48·425s
16	Derek Warwick	GB	Elf RENAULT RE50	M	Renault EF4	Equipe Renault Elf	1m 48·576s	1m 48·382s
17	Marc Surer	CH	ARROWS A7	G	BMW M12/13	Barclay Nordica Arrows BMW	1m 56·450s	1m 51·475s
18	Thierry Boutsen	B	ARROWS A7	G	BMW M12/13	Barclay Nordica Arrows BMW	1m 52·144s	1m 51·551s
19	Ayrton Senna	BR	TOLEMAN TG184	M	Hart 415T	Toleman Group Motorsport	1m 49·395s	1m 49·831s
21	Huub Rothengatter	NL	SPIRIT 101	P	Hart 415T	Spirit Racing	1m 56·112s	2m 00·118s
22	Riccardo Patrese	I	Benetton ALFA ROMEO 184T	G	Alfa Romeo 183T	Benetton Team Alfa Romeo	1m 52·769s	1m 54·665s
23	Eddie Cheever	USA	Benetton ALFA ROMEO 184T	G	Alfa Romeo 183T	Benetton Team Alfa Romeo	1m 54·802s	1m 51·950s
24	Piercarlo Ghinzani	I	Kelemata OSELLA FA1F	P	Alfa Romeo 183T	Osella Squadra Corse	1m 59·505s	1m 54·546s
25	François Hesnault	F	LIGIER Loto JS23	M	Renault EF4	Ligier Loto	1m 53·985s	1m 51·872s
26	Andrea de Cesaris	I	LIGIER Loto JS23	M	Renault EF4	Ligier Loto	1m 50·338s	1m 50·117s
27	Michele Alboreto	I	Fiat FERRARI 126C4	G	Ferrari 126C	Scuderia Ferrari SpA	1m 49·782s	1m 48·847s
28	René Arnoux	F	Fiat FERRARI 126C4	G	Ferrari 126C	Scuderia Ferrari SpA	1m 50·830s	1m 49·857s
30	Jo Gartner	A	Kelemata OSELLA FA1F	P	Alfa Romeo 183T	Osella Squadra Corse	1m 58·457s	1m 55·594s

		Fri pm Hot, dry	Sat pm Warm, dry

Friday morning and Saturday morning practice sessions not officially recorded.

G – Goodyear, M – Michelin, P – Pirelli.

Starting grid

7 PROST (1m 47·012s)
McLaren

    11 DE ANGELIS (1m 47·065s)
    Lotus

16 WARWICK (1m 48·382s)
Renault

    15 TAMBAY (1m 48·425s)
    Renault

1 PIQUET (1m 48·584s)
Brabham

    27 ALBORETO (1m 48·847s)
    Ferrari

8 LAUDA (1m 48·912s)
McLaren

    2 FABI (1m 49·302s)
    Brabham

19 SENNA (1m 49·395s)
Toleman

    28 ARNOUX (1m 49·857s)
    Ferrari

26 DE CESARIS (1m 50·117s)
Ligier

    5 LAFFITE (1m 50·511s)
    Williams

14 WINKELHOCK (1m 50·686s)
ATS

    17 SURER (1m 51·475s)
    Arrows

18 BOUTSEN (1m 51·551s)
Arrows

    12 MANSELL (1m 51·715s)
    Lotus

25 HESNAULT (1m 51·872s)
Ligier

    23 CHEEVER (1m 51·950s)
    Alfa Romeo

6 ROSBERG (1m 52·003s)
Williams

    22 PATRESE (1m 52·769s)
    Alfa Romeo

24 GHINZANI (1m 54·546s)
Osella

    9 ALLIOT (1m 55·505s)
    RAM

30 GARTNER (1m 55·594s)
Osella

    21 ROTHENGATTER (1m 56·112s)
    Spirit

10 PALMER (1m 56·797s)
RAM

    3 JOHANSSON (1m 59·461s)
    Tyrrell

Did not start:
4 Mike Thackwell (Tyrrell), 1m 59·516s, did not qualify.

Results and retirements

Place	Driver	Car	Laps	Time and Speed (mph/km/h)/Retirement	
1	Alain Prost	McLaren-TAG t/c V6	44	1h 24m 43·210	131·608/211·803
2	Niki Lauda	McLaren-TAG t/c V6	44	1h 24m 46·359s	131·544/211·7
3	Derek Warwick	Renault t/c V6	44	1h 25m 19·633s	130·674/210·3
4	Nigel Mansell	Lotus-Renault t/c V6	44	1h 25m 34·873s	130·301/209·7
5	Patrick Tambay	Renault t/c V6	44	1h 25m 55·159s	129·742/208·8
6	René Arnoux	Ferrari t/c V6	43		
7	Andrea de Cesaris	Ligier-Renault t/c V6	43		
8	François Hesnault	Ligier-Renault t/c V6	43		
9	Stefan Johansson	Tyrrell-Cosworth V8	42		
10	Huub Rothengatter	Spirit-Hart t/c 4	40		
	Manfred Winkelhock	ATS-BMW t/c V8	31	Turbo boost/gearbox	
	Eddie Cheever	Alfa Romeo t/c V8	29	Engine	
	Teo Fabi	Brabham-BMW t/c 4	28	Lost boost	
	Nelson Piquet	Brabham-BMW t/c 4	23	Gearbox pinion bearing	
	Riccardo Patrese	Alfa Romeo t/c V8	16	Metering unit	
	Piercarlo Ghinzani	Osella-Alfa Romeo t/c V8	14	Electrics	
	Jo Gartner	Osella-Alfa Romeo t/c V8	13	Turbo	
	Michele Alboreto	Ferrari t/c V6	13	Engine misfire	
	Jonathan Palmer	RAM-Hart t/c 4	11	Turbo	
	Keke Rosberg	Williams-Honda t/c V6	10	Electrics	
	Jacques Laffite	Williams-Honda t/c V6	10	Engine	
	Thierry Boutsen	Arrows-BMW t/c 4	8	Oil pressure	
	Elio de Angelis	Lotus-Renault t/c V6	8	Turbo	
	Philippe Alliot	RAM-Hart t/c 4	7	Overheating	
	Ayrton Senna	Toleman-Hart t/c 4	4	Accident (rear wing failure)	
	Marc Surer	Arrows-BMW t/c 4	1	Turbo	

Fastest lap: Prost, on lap 31, 1m 53·538s, 133·915mph/215·515km/h (record).
Previous lap record: René Arnoux (F1 Ferrari 126C3 t/c V6), 1m 53·938s, 133·444mph/214·758km/h (1983).

Past winners

Year	Driver	Nat	Car	Circuit	Distance miles/km	Speed mph/km/h
1950*	Alberto Ascari	I	2·0 Ferrari 166	Nürburgring North	266·78/364·96	77·75/125·13
1951	Alberto Ascari	I	4·5 Ferrari 375	Nürburgring North	283·47/456·20	83·76/134·80
1952	Alberto Ascari	I	2·0 Ferrari 500	Nürburgring North	255·12/410·58	82·20/132·29
1953	Giuseppe Farina	I	2·0 Ferrari 500	Nürburgring North	255·12/410·58	83·91/135·04
1954	Juan Manuel Fangio	RA	2·5 Mercedes-Benz W196	Nürburgring North	311·82/501·82	82·87/133·37
1956	Juan Manuel Fangio	RA	2·5 Lancia-Ferrari D50	Nürburgring North	311·82/501·82	85·45/137·52
1957	Juan Manuel Fangio	RA	2·5 Maserati 250F	Nürburgring North	311·82/501·82	88·82/142·94
1958	Tony Brooks	GB	2·5 Vanwall	Nürburgring North	212·60/342·15	90·31/145·34
1959	Tony Brooks	GB	2·4 Ferrari Dino 256	Avus	309·44/498·00	145·35/230·70
1960*	Jo Bonnier	S	1·5 Porsche 718	Nürburgring South	154·04/247·90	80·23/129·12
1961	Stirling Moss	GB	1·5 Lotus 18/21-Climax	Nürburgring North	212·60/342·15	92·30/148·54
1962	Graham Hill	GB	1·5 BRM P57	Nürburgring North	212·60/342·15	80·35/129·31
1963	John Surtees	GB	1·5 Ferrari 156	Nürburgring North	212·60/342·15	95·83/154·22
1964	John Surtees	GB	1·5 Ferrari 158	Nürburgring North	212·60/342·15	96·58/155·43
1965	Jim Clark	GB	1·5 Lotus 33-Climax	Nürburgring North	212·60/342·15	96·76/160·55
1966	Jack Brabham	AUS	3·0 Brabham BT19-Repco	Nürburgring North	212·60/342·15	86·75/139·61
1967	Denny Hulme	NZ	3·0 Brabham BT24-Repco	Nürburgring North	212·60/342·15	101·41/163·20
1968	Jackie Stewart	GB	3·0 Matra MS10-Ford	Nürburgring North	198·65/319·69	85·71/137·94
1969	Jacky Ickx	B	3·0 Brabham BT26A-Ford	Nürburgring North	198·65/319·69	108·43/174·50
1970	Jochen Rindt	A	3·0 Lotus 72-Ford	Hockenheim	210·92/339·44	124·07/199·67
1971	Jackie Stewart	GB	3·0 Tyrrell 003-Ford	Nürburgring North	170·27/274·02	114·45/184·19
1972	Jacky Ickx	B	3·0 Ferrari 312B-2/72	Nürburgring North	198·65/319·69	116·62/187·68
1973	Jackie Stewart	GB	3·0 Tyrrell 006-Ford	Nürburgring North	198·65/319·69	116·79/187·95
1974	Clay Regazzoni	CH	3·0 Ferrari 312B-3/74	Nürburgring North	198·65/319·69	117·33/188·82
1975	Carlos Reutemann	RA	3·0 Brabham BT44B-Ford	Nürburgring North	198·65/319·69	117·73/189·47
1976	James Hunt	GB	3·0 McLaren M23-Ford	Nürburgring North	198·65/319·69	117·18/188·59
1977	Niki Lauda	A	3·0 Ferrari 312T-2/77	Hockenheim	198·27/319·08	129·57/208·53
1978	Mario Andretti	USA	3·0 JPS Lotus 79-Ford	Hockenheim	189·83/305·51	129·41/208·26
1979	Alan Jones	AUS	3·0 Williams FW07-Ford	Hockenheim	189·83/305·51	134·27/216·09
1980	Jacques Laffite	F	3·0 Ligier JS11/15-Ford	Hockenheim	189·83/305·51	137·22/220·83
1981	Nelson Piquet	BR	3·0 Brabham BT49C-Ford	Hockenheim	189·83/305·51	132·53/213·29
1982	Patrick Tambay	F	1·5 Ferrari 126C2 t/c	Hockenheim	190·05/305·86	130·43/209·90
1983	René Arnoux	F	1·5 Ferrari 126C3 t/c	Hockenheim	190·05/305·86	130·81/210·52
1984	Alain Prost	F	1·5 McLaren MP4/2-TAG t/c	Hockenheim	185·83/299·07	131·61/211·80

* Non-championship (Formula 2)

Circuit data

Hockenheim-Ring, near Heidelberg
Circuit length: 4·2234 miles/6·797 km
Race distance: 44 laps, 185·83 miles/299·068 km
Race weather: Warm, dry

Fastest laps

Driver	Time	Lap
Alain Prost	1m 53·538s	31
Niki Lauda	1m 53·778s	29
Nelson Piquet	1m 54·328s	6
Nigel Mansell	1m 54·466s	33
Keke Rosberg	1m 54·529s	7
Patrick Tambay	1m 54·583s	33
Elio de Angelis	1m 54·776s	7
Derek Warwick	1m 55·024s	37
Teo Fabi	1m 55·062s	23
René Arnoux	1m 55·668s	32
Ayrton Senna	1m 55·712s	4
Jacques Laffite	1m 56·176s	4
Michele Alboreto	1m 56·930s	4
Thierry Boutsen	1m 57·142s	7
Eddie Cheever	1m 57·460s	18
Riccardo Patrese	1m 58·257s	7
François Hesnault	1m 58·421s	7
Piercarlo Ghinzani	1m 58·425s	7
Andrea de Cesaris	1m 58·588s	5
Manfred Winkelhock	1m 58·658s	6
Jo Gartner	1m 59·567s	7
Stefan Johansson	2m 00·730s	36
Jonathan Palmer	2m 01·116s	7
Philippe Alliot	2m 02·203s	2
Huub Rothengatter	2m 03·195s	2
Marc Surer	3m 02·645s	1

Points

WORLD CHAMPIONSHIP OF DRIVERS

1	Alain Prost	43·5 pts
2	Niki Lauda	39
3	Elio de Angelis	26·5
4	René Arnoux	24·5
5	Derek Warwick	23
6	Keke Rosberg	20
7	Nelson Piquet	18
8	Michele Alboreto	11
9=	Patrick Tambay	9
9=	Nigel Mansell	9
11	Ayrton Senna	8
12	Jacques Laffite	4
13=	Eddie Cheever	3
13=	Riccardo Patrese	3
13=	Teo Fabi	3
16=	Andrea de Cesaris	2
16=	Piercarlo Ghinzani	2
18	Thierry Boutsen	1
*	Martin Brundle	8
*	Stefan Bellof	5

CONSTRUCTORS' CUP

1	McLaren	82·5 pts
2=	Ferrari	35·5
2=	Lotus	35·5
4	Renault	32
5	Williams	24
6	Brabham	21
7	Toleman	8
8	Alfa Romeo	6
9=	Ligier	2
9=	Osella	2
11	Arrows	1
*	Tyrrell	13

* Points removed by FISA Executive Committee.

Johansson drove a spirited if lonely race into ninth place.

Lap chart

1st LAP ORDER	1	2	3	4	5	6	7	8	9	10	11	12	13	14	15	16	17	18	19	20	21	22	23	24	25	26	27	28	29	30	31	32	33	34	35	36	37	38	39	40	41	42	43	44
11 E. De Angelis	11	11	11	11	11	11	11	1	1	1	1	1	1	1	1	1	1	1	1	1	1	7	7	7	7	7	7	7	7	7	7	7	7	7	7	7	7	7	7	7	7	7	7	7
7 A. Prost	7	7	7	7	7	7	7	7	7	7	7	7	7	7	7	7	7	7	7	7	7	8	8	8	8	8	8	8	8	8	8	8	8	8	8	8	8	8	8	8	8	8	8	8
1 N. Piquet	1	1	1	1	1	1	1	16	8	8	8	8	8	8	8	8	8	8	8	8	8	1	16	16	16	16	16	16	16	16	16	16	16	16	16	16	16	16	16	16	16	16	16	16
16 D. Warwick	16	16	16	16	16	16	16	16	16	16	16	16	16	16	16	16	16	16	16	16	16	2	2	2	2	15	15	15	15	15	12	12	12	12	12	12	12	12	12	12	12	12	12	12
15 P. Tambay	15	19	19	19	8	8	8	6	16	16	2	2	2	2	2	2	2	2	2	2	2	15	15	15	15	12	12	12	12	12	15	15	15	15	15	15	15	15	15	15	15	15	15	15
19 A. Senna	19	15	15	8	2	2	6	2	2	2	15	15	15	15	15	15	15	15	15	15	15	12	12	12	12	2	28	28	28	28	28	28	28	28	28	28	28	28	28					
27 M. Alboreto	27	8	8	2	6	6	2	15	15	15	28	28	28	28	28	28	12	12	12	12	12	28	28	28	28	26	26	26	26	26	25	25	26	25	25	25	26	26	26	26				
8 N. Lauda	8	27	2	15	15	15	5	5	28	12	12	12	12	12	12	12	28	28	28	28	1	23	23	23	23	25	25	25	25	26	26	26	25	26	26	26	25	25	25	25				
2 T. Fabi	2	2	27	27	27	27	28	28	28	28	2	23	23	23	23	23	23	23	23	23	23	26	26	26	26	3	3	3	3	3	3	3	3	3	3	3	3	3	3	3				
26 A. de Cesaris	26	26	28	6	28	28	5	12	12	23	23	25	25	26	26	26	26	26	26	25	26	26	26		25	25	25	25	25	3	21	21	21	21	21	21	21	21	21	21				
28 R. Arnoux	28	28	6	28	5	5	27	18	23	25	26	25	25	25	25	25	25	26	25	25	25				14	14	14	14	14	3	14	14	14											
14 M. Winkelhock	14	6	26	5	26	12	12	26	26	14	14	14	14	14	14	14	14	14	14	14	14	3	3	3	3	14	21																	
23 E. Cheever	23	14	14	26	12	26	26	23	14	14	24	24	24	24	24	22	22	3	21	21	21	21	21																					
5 J. Laffite	5	23	5	12	14	14	18	14	25	24	22	22	22	22	22	3	3	21	21	21	21	21																						
12 N. Mansell	12	5	23	14	23	18	23	25	24	22	30	30	30	3	21	21																												
6 K. Rosberg	6	12	12	23	18	23	14	27	22	5	3	3	21																															
25 F. Hesnault	25	25	25	18	25	25	25	24	30	21	21	21																																
22 R. Patrese	22	22	18	25	22	22	22	22	10	10	10	27	27																															
24 P. Ghinzani	24	24	22	22	24	24	24	30	3	3	27																																	
30 J. Gartner	30	18	24	24	30	30	30	10	21	21																																		
18 T. Boutsen	18	30	30	30	10	10	10	3	27	27																																		
9 P. Alliot	9	9	10	3	3	3	21																																					
3 S. Johansson	3	10	9	3	21	21	21	11																																				
10 J. Palmer	10	3	3	9	9	9	9																																					
21 H. Rothengatter	21	21	21	21																																								
17 M. Surer	17																																											

181

Grosser Preis von Österreich

IT had been thirteen successful years since Niki Lauda made his Grand Prix debut on his home soil, an inauspicious and singularly unspectacular first Formula 1 drive, ending in retirement, at the wheel of a "renta drive" works March 711. In the years that followed there were to be a couple of World Championships, not to mention world-wide fame and acclaim, awaiting the toothy youngster from Vienna, but never, so it seemed, victory in his home Grand Prix. The nearest he had managed was a distant second in 1977 behind Alan Jones's Shadow DN8 – a result achieved at the wheel of a Ferrari 312T2 and rounded off by a blazing row with Mauro Forghieri.

This time, be it whispered, Niki Lauda looked as though he had the Austrian Grand Prix in the palm of his hand. Team-mate Prost had spun off, falling foul of an oil slick dropped by Elio de Angelis's stricken Lotus 95T, and reigning World Champion Nelson Piquet had eased his pace to conserve badly wearing rear Michelins. On lap 40, with only 11 left to run, Lauda had scythed ahead of the Brazilian's Brabham and now only had to cruise home to that long-awaited first Österreichring victory.

Suddenly, it all seemed to go wrong. Plunging down the long left-hander into the *Texaco-Schikane*, Niki suddenly flung up his arm. A Brabham whisked past him! It was all over. The crowds in the grandstands half rose to their feet, groaning with disappointment. But wait, Niki was still running. The Brabham had been Fabi's and their hero was still in the lead . . .

"I was hard on the throttle in fourth gear when there was an enormous 'bang' as the gear broke," reflected Lauda after the race was over, "I thought, well, that's the end of that, and I began to slow, looking for somewhere to park it. Then I began to fish around to see if there were any other gears still working. I got third, then I found fifth . . . so I thought, let's go on and see how far we get . . ." Niki lost the best part of seven seconds in a single lap, but managed to nurse his McLaren those last crucial ten laps to win the Austrian Grand Prix, consolidating his position at the head of the World Championship table.

Nelson Piquet, secure in second place, simply reckoned that Niki was rolling it off, cruising home. He had no idea that the Austrian was nursing that ailing gearbox and praying for an easy run. So the Brabham team leader cruised home some 24 seconds behind the winning McLaren. Arguably, it was the biggest misjudgement of Nelson Piquet's career: if he had kept up the pressure over those final few laps he might have put Niki under too much strain. As it was, Lauda was able to ease his way home to, possibly, the most inwardly satisfying victory of all.

ENTRY AND PRACTICE

Frequently, the Austrian Grand Prix turns out to be a crucial turning point on the World Championship calendar. The 1983 race marked Renault's most recent Grand Prix triumph thanks to the efforts of Alain Prost and, more importantly, it was the event at which the Frenchman came to fully appreciate the Brabham-BMW potential. Although he emerged victorious, the days immediately after the race sowed the seeds of discontent which would eventually lead to his departure from the team at the end of the season. Prost went straight back and told Renault that, unless they stepped up the pace of engine development, they would lose the Championship to the Brazilian. And, as things turned out, Prost's prediction proved totally correct.

This year, when the teams returned to the super-fast 3.692-mile Österreichring, Alain Prost and team-mate Niki Lauda were jousting, apparently alone, for the '84 Championship title. Piquet had long faded from the overall equation thanks to that apparently endless run of mechanical problems, punctuated only by those brilliant victories at Detroit and Montreal, but there was no way that he could be ignored on a race-to-race basis. Although Nelson's chances of retaining the Championship had virtually slipped away with his retirement at Hockenheim, he was destined to be the most enduring thorn in the McLaren team's

flesh throughout the Austrian GP weekend.

During first qualifying on Friday the McLarens were quickest, Prost marginally ahead of Lauda, with Nelson lurking in third place as the only other competitor to breach the 1m 27s barrier. Then, on Saturday afternoon, pit lane onlookers were treated to a classic demonstration of the cool, controlled Piquet/Gordon Murray partnership. On his first set of Michelin qualifiers, Piquet ripped on to the front row alongside Prost. Then he pulled into the pits and sat, his BT53 fitted out with its second set of qualifiers, awaiting the signal from Brabham's chief designer. Meanwhile, in the cool of the Brabham garage his mechanics and Michelin tyre technicians were examining the tyres from that first run, selecting the two best surviving covers to match with the two best survivors from the second set – just in case Nelson might need a third bite at the cherry. He didn't! On his second set he slammed round in 1m 26.173s to throw pole position beyond the reach of his rivals.

"The car feels pretty good, but those McLaren drivers are having an easier ride," mused Nelson at the end of the day, "we may be strong in qualifying, but I don't underestimate just how difficult it will be to beat them. They will be in really strong shape come race day." A succession of minor, trifling problems bugged the McLaren team's progress on Friday, but a 1m 26.03s was good enough to stand Prost as quickest overall. On Saturday afternoon Alain's defence of his pole position was badly

compromised when his race car's engine failed and, before he could get into the swing of things with the team's spare car, Andrea de Cesaris and Elio de Angelis had both suffered major engine failures and doused the track surface with oil.

Lauda complained about excessive oversteer on his first timed run, waiting in the pit lane until Prost returned from his first run in the spare to report on the state of the track surface. Prost was surprised that it did not feel too bad – "the only real problem is a big patch on the entrance to the chicane at the top of the hill" – but at the end of the day neither McLaren driver managed to improve on his best Friday times. Alain was held up in the traffic and Lauda was late out for his second qualifying run after problems with a slightly sticking throttle return spring. Prost hung on to second place with Lauda's 1m 26.715s earning him fourth place on the outside of row two.

Slipping into third place on the grid after a splendid effort during final qualifying was Goodyear's best-placed runner Elio de Angelis. Despite the fact that Akron's qualifying rubber was even more marginal than Michelin's, Elio managed to keep his tyres in just about one piece as he recorded a last-moment 1m 26.318s. The Italian managed this superb effort despite the tyres losing grip badly on the last corner of the lap plus the fact that he was still running a rather tired Renault V6 which had a good few hundred miles' use behind it – including a test session at Donington the previous

Niki Lauda was forced to borrow his team-mate's overalls for the race after the zip on the Austrian's driving suit had broken. Nelson Piquet sees the funny side but Lauda had the last laugh, the McLaren driver winning his home Grand Prix in spite of losing fourth gear. Had Piquet realised Lauda's dilemma, then the Brabham driver might have won instead of driving conservatively into second place.

week in the hands of F3 man-of-the-moment Johnny Dumfries.

Elio's success came at the end of two practice sessions which had started on a pessimistic note the previous day. On Friday his 95T not only blew its engine early during the untimed morning stint, but when Elio took over the spare car it was not long before he spun off wildly into one of the many cornfields which flank the Österreichring. When the Lotus was retrieved it looked more like a combine harvester than a Grand Prix racing car . . .

Team-mate Nigel Mansell, occupant of third place on the previous year's Austrian GP grid at the wheel of a Pirelli-shod Lotus 94T, had a less successful time than his Italian colleague. Wary about possible engine problems in the wake of Elio's morning failure, the team ran very conservative turbo boost pressure on Nigel's car during first qualifying which left his 95T a bit breathless when it came to straight line speed. "But it handles really well," grinned the Englishman, "I can't fault it in that area!"

On Saturday morning Nigel suffered a major engine failure which meant that Bob Dance and his mechanics had their work cut out installing a fresh V6 in time for the final session, but this was duly completed with a few minutes to spare and Mansell went out for a final effort at matching his previous year's grid position. No chance. Mid-way round the dauntingly fast *Boschkurve*, the Lotus's rear Goodyears began blistering badly and an eighth quickest 1m 27.558s was all he could manage.

Determined to mark the anniversary of the team's last win on a successful note, Derek Warwick and Patrick Tambay were both feeling in a confident mood at the wheel of their Renault RE50s, the Frenchman quickly satisfying himself that he preferred the spare chassis to his own race car and settling down to work with that throughout the weekend. Both men had a touch too much understeer for their liking on Friday, but Tambay was brimful of confidence after his first qualifying run on Saturday, begging Gerard Larrousse to leave the car as it was for his second stab at a top grid position.

However, Larrousse was absolutely convinced that a *banzai* run was essential, so the turbo boost pressure was cranked up and Patrick could scarcely believe the way in which the RE50 came off the *Boschkurve* on his "warm up" lap. Convinced he had the potential to get on to the front row, the Frenchman hurtled into his qualifying lap with an empty track immediately in front of him, but the engine failed spectacularly in a cloud of oil and water at the top of the hill beyond the pits, leaving him with a fifth fastest 1m 26.748s under his belt.

Warwick survived a spectacular close shave with Niki Lauda on Friday as he exited the *Boschkurve*. "I was just warming up, wiping my vizor actually," explained Derek, "and Niki came out of the corner on his quick lap . . ." Fortunately Warwick did not move suddenly in any direction, so Niki was able to nail his way through on the right-hand side, his two wheels shaving the grass as he did so. After the session the two men met up and commiserated with each other over what they both agreed was a character building incident!

By opting for a steady drive without pit stops, Michele Alboreto salvaged third place out of a miserable season for Ferrari. The Italian team continued to play around with various aerodynamic and suspension configurations in a bid to find additional grip from their Goodyears. Alboreto laps Jonathan Palmer as the RAM heads for an encouraging ninth place *(right)*.
Never having driven a Formula 1 turbo before, Gerhard Berger gave a good account of himself in the second ATS *(below)*.
Niki Lauda won his home Grand Prix for the first time and moved to the head of the championship *(bottom)*.

Warwick qualified just behind Tambay on 1m 27.123s, slightly disappointed at the level of power his engine was producing during final qualifying, but reasonably optimistic for the race. Teo Fabi's Brabham BT53 paired with Mansell on the fourth row of the grid, the Italian having to use Piquet's car after Nelson had finished with it on Friday afternoon after spinning off at the *Rindtkurve* during the unofficial session, ripping two wheels off his BT53 in the process. It was back together for Saturday and Teo managed a 1m 27.201s to repay the mechanics' efforts.

Over in the Williams camp Keke Rosberg was not really making a great deal of progress with the unloved FW09B, recording a ninth quickest 1m 28.760s and remarking "it just feels slow – I think we lost some turbo boost pressure". Two places behind the Flying Finn came his team-mate Jacques Laffite, who had matched Rosberg's testing times at the Österreichring. But loss of fuel pressure and heavy traffic during the final session prevented him from improving on 1m 29.228s.

Toleman still had not nominated anybody to stand in for the injured Johnny Cecotto, leaving Ayrton Senna with the pick of the available machinery throughout the weekend. The new lad's basic problem amounted to having a race car which handled well, but was equipped with an engine that would not rev. properly – and a spare car which had a good engine but which did not handle as well. After Friday's morning session the electronic management system was taken off the race car and transferred to the spare – with the result that this car then pulled so willingly that Senna found himself over-revving in top gear. However, as the chassis did not feel as well balanced as the race car, Senna was not a happy man.

Virtually the same problem repeated itself on Saturday morning when the race car's engine lost 300rpm during the course of the unofficial 90-minute session. Ayrton successfully persuaded the team *not* to try switching the spare car's engine into the race chassis during the lunch break, worried that time would run out before the task was completed, so he stayed with the race car and qualified 10th on 1m 29.200s. The engines were swapped in time for the race.

These were but minor problems when compared with the dramas besetting Ferrari, however. Experimenting with endless combinations of rear suspension configurations, exhaust arrangement, undertrays and wheelbase dimensions, the abiding problem was dire lack of Goodyear grip. Arnoux was almost distraught with frustration. "No balance, understeer in, oversteer out. Hopeless!" he shrugged. Alboreto wrestled his way round to a 1m 29.694s to take 12th place on the grid with Arnoux way back in 15th slot with 1m 31.000s.

Ferrari's embarrassment was undoubtedly heightened by the proximity of the 126C4s to the pair of Alfa Romeo 184Ts on the starting grid. In spite of the fact that these rival Italian machines were back on their original mechanical fuel injection for this race, and survived two days of mechanical mayhem throughout practice, Riccardo Patrese managed a 1m 30.736s for 13th place on the grid – despite suffering a piston breakage on

Friday and turbo failure on Saturday. Team-mate Eddie Cheever had "two proper timed laps on each day" whilst running the gauntlet of gearbox problems and engine maladies, a blown piston finally rounding off his efforts on Saturday afternoon shortly after he had bagged a 1m 31.045s for 16th position in the line-up.

Thierry Boutsen had to use his spare car to grab 17th place on the grid after crashing his own Arrows A7 at the chicane beyond the pits, damaging its left-hand suspension in the process, while Marc Surer's similar car was plagued by a frustrating degree of understeer, preventing him from improving on a 19th fastest 1m 31.189s.

Gunter Schmid decided to field F3 runner Gerhard Berger in his second ATS D7, notwithstanding the fact that the team barely had enough in the way of spares to run a single car for Winkelhock. The young Austrian acquitted himself very respectably and might have improved on his 20th place on the grid had not the irate Manfred taken over his car for the Friday session after his own machine suffered a succession of gearbox and fuel pressure maladies. Winkelhock's 1m 30.853s, 14th quickest, was achieved as much out of bad temper as anything else on Saturday afternoon once his own race car was repaired again!

Andrea de Cesaris joined in the fashionable pastime of blowing Renault V6s apart, the volatile Italian suffering major failures in both qualifying sessions on his way to a 1m 31.588s, 16th quickest. Team-mate Hesnault plainly did not look at home on the fast sweeps of the circuit, acute understeer keeping his time down to a lowly 1m 32.270s.

In the Osella camp a spate of engine failures left only a single car serviceable for the final session, this enabling Austrian new boy Jo Gartner to pip his more experienced team-mate Piercarlo Ghinzani to 22nd on the grid, while RAM's Jonathan

Teo Fabi stalled on the line but a charge back to fourth place fully vindicated his decision to abandon CART racing and concentrate fully on Formula 1 (below).

Palmer had to call it a day on 1m 34.128s when his misfiring machine jammed its gearbox with broken gear selectors. On the final row of the grid were Alliot in the second RAM and Rothengatter's Spirit, the Dutchman's car suffering a con-rod breakage on Friday afternoon after Huub suspected something had not been quite right during the morning. He finally squeezed on to the grid using a Hart 415T borrowed from the RAM organisation, thereby consigning both Tyrrell 012s to the ranks of non-qualifiers. Bellof would not have been permitted to start anyway, even if he had qualified on lap times: a spot weight check at the pit lane entrance during that final session revealing his Tyrrell to be 3kg beneath the weight limit. The amiable German was thus excluded from the meeting, although the ultimate effect was the same for the hard-trying Stefan Johansson who had been displaced in the dying moments of that final hour by Rothengatter's last-ditch effort.

RACE

As the enormous crowd continued to file its way into the spectacular Österreichring, now conclusively established as the fastest Formula 1 circuit in the business, Alain Prost and Niki Lauda underlined their strength by setting quickest times in the race morning warm-up session. However, things were not all routine and straightforward in the McLaren pit for Prost complained that his newly installed TAG turbo was showing the first signs of serious overheating: immediately the mechanics set to work installing yet another fresh V6 in time for the start of the race. Piquet, meanwhile, was worried about a "soft" brake pedal and Winkelhock's horrid weekend was finally rounded off in appropriate fashion when his ATS's rebuilt gearbox broke during the warm-up, probably the result of incorrectly machined internals, and he was relegated to the role of spectator before the Austrian Grand Prix even started!

The next problem occurred when the cars were sitting on the grid, having completed the parade lap, all ready to start the race. As Derek Ongaro pressed the button to flick the starting lights from red to green, he saw both Elio de Angelis and Huub Rothengatter fling up their hands to indicate that they would not be moving. Ongaro hit the "abort" button which should switch on flashing orange lights, but an electrical malfunction in the control system meant that the green was displayed briefly before the flashing orange came up. In that split-second half the grid decided to go, seriously – and half realised that the start had been aborted. Tambay and Laffite decided that the best thing to do was to stop behind de Angelis's stationary Lotus while the pack scattered around them in all directions, while, somewhat ironically, Rothengatter got going only to spin off on the opening lap. Elio, Patrick and Jacques eventually staggered away, but this "first race" was over as quickly as it started. The first lap was discounted, refuelling was permitted and everybody rejoined the grid for another attempt at the full 51-lap distance.

As at the original start, Prost got off the line first, but Piquet elbowed his way into the lead in uncompromising style as they scrambled into that first chicane, with Tambay, running a suicidally

AUGUST:

John Player Team Lotus gives test drive to Johnny Dumfries at Donington.

Mike Thackwell demonstrates Cosworth rev-limiter, suitable for proposed Formula 3000, on Williams FW08 at Donington.

Guy Edwards retires from race driving.

Cale Yarborough wins IROC Championship and $150,000.

TAG Turbo Engines confirm continuation of exclusive deal with Marlboro McLaren International.

Eddie Cheever re-signs with Euroracing Alfa Romeo.

David Yorke, aged 70, former team manager with Vanwall and JW Automotive, dies peacefully in Zeltweg.

The most promising combination of 1984. Ayrton
Senna developed his talent with the equally
competitive Toleman-Hart TG184.
Photo: Paul Henri Cahier

soft choice of Michelins, right on their tail. Gartner
managed to swipe Berger's ATS into a lurid slide as
they went into the braking area for that first corner,
but Gerhard *just* retained control, while his
compatriot went on to push Ghinzani on to the
grass a couple of hundred yards further on!

At the end of the first lap the field had a distinctly
familiar look about it, Piquet and Prost already
edging away slightly from Tambay with Lauda
settling down to his customary charge from sixth
place behind Warwick and de Angelis. Behind the
Austrian came Senna, Mansell, Rosberg, Alboreto,
Arnoux, Patrese, Cheever, Laffite, Boutsen, de
Cesaris, Gartner, Palmer, Berger, Alliot, Ghinzani, Surer, Rothengatter and a disappointed Fabi,
the diminutive Italian having blotted his copybook
and stalled his Brabham as the race got under way.

With half a dozen laps completed it looked as
though Piquet was on the verge of breaking the
McLaren challenge, Nelson having opened an
advantage of just under two seconds. What we did
not know, of course, was that Prost's fourth gear
had started to play up and the plucky Frenchman
was driving for much of every daunting lap with
one hand on the wheel – the other holding his
McLaren in fourth gear. At the start of lap 9 Lauda
moved on to Tambay's tail and deprived the
Frenchman of third place as they sped out of the
Boschkurve, the Austrian taking an ambitious and
successful run round the outside on the fast
left-hander which followed, Tambay by now also
handicapped by a slightly sticking throttle.

By this time Patrick's choice of "hot" Michelin
"5s" and "10s" was proving predictably marginal
and he scuttled into the pit lane on lap 10 for
replacement rubber. That little delay dropped him
to 10th, but he was soon in the groove again and
steadily making up time.

Early casualties included both Osellas, Ghinzani with gearbox failure (the result of being hit by
Gartner?) and Jo himself with a well-cooked Alfa
V8. Lap 12 was marked by Laffite's departure from
the fray with an expensively ventilated Honda V6
smoking away in the back of his Williams, while
Rosberg came in to ask whether *anything* could be
done to counter the appalling understeer his
FW09B was displaying. Fresh Goodyears were
fitted and more nose wing wound on, but it was all
in vain. At the end of lap 15 Keke came trailing in
to report that the car was "totally impossible to
drive". Brushing aside speculation as to what it
must have been like to elicit such a trenchant
reaction from the normally placid Rosberg, the car
was pushed away . . . shortly afterwards a slowly
deflating front tyre was discovered. Perhaps a front
wheel rim had been slightly porous.

By lap 14 Senna was up on Warwick's tail,
challenging for fifth place, but Derek handed him
the position on a plate when he too aimed his
Renault into the pit lane for replacement rubber.
This left Ayrton as the Toleman meat in a Lotus
sandwich, but none of this trio lasted until the
finish. Mansell's Lotus expired on lap 33 with
engine failure while Senna succumbed to a similar
problem three laps later. By this time, however, de
Angelis's departure from the race had made a
dramatic impact on its potential outcome.

On lap 28 the Italian's engine expired expen-

sively just as it had done at Hockenheim, flames
and oil smoke licking round the engine compartment in the process. Elio had been troubled by a
misfire for several laps and, worried that this might
be the eventual outcome, wound down the turbo
boost pressure in an attempt to conserve the V6. It
was all too late and, when the engine did finally let
go, de Angelis chose to stagger back to the pits
rather than showing consideration for his colleagues by parking the black and gold oil bowser at
the side of the track.

The marshals at the *Rindtkurve*, the downhill
right-hander before the pits, were slow in getting
the oil flags out and Prost, still steering with one
hand and holding his McLaren in fourth gear at
that point on the circuit, never had a chance . . .
Piquet, with two hands on the wheel, almost lost
his Brabham, but when the Frenchman hit the oil
his MP4/2 pirouetted off the circuit almost before
he had a chance to slam on even a touch of opposite

lock. McLaren No. 7 shuddered to a halt on the
outside of the corner, its engine stalled. Prost
climbed out sadly and walked back to the paddock.

This left Lauda a clear track to move up on to
Piquet's tail, a task aided by the fact that the
leading Brabham was wearing its rear tyres quite
badly and Niki's aggressive approach to the
ensuing battle for the lead was really quite
remarkable. The Austrian "veteran" tried every
trick in the book as he wore down Nelson's
resistance, attempting to box him in behind slower
cars, darting this way and that in his slipstream
looking for any way through.

On lap 39 Nelson got into a heart-stopping slide
as he came up to lap Alboreto's Ferrari and this
convinced the Brazilian that any further resistance
was futile. Niki nipped by into the lead and Nelson
just sat and watched the McLaren disappear into
the distance. Just over three laps later came that
enormous "bang" from the McLaren's transmis-

sion as fourth gear broke and, for the remainder of the race, Niki was nursing his car along as quickly as he dared, unaware that a dog-ring tooth had smashed its way into the side of the gearbox casing. Had the tooth come out the other side, then the gearbox almost certainly would have lost its oil . . .

Lauda's winning margin was just under 24s at the chequered flag, but his problems were such that both Alboreto, who finished third, and Fabi, who climbed back to take a good fourth place after his earlier error, managed to un-lap themselves from the winning McLaren. In a race for fifth place Thierry Boutsen just beat Arrows A7 team-mate Marc Surer to the line in a sprint from the final corner, the Swiss having taken the spare car after his race machine had shown signs of a serious misfire on the warm-up lap.

René Arnoux, delayed by a pit stop to see if fresh Goodyears would give his Ferrari C4 any more grip (they didn't) finished a lapped seventh ahead of

François Hesnault's Ligier and Jonathan Palmer's RAM. Riccardo Patrese looked as though he was heading for some points until he forgot to turn the turbo boost down over the last three laps – and his tanks ran dry three laps from home, much to the amusement of team-mate Eddie Cheever who had earlier retired with engine failure. He was classified 10th ahead of the dogged Alliot and the plucky Berger, the Austrian making a precautionary stop shortly before the end when the low fuel warning light started blinking. A fresh set of Pirellis was fitted and he was eventually classified 12th, after stopping with gearbox trouble.

Meanwhile, what of the Renault challenge? After their pit stops, both Tambay and Warwick succumbed to engine failures, the Englishman as early as lap 18 when the water injection packed up, while Patrick survived, running very quickly and competitively, until he was sidelined from third place on lap 43. His was a cruel reward: if Tambay

had continued to the end, he just might have been in with a chance of victory.

Huub Rothengatter was still running, some 28 laps behind, after a lengthy pit visit to replace a fractured exhaust system, while fuel metering unit problems sidelined de Cesaris's Ligier.

Thus the seemingly fickle pendulum of McLaren International fortunes had swung Lauda's way on a day when the famous Austrian had Lady Luck doubly on his side. "Nine more points in the bank, that's what's important," he grinned. But victory on home soil had definitely given the day's success just a dash more sparkle and spice, even for the hard-bitten Viennese. What's more, it had endorsed Ron Dennis's view that the Championship between these two "will be resolved by some minor problem, a minor incident, rather than any great victory on the track." Alain Prost, cursing that gearbox and the oil slick, must have known *precisely* what his Boss meant!　AH

Entries and practice times

No.	Driver	Nat	Car	Tyre	Engine	Entrant	Practice 1	Practice 2
1	Nelson Piquet	BR	Parmalat BRABHAM BT53	M	BMW M12/13	MRD International	1m 26·928s	**1m 26·173s**
2	Teo Fabi	I	Parmalat BRABHAM BT53	M	BMW M12/13	MRD International	1m 29·893s	**1m 27·201s**
3	Stefan Johansson	S	TYRRELL 012	G	Ford Cosworth DFY	Tyrrell Racing Organisation	1m 37·292s	**1m 36·282s**
4	Stefan Bellof	D	TYRRELL 012	G	Ford Cosworth DFY	Tyrrell Racing Organisation	**1m 37·535s**	*1m 37·893s
5	Jacques Laffite	F	WILLIAMS FW09B	G	Honda RA 163–E	Williams Grand Prix Engineering	1m 29·228s	1m 29·012s
6	Keke Rosberg	SF	WILLIAMS FW09B	G	Honda RA 163–E	Williams Grand Prix Engineering	**1m 28·760s**	1m 27·098s
7	Alain Prost	F	Marlboro McLAREN MP4/2	M	TAG P01 (TTE P01)	Marlboro McLaren International	**1m 26·203s**	1m 27·098s
8	Niki Lauda	A	Marlboro McLAREN MP4/2	M	TAG P01 (TTE P01)	Marlboro McLaren International	**1m 26·715s**	1m 27·312s
9	Philippe Alliot	F	RAM 02	P	Hart 415T	Skoal Bandit Formula 1 Team	1m 34·495s	1m 44·304s
10	Jonathan Palmer	GB	RAM 02	P	Hart 415T	Skoal Bandit Formula 1 Team	1m 34·622s	**1m 34·128s**
11	Elio de Angelis	I	John Player Special LOTUS 95T	G	Renault EF4	John Player Team Lotus	1m 27·531s	**1m 26·318s**
12	Nigel Mansell	GB	John Player Special LOTUS 95T	G	Renault EF4	John Player Team Lotus	1m 28·430s	**1m 27·558s**
14	Manfred Winkelhock	D	ATS D7	P	BMW M12/13	Team ATS	1m 33·276s	**1m 30·853s**
15	Patrick Tambay	F	Elf RENAULT RE50	M	Renault EF4	Equipe Renault Elf	1m 27·748s	**1m 26·748s**
16	Derek Warwick	GB	Elf RENAULT RE50	M	Renault EF4	Equipe Renault Elf	1m 27·928s	**1m 27·123s**
17	Marc Surer	CH	ARROWS A7	G	BMW M12/13	Barclay Nordica Arrows BMW	1m 31·701s	**1m 31·655s**
18	Thierry Boutsen	B	ARROWS A7	G	BMW M12/13	Barclay Nordica Arrows BMW	1m 31·255s	**1m 31·189s**
19	Ayrton Senna	BR	TOLEMAN TG184	M	Hart 415T	Toleman Group Motorsport	1m 29·463s	**1m 29·200s**
21	Huub Rothengatter	NL	SPIRIT 101	P	Hart 415T	Spirit Racing		**1m 35·605s**
22	Riccardo Patrese	I	Benetton ALFA ROMEO 184T	G	Alfa Romeo 183T	Benetton Team Alfa Romeo	1m 30·966s	**1m 30·736s**
23	Eddie Cheever	USA	Benetton ALFA ROMEO 184T	G	Alfa Romeo 183T	Benetton Team Alfa Romeo	1m 31·250s	**1m 31·045s**
24	Piercarlo Ghinzani	I	Kelemata OSELLA FA1F	P	Alfa Romeo 183T	Osella Squadra Corse	**1m 33·172s**	–
25	François Hesnault	F	LIGIER Loto JS23	M	Renault EF4	Ligier Loto	1m 32·582s	**1m 32·270s**
26	Andrea de Cesaris	I	LIGIER Loto JS23	M	Renault EF4	Ligier Loto	1m 36·771s	**1m 31·588s**
27	Michele Alboreto	I	Fiat FERRARI 126C4	G	Ferrari 126C	Scuderia Ferrari SpA	**1m 29·694s**	1m 30·000s
28	René Arnoux	F	Fiat FERRARI 126C4	G	Ferrari 126C	Scuderia Ferrari SpA	**1m 31·003s**	1m 31·313s
30	Jo Gartner	A	Kelemata OSELLA FA1F	P	Alfa Romeo 183T	Osella Squadra Corse	1m 35·212s	**1m 33·019s**
31	Gerhard Berger	A	ATS D7	P	BMW M12/13	Team ATS	**1m 31·904s**	–

Friday morning and Saturday morning practice sessions not officially recorded.

* Time disallowed

Fri pm — Warm, dry
Sat pm — Hot, dry

G – Goodyear, M – Michelin, P – Pirelli.

Starting grid

1 PIQUET (1m 26·173s)
Brabham

    7 PROST (1m 26·203s)
    McLaren

11 DE ANGELIS (1m 26·318s)
Lotus

    8 LAUDA (1m 26·715s)
    McLaren

15 TAMBAY (1m 26·748s)
Renault

    16 WARWICK (1m 27·123s)
    Renault

2 FABI (1m 27·201s)
Brabham

    12 MANSELL (1m 27·558s)
    Lotus

6 ROSBERG (1m 28·760s)
Williams

    19 SENNA (1m 29·200s)
    Toleman

5 LAFFITE (1m 29·228s)
Williams

    27 ALBORETO (1m 29·694s)
    Ferrari

22 PATRESE (1m 30·736s)
Alfa Romeo

    *14 WINKELHOCK (1m 30·853s)
    ATS

28 ARNOUX (1m 31·003s)
Ferrari

    23 CHEEVER (1m 31·045s)
    Alfa Romeo

18 BOUTSEN (1m 31·189s)
Arrows

    26 DE CESARIS (1m 31·588s)
    Ligier

17 SURER (1m 31·655s)
Arrows

    31 BERGER (1m 31·904s)
    ATS

25 HESNAULT (1m 32·270s)
Ligier

    30 GARTNER (1m 33·019s)
    Osella

24 GHINZANI (1m 33·172s)
Osella

    10 PALMER (1m 34·128s)
    RAM

9 ALLIOT (1m 34·495s)
RAM

    21 ROTHENGATTER (1m 35·605s
    Spirit

Results and retirements

Place	Driver	Car	Laps	Time and Speed (mph/km/h)/Retirement	
1	Niki Lauda	McLaren-TAG t/c V6	51	1h 21m 12·851s	139·11/223·883
2	Nelson Piquet	Brabham-BMW t/c 4	51	1h 21m 36·376s	138.44/222.8
3	Michele Alboreto	Ferrari t/c V6	51	1h 22m 01·849s	137.75/221·7
4	Teo Fabi	Brabham-BMW t/c 4	51	1h 22m 09·163s	137·50/221·3
5	Thierry Boutsen	Arrows-BMW t/c 4	50		
6	Marc Surer	Arrows-BMW t/c 4	50		
7	René Arnoux	Ferrari t/c V6	50		
8	François Hesnault	Ligier-Renault t/c V6	49		
9	Jonathan Palmer	RAM-Hart t/c 4	49		
10	Riccardo Patrese	Alfa Romeo t/c V8	48	Out of fuel	
11	Philippe Alliot	RAM-Hart t/c 4	48	Gearbox	
12	Gerhard Berger	ATS-BMW t/c 4	48	Gearbox	
	Patrick Tambay	Renault t/c V6	42	Engine	
	Ayrton Senna	Toleman-Hart t/c 4	35	Oil pressure	
	Nigel Mansell	Lotus-Renault t/c V6	32	Engine	
	Alain Prost	McLaren-TAG t/c V6	28	Spun off	
	Elio de Angelis	Lotus-Renault t/c V6	28	Engine	
	Huub Rothengatter	Spirit-Hart t/c 4	23	Running, not classified	
	Eddie Cheever	Alfa Romeo t/c V8	18	Engine	
	Derek Warwick	Renault t/c V6	17	Engine	
	Andrea de Cesaris	Ligier-Renault t/c V6	15	Fuel injection	
	Keke Rosberg	Williams-Honda t/c V6	15	Handling	
	Jacques Laffite	Williams-Honda t/c V6	12	Engine	
	Jo Gartner	Osella-Alfa Romeo t/c V8	6	Engine	
	Piercarlo Ghinzani	Osella-Alfa Romeo t/c V8	4	Gearbox	

Fastest lap: Lauda, on lap 23, 1m 32·882s, 143·105mph/230·305km/h.
Lap record: René Arnoux (F1 Renault RE t/c V6), 1m 32·53s, 143·659mph/231·197km/h.

Past winners

Year	Driver	Nat	Car	Circuit	Distance miles/km	Speed mph/km/h
1963*	Jack Brabham	AUS	1·5 Brabham BT7-Climax	Zeltweg	159·07/ 256·00	96·34/115·04
1964	Lorenzo Bandini	I	1·5 Ferrari 156	Zeltweg	208·78/ 336·00	99·20/159·65
1965	Jochen Rindt	A	3·3 Ferrari 250LM	Zeltweg	198·84/ 320·00	97·13/156·32
1966†	Gerhard Mitter/ Hans Herrmann	D	2·0 Porsche 906	Zeltweg	312·18/ 502·40	99·68/160·42
1967†	Paul Hawkins	AUS	4·7 Ford GT40	Zeltweg	312·18/ 502·40	95·29/153·35
1968†	Jo Siffert	CH	3·0 Porsche 908/02 Spyder	Zeltweg	312·18/ 502·40	106·86/171·97
1969†	Jo Siffert/ Kurt Ahrens	CH D	4·5 Porsche 917		624·40/1004·87	115·78/186·33
1970	Jacky Ickx	B	3·0 Ferrari 312B-1/70	Österreichring	220·38/ 354·67	129·27/208·04
1971	Jo Siffert	CH	3·0 BRM P160	Österreichring	198·34/ 319·20	131·64/211·85
1972	Emerson Fittipaldi	BR	3·0 JPS/Lotus 72-Ford	Österreichring	198·34/ 319·20	133·29/214·51
1973	Ronnie Peterson	S	3·0 JPS/Lotus 72-Ford	Österreichring	198·34/ 319·20	133·99/215·64
1974	Carlos Reutemann	RA	3·0 Brabham BT44-Ford	Österreichring	198·34/ 319·20	134·09/215·80
1975	Vittorio Brambilla	I	3·0 March 751-Ford	Österreichring	106·12/ 170·78	110·30/177·51
1976	John Watson	GB	3·0 Penske PC4-Ford	Österreichring	198·29/ 319·11	132·00/212·41
1977	Alan Jones	AUS	3·0 Shadow DN8-Ford	Österreichring	199·39/ 320·89	122·98/197·91
1978	Ronnie Peterson	S	3·0 JPS/Lotus 79-Ford	Österreichring	199·39/ 320·89	118·03/189·95
1979	Alan Jones	AUS	3·0 Williams FW07-Ford	Österreichring	199·39/ 320·89	136·52/219·71
1980	Jean-Pierre Jabouille	F	1·5 Renault RS t/c	Österreichring	199·39/ 320·89	138·69/223·20
1981	Jacques Laffite	F	3·0 Ligier JS17-Matra	Österreichring	195·70/ 314·95	134·03/215·70
1982	Elio de Angelis	I	3·0 Lotus 91-Ford	Österreichring	195·70/ 314·95	138·07/222·20
1983	Alain Prost	F	1·5 Renault RE40 t/c	Österreichring	195·70/ 314·95	138·87/223·49
1984	Niki Lauda	A	1·5 McLaren MP4/2 t/c	Österreichring	188·31/ 303·06	139·11/223·88

* Non-championship (Formula 1)
† Sports car race

Did not start:
*14 Winkelhock (ATS), broken gearbox; unable to effect repairs after race morning warm-up due to shortage of parts.
3 Johansson (Tyrrell), 1m 36·282, did not qualify.
4 Bellof (Tyrrell), found to be 3 kilos under minimum weight limit during final practice session; excluded from meeting. With a best time of 1m 37·535s, Bellof would not have qualified in any case.

Circuit data

Österreichring, near Knittelfeld
Circuit length: 3·692 miles/5·9424 km
Race distance: 51 laps, 188·313 miles/303·062 km
Race weather: Warm, dry

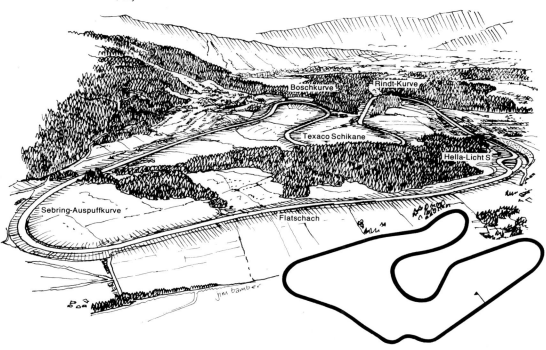

Fastest laps

Driver	Time	Lap
Niki Lauda	1m 32·882s	23
Patrick Tambay	1m 33·056s	17
Nelson Piquet	1m 33·074s	12
Alain Prost	1m 33·081s	22
Elio de Angelis	1m 33·227s	11
Teo Fabi	1m 34·342s	38
Ayrton Senna	1m 34·348s	6
Nigel Mansell	1m 34·401s	27
Derek Warwick	1m 34·469s	7
Michele Alboreto	1m 34·821s	47
Marc Surer	1m 35·209s	40
Jacques Laffite	1m 35·240s	11
Riccardo Patrese	1m 35·659s	20
René Arnoux	1m 35·846s	35
Keke Rosberg	1m 35·944s	4
Thierry Boutsen	1m 36·105s	40
Eddie Cheever	1m 36·197s	16
Gerhard Berger	1m 36·914s	15
Andrea de Cesaris	1m 36·976s	5
Jonathan Palmer	1m 37·626s	38
François Hesnault	1m 37·906s	4
Philippe Alliot	1m 39·245s	17
Piercarlo Ghinzani	1m 39·297s	3
Jo Gartner	1m 40·359s	2
Huub Rothengatter	1m 41·317s	13

Points

WORLD CHAMPIONSHIP OF DRIVERS

1	Niki Lauda	48 pts
2	Alain Prost	43·5
3	Elio de Angelis	26·5
4	René Arnoux	24·5
5	Nelson Piquet	24
6	Derek Warwick	23
7	Keke Rosberg	20
8	Michele Alboreto	15
9=	Patrick Tambay	9
9=	Nigel Mansell	9
11	Ayrton Senna	8
12	Teo Fabi	6
13	Jacques Laffite	4
14=	Eddie Cheever	3
14=	Riccardo Patrese	3
14=	Thierry Boutsen	3
17=	Andrea de Cesaris	2
17=	Piercarlo Ghinzani	2
19	Marc Surer	1

CONSTRUCTORS' CUP

1	McLaren	91·5 pts
2	Ferrari	39·5
3	Lotus	35·5
4	Renault	32
5	Brabham	30
6	Williams	24
7	Toleman	8
8	Alfa Romeo	6
9	Arrows	4
10	Ligier	2
11	Osella	2

Lap chart

1st LAP ORDER		1	2	3	4	5	6	7	8	9	10	11	12	13	14	15	16	17	18	19	20	21	22	23	24	25	26	27	28	29	30	31	32	33	34	35	36	37
1	N. Piquet	1	1	1	1	1	1	1	1	1	1	1	1	1	1	1	1	1	1	1	1	1	1	1	1	1	1	1	1	1	1	1	1	1	1	1	1	1
7	A. Prost	7	7	7	7	7	7	7	7	7	7	7	7	7	7	7	7	7	7	7	7	7	7	7	7	7	7	7	8	8	8	8	8	8	8	8	8	8
15	P. Tambay	15	15	15	15	15	15	15	15	8	8	8	8	8	8	8	8	8	8	8	8	8	8	8	8	8	8	8	19	19	19	15	15	15	15	15	15	15
16	D. Warwick	16	16	8	8	8	8	8	8	15	11	11	11	11	11	11	11	11	11	11	11	11	11	11	11	11	19	15	15	15	19	19	19	19	27	27		
11	E. De Angelis	11	8	16	16	16	16	16	16	11	15	16	16	16	16	16	19	19	19	19	19	19	19	19	19	19	11	12	12	12	12	27	27	27	2	2		
8	N. Lauda	8	11	11	11	19	19	19	11	16	16	19	19	19	19	19	12	12	12	12	12	12	12	12	12	12	15	27	27	27	27	2	2	2	22	22		
19	A. Senna	19	19	19	19	11	11	11	19	19	19	12	12	12	12	12	16	15	15	15	15	15	15	15	15	15	12	2	2	2	2	22	22	22	18	18		
12	N. Mansell	12	6	6	6	6	6	6	6	6	6	27	27	15	15	15	27	27	27	27	27	27	27	27	27	27	22	22	22	22	18	18	18	17	17			
6	K. Rosberg	6	12	12	12	12	12	12	12	12	27	5	15	15	27	27	23	2	2	2	2	2	2	2	2	2	18	18	18	18	17	17	17	28	28			
27	M. Alboreto	27	27	27	27	27	27	27	27	27	5	15	28	23	23	23	23	16	22	22	22	22	22	22	22	22	22	17	17	17	28	28	28	25	25			
28	R. Arnoux	28	28	28	28	28	28	28	5	5	6	28	23	22	22	22	22	2	28	28	28	28	28	18	18	18	18	18	18	28	28	28	25	25	25	31	31	
22	R. Patrese	22	22	23	23	23	23	5	28	28	28	23	22	2	2	2	2	22	18	18	18	18	28	28	28	28	17	25	25	25	31	31	31	10	10	10		
23	E. Cheever	23	23	5	5	5	5	23	23	23	23	22	2	18	28	28	28	28	23	17	17	17	17	17	17	17	28	28	31	31	31	31	9	9	9	9		
5	J. Laffite	5	5	22	22	22	22	22	22	22	22	18	2	18	18	18	18	17	17	25	25	25	25	25	25	25	9	9	9	9	10	10	10					
18	T. Boutsen	18	18	18	18	18	18	18	18	18	2	26	31	31	31	17	17	25	31	31	31	31	31	31	31	31	10	10	10	10								
26	A. De Cesaris	26	26	26	26	26	26	26	26	2	26	31	17	17	17	31	31	10	10	10	10	9	9	9	9	9												
30	J. Gartner	30	30	30	31	31	31	31	2	26	31	17	25	25	25	25	25	10	9	9	9	10	10	10	10	10												
10	J. Palmer	10	10	31	10	10	2	2	31	31	31	17	25	10	10	10	10	9	21	21	21	21	21															
31	G. Berger	31	31	10	30	2	10	25	25	17	17	25	5	26	26	9	9	9	21																			
9	P. Alliot	9	24	24	17	25	25	17	17	25	25	10	10	9	9	26	21	21																				
24	P. Ghinzani	24	17	17	25	17	17	10	10	10	10	9	9	6	6	6																						
17	M. Surer	17	25	2	30	9	9	9	9	9	9	6	6	21	21																							
21	H. Rothengatter	21	9	2	9	9	30	21	21	21	21	21																										
25	F. Hesnault	25	21	9	24	21	21																															
2	T. Fabi	2	2	21	21																																	

38	39	40	41	42	43	44	45	46	47	48	49	50	51
1	1	8	8	8	8	8	8	8	8	8	8	8	8
8	8	1	1	1	1	1	1	1	1	1	1	1	1
15	15	15	15	15	27	27	27	27	27	27	27	27	27
27	27	27	27	27	2	2	2	2	2	2	2	2	2
2	2	2	2	2	22	22	22	22	22	22	18	18	
22	22	22	22	22	18	18	18	18	18	18	17	17	
18	18	18	18	18	17	17	17	17	17	17	28	28	
17	17	17	17	17	28	28	28	28	28	28	25		
28	28	28	28	28	25	25	25	25	25	25	10		
25	25	25	25	25	10	10	10	10	10	10	10		
31	31	31	31	31	10	31	9	9	9	9			
10	10	10	10	31	9	31	31	31	31	31			
9	9	9	9	9									

Grote Prijs van Nederland

Had Niki Lauda made a better start, things might have been different. Had he not been pushed down to tenth place instead of keeping in touch with Alain Prost, then his gamble might have paid off; the result might have been Lauda first and Prost second, instead of the other way round.

Before the race, Lauda had agonised over the choice of tyres. Once again, Prost was on pole while Lauda was a couple of rows further back. Using the German Grand Prix as a yardstick, it was clear that Lauda would not catch his McLaren team-mate on speed alone. He had to find an advantage elsewhere and the only solution was tyres. With Prost choosing a conservative compound all round, Lauda had no alternative but to opt for a softer mix.

Thanks to struggling off the line, Lauda was forced to use that advantage on a greasy track as he worked his way through the field. By the time he got to within striking distance of Prost, the edge had gone. Prost simply pulled away and Lauda was helpless to prevent the championship lead from shrinking to one and a half points.

There had been the almost customary challenge from Nelson Piquet, the Parmalat Brabham leading by four to five seconds and looking reasonably comfortable until an loose oil union meant retirement after 10 laps.

Third – and the only other driver to run the full 71 laps – was Nigel Mansell, the JPS Lotus driver cocking a snook at his team on a day when they announced the signing of Ayrton Senna for 1985. It had been a well-judged performance – which was more than could be said for the handling of the Senna affair. Running gently at the start, the better to conserve the latest Goodyear race tyres, Mansell moved forward to deal aggressively with team-mate Elio de Angelis and Keke Rosberg. The Williams-Honda, as high as third at one stage, eventually ended an encouraging race by running out of fuel with a few laps remaining.

With de Angelis finishing fourth, the remaining points went to Teo Fabi's Brabham and the Renault of Patrick Tambay, the Frenchman deserving better after losing fifth gear with 20 laps remaining.

In truth, however, the rest were nowhere when compared to the red and white domination at the front. And, to rub it in, Marlboro McLaren International established a new record by taking their ninth victory of the season. The previous mark of eight wins in a season had been set by Lotus in 1978, largely through the efforts of Mario Andretti with Ronnie Peterson dutifully supporting the man who was to become World Champion.

In 1984, it was 'may the best man win' and Prost's victory made it five – four in his favour. He was justifiably pleased with a performance which had been perfect in every respect. It proved he was able to withstand the pressure. Had Lauda made a better start, however, the pressure might have been greater still.

ENTRY AND PRACTICE

After practice had finished, John Barnard expressed surprise at winning pole position in the face of BMW qualifying boost. But there, at the top of the list, sat Alain Prost with a time some two tenths quicker than the best Nelson Piquet could manage. The McLaren was not as quick in a straight line but there was no shortage of traction out of the corners when compared to the more ragged performance of the Brabham.

On Friday, Nelson had been the quicker of the two although Prost was not unduly concerned. He had been running the smaller 'race' turbos and, in addition, a leaking intercooler pipe had meant a loss of boost. For Saturday, the larger turbochargers were in place, giving more power if slightly less response but, on his first set of tyres, Prost looked to be in difficulties since he was one second away from pole. On with the second set, two warm-up laps and then, in his own words, an almost perfect lap, 1.4 seconds quicker than the previous day.

Piquet had already been out in his spare car but, since the engine was down on power, he switched to the race chassis for his second run. The Brabham bottomed coming through the right-hander before *Hugenholtzbocht* and the resulting high-speed spin ended Nelson's efforts to reclaim pole position.

There was, however, another combination capable of taking pole. The Lotus/Renault/Goodyear package may have been no match for the McLaren/TAG/Michelin combination but that

did not prevent Elio de Angelis from showing his undoubted skill. Second fastest on Friday, Elio went out in the closing minutes of practice but his best efforts to keep a place on the front row fell short by one hundredth of a second. None the less, Goodyear were pleased since the Italian was to be their only representative in the top six.

McLaren – Brabham – Lotus; one – two – three. But what of their team-mates? Niki Lauda, *very* impressed by Prost's final lap, was down in sixth place and disappointed to be that far back! On Friday, his 'Österreichring' engine had finally lost its edge while, on Saturday, Herr Lauda almost lost his cool after being blocked on both his fastest laps. Given the competitive state of his car in race trim, sixth place should not have been a problem. Except that Prost would be sitting in a similar car – on the front row.

Teo Fabi, fastest through the official speed trap on both days (188.421 mph in the final session), could manage no better than 10th place, indicating, perhaps, that sheer horsepower was no good unless the chassis and driver were capable of extracting the maximum. Nigel Mansell was the first to agree that he had a potentially excellent chassis at his disposal but a series of niggling problems prevented the Englishman from making the most of it. On Friday, poor throttle response made smooth cornering difficult while, on Saturday, an electrical fault caused the engine to cut out in the middle of his final run. An improvement

while using his first set of qualifiers had given Mansell 12th place.

Further up the grid, the Renaults of Derek Warwick and Patrick Tambay were fourth and fifth, the Frenchman using the team's spare car to improve on 15th place from Friday. Tambay had found chassis number 9 difficult to balance from the moment it made its first appearance at Hockenheim and, by switching engines and concentrating on the T-car, Patrick felt he was making progress at last. Warwick, suffering from a stomach upset on Friday, was happy with his car on full tanks but, apart from traffic problems, he was slightly disappointed with his performances during qualifying.

The first signs of an improvement within Williams came on Friday afternoon when Keke Rosberg was fastest for a short period. While running his second set of tyres, a rubber collar came adrift and found its way into the turbocharger unit just as he powered on to the main straight. Keke slipped to fourth place and, by the end of Saturday's practice, he was seventh. One of his laps had been spoiled by a brake-locking moment as he came across Lauda trundling alongside Alliot, the Austrian glaring at the RAM driver in silent disapproval over an earlier move by the Frenchman. Rosberg had little sympathy for either party. Jacques Laffite, full of fire, improved considerably on Saturday to take eighth place, just over one tenth behind his team-mate.

Record breaking team: Alain Prost receives a
welcome from the McLaren team as they celebrate
their ninth win of the season, breaking the previous
record set by Lotus in 1978.

With four cars and a variety of suspension arrangements on hand, Ferrari appeared to be in disarray once more although their straightline speed seemed healthy enough. The problem continued to be transmitting that power out of the corners but Arnoux favoured new tubular rear suspension wishbones along with the longer wheelbase. The wishbones were fitted to Alboreto's car for Saturday and the Italian improved by a second to take ninth place. Arnoux, however, was out of luck throughout practice. On Friday, a turbo failure restricted him to one qualifying attempt while, during the final session, trouble with a faulty heat exchanger meant he was unable to improve, René finally finishing in 15th place.

Thierry Boutsen took one of his best grid positions of the season, the Arrows-BMW handling better than of late and giving the Belgian driver 11th place and a chance of another finish in the points. Marc Surer, his car understeering terribly, was back in 19th spot thanks to a misfire forcing the Swiss to use the team's spare chassis on Saturday.

Ayrton Senna was down in 13th place but high in the headlines. The mood in the Toleman camp was frosty, to say the least, when Lotus made public their agreement with the Brazilian driver for 1985. This news did not go down well with Toleman who believed *they* had a contract with Senna for 1985. Senna, for his part, said he simply wanted to get on with his racing but a misfire on Friday and difficulty making his qualifying tyres work on Saturday prevented him from taking the pole position which, clearly, could not come soon enough for the talented South American.

Andrea de Cesaris took 14th place for Ligier on Saturday afternoon. During the course of the final session, the team lost another engine, Andrea thoughtfully dropping oil at the hairpin and causing his team-mate to back off in the middle of his quick lap. François Hesnault eventually took 20th place. Manfred Winkelhock had to contend with fluctuating boost pressure throughout practice, the ATS driver finishing just ahead of Eddie Cheever and Riccardo Patrese, neither of whom could find any improvement during the final session. While the handling of the Alfa Romeos was good, the Benetton cars were well down the list when it came to recording straight line speed. In addition, Cheever had *two* blown engines on Friday, Patrese taking his turn to suffer a blown turbo on Saturday.

Piercarlo Ghinzani had a similar problem, almost at the same time, on his Osella, the Italian qualifying 21st, just a couple of places ahead of his team-mate, Jo Gartner. Splitting the Osellas, Jonathan Palmer was pleased with the handling of his RAM and finished practice over half a second quicker than Philippe Alliot. Stefan Bellof was the quicker of the Tyrrell drivers, the German benefitting from a six-speed gearbox which was not fitted to Stefan Johansson's car. With an obvious straight-line speed disadvantage, it was no surprise to see the Cosworth cars in 24th and 25th places despite energetic performances from both drivers, but Huub Rothengatter was disappointed to find himself at the bottom of the list on both days.

This would be the most important race of the year for the lanky Dutchman but problems with

Nelson Piquet comfortably led the opening laps until his BMW lost its oil. Piquet's attempts to win pole from Prost ended in a spin.

August:
FISA confirm official European Championship for Formula 3000 in 1985.

Lotus announce signing of Ayrton Senna for 1985 and 1986.

FIA Court of Appeal confirm $6000 fine on Nigel Mansell for his part in startline accident at Detroit but waive 'probationary period' which could have resulted in ban had Mansell been involved in further incidents.

low turbo boost and severe understeer on the Spirit-Hart meant he was unable to utilise his local knowledge to the full. Indeed, in perhaps an over-enthusiastic moment on Friday, Huub crashed at the fast right-hander leading on to the pit straight. With FISA continuing to assume the Tyrrells were not part of the World Championship, however, Rothengatter was allowed to become the 27th starter in what should have been a 26-car field.

RACE

In spite of the almost predictable nature of the race result, a vast crowd flocked to the sand dunes to make the most of a fine, warm day. The paddock had been rejigged to give the teams more room in which to work and, in keeping with the increasingly common 'isolation' policy favoured by FOCA, members of the paying public were denied access to the inner areas. And yet vast numbers were crammed into areas which, it would seem, had not been designed to cope with the sport's burgeoning popularity. As a result, there was an accident which could have been tragic.

Shortly before the warm-up was due to com-
mence, a staircase serving the balcony at the rear of the pits collapsed. Girders crashed into the rear of the RAM and Arrows pits, injuring many spectators, most of whom had been on the staircase at the time. One or two were seriously injured and it was miraculous that only a few had been standing beneath the structure when it gave way.

When the warm-up finally got under way, it came as no surprise to see the McLarens at the top of the list, followed by de Angelis, Fabi, Senna, Mansell, Arnoux and Piquet. Warwick and Tambay were 10th and 11th, the excellent handling on full tanks having mysteriously disappeared. Now the head-scratching began, Lauda entering into deep discussion with his engineer, Steve Nichols, and the men from Michelin. With Prost opting for '10s' all round, Lauda gambled on running the softer '05s' on the right-hand side. He had nothing to lose except, perhaps, a championship lead of four and a half points.

All that hard work, however, was more or less thrown away at the start when Lauda struggled off the line after allowing his revs to drop. By the end of the first lap, he was in ninth place and facing the prospect of a busy few laps before he could even think about getting on terms with Prost. Alain, for his part, was second, a few lengths behind Piquet, the Brabham-BMW having powered off the line and opened an immediate advantage.

Piquet continued to extend his lead but Prost was not unduly worried since he knew that Piquet was running the same tyre combination as Lauda. Besides, there was a fine spray of oil coming from the BMW . . .

After five laps, they had opened a gap of as many seconds on Rosberg, the Williams driver showing his usual aggression by taking third place from Tambay. De Angelis was fifth and coming under pressure from Lauda, the Austrian having dis-

THE TYRRELL SCANDAL

In the days following the Dutch Grand Prix, an FIA Court of Appeal supported the ban, imposed by FISA in July, on the Tyrrell Racing Organisation. The Court, convened in Paris, ruled that the team should take no further part in the 1984 Grand Prix season, in addition to being excluded from the 1984 Championship as a whole.

The original charges were based on an analysis of the contents of the water tank on Martin Brundle's Tyrrell which finished second in the Detroit Grand Prix. (The water, which was pumped from the tank to a spraying mechanism over the engine air intake trumpets, was topped up during a pit stop in the middle of the race.)

After the Grand Prix, the first six cars were inspected in the usual way, SCCA officials taking samples of petrol from the fuel tank and water from the 13-litre reservoir. A quantity of small lead balls, claimed by Tyrrell to be ballast, were found in the tank. Samples were made available to Tyrrell and FISA. Tyrrell, believing the water was nothing more than "Detroit water" did not bother to take his sample.

When Tyrrell was called before a FISA Executive Committee Meeting in July, he was told that the water sample contained 27.5 per cent Aromatics. He was alleged to have broken the rules on four counts: by taking on fuel during the race; using fuel which did not comply with the regulations; equipping the car with fuel lines which were not to the correct specification; and using lead ballast which was not fixed to the car in the prescribed manner.

Subsequent inquiries by Tyrrell revealed that there was, in fact, less than one per cent hydrocarbon content in the water. Contact with the research organisation in France, which carried out the analysis for FISA, indicated that the contaminants amounted to a mere .0005 per cent – 96 per cent of which was Dimethyl Formamide, a common solvent which, according to the analysts, was likely to have arrived there at the time of sampling. It was evident that FISA had wrongly interpreted their analysis.

However, mistake or not, the FIA Court of Appeal chose to ignore Tyrrell's weighty evidence by switching the charges. Tyrrell was now guilty on three counts: the presence of hydrocarbons in the water; unsecured mobile ballast; holes existing in the flat bottom of the car.

On the subject of hydrocarbons, FISA said "From the sampling conducted at the end of the Detroit Grand Prix on 24 June 1984, analyses made by various laboratories revealed – be they *infinitesimal* (our italics) traces – the forbidden presence of hydrocarbons."

Tyrrell did not know, and probably will never know, how the infinitesimal amount of hydrocarbon came to be there. A possibility was the fact that the water had been transported to the pits in one of the team's fuel churns.

On the subject of 'insecured mobile ballast', the onus was on Tyrrell to satisfy the scrutineers that the car complied with the regulations at all times. Tyrrell proved to the Court that there was provision for the scrutineers to place a seal across the opening of the tank and they were at liberty to do so before the start of any race.

The Court made a lengthy reference to figures which inferred that Tyrrell was running without water for part of the French Grand Prix and stopped his car four laps from the end for no other reason than to take on ballast. Tyrrell proved conclusively to the Court of Appeal that those calculations were incorrect. This appears to have been overlooked in the final judgement.

The regulations required ballast to be secured in such a way that tools were required for its removal; Tyrrell argued that the ballast could not be removed without the aid of tools.

There was the suggestion by FISA that Tyrrell had been using fuel additives in the first half of the race, flushing them out at the pit stop and adding ballast at the same time. Tyrrell later commented: "If that is so, then why has not a trace of any additive which would increase horsepower – such as nitromethane – been found. And if we were running with additives *and* running light before the pit stop, you would

expect our lap times afterwards to be dramatically slower, wouldn't you? After all, the claim is that the additives were flushed away at the stop and the car's weight increased."

Analysis of Longines lap times revealed that the Tyrrells were often faster *after* their pit stops than they were before and the slower times after the stop at Detroit were due to slower track conditions which affected the lap times of every competitor.

The holes referred to during the previously unheard-of business of revising charges in a Court of Appeal were a reference to two drain holes in the flat bottom of the monocoque to allow air to escape during the high-pressure refilling process. The holes did breach the 'flat bottom' rule but Patrick Head of Williams gave evidence to the effect that they could have absolutely no discernible effect upon the car's aerodynamics. John Barnard of McLaren sent an affidavit to the same effect.

The Court of Appeal judges, Dr. C Vaquer (Argentina), Dr. P. Weissenburger (Austria), Mr. Roberti de Winghe (Belgium), Mr Hubert Boquis (France), Dr. Piero Dino Dini (Italy), Dr. J. Macedo e Cunha (Portugal) and Mr. Manos Remvikos (Greece) were unmoved and an outrageously severe and unprecedented penalty was confirmed.

The RACMSA did not come to Tyrrell's aid, Mr. Peter Cooper claiming that there were wider issues at stake. It is our view that there can be no 'wider issue' than a British team being denied its livelihood by what appears to be nothing more than suspicion.

Apart from being branded a cheat, the costs to Tyrrell were enormous. The loss of 13 points also meant the loss of subsidised FOCA travel in 1985 and this was merely the start of the crippling effects of the judgement.

Why had FISA been so harsh? There were no obvious reasons. However, Tyrrell had been the only objector in the move to change the rules and retain the 220-litre fuel limit rather than reducing the capacity further to 195 litres. With Tyrrell removed from the scene, there would be unanimity when the votes were cast . . .

Closed doors and closed minds: Tyrrell presented his appeal to the FIA – and was roundly defeated.

pensed with Alboreto, Laffite and Warwick in quick succession. Warwick had been helpless since a lack of boost meant poor straightline speed and Alboreto was shortly to post the first retirement when he pulled into the pits with engine failure.

By lap nine, Lauda had caught and passed de Angelis and Tambay and the Austrian was lapping a few tenths faster than Prost. Since Alain had dropped to around five seconds behind Piquet's leading Brabham, it was clear that Lauda's tyre combination was superior on what was rapidly becoming an oily track. And much of that oil was dripping from a loose union on the leading car.

After 10 laps, there was no oil left, Piquet pulling off when his pressure gauge registered an ominous fall. It was a most unfortunate retirement since Nelson had been running comfortably, the Brazilian setting a time half-a-second faster than anyone else – on his second lap.

At the end of 11 laps, Prost led Rosberg by eight seconds but, one lap later and it was a McLaren one-two, Lauda having passed the Williams under braking at *Tarzan*. Now we had a battle of tactics. Would Lauda's gamble pay off? Judging by the lap times which followed, the answer seemed to be in the affirmative.

Lap	Prost	Lauda
12	1m 23.072s	1m 22.950s
13	1m 21.789s	1m 21.834s
14	1m 22.047s	1m 20.977s
15	1m 21.324s	1m 20.983s
16	1m 23.053s	1m 20.594s
17	1m 21.759s	1m 22.359s
18	1m 21.599s	1m 20.599s
19	1m 21.205s	1m 21.107s
20	1m 21.151s	1m 20.685s
21	1m 21.514s	1m 20.646s
22	1m 21.314s	1m 21.061s
23	1m 21.765s	1m 21.570s

The gap between the two was now 4.1 seconds and, during the course of the next few laps, it came down further, Lauda hovering a car's length behind on lap 25. Suddenly Prost realised what was happening.

For some reason best known to himself, Prost had misread his pit signals. Assuming the gap of 17 seconds to Rosberg meant the Williams was a distant second, Prost had eased off slightly once Piquet had retired. Now he had the red and white number eight looming in his mirrors and it was clear he was under threat from the man he feared most. Prost put the hammer down.

Lap	Prost	Lauda
24	1m 20.538s	1m 20.889s
25	1m 23.270s	1m 21.607s
26	1m 20.933s	1m 22.076s
27	1m 20.992s	1m 20.783s
28	1m 21.802s	1m 22.000s
29	1m 20.995s	1m 22.083s
30	1m 21.405s	1m 20.885s

Now it became questionable whether Lauda could make his tyres last at this pace. And the race had yet to reach the half-way mark.

One thing was sure; the McLarens would not be troubled by Rosberg. In a bid to halt the rash of piston failures, the Honda was set to run rich but the trade-off in fuel consumption was going to be costly. A gauge in the cockpit told Rosberg of the impending problem and he turned the boost down accordingly. It made little difference. He could merely sit and wait. In the meantime, he was a comfortable third.

Tambay was fourth, having survived an attack from de Angelis before the Lotus lost ground thanks to being rudely chopped by Manfred Winkelhock as the Italian tried to lap the ATS on lap 20. There was to be a major reshuffle four laps later when Laffite, lying an excellent sixth after taking Warwick, suffered a major engine failure. The Honda V6 blew itself to bits, dumping its oil in Warwick's path and sending the Renault into a spin. Winkelhock was also caught out by the trail of Mobil and neither he nor Warwick was able to restart.

All of which let René Arnoux into sixth place but he was soon to be demoted to seventh by Nigel Mansell, the Lotus driver getting into his stride after being held up by Lauda at the start and then taking it easy on full tanks in order to conserve his tyres. Teo Fabi would have been running in the top six had he not indulged in a spin at *Tarzan*, the Italian locking his rear brakes as he struggled to slow the Brabham with a right foot made painful by excessive temperatures filtering through from the oil cooler.

There were no mistakes from Prost, as Lauda would testify after the race. Having caught his

team-mate's attention, Lauda hung on as Prost continued to lap quickly and crisply.

Lap	Prost	Lauda
31	1m 20.830s	1m 20.972s
32	1m 20.688s	1m 20.563s
33	1m 20.285s	1m 20.707s
34	1m 20.309s	1m 20.582s
35	1m 20.340s	1m 21.118s
36	1m 20.565s	1m 20.574s
37	1m 20.414s	1m 20.470s
38	1m 21.050s	1m 20.856s
39	1m 20.567s	1m 20.742s
40	1m 21.859s	1m 21.071s

We had reached the turning point. Lap 37 would be Lauda's quickest of the race and yet, at the end of lap 40, the gap between the two was 4.6 seconds. Prost had made the correct tyre choice after all. Lauda would finish second.

The finishing order of the Lotus team remained in doubt, however, as Mansell closed on de Angelis's fifth place. It became a battle for fourth when Tambay's excellent run was halted by a 15-second stop for tyres, the Renault driver rejoining in ninth place to follow Fabi through as the Brabham worked his way back into the points by passing Patrese and then Arnoux.

In terms of lap times, Lauda may have accepted second best to Prost but the chances of a win for the Austrian suddenly came alive as the leaders caught the Lotus duo, now battling for third place since they had caught Rosberg as he nursed his thirsty Williams as quickly as he dared.

On lap 52, de Angelis thought about outbraking Rosberg into *Tarzan* but decided against it at the last moment – by which time Mansell had pulled alongside his team-mate and proceeded to run round the outside while Elio became stuck behind the Williams. Watching with a certain amount of apprehension – Lauda was only 12 seconds or so in arrears – Prost then nipped past de Angelis as they accelerated out of the corner and the McLaren driver waited for the next move as Mansell began an immediate attack on Rosberg.

End of the next lap – same place. This time Mansell made a run down the inside of the Williams, the bumps in the braking area throwing the Lotus off-line briefly. But he had the corner – and third place. Prost waited until *Hunserug* before taking Rosberg, only to find the Williams accelerating ahead of the McLaren after Prost had got out of shape momentarily. By the end of the lap, however, the leader was safely by and on his way towards lapping Mansell. A busy few laps!

Further back, Tambay had taken Fabi to assume sixth place but the sudden loss of fifth gear meant the Brabham was back in front on lap 53. Arnoux was next with Boutsen following closely, the Ferrari driver about to indulge in a most irresponsible piece of driving as he made the decision to stop for tyres at the end of lap 59. Without warning, Arnoux slowed suddenly before swinging into the pit lane. Boutsen, a few yards behind, was suddenly confronted with a close-up of the 'Agip' signs on Arnoux's rear wing. The right-front wheel of the Arrows was almost ripped off as Boutsen's car reared into the air before,

fortunately, landing squarely on the track, the Belgian more or less a passenger as he rolled safely to a halt.

Arnoux rejoined but was to retire eventually when the Ferrari stopped with electrical trouble out on the circuit. The field dwindled further when Patrese's Alfa Romeo blew up, not long before Eddie Cheever would bring his Alfa to a halt with empty tanks. This was the end of another good drive from the American who had been pushed off the track during the first lap and then spent the rest of the race climbing back through the field before stopping for tyres. And finally, Rosberg crept into the pits with three laps to go . . .

The Ligiers and the Tyrrells had engaged in their inter-team battles, de Cesaris retiring with engine failure to leave Hesnault to finish in a lonely seventh place. Johansson, running non-stop, came off best to finish eighth after Bellof had stopped at half-distance and resumed with fresh tyres to take ninth place. Behind the Tyrrells came the RAM team, Jonathan Palmer and Philippe Alliot running steadily to give the team 11th and 12th places. For John Macdonald, four finishes in two races marked a major turning point.

For McLaren, their third one-two marked, not so much a turning point, more a result which we had come to expect. It was merely a question of in which order Alain Prost and Niki Lauda would cross the finishing line. Or, to be more precise, which of the two would make the correct choice of tyres on the day. Their domination was as closely defined as that.   MH

Elio de Angelis led the Goodyear challenge during practice at Zandvoort but the JPS-Lotus driver eventually finished fourth behind his team-mate, Nigel Mansell.
Photo: Bernard Asset/Agence Vandystadt

Entries and practice times

No.	Driver	Nat	Car	Tyre	Engine	Entrant	Practice 1	Practice 2
1	Nelson Piquet	BR	Parmalat BRABHAM BT53	M	BMW M12/13	MRD International	1m 13·872s	1m 13·953s
2	Teo Fabi	I	Parmalat BRABHAM BT53	M	BMW M12/13	MRD International	1m 16·607s	1m 15·338s
3	Stefan Johansson	S	TYRRELL 012	G	Ford Cosworth DFY	Tyrrell Racing Organisation	1m 20·959s	1m 20·236s
4	Stefan Bellof	D	TYRRELL 012	G	Ford Cosworth DFY	Tyrrell Racing Organisation	1m 20·861s	1m 20·092s
5	Jacques Laffite	F	WILLIAMS FW09B	G	Honda RA 163–E	Williams Grand Prix Engineering	1m 16·659s	1m 15·231s
6	Keke Rosberg	SF	WILLIAMS FW09B	G	Honda RA 163–E	Williams Grand Prix Engineering	1m 15·137s	1m 15·117s
7	Alain Prost	F	Marlboro McLAREN MP4/2	M	TAG P01 (TTE P01)	Marlboro McLaren International	1m 14·946s	1m 13·567s
8	Niki Lauda	A	Marlboro McLAREN MP4/2	M	TAG P01 (TTE P01)	Marlboro McLaren International	1m 15·556s	1m 14·866s
9	Philippe Alliot	F	RAM 02	P	Hart 415T	Skoal Bandit Formula 1 Team	1m 21·387s	1m 20·270s
10	Jonathan Palmer	GB	RAM 02	P	Hart 415T	Skoal Bandit Formula 1 Team	1m 19·849s	1m 19·598s
11	Elio de Angelis	I	John Player Special LOTUS 95T	G	Renault EF4	John Player Team Lotus	1m 14·027s	1m 13·883s
12	Nigel Mansell	GB	John Player Special LOTUS 95T	G	Renault EF4	John Player Team Lotus	1m 16·533s	1m 15·811s
14	Manfred Winkelhock	D	ATS D7	P	BMW M12/13	Team ATS	1m 17·760s	1m 16·450s
15	Patrick Tambay	F	Elf RENAULT RE50	M	Renault EF4	Equipe Renault Elf	1m 17·013s	1m 14·566s
16	Derek Warwick	GB	Elf RENAULT RE50	M	Renault EF4	Equipe Renault Elf	1m 15·184s	1m 14·405s
17	Marc Surer	CH	ARROWS A7	G	BMW M12/13	Barclay Nordica Arrows BMW	1m 17·534s	1m 17·368s
18	Thierry Boutsen	B	ARROWS A7	G	BMW M12/13	Barclay Nordica Arrows BMW	1m 16·595s	1m 15·735s
19	Ayrton Senna	BR	TOLEMAN TG184	M	Hart 415T	Toleman Group Motorsport	1m 16·951s	1m 15·960s
21	Huub Rothengatter	NL	SPIRIT 101	P	Hart 415T	Spirit Racing	1m 24·771s .	1m 21·063s
22	Riccardo Patrese	I	Benetton ALFA ROMEO 184T	G	Alfa Romeo 183T	Benetton Team Alfa Romeo	1m 17·124s	1m 17·402s
23	Eddie Cheever	USA	Benetton ALFA ROMEO 184T	G	Alfa Romeo 183T	Benetton Team Alfa Romeo	1m 16·991s	1m 17·855s
24	Piercarlo Ghinzani	I	Kelemata OSELLA FA1F	P	Alfa Romeo 183T	Osella Squadra Corse	1m 22·472s	1m 19·454s
25	François Hesnault	F	LIGIER Loto JS23	M	Renault EF4	Ligier Loto	1m 18·469s	1m 17·905s
26	Andrea de Cesaris	I	LIGIER Loto JS23	M	Renault EF4	Ligier Loto	1m 17·897s	1m 16·070s
27	Michele Alboreto	I	Fiat FERRARI 126C4	G	Ferrari 126C	Scuderia Ferrari SpA	1m 16·248s	1m 15·264s
28	René Arnoux	F	Fiat FERRARI 126C4	G	Ferrari 126C	Scuderia Ferrari SpA	1m 16·121s	1m 16·200s
30	Jo Gartner	A	Kelemata OSELLA FA1F	P	Alfa Romeo 183T	Osella Squadra Corse	1m 21·655s	1m 20·017s

Friday morning and Saturday morning practice sessions not officially recorded.

G – Goodyear, M – Michelin, P – Pirelli.

Fri pm — Hot, dry
Sat pm — Hot, dry

Starting grid

1 PIQUET (1m 13·872s) Brabham

7 PROST (1m 13·567s) McLaren

16 WARWICK (1m 14·405s) Renault

11 DE ANGELIS (1m 13·883s) Lotus

8 LAUDA (1m 14·866s) McLaren

15 TAMBAY (1m 14·566s) Renault

5 LAFFITE (1m 15·231s) Williams

6 ROSBERG (1m 15·117s) Williams

2 FABI (1m 15·338s) Brabham

27 ALBORETO (1m 15·264s) Ferrari

12 MANSELL (1m 15·811s) Lotus

18 BOUTSEN (1m 15·735s) Arrows

26 DE CESARIS (1m 16·070s) Ligier

19 SENNA (1m 15·960s) Toleman

14 WINKELHOCK (1m 16·450s) ATS

28 ARNOUX (1m 16·121s) Ferrari

22 PATRESE (1m 17·124s) Alfa Romeo

23 CHEEVER (1m 16·991s) Alfa Romeo

25 HESNAULT (1m 17·905s) Ligier

17 SURER (1m 17·368s) Arrows

10 PALMER (1m 19·598s) RAM

24 GHINZANI (1m 19·454s) Osella

4 BELLOF (1m 20·092s) Tyrrell

30 GARTNER (1m 20·017s) Osella

9 ALLIOT (1m 20·270s) RAM

3 JOHANSSON (1m 20·236s) Tyrrell

*21 ROTHENGATTER (1m 21·063s) Spirit

* Rothengatter given special dispensation to join 26-car grid due to doubts over eligibility of Tyrrell team pending FIA Court of Appeal.

Results and retirements

Place	Driver	Car	Laps	Time and Speed (mph/km/h)/Retirement	
1	Alain Prost	McLaren-TAG t/c V6	71	1h 37m 21·468s	115·606/186·050
2	Niki Lauda	McLaren-TAG t/c V6	71	1h 37m 31·751s	115·388/185·7
3	Nigel Mansell	Lotus-Renault t/c V6	71	1h 38m 41·012s	114·083/183·6
4	Elio de Angelis	Lotus-Renault t/c V6	70		
5	Teo Fabi	Brabham-BMW t/c 4	70		
6	Patrick Tambay	Renault t/c V6	70		
7	François Hesnault	Ligier-Renault t/c V6	69		
8	Stefan Johansson	Tyrrell-Cosworth V8	69		
9	Stefan Bellof	Tyrrell-Cosworth V8	69		
10	Keke Rosberg	Williams-Honda t/c V6	68	Out of fuel	
11	Jonathan Palmer	RAM-Hart t/c 4	67		
12	Philippe Alliot	RAM-Hart t/c 4	67		
13	René Arnoux	Ferrari t/c V6	66	Electrics	
14	Jo Gartner	Osella-Alfa Romeo t/c V8	66		
15	Eddie Cheever	Alfa Romeo t/c V8	65	Out of fuel	
	Thierry Boutsen	Arrows-BMW t/c 4	59	Accident with Arnoux	
	Huub Rothengatter	Spirit-Hart t/c 4	53	Throttle cable	
	Riccardo Patrese	Alfa Romeo t/c V8	51	Engine	
	Andrea de Cesaris	Ligier-Renault t/c V6	31	Engine	
	Jacques Laffite	Williams-Honda t/c V6	23	Engine	
	Derek Warwick	Renault t/c V6	23	Spun off on Laffite's oil	
	Manfred Winkelhock	ATS-BMW t/c 4	22	Spun off	
	Ayrton Senna	Toleman-Hart t/c 4	19	Engine	
	Marc Surer	Arrows-BMW t/c 4	17	Wheel bearing	
	Nelson Piquet	Brabham-BMW t/c 4	10	Oil pressure/loose oil union	
	Piercarlo Ghinzani	Osella-Alfa Romeo t/c V8	8	Fuel pump	
	Michele Alboreto	Ferrari t/c V6	7	Engine	

Fastest lap: Arnoux, on lap 64, 1m 19·465s, 119·693mph/192·628km/h.
Lap record: René Arnoux (F1 Renault RE t/c V6), 1m 19·35s, 119·867mph/192·907km/h (1980).

Past winners

Year	Driver	Nat	Car	Circuit	Distance miles/km	Speed mph/km/h
1949*	Luigi Villoresi	I	1·5 Ferrari 125 GP s/c	Zandvoort	104·22/167·72	77·09/124·06
1950*	Louis Rosier	F	4·5 Lago-Talbot	Zandvoort	234·49/377·37	76·63/123·32
1951*	Louis Rosier	F	4·5 Lago-Talbot	Zandvoort	234·49/377·37	78·45/126·26
1952	Alberto Ascari	I	2·0 Ferrari 500	Zandvoort	234·49/377·37	81·13/130·53
1953	Alberto Ascari	I	2·0 Ferrari 500	Zandvoort	234·49/377·37	81·05/130·43
1955	Juan Manuel Fangio	RA	2·5 Mercedes-Benz W196	Zandvoort	260·54/419·30	89·65/144·27
1958	Stirling Moss	GB	2·5 Vanwall	Zandvoort	195·41/314·48	93·93/151·17
1959	Jo Bonnier	S	2·5 BRM P25	Zandvoort	195·41/314·48	93·46/150·42
1960	Jack Brabham	AUS	2·5 Cooper T53 Climax	Zandvoort	195·41/314·48	96·27/154·93
1961	Wolfgang von Trips	D	1·5 Ferrari Dino 156	Zandvoort	195·41/314·48	96·23/154·83
1962	Graham Hill	GB	1·5 BRM P57	Zandvoort	208·43/335·44	95·44/153·60
1963	Jim Clark	GB	1·5 Lotus 25-Climax	Zandvoort	208·43/335·44	97·53/156·96
1964	Jim Clark	GB	1·5 Lotus 25-Climax	Zandvoort	203·43/335·44	98·02/157·74
1965	Jim Clark	GB	1·5 Lotus 33-Climax	Zandvoort	208·43/335·44	100·87/162·33
1966	Jack Brabham	AUS	3·0 Brabham BT19-Repco	Zandvoort	234·49/377·37	100·10/161·11
1967	Jim Clark	GB	3·0 Lotus 49-Ford	Zandvoort	234·49/377·37	104·45/168·09
1968	Jackie Stewart	GB	3·0 Matra MS10-Ford	Zandvoort	234·49/377·37	84·66/136·25
1969	Jackie Stewart	GB	3·0 Matra MS80-Ford	Zandvoort	234·49/377·37	111·04/178·71
1970	Jochen Rindt	A	3·0 Lotus 72-Ford	Zandvoort	208·43/335·44	112·96/181·78
1971	Jacky Ickx	B	3·0 Ferrari 312B-2/71	Zandvoort	182·38/293·51	94·06/151·38
1973	Jackie Stewart	GB	3·0 Tyrrell 006-Ford	Zandvoort	189·07/304·27	114·35/184·02
1974	Niki Lauda	A	3·0 Ferrari 312B-3/74	Zandvoort	196·94/316·95	114·72/184·62
1975	James Hunt	GB	3·0 Hesketh 308-Ford	Zandvoort	196·94/316·95	100·48/177·80
1976	James Hunt	GB	3·0 McLaren M23-Ford	Zandvoort	196·94/316·95	112·68/181·35
1977	Niki Lauda	A	3·0 Ferrari 312T-2/77	Zandvoort	196·94/316·95	116·12/186·87
1978	Mario Andretti	USA	3·0 JPS/Lotus 79-Ford	Zandvoort	196·94/316·95	116·92/188·16
1979	Alan Jones	AUS	3·0 Williams FW07-Ford	Zandvoort	196·94/316·95	116·62/187·67
1980	Nelson Piquet	BR	3·0 Brabham BT49-Ford	Zandvoort	190·23/306·14	116·19/186·99
1981	Alain Prost	F	1·5 Renault RE t/c	Zandvoort	190·23/306·14	113·71/183·00
1982	Didier Pironi	F	1·5 Ferrari 126C2 t/c	Zandvoort	190·23/306·14	116·38/187·30
1983	René Arnoux	F	1·5 Ferrari 126C3 t/c	Zandvoort	190·23/306·14	115·64/186·10
1984	Alain Prost	F	1·5 McLaren MP4/2-TAG t/c	Zandvoort	187·59/301·89	115·60/186·05

* Non-championship

Circuit data

Circuit van Zandvoort, near Haarlem
Circuit length: 2·642 miles/4·252 km
Race distance: 71 laps, 187·586 miles/301·892 km
Race weather: Warm, dry

Fastest laps

Driver	Time	Lap
René Arnoux	1m 19·465s	64
Alain Prost	1m 20·063s	45
Niki Lauda	1m 20·470s	37
Patrick Tambay	1m 20·585s	41
Teo Fabi	1m 20·861s	36
Nelson Piquet	1m 20·942s	2
Eddie Cheever	1m 21·203s	55
Michele Alboreto	1m 21·442s	3
Elio de Angelis	1m 21·455s	22
Nigel Mansell	1m 21·463s	28
Thierry Boutsen	1m 21·516s	43
Keke Rosberg	1m 21·593s	4
Ayrton Senna	1m 21·683s	7
Jacques Laffite	1m 21·898s	22
Derek Warwick	1m 22·203s	3
Riccardo Patrese	1m 22·486s	34
Andrea de Cesaris	1m 22·668s	10
Jonathan Palmer	1m 22·835s	35
Marc Surer	1m 23·141s	14
François Hesnault	1m 23·153s	10
Jo Gartner	1m 23·615s	29
Stefan Bellof	1m 23·740s	53
Manfred Winkelhock	1m 23·934s	9
Stefan Johansson	1m 24·071s	46
Philippe Alliot	1m 24·517s	55
Huub Rothengatter	1m 24·562s	34
Piercarlo Ghinzani	1m 25·656s	6

Points

WORLD CHAMPIONSHIP OF DRIVERS

1	Niki Lauda	54 pts
2	Alain Prost	52·5
3	Elio de Angelis	29·5
4	René Arnoux	24·5
5	Nelson Piquet	24
6	Derek Warwick	23
7	Keke Rosberg	20
8	Michele Alboreto	15
9	Nigel Mansell	13
10	Patrick Tambay	10
11=	Ayrton Senna	8
11=	Teo Fabi	8
13	Jacques Laffite	4
14=	Eddie Cheever	3
14=	Riccardo Patrese	3
14=	Thierry Boutsen	3
17=	Andrea de Cesaris	2
17=	Piercarlo Ghinzani	2
19	Marc Surer	1
*	Martin Brundle	8
*	Stefan Bellof	5

CONSTRUCTORS' CUP

1	McLaren	106·5 pts
2	Lotus	42·5
3	Ferrari	39·5
4	Renault	33
5	Brabham	32
6	Williams	24
7	Toleman	8
8	Alfa Romeo	6
9	Arrows	4
10=	Ligier	2
10=	Osella	2
*	Tyrrell	13

* Points removed by FISA Executive Committee.

Lap chart

1st LAP ORDER	1	2	3	4	5	6	7	8	9	10	11	12	13	14	15	16	17	18	19	20	21	22	23	24	25	26	27	28	29	30	31	32	33	34	35	36	37
1 N. Piquet	1	1	1	1	1	1	1	1	1	1	1	7	7	7	7	7	7	7	7	7	7	7	7	7	7	7	7	7	7	7	7	7	7	7	7	7	7
7 A. Prost	7	7	7	7	7	7	7	7	7	7	7	6	8	8	8	8	8	8	8	8	8	8	8	8	8	8	8	8	8	8	8	8	8	8	8	8	8
15 P. Tambay	15	15	15	15	6	6	6	6	6	6	6	8	6	6	6	6	6	6	6	6	6	6	6	6	6	6	6	6	6	6	6	6	6	6	6	6	6
11 E. De Angelis	11	11	11	6	15	15	15	15	8	8	15	15	15	15	15	15	15	15	15	15	15	15	15	15	15	15	15	15	15	15	15	15	15	15	15	15	11
6 K. Rosberg	6	6	6	11	11	11	11	8	15	15	11	11	11	11	11	11	11	11	11	11	11	11	11	11	11	11	11	11	11	11	11	11	11	11	11	12	12
16 D. Warwick	16	16	16	16	16	8	8	11	11	11	16	16	16	16	16	16	16	16	16	5	5	5	28	28	12	12	12	12	12	12	12	12	12	12	12	15	15
5 J. Laffite	5	5	5	5	8	16	16	16	16	16	5	5	5	5	5	5	5	5	5	16	16	16	12	12	28	28	28	28	28	28	28	28	28	28	28	28	28
27 M. Alboreto	27	8	8	8	5	5	5	5	5	5	2	2	2	2	2	2	2	2	2	2	2	28	28	18	18	18	18	18	18	18	18	18	22	22	22	22	22
8 N. Lauda	8	27	27	27	27	27	19	19	19	2	19	19	19	19	19	19	19	19	19	28	28	18	12	22	22	22	22	22	22	22	22	18	18	18	18	2	
18 T. Boutsen	18	18	2	19	19	19	2	2	2	19	28	28	28	28	28	28	28	28	18	18	18	12	18	26	26	26	26	26	2	2	2	2	2	2	2	18	
2 T. Fabi	2	2	18	2	2	28	28	28	28	18	18	18	18	18	18	18	18	18	12	12	12	2	22	2	2	2	2	2	26	23	23	23	23	23	23	23	23
19 A. Senna	19	19	19	18	28	28	18	18	18	18	12	12	12	12	12	12	12	12	22	22	22	26	25	25	25	25	25	25	25	25	25	25	25	25	25	25	25
28 R. Arnoux	28	28	28	28	18	18	12	12	12	12	22	22	22	22	22	22	22	22	26	26	26	25	23	23	23	23	23	23	25	3	3	3	3	3	3		
12 N. Mansell	12	12	12	12	12	12	22	22	22	22	26	26	26	26	26	26	26	26	25	25	25	2		3	3	3	3	3	3	4	4	4	4	4	4		
22 R. Patrese	22	22	22	22	22	22	26	26	26	26	17	17	17	17	17	17	25	25	25	23	23	23	23		4	4	4	4	4	4	9	9	9	9	9		
17 M. Surer	17	17	17	17	17	17	17	17	17	17	25	25	25	25	25	25	23	23	23	3	3		3	30	9	9	9	9	9	9	30	30	30	30	30		
25 F. Hesnault	25	25	25	26	26	26	25	25	25	25	4	4	23	23	23	23	3	3	3		4	4	4	9	10	10	10	10	10	10	10	10	10	10	10		
24 P. Ghinzani	24	24	26	25	25	25	4	4	4	4	3	3	4	4	3	3	4	4		30	30	30	30	10	21	30	30	30	30	30	30	21	21	21	21		
26 A. De Cesaris	26	26	24	24	24	24	3	3	3	23	23	3	3	4	4	17		30	30	14	14	14	9	21	30	21	21	21	21	21							
3 S. Johansson	3	4	4	4	4	4	24	24	23	3	30	30	30	30		30	14	14	9	9	9	10															
4 S. Bellof	4	3	3	3	3	23	23	30	30	9	9	9	9		9	9	10	10	10	21																	
21 H. Rothengatter	21	21	30	30	30	30	30	9	9	10	10	10	10		14	14	14	10	10	21	21	21															
30 J. Gartner	30	30	21	21	23	23	21	9	10	10	14	14	14		10	10	10	21	21																		
9 P. Alliot	9	9	23	23	21	21	9	21	21	14	21	21		21	21	21	21																				
10 J. Palmer	10	10	9	9	9	9	9	10	10	14	21																										
23 E. Cheever	23	23	10	10	10	10	27	14																													
14 M. Winkelhock	14	14	14	14	14	14	14																														

38	39	40	41	42	43	44	45	46	47	48	49	50	51	52	53	54	55	56	57	58	59	60	61	62	63	64	65	66	67	68	69	70	71
7	7	7	7	7	7	7	7	7	7	7	7	7	7	7	7	7	7	7	7	7	7	7	7	7	7	7	7	7	7	7	7	7	7
8	8	8	8	8	8	8	8	8	8	8	8	8	8	8	8	8	8	8	8	8	8	8	8	8	8	8	8	8	8	8	8	8	8
6	6	6	6	6	6	6	6	6	6	6	6	6	6	6	12	12	12	12	12	12	12	12	12	12	12	12	12	12	12	12	12	12	12
11	11	11	11	11	11	11	11	11	11	11	11	11	11	11	12	6	6	6	6	6	6	6	6	6	6	6	6	6	11	11	11		
12	12	12	12	12	12	12	12	12	12	12	12	12	12	11	11	11	11	11	11	11	11	11	11	11	11	11	11	11	6	2	2		
28	28	28	28	28	28	28	28	2	2	2	2	2	15	15	15	2	2	2	2	2	2	2	2	2	2	2	2	2	15	15			
22	22	2	2	2	2	2	2	15	15	15	15	15	2	15	15	15	15	15	15	15	15	15	15	15	15	15	15	15	25	25			
2	2	22	22	22	15	15	15	28	28	28	28	28	28	28	28	28	28	28	28	28	18	28	28	28	28	28	28	25	25	3			
15	15	15	15	15	22	22	22	22	22	22	22	22	18	18	18	18	18	18	18	18	28	23	23	23	23	23	25	3	3	3			
23	23	18	18	18	18	18	18	18	18	18	18	18	23	23	23	23	23	23	23	23	25	25	25	25	25	25	3	4	4				
18	18	23	23	23	23	23	23	23	23	23	23	23	25	25	25	25	25	25	3	3	3	3	3	3	3	4	10						
25	25	25	25	25	25	25	25	25	25	25	25	25	3	3	3	3	3	3	4	4	4	4	4	4	10	9							
3	3	3	3	3	3	3	3	3	3	3	3	3	4	4	4	4	4	4	10	10	10	10	10	10	9								
4	4	4	4	4	4	4	4	4	4	4	10	10	10	10	10	10	10	9	9	9	9	9	9	30									
30	30	30	30	30	30	30	30	30	30	30	30	30	30	30	30	30	9	30	30	30	30	30	30										
9	9	9	10	10	10	10	10	10	10	10	9	9	9	9	9	9	9	9	9	9	9	30											
10	10	10	9	9	9	9	9	9	9	9	21	21																						
21	21	21	21	21	21	21	21	21	21	21																							

Tyrrell: absent from the last three races of the 1984 season.

Gran Premio d'Italia

On the evening prior to the Italian Grand Prix, the McLaren International team went through its customary even-handed routine when it came to the task of selecting its freshly prepared TAG turbo engines to be installed for the following day's race. The two engines were lined up against the wall in the garage, the end which bears their identifying numbers facing inwards: one of the chief mechanics made his random choice and the engines were installed in the two cars. All routine stuff . . .

Just over twelve hours later, on Sunday morning, the team's pits were the scene of agitated debate. Niki Lauda, his face screwed up into an apprehensive scowl, shook his head. "Honestly," he said, "if Alain doesn't mind running the spare, I would *really* like to run my car . . ." During the half-hour warm-up session both the MP4/2 race cars had suffered loss of power, fluctuating boost pressure and water leaks. Ron Dennis and John Barnard had suggested that Niki might like to run the spare as work had already started on changing Prost's V6 by the time Niki's failed. The Rat shook his head again. No, he really didn't like the idea. He wanted a fresh engine in his race car. Prost, obliging as ever, and knowing that he had won in the past with the spare, offered no objection. Niki's engine was changed, Alain raced the spare which itself had also received a fresh TAG turbo on Saturday night.

By such tiny quirks of fate are the outcomes of World Championships affected – perhaps even decided altogether. Prost started from the front row of the grid alongside pole-winner Nelson Piquet's Brabham BT53: he was challenging for the lead at the start of lap four when his TAG turbo expired in an expensive cloud of smoke, a rod punched firmly through its cylinder block. Niki, who qualified fourth and drove his characteristically strategic race, emerged with his fifth victory of the season – in a race which had initially seemed likely to take place without his patronage! On Saturday morning he had slipped a disc in his back and set his qualifying time in excruciating pain during the afternoon. Intensive overnight physiotherapy from Willi Dungl was the only thing that saved the situation and allowed Lauda to take part.

Piquet led initially, of course, but a BMW engine failure cost him his race – this time after it had pumped out all its coolant thanks to Nelson running over a kerb and splitting the water radiator. That left Patrick Tambay, using a high compression development engine in his Renault RE50, leading the pack from Teo Fabi's Brabham BT53 and the ever-watchful Lauda. Niki watched, waited and sized everything up. On lap 40 he slammed past Fabi to take second place. On lap 43 he slipped ahead of Tambay's Renault into the lead, a task immeasurably aided by the fact that Patrick was suffering with a stiffening throttle linkage which almost immediately broke once Niki had overtaken him. The previous lap saw Fabi out, all the Brabham's oil having leaked away, so Lauda just stroked it home by over 20s from Michele Alboreto's Ferrari 126C4, the only other car on the same lap.

It all looked so absurdly simple . . .

ENTRY AND PRACTICE

For the first time in years, the Monza crowd faced the prospect of an Italian Grand Prix in which its beloved scarlet Ferraris were *not* forces with which to be reckoned. Although the Maranello marque had not won on home soil since the historic Scheckter-Villeneuve 1-2 here five years ago, on every occasion the Prancing Horse has been represented at this hallowed home of Italian motor racing, its cars have been front-running contenders. Even what looked like frantic, last-moment modifications resulting in the production of a revised car, the C4 'M2', could not change the inexorable course of the 1984 season in favour of the customary McLaren/Brabham confrontation. With two *green* liveried Alfa Romeo 184Ts (what kind of heresy was this?) outqualifying Enzo's cars, the only worthwhile interest for the vocal Italian fans was to see whether Lotus's Elio de Angelis could hang on to the final sliver of a Championship chance. A vain hope in the path of the McLaren-TAG steamroller!

Notwithstanding the intervention of a rain shower or two on Friday afternoon, a climatic factor which briefly catapulted a Ferrari C4, albeit an unmodified spare C4, up to fourth place in the hands of Michele Alboreto, the front two rows of the grid were "standard '84". In the Brabham camp things were running in routine fashion with Nelson Piquet managing second quickest time on Friday afternoon, behind de Angelis, before throwing pole beyond reach the following day with a superb 1m 26.584s. His Friday efforts were slightly compromised when his "qualifying spare" broke its engine after the Brazilian's first run, forcing Nelson to switch to his race-designated BT53 to turn a 1m 28.709s – not exceptionally quick owing to several very damp patches still remaining under the trees. On Saturday his best time came on his first run on soft rubber as his "sprint" machine suffered turbo failure on the first lap of its second run. As a precaution, he went out again for another try in his race car, but the fact that he couldn't improve did not matter in the least. Nobody matched his pole time, although Prost got close.

The Frenchman, out to sustain the momentum of his recent Zandvoort success as the season moved into its crucial, final phase, was in splendid form, no question. After his race MP4/2 suffered engine problems on Saturday morning, Alain switched to the spare and scorched round in 1m 26.671s to wrap up second place on the grid: this

Renault were in trouble again at Monza. Derek
Warwick (pictured) retired with engine trouble while
Patrick Tambay's superb run at the front was halted
by a broken throttle cable.
Photo: Bernard Asset/Agence Vandystadt.

SEPTEMBER:
Williams sign Nigel Mansell for 1985.
*Rick Mears injured during qualifying for CART
race at Sanair, near Montreal.*
Gustav Brunner leaves Euroracing and joins RAM.

was almost two seconds quicker than Niki Lauda
was to manage for fourth slot on the grid, but Niki
had other, more immediate problems, on his mind
by the end of Saturday morning unofficial practice.

Tweaking his McLaren through one of the faster
ess-bends, Niki suddenly felt a searing pain in his
back, possibly as he was jolted slightly within what
is, for him, a capacious cockpit. He pulled into the
pits and had to be helped from the car in sheer
agony. Trainer Willi Dungl was immediately
summoned and a quick examination revealed that
Niki had slipped a disc in his back – a problem that
is apparently not new to him. For a short while this
looked as though it might be the unexpected
"outside factor" which Ron Dennis has been for so
long predicting would decide the destiny of the
Championship between his two drivers. There
were rumours that Niki would withdraw from the

race. Bravely, he strapped himself back into the
cockpit of his MP4/2 and slammed round to record
that fourth quickest 1m 28.533s. Then it was back
to his hotel for more massage and early to bed: he
would take part in the race morning warm-up and
then decide whether he would race . . .

Splitting those McLarens, Elio de Angelis was in
a fine mood. His Lotus 95T was performing
perfectly, although he reckoned that the engine lost
its edge between Friday and Saturday qualifying.
Quickest on Friday, an achievement which
brought some smiles to the faces of Goodyear's
personnel, Elio reckoned he could have held on to
pole if "the engine had responded to high boost as
well as it did yesterday." The Italian also had the
sole revised heavy-duty Lotus-developed gearbox
available, incorporating a strengthened outer
casing, revised lubrication system and Hewland

DGB internals. It was hoped that the new unit
would prevent any repeat of the transmission
problems which had bugged the team – a vain
hope, as things turned out.

Behind the first four regulars, Teo Fabi was
really getting into his stride at the wheel of the
second Brabham BT53, at last producing the kind
of form many people had predicted of him. His fifth
quickest 1m 28.587s was achieved with an engine
that seemed reluctant to pull its full quota of revs in
top gear. Understandably, the diminutive Italian
was delighted.

By contrast, Nigel Mansell, on the home run
with Team Lotus and on the verge of clinching an
'85 deal with Williams, had a less happy time.
From the word go on Friday his engine was cutting
out intermittently and, although he briefly shot up
to third place during the height of Saturday's

But for a wheel-bearing failure, Stefan Johansson would have taken third place at the end of his first drive for Toleman. The Swede nursed his car across the line to finish fourth after an excellent charge from the back of the field.

jousting, he was back in seventh place on 1m 28.969s by the time the dust settled. On Friday he had prompted a dark look from Niki Lauda when he stayed out too long on a qualifying run, ran out of fuel and left his Lotus parked right on the fast line at one point round the circuit. "I had to swerve on to the wet to avoid it," frowned Lauda, "why the hell he couldn't have steered it on to the grass when he realised it was stopping I just can't imagine!"

Over at Williams there was a grade one row brewing right in the middle of a Grand Prix weekend. Keke Rosberg, never one to hide his own personal light under a bushel, simply exploded with indignation when he heard that Frank had done the deal with Mansell and the Finn spent much of the weekend telling anybody who would listen that he did *not* approve of this nomination.

Rosberg's Friday efforts with the Williams FW09B were hampered by an engine failure in his race car mid-way through qualifying, but on Saturday he got the inherent understeer reasonably well under control to record a 1m 28.818s which was good enough for a third row start. Jacques Laffite, saddened at the prospect of leaving the Williams team, recorded 13th quickest 1m 30.578s, although he was not particularly happy about the performance of the Williams-Honda with a full fuel load.

For the Renault-Elf team, Monza qualifying was an unremitting nightmare with an endless catalogue of problems, culminating with all three RE50s encountering engine malfunctions during Saturday qualifying. Patrick Tambay opted to concentrate his efforts on the team's spare chassis which he personally preferred. His Friday qualifying efforts were upset when Gerard Larrousse sent him out earlier than Patrick reckoned ideal and the Frenchman spun wildly on a damp patch as he turned into the *Curva Grande*. "I was just left sitting there in the middle of the circuit, waiting for something to happen," Tambay reflected, "there was no question of the marshals helping me to start or the session being stopped – not like the old days at Ferrari!"

After hurrying back to the pits to take over his former race car (now doing service as the spare), his efforts were thwarted again when it suffered turbo failure. This seemingly unending series of disappointments continued throughout the following afternoon: the race car suffered another turbo failure, so he was left to do his eighth quickest 1m 29.253s in the spare which, as Derek Warwick was to discover, was badly down on revs. Derek, who freely confessed to hating "all this scrambling over kerbs and manhandling the bloody thing around this place", highlighted Friday practice with a big spin braking for the first chicane – "I'd forgotten to readjust the brake balance from its wet settings" – and also qualified in the spare after his own race car developed a misfire. Under the circumstances, a 12th fastest 1m 30.113s was not too bad.

The Alfa Romeo 184Ts emerged at Monza sporting waisted McLaren-style rear ends, said to be developed from designs that Gerard Ducarouge "left in the drawer" on his departure from the team early last year! Whether through an ability to run with less rear wing as a result of this alteration, or simply because the modification improved the air

flow to the turbochargers, both Eddie Cheever and Riccardo Patrese pronounced themselves delighted with the revised cars. Aside from slight concern over rising oil temperatures, the Alfas were pulling slightly more revs in top gear – and sprinted up to maximum speed appreciably quicker. Patrese was tenth on the grid on 1m 29.382s with Eddie alongside him, a fraction slower.

Frankly, Ferrari was in a bit of a mess. Although the Commendatore had enthusiastically endorsed his faith in both Mauro Forghieri and Harvey Postlethwaite at a press conference the previous week, neither of the Scuderia's senior Formula 1 engineers was to be seen at Monza, an amazing development. Forghieri had decided to stay at the factory "and let them get on with it" while Harvey, perhaps anxious not to be seen doing anything that might be construed as usurping his colleague's status, took a holiday in England.

The team turned up with four cars, two to regular long wheelbase C4 specification and a pair of the mysteriously dubbed "M2s". The new cars had the fashionable waisted rear bodywork, a change which involved resiting the water and oil radiators, while the rear suspension had been revised yet again. The merits of this revised configuration were never conclusively proved. Alboreto wound up using Arnoux's regular C4 spare after his M2 lost turbo boost pressure on Friday and his spare broke its gearbox. On Saturday Michele's M2 suffered an engine failure, so it was back to his own "regular" C4 to qualify 11th on 1m 29.810s. Arnoux concentrated on the M2 for most of the two sessions, consistently complaining about lack of Goodyear grip: he qualified 14th on 1m 30.695s. Eventually it was decided not to race the M2s after a worrying transmission vibration developed and both drivers went to the start in their spare cars.

Although Ligier's revamped JS23B had been tested briefly at Paul Ricard the previous week, it was deemed too new to be raced at Monza, so the Italian and his team-mate François Hesnault appeared in their regular Renault-engined cars. Andrea qualified a rather disappointed 16th on 1m 31.198s, while Hesnault was quite pleased with himself on this occasion, barely a tenth of a second behind in 18th spot.

Marc Surer headed the Arrows effort with a 15th quickest 1m 31.108s, set on Friday: the Swiss driver was unable to improve on Saturday after pick-up problems with his freshly-installed BMW engine. Thierry Boutsen, equipped with a brand new chassis (A7/4) to replace the one wrecked in his frightening collision with Arnoux at Zandvoort, had a troubled couple of days, starting off on the wrong foot when his new machine speared off into the barrier under hard braking for one of the chicanes. The turbo wastegate had come loose, the exhaust pipe had pivoted round slightly as a result and melted a rear brake pipe, causing the bewildered Belgian to plunge off the road. The car was repaired for Saturday and Boutsen did a 1m 31.342s 19th place.

Splitting the two Ligier JS23s was Toleman debutant Stefan Johansson, the amiable Swede drafted in to take Ayrton Senna's place in the wake of litigation following the announcement of the

Brazilian's move to Lotus for 1985. After recording a respectable tenth quickest time on Friday, Johansson was very depressed by the apparently sudden development of an alarming high speed oversteer which kept him down in 17th place with a 1m 31.203s. Only when it was decided to switch the race car's engine to the spare TG184 for Stefan to use in the Grand Prix was the problem pinpointed: the race car had a broken engine mounting bobbin which was allowing the engine to flex slightly, causing the handling imbalance.

Gerhard Berger was given another outing in the second ATS, the promising Austrian qualifying 20th on 1m 31.549s, while regular team driver Manfred Winkelhock got his weekend off to a good start when his D7 broke a rear suspension rose joint and spun him off very violently on Friday morning. Frontal damage to the monocoque was repaired and he managed to squeeze in a 1m 32.866s on Saturday before gearbox trouble intervened.

Rounding off the last two rows of the grid was Piercarlo Ghinzani, who qualified alongside Winkelhock, then Alliot's RAM, Jo Gartner's Osella, Huub Rothengatter's Spirit 101B and Palmer's RAM. On Friday afternoon both Osella drivers had to share the team's spare FA1F after a sticking

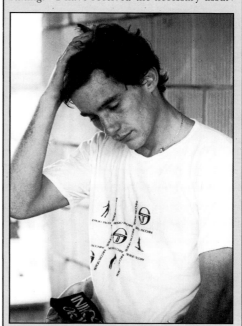

AYRTON Senna, the revelation of the 1984 season, was unemployed at Monza. The Brazilian had been suspended by the Toleman team in the light of an announcement by Lotus at Zandvoort that Senna would be driving for them in 1985 and 1986. Toleman were incensed, not so much by the fact that Senna wanted to leave, but by the manner in which the negotiations had been carried out.

Senna had agreed to a three-year deal with Toleman at the beginning of the season and the contract contained a 'buy out' clause which stipulated that a certain sum should be paid to Toleman before any negotiations could take place. According to Toleman, not only had Senna not paid the money, he had also continually denied that he was negotiating with Lotus.

Matters had reached a head at Zandvoort when Lotus announced, as a secondary paragraph in a press release confirming the continuation of sponsorship from John Player Special, that Senna had 'completed contractual terms with JPS Team Lotus. The additional line: 'He (Senna) will, of course, continue to drive for Toleman for the rest of the season' threw Alex Hawkridge into a predictable fury. The meaning was clear but the choice of words was as ill-conceived as the poorly handled negotiations.

Peter Warr attempted to distance himself from the impending row with Toleman by stating: "I have received the necessary assurances from Ayrton Senna that he will be able to fulfil the obligations and undertakings he has given us in the contract he signed with us . . . It is important to stress that our contract is with Ayrton Senna. We have no links with Toleman."

A rather bewildered Senna was present at Monza where he issued a formal statement repudiating many of the points made by Toleman. By now, observers were growing weary of the consequences of what appeared to be an appalling piece of bargaining.

Senna summed it up best when he said: "I intended to keep quiet about the whole thing and deal with the people who were involved at Toleman. I don't want any more aggravation. I just want to go motor racing."

And, on that note, he went up to the Brazilian television commentary position and watched Stefan Johansson turn on a brilliant performance in a car which, clearly, had done much for Senna's flourishing reputation. . . .

throttle sent Gartner into the guard rail exiting the *Variante Ascari* and Ghinzani's machine blew its engine: they were both back in their regular machines the following afternoon. In the RAM camp Palmer had to qualify Alliot's car once the Frenchman had finished with it on Saturday afternoon, his efforts in his regular car hampered by two successive rough-running engines, one of which showed signs of a porous block.

The only non-qualifier was the luckless Pierluigi Martini, drafted in by financial considerations to drive the second Toleman TG184: lack of experience with the car resulted in the diminutive Italian doing his reputation no good at all and he failed to make the race.

RACE

As the crowds filed into the autodrome on Sunday morning, the pit lane was a scene of frenzied activity following the half-hour warm-up session. Apart from the McLaren mechanics sweating to change Lauda's engine, the Williams team was in a similarly fraught situation with two engine breakages on its hands. A fresh Honda V6 was installed in Rosberg's FW09B while Laffite was allocated the spare car for the race. Both Ferrari drivers were

in their *mulettas*, Warwick opted for the spare Renault as his own RE50 had developed a misfire, Toleman was busy swapping engines around from race to spare car for Johansson, Winkelhock was fuming as his ATS D7 did not want to engage anything but fourth and fifth while Surer came into the pits at the end of the final warm-up lap to complain that his Arrows A7 would not rev properly. The Swiss was still in the pit lane when the starting signal was given and joined in as the pack completed the opening tour!

When the starting signal was given Elio de Angelis made the getaway of his career, fish-tailing his Lotus 95T between the two front row cars to nose into the lead as the pack sprinted for the first chicane. Mansell was similarly quick off the mark, but Piquet's BMW power eventually told and the outgoing World Champion just managed to beat the Italian into the first complex. From that point onwards the Brazilian just bounded away into the lead, bursting out from *Parabolica* to complete that opening lap several lengths clear of Prost and Tambay, both of whom had surged past de Angelis in the previous couple of miles.

Fabi led the pursuit in fifth place with Lauda next up, then Mansell, Patrese, Rosberg, Cheever,

Patrick Tambay drove superbly, the Renault driver taking the lead once Nelson Piquet had retired. Tambay held off an attack from Teo Fabi, the Italian storming through the field after an early spin. Fabi stopped when an oil union broke but Tambay was unable to hold off Niki Lauda's McLaren when the Renault's throttle cable began to break, causing the Frenchman to retire eight laps from the end.

Alboreto, Warwick and the rest. Johansson had well and truly fluffed his start and was right down amongst the tail enders, while Winkelhock was not even in the race: the furious German had found that his ATS *still* only had fourth and fifth gear available as he accelerated away on the warm-up lap. When he returned to the grid, with a racing start obviously out of the question, he parked at the back, hopped out and walked away . . . it was the second race this season that gearbox problems had sidelined the amiable German before the start.

Coming out of the first Lesmo right-hander on the second lap, Piquet dropped his left-rear wheel over the kerb, managed to catch the ensuing heart-stopping slide, but allowed Prost and Tambay to ease up on to his tail as they completed the tour. This was clearly going to be the main issue of the race, and Prost was soon right on Piquet's tail, sizing up the Brabham with a view to nipping by early on in the contest, but as the Frenchman completed his third lap the McLaren began to spew out an ominous trail of oil smoke, heralding a mortally damaged TAG turbo. Into the first chicane Prost slowed dramatically, boxing in Tambay and throwing copious quantities of lubricant all over the Renault driver's vizor, before pulling off on to the grass. As Niki Lauda passed Prost's stricken car he realised that his paramount task was to collect *some* World Championship points, not necessarily win: the Austrian wound down the turbo boost pressure and sat back in fourth place to await developments.

Fabi quickly hauled his way up on to Tambay's tail but, mid-way round lap eight, got carried away under braking for one of the chicanes and spun. To the little Italian's credit he neither allowed his BT53 to touch the guard rail (which looms very close at that point!), nor did he stall the engine. He quickly recovered and completed the lap in eighth place, charging for all he was worth.

Piquet clearly had an edge over the field, but Tambay for once had a Renault V6 capable of matching a BMW four-cylinder on this occasion and was hanging on, comfortably in touch, as the leaders completed their tenth lap. Lauda was third, with Alboreto next in front of de Angelis, the recovering Fabi, Cheever (now the best placed Alfa following an excursion into a sand trap which dropped Patrese well down the field), Warwick and Laffite. Ferrari's challenge was blunted when Arnoux's gearbox failed on lap six and left René stranded out on the circuit.

By lap 13 Tambay was making up time slightly on the leading Brabham and, as Piquet came rushing down to *Parabolica* on lap 15, the BT53 emitted a worrying puff of smoke. It was the beginning of the end – yet again – for Nelson's efforts and, as the two cars raced past the pits at the end of the lap, Tambay pulled out and outbraked the obviously sickening Brabham into the first chicane. Nelson cruised round to the pits where he retired at the end of lap 16. (It was thought that the early trip across a kerb had split a water radiator, the BMW then losing its coolant during the next few laps.)

Now the complexion of the whole affair had changed dramatically, with both front row qualifiers out of the equation. Tambay was left with a 5.8s advantage over Fabi, who had just nipped past Lauda, but there was an inexorable aura of the inevitable exuded by McLaren number eight as the Austrian paced himself confidently along in the wake of the keen little Italian!

Elio de Angelis's promising run had faded early, his Goodyears clearly no match for the leaders' Michelins, but his new gearbox also wilted under the strain and, after slowing to a crawl at the end of lap 14, he retired a lap later with second and fourth ratios totally inoperative. Just to add to Lotus's displeasure, Nigel Mansell went skating off on oil dropped by Andrea de Cesaris's blowing-up Ligier and got his 95T irretrievably bogged down in a sand trap mid-way round lap 14 – a fate shared by Hesnault, incidentally! In fact, by this time Goodyear's runners were becoming significantly depleted as both Rosberg and Laffite had ground to a halt on laps nine and 11 respectively, their Honda engines having expired yet again.

By lap 20 it was becoming clear that Fabi and Lauda were pulling up on to Tambay's tail, the gap shrinking steadily each time round. Niki had made a few preliminary forays against Fabi, poking the nose of his McLaren out of the Brabham's slipstream from time to time, testing Teo's defences, but by lap 25 Lauda realised that he was going to have to get serious. For the next six laps the first three cars were nose-to-tail with Tambay coming under as much attack from Fabi as the Brabham driver was from Lauda. But Patrick was soon to feel the first signs of the problem that would eventually lead to his retirement . . .

On lap 33, as the leaders weaved their way in and out of the backmarkers, Tambay became conscious that the Renault's throttle pedal was getting slightly stiffer to operate. It was also slow to return, so although it was not exactly sticking open, it *was* giving him plenty to think about. By lap 30 Warwick, who had earlier been boxed in badly behind a weaving Cheever, had convincingly consolidated fifth place behind Alboreto, leaving

Johansson back in seventh place, ducking, diving and cursing in the Toleman as he sought to find a path ahead of the unhelpful Eddie.

It was becoming clear that Lauda was going to have an enormous amount of hard work to do if he was going to wrest the lead, but the way in which he finally forced his way into second place, overtaking Fabi with his two right-hand wheels almost shaving the grass on the straight down to *Parabolica* on lap 42, indicated that Niki is no softy. A lap later he surged ahead of Tambay coming out of the pre-Lesmo chicane, but Patrick's throttle was by now giving him real trouble and, as he changed up to fourth coming out of *Parabolica* at the end of the lap, the throttle cable broke at the engine end of the linkage. The bitterly disappointed Tambay coasted down the outside of the pit wall before symbolically abandoning the RE50 right next to the Renault crew: he had done his bit and the car had let him down. Fabi's race had finished in front of the pits on lap 44 after a broken oil pipe had caused the loss of all his engine's lubricant.

With only eight laps left to run, Lauda had it in the bag. Taking no chances, he cruised home to his fifth win of the season, still with well over 20s in hand over the hard-trying Alboreto who was cheered to the echo as he crossed the line to collect six Championship points. But behind the Italian, there had been mechanical carnage on a grand scale. Cheever's earlier antics had taken such a toll on the Alfa's fuel consumption that it ran out six laps from the flag. Johansson would have inherited third had he not dived into the pits to investigate a worrying vibration from the Toleman's rear end: the problem was a failing wheel bearing, so he was sent back into the race to nurse the car home fourth. Patrese inherited third as a result of Stefan's pause, while Ghinzani's Osella fell prey to the Alfa fuel consumption bug and its tank ran dry with three laps left – handing fifth to team-mate Gartner, the Austrian just staggering up to the line with the aid of the electric pump sucking up the last few dregs in the system.

Gerhard Berger survived to finish sixth, the Austrian struggling without fourth gear since lap 15, although both he and Gartner were ineligible to score points since ATS and Osella had entered just one car each for the World Championship. Ghinzani was classified seventh ahead of Rothengatter, the retired Cheever and Thierry Boutsen who had struggled on to the end despite a couple of pit stops in his Arrows A7. Surer had succumbed to engine trouble while Warwick, holding back slightly in fifth place owing to a chassis vibration, switched off when the oil pressure warning light began to flicker on lap 32.

After the drama was all over, Lauda's biggest remaining problem was fighting his way through the paddock crowds to his helicopter, still wincing slightly with the discomfort of his troublesome back. Prost simply sat and reflected philosophically on the unpredictable way the cards fall in the Grand Prix game. If only he had *insisted* that *his* car had undergone that engine change, the Championship points table might have told a very different story.

If only. . . .   AH.

If only . . . Prost's engine failure after three laps.

Entries and practice times

No.	Driver	Nat	Car	Tyre	Engine	Entrant	Practice 1	Practice 2
1	Nelson Piquet	BR	Parmalat BRABHAM BT53	M	BMW M12/13	MRD International	1m 28·709s	**1m 26·584s**
2	Teo Fabi	I	Parmalat BRABHAM BT53	M	BMW M12/13	MRD International	1m 29·383s	**1m 28·587s**
5	Jacques Laffite	F	WILLIAMS FW09B	G	Honda RA 163–E	Williams Grand Prix Engineering	1m 32·091s	**1m 30·578s**
6	Keke Rosberg	SF	WILLIAMS FW09B	G	Honda RA 163–E	Williams Grand Prix Engineering	1m 33·386s	**1m 28·818s**
7	Alain Prost	F	Marlboro McLAREN MP4/2	M	TAG P01 (TTE P01)	Marlboro McLaren International	1m 29·854s	**1m 26·671s**
8	Niki Lauda	A	Marlboro McLAREN MP4/2	M	TAG P01 (TTE P01)	Marlboro McLaren International	1m 30·142s	**1m 28·533s**
9	Philippe Alliot	F	RAM 02	P	Hart 415T	Skoal Bandit Formula 1 Team	1m 37·186s	**1m 34·120s**
10	Jonathan Palmer	GB	RAM 02	P	Hart 415T	Skoal Bandit Formula 1 Team	1m 36·876s	**1m 35·412s**
11	Elio de Angelis	I	John Player Special LOTUS 95T	G	Renault EF4	John Player Team Lotus	1m 28·014s	**1m 27·538s**
12	Nigel Mansell	GB	John Player Special LOTUS 95T	G	Renault EF4	John Player Team Lotus	1m 31·715s	**1m 28·969s**
14	Manfred Winkelhock	D	ATS D7	P	BMW M12/13	Team ATS	2m 00·593s	**1m 32·866s**
15	Patrick Tambay	F	Elf RENAULT RE50	M	Renault EF4	Equipe Renault Elf	1m 31·532s	**1m 29·253s**
16	Derek Warwick	GB	Elf RENAULT RE50	M	Renault EF4	Equipe Renault Elf	**1m 30·113s**	1m 30·569s
17	Marc Surer	CH	ARROWS A7	G	BMW M12/13	Barclay Nordica Arrows BMW	**1m 31·108s**	1m 31·513s
18	Thierry Boutsen	B	ARROWS A7	G	BMW M12/13	Barclay Nordica Arrows BMW	1m 32·636s	**1m 31·342s**
19	Stefan Johansson	S	TOLEMAN TG184	M	Hart 415T	Toleman Group Motorsport	1m 31·207s	**1m 31·203s**
20	Pierluigi Martini	I	TOLEMAN TG184	M	Hart 415T	Toleman Group Motorsport	1m 38·312s	**1m 35·840s**
21	Huub Rothengatter	NL	SPIRIT 101	P	Hart 415T	Spirit Racing	1m 38·255s	**1m 34·719s**
22	Riccardo Patrese	I	Benetton ALFA ROMEO 184T	G	Alfa Romeo 183T	Benetton Team Alfa Romeo	1m 30·710s	**1m 29·382s**
23	Eddie Cheever	USA	Benetton ALFA ROMEO 184T	G	Alfa Romeo 183T	Benetton Team Alfa Romeo	1m 32·365s	**1m 29·797s**
24	Piercarlo Ghinzani	I	Kelemata OSELLA FA1F	P	Alfa Romeo 183T	Osella Squadra Corse	**1m 33·456s**	1m 33·562s
25	François Hesnault	F	LIGIER Loto JS23	M	Renault EF4	Ligier Loto	1m 32·779s	**1m 31·274s**
26	Andrea de Cesaris	I	LIGIER Loto JS23	M	Renault EF4	Ligier Loto	1m 32·014s	**1m 31·198s**
27	Michele Alboreto	I	Fiat FERRARI 126C4	G	Ferrari 126C	Scuderia Ferrari SpA	**1m 29·810s**	1m 30·069s
28	René Arnoux	F	Fiat FERRARI 126C4	G	Ferrari 126C	Scuderia Ferrari SpA	1m 31·495s	**1m 30·695s**
30	Jo Gartner	A	Kelemata OSELLA FA1F	P	Alfa Romeo 183T	Osella Squadra Corse	1m 37·123s	**1m 34·472s**
31	Gerhard Berger	A	ATS D7	P	BMW M12/13	Team ATS	1m 33·161s	**1m 31·549s**

Friday morning and Saturday morning practice sessions not officially recorded.

G – Goodyear, M – Michelin, P – Pirelli.

	Fri pm	Sat pm
	Warm, damp/dry	Hot, dry

Starting grid

1 PIQUET (1m 26·584s)
Brabham

7 PROST (1m 26·671s)
McLaren

11 DE ANGELIS (1m 27·538s)
Lotus

8 LAUDA (1m 28·533s)
McLaren

2 FABI (1m 28·587s)
Brabham

6 ROSBERG (1m 28·818s)
Williams

12 MANSELL (1m 28·969s)
Lotus

15 TAMBAY (1m 29·253s)
Renault

22 PATRESE (1m 29·382s)
Alfa Romeo

23 CHEEVER (1m 29·797s)
Alfa Romeo

27 ALBORETO (1m 29·810s)
Ferrari

16 WARWICK (1m 30·113s)
Renault

5 LAFFITE (1m 30·578s)
Williams

28 ARNOUX (1m 30·695s)
Ferrari

17 SURER (1m 31·108s)
Arrows

26 DE CESARIS (1m 31·198s)
Ligier

19 JOHANSSON (1m 31·203s)
Toleman

25 HESNAULT (1m 31·274s)
Ligier

18 BOUTSEN (1m 31·342s)
Arrows

31 BERGER (1m 31·549s)
ATS

*14 WINKELHOCK (1m 32·866s)
ATS

24 GHINZANI (1m 33·456s)
Osella

9 ALLIOT (1m 34·120s)
RAM

30 GARTNER (1m 34·472s)
Osella

21 ROTHENGATTER (1m 34·719s)
Spirit

10 PALMER (1m 35·412s)
RAM

Did not start:
20 Martini (Toleman), 1m 35·840s, did not qualify
*14 Winkelhock (ATS), gearbox trouble during warm-up lap

Results and retirements

Place	Driver	Car	Laps	Time and Speed (mph/km/h)/Retirement	
1	Niki Lauda	McLaren-TAG t/c V6	51	1h 20m 29·065s	137·021/220·514
2	Michele Alboreto	Ferrari t/c V6	51	1h 20m 53·314s	136·329/219·4
3	Riccardo Patrese	Alfa Romeo t/c V8	50		
4	Stefan Johansson	Toleman-Hart t/c 4	49		
5	Jo Gartner	Osella-Alfa Romeo t/c V8	49		
6	Gerhard Berger	ATS-BMW t/c 4	49		
7	Piercarlo Ghinzani	Osella-Alfa Romeo t/c V8	48	Out of fuel	
8	Huub Rothengatter	Spirit-Hart t/c 4	48		
9	Eddie Cheever	Alfa Romeo t/c V8	45	Out of fuel	
10	Thierry Boutsen	Arrows-BMW t/c 4	45		
	Patrick Tambay	Renault t/c V6	43	Throttle cable	
	Teo Fabi	Brabham-BMW t/c 4	43	Engine/broken oil union	
	Marc Surer	Arrows-BMW t/c 4	43	Engine	
	Derek Warwick	Renault t/c V6	31	Oil pressure	
	Jonathan Palmer	RAM-Hart t/c 4	20	Oil pressure	
	Nelson Piquet	Brabham-BMW t/c 4	15	Engine/split water radiator	
	Elio de Angelis	Lotus-Renault t/c V6	14	Gearbox	
	Nigel Mansell	Lotus-Renault t/c V6	13	Spun off	
	Jacques Laffite	Williams-Honda t/c V6	10	Turbo	
	Keke Rosberg	Williams-Honda t/c V6	8	Engine	
	Andrea de Cesaris	Ligier-Renault t/c V6	7	Engine	
	François Hesnault	Ligier-Renault t/c V6	7	Spun off	
	Philippe Alliot	RAM-Hart t/c 4	6	Electrics	
	René Arnoux	Ferrari t/c V6	5	Gearbox	
	Alain Prost	McLaren-TAG t/c V6	4	Engine	

Fastest lap: Lauda, on lap 42, 1m 31·912s, 141·158mph/227·173km/h (record).
Previous lap record: René Arnoux (F1 Renault RE30B t/c), 1m 33·619, 138·585mph/223·031km/h 1982.

Past winners

Year	Driver	Nat	Car	Circuit	Distance miles/km	Speed mph/km/h
1950	Giuseppe Farina	I	1·5 Alfa Romeo 158 s/c	Monza	313·17/504·00	109·70/176·54
1951	Alberto Ascari	I	4·5 Ferrari 375	Monza	313·17/504·00	115·52/185·92
1952	Alberto Ascari	I	2·0 Ferrari 500	Monza	313·17/504·00	110·04/177·09
1953	Juan Manuel Fangio	RA	2·0 Maserati A6SSG	Monza	313·17/504·00	110·68/178·13
1954	Juan Manuel Fangio	RA	2·5 Mercedes-Benz W196	Monza	313·17/504·00	111·98/180·22
1955	Juan Manuel Fangio	RA	2·5 Mercedes-Benz W196	Monza	310·69/500·00	128·49/206·79
1956	Stirling Moss	GB	2·5 Maserati 250F	Monza	310·69/500·00	129·73/208·79
1957	Stirling Moss	GB	2·5 Vanwall	Monza	310·84/500·25	129·73/208·79
1958	Tony Brooks	GB	2·5 Vanwall	Monza	250·10/402·50	121·21/195·08
1959	Stirling Moss	GB	2·5 Cooper T45-Climax	Monza	257·25/414·00	124·38/200·18
1960	Phil Hill	USA	2·4 Ferrari Dino 246	Monza	310·69/500·00	132·06/212·53
1961	Phil Hill	USA	1·5 Ferrari Dino 156	Monza	267·19/430·00	130·11/209·39
1962	Graham Hill	GB	1·5 BRM P57	Monza	307·27/494·50	123·62/198·94
1963	Jim Clark	GB	1·5 Lotus 25-Climax	Monza	302·27/494·50	127·74/205·58
1964	John Surtees	GB	1·5 Ferrari 158	Monza	278·68/448·50	127·77/205·63
1965	Jackie Stewart	GB	1·5 BRM P261	Monza	271·54/437·00	130·46/209·96
1966	Ludovico Scarfiotti	I	3·0 Ferrari 312/66	Monza	242·96/391·00	135·92/218·75
1967	John Surtees	GB	3·9 Honda RA300	Monza	242·96/391·00	140·50/226·12
1968	Denny Hulme	NZ	3·0 McLaren M7A-Ford	Monza	242·96/391·00	145·41/234·02
1969	Jackie Stewart	GB	3·0 Matra MS80-Ford	Monza	242·96/391·00	146·97/236·52
1970	Clay Regazzoni	CH	3·0 Ferrari 312B-1/70	Monza	242·96/391·00	147·08/236·67
1971	Peter Gethin	GB	3·0 BRM P160	Monza	196·51/316·25	150·75/242·62
1972	Emerson Fittipaldi	BR	3·0 JPS/Lotus 72-Ford	Monza	197·36/317·63	131·61/211·81
1973	Ronnie Peterson	S	3·0 JPS/Lotus 72-Ford	Monza	197·36/317·63	132·63/213·45
1974	Ronnie Peterson	S	3·0 JPS/Lotus 72-Ford	Monza	186·76/300·56	135·10/217·42
1975	Clay Regazzoni	CH	3·0 Ferrari 312T/75	Monza	186·76/300·56	135·48/218·03
1976	Ronnie Peterson	USA	3·0 March 761-Ford	Monza	187·41/301·60	124·12/199·75
1977	Mario Andretti	USA	3·0 JPS/Lotus 78-Ford	Monza	187·41/301·60	128·01/206·02
1978	Niki Lauda	A	3·0 Brabham BT46-Alfa Romeo	Monza	144·16/232·00	128·95/207·53
1979	Jody Scheckter	ZA	3·0 Ferrari 312T-4	Monza	180·20/290·00	131·85/212·18
1980	Nelson Piquet	BR	3·0 Brabham BT49-Ford	Imola	186·41/300·00	113·98/183·44
1981	Alain Prost	F	1·5 Renault RE30 t/c	Monza	187·40/301·60	129·87/209·00
1982	René Arnoux	F	1·5 Renault RE30B t/c	Monza	187·40/301·60	136·39/219·50
1983	Nelson Piquet	BR	1·5 Brabham BT52B-BMW t/c	Monza	187·40/301·60	136·18/217·55
1984	Niki Lauda	A	1·5 McLaren MP4/2-TAG t/c	Monza	183·80/295·80	137·02/220·51

Circuit data

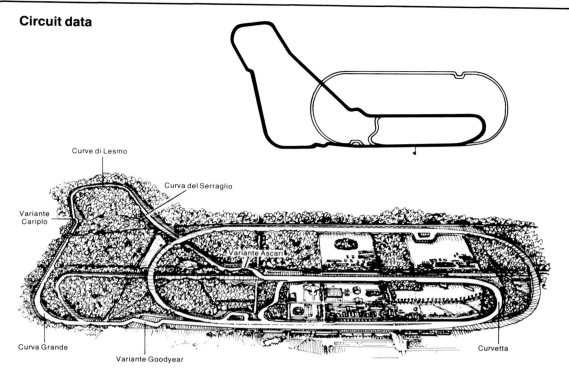

Curve di Lesmo
Curva del Serraglio
Variante Cariplo
Variante Ascari
Curva Grande
Variante Goodyear
Curvetta

Autodromo Nazionale di Monza, near Milan
Circuit length: 3·6039 miles/5·80 km
Race distance: 51 laps, 183·801 miles/295·800 km
Race weather: Hot, dry

Lap chart

1ST LAP ORDER		1	2	3	4	5	6	7	8	9	10	11	12	13	14	15	16	17	18	19	20	21	22	23	24	25	26	27	28	29	30	31	32	33	34	35	36	37
1	N. Piquet	1	1	1	1	1	1	1	1	1	1	1	1	1	1	15	15	15	15	15	15	15	15	15	15	15	15	15	15	15	15	15	15	15	15	15	15	15
7	A. Prost	7	7	7	15	15	15	15	15	15	15	15	15	15	15	8	2	2	2	2	2	2	2	2	2	2	2	2	2	2	2	2	2	2	2	2	2	2
11	E. De Angelis	11	15	15	2	2	2	2	8	8	8	8	8	8	8	2	8	8	8	8	8	8	8	8	8	8	8	8	8	8	8	8	8	8	8	8	8	8
15	P. Tambay	15	11	2	8	8	8	8	27	27	27	27	2	2	2	27	27	27	27	27	27	27	27	27	27	27	27	27	27	27	27	27	27	27	27	27	27	27
2	T. Fabi	2	2	8	11	11	11	27	11	11	11	2	27	27	27	23	23	23	16	16	16	16	16	16	16	16	16	16	16	16	23	23	23	23	23	23
8	N. Lauda	8	8	11	27	27	27	11	23	23	2	11	11	23	23	16	16	16	23	23	23	23	23	23	23	23	23	23	23	23	19	19	19	19	19	19
12	N. Mansell	12	12	12	12	12	23	23	16	2	23	23	23	16	16	19	19	19	19	19	19	19	19	19	19	19	19	19	19	19	17	17	17	17	17	17
22	R. Patrese	22	22	27	23	23	12	16	2	16	16	16	16	19	19	1	22	22	22	22	22	22	22	22	22	17	17	17	22	22	22	22	22
23	E. Cheever	23	27	23	16	16	16	6	6	12	5	12	12	12	11	18	22	24	24	24	24	17	17	17	17	17	22	22	22	22	24	24	24	**24**	**24**
6	K. Rosberg	6	23	16	6	6	6	12	12	5	12	19	19	19	18	22	24	17	17	17	17	24	24	24	24	24	24	24	24	**30**	30	30	30	30	30
27	M. Alboreto	27	6	22	26	28	5	5	5	19	19	18	18	22	24	17	17	17	18	18	18	18	18	18	18	**30**	30	30	30	30	21	31	31	31	31
16	D. Warwick	16	16	6	28	26	26	26	19	18	18	22	22	24	17	18	18	18	18	**30**	30	30	30	30	30	21	31	21	21	21	21	21
26	A. De Cesaris	26	26	26	5	5	19	19	18	22	22	24	24	17	**30**	31	10	10	10	21	21	21	21	21	21	31	18	18	18	18	18	18
28	R. Arnoux	28	28	28	22	22	22	18	22	24	24	17	17	**30**	31	10	21	21	31	31	31	31	31	31	31	18						
5	J. Laffite	5	5	5	18	19	18	22	24	17	17	**30**	30	31	10	10	21	31	31	10												
18	T. Boutsen	18	18	18	19	18	24	24	17	31	30	5	31	31	10	21	21															
19	S. Johansson	19	19	24	24	24	25	25	31	30	31	31	10	10	21	11																
25	F. Hesnault	25	25	19	25	25	31	17	30	10	21	21	21	21																		
24	P. Ghinzani	24	24	25	31	31	30	31	10	21	10	10																				
31	G. Berger	31	31	31	30	30	17	30	21																							
30	J. Gartner	30	30	30	9	9	9	10	26																							
9	P. Alliot	9	9	9	21	17	10	21																								
21	H. Rothengatter	21	21	21	17	21	21																									
10	J. Palmer	10	10	10	10	10																										
17	M. Surer	17	17	17																												

38	39	40	41	42	43	44	45	46	47	48	49	50	51
15	15	15	15	15	8	8	8	8	8	8	8	8	8
2	2	8	8	8	15	15	27	27	27	27	27	27	27
8	8	2	2	2	2	27	22	22	22	22	22	22	
27	27	27	27	27	27	23	19	19	24	24	19		
23	23	23	23	19	19	19	22	24	19	19	30		
19	19	19	19	23	23	17	24	30	30	30	31		
17	17	17	17	17	17	22	30	31	31	31			
22	22	22	22	22	22	24	31	21	21	21			
24	24	24	24	24	24	30	21						
30	30	30	30	30	30	31	18						
31	31	31	31	31	31	21							
21	21	21	21	21	21	18							
18	18	18	18	18	18								

Fastest laps

Driver	Time	Lap
Niki Lauda	1m 31·912s	42
Teo Fabi	1m 32·418s	22
Patrick Tambay	1m 32·433s	39
Michele Alboreto	1m 33·159s	43
Thierry Boutsen	1m 33·280s	36
Derek Warwick	1m 33·359s	27
Eddie Cheever	1m 33·666s	30
Stefan Johansson	1m 33·867s	23
Nelson Piquet	1m 34·076s	7
Marc Surer	1m 34·657s	26
Nigel Mansell	1m 34·907s	13
Keke Rosberg	1m 35·245s	4
Jacques Laffite	1m 35·268s	8
René Arnoux	1m 35·453s	5
Riccardo Patrese	1m 35·574s	27
Alain Prost	1m 35·604s	3
Elio de Angelis	1m 35·900s	13
Piercarlo Ghinzani	1m 36·036s	26
Andrea de Cesaris	1m 36·893s	7
Jo Gartner	1m 37·278s	22
François Hesnault	1m 37·300s	4
Gerhard Berger	1m 37·748s	5
Huub Rothengatter	1m 38·351s	21
Philippe Alliot	1m 38·647s	5
Jonathan Palmer	1m 38·967s	15

Points

WORLD CHAMPIONSHIP OF DRIVERS

1	Niki Lauda	63 pts
2	Alain Prost	52·5
3	Elio de Angelis	29·5
4	René Arnoux	24·5
5	Nelson Piquet	24
6	Derek Warwick	23
7	Michele Alboreto	21
8	Keke Rosberg	20
9	Nigel Mansell	13
10	Patrick Tambay	10
11=	Ayrton Senna	8
11=	Teo Fabi	8
13=	Riccardo Patrese	7
14	Jacques Laffite	4
15=	Eddie Cheever	3
15=	Thierry Boutsen	3
15=	Stefan Johansson	3
18=	Andrea de Cesaris	2
18=	Piercarlo Ghinzani	2
20=	Marc Surer	1
*	Martin Brundle	8
*	Stefan Bellof	5

CONSTRUCTORS' CUP

1	McLaren	115·5 pts
2	Ferrari	45·5
3	Lotus	42·5
4	Renault	33
5	Brabham	32
6	Williams	24
7	Toleman	11
8	Alfa Romeo	10
9	Arrows	4
10	Osella	2
11	Ligier	2
*	Tyrrell	13

* Points removed by FISA Executive Committee

Grosser Preis von Europa

Niki Lauda arrived at the new Nürburgring knowing that victory in the European Grand Prix would give him the World Championship for the third time – regardless of the result achieved by Alain Prost in the final round at Estoril. Prost, for his part, had to win in Germany in order to keep his title hopes alive.

Those were the final parameters of a championship which had been the property of Marlboro McLaren since the series began in Brazil and, as ever, the team management let fate rather than team orders decide the outcome. It was almost a foregone conclusion that *one* of their cars would win the race . . .

On October 7, Prost continued the winning process by taking a victory which had been pre-ordained in part by the weather and a run of bad luck for Lauda during practice. Lauda finished fourth in the race but it was Prost's dominant performance at the front which ensured that the championship would be decided in Portugal.

He led from start to finish, having survived an accident during the morning warm-up and been beaten only by the Parmalat Brabham-BMW of Nelson Piquet during practice. The World Champion, playing out the last few weeks of his reign, was troubled by a baulky gearbox and fell behind the Renault-Elf of Patrick Tambay, the Frenchman turning on another fine drive only to be robbed by an engine misfire.

Piquet should have finished second but a tense struggle with Michele Alboreto, which saw both drivers set an identical lap record – on the same lap, resulted in the Brabham and Ferrari running out of fuel on the last lap, Michele passing Nelson before the final corner, only to have the Ferrari falter and almost lose the place as Piquet made a last desperate surge towards the line.

Had the race been half a mile longer, Lauda might have finished second and earned the six points which would have more or less assured him of the title. Indeed, had he not spun while trying to lap a backmarker, Lauda would have overtaken the Brabham and Ferrari as they struggled towards the line but the misjudgement on Lauda's part merely heightened Prost's majestic drive at the front.

By making a clean start, Prost had steered clear of a shunt involving five cars at the first corner. No one was hurt but the incident, at the safest circuit in the world, underlined the fact that motor racing can never be hazard-free. In the same way, the performance of the McLaren drivers illustrated the part fate has to play in the winning of any championship. At the Nürburgring, it was Prost's turn to come good following his early retirement at Monza.

ENTRY AND PRACTICE

As might have been expected, the Germans had polished the new Nürburgring to perfection. The circuit may have lacked character and challenge but it was well prepared and lacked nothing when it came to safety and facilities. And, at precisely 10 a.m. on Friday morning, practice began.

At 10.05, Alain Prost spun. Caught out by a damp track, he had applied the power too soon at the first corner but it was to be one of the few things to go wrong for the Frenchman during practice although the atmosphere did become rather tense in the McLaren garage on Friday afternoon.

From the word go, Prost had experienced problems with engine pick-up at the lower end of the rev band. The team tried four times to make suitable adjustments and a change of turbo and fuel pump at lunch-time encroached on the official session. That should not have been a problem but Prost's anxious glances at the threatening sky told of impending rain. Work was completed at 1.20 p.m. – just as the first spots sprinkled onto the track. And Nelson Piquet had already been round to set what looked like being a safe overnight pole.

The Brabham team had been well prepared. Apart from having a new chassis, Piquet was also running revised profiles to the rear wing and the Brazilian was first out of the pits, recording his time on his second set of qualifiers. By the time Prost took to the track, the surface was greasy and he could only return to the pits in the hope that the shower would soon pass.

For 20 minutes or so, the circuit was quiet but it

soon became clear that the final 15 minutes of practice would be reasonably dry. And, with that, the place became alive as almost the entire field emptied onto the track, desperate to produce a time in case the fickle Eifel weather dumped more rain during final practice on Saturday. Piquet, having had the circuit more or less to himself, looked secure.

Prost joined the scramble and was fortunate enough to find some space in which to cut a lap good enough for second place. His problems, such as they were, were insignificant when compared to those being experienced in the other half of the McLaren garage.

Lauda's day had started badly. His first lap (in the spare car) had been halted by a problem with a revised wiring loom and he immediately switched to his race chassis – only to find that a leaking gearbox seal was allowing oil to seep onto the clutch. The sum total of his morning's work was four laps and he reluctantly began practice with the spare chassis while the gearbox repairs were carried out.

The plan was to use one set of qualifiers and then fit the second set to the race car when it was ready. With the advent of rain, Lauda changed his mind and asked for his second set immediately, completely wasting them on a damp track. It turned out to be a panic measure since he was to set his fastest time in the final dry period, a combination of the best of both sets of qualifiers being worth a mere 15th place. Lauda was not at all happy and his hopes of improving on Saturday were to be dashed by constant rain in the last session. Friday's

practice, therefore, would determine the grid. Nelson Piquet had just earned his eighth pole position of the season.

For a long time, Patrick Tambay had held second fastest time, the Frenchman sticking to the older '02' chassis in preference to '09'. Both cars were fitted with the 'standard' fuel injection rather than the electronic system entrusted to Warwick but Tambay spent some time experimenting with carbon fibre brakes. This accounted for a spin in the wet on Saturday morning, Patrick failing to warm the brakes sufficiently and paying for his mistake by damaging the right-rear corner of the car against the barrier. Prost's late run on Friday put Tambay into third place on the grid.

Warwick was seventh, and the fact that he set the time in the spare chassis gave some indication of the trouble experienced with the electronic injection on his race car. Renault had tested the system, a mixture of Weber/Marelli injectors in conjunction with Renault electronic control, at Ricard and found it satisfactory but a continual loss of boost hampered progress on Friday morning. This was traced later to a leaking intercooler but not before Warwick had been assigned the spare car which presented problems with third gear. Warwick compounded that by spinning while trying to move out of Tambay's way and the resulting flat-spot (on his second set of qualifiers) made life very uncomfortable as he went on to set what would be his best time.

Keke Rosberg recorded his fastest lap as he crossed the line with a Honda engine which had blown up a few seconds before. That was right at

Ayrton Senna's Toleman-Hart: one of five cars involved in separate incidents at the first corner. Eddie Cheever revived the rotating visor favoured by Graham Hill, among others, during wet practice sessions. The Alfa Romeo driver was quick, as ever, in the miserable conditions on Saturday afternoon but his race would end in yet another retirement.

the end of a practice session which had seen Keke put up his usual spirited performance with a car which switched abruptly from understeer to oversteer as the narrow rev band of the Honda V6 came into play. Jacques Laffite had a new chassis at his disposal but low boost pressure during the brief period when the track was dry meant 14th place, just in front of Lauda.

The Ferraris of Alboreto and Arnoux were fifth and sixth, the red cars running in the latest 'M2' McLaren-type configuration seen, but not raced, at Monza. Apart from having to cope with excessive understeer, both drivers were happy with the progress which had been made, Alboreto saying that the cars were more progressive, particularly in the wet when he set seventh fastest time while running full tanks on Saturday afternoon. Once again, Mauro Forghieri was conspicuous by his absence, the engineer remaining at the factory to work on the proposed four-cylinder engines.

As had been the case at the beginning of the season, Lotus dominated early testing when teams visited the new Nürburgring for the first time. However, Elio de Angelis's luck was rock bottom – rather like his grid position. On his first lap on Friday afternoon (in the T-car), the turbo failed. Switching to his race chassis, the same thing happened and Elio sat out the wet part of the session while a replacement turbo was fitted to the spare. Jumping into that for the dry laps at the end of practice, de Angelis could scarcely believe it when a turbo failed yet again, the Italian crossing the line to set 23rd fastest time with the rear of the Lotus on fire.

It was left to Nigel Mansell, eighth fastest, to carry the immediate hopes of the JPS team, the Englishman having nipped out at the start of practice to set his time on his first set of qualifiers. Attempts at improving later on were spoiled when Mansell spun in the damp conditions.

Riccardo Patrese took a place on row five with the first of the Benetton Alfa Romeos, Eddie Cheever finishing practice in 13th place. The spare 184T had been fitted with a special qualifying engine, the idea being to give it to Patrese on Friday while Cheever would take his turn on Saturday. Rain, of course, denied Cheever his opportunity to make the most of the additional power but Patrese was to be out of luck too, a turbo failure before he could put in a quick lap on Friday forcing the Italian to use his race car during the final crowded minutes.

A change of engine on Friday meant Teo Fabi missed the dry start to the timed session and, when he did get going, fluctuating boost pressure meant 10th place with a time over three seconds slower than his Brabham team-mate. Thierry Boutsen took 11th place in the closing minutes of practice while, on Saturday morning, he spun and tangled with the Ligier of Hesnault. Marc Surer, five places behind Boutsen, set his time at the beginning of the Friday session and the Barclay Arrows driver was disappointed at not having made the most of the track when it was at its best.

Although the legal proceedings between Toleman and Senna were continuing apace, the Brazilian driver was reinstated after being suspended at Monza. Brian Hart had brought along an engine fitted with a larger Holset turbo and Senna confessed to being very impressed with the top-end power. However, any chance of worthwhile tests being carried out on Friday morning were halted by a broken wire in the electronic control box. In the afternoon, Senna used his race car to take 12th place while Stefan Johansson was forced to use the spare after a distributor rotor arm had broken on his own car. However, the Swede was destined to complete just one timed lap, the engine on the T-car refusing to fire and, when it did, it popped and banged to such an extent that Johansson completed just one lap and ended the day at the bottom of the time sheet. Fortunately for Stefan, an entry of 26 cars meant there was no danger of him failing to qualify.

After unsatisfactory tests prior to the Italian Grand Prix, Ligier finally gave their revised car – the JS23B – an official airing. Featuring pushrod suspension (which required ungainly bodywork to cover the upper pick-up points at the front) and revised intercoolers, the Loto and Antar sponsored car offered little improvement although Andrea de Cesaris stuck with it throughout most of practice and took 17th place, only three-tenths quicker than Hesnault.

The usual state of disarray within ATS reached new heights this weekend. Gunter Schmid had dismissed Manfred Winkelhock earlier in the week and then Gerhard Berger smashed a D7 against the guardrail on Friday morning. Then, Winkelhock arrived in the paddock with a court injunction which entitled him to confiscate the stock of ATS Formula 1 cars in lieu of money owed to the German driver. In the event, this was not necessary since a representative of the team was able to prove that DM251,000 had already been deposited at the High Court in Mannheim. Practice continued. Berger, now in the spare chassis, qualified in 18th place after a further two spins. In all, an eventful few days for ATS . . .

Piercarlo Ghinzani's Osella showed rear end modifications which followed the familiar McLaren trend, the Italian qualifying in 20th place while Jo Gartner took 22nd spot after experiencing problems with fourth gear. The Kelemata Osellas were split by Jonathan Palmer's Skoal Bandit RAM-Hart, the English driver losing out on Friday by running his harder set of Pirelli qualifiers when the track was dry and using his softer tyres just as the rain began to fall. Philippe Alliot broke a turbo on Friday morning and split his qualifying runs before and after the rain in the afternoon. His last lap was worth 25th place behind the Spirit-Hart of Mauro Baldi. Financial considerations saw the Italian return to the team for the first time since Monaco and plans to run a second car for Rothengatter came to nothing. Modifications to the second chassis included revised aerodynamics and a wheelbase lengthened by four inches, these having been tested in England by Baldi during the break after Monza.

Parked alongside the Spirit would be de Angelis while just behind them lurked Johansson. With Lauda few rows ahead of those two chargers, a busy first lap was in store. And there was the chance that it might rain . . .

RACE

Contrary to expectations, it neither rained nor snowed on race morning. When the calendar was announced earlier in the year, there had been gloomy predictions for the Nürburgring in October but, on Sunday morning, the sun shone. Gone, then, was the wild card which could upset form although Alain Prost did his best to add a degree of uncertainty to what looked like another victory for the Frenchman.

Arriving at the Romer Curve a shade too fast, Prost slid onto a wet kerb and was suddenly spinning across the grass. He managed to avoid the safety barrier but the McLaren then collected a course car which was parked just beyond the end of the armco. The Volkswagen Passat came off badly as the left-rear corner of Prost's car slammed into it. Prost hopped out and immediate inspection revealed a broken wheel. The rest of the McLaren

Aiming for yet another pole – his eighth of the season – Nelson Piquet prepares to practise.

looked to be intact. But was it? The suspension – perhaps, even, the tub – could have been weakened by the impact. It was a psychological blow for Prost as Lauda sped by to set the fastest time in the warm-up.

With the spare car on wet settings (for Lauda), Prost's mechanics set to work and not only replaced what components they could but changed the engine as well since the TAG-Porsche, freshly installed the night before, had been losing water.

Elsewhere, Derek Warwick prepared to use the T-car after further problems with the electronic injection while Tambay was in better heart, having just set second fastest time. Lauda continued to be the focus of heavy attention, the Austrian being harassed to such an extent that he was unable to visit a toilet in the pit lane without a battery of photographers waiting by the door. Not even the ruse of using the 'Ladies' loo would shake off his pursuers. Lauda, of course, was scarcely bothered. He had other things on his mind. Like the start, for instance . . .

The betting had been that Prost would spend the first few laps dealing with Piquet while Lauda charged through from the eighth row but, as the field rushed towards the first corner, it was Tambay who came forward to challenge the McLaren. Piquet had made a comparatively slow start from pole and Prost just managed to stop the Renault from running round the outside to take the lead. Then, a few seconds later, all hell broke loose.

Five cars were involved in three separate incidents, the first being sparked off when Senna rode over the back of Rosberg's car, leaving bits of Michelin on the side of the Williams cockpit. Senna said he had been squeezed out; others suggested he had left his braking too late while one observer reckoned he had been nudged. At the same time, Berger completed a rather wild weekend by getting sideways and collecting Surer, Fabi and Ghinzani making contact as a result. Everyone, with the exception of Fabi, abandoned their cars, the Brabham driver eventually receiving a tow as the leaders came into sight once more.

Prost had pulled out a second on Tambay. Then followed Piquet, Warwick, Alboreto, Arnoux, Patrese, Cheever and . . . Lauda. Somehow, Niki had managed to avoid the chaos – as had de Angelis (11th behind Boutsen) and Johansson (14th behind Hesnault and de Cesaris). Lauda's plan, of course, was to stop Prost from cutting the points deficit as much as possible and, assuming the Frenchman was going to win, Lauda needed to score as many points as he could.

From ninth place at the end of lap one, he moved ahead of the Alfa Romeos on successive laps and took sixth place from Arnoux on lap five. One vital point secure.

His progress from that point on was not so rapid since he came across a furious battle for fourth place between Warwick and Alboreto. The three cars circulated together for ten laps, Alboreto

trying to take Warwick on the outside as they completed lap 17. The Renault driver, not a man to be trifled with, held his ground, forcing Alboreto to back off slightly as they left the Castrol 'S' after the pits. Almost immediately, Lauda was on the attack, trying to force his way alongside the Ferrari under braking for the next left-hander. Alboreto would have none of it.

Prost, meanwhile, had continued to pull away from Tambay, setting the fastest lap of the race so far on lap four and opening a gap of 14 seconds within 20 laps. Piquet, having kept the Renault in sight, began to drop back although he was safely ahead of the continuing struggle for fourth place. Then, on lap 22, an incident which brought an increasingly processional race to life.

Warwick, Alboreto and Lauda were working their way through the backmarkers when they came across a battle for 17th place between Gartner and Baldi. The Spirit had let Warwick through at the Veedol chicane and left the door open on the approach to the last corner. Alboreto went for the inside line and, Lauda, believing there was enough room for him as well, tried to follow.

Suddenly the McLaren twitched as the rear brakes locked and sent Lauda into a spin. The Austrian emerged from the tyre smoke, having completed a 360-degree gyration on the grass – fortunately, with his engine still running. Selecting a gear, he was on his way, collecting his thoughts while defending his sixth place from an attentive Elio de Angelis.

The Lotus driver had made excellent progress from the penultimate row of the grid and he was keen to make the most of Lauda's misfortune. The spin had flat-spotted Niki's tyres but his composure was such that he actually began to pull away from the Lotus, setting new lap records as he did so! He would report later that the initial effect of the spin was not serious but, as the race wore on so, too, did the rubber on his Michelins, exacerbating the flat-spots and increasing the vibrations. In the meantime, he could merely hope for problems to strike those in front of him.

A threat from behind was removed on lap 26 when de Angelis suffered a turbo failure not long after Johansson had stopped with an overheating problem which had begun to trouble the Swede after about five laps. A faulty water pump was later discovered to have been the culprit but, for the time being, that was the end of the European Grand Prix for Toleman. The weekend was soon over for Williams as well, Laffite retiring on lap 27 with engine trouble.

The lap chart remained unchanged except for the progress of Nigel Mansell. The Lotus driver had made a slow start and was further delayed by the mêlée at the first corner. At the end of the first lap he was 20th but soon began to climb through the field, working his way past the Alfas and into eighth place on lap 33. Arnoux, his engine misfiring slightly, was next to fall and Mansell moved into the top six thanks to a problem for Patrick Tambay.

The Renault had been running superbly, unable to keep pace with Prost but comfortably holding second place as Piquet struggled with a stiff gearchange. Then, on lap 40, the gap between the two began to shrink and, three laps later, the Brabham was second. An engine misfire on left-handers meant Tambay was powerless to stop Warwick, Alboreto and Lauda from steaming by and, on lap 44, his race was over, the Frenchman stopping at the pits for good. Lauda was fifth; two vital championship points.

Further back, the field had been decimated by a rash of mechanical failures, Cheever stuttering to a halt with no fuel pressure and the entire RAM team stopping within minutes with turbo failures.

Mansell was the next to go, his race ending abruptly when the Renault V6 exploded as he powered away from the Veedol chicane in fourth gear. The Lotus spun to a halt at the following right-hander and Mansell was quickly out of the cockpit since there was a fair amount of smoke billowing from around the engine bay. It took some time for a marshal to approach with a fire extinguisher and Mansell had to show the man where to direct it now that flames were erupting around the hot turbo.

British hopes were finally dashed when Warwick's engine began to sound rough and Alboreto and Lauda passed the Renault with ease. An overheating engine would eventually lead to a valve failure and, like his team-mate, Warwick would have nothing to show for an excellent drive made difficult by the mediocre handling of the T-car. Fabi, certain to be disqualified because of assistance received at the first corner, saved the officials any embarrassment by retiring the Brabham with gearbox failure and a steady run from Gartner would end seven laps from the finish, the Osella out of fuel even though Jo had cut his revs and was motoring gently at the back of the field.

Prost was doing much the same at the front but the announcement of fastest lap to both Piquet and Alboreto (with an identical time on the same lap!) gave some indication of Piquet's efforts (with a baulky gearchange) to save second place from the advances of a Ferrari with a blistered left-rear tyre. As Prost crossed the line to wave both arms with a mixture of jubilation and relief, it seemed certain that the six points would go to Piquet.

However, the Brabham began to stutter on the climb towards the last corner and Alboreto surged past. Then, swinging onto the home straight, the Ferrari coughed, jerked forward and then cut out completely. Piquet, weaving the Brabham from side to side in a bid to pick up the last dregs of fuel, made a sudden surge forward but then he too was powerless, the BT53 coasting across the line a few feet behind the Ferrari.

Arnoux and Patrese, in fifth and sixth places respectively, just made it to the finish while de Cesaris, short of brakes, took seventh place and Baldi claimed eighth after Boutsen had stopped when the electrics failed on his last lap. The Arrows driver, having made a pit stop for tyres on lap 14, had been without a clutch for most of the race although he was eventually classified ninth ahead of Hesnault.

And Lauda was fourth; three vital points. He would have liked more, of course, since the result meant a fight to the finish at Estoril. Lauda had driven in his usual conservative manner towards the end although, in retrospect, that might have been a mistake. Had he pressed on instead of consolidating fourth place, he would have been close enough to take advantage of Alboreto and Piquet as they free-wheeled across the line.

Lauda, of course, had taken it easy because of the flat-spots on his tyres. They had been caused by a spin. He had spun because he was working his way from a starting position dictated largely by mechanical problems and the weather. Prost on the other hand, said he had never know his car feel better in a race. Fate had played its part – as the McLaren International management said it would. **MH**

Alain Prost received an unexpected bonus two days after the European Grand Prix. A decision by FISA to adjust the championship scores in the light of the Tyrrell disqualification meant that Prost gained an extra point and closed the gap on Lauda to just 3½ points.

Initially, the points earned by Tyrrell were simply removed from the table without moving the remaining drivers into the places vacated by Brundle and Bellof. It took FISA a few weeks to study the effect of a such a wholesale change and it can hardly be a coincidence that the prospective French World Champion should benefit whereas Lauda, conveniently, did not.

Prost finished fifth in Detroit but now moved into fourth place to score three points rather than two as the result of Brundle's disqualification from second place. Other drivers to benefit were de Angelis (an extra ½ point at Monac o and two points at Detroit), Arnoux (½ point at Monaco), Alboreto (½ at Rio), Senna (1 point at Zolder), Fabi (1 point at Detroit) Laffite (1 point at Detroit), Boutsen (1 point at Rio and Imola) and de Cesaris (1 point at Imola).

In the Constructors' Championship, Lotus came off best with 2½ points, although Ferrari, their main rival for second place on the table, gained 1 point.

A sensible drive by Michele Alboreto gave Ferrari second place. The Italian struggling across the line to beat Piquet as they ran out of fuel. In the background the Schloss Nürburg and the start of the North Curve.

Perhaps their biggest mistake was to construct the new Nürburgring alongside the old. Comparisons were inevitable and, with the 14.2-mile *Nordschleife* peeling off into the Hatzenbach forest just behind the new paddock, the latest version could not avoid being branded bland and boring.

Of course, it was a model of safety and no one in their right mind would criticise the circuit for that. It was built to the highest standards; excellent internal roads for rescue vehicles, a smooth track surface, perfect grading and drainage, copious spectator tribunes, spacious pits and paddock. It was easy to see where the £18m (the majority provided by the Federal Government) had been spent. But the feeling was that the money had been wasted.

Vast sums, for instance, had been poured into excavations and earth moving when, all along, the planners had been working in a natural terrain which other circuit builders had spent small fortunes trying to recreate. The result was a clinical collection of constant radius corners the like of which could be found at any modern motodrome. This, most certainly, was not the Nürburgring.

It was textbook stuff, dreamed up with the aid of a computer and executed with all the thoroughness one had come to expect from the Germans. But it was not a *challenge*. It did not set the adrenalin flowing in the way that Spa-Francorchamps thrilled drivers and spectators alike. Indeed, it seemed a pity that the

fine blend of old and new just across the Belgian border had not served as an example of how to keep pace with modern technology without losing sight of what motor racing is all about.

Construction of the new Nürburgring began in November 1981 and, at first, it seemed the abandoned South circuit could be incorporated. However, we should have known better when they said spectators could see most of the new circuit from any given point.

Indeed they can. But, as for feeling part of the action, they may as well stay at home. In fact, many did on October 7.

To make matters worse, the racing was boring. This was due in part to the absence of a vital ingredient on any circuit which hopes to promote close racing: a long straight fed by a fast curve and ending with a second gear corner. You can have all the run-off area you like. You also have *overtaking*.

Then, the final irony. It is all very well building a 'safe' circuit but you may as well abandon it if it is not peopled by efficient marshals. When Nigel Mansell spun off, his Lotus smouldered for quite some time before a marshal arrived with an extinguisher. Even then, Mansell had to inject some urgency into the situation and direct operations.

In case you have forgotten, one of the reasons Grand Prix racing chose not to return to the old Nürburgring after 1976 was the length of time it took marshals to reach and deal with a driver in trouble . . .

Entries and practice times

No.	Driver	Nat	Car	Tyre	Engine	Entrant	Practice 1	Practice 2
1	Nelson Piquet	BR	Parmalat BRABHAM BT53	M	BMW M12/13	MRD International	**1m 18·871s**	1m 43·988s
2	Teo Fabi	I	Parmalat BRABHAM BT53	M	BMW M12/13	MRD International	**1m 22·206s**	1m 45·075s
5	Jacques Laffite	F	WILLIAMS FW09B	G	Honda RA 163–E	Williams Grand Prix Engineering	**1m 22·613s**	–
6	Keke Rosberg	SF	WILLIAMS FW09B	G	Honda RA 163–E	Williams Grand Prix Engineering	**1m 20·625s**	1m 43·619s
7	Alain Prost	F	Marlboro McLAREN MP4/2	M	TAG P01 (TTE P01)	Marlboro McLaren International	**1m 19·175s**	1m 40·693s
8	Niki Lauda	A	Marlboro McLAREN MP4/2	M	TAG P01 (TTE P01)	Marlboro McLaren International	**1m 22·643s**	1m 40·392s
9	Philippe Alliot	F	RAM 02	P	Hart 415T	Skoal Bandit Formula 1 Team	**1m 30·259s**	1m 53·587s
10	Jonathan Palmer	GB	RAM 02	P	Hart 415T	Skoal Bandit Formula 1 Team	**1m 25·050s**	1m 51·449s
11	Elio de Angelis	I	John Player Special LOTUS 95T	G	Renault EF4	John Player Team Lotus	**1m 26·161s**	1m 39·762s
12	Nigel Mansell	GB	John Player Special LOTUS 95T	G	Renault EF4	John Player Team Lotus	**1m 21·710s**	1m 40·705s
15	Patrick Tambay	F	Elf RENAULT RE50	M	Renault EF4	Equipe Renault Elf	**1m 19·499s**	–
16	Derek Warwick	GB	Elf RENAULT RE50	M	Renault EF4	Equipe Renault Elf	**1m 21·571s**	1m 44·289s
17	Marc Surer	CH	ARROWS A7	G	BMW M12/13	Barclay Nordica Arrows BMW	**1m 22·708s**	1m 45·319s
18	Thierry Boutsen	B	ARROWS A7	G	BMW M12/13	Barclay Nordica Arrows BMW	**1m 22·248s**	1m 44·642s
19	Ayrton Senna	BR	TOLEMAN TG184	M	Hart 415T	Toleman Group Motorsport	**1m 22·439s**	1m 43·747s
20	Stefan Johansson	S	TOLEMAN TG184	M	Hart 415T	Toleman Group Motorsport	**1m 41·178s**	1m 43·881s
21	Mauro Baldi	I	SPIRIT 101	P	Hart 415T	Spirit Racing	**1m 28·137s**	1m 45·814s
22	Riccardo Patrese	I	Benetton ALFA ROMEO 184T	G	Alfa Romeo 183T	Benetton Team Alfa Romeo	**1m 21·937s**	1m 41·724s
23	Eddie Cheever	USA	Benetton ALFA ROMEO 184T	G	Alfa Romeo 183T	Benetton Team Alfa Romeo	**1m 22·525s**	1m 41·285s
24	Piercarlo Ghinzani	I	Kelemata OSELLA FA1F	P	Alfa Romeo 183T	Osella Squadra Corse	**1m 24·699s**	1m 42·746s
25	François Hesnault	F	LIGIER Loto JS23	M	Renault EF4	Ligier Loto	**1m 23·322s**	1m 44·420s
26	Andrea de Cesaris	I	LIGIER Loto JS23	M	Renault EF4	Ligier Loto	**1m 23·034s**	1m 42·362s
27	Michele Alboreto	I	Fiat FERRARI 126C4	G	Ferrari 126C	Scuderia Ferrari SpA	**1m 20·910s**	1m 41·878s
28	René Arnoux	F	Fiat FERRARI 126C4	G	Ferrari 126C	Scuderia Ferrari SpA	**1m 21·180s**	1m 42·457s
30	Jo Gartner	A	Kelemata OSELLA FA1F	P	Alfa Romeo 183T	Osella Squadra Corse	**1m 26·156s**	1m 48·214s
31	Gerhard Berger	A	ATS D7	P	BMW M12/13	Team ATS	**1m 23·116s**	1m 44·899s

		Fri pm	Sat pm
		Cold, dry	Cold, wet

Friday morning and Saturday morning practice sessions not officially recorded.

G – Goodyear, M – Michelin, P – Pirelli.

Starting grid

	1 PIQUET (1m 18·871s) Brabham
7 PROST (1m 19·175s) McLaren	
	15 TAMBAY (1m 19·499s) Renault
6 ROSBERG (1m 20·652s) Williams	
	27 ALBORETO (1m 20·910s) Ferrari
28 ARNOUX (1m 21·180s) Ferrari	
	16 WARWICK (1m 21·571s) Renault
12 MANSELL (1m 21·710s) Lotus	
	22 PATRESE (1m 21·937s) Alfa Romeo
2 FABI (1m 22·206s) Brabham	
	18 BOUTSEN (1m 22·248s) Arrows
19 SENNA (1m 22·439s) Toleman	
	23 CHEEVER (1m 22·525s) Alfa Romeo
5 LAFFITE (1m 22·613s) Williams	
	8 LAUDA (1m 22·643s) McLaren
17 SURER (1m 22·708s) Arrows	
	26 DE CESARIS (1m 23·034s) Ligier
31 BERGER (1m 23·116s) ATS	
	25 HESNAULT (1m 23·322s) Ligier
24 GHINZANI (1m 24·699s) Osella	
	10 PALMER (1m 25·050s) RAM
30 GARTNER (1m 26·156s) Osella	
	11 DE ANGELIS (1m 26·161s) Lotus
21 BALDI (1m 28·137s) Spirit	
	9 ALLIOT (1m 30·259s) RAM
20 JOHANSSON (1m 41·178s) Toleman	

Results and retirements

Place	Driver	Car	Laps	Time and Speed (mph/km/h)/Retirement	
1	Alain Prost	McLaren-TAG t/c V6	67	1h 35m 13·284s	119·148/191·751
2	Michele Alboreto	Ferrari t/c V6	67	1h 35m 37·195s	118·682/191·0
3	Nelson Piquet	Brabham-BMW t/c 4	67	1h 35m 38·206s	118·619/190·9
4	Niki Lauda	McLaren-TAG t/c V6	67	1h 35m 56·370s	118·247/190·3
5	René Arnoux	Ferrari t/c V6	67	1h 36m 14·714s	117·874/189·7
6	Riccardo Patrese	Alfa Romeo t/c V8	66		
7	Andrea de Cesaris	Ligier-Renault t/c V6	65		
8	Mauro Baldi	Spirit-Hart t/c 4	65		
9	Thierry Boutsen	Arrows-BMW t/c 4	64	Electrics/ignition	
10	François Hesnault	Ligier-Renault t/c V6	64		
11	Derek Warwick	Renault t/c V6	61	Overheating/broken valve	
	Jo Gartner	Osella-Alfa Romeo t/c V8	60	Fuel feed	
	Teo Fabi	Brabham-BMW t/c 4	57	Gearbox	
	Nigel Mansell	Lotus-Renault t/c V6	51	Engine	
	Patrick Tambay	Renault t/c V6	47	Fuel feed	
	Eddie Cheever	Alfa Romeo t/c V8	37	Fuel pump	
	Philippe Alliot	RAM-Hart t/c 4	37	Turbo	
	Jonathan Palmer	RAM-Hart t/c 4	35	Turbo	
	Jacques Laffite	Williams-Honda t/c V6	27	Engine	
	Elio de Angelis	Lotus-Renault t/c V6	25	Turbo	
	Stefan Johansson	Toleman-Hart t/c 4	17	Overheating	
	Keke Rosberg	Williams-Honda t/c V6	0	Accident	
	Gerhard Berger	ATS-BMW t/c 4	0	Accident	
	Marc Surer	Arrows-BMW t/c 4	0	Accident	
	Piercarlo Ghinzani	Osella-Alfa Romeo t/c 4	0	Accident	
	Ayrton Senna	Toleman-Hart t/c 4	0	Accident	

Fastest lap: Piquet and Alboreto, on lap 62, 1m 23·146s, 122·196mph/196·656km/h (record).
Previous lap record: Not given.

Past winners

Year	Driver	Nat	Car	Circuit	Distance miles/km	Speed mph/km/h
1983	Nelson Piquet	BR	1·5 Brabham BT52B-BMW t/c	Brands Hatch	198·63/319·67	123·16/198·21
1984	Alain Prost	F	1·5 McLaren MP4/2-TAG t/c	Nürburgring	189·09/304·31	119·15/191·75

Circuit data

Nürburgring, near Koblenz
Circuit length: 2·822 miles/4·542km
Race distance: 67 laps, 189·091 miles/304·314 km
Race weather: Cold, dry

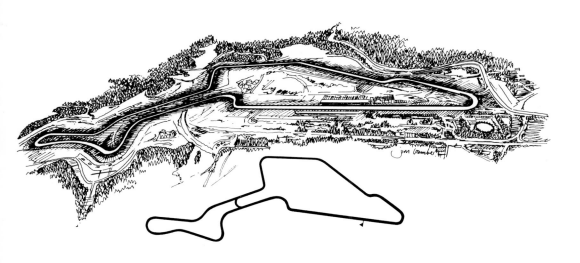

Fastest laps

Driver	Time	Lap
Nelson Piquet	1m 23·146s	62
Michele Alboreto	1m 23·146s	62
Niki Lauda	1m 23·729s	48
Nigel Mansell	1m 23·978s	48
René Arnoux	1m 24·169s	61
Alain Prost	1m 24·182s	30
Derek Warwick	1m 24·211s	46
Patrick Tambay	1m 24·671s	31
Teo Fabi	1m 24·814s	15
Eddie Cheever	1m 25·512s	36
Riccardo Patrese	1m 25·644s	37
Jacques Laffite	1m 25·687s	19
Elio de Angelis	1m 25·836s	22
Thierry Boutsen	1m 25·908s	49
Andrea de Cesaris	1m 26·378s	25
Mauro Baldi	1m 26·680s	65
Stefan Johansson	1m 26·943s	11
Jo Gartner	1m 28·249s	32
François Hesnault	1m 28·276s	49
Jonathan Palmer	1m 30·415s	13
Philippe Alliot	1m 30·480s	19

Points
(Adjusted in accordance with FISA decision on 9 October 1984 to amend results by moving drivers into positions vacated by disqualified Tyrrell drivers.)

WORLD CHAMPIONSHIP OF DRIVERS

1	Niki Lauda	66 pts
2	Alain Prost	62·5
3	Elio de Angelis	32
4	Nelson Piquet	28
5	Michele Alboreto	27·5
6	René Arnoux	27
7	Derek Warwick	23
8	Keke Rosberg	20·5
9	Nigel Mansell	13
10	Patrick Tambay	11
11=	Ayrton Senna	9
11=	Teo Fabi	9
13	Riccardo Patrese	8
14=	Jacques Laffite	5
14=	Thierry Boutsen	5
16=	Eddie Cheever	3
16=	Stefan Johansson	3
16=	Andrea de Cesaris	3
19	Piercarlo Ghinzani	2
20	Marc Surer	1
*	Martin Brundle	8
*	Stefan Bellof	5

CONSTRUCTORS' CUP

1	McLaren	128·5 pts
2	Ferrari	54·5
3	Lotus	45
4	Brabham	37
5	Renault	34
6	Williams	25·5
7=	Toleman	12
7=	Alfa Romeo	11
9	Arrows	6
10	Ligier	3
11	Osella	2
*	Tyrrell	13

* Points removed by FISA Executive Committee

Lap chart

1ST LAP ORDER	1	2	3	4	5	6	7	8	9	10	11	12	13	14	15	16	17	18	19	20	21	22	23	24	25	26	27	28	29	30	31	32	33	34	35	36	37
7 A. Prost	7	7	7	7	7	7	7	7	7	7	7	7	7	7	7	7	7	7	7	7	7	7	7	7	7	7	7	7	7	7	7	7	7	7	7	7	7
15 P. Tambay	15	15	15	15	15	15	15	15	15	15	15	15	15	15	15	15	15	15	15	15	15	15	15	15	15	15	15	15	15	15	15	15	15	15	15	15	15
1 N. Piquet	1	1	1	1	1	1	1	1	1	1	1	1	1	1	1	1	1	1	1	1	1	1	1	1	1	1	1	1	1	1	1	1	1	1	1	1	1
16 D. Warwick	16	16	16	16	16	16	16	16	16	16	16	16	16	16	16	16	16	16	16	16	16	16	16	16	16	16	16	16	16	16	16	16	16	16	16	16	16
27 M. Alboreto	27	27	27	27	27	27	27	27	27	27	27	27	27	27	27	27	27	27	27	27	27	27	27	27	27	27	27	27	27	27	27	27	27	27	27	27	27
28 R. Arnoux	28	28	28	28	8	8	8	8	8	8	8	8	8	8	8	8	8	8	8	8	8	8	8	8	8	8	8	8	8	8	8	8	8	8	8	8	8
22 R. Patrese	22	22	8	8	28	28	28	28	28	28	28	28	28	28	28	11	11	11	11	11	11	11	11	11	11	28	28	28	28	28	28	28	28	28	28	28	28
23 E. Cheever	23	8	22	22	22	22	22	22	22	22	22	22	11	11	11	28	28	28	28	28	28	28	28	28	22	22	22	22	22	22	12	12	12	12	12	12	12
8 N. Lauda	8	23	23	23	23	23	23	23	23	11	11	11	22	22	22	22	22	22	22	22	22	22	22	23	23	23	23	12	12	12	22	22	22	22	22	22	22
18 T. Boutsen	18	11	11	11	11	11	11	11	11	23	23	23	23	23	23	23	23	23	23	23	23	23	23	12	12	12	12	23	23	23	23	23	23	23	23	23	23
11 E. De Angelis	11	18	18	18	18	18	18	18	18	18	18	18	26	26	12	12	12	12	12	12	12	12	12	26	26	26	26	26	26	26	26	26	26	26	26	26	26
25 F. Hesnault	25	26	26	26	26	26	26	26	26	26	26	20	12	26	26	26	26	26	26	26	26	25	5	5	18	18	18	18	18	18	18	18	18				
26 A. De Cesaris	26	20	20	20	20	20	20	20	20	20	20	20	12	20	20	5	5	5	5	5	5	5	25	18	25	25	25	25	25	25	25	25	25				
20 S. Johansson	20	25	25	25	25	25	12	12	12	12	12	12	18	5	5	25	25	25	25	25	25	18	25	21	21	21	21	21	21	21	2	2	2	2			
10 J. Palmer	10	10	10	12	12	12	25	25	25	5	5	5	5	20	20	20					18	18	18	18	18	21	21	30	30	30	30	2	21	21	21	21	
30 J. Gartner	30	30	30	10	5	5	5	5	5	5	5	25	25	25	25	30	30	30	30	30	30	30	30	30	30	30	30	2	2	2	2	30	30	30	30	30	
21 M. Baldi	21	21	12	30	10	10	10	10	10	30	30	30	30	30	30	21	21	18	21	21	21	21	21	21	30	2	2	10	10	10	10	10	10	10	9	9	
9 P. Alliot	9	5	21	5	30	30	30	30	21	21	21	21	21	21	18	18	21	10	2	2	2	2	2	2	10	10	9	9	9	9	9	9	9	9			
5 J. Laffite	5	12	5	21	21	21	21	21	10	10	10	10	10	10	10	10	10	2	10	10	10	10	10	10	9	9											
12 N. Mansell	12	9	9	9	9	9	9	9	9	9	9	9	9	9	9	2	2	9	9	9	9	9	9	9													
2 T. Fabi	2	2	2	2	2	2	2	2	2	2	2	2	2	2	9	9																					

38	39	40	41	42	43	44	45	46	47	48	49	50	51	52	53	54	55	56	57	58	59	60	61	62	63	64	65	66	67
7	7	7	7	7	7	7	7	7	7	7	7	7	7	7	7	7	7	7	7	7	7	7	7	7	7	7	7	7	7
15	15	15	15	15	1	1	1	1	1	1	1	1	1	1	1	1	1	1	1	1	1	1	1	1	1	1	1	1	27
1	1	1	1	1	15	16	16	16	16	16	27	27	27	27	27	27	27	27	27	27	27	27	27	27	27	27	27	27	1
16	16	16	16	16	16	27	27	27	27	27	16	16	16	16	16	16	8	8	8	8	8	8	8	8	8	8	8	8	8
27	27	27	27	27	27	15	8	8	8	8	8	8	8	8	8	8	16	16	16	16	16	16	28	28	28	28	28	28	28
8	8	8	8	8	8	8	15	12	12	12	12	12	12	28	28	28	28	28	28	28	28	28	22	22	22	22	22		
28	12	12	12	12	12	12	12	28	28	28	28	28	22	22	22	22	22	22	22	22	22	22	26	26	26	26			
12	28	28	28	28	28	22	22	22	22	22	22	26	26	26	26	26	26	26	26	26	26	18	18	18	21				
22	22	22	22	22	22	26	26	26	26	18	18	18	18	18	18	18	21	21	21	21									
26	26	26	26	26	26	26	18	18	18	18	18	2	2	2	2	2	21	21	21	21	25	25	25						
18	18	18	18	18	18	18	2	2	2	2	2	21	21	21	21	21	25	25	25	25									
2	2	2	2	2	2	2	15	25	25	25	21	21	25	25	25	25	30	30	30										
25	25	25	25	25	25	25	25	21	21	21	25	25	30	30	30	30	30												
21	21	21	21	21	21	21	21	15	30	30	30	30																	
30	30	30	30	30	30	30	30	30	30	30																			

Grande Premio de Portugal

IN a consummate act of generosity, Alain Prost stepped from the Portuguese Grand Prix winner's rostrum and invited team-mate Niki Lauda to assume the premier position on the podium. Lauda grinned broadly and hugged his colleague, his face wearing a smile of genuine pleasure that the Austrian reserves for increasingly rare public occasions. Watching from the touchlines, one felt sympathy for them both, funnily enough. There was Prost, the man who had now won seven Grand Prix victories in a season, being beaten to the Championship by his team-mate who had won a "mere" five races. Yet somehow, in a strange, indefinable way, one was suddenly aware of how much that third Championship meant to Niki Lauda: it was almost as if he had finally achieved a symbolic goal of self-justification, the bottom line which had finally made his return to the sport worthwhile. It was his great moment, yet one was perhaps sorry for the way in which it had to be compromised by the stark, oh-so-public knowledge that his team-mate was the quicker, more effective driver in the McLaren team.

Unquestionably, the 1984 Portuguese Grand Prix was a great motor race, a fascinating finale to the Championship season which saw battles raging throughout the top ten for much of its 70-lap distance. We saw Nelson Piquet starting from pole position, yet again, only to spin on the opening lap, and effectively, hand the initiative to Prost on a plate. We saw Keke Rosberg hold his bucking bronco of a Williams FW09B in the lead for eight-and-a-bit heart-stopping laps. Ayrton Senna consolidated his brilliant reputation with a magnificent third for Toleman and Stefan Johansson proved he is a worthy successor to the Brazilian as the English team's number one by holding Niki Lauda at bay for many, many laps.

At the end of the afternoon, however, it was game to Prost, but set and match to the second-placed Lauda. The last remaining obstacle to the realisation of Niki's championship aspirations fell away on lap 52 when Nigel Mansell lost a magnificent second place after his Lotus 95T suffered a sudden brake failure. Thus, for the last 18 laps of the race, Prost knew that he had won and lost all at the same time. Lauda's second place salvaged the Championship for him by half a point, justifiably the closest margin in history in view of the two drivers' achievements throughout McLaren's record-breaking 1984 season.

ENTRY AND PRACTICE

There had been speculation as to whether Estoril would be ready to host its first World Championship Formula 1 event, rumours filtering back from Portugal suggesting that updating work at the tight little autodrome, situated up in the hills behind the picturesque fishing village of Cascais, was falling worryingly behind schedule. But with Bernie Ecclestone's FOCA-promoted momentum behind it, somehow everything was *just* ready in time, but although the paddock and garage facilities turned out to be suitably impressive, the overall impression of the place was just a little "scrappy" with several areas in need of tightening up before the Championship circus returns for the third round of the 1985 series. On the whole, though, it was good for Formula 1 to be seen in yet another "new" European country. There were three Portuguese Grands Prix between 1958 and '60, but this was the first time that contemporary Formula 1 cars had raced in Portugal.

The redevelopment work had precluded any sort of official pre-event testing apart from a two-hour blast on the Thursday prior to official qualifying, the bumpy, demanding and challenging autodrome being totally new to many drivers, although several like Cheever, Rosberg and Patrese recalled hectic Formula 2 battles there in their struggle up the ladder to Grand Prix stardom. Most people agreed that Estoril was a good track, a trifle narrow in places, and with a wide variation in run-off areas. In this respect there seemed to be a few strange anomalies: two very slow corners were provided with run-offs the size of Brighton Beach while a couple of dauntingly fast corners had no run-offs at all!

As far as the entry was concerned, Renault decided to give Philippe Streiff a crack behind the wheel of their RE50, the French novice ran as a "team within a team", apart from the two regular contenders, while poor Teo Fabi had to return suddenly to Italy when the sad news of his father's death was communicated to him on Thursday night. This meant that only a single Brabham BT53 practised on Friday while stand-in Manfred Winkelhock battled with the vagaries of the weather and airline timetables to find his way down from Frankfurt to Lisbon. Even though bad weather delayed the first qualifying session quite considerably, Winkelhock none the less arrived in the paddock a few minutes too late to try a BT53 before Saturday morning.

Talking of Brabhams, possibly the most fascinating development in that camp was the first public appearance of a fully-developed onboard television camera on the spare BT53, a neat little device weighing a mere 3kg complete with its power pack and aerial. Mounted in a position that gives an "over the shoulder" view of the cockpit, the first pictures showed its exciting possibilities, but interference with the signal from the bridges on the circuit meant that it was eventually put away for another day. It is three years since development of this unit began and now the television people are tantalisingly close to opening a new dimension in Grand Prix coverage. There will be no secrets for drivers to keep in future . . .

Friday's practice was delayed when a flash flood turned the whole circuit (apart from the tarmac Formula 1 paddock) into something akin to the Brands Hatch car park after an early Spring monsoon! The untimed session was delayed and eventually timed qualifying was scheduled to take place an hour and a half late, keeping up the nerve-wracking pressure on Championship contenders Alain Prost and Niki Lauda, both of whom seemed to be more in control of their emotions than the inevitable gaggle of sensation-seeking photographers and journalists who pestered them both morning, noon and, one understands, night as well!

When the first hour-long qualifying session did get under way, the track had dried briefly, but there were the first signs of rain returning and anybody who was out and ready for a quick lap at the very start could count himself in good shape. Immediately the pit gate was open, Stefan Johansson stormed out at the wheel of his Toleman TG184 and blasted round in a splendid 1m 28.891s, "despite the fact that I was all over the place, hanging on for dear life because, although I was on slicks, I could see the spots of rain building up on my vizor all the way round."

Similarly prompt about getting on to the circuit were the two Osella drivers, with the result that when the session was stopped after eight minutes to retrieve the wreckage of Gerhard Berger's ATS D7, comprehensively rattled along one of the unyielding guard rails, the order at the head of the grid read Johansson, Ghinzani, Gartner!

Berger's accident had demolished a section of guard rail as well as showering one unfortunate marshal with hefty stones, so it took quite a while to get everything cleared up and by the time the cars returned to the circuit it was absolutely saturated. For the balance of that hour, the amiable Johansson spent most of his time doing a rain dance in the Toleman pit, willing it to rain just long enough to sustain his position at the head of the practice times but, unfortunately, his prayers were not to be answered.

In the closing stages the racing line dried out sufficiently for a slick-tyred Alain Prost to set the tone of the weekend's proceedings with a worthwhile 1m 28.276s and it seemed as though Lauda might match this before the rather disgruntled Austrian found himself called into the pits rather sooner than he expected. This meant that he lost second place to the hard-charging Elio de Angelis, whose confident opposite-lock slides in the pouring rain were enough to raise the hairs on the back of your neck . . . Lauda wound up third ahead of the disappointed Johansson's earlier time, but the whole affair did not really mean much and, when Saturday qualifying took place in dry conditions, the grid quickly assumed its regular 1984 appearance.

Fed up with his string of mechanical retirements throughout the season, Nelson Piquet's spirit was clearly intact and he resolved that he would win this final race of the season, whatever effect it might have on the outcome of the Championship battle between those two McLaren men. Brabham chief mechanic Charlie Whiting simply said "put your money on Nelson," with a knowing wink that seemed to be more than simply his normally enthusiastic team loyalty. When qualifying seriously got under way, Piquet took his qualifying spare BT53 and, despite the need to change a turbo mid-way through the session, he slammed round in an impressive 1m 21.703s, being easily quickest through the speed trap at just over 191mph. Prost joined him on the front row with 1m 21.774s, but Lauda wound up way back in 11th position on 1m 23.183s.

Niki finished the session in a pretty irritated frame of mind. By his own admission he ruined his chances on his first set of qualifiers when he spun up an escape road after overbraking, flat-spotting all four Michelins in the process. But he was also worried about a clattering from the valve gear of his TAG turbo engine and came in to ask for advice about what the problem might be before going out on his second run.

"I told them it was making quite worrying noises," said Niki later, "but the Porsche people told me that it was nothing to worry about, just the gears at the front of the camshaft clattering away. So I went out on my second run and the engine just lost about 300rpm at the top. There was just no way I could turn a decent time." He thought for a moment and then added, "I'm going to need a *lot* of luck tomorrow, no question of that." This sort of technical problem, routine and unavoidable to those in the business, none the less got the Austrian "purple press" stoked up into a right old lather and by the end of the weekend ridiculous suggestions were being made to the effect that Lauda's car was being deliberately "knobbled" in an attempt to ensure that Prost won the Championship. When Niki was confronted by these stories, his face simply contorted slightly in a mixture of pained despair. In his view, the rumours were not even worth commenting on . . .

Revelling in the luxury of the latest specification Michelins for the first time, the Toleman team was rounding off its season on the highest possible note with both its drivers well on the pace. Ayrton Senna proved nothing short of sensational as he swept round in 1m 21.936 to grab third place in the line-up, Johansson's TG184 only qualifying tenth after its Hart 415T developed an irritating misfire every time the boost pressure was turned up. Stefan was marginally quicker than the Brazilian on race tyres, though, so the team faced the Portuguese Grand Prix with enormous optimism.

By contrast, optimism, was not to the forefront in the Williams camp where Keke Rosberg worked his way steadily through a diet of disaster which lasted right up until the dying moments of the final qualifying session. In Friday's rain-soaked session his race car suffered a turbo failure and the spare rolled to a halt out on the circuit with exactly the same problem. Unfortunately, as it expired, the Finn's second Williams-Honda doused the already slippery track surface with a hefty dose of oil, sending team-mate Jacques Laffite's FW09B spinning helplessly into Streiff's Renault which had itself spun on the right-hander after the pits and stood, broadside to the traffic, almost blocking the circuit. Fortunately nobody was hurt in this right old shambles, and both cars were repairable for Saturday, but it left the Williams team more than slightly dejected.

For Saturday both cars had fresh turbochargers fitted, but Rosberg's race machine pumped out its water during the untimed session which meant a fresh Honda V6 had to be installed for final qualifying. This swap took longer than had been hoped, with the result that Keke did not get out until about 15 minutes from the end – only for the car to expire on its first serious lap in another huge cloud of smoke. At this moment Keke was 27th overall, the sole non-qualifier and he had pretty well reached the end of his tether.

Walking calmly back to the pits – "I knew the problem and I wasn't about to get myself into a state by *running*" – Rosberg was strapped into the spare FW09B and went out on to the circuit with about two-and-a-half minutes left. The Williams team was on tenterhooks, but it had no call to worry. In one of those truly memorable, historic, laps of racing history, Rosberg wound that Williams-Honda round his little finger and, in a single, dynamic effort, hurled round to record a stunning 1m 22.049s. One lap had promoted him from 27th to fourth! It was unbelievable ... possibly the single most exciting lap of the entire weekend.

Elio de Angelis and Nigel Mansell paired up for Lotus together on the third row, the Italian consigned to using the spare car for final qualifying and the race after Streiff shut the door on him during Saturday morning's session. "I don't know what the hell he thought he was doing," grumbled Elio, "FISA ought to think a bit more carefully before it issues Super Licences to people like that ..." The impact broke the Lotus's right-front suspension, ripping the pick-up point out of the monocoque, so there was no question of using that car again in Portugal.

Over at Renault Patrick Tambay emerged fastest of the three runners, qualifying his RE50 on the inside of row four with a 1m 22.801s, two places ahead of Derek Warwick who had a somewhat troubled time. In Friday's wet session Derek's RE50 blew both its turbos, so he took the spare and knocked the nose off in a spin trying to pass one of the Alfas: by the time this was repaired, he found that he was out of time. On Saturday he found his car "a real handful, impossible to work into any sort of rhythm." He blamed Arnoux for messing up his quickest run – "as usual, what's the matter with him?" – and wound up with a 1m 22.686s. Streiff, showing a commendable blend of enthusiasm and restraint, qualified a very respectable 13th on 1m 24.089s, adding "I haven't quite got used to the technique of qualifying rubber ... If I'd been allowed another set, I feel I could have sliced off another second ..."

Michele Alboreto split the two regular works Renaults, expressing himself "encouraged" by the performance of the Ferrari C4 M2 which was being presided over by Harvey Postlethwaite throughout practice. René Arnoux was way out of contention, a split turbocharger intercooler ruining his efforts on Saturday, a similar problem to that which kept

Winkelhock out of contention in the second Brabham BT53.

Amongst the also-rans, the Alfas were just in their regular places, Patrese taking time off to charge a guard rail on Saturday, while the revised fuel feed system in Cheever's 184T seemed to take a dislike to pre-cooled fuel and the car developed a misfire as a result, obliging Eddie to take the spare. Laffite's Williams qualified 15th on 1m 24.437s ahead of Surer, Arnoux and Boutsen, both Arrows drivers commenting that their qualifying tyres had lost grip unusually early and they both complained of a hard time in heavy traffic.

Winkelhock's efforts only earned him 19th place, the German beaming at the thought of racing a car that wouldn't give trouble after a few laps, while de Cesaris and Hesnault seemed to be getting nowhere in the Ligier JS23s, Andrea trying the 'B' spec. car yet again. Completing the grid were Ghinzani, Berger in the ATS D7, his spare pressed into use after Friday's accident, Gartner, Baldi's Spirit 101B and the RAM 02s of Palmer and Alliot. The Frenchman was originally the sole non-qualifier, but the stewards of the meeting allowed him to start as 27th runner in view of the fact that Winkelhock was a late substitution and not an originally nominated driver.

RACE

It seemed that the local Portuguese population was easily able to resist the temptation offered by the return of Formula 1 following a 24-year absence, because the crowd which flocked into the Estoril autodrome was disappointingly small – just over 44,000. As a consequence, access up the small rural roads was not as difficult as expected and there were great empty spaces in the several large grandstands which had been erected round the track.

The Championship battle was building up to its grand finale and Lauda's experience in the warm-up was true to typical McLaren International style. He set quickest time, but his TAG engine (newly installed on Saturday night) developed a water leak, so yet another new engine was produced to replace it. Time and again this season one or other of the McLarens has been afflicted with major mechanical problems in the race morning warm-up session. And time and again the cars have run through the race without missing a beat. Estoril was to be no exception.

With an electric atmosphere of anticipation hanging over the grid after the parade lap, the cars paused, Derek Ongaro switched the lights from red to green and the final Grand Prix of the '84 season was under way. Prost was moving first, cutting across in front of Piquet, but from the second row it was Rosberg who erupted down the outside to snatch the lead going into the first right-hander, with Mansell making a terrific start from the third row to follow him round into an initial second place. This was a real turn up for the books and the apparently unpredictable nature of the contest was underlined when Piquet, irritated after his poor start and Prost's positive action, got off-line and spun on the opening lap, dropping to the tail of the field before he could resume.

Rosberg's bucking, weaving and bouncing Williams-Honda came slamming through over the bumps to lead the opening lap by half a dozen lengths from Mansell, with Prost a close third, then Senna, Alboreto, de Angelis, Tambay, Warwick, Johansson, Cheever and Lauda. Niki, quite clearly, had a great deal of work ahead of him.

Mid-way round the second lap Mansell slid wide on a tight left-hander, allowing Prost through to second place, while Lauda nipped ahead of Cheever and began to start looking for a way through in front of Tambay. Rosberg was giving it everything he'd got at the head of the field, but there was no way that the Williams FW09B was any match for a smoothly-driven McLaren MP4/2 and it took Prost only another couple of laps before he was right up on Keke's gearbox. However, Alain could not afford to take any more risks than Lauda in this crucial race, so it took him until the start of lap nine before he nailed the Williams cleanly up the inside at the end of the start/finish straight,

nipping by into the lead as Keke almost locked his rear wheels on the outside line in one final gesture of bitter defiance.

From that point onwards the outcome of the Portuguese Grand Prix was never in doubt. In another splendid demonstration of precision driving, Prost the perfectionist stamped his mastery on the entire event, sailing serenely home to his seventh victory of the year. Twenty-one years earlier, Jim Clark's tally of seven victories had been sufficient to win the Scot his first Championship title by a mile. This one would be lost by Prost by a tantalising, frustrating, minúscule margin ...

With Prost running away at the head of the field, Mansell eventually finding a way past Rosberg, none too easily one might add, for Keke was intent on sending a none-too-discreet message to the Englishman as to who will be team leader at Williams next year. They banged wheels when Rosberg slammed the door in Mansell's face the lap before Nigel finally made it through into second place at the start of lap 12.

Tambay was gradually dropping away from the leading bunch now, frustrated at the way in which his newly-installed electronic injection engine was performing, so Lauda got through to ninth at the end of lap six before hitting some real problems. Immediately ahead of him were Alboreto, Warwick, de Angelis and Johansson, although Derek was eliminated from the equation on lap 13 when he spun as he attempted to outbrake the Ferrari resuming well down the field after a stop to change his ruined Michelins. Mansell was hanging on valiantly in second place, Rosberg was still keeping Senna at bay while Alboreto did everything in his power to haul up on to the Toleman's tail. Meanwhile Stefan was trying to work out a way round de Angelis and Lauda had started to feel rather anxious with all these determined young lads ahead of him.

Senna successfully deposed Rosberg on lap 19 while badly wearing tyres (the wrong choice) and loss of power on the straights dropped de Angelis out of the picture, allowing Johansson and Lauda to move up on to Alboreto's tail. Niki was having a look down the inside of just about every corner all

Despite one or two spins, Philippe Streiff acquitted himself well in a third works Renault.

OCTOBER:

Monaco Grand Prix omitted from provisional calendar for 1985.

General Motors announce plans for V8 engine for Indycar racing.

Ivan Capelli (Martini MK42-Alfa Romeo) wins the last European Formula 3 Championship.

FISA announce technical change: no chilled fuel in 1985; fuel capacity reduced to 195 litres in 1986 and 180 litres in 1988 when maximum engine capacity will be reduced from 1500 to 1200cc.

the way round the circuit as he weighed up the possibility of passing Johansson, but the Swede was driving brilliantly, making not the smallest slip which would allow Niki to get his McLaren alongside.

"I simply couldn't believe the speed of that Toleman on the straight," said Niki afterwards, "I eventually had to wind my boost up to well beyond qualifying level and go down the outside of him into a tricky left-hander . . . as I came across in front of him, I tagged his nose which was a bit unfortunate . . ." Stefan, who had been wondering why the hell Lauda had been sitting on his tail for lap after lap, not making, in his view, any serious effort to come past, shared Niki's view of the situation. "Unfortunate? I was livid," he grinned at the end of the race. This slight contact meant that Johansson lost the best part of two laps in the pits having the nose wing replaced: on his return to the fray he set the third quickest lap of the race, behind the two McLarens. For certain he would have otherwise been fourth behind team-mate Senna.

Lauda kept the boost pressure up to pass Alboreto into third place within a lap of overtaking Johansson and, suddenly, Prost's advantage did not seem so secure. Lauda had the best part of half a minute to make up if he was to catch Mansell for second place and, after trouble with some obstructive backmarkers, for a time it looked as though Niki would be unable to pull it off. As things turned out, he was spared the necessity of doing so. Mansell's brilliant drive came to an end when he spun abruptly and crawled in to retire with no brakes at the end of lap 52. Close examination revealed that one of the front calipers had popped out of one of its pistons, the fluid had leaked away and that was the end of Nigel's great effort. "I could cry, I'm so upset," he confessed.

Alain Prost's most enduring nightmare had finally come true. With 18 laps to go his team-mate was holding second place and the two McLarens ran out the race in team formation with Niki grasping his third Championship title by that impossibly narrow margin of half a point. Into third place came Ayrton Senna, underlining his supreme talent and the excellence of the Toleman-

Hart combination, while Rosberg's Williams blew its engine on lap 40, allowing Alboreto to take fourth after recovering from a spin as he tried to get on terms with Senna. De Angelis managed to unlap himself shortly before the finish to take fifth, while a furious Patrick Tambay was displaced from sixth by a recovering Nelson Piquet who had earlier stopped for fresh Michelins and then charged back into contention. The Renault pit failed to notice his progress and, thinking Patrick was comfortably ahead of Patrese's Alfa, did not realise that Piquet was the man they should be watching for.

Patrese was, in fact, eighth ahead of Arnoux, the Frenchman having performed "miserably" by his own admission, while Winkelhock was 10th after losing second gear 20 laps from the end. Johansson was a dejected 11th from de Cesaris, Berger and Laffite, Jacques making two pit stops to deal with lifting bodywork that was trying to blow off his Williams, eventually continuing to the finish minus his engine cover.

Almost unnoticed in the tense battle for the Championship, both RAMs and both Arrows had failed to make the distance. Alliot was out early with engine trouble while Palmer succumbed to a gearbox problem, Surer was sidelined with electrical failure and Boutsen broke a driveshaft. Warwick and Streiff both had spins (Derek's second when he was trying to pass Piquet later in the race) before their Renaults stopped with gearbox failure and a broken driveshaft respectively, while Ghinzani's Osella suffered a spectacular engine blow-up and team-mate Gartner ran out of fuel five laps from the end. Finally, Mauro Baldi was four laps behind in 15th place after completing the last lap and a half with a deflated rear tyre.

Suddenly, it was all over. The man who had opened the season on a high note with a win at Rio closed it in a similarly successful vein with victory in Portugal. In between, he had stamped his mastery on Formula 1: there was rarely a race in which he had not been a major, potentially winning factor, and yet he had lost the Championship to his admittedly talented team-mate, a man who had never beaten him fair and square in a straight fight!

AH

Rain stopped play on Friday. Jackie Oliver and Marc Surer ponder their future together after a difficult year sorting the Arrows A7-BMW.

Grande Premio de Portugal, October 21/statistics

Entries and practice times

No.	Driver	Nat	Car	Tyre	Engine	Entrant	Practice 1	Practice 2
1	Nelson Piquet	BR	Parmalat BRABHAM BT53	M	BMW M12/13	MRD International	1m 30·889s	**1m 21·703s**
2	Manfred Winkelhock	D	Parmalat BRABHAM BT53	M	BMW M12/13	MRD International	—	**1m 25·289s**
5	Jacques Laffite	F	WILLIAMS FW09B	G	Honda RA 163–E	Williams Grand Prix Engineering	1m 39·696s	**1m 24·437s**
6	Keke Rosberg	SF	WILLIAMS FW09B	G	Honda RA 163–E	Williams Grand Prix Engineering	1m 32·269s	**1m 22·049s**
7	Alain Prost	F	Marlboro McLAREN MP4/2	M	TAG P01 (TTE P01)	Marlboro McLaren International	1m 28·276s	**1m 21·774s**
8	Niki Lauda	A	Marlboro McLAREN MP4/2	M	TAG P01 (TTE P01)	Marlboro McLaren International	1m 28·837s	**1m 23·183s**
9	Philippe Alliot	F	RAM 02	P	Hart 415T	Skoal Bandit Formula 1 Team	1m 34·839s	**1m 30·406s**
10	Jonathan Palmer	GB	RAM 02	P	Hart 415T	Skoal Bandit Formula 1 Team	1m 40·344s	**1m 29·397s**
11	Elio de Angelis	I	John Player Special LOTUS 95T	G	Renault EF4	John Player Team Lotus	1m 28·428s	**1m 22·291s**
12	Nigel Mansell	GB	John Player Special LOTUS 95T	G	Renault EF4	John Player Team Lotus	1m 32·986s	**1m 22·319s**
15	Patrick Tambay	F	Elf RENAULT RE50	M	Renault EF4	Equipe Renault Elf	1m 29·409s	**1m 22·583s**
16	Derek Warwick	GB	Elf RENAULT RE50	M	Renault EF4	Equipe Renault Elf	1m 34·003s	**1m 24·688s**
17	Marc Surer	CH	ARROWS A7	G	BMW M12/13	Barclay Nordica Arrows BMW	1m 34·809s	**1m 25·115s**
18	Thierry Boutsen	B	ARROWS A7	G	BMW M12/13	Barclay Nordica Arrows BMW	1m 30·077s	**1m 21·936s**
19	Ayrton Senna	BR	TOLEMAN TG184	M	Hart 415T	Toleman Group Motorsport	1m 28·891s	**1m 22·942s**
20	Stefan Johansson	S	TOLEMAN TG184	M	Hart 415T	Toleman Group Motorsport	1m 36·483s	**1m 29·001s**
21	Mauro Baldi	I	SPIRIT 101	P	Hart 415T	Spirit Racing	1m 37·154s	**1m 24·048s**
22	Riccardo Patrese	I	Benetton ALFA ROMEO 184T	G	Alfa Romeo 183T	Benetton Team Alfa Romeo	1m 34·809s	**1m 24·235s**
23	Eddie Cheever	USA	Benetton ALFA ROMEO 184T	G	Alfa Romeo 183T	Benetton Team Alfa Romeo	1m 31·336s	**1m 26·840s**
24	Piercarlo Ghinzani	I	Kelemata OSELLA FA1F	P	Alfa Romeo 183T	Osella Squadra Corse	1m 34·233s	**1m 26·701s**
25	François Hesnault	F	LIGIER Loto JS23	M	Renault EF4	Ligier Loto	1m 33·398s	**1m 26·082s**
26	Andrea de Cesaris	I	LIGIER Loto JS23	M	Renault EF4	Ligier Loto	1m 31·192s	**1m 22·686s**
27	Michele Alboreto	I	Fiat FERRARI 126C4	G	Ferrari 126C	Scuderia Ferrari SpA	1m 36·634s	**1m 24·848s**
28	René Arnoux	F	Fiat FERRARI 126C4	G	Ferrari 126C	Scuderia Ferrari SpA	1m 33·540s	**1m 28·229s**
30	Jo Gartner	A	Kelemata OSELLA FA1F	P	Alfa Romeo 183T	Osella Squadra Corse	1m 44·966s	**1m 28·106s**
31	Gerhard Berger	A	ATS D7	P	BMW M12/13	Team ATS	1m 37·280s	**1m 24·089s**
33	Philippe Streiff	F	Elf RENAULT RE50	M	Renault EF4	Equipe Renault Elf		

Thursday afternoon, Friday morning and Saturday morning practice sessions not officially recorded.

Fri pm	Sat pm
Cool, dry, wet, then dry	Warm, dry

G – Goodyear, M – Michelin, P – Pirelli.

Starting grid

1 PIQUET (1m 21·703s)
Brabham

7 PROST (1m 21·774s)
McLaren

19 SENNA (1m 21·936s)
Toleman

6 ROSBERG (1m 22·049s)
Williams

11 DE ANGELIS (1m 22·291s)
Lotus

12 MANSELL (1m 22·319s)
Lotus

15 TAMBAY (1m 22·583s)
Renault

27 ALBORETO (1m 22·686s)
Ferrari

16 WARWICK (1m 22·801s)
Renault

20 JOHANSSON (1m 22·942s)
Toleman

8 LAUDA (1m 23·183s)
McLaren

22 PATRESE (1m 24·048s)
Alfa Romeo

33 STREIFF (1m 24·089s)
Renault

23 CHEEVER (1m 24·235s)
Alfa Romeo

5 LAFFITE (1m 24·437s)
Williams

17 SURER (1m 24·688s)
Arrows

28 ARNOUX (1m 24·848s)
Ferrari

18 BOUTSEN (1m 25·115s)
Arrows

2 WINKELHOCK (1m 25·289s)
Brabham

26 DE CESARIS (1m 26·082s)
Ligier

25 HESNAULT (1m 26·701s)
Ligier

24 GHINZANI (1m 26·840s)
Osella

14 BERGER (1m 28·106s)
ATS

30 GARTNER (1m 28·229s)
Osella

21 BALDI (1m 29·001s)
Spirit

10 PALMER (1m 29·397s)
RAM

9 ALLIOT (1m 30·406s)
RAM

Results and retirements

Place	Driver	Car	Laps	Time and Speed (mph/km/h)/Retirement	
1	Alain Prost	McLaren-TAG t/c V6	70	1h 41m 11·753s	112·182/180·540
2	Niki Lauda	McLaren-TAG t/c V6	70	1h 41m 25·178s	111·909/180·1
3	Ayrton Senna	Toleman-Hart t/c 4	70	1h 41m 31·795s	111·784/179·9
4	Michele Alboreto	Ferrari t/c V6	70	1h 41m 32·070s	111·784/179·9
5	Elio de Angelis	Lotus-Renault t/c V6	70	1h 42m 43·922s	110·479/177·8
6	Nelson Piquet	Brabham-BMW t/c 4	69		
7	Patrick Tambay	Renault t/c V6	69		
8	Riccardo Patrese	Alfa Romeo t/c V8	69		
9	René Arnoux	Ferrari t/c V6	69		
10	Manfred Winkelhock	Brabham-BMW t/c 4	69		
11	Stefan Johansson	Toleman-Hart t/c 4	69		
12	Andrea de Cesaris	Ligier-Renault t/c V6	69		
13	Gerhard Berger	ATS-BMW t/c 4	68		
14	Jacques Laffite	Williams-Honda t/c V6	67		
15	Mauro Baldi	Spirit-Hart t/c 4	66		
16	Jo Gartner	Osella-Alfa Romeo t/c V8	65	Out of fuel	
17	Eddie Cheever	Alfa Romeo t/c V8	64		
	Piercarlo Ghinzani	Osella-Alfa Romeo t/c V8	60	Engine	
	Nigel Mansell	Lotus-Renault t/c V6	52	Lost brake fluid/spun off	
	Derek Warwick	Renault t/c V6	51	Gearbox	
	Philippe Streiff	Renault t/c V6	48	Driveshaft	
	Keke Rosberg	Williams-Honda t/c V6	39	Engine	
	François Hesnault	Ligier-Renault t/c V6	31	Electrics	
	Thierry Boutsen	Arrows-BMW t/c 4	24	Driveshaft	
	Jonathan Palmer	RAM-Hart t/c 4	19	Gearbox	
	Marc Surer	Arrows-BMW t/c 4	8	Electrics	
	Philippe Alliot	RAM-Hart t/c 4	2	Engine	

Fastest lap: Lauda, on lap 51, 1m 22·996s, 117·242mph/188·683km/h (record).
Previous lap record: Derek Daly (F2 Chevron B40-Hart), 1m 34·16s, 103·341mph/166·312km/h (1977).

Past winners

Year	Driver	Nat	Car	Circuit	Distance miles/km	Speed mph/km/h
1958	Stirling Moss	GB	2·5 Vanwall	Oporto	233·01/375·00	105·03/169·03
1959	Stirling Moss	GB	2·5 Cooper T51-Climax	Monsanto	209·00/336·35	95·32/153·40
1960	Jack Brabham	AUS	2·5 Cooper T53-Climax	Oporto	256·31/412·50	109·27/175·85
1984	Alain Prost	F	1·5 McLaren MP4/2-TAG t/c	Estoril	189·21/304·50	112·18/180·54

Circuit data

Autodromo do Estoril
Circuit length: 2·703 miles/4·350 km
Race distance: 70 laps, 189·207 miles/304·500 km
Race weather: Hot, dry

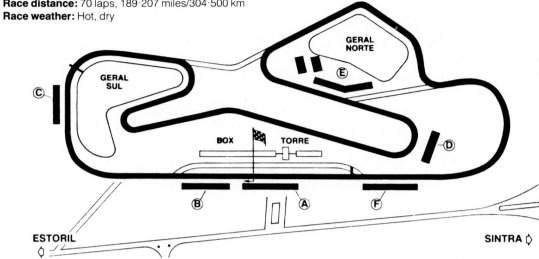

Fastest laps

Driver	Time	Lap
Niki Lauda	1m 22·996s	51
Alain Prost	1m 23·452s	39
Stefan Johansson	1m 24·053s	51
Michele Alboreto	1m 24·148s	68
Nigel Mansell	1m 24·267s	47
Nelson Piquet	1m 24·275s	39
Ayrton Senna	1m 24·373s	46
Jacques Laffite	1m 24·507s	55
Derek Warwick	1m 25·309s	20
Patrick Tambay	1m 25·506s	37
Keke Rosberg	1m 25·667s	37
Elio de Angelis	1m 25·680s	45
René Arnoux	1m 25·711s	53
Eddie Cheever	1m 26·020s	33
Riccardo Patrese	1m 26·173s	43
Manfred Winkelhock	1m 26·404s	63
Gerhard Berger	1m 26·601s	59
Andrea de Cesaris	1m 26·806s	36
Philippe Streiff	1m 26·874s	43
Jo Gartner	1m 27·169s	58
Thierry Boutsen	1m 27·725s	24
Mauro Baldi	1m 27·772s	48
Piercarlo Ghinzani	1m 28·410s	42
Marc Surer	1m 28·635s	7
François Hesnault	1m 29·219s	19
Jonathan Palmer	1m 30·711s	6
Philippe Alliot	1m 35·542s	2

Points

WORLD CHAMPIONSHIP OF DRIVERS

1	Niki Lauda	72 pts
2	Alain Prost	71·5
3	Elio de Angelis	34
4	Michele Alboreto	30·5
5	Nelson Piquet	29
6	René Arnoux	27
7	Derek Warwick	23
8	Keke Rosberg	20·5
9=	Nigel Mansell	13
9=	Ayrton Senna	13
11	Patrick Tambay	11
12	Teo Fabi	9
13	Riccardo Patrese	8
14=	Jacques Laffite	5
14=	Thierry Boutsen	5
16=	Eddie Cheever	3
16=	Stefan Johansson	3
16=	Andrea de Cesaris	3
19	Piercarlo Ghinzani	2
20	Marc Surer	1
*	Martin Brundle	8
*	Stefan Bellof	5

CONSTRUCTORS' CUP

		Points
1	McLaren	143·5 pts
2	Ferrari	57·5
3	Lotus	47
4	Brabham	38
5	Renault	34
6	Williams	25·5
7	Toleman	16
8	Alfa Romeo	11
9	Arrows	6
10	Ligier	3
11	Osella	2
*	Tyrrell	13

* Points removed by FISA Executive Committee and remaining finishing positions for races in question subsequently adjusted accordingly.

Lap chart

1st LAP ORDER — Laps 1–37

1st LAP ORDER	1	2	3	4	5	6	7	8	9	10	11	12	13	14	15	16	17	18	19	20	21	22	23	24	25	26	27	28	29	30	31	32	33	34	35	36	37
6 K. Rosberg	6	6	6	6	6	6	6	6	7	7	7	7	7	7	7	7	7	7	7	7	7	7	7	7	7	7	7	7	7	7	7	7	7	7	7	7	7
12 N. Mansell	12	7	7	7	7	7	7	7	6	6	6	12	12	12	12	12	12	12	12	12	12	12	12	12	12	12	12	12	12	12	12	12	12	12	12	12	12
7 A. Prost	7	12	12	12	12	12	12	12	12	12	12	6	6	6	6	6	6	6	19	19	19	19	19	19	19	19	19	19	19	19	19	19	8	8	8	8	8
19 A. Senna	19	19	19	19	19	19	19	19	19	19	19	19	19	19	19	19	19	19	6	6	6	6	6	6	6	6	6	6	6	8	6	19	19	19	19	19	19
27 M. Alboreto	27	27	27	27	27	27	27	27	27	27	27	27	27	27	27	27	27	27	27	27	27	27	27	27	27	27	27	8	8	6	8	6	6	6	6	6	6
11 E. De Angelis	11	11	11	11	11	11	11	11	11	16	16	16	11	11	11	11	11	20	20	20	20	20	20	20	20	8	27	27	27	27	27	27	27	27	27	27	27
15 P. Tambay	15	16	16	16	16	16	16	16	16	11	11	11	20	20	20	20	8	8	8	8	8	8	8	20	15	15	15	15	15	15	15	15	15				
16 D. Warwick	16	15	15	15	20	20	20	20	20	20	20	8	8	8	8	11	11	15	15	15	15	15	15	15	11	11	11	11	11	11	11	11	11	11	11		
20 S. Johansson	20	20	20	20	15	8	8	8	8	8	8	15	15	15	15	15	15	11	11	11	11	11	11	11	11	20	22	22	22	22	22	22	22	22	22	22	22
23 E. Cheever	23	23	8	8	8	15	15	15	15	15	15	23	23	23	23	23	23	23	23	23	23	23	23	2	2	2	2	2	2	2	2	2	2	2	2	2	2
8 N. Lauda	8	8	23	23	23	23	23	23	23	23	23	22	22	22	22	22	22	22	22	22	22	22	22	22	22	2	2	26	26	26	26	26	26	26	26	26	26
22 R. Patrese	22	22	22	22	22	22	22	22	22	22	22	18	18	18	18	18	18	18	18	18	18	18	2	2	26	26	26	28	28	28	1	1	1	1	1		
18 T. Boutsen	18	18	18	18	18	18	18	18	18	18	18	2	2	2	2	2	2	2	2	2	2	2	26	26	1	28	28	1	1	1	28	28	28	28	28		
17 M. Surer	17	2	2	2	2	2	2	2	2	2	2	16	26	26	26	26	26	26	26	26	26	26	1	1	23	1	1	25	14	14	16	16	16	16	16		
2 M. Winkelhock	2	17	17	17	17	17	17	26	26	26	26	5	5	5	5	5	1	1	1	1	16	16	16	16	28	25	25	14	14	14	14	14	14	14	14		
28 R. Arnoux	28	28	28	28	28	28	28	28	28	5	5	5	33	33	1	1	1	16	16	16	16	28	25	25	14	14	24	21	21	21	21	21	21	21	21		
26 A. De Cesaris	26	26	26	26	26	26	26	26	5	5	28	33	33	1	1	33	33	16	5	33	28	28	25	25	14	24	24	21	24	30	30	30	30	30	30		
33 P. Streiff	33	33	33	33	33	33	33	33	33	28	28	28	28	28	16	33	28	5	25	25	14	14	24	21	16	30	30	24	24	24	24	33					
5 J. Laffite	5	5	5	5	5	5	5	5	1	1	1	1	1	16	16	16	28	28	28	25	14	14	14	24	21	30	16	30	25	33	33	33	33	33	24		
25 F. Hesnault	25	25	25	25	25	25	1	25	25	25	25	25	25	25	25	25	25	14	24	24	21	30	16	30	33	20	20	20	20	20							
14 G. Berger	14	14	14	14	14	14	1	25	14	14	14	14	21	21	21	21	21	21	30	16	33	33	33	33	5	5	5	5	5								
24 P. Ghinzani	24	24	24	24	24	24	14	14	24	24	24	24	24	24	24	24	24	21	30	30	33	33	5	5	23	23	23	23	23	23							
30 J. Gartner	30	30	30	30	1	1	24	24	30	30	30	30	30	21	21	21	21	30	33	33	5	5	5	23	23	23											
21 M. Baldi	21	21	21	1	30	30	30	30	21	21	21	21	30	30	30	30	5	5	5	5																	
10 J. Palmer	10	10	10	10	21	10	10	21	10	10	10	10	10	10	10	10	10	10	10																		
9 P. Alliot	9	9	1	10	10	21	21	10																													
1 N. Piquet	1	1																																			

Laps 38–70

38	39	40	41	42	43	44	45	46	47	48	49	50	51	52	53	54	55	56	57	58	59	60	61	62	63	64	65	66	67	68	69	70
7	7	7	7	7	7	7	7	7	7	7	7	7	7	7	7	7	7	7	7	7	7	7	7	7	7	7	7	7	7	7	7	7
12	12	12	12	12	12	12	12	12	12	12	12	12	8	8	8	8	8	8	8	8	8	8	8	8	8	8	8	8	8	8	8	8
8	8	8	8	8	8	8	8	8	8	8	8	8	19	19	19	19	19	19	19	19	19	19	19	19	19	19	19	19	19	19	19	19
19	19	19	19	19	19	19	19	19	19	19	19	19	27	27	27	27	27	27	27	27	27	27	27	27	27	27	27	27	27	27	27	27
6	27	27	27	27	27	27	27	27	27	27	27	27	11	11	11	11	11	11	11	11	11	11	11	11	11	11	11	11	11	11	11	11
27	6	15	15	15	15	11	11	11	11	11	11	11	11	15	15	15	15	15	15	15	15	15	15	15	1	1	1	1	1	1	1	1
15	15	11	11	11	11	15	15	15	15	15	15	15	12	22	22	1	1	1	1	1	1	1	1	15	15	15	15	15	15	15	15	15
11	11	22	22	22	22	22	22	22	22	22	22	22	1	1	22	22	22	22	22	22	22	22	22	22	22	22	22	22	22	22	22	22
22	22	2	2	2	2	2	2	2	2	2	2	1	2	2	2	2	2	2	2	2	2	2	2	2	2	2	2	2	2	2	2	28
2	2	26	26	26	26	26	26	26	26	26	1	2	2	26	26	26	26	26	26	26	26	26	26	26	26	26	26	28	28	28	2	
26	26	1	1	1	1	1	1	1	1	1	2	2	26	26	28	28	28	28	28	28	28	28	28	28	28	28	28	28	2			
1	1	28	28	28	28	28	28	28	28	28	28	28	20	20	20	20	20	20	20	20	20	20	20	20	20	20	20	20	26			
28	28	16	16	16	16	16	16	16	16	16	16	16	16	30	30	30	30	30	30	30	30	30	30	30	14	14	14					
16	16	14	14	14	14	14	14	14	14	14	14	16	20	20	14	14	14	14	14	14	14	14	14	14	5	5						
16	14	30	30	30	30	30	30	30	20	20	14	14	30	21	21	21	21	21	21	21	5	5	5	5	21							
14	30	30	30	30	30	30	20	20	14	14	30	33	33	33	33	30	30	5	5	21	21	21	21									
30	30	21	21	21	21	20	20	20	33	33	33	21	21	24	24	24	24	24	24	24	24	24	23	23								
21	21	21	21	21	21	21	21	24	24	5	23	23	23	23	23	23	23	23	23													
33	33	20	20	21	21	21	21	21	24	24	24	5	23	23	23	23	23	23	23														
24	24	24	24	24	24	24	24	24	24	5	5	23																				
20	20	5	5	5	5	5	5	5	5	23	23	23																					
5	5	23																														
23	23																															

Andretti on form

American Review by Gordon Kirby

Although beaten comprehensively by Lola on the road circuits, March supplied 30 of the 33 starters at Indy (an all-time record for a single manufacturer).

At 44, Mario Andretti remains as intense and hungry a race driver as ever. Six years after winning the World Championship and fifteen years after his last American national championship, Andretti was the dominant figure in CART's 16-round 1984 Indy Car World Series.

On *Autocourse's* deadline, with three races still to go, Andretti had won six times, led 479 of the 1,860 laps run to that point and started seven races from the pole. There were mathematical chances that either Tom Sneva, Danny Sullivan or Bobby Rahal could beat Andretti to the Indycar championship but the formal outcome of the point contest couldn't muddy the fact that Andretti was clearly the man of the year in American racing.

In the eight road races on the Indycar schedule Andretti was fearsome, winning at Long Beach, the Meadowlands, Road America and Mid-Ohio and starting from the pole for all six road races run at the time of writing. On the ovals he was less dominant but always on the pace. He won both races on the ultra-fast Michigan International Speedway, beating Indianapolis track record holder Tom Sneva in the mid-summer 500-miler and again in the autumn sprint race over 200 miles.

Andretti did all this at the wheel of an all-new Lola, typenumbered the T800. Built to exacting new standards in Huntington, the T800 was constructed around a high-sided honeycomb aluminium chassis and designed by widely-experienced English F1 designer Nigel Bennett and CanAm-trained American Tony Cicale. The car was elegant and effective with a completely different underbody, tail section and rear suspension package for the superspeedways. The T800 was also very close to the 1,500 lb weight limit, tipping the scales more than 100 lbs lighter than most Marches.

It was of course, this other English constructor which furnished cars to fully ninety per cent of the Indycar field in 1984. March's fifth-generation 84C proved to be an excellent speedway car, even in virtually "stock" form. However, it took a lot of weight paring and some rear suspension changes to make an 84C competitive with a T800 Lola on road courses – particularly the stop-and-go variety which predominate among CART's 50/50 philosophy of ovals versus road races.

Fastest of the March runners were Mayer Motor Racing (Tom Sneva, with Howdy Holmes as number two), Penske Racing (Rick Mears, Al Unser Sr, Johnny Rutherford and at the last two races, Mike Thackwell) and True-sports (Bobby Rahal). Others able to produce results with Marches included Galles Racing (Al Unser Jr), the Kraco Stereos team (Michael Andretti and Geoff Brabham) and Bignotti-Cotter Racing (Roberto Guerrero). With Penske and Patrick teams joining the March fold early in the season and Rick Mears subsequently winning the Indianapolis 500 with no fewer than thirty March-mounted starters (an all-time record for a single manufacturer) in the 33-car field, the year was a hectic success for March Engineering.

In the results box however, March was blown off by Lola with the all-powerful Andretti finding himself joined at Indianapolis by the first privately-run T800. The car was bought by Doug Shierson who decided to put aside his own neat but unsuccessful car and put Danny Sullivan in a hurriedly-built new Lola for the 500. Sullivan crashed in the race but the following month Shierson's team began to hit their stride and Sullivan went on to win three races during July, August and September, becoming a late-season contender for the championship.

PUTTING IT ALL TOGETHER

Nevertheless the 1984 Indy Car season proved primarily that Mario Andretti is as sharp and aggressive a personality as automobile racing has ever witnessed. Much in the way that he was an integral part of the 1978 World Championship-winning Lotus team and the Lotus 79, so Andretti impelled the germination of the Lola T800 and gave direction to the Newman/Haas team owned by the odd-couple combination of actor/racer Paul Newman and veteran CanAm/F5000 team owner Carl Haas.

Haas has been Lola Cars' American agent and a partner with Eric Broadley for fifteen years. Based in Chicago, his team carried off three Formula 5000 championships and four CanAm titles before the respective demise of those SCCA-sanctioned series. At the end of 1983 Haas got together with fellow CanAm team owner Paul Newman to run an Indycar team for Andretti with the driver having considerable power to oversee the hiring of key personnel. Budweiser, Anheuser-Busch Breweries massive-selling keynote brand, had been the prime sponsor of Newman's CanAm team since 1978, and the brewery came along to back the new team.

The first car was called a T700 and it was something of bitza put together around many existing Lola components. The team made a lot of progress with the car however and by the end of the season Andretti was one of the strongest race-for-race contenders and was also beginning to win on a regular basis.

By that time Nigel Bennett had joined the operation to design a completely new car with Haas bringing in a partner, John Jellinek, to help finance the T800 project. Andretti and the first car were out and running by early February and at the Long Beach season-opener the team got the drop on everyone by scoring a well-sorted, troublefree, flag-to-flag win over a decimated field.

Round two was run on the irregular, one-mile oval on the outskirts of Phoenix, in Arizona. Andretti was outpaced on the little oval by Tom Sneva in Mayer Motor Racing's March 84C and in the race Andretti first ran out of fuel and then broke a driveshaft while leaving the pits.

Three weeks later everyone converged on Indianapolis for three weeks of Gasoline Alley Fever. From the start of practice Andretti was on the pace and by mid-week, before the first qualifying weekend, it was clear Andretti and the new Lola were setting the pace. Before the week was out he had set a new, unofficial (only qualifying runs are "official" at Indianapolis) one lap record in 42.37 secs, for an average of 212.414 mph.

On Pole Day however, bad luck overtook Andretti. A curious electrical fault which had first shown its head the day before, caused the Lola's engine to lose revs and then cut out altogether on the last lap. The engine finally stopped running coming off the last corner on Andretti's fourth and final qualifying lap so that he coasted across the line fast enough only for sixth place on the starting grid.

In the race Andretti jumped into the battle for the lead and moved ahead during the first round of pit stops. For thirty laps or so the red Lola set the pace but then Andretti ran into trouble with his boost control which contrived to keep him under-boosted so that the car was short of revs down the straight. The relentless little man hung on however, keeping himself on the same lap as leaders Mears and Sneva until he got overanxious during a pit stop with just over one hundred miles to go and ran into Josele Garza's car, terminally damaging the front of the Lola.

On the one-mile oval at Milwaukee the following week, Andretti's luck wasn't much better. Unable to match Mears and Sneva he was fighting for third before a disastrous pit stop saw him lose a wheel. He finally finished eighth, four laps behind.

Two weeks later in Oregon for a 200-mile road race on the tight 1.9-mile Portland Raceway, Andretti started from the pole only to run almost immediately into overheating problems from a holed water radiator. At the inaugural Meadowlands Grand Prix two weeks later, Andretti was dominant once again, starting from the pole and this time winning convincingly from Sullivan's Lola. For the rest of the year Andretti was to be a major factor in every race.

At the lakeside Cleveland airport race he again qualified fastest and led the early going. In the middle stages of the race he chased Bobby Rahal and was a close second when another electrical fault left him stranded out on the course. Two weeks later at the Michigan 500 he took his first oval track pole position of the year and drove a great race to beat Tom Sneva to the flag after losing a lap early in the race because of a loose plug wire.

On the 4.0-mile Road America road course in Wisconsin in early August, Andretti was again in command. Starting from the pole for the sixth time he led the early going and dogged Danny Sullivan's tracks through the middle of the race before coming home to his fourth win of the year after Sullivan's car caught fire.

The Pocono 500 was next and Andretti was outqualified by Mears and Rahal although he was still on the front row. In the race he chased Mears through the opening laps before more exasperating electrical problems slowed him down and brought him into the pits. After losing many laps trying to repair the problem Andretti finally dropped out when an oil fitting at the bottom of the engine broke and the engine blew up.

A 200-miler on the busy, 2.5-mile Mid-Ohio road course followed. This was one of those races dominated entirely by Andretti. He was on the pole by a clear second and ran away to win by half a minute from Rahal. The victory at Mid-Ohio put him on top of the point standings, closely pursued by Sneva and Mears with Sullivan a more remote fourth in the points table.

The season's twelfth race was run the following weekend on a furiously tight, 0.876-mile tri-oval outside Montreal. It was the first time Indycars had raced on the little track and the first time they had been to the province of Quebec in fifteen years. Unfortunately things started on a sour note when Rick Mears crashed heavily during the opening practice session.

In a self-admitted error Mears drove into the side of Corrado Fabi's car. He was launched into the air and driven hard into a guardrail which momentarily trapped the nose of his car and tore apart the front bulkhead. Both of Mears' feet were badly broken in the accident and he was expected to spend six months or more recovering and rehabilitating himself.

Mears' crash removed Penske Racing from championship contention so that for only the second time in the past nine years the team would not be Indycar champions. It also meant Sneva was the only real opposition faced by Andretti although Sullivan and Rahal were still hanging in.

Andretti qualified fourth and ran third behind Rahal and Sullivan in the opening laps at Sanair. After barely twenty miles however, he clipped Ed Pimm's Eagle while trying to lap him. The incident knocked Andretti's suspension out of line and after a long race he made it into seventh place, three laps behind winner Sullivan.

The last race run before the time of writing was the 200-mile sprint race at Michigan International Speedway. The pace was substantially quicker than at the 500-miler two months earlier with Johnny Rutherford qualifying on the pole in the injured Mears' car at better than 215 mph! Andretti started third behind Sneva, but the race was postponed until the following day after the combination of rain showers and a giant crash by Derek Daly closed down the fearfully fast speedway for the day. Rutherford, Sneva, Andretti, Al Unser Sr, Rahal, Al Unser Jr and Danny Ongais all featured in the battle for the lead the following day but at the end Andretti was out front with Sneva making a last minute bid to pass only to be foiled by the race finishing under a yellow flag when Rutherford crashed with only four laps to go.

Andretti's sixth win of the year put him 15 points clear of Sneva with Sullivan (an uncompetitive ninth in the MIS 200-miler) 37 points behind and Rahal trailing by a further 16 points. CART's point system awards twenty points for a win, 16 for a second, 14 for third and so on down to a single point for twelfth place. There's also a bonus point apiece for pole position and the driver who leads the most laps in each race.

Mario and Moët united again. Mario Andretti proved he had lost none of his winning ways, both on and off the track *(top)*.
Sharp and aggressive as ever, 44-year-old Mario Andretti dominated the road circuits with the Hass Lola T800.

Mark Clifford.

John Townsend.

221

SNEVA'S CHALLENGE

Sneva obviously had a real chance to beat Andretti although he *had* to finish strongly at Phoenix. The last two races took place at the fast Laguna Seca road course in northern California and the five-cornered, flat 1.25-mile track in Caesars Palace's Las Vegas parking lot and Sneva's record on both of those tracks was less than impressive.

Nor had Sneva been truly impressive over the course of the season. Driving with Texaco sponsorship in Teddy Mayer and Tyler Alexander's reborn Indycar team, Sneva was tenaciously fast in all oval races and certainly did a better job of road racing than ever before. Overall, however, his results paled in the face of Andretti's record. Sneva won only two of the 13 races run at the time of writing, both victories coming on the one-mile ovals at Phoenix, in April, and Milwaukee, in June. Sneva led from the pole at Phoenix and won at Milwaukee when Mears blew up on the last lap.

He was also on the pole at Indianapolis with a new track record of 210.029 mph (2 mins 51.405 secs for the four laps or ten miles). In the race he was Mears' prime competition until dropping out with only 32 laps to go when a CV joint broke. At both of the races at Michigan, Sneva was right on the pace, starting both races from the front row and finishing hard on Andretti's tail on each occasion. At the Pocono 500 he ran into handling problems because of a fading shock absorber and finished fourth, some five seconds behind the three-way battle to the flag between Sullivan, Mears and Rahal.

On the road race portion of the schedule however, Sneva was completely eclipsed by Andretti. Better as his road racing technique most certainly was, he could only amass a distant third at Long Beach (won by Andretti), a fourth place at Portland (Andretti DNF), a fifth at the Meadowlands (won by Andretti), and a seventh at Mid-Ohio (also won by Andretti).

In addition to running Sneva, Mayer Motor Racing ran March 84C in all races for Howdy Holmes. In his fifth year of Indycar racing, the one-time Formula Atlantic champion ran well at the beginning of the year and then seemed to taper off. He was a strong second to team-mate Sneva at Phoenix in April and started from the front row at Indianapolis, qualifying second only to Sneva.

MEARS' COSTLY ERROR

Despite Andretti being the dominant man last season and the Mayer/Alexander team having such a good first year of operation, it remained that Penske Racing was still rated at the top of the pile. Mears was in keen contention for the championship when he crashed after putting together another solid record of finishes spiced by some excellent speedway performances. He ran well if not brilliantly in road races – much better than Sneva – and as ever he and his faithful crew of mechanics combined to produce the most relentless finishing record of all. The team started the year with the latest Penske chassis – the PC12 – but after two uncompetitive races which ended in retirement for both Mears and team-mate Al Unser Sr, Penske took the decision to switch to a full fleet of Marches for Indianapolis. Mears qualified on the front row and won the 500 in fine style with Unser finishing a distant third. Thereafter Mears finished every other race he started in 1984.

He was on the pole at Milwaukee and had the race in his pocket before his engine started to give out. It finally blew up on the last lap although he still coasted home in second place. Three road races followed and Mears had a tough time. He ran well in each of the races, usually hanging in there among the top six but at Portland he had to stop to repair a broken tailwing and at the Meadowlands he spun and lost time in two incidents with other cars. He made it home in tenth place (3 pts) in both races. At the Cleveland airport race he finished fourth, driving to finish after spinning in qualifying and starting near the back of the field.

In the Michigan 500 Mears had trouble with a leaky "Pop-off" valve but hung in there all the way finishing third, barely four seconds behind the

battling Andretti-Sneva duo. At Road America he was fourth, lapped and on seven cylinders at the finish. For the Pocono 500 he qualified on the pole, breaking Andretti's string of five consecutive poles. He led much of the race in company with Sneva and Bobby Rahal and ten laps from the end it looked as if Mears was going to hold-off Rahal to win. Both of them were too conservative with their boost gauges in the final laps however, as their fuel warning lights began to flash. The result was that an on-form and aggressive Danny Sullivan charged by both of them to beat Mears home by 0.27 of a second with Rahal another half a second behind in third place.

Mears qualified second to Andretti at the Mid-Ohio road race and finally finished fifth after stalling in the pits on one occasion. The next race was on the tiny Sanair trioval in southern Quebec and it was there that Mears made a very uncharacteristic, overzealous mistake barely half an hour into the first practice session.

Looking hard to find a way around Rahal, he misjudged the rate of acceleration of Corrado Fabi's Lola. Mears' left-rear wheel clipped Fabi's right-front as he tried to slot across Fabi's nose. The Penske/March bounced over Fabi's nose, smacked back against the road surface and cannoned into the inside row of the guardrail – all this directly in front of the pits. The front of the car slammed underneath the guardrail and a retaining post came out of the ground so that the front of the car was torn open. Mears' feet were smashed badly in the accident and his pursuit of a fourth Indycar championship was suddenly stopped short.

Mears underwent a series of operations to his feet and spent five weeks in hospital before beginning a long rehabilitation programme. At press time Mears was saying all the repair work to his shattered feet had gone better than expected and he was quietly hoping to be able to begin driving again by the start of the '85 season.

Penske filled Mears' shoes for a series of three speedway races with out-of-work veteran Johnny Rutherford while Formula 2 Champion Mike Thackwell was down to drive the car in the last two "road races" of the season. In qualifying for the September 200-miler at MIS, Rutherford put the Pennzoil-backed Penske/March on the pole at an all-time qualifying speed record of 215.189 mph (33.459 secs for one lap of the high-banked, 2.0-mile superspeedway).

1983 champion Al Unser Sr continued as Mears' teammate in 1984. He had nothing like the season he enjoyed in '83 however, finishing neither as regularly nor as well. Nevertheless Unser did a workmanlike job and was very competitive toward the end of the year as the Penske team figured out how to get the most from their Marches. A very popular man with the Penske team, it appeared at the time of writing that Unser would stay with Penske Racing for another year, shouldering the winter test program of March and Penske chassis while Mears recovers.

SULLIVAN AND RAHAL

In addition to Andretti, Sneva and Mears, the other two leading contenders over the course of last year's Indycar championship were Danny Sullivan and Bobby Rahal. Sullivan was very successful in his first full year of Indycar racing after doing three races – Indianapolis included- in 1982. Rahal was in his third season as an Indycar driver, continuing with motel chain owner Jim Trueman's keenly-organised, March-equipped team.

After driving F1 for Ken Tyrrell in 1983, Sullivan jumped to Indycars when Tyrrell was unable to find a turbo engine. In America, Doug Shierson offered Sullivan an all-new car and a strong sponsor in Domino's Pizza, a booming nationwide home delivery chain. Johnny Rutherford was supposed to partner Sullivan in the 500-mile races but Shierson's new car proved to be a no-hoper and at Indianapolis, as Sullivan and Rutherford struggled to get up to qualifying speed, Shierson scrapped the project and bought a Lola T800 for Sullivan.

Rutherford finally qualified for the race in a third Gilmore/Foyt car and later drove for Foyt in the Michigan and Pocono 500s before filling-in for

Mears in three late-season speedway races. Sullivan qualified comfortably on the second weekend at Indianapolis and despite crashing the hurriedly-built Lola in the race he went on to have his most successful racing season to date.

Sullivan won his first Indycar race at Cleveland in July after Rahal's car broke a gearbox and he then came through to win in fine style at Pocono and Sanair. He also finished second to Andretti at the Meadowlands and battled with the man at Road America before a fuel fire stopped him. At Mid-Ohio Sullivan was third behind Andretti and Rahal, all of which put him well in the hunt in the points table. He was notably uncompetitive in both races at MIS but with three races to go on tracks that should have suited his style, Sullivan had a realistic chance at winning the championship.

Bobby Rahal's chances were considerably more remote after a year in which he was fast on all types of tracks but rarely enjoyed a troublefree race. At the time of writing Rahal had not won a race in 1984. With March engineer Adrian Newhy joining the Truesports team in place of American engineer Lee Dykstra, Rahal's Marches quickly developed into the most unique and effective 84Cs in the garage. The cars were lightened (one by as no less than 140 lbs!) and there were all manner of special pieces and set-ups to suit different tracks.

After a slow start to the season Rahal and the Truesports team became a major factor at every race. Rahal led at Portland before stopping because of a transmission failure. He chased hard after Andretti at the Meadowlands before spinning and stalling. At Cleveland he passed Andretti and seemed to have him beaten before the Lola dropped out. Sullivan tried to catch Rahal near the end of the race but was also rebuffed only to watch Rahal pull off with eight laps to go because of another transmission failure.

At the Michigan 500 Rahal was in fine form and was leading strongly from Andretti, Sneva and Mears only to be eliminated through no fault of his own in a multiple crash with less than eighty miles to go. Then, at long last, came a series of good finishes. Rahal was second to Andretti at Road America. In the Pocono 500 he was a real contender and finished a very close third. At Mid-Ohio he outpaced everyone else to finish second to Andretti once again.

Rahal was on the pole at Sanair, led much of the race and finished second to Sullivan after blistering his tyres. Two weeks later at Michigan he was in the middle of the race for the lead all the way and finished a closing fifth, within range of winner Andretti after mid-race tyre troubles. Not an outrageously successful year but one that was very satisfying to Rahal from the point of view of across-the-board competitiveness.

JUNIORS

The only other man to win a race at the time of writing beyond those already described was Al Unser Jr. In his second season of Indycar racing young Unser scored his first Indycar victory, at the Portland, Oregon road race in June. The rest of his season was almost entirely devoid of results however, although he was often fast and was a real contender at Indianapolis, and elsewhere, before hitting trouble.

Unser, 22, continued to drive for Albuquerque businessman Rick Galles who had nurtured the second generation driver through Super Vee and CanAm championships into Indycars in 1983. Equipped with Marches, the team were one of four who did most of March's winter testing and young Unser was quick in the early part of the season before the team seemed to lose their way in mid-summer. In early September crew chief Huey Absalom departed the team and at the end of the

Rick Mears gave Roger Penske victory at Indy but crashed in Quebec when in contention for the CART championship *(top)*.
Danny Sullivan, in his first full season of Indycar racing, won at Cleveland and was usually on the pace with his Shierson Lola T800.

month the disenchanted Unser signed with Roy Winkelmann's new Lotus Indycar team for 1985.

Another highly-rated second generation driver to make a real impression last year was Michael Andretti, 22 on October 5th. Mario's son completed his first full Indycar season last year. He was the Formula Atlantic champion in 1983 and also started three, end-of-season Indycar races. Driving for the well-equipped Kraco Stereos team, Michael quickly found his feet and last year he was often very competitive.

At Indianapolis the youngster qualified on the second row and finished fifth, despite a broken side-pod. In company with Roberto Guerrero, he was selected as the race's co-Rookie-of-the-Year. Michael also battled for the lead at Portland in June, and again at Sanair in September. At the time of writing young Andretti had collected a trio of third place results and was heading for a top six finish in the point table.

Team-mate Geoff Brabham, CanAm champion in 1981, had a tough time with the second Kraco March although he was often around at the finish. He was second at Long Beach and Portland and finished third at the Meadowlands. With three races to go Brabham was well-placed for an overall finish in the top ten.

ROOKIES

Former Formula 1 driver Roberto Guerrero moved into Indycars with a reorganised version of the 1983 Indy 500-winning (Tom Sneva at the wheel) Bignotti-Cotter team. Mo Nunn moved in as team manager of the Bignotti-Cotter operation and Guerrero had a good rookie season that was spoiled by poor reliability. Nevertheless he finished an excellent second at Indianapolis and was fifth in the Michigan 500, despite spinning in both races. With three races to go Guerrero was narrowly leading CART's rookie point standings ahead of Emerson Fittipaldi (!) Al Holbert and Jacques Villeneuve.

Sportscar veteran Holbert tried his hand at Indycars with Alex Morales's small, March-equipped team. Holbert was fourth at Indy in what was to be his best finish of the year. He was never much more than a mid-field runner and also had the worst finishing record of any regular starter.

CanAm champion in 1983, Villeneuve tackled his rookie year of Indycars with a well-financed, all-Canadian team. He missed half a dozen races after crashing heavily in practice at Indianapolis and again during practice for the Michigan 500. Villeneuve returned to action at Sanair in September and had his best race to date, running strongly with the leaders until tyre problems dropped him down the field.

Two-time World Champion Fittipaldi made a comeback to racing at the Miami GP IMSA race in February and started the Indycar season with a new team owned by a certain Pepe Romero. Fittipaldi finished fifth at Long Beach but the team had serious organisational problems and after qualifying near the back of the field at Indy and falling by the wayside after only 37 laps – the race's second retirement – the Brazilian departed the operation which soon folded. Fittipaldi later reappeared for two mid-season races in another privately-run March. He showed well in both races before being stopped by mechanical failure. In August, after a test session at Road America, Fittipaldi signed with oil man Pat Patrick's team for 1985, subsequently starting a number of end-of-season races as a stand-in for the injured Chip Ganassi.

ALSO-RANS

Like the Penske team, Patrick's operation quickly forsook their own cars early in the 1984 season to concentrate on running Marches. Veteran Gordon Johncock continued to lead the team, coming back from a big crash in the '83 Michigan 500 which broke both of his legs. At Indianapolis, Johncock crashed again however, breaking a bone in his left leg although doggedly returning to action at Milwaukee the following weekend. The rest of Johncock's year was littered however, with mechanical failures and more crashes. His best and only real result of the year was a tyre-troubled fourth in the Michigan 500.

Chip Ganassi was Johncock's team-mate for most of the year but he too suffered from terrible reliability as well as a rotten turn of luck. He was a distant second to Sullivan in the Cleveland airport race but had a big crash two weeks later in the Michigan 500. Ganassi lost control, crashing into Al Unser Jr and the inner guardrail before flipping down the backstretch. A severe concussion and broken hand put him out of action for three months and he was scheduled to return to work for Patrick at the season's last three races.

The Forsythe team, which had done so much with Teo Fabi in 1983, had a luckless '84 season. Fabi started the year with the team but his Formula 1 drive for Brabham was clearly what he preferred as he rapidly lost interest in Indycars. Following a couple of uninspired performances Fabi left the team in July and was replaced by Kevin Cogan. Cogan was very fast in the early laps of the Michigan 500 before handling troubles intervened and then he crashed while practising at Pocono, breaking both heels. For the last five races of the season Corrado Fabi stepped into the team's new Lola, hoping to emulate his brother's success of the previous year.

Another operation to have a frustrating time was the Provimi Veal-backed team which ran ex-Formula 1 man Derek Daly and Tony Bettenhausen in Marches. Organisational problems hamstrung the team through the first part of the year and then Bettenhausen was benched at mid-season after a series of poor showings. Daly was quick in most road races, finishing fourth at Portland and running well before mechanical failures at the Meadowlands and Mid-Ohio. He crashed heavily and horrifically at MIS in September however, smashing his left leg and also breaking his right leg and left hand.

Mexican Josele Garza often went well in the tightly-budgeted Machinists' Union March 84C while another quick runner on occasion was Scott Brayton, who tried a turbo Buick V6 at Indianapolis. Appearing only infrequently last season was A. J. Foyt who continued with a fleet of new Marches, also running old friend George Snider and fellow Texan Johnny Rutherford at Indianapolis. Now 49, Foyt was never a real factor in any of his four starts, although he did lead fourteen laps under the yellow flag at the Michigan 500.

Continuing to fight the tide of English-built March and Lola chassis was Dan Gurney who fielded a normally-aspirated, Pontiac-powered Eagle for a variety of drivers. Michael Chandler started the season in the car but after a great season-opening performance at Long Beach he crashed during practice at Indy and took a blow to the head which sidelined him for the rest of the year.

Kevin Cogan took over from Chandler after the miserable demise of Guy Ligier's abortive Indycar effort. Cogan drove in six races for Gurney before moving on to the more attractive Forsythe team. In turn, he was replaced by Super Vee champion Ed Pimm who completed the year in the Eagle which was underpowered and also lacked downforce in comparison to full-sidepodded, Cosworth-powered Lolas and Marches. Gurney will be back next year with Pimm at the wheel of a more conventional, Cosworth-powered, "tunnel-car" Eagle.

Cosworth's 2.65 litre, low-boost turbo DFX V8 continued to dominate in Indycar racing, winning all the 1984 races. The engine won its 100th Indycar race at Cleveland in July and powered at least ninety per cent of the field in all races. Buick and Chevrolet experimented with turbo V6 "stock blocks" (permitted 48 more cubic inches than a Cosworth) while Gurney and a few other die-hards continued to fly the fading, normally-aspirated "stock-block" flag.

THE SAFETY ISSUE

There were of course many leg injuries in Indycar races last year. Most of these came in big, wall-banging accidents on super-speedways. Among those to break legs, feet or ankles in 1984 were Rick Mears, Kevin Cogan, Gordon Johncock, Derek Daly, Jacques Villeneuve and Steve Krisiloff. Also injured in accidents were Mike Chandler,

David Hutson.

Robert Harmeyer.

Patrick Bedard and Chip Ganassi while Al Unser Jr, Pancho Carter, John Paul Jr and others enjoyed narrow escapes from wild tumbles.

In September, USAC (on behalf of the Indianapolis Motor Speedway) and CART made their own separate announcements on the same day of 'safety-oriented'' rule changes for 1985. In an attempt to reduce speeds on superspeedways the cars will be required to run with a two-inch gap between the base of the sidepods and the bottom plane of the chassis. This two-inch gap rule and USAC's 47 ins Hg manifold pressure ruling will be in effect not only at Indianapolis but also in the CART races at Michigan and Pocono. In all other CART races (short tracks and road courses), the organization's 1983 rules (48 ins Hg manifold pressure and one-inch gaps) will continue to apply.

USAC have also announced their intentions to adopt flat-bottomed cars in 1986 although this is still a matter of hot debate. Also under attack is the question of reduced engine power, particularly by Mario Andretti who insists that the cars need more power, as well as less downforce, in order to improve the safety situation on superspeedways. The one man who could legitimately lay claim to the title of "World's Most Accomplished Racing Driver", Andretti says the biggest "safety problem" faced by Indycar racing is that the cars can be driven around the Indianapolis and Michigan Speedways (clearly, on the record, the most dangerous tracks by far) flat-out.

"It is this absolute momentum thing that we have to get rid of," says Andretti. "We need to have enough power versus ground-effect so that we have to get off the throttle and drive the cars into the corners. We need more power, not less. That will make the cars more driveable. It will separate the drivers and it will give us a chance to react.

"If they don't listen to us drivers on this matter, if they don't begin to look at this situation in the real light of day, they are heading for a confrontation. A lot of good things have happened in Indycar racing in the past few years and because of that I don't want to force a confrontation but if the management at the Indianapolis Motor Speedway don't listen to us about this, that's what they are going to get."

Also required under CART's 1985 rules, and this is something Andretti heartily agrees with, is an extension to the front bulkheads in all cars. This extension must enclose the brake and clutch master cylinders (which may not be mounted on this additional bulkhead) and be located at least six inches ahead of the conventional forward face of the front bulkhead. Hopefully this structure will help protect drivers' feet. Meanwhile the fearsome implications of a big crash on a superspeedway in a powerful single-seater remain a harsh fact of an Indycar driver's life.

MANAGEMENT IN ABSENTIA

As competitive as CART's Indycar championship has become over the last couple of years, it is a very sobering thing to look around outside the world of Indycar racing at the rest of the single-seater formulae in North America. The plain facts are that after years of mismanagement of Sprint car/Dirt car racing by USAC and of Formula Atlantic/Formula 5000/CanAm racing by the SCCA, the training grounds for Indycar racing are in desperately bad shape. Once he is out of Formula Ford, a driver has nowhere to go other than the wildly-expensive Super Vee category.

Sprint car racing, while continuing to provide great Saturday night entertainment throughout the mid and southwestern parts of the country, is no longer part of the road to Indianapolis, or any place else for that matter. USAC's already-weakened series has faded rapidly in the past five years and has been clearly surpassed by the

A.J. Foyt, pictured in his March made only fleeting appearances during the CART season (top).
The Group 44 Jaguar team helped make IMSA racing the 'one bright spot' in the world of American road racing.

225

nationwide World of Outlaws series. Even so, top WoO drivers like Steve Kinser and Sammy Swindell have found themselves stuck, with nowhere to go. Some of them like Swindell, have begun to move into stock car racing, aiming for NASCAR's Grand National circuit because the techniques, demographics, audiences and cultural background, if you will, of stock car racing are much more akin to sprint car driver than the world of contemporary Indycar racing.

The most successful category at nurturing American talent in the last ten years has been Formula Atlantic. It was out of that fine category that we saw drivers develop like Gilles Villeneuve, Bobby Rahal, Kevin Cogan, Danny Sullivan, Geoff Brabham, not to mention Keke Rosberg and others. Never properly embraced by the SCCA for fear it would damage their insipidly-directed CanAm series, Formula Atlantic survived in Canada and now lives on, ever closer to death's door, as a regional series on the west coast thanks to some hardy devotees.

Super Vee remains as the only training ground in America although its ranks have been strafed by a lack of cost controls. A budget for a championship-chasing season now tops the quarter of a million dollar mark! For the past four years the Super Vee series has run primarily as a support race at Indycar events. The '84 series quickly boiled down to a three-way battle between Dutchman Arie Luyendyk, New Jerseyite Chip Robinson and Canadian Ludwig Heimrath Jr. By mid-season the championship had focused into a head-to-head confrontation between Luyendyk and Robinson with Luyendyk establishing himself as a clear favourite at the time of writing.

CanAm racing, which had dwindled in recent years from a premier category to that of a training ground, debilated even further in 1984. Despite the well-intentioned but past-the-point-of-no-return attempts to salvage the series by Dallas GP promoter Don Walker, the series reached new lows with twelve and thirteen-car fields and only one or two drivers of any reputation. Irishman Michael Roe dominated the proceedings with Walker's own VDS-Chevrolet and Scotsman Jim Crawford played the bridesmaid role in Bob Fernley's March-based car.

The SCCA's strongest card was the TransAm series which has enjoyed something of a renaissance over the past three years. As in 1983, the TransAm boasted big fields and affordable, competitive racing. Although its "market penetration" was small, the TransAm continued to be an artistic success and last year Ford managed to turn the tables on Chevrolet for once, with Ford Capri-mounted drivers Tom Gloy and Greg Pickett battling for the championship.

Other drivers to impress in the TransAm included Willy T. Ribbs, who joined Pickett as a team-mate after departing the 93-championship winning Budweiser DeAtley/Chevrolet team following disputes with the team owner and other drivers. Ribbs got the last laugh as the Ford he stepped into enabled him to win races and contend for the championship while the DeAtley team had a frustratingly uncompetitive time with their brand new Corvettes. '83 TransAm champion David Hobbs never figured in the '84 title chase with the ungainly Corvettes nor did highly-touted young team-mate Darin Brassfield.

MR. BISHOP'S DELIGHT

The one real bright spot in the world of American road racing continued to be John Bishop's International Motor Sports Association. IMSA has now thoroughly supplanted the SCCA as the premier road racing organising club in the USA and last year their flagship category began to come good after a few years of struggling to get off the ground. One of the reasons behind the expanded strength of GTP racing (literally, GT Prototype) was the arrival on the scene of British chassis constructors. March, Lola and Argo built a variety of cars to challenge the traditional fleet of customer Porsches while Bob Tullius' Group 44 Jaguar team continued to compete in most races with their XJR5 which also made the trip to Le Mans in 1984.

The 17-race Camel GT championship went however, to Floridian Randy Lanier who fielded a pair of Blue Thunder Racing March 84G-Chevrolets in most races for himself and Bill Whittington. The latter is widely-experienced in IMSA and Indycar racing and was the co-winner at Le Mans in 1979 with brother Don and German Klaus Ludwig. After a slow start to the season Lanier and Whittington began to sweep the boards, handily defeating the Porsche 962 combination of Derek Bell and '83 champion Al Holbert. Other contenders included South African Sarel van Der Merwe who drove Porsche and Chevy-engined Marches as well as a 962. John Paul Jr was also a major factor in many late-season races with another Chevy-powered March while veteran Brian Redman was part of Tullius' two-car Jaguar effort.

IMSA's real strength lay in their other categories for small capacity or strictly-limited "stock car"-type sedans. At most IMSA meetings there were four support races to back-up the Camel GT race, providing a full day's racing for the spectator as well as some neatly-packaged trade and aftermarket sponsorships.

REAL AMERICAN HEROES

Meanwhile the meat and potatoes of American motor racing continued to be about short-track stock car racing in all its many shapes and guises. NASCAR is the leading stock car racing organising body in the USA and in the past few years Bill France's group has moved deliberately to expand their already untouchable position.

With flagship sponsor Winston cigarettes providing the backing, NASCAR has started to expand and improve their series for Late Model Sportsmen and Modified stock cars. More and more tracks have signed-on as NASCAR affiliates during this well-planned push and the Daytona Beach-based organisation now has considerable control of the grass roots of stock car racing. While the "farm system" in road racing and Indycar racing has become almost non-existent, stock car racing has become an exceedingly broad-based, strong business, unlike any other form of motor sport anywhere in the world.

At the top of the tree, the Winston Cup Grand National championship is closer, more competitive than ever. The American media covers the 30-race series more extensively and widely than any other type of racing and in the minds of most followers of automobile racing in the USA, the Grand National championship is the one that counts.

For much of the season the 1984 Grand National championship witnessed a five-way battle for the title although as the season wound down the points battle focussed itself on three men – Terry Labonte, Harry Gant and Dale Earnhardt – with the never-say-die Darrell Waltrip as an outsider. '83 champion Bobby Allison never really figured as a championship threat in 1984 although he did win a couple of races and was ranked sixth in the championship at the time of writing, with five races still to go.

Labonte, 27, was in his sixth year of Grand National racing and with former Petty Enterprises crew chief Dale Inman running his team, he was a persistent finisher and leading frontrunner all year long. After 25 races Labonte had won two and finished second or third in ten more races. Driving Billy Hagan's Chevrolets, the young Texan was quiet and unassuming, in sharp contrast to talkative triple champion Waltrip and argumentative '83 champion Allison.

A high point of the '84 Grand National season came at Daytona in the mid-summer heat of July when Richard Petty celebrated his 46th birthday by winning the Firecracker 400. It marked his 200th Grand National victory, coming after 26 years and 944 races!

NASCAR continued to be the 'meat and potatoes' of American motor racing.

Robert Harmeyer.

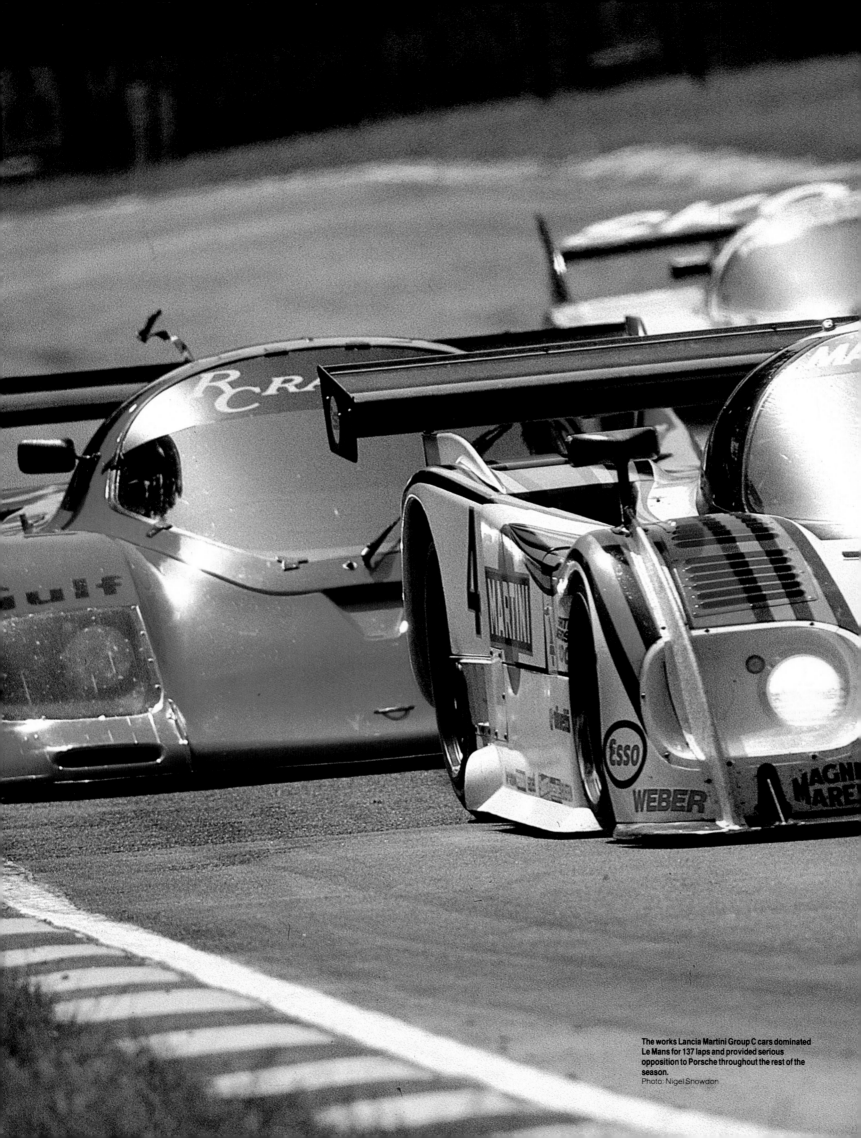

The works Lancia Martini Group C cars dominated
Le Mans for 137 laps and provided serious
opposition to Porsche throughout the rest of the
season.
Photo: Nigel Snowdon

Status quo

1984 FIA World Endurance Championships
by Quentin Spurring, Editor, *Autosport*

World Championship sports car racing marked time in 1984. Three factors – uncertainty about future regulation changes, the dominance of Porsche, and the perennial shortage of finance for private teams – served to restrict car development, and not even Porsche and Lancia, the series stalwarts, came up with anything significantly different. Porsche fielded a full factory Group C team for the third season and it continued to dominate both Lancia and the privateer Porsche pack, so that the status quo was very firmly maintained.

FISA's inconsistency over the regulations was the most damaging of the restrictive factors. Since the start of the Group C formula in 1982, FISA's preoccupation had rightly been to achieve a sports car racing category with identical vehicle rules on either side of the Atlantic. In both 1982 and 1983, the American body IMSA, having rejected the fuel economy aspect of the new FIA class, had established a successful national series in which the cars were raced to a set of rules regulating engine sizes and types against vehicle weights. There seemed little prospect of rationalisation between FIA Group C and IMSA GTP and, when FISA announced a 15% reduction in the Group C fuel allowance for 1984, the rift deepened further.

Just before the season began, FISA announced a so-called compromise solution to the problem which stunned the WEC teams. Essentially, FISA intended to turn 1984 into an interim season, pending an almost wholesale sell-out to IMSA in 1985.

For 1984 – the season only six weeks away when FISA dropped its bombshell – the imminent 15% reduction in fuel would be scrapped, and the series opened to cars complying with all the IMSA classes, namely GTP, GTX (similar to the old Group 5), GTO and GTU (like the old Group 4). For this season only, said FISA, the WEC cars would be raced to the 1982-83 fuel consumption rules, but in 1985 the entire fuel allocation concept would go. It would be replaced by set of rules similar to the IMSA engine/weight format, under which all cars would have to comply with the IMSA footwell regulations. These stipulate that the driver's feet must be located behind a line drawn between the front wheel centres. Neither the Porsche 956 nor the Lancia LC2 would comply. Not only that, but their engines would also be oversize . . .

Porsche's reaction to this extraordinary decision was to withdraw its factory team and drivers from Le Mans. This move was not made lightly, for the company had fielded a works team in the 24 Hours every year since 1951 (except 1975). The motive was to protest in the strongest terms available against FISA's disregard of the stability rules.

In anticipation of the 15% reduction in fuel allowance, Porsche had invested a large sum of money in new engine management research with Bosch over the winter. The company not only saw this investment largely going to waste, but also contemplated massive cost – to both the works team and the customers – as both chassis and engines became ineligible. In addition, Porsche engineers were concerned about the financial and safety aspects of getting into an inevitable power race with Lancia.

FISA at first declined to react to Porsche's initiative, save by setting up a working group to study methods of controlling power. This group made little progress and, in July (after Le Mans), FISA did finally make another U-turn. The governing body announced that the 15% fuel reduction would be implemented in 1985. So would the revised chassis rules, but cars built before 1 January, 1985, would remain eligible to compete in the WEC until 1987. This compromise was accepted by all the teams.

Other changes to the rules in 1984 included the abolition of the nonsensical limitation on the number of fuel stops, which allowed team managers greatly increased flexibility in their race strategy. The minimum weight of the Group C1 cars was increased by 50 kilos to 850, so as to bring them more closely into line with the American GTP entries which were expected, but which did

not materialise (except at Le Mans). And the Junior class was renamed 'Group C2', and the cars permitted to have full, 100-litre capacity fuel tankage, so as to increase their competitiveness in overall terms.

The WEC races numbered eleven, and the European series was scrapped so that there were just the two championships, for Makes and Drivers. The races at Monza, Silverstone, Le Mans, Nürburgring, Mosport, Spa-Francorchamps, Fuji and Kyalami counted towards both series; those at Brands Hatch, Imola and Sandown towards the Drivers title only. In terms of numbers if not variety, support was strong. As always, Le Mans was the most popular race, with 53 starters, but Silverstone had 43 and the Nürburgring 42, Monza and Fuji 34 each. On the other hand, Mosport and Kyalami were both very poorly supported.

Porsche wrapped up the Makes title yet again

very early in the game, with Alba-Giannini achieving a second successive Group C2 trophy, with BMW claiming the Group B title. The Drivers championship chase went down to the wire between factory Porsche drivers Stefan Bellof and Jochen Mass, and was resolved at the new Sandown fixture in Australia after this review went to press.

As to the C1 cars themselves, the works Porsche team conducted relatively little development, but the privateers became very active in this area. Most of them conducted their own aerodynamic research, the GTI and Joest teams producing the most effective packages. The GTI team even constructed its own aluminium honeycomb chassis. Joest and Fitzpatrick came to reject the inflexibility of the pre-programmed Bosch Motronic 2.6-litre customer engine, and on occasion raced with mechanical-control 3-litre power plants. The Porsche teams' season, in fact, began

Henri Pescarolo took a popular win at Le Mans with Klaus Ludwig in the absence of the works Porsche team.
Photo: Keith Sutton.

factory cars failed even to win the races missed by the works Porsches, and the privateer teams of Joest (the great prize of Le Mans), GTI (Brands Hatch) and Brun (Imola) scored valuable victories during the season.

However, all the other races fell to Rothmans Porsche, the factory team. Having been beaten both in 1982 and in 1983, the works cars won every race they seriously contested, a fact which was of no benefit for the image of the World Endurance Championships. Under the more stringent fuel consumption rules next year, other marques should be more competitive, and Jaguar, Aston Martin, Toyota, Nissan and Mazda are all seeking to increase their involvement with the series. If they can challenge Porsche, along with Lancia, then the WEC is set to continue its expansion after a season of little progress caused, to a large extent, by FISA's vacillation over the rules. First, however, the governing body must realise that World series sports car racing may never attain its former status if it continues to lack the fundamental qualities of effective administration and strong promotion.

THE TEAMS

The factory Porsche team, directed by Peter Falk and managed by Norbert Singer, raced for a third season in the colours of the Rothmans cigarette company and, as always, was supported by constant tyre development by Dunlop. Because its resources were stretched over the winter by the demand for 'customer' cars (both for the WEC and for the American IMSA series), the Weissach R&D division did not build new chassis for its 1984 racing effort, but relied on its 1983 cars. Before the start of the new season, there was also very little technical development, except the work with Bosch on the engine management systems, and testing of an ingenious, electronically controlled, double-clutch transmission. Nevertheless, the works team maintained its performance advantage, with clearly more powerful engines than those available to the privateers, and a subtly different aerodynamic package.

Up to and including Fuji, the team's record was as impressive as ever. It secured a victory in every event contested except Imola, where it was race-testing the new transmission. From the first 14 race starts, there was just this one retirement, which says it all.

Yet the team's domination was not quite total, even though the race results suggest otherwise. There were only four pole positions, and only three one-two finishes. The victories at Silverstone and the Nürburgring were fortuitously achieved, and few race days were easy for the Rothmans Porsche drivers.

The team retained its 1983 line-up of regulars, namely Jacky Ickx (the 1983-84 World Champion), Jochen Mass, Stefan Bellof and Derek Bell. As well as these, John Watson and Vern Schuppan raced works cars on occasion, and Alan Jones was due to do so at Sandown when this was written. All season in the two regular cars – pit-signalled 'BEL' and 'MIX' – Bellof was a little quicker than Bell, and Mass a mite faster than Ickx. But generally the BEL pairing was superior, and it was Bellof who secured all the team's pole positions. It was also his outstanding ability to drive spectacular first-stint charges that put this car into very strong positions.

The young German drove one of these from the pole at Monza, and here the BEL car led from start to finish. To finish second, 24 seconds behind, the MIX entry had first to overcome the Canon Porsche private car and also one of the works Lancias, both of which were then delayed. After the race, the winning car was judged to be one kilo under the weight limit, and disqualified. Porsche protested the Monza weighbridge and, three months later, the CSAI reinstated the car.

At Silverstone, where Lancia claimed the pole, both the works Porsches were dominated by the Canon car until the private entry was again

delayed. The lead passed to MIX and it stayed that way, for BEL was delayed first when, in an uncharacteristic mistake, a mechanic failed to secure a wheel, and second when the oil cooler ruptured, costing Bell some 20 minutes. It could finish only tenth.

Missing Le Mans, it was two months before the works team raced again, and Bellof landed another pole as the Group C cars raced on the new Nürburgring for the first time. The 30th ADAC 1000 Kms may have shifted to a new and less demanding venue, but it certainly produced the best of the 1984 races in which the factory team was involved, and the closest finish.

Bellof led away as usual but, his car understeering, he was soon passed by private cars from the Brun and Canon teams, with Mass fourth. BEL resumed the lead during the first pit stops and MIX gained third place, only to pick up a puncture. Then BEL lost the lead again, to the Canon car.

At two hours, it rained heavily. The Canon team misjudged its tyre stop, the Brun car crashed out, and the lead passed back to the BEL works car. In the rain, however, Bellof lost out to the better-tyred Skoal Bandit Porsche of Boutsen/Hobbs and, in trying to keep up, he went off the road, damaging a wheel. Later, he had to make another stop when a vane from a wheel centre broke off, puncturing the tyre.

Fortunately for the works team, the JFR 956B had a long stop when the engine was slow in restarting, and then the track dried with about 80 laps still to go. Gradually, BEL reeled in the Bandit and, after both teams had made late fuel stops, Bellof repassed Hobbs to take the lead only five laps from the finish. The winning margin was extended to 15 seconds when Hobbs collided with a backmarker while trying to respond. Although it made no formal protest, the JFR team accused Rothmans Porsche of exceeding Bellof's maximum individual driver time (two-thirds distance). MIX, meanwhile, lost out because of two extra-long front pad changes and a misfire, and finished seventh.

From that breathless Nürburgring race, the works team flew to Canada for the poorly supported Mosport 1000, which the MIX crew won as it liked. Bellof again took the pole and built up a lead of 40 seconds, but this was wiped out under a yellow. Then the alternator drive sheared, and thereafter the car struggled through a succession of new batteries. Both drivers strove hard to eliminate this disadvantage, and the car survived a flash fire in the pits, but in the end it was no fewer than 32 laps behind its untroubled sister entry, albeit in fourth place.

Back in Europe for the popular Spa 1000 fixture, the works team was again outqualified (this time by Boutsen's Bandit) but Bellof drove an exceptional first stint again to establish BEL way out in front. Yet the Anglo-German pairing was fortunate to win this race, for four reasons. First, a spinning backmarker came perilously close to take Bellof off the road. Second, Bellof, short on stopping power, had to use the escape road at the chicane, and then rejoined the circuit illegally; normally there is a time penalty for this offence, but in Belgium he was merely fined. Third, when the car suffered a detached front brake caliper towards the end, it happened near the pits and Stefan lost little time. And fourth, for most of the race the MIX entry nursed an intermittent misfire.

When the Boutsen/Hobbs privateer lost its engine though, it secured second place only 58 seconds behind, and the team's second one-two of the series. Rothmans Porsche ran a third car here, for Watson/Schuppan, but all day it struggled with an alternator failure and finished sixth, five laps down.

For the works team, Imola was a non-event. Ickx/Watson tried the new trick gearbox in a solo entry, but two of the twin-clutch units broke during practice, and the third on the very first lap of the race.

Far and away the team's most powerful performance came at Fuji, where Porsche are always anxious to dominate in front of the massive crowd of impressionable Japanese sports car

with a worrying series of engine failures – 16 at the first two races! – which was halted in the end by adjustments to the ignition systems.

Porsche sold four B-specification cars for the WEC, featuring lighter chassis and bodywork and improved steering geometry, but no more were made because of the proposed chassis rule changes. These also led the Fitzpatrick team to race an IMSA-legal type 962 Porsche as a Group C entry. Fitzpatrick also tried to find a performance advantage by using a tyre supplier other than the dominant Dunlop, and this team and Kremer were responsible for bringing Goodyear, Yokohama and Bridgestone into the WEC Porsche business. Avon and BF Goodrich were also actively and successfully involved in the series.

Lancia carried out a lot of car development (including a new 3-litre, Weber-Marelli managed engine) but the cars remained unreliable, with just seven finishes from the first 14 starts. The Italian

enthusiasts. No other car was in the same class and Bellof, from pole again, quickly defined a big lead. MIX was again the less reliable and had an unscheduled stop with a badly chunked rear tyre. Mass then lost half a lap under the yellow and the car was also black-flagged for a stop-and-go penalty because he had inadvertently passed a backmarker during this period. Still giving aggressive chase during the final stints, Ickx then had to back off with a braking problem, leaving Watson to make good the first sports car championship victory of his career, by 32 seconds.

As in 1983, the works drivers dominated the Drivers championship, although Bellof and Mass, who were left to fight out the title in the final round at Sandown, increased their points scores by racing for private teams when Rothmans Porsche missed the Drivers-only rounds at Brands Hatch and Imola. Neither Ickx nor Bell did this, and the latter dropped out of the series (missing Fuji) because he wished to concentrate on the more lucrative IMSA championship.

The leading private Porsche teams were those of Joest, GTI/Canon, Brun, Fitzpatrick and Kremer. All had their moments during the season, but as things turned out the factory team again made such a meal of the WEC series that precious few crumbs were left for the privateers. It did leave, however, the prestige result of the sports car racing year – victory at Le Mans – and this fell to Joest Racing.

Reinhold Joest's German based team, sponsored by New Man fashion and Pierlant sparkling wine, ran singleton entries except at Le Mans, and its regular drivers were Henri Pescarolo, Stefan Johansson and Klaus Ludwig. Jochen Mass drove for the Joest team in the German national series, which included Brands Hatch and Imola.

Managed by Domingos Piedade, the team ran its older type 956 car at Monza (engine failure) and Silverstone (second) before getting its new type 956B just before the 24 Hours. It was qualified fourth behind two works Lancias and its older sister car, driven by Johansson, and then it set off for an extraordinary debut race.

Pescarolo was in the pits only 11 minutes after the start, and two stops to correct fluctuating fuel pressure cost five minutes. The New Man 956B rejoined dead last. Three and a half hours later, Ludwig was back in the pits for 14 minutes while his mechanics repaired the left front suspension.

But you never say die at Le Mans. With consistently fast driving, Henri and Klaus took fullest advantage of the inevitable mechanical delays to cars ahead, so that they were able to move into the top ten during the sixth hour, and into the top five just before half-distance. At ten minutes past seven on the Sunday morning, they went into the lead . . .

There were two more scares, both during the 17th hour of the great marathon, and both further suspension breakages costing a total of 21 minutes at rest. But by this time the main challengers had all fallen by the wayside. It was a famous victory, Pescarolo's fourth at Le Mans, Ludwig's second. The only cloud on the team's horizon was that Johansson had got on some oil, and crashed the sister car.

The Joest 956B was as competitive thereafter, but less spectacularly successful, and more than once the team struggled with the aerodynamics. At the Nürburgring, Ayrton Senna accepted an invitation to drive it, but an inoperable clutch dropped it to an eighth place finish. It ran Brands and Imola in the livery of Blaupunkt hi-fi (the team's German series sponsor), finishing respectively second and third for Mass and Pescarolo. The Joest team also fielded the older 956 at Spa (ignition failure) and Fuji (fourth), but again the team failed to mount an effective Drivers title challenge for the veteran Pescarolo, showing signs of running short of finance towards the end of the year.

Like Joest, Richard Lloyd's GTI Engineering team evolved its own aerodynamics, designing a neat, one-piece underbody for its type 956, similar to the factory cars' but with the cooling air extractor vents on either side of the gearbox instead of actually within the engine bay. From the start of

the season, the Jonathan Palmer/Jan Lammers combination was very competitive, never once failing to qualify outside the top six, and leading five races.

The Keith Greene managed, Canon sponsored GTI car split the works Porsches at Monza until delayed by a broken suspension top rocker, finishing fifth. At Silverstone – where it was based – it dominated its home race in outstanding fashion and was leading by a minute when an oil line split, recovering to finish fifth once more. Le Mans was a race the team will wish to forget, for all manner of things went wrong, and its team manager was hurt in an incident in the overcrowded pit lane, but fourth place resulted from another competitive run at the Nürburgring, and then came Brands Hatch.

Here the car was equipped with an extra aerofoil mounted on twin stalks above the nosecone, and a new, twin-tier rear Ubezio wing. This package eliminated the understeer so characteristic of the

Porsche 956 on certain types of circuit, and set a fashion copied by almost all other teams in subsequent races (with the very noticeable exception of the factory team). Palmer and Lammers utterly dominated the race, leading from pole position for the entire distance, troubled only in the last hour by a recalcitrant gearbox.

Missing Mosport, the British team spent the time readying a brand new car for Spa. Lloyd, believing that a performance advantage was to be had if he could field a more rigid chassis, commissioned Nigel Stroud to design an all-new monocoque made from honeycomb (rather than sheet) aluminium, and featuring pushrod front suspension. Testing went well, but in Belgium the new car was the first retirement due to a big crack in the gearbox bellhousing: it seemed that the extra chassis rigidity was putting unaccustomed loads through the standard components. There were more chassis problems at Imola and Fuji, both

Of the regular front runners, though, the team with the most mechanical misfortune was John Fitzpatrick Racing, which ran two cars sponsored by Skoal Bandit, the US produced smokeless tobacco. The usual drivers were Thierry Boutsen, David Hobbs, Rupert Keegan and Guy Edwards, the last-named replaced by Franz Konrad when he retired mid-season. JFR was the first team to get a new 956B but was off the top pace during the first part of the season, with its Yokohama tyre deal. The situation was improved by a switch to Goodyears at the Nürburgring and, indeed, Boutsen/Hobbs came tantalisingly close to winning there, for the American supplier's were the best wet-weather tyres. The Skoal Bandit 956B finished eighth at Silverstone and a fighting third (after leading) at Le Mans, but was otherwise afflicted too many times by mechanical failures. Broken engines at Spa and Imola caused the team to scratch from Fuji.

With an eye on the next season's chassis rules, JFR cancelled its order for another 956B and instead ordered a 1985-legal type 962 IMSA GTP car, which was fitted with the Group C flat-bottom area and 2.6 Motronics engine. Keegan/Edwards switched to this new car at Le Mans, but the long wheelbase chassis handled less well, and again there were mechanical failures. Third place was achieved at Brands Hatch but more disappointment followed at Mosport and Spa, and then the team decided to revert to its 956 spare car for the remaining races.

Keegan/Edwards had also driven the first two races with this car (finishing third at Silverstone) before the 962 arrived, and the 956 was leased to Team Australia for Le Mans, where it was crashed by Perkins. Later on, it finished sixth at Brands and second at Imola. JFR's other 1983 chassis was used as a third race entry at the first two events, without success, and then sold to Paul Vestey, and run at Le Mans by Charles Ivey Racing.

The Kremer Porsche Racing team, as in 1983, ran a fully professional operation hampered by lack of funds, taking its sponsorship on a race-to-race basis. The Kremer brothers, Erwin and Manfred, also switched to Goodyear mid-series (from Dunlop). The German team's new 956B arrived at Le Mans and, sponsored by Kenwood hi-fi, was raced very competitively by Vern Schuppan/Alan Jones/Jean-Pierre Jarier, leading the race but then dropping to sixth place after a collision and engine problems. Its only other race was the Nürburgring, where it was fifth in the hands of Manfred Winkelhock/Marc Surer.

The Kremers' older 956 was more often in use and retired only at Mosport (gearbox), securing fourth place finishes at Brands and Imola. It would have finished higher than fifth at Fuji had Winkelhock/Mike Thackwell not been driving a second and more off the pace, on Bridgestone tyres. As well as the drivers mentioned, the Kremer team used a dozen others during the season, an indication of its financial position.

The other regulars were the type 956 cars owned by Dieter Schornstein and Reinhold Obermaier, the latter's car co-owned by Jurgen Laessig. Schornstein's Team Aachen entry was run for him by the Joest team again and sponsored by New Man, while that of Obermaier Racing was backed

times with the front suspension pickup points. However, the team would have won at Imola had its Motronic engine computer behaved itself; instead, it had to stage a fuel economy run in the last two hours, finishing second after leading most of the distance. A collapsed noseframe and a seized wheelbearing delayed it badly at Fuji.

Another team to secure a WEC victory in 1984 was the emerging, Swiss owned Brun Motorsport whose drivers included three quick Germans: Harald Grohs, Hans-Joachim Stuck (clashing touring car commitments to BMW permitting) and, when not working for the factory team, Stefan Bellof. Sponsorship came from a variety of companies including Swatch, Schiesser underwear and Jaegermeister beer, in whose livery Imola was magnificently won.

Stuck collided with a backmarker before half-way, causing a delay in the pits while the noseframe was repaired, but he and Bellof charged very hard

indeed to make up the lost time, and were in a strong position to overhaul the Canon 956 when it ran short of fuel. The Brun 956B assumed the lead six laps from the end and won by half a minute. The car was always a contender after an inauspicious debut at Silverstone (delayed by a lost wheel). It was a strong fourth at Le Mans and then led at the Nürburgring before being crashed in the rain by Stuck. It was also fifth at Brands Hatch and third at Spa.

As well as hiring a 956 from the rival Kremer team on two occasions, Walter Brun's team also fielded a 956 for the rapid Oscar Larrauri/ Massimo Sigala, sponsored by Gaggia coffee machines. The season began with Larrauri's heavy accident at Monza, when attempting a rash overtaking manoeuvre on Boutsen's JFR Porsche, but after that these drivers were increasingly competitive if unlucky with reliability, the best result – fourth – coming at Spa.

by the rival fashion company, Boss. Both lacked development and they were raced with circumspection, always going for the finish. The New Man car achieved this every time out, but the Boss 956 started its season with three non-finishes, two of these caused by detached road wheels.

US entrant Preston Henn entered a 956 and a 962 for Le Mans, and the former finished a game second in the hands of Jean Rondeau/John Paul Jnr. It was then sold to the Japanese 'From A' team and entered for Fuji, but went out with broken transmission. Another of the Japanese entered Porsches was the Team Trust/Iseki entry, expertly prepared by Nova Engineering, and it was very impressive. Driven by Vern Schuppan/Hans-Joachim Stuck, it came third behind the factory cars for the second successive year.

Taken as a group, the privately entered Porsches enjoyed an unexpectedly better season than the factory Lancia team, which was again a disappointment, its cars always quick and usually unreliable. Like Porsche, the Martini aperitif sponsored Lancia team under Cesare Fiorio decided to retain its 1983 chassis, although the cars were extensively modified over the winter. The suspension – originally designed around Pirelli radial tyres – was reworked to suit Dunlop crossplies, the aerodynamics were improved, and the Hewland gearboxes were replaced by purpose-made, Abarth-cased units. In addition, the electronic computer control for the 2.6-litre, V8 engines was so effectively improved by Weber-Marelli that the team commissioned new engines of 3-litre capacity from Ferrari. As before, Maranello supplied the power units and they were race-prepared by Lancia engineers in Turin.

Early in the season, Lancia Martini lost its longtime chief engineer, Gianni Tonti, to the Alfa Romeo Formula 1 effort, and he was replaced by the head designer of Abarth, Pierpaolo Messori. He affected more aerodynamic improvements and was on hand at Le Mans, where the 3-litre 308C engines were raced for the first time.

Lancia Martini's regular drivers were Bob Wollek (the 1983 European Endurance Champion in a Porsche), Riccardo Patrese, Paolo Barilla, Sandro Nannini and Mauro Baldi. The team normally ran two cars and also supported the Jolly Club Lancia which was similar in specification, sponsored by the Totip lottery, and raced without success in the first three races by Beppe Gabbiani and Pierluigi Martini.

The cars were very powerful – with upwards of 700bhp for qualifying, perhaps 650bhp for the races, the V8 engine was more than a match for the Porsche flat-six – and the team secured two pole positions, Patrese at Silverstone, Wollek at Le Mans. But on race day such a wide variety of things went wrong that weak preparation is the only conclusion, and there are obvious doubts about Lancia's ability to mount a serious challenge in both Endurance racing and rallying.

Patrese/Wollek, the team's best combination, were put out at Monza by a fire in the pits caused by an oil leak, and at Silverstone by an obscure turbocharger oiling fault, while the Barilla/Baldi pairing finished both races with a sick engine, albeit third and fourth respectively. Like the winning Porsche, their car was found to be underweight at Monza (five kilos) and disqualified, but it was reinstated because of doubts about the weighbridge.

Without a doubt, the high point of the team's season came at Le Mans, where its performance was wildly unexpected. Eleven hours after the start, no less, the works Lancias had established an apparently solid one-two, holding all the private Porsches at bay. But the leading Barilla/Baldi LC2 (co-driven here by Hans Heyer) then stripped its fifth gear pinion. It later retrieved a position in the top six, but was eventually retired when the engine failed. The Wollek/Nannini Lancia took up the running and was still leading over five hours later when it, too, lost fifth gear. The repair cost almost an hour and eighth place was the outcome.

Yet Le Mans did much for the team's morale. The drivers expected a win later in the season, but yet more mechanical failures and some accidents

intervened. Nannini/Barilla finished third at the Nürburgring, putting Barilla into contention for the Drivers championship, but he then spoiled his chances with heavy accidents at Brands and Imola, and in any case the team achieved no other high placings. The confidence turned to disillusionment, and Lancia missed Mosport, Spa and Fuji from its schedule. In November (after this review was written), Fiorio tried to salvage something from 1984 by sending two cars to Kyalami, a race supported by no other competitive Group C1 teams after the South African organisers had been unable to offer any realistic financial incentive.

The Porsches and Lancias composed virtually the entire C1 class at all the WEC races with the exceptions of Le Mans and Mount Fuji. There was a good deal of welcome variety in the 24 Hours, notably from Jaguar and Aston Martin, two famous names big in sports car racing history.

The Jaguar contenders were the Lee Dykstra designed, XJR-5 GTP cars from Bob Tullius's Group 44 Racing team, which were very competitive in the IMSA series and which had official factory support in terms of engine development. The immaculately prepared cars were powered by 6-litre race versions of the familiar stockblock V12, normal induction units with only two valves per cylinder but with Lucas Micos engine management. With Brian Redman and John Watson among the drivers, the white Jaguars had enormous patriotic support from the 20,000 British fans at Le Mans, but they were a little underpowered (600bhp) and slightly overweight, and relied on impressive fuel economy to get a result. In the event, this was enough only to allow one of the cars to lead for a lap during the first round of pit stops, but nevertheless the cars showed very well. Both ran in the top six for many hours. One was crashed by Tony Adamowicz when a tyre went down, and the other finally broke its gearbox, but it was an interesting Le Mans debut, auguring well for the future.

GROUP C2

The renamed Junior category resulted in another title for Alba Giannini, but it was far more competitive than in 1983.

Using a carbon fibre chassis designed and built by Giorgio Stirano, and 1.8-litre, four-valve, four-cylinder engines built by Carlo Facetti, the whole operation funded by Facetti's regular co-driver Martino Finotto, the 'works' Alba team failed to win the class. Its 1983 car, in the hands of a private team and sponsored by Duracell batteries, scored the maxima for the marque at Silverstone and when it finished third overall at Mosport. The Alba Giannini reaction to considerably increased competition was decreased reliability, and it was as well that two cars were raced. Neither would the Italian cars have claimed the C2 championship had some of the other teams conducted a full season.

Jim Busby's American based GTP team, sponsored by BF Goodrich and using that company's street construction radial tyres, did only four WEC races but won the class twice, including the prestige result of the season at Le Mans where one of its Mazda rotary engined Lola T-616 cars finished tenth overall. The Lolas had a hundred horsepower less than their rivals but were extremely reliable.

Gordon Spice's British team ran its neat, 3.3 Cosworth powered Tiga GC-84, backed by Waspeze, on five occasions and won the class four times, but these wins included the Drivers-only events at Brands and Imola.

And no one supposed that the straight-six BMW type M88 engine could live on the C2 fuel allocation until Fuji, when Kiyoshi Fukui's Auto-Beaurex team won with ease with its 3.5-litre Lotec.

Other cars to show well in C2 included the latest Gebhardts (with BMW and Cosworth engines) and, until crashed mid-season in a non-championship race, the revived Ecurie Ecosse team's Ecosse-Cosworth. The Kelmar team ran a Cosworth engine in an Alba chassis and went well on occasion, as did the works Mazda team with its latest type 727C rotary powered device. Other competitors included another Tiga with a loaned Ford RS1700T research engine, various Rondeaus and cars from ADA, March and Sthemo.

GROUP B

Very few IMSA GTO cars were raced to take advantage of FISA's rule change, and none at all from IMSA GTU, so the only production-based racers were BMW M1s and various Porsches, 924s, 928s and 930s. The BMWs exploited their big power advantage and dominated the class, with Jens Winther's Team Castrol entry a prominent category winner.

In 1985, the new four-wheel drive Porsche and Ferrari GTO are supposed to be entering the arena, but doubts are beginning to emerge about their ability to qualify in view of the growing numbers of Group C Prototype cars available.

After a shakedown at Silverstone, two Nimrod Aston Martin C1 cars were entered in France, officially backed by the factory this time and with sponsorship from Bovis construction. A Tickford developed, turbo version of the 5.3-litre stockblock V8 was not ready in time, but the modified and lightened car of Ray Mallock/Drake Olson outqualified the Jaguars. But the seventh hour of the race brought disaster.

At this point, both Nimrods were badly damaged in a tragic accident at the Mulsanne kink. John Sheldon, for some reason still unproved, lost his car and crashed very heavily at over 200mph, the debris killing a marshal and injuring another. Olson, following, swerved to avoid the wreckage and also crashed. He was unhurt, but poor Sheldon received serious injuries, including hands burned by the fire that resulted.

Also at Le Mans, the latest version of the French-built WM was briefly but memorably impressive. In one of the cars, powered by a race version of the Peugeot V6 engine with two turbochargers, team owner Roger Dorchy struck a blow for France by leading in the first few laps, before being delayed by contact with the barrier.

A few more C1 cars – a Sehcar-Porsche, a Rondeau-Cosworth, Chuck Graemiger's promising but under-financed carbon fibre Cheetah Aston Martin – appeared sporadically, but nothing very different appeared in the WEC until the Fuji race. The Japanese national Group C series is quite strong and has healthy manufacturer involvement. Particularly interesting were the latest Dome chassis, powered by turbo Toyota four-cylinder engines, which were a match for the private Porsches for much of the distance. Nissan also ran quasi-works four-cylinder turbos in a March 84G and in Japanese constructed LM-04 chassis, while Mazda raced for the first time with a turbo version of the type 13B rotary engine, producing as much power as the Toyota and Nissan (550bhp) from only 1.3 litres.

The European Touring Car Championship race series took on a new lease of life in 1983, and the trend continued for 1984.

The twelve race locations were the same, all being to the specified 500km or 3.5hr with the exception of the daddy of them all, *Les 24 heures de Francorchamps*, which really ought to have its own scale of bonus points for the drivers' *and the* makers' championships.

The Nürburgring 6-hour is no more; on the new circuit, 500km was quite enough for most people. The Mugello fixture was snatched from early summer and placed in late autumn; it had not taken place when these words were written. There will be a new autumn race for 1985, at Estoril, Portugal, and a Swedish round is expected to bring the number of races up to fourteen – making the ETC series even more international.

The main features of 1984? Frequent close finishes: Only a few races in mid-season gave the premature suggestion of a Jaguar steamroller. Peace in our time: As predicted in the last edition of *Autocourse* a Technical Delegate attended every race, with the result that inter-team disputes virtually disappeared. (Marcel Servais of Belgium went about his business of meeting makers, entrants, and organisers with just the right combination of tact and firmness.) The third main feature was that more and more people were giving ETC the attention it deserves as one of the best championships on any calendar.

Rain played a big part in the spring and autumn races, especially Monza and Vallelunga in April, and Silverstone and Zolder in September. It certainly worked against the favourites, the TWR/Motul Jaguars, which lost three of those four.

Monza set the scene. The duel between Helmut Kelleners/Gianfranco Brancatelli (BMW Italia Eggenberger CSi) and Tom Walkinshaw/Hans Heyer began there on 1st April and did not end until 23rd September. Kelleners and Walkinshaw had new regular partners. Brancatelli, fast and fiery, proved a good partner for the reliable, persistent Kelleners who was champion in 1980, 1981 and 1982. Hans Heyer, also German *and a* former champion (in 1974, for Ford), was Tom Walkinshaw's new driving mate in the official Jaguar team, now boosted to three cars. At Monza, Walkinshaw waltzed up the wet pit lane as he started his final stint. The Jaguars normally need two pit stops to the BMW's one, and there was some catching up to do. It was here, in 1983, that Walkinshaw's first real chance for the championship had been lost; the team boss was all the more determined to gain the psychological advantage this time. One by one, he picked off the BMWs, finally putting Kelleners in his spray with twelve laps to go. Those who braved the elements were rewarded with a fine race, and the particular memory of a big black box which had chased the Jaguars and then overtaken them one by one before losing time at a pit stop. Thomas Lindström's turbocharged Volvo did not yet have water

injection, but it impressed everyone. Embarrassed might be a better word. It's all very well seeing Rovers and Volvos running together (it might be argued); likewise BMWs and Jaguars – but to see cars from such diverse market groups competing against one another, seemed incredible. To others, perhaps; but not to the charming Swedes. Someone said, almost mockingly: "They'll be winning soon". He was right.

Early in the season, however, the Volvo teams from Sweden and Belgium were still having problems. Ulf Granberg's 240 Turbo did lead for some time at Vallelunga – a week after Monza and just as wet. Tyre choice and timing played a big part here. The Belgian Juma Bastos BMW of Alain Cudini and Dany Snobeck survived another car landing on top of it to win from rain specialist Hans-Joachim Stuck, now driving as regular co-driver with defending champion Dieter Quester in the works/Schnitzer BMW team. Walkinshaw and Heyer took a useful 3rd place. On the whole it was to be a year of crashes for the "Belgian" BMWs.

That brilliant and very balanced personality, Win Percy, had become a valued regular worker-driver for the 1984 Jaguar team. At Donington, where it was actually dry and sunny, he and Chuck Nicholson scored a neat Jaguar home victory. Then it was a trek to Sicily, where Martin Brundle and Enzo Calderari won from their team-mates. It was the first Jaguar 1-2-3 demonstration for years – and in unusually difficult circumstances, because of blinding swarms of flies. Brundle was to have driven in other races not clashing with Grands Prix, but his accident in America prevented this. David Sears, son of former UK saloon car champion Jack Sears, proved a worthy team member for the rest of the season – sometimes having to sit out a race if someone else was put in to drive 'his' car, but collecting two 2nds and a 3rd with Calderari none the less.

The Czechoslavak and Austrian rounds put Jaguar in command, but the tables were turned at the *Neue Nürburgring* in July, when the ever-present Kelleners and Brancatelli gave BMW their second win of the year while Jaguar were in all kinds of trouble. (It was here that Heyer did not score his marks for coming 5th, because he had driven one of the other Jaguars before it broke down; thus Walkinshaw retained his championship lead, ten points ahead of his co-driver.) Volvos led again here, but so did the Austin Rover Group's big V8-engined saloons; indeed, it looked as if the poor form shown by the Rovers would be a thing of the past; but 2nd place here proved a flash in the pan. Somehow, they never got going in the way they did on their few 1983 appearances. Their speed early in some races was very impressive; only at the Nürburgring was it sustained.

If there was one race that everyone wanted to win it was the 24-hour one at Spa Francorchamps. The faster Volvos stayed at home for more development work. Jaguar led, then BMW, then

Rover. Only two Jaguars were taking part, and one crashed in the wet of the evening. The other, driven by strong men Walkinshaw, Heyer, and Percy ran steadily through a foggy night, a damp morning and dry sunny day to score a victory of the type traditional to Coventry – while a myriad BMWs made mistakes.

Confidence at Silverstone was shattered by an almost freak thunderstorm halfway through the TT. The Jaguars were leading – 1, 2, 3 – all having refuelled once, and the BMWs were about to make their single pit stops, when the heavens opened. Lady Luck took over (with the help of a bit of pit-politics and the pace-car driver); but everyone praised Brancatelli's final fling, and Walkinshaw's brave effort with a misfiring (and ultimately broken) engine. The bad luck and the good were shared fairly evenly; as in 1983, it was a Silverstone cliffhanger – and it kept BMW in the title chase. So, it was unfortunate that at Zolder Brancatelli should damage the Eggenberger BMW's rear end; Walkinshaw paced himself to a simple finish thereafter. Up front, the Schnitzer BMW was working hard, just as it had done all season – but it was to be Volvo's day. Ulf Granberg and Robert Kvist drove hard through rain and shine to score Volvo's first victory in a major international event since the 1960s, when the PV544 and 122S compacts were winning tough rallies like the Safari and the Acropolis. Even now, those who 'typecast' the Volvo as 'green welly' or just plain boring can hardly believe the evidence of 1984. If the doubters are still in doubt by 1985, it will be surprising – for Zolder 1984 was just a beginning for the company that is fighting to remove its Staid Swede image. Volvo *will* have more cars and more wins.

As for Tom Walkinshaw, he kept the championship lead he had had since Monza, and became the first British ETC champion since the 1960s – just twenty-one years after another Jaguar driver, Peter Nöcker, had won the inaugural series. Hans Heyer, truly the co-winner, claimed the runner-up slot for Jaguar. Third place downwards would not be known until after Mugello.

In the manufacturers' table, Jaguar led the over-2.5-litre class comfortably from BMW, Volvo, Rover, and Toyota (whose Supra did well at Spa and is sure to make dramatic strides in 1985).

The middle ground is Alfa territory, and once again the GTV6 was virtually unopposed; in the 1 to 1.6-litre category, VW made a late attack on Toyota.

If more of the organisers would do more to publicise or even give names to their events, and in certain cases get down to printing decent race programmes; *if* there could be fewer clashes with other major events; then more spectators might attend these excellent competitions which certainly contain more than enough excitement to make TV features (of the 'edited highlights' type) worthwhile for those who stay at home at weekends. These things take time. Group A's time must be pretty soon, if not NOW.

Jaguar and Tom Walkinshaw came out on top in the European Touring Car Championship, Walkinshaw becoming the first British ETC Champion since 1963.

Jaguar wins.. but it's no walkover

European Championships for 'Group A' touring cars and drivers
by Andrew Whyte

Volkswagen supplied Johnny Dumfries with an engine which was reliable and powerful enough to give the young British driver the edge over his rivals in the British Formula 3 Championship.
Photos: Nigel Snowdon

Whatever happened in 1984, 1983's Formula 3 season in Britain was going to be a hard act to follow, after the titanic battles between Formula 1 graduates Ayrton Senna and Martin Brundle. In truth, 1984 wasn't too bad, but sadly it became the year of What Might Have Been.

What would have happened had Johnny Dumfries had to face Ross Cheever's fullblown challenge *throughout* the season, instead of over just the latter half?

As it was, the talented Earl of Dumfries confirmed what was suspected at the end of 1983: Put him in the right team and he could be champion. Entrant Dave Price had been around Formula 3 more years than most. With BP support in 1982 Brundle had shown promise with him, but Martin's lack of experience at the time denied its fulfillment. In 1983 Calvin Fish had been all but swallowed by the pressures on him, winning only at Oulton Park.

This year there seemed a whole new sense of purpose within Dave Price Racing, as if its very *raison d'être* had been examined minutely. Like a boxer anxious to get an important fight won early, Dumfries came out fists flailing when the Marlboro British series got underway in March. By late May he had successfully demoralised most of his rivals with three straight wins, one second and another hat-trick. Interspersed was victory in the European series, and for some time the young Scot seemed on target to become the only driver to win both titles.

There were interludes in the British series when other lights shone, however. At Silverstone's GP circuit on March 11 Briton Andrew Gilbert-Scott, winner of the 1983 Formula Ford Festival, took a splendid victory on the road in a Murray Taylor Ralt VW backed by Racing for Britain. But he had anticipated the start and was penalised, even though his indiscretion had reaped no benefit. Ever troubled by financial worries, Andrew thereafter appeared to let the money side of things affect his driving. When he ran out of funds he left Taylor, transferring to occasional races in Richard Trott's Ralt-Toyota.

I am sure we have seen only a glimpse of Gilbert-Scott's true ability in 1984; hopefully a ride in the right car and team next year will see him reap his just reward.

The first man officially to topple Dumfries was another Brit, bluff Yorkshireman Russell Spence. When Dave Scott initially decided *not* to go Formula 3 again after all, having purchased a new Ralt VW at the start of the year, Dave Scott Snr allowed Glenn Waters to run the car with another driver, Spence securing enough backing for a season. He came to Formula 3 with strong FF2000 showings behind him and a reputation as a bit of a hellraiser off the track. He soon got down to work and after an impressive but spin-spoiled performance which lost *him* that Silverstone GP circuit win, he took victory at Zolder when the series made its first of three very successful forays abroad. Thereafter he was usually on the pace, only Thruxton seeming his bogey circuit. He took two more wins, at Donington in July and Oulton Park in August and established himself as a firm runner-up in the title chase. Perhaps that was why

the latter half of his season went slightly awry. With three races to go he needed victory and the point for fastest lap in each if he was to beat Dumfries, who needed only one sixth. A series of incidents with other runners reached a head at Brands Hatch in September when he was excluded from third place after a brush with Spaniard Carlos Abella.

Spence shows occasional inconsistency and possibly tackles his racing less seriously than he might. If he can avoid such lapses he could well take the crown in 1985.

After Martin Brundle's success with Eddie Jordan Racing in 1983, it seemed Canadian Allen Berg had a strong foundation on which to base his 1984 campaign, but he started badly by spinning in his pursuit of Dumfries at Silverstone. He blotted his copybook again at Thruxton with the sort of move at the chicane one would expect of a Formula 3 novice rather than a man of his experience but then he settled down to emerge again as a quick, fearless competitor. Frankly, though, a Berg victory would have been a surprise rather than an expectation, although he showed the potential to break out of the bridesmaid role at Silverstone on rainy Bank Holiday Monday in May. He had Dumfries well sewn up only to lose out as his wet weather tyres overheated as the track dried and Mario Hytten and Tony Trevor swept ahead in their slick-shod Ralts. Like Berg, Hytten proved able if not startling, that Silverstone win being the high point of his year with Murray Taylor Racing. He and Berg were also hampered by financial worries and initially Mario was overshadowed by team-mates Gilbert-Scott and New Zealander Paul Radisich. The latter took pole at Thruxton early on, in his first Formula 3 season, only to be punted off in the race by Berg. Like Briton Trevor, he showed promise on other occasions, but both fell by the wayside when their funds became exhausted.

Carlos Abella was disappointing, stepping in to a drive with Dick Bennetts and West Surrey Racing after Roberto Moreno accepted a Formula 2 Ralt drive at the last minute. With one of the best teams in the business, Carlos couldn't quite muster that last ounce of pace his previous Formula 3 showings suggested he possessed. Team-mate Gary Evans had a learning year but showed promise by leading at Oulton in August, while ex-F2 runner Dave Scott *did* return to the formula late in the season and showed his old form, although one wonders just what the future holds for this former shooting star.

Ultimately, the man who emerged to challenge Dumfries most strongly was American Cheever, 20 year-old brother of Alfa Romeo Grand Prix team member Eddie. Initially, Ross van Valour Racing's 1983 Ralt RT3 and showed sufficient panache to merit close attention. From the moment he got a 1984 specification model in July, he was right on the pace. Young, fast and eminently quotable, he established a reputation as a hard man on the track and for a spell was the man most likely to be at the centre of any contretemps. Then he went abroad for the series' second continental sojourn at Spa-Francorchamps, and won. He followed that with wins at Zandvoort (where he pushed Spence

What might have been…

by David Tremayne, Editor, *Motoring News*

into passing the pace car!) and Brands Hatch, the latter a copybook performance.

The natural talent is there and Cheever has already signed for a second year with John Upton's blossoming team. If you fancy the odd bet, you might care to have a flutter on the crew-cut Yank winning the 1985 title . . .

Also in Britain, the newly introduced Class B category for cars over one year old and not modified beyond strict allowances, helped bury the 1983 spectre of small grids, and provided some of the best racing. Keith Fine emerged champion in his ex-Murray Taylor Racing Ralt VW run by MAS Promotions, his driving showing an impressive blend of speed and smoothness right from the start. He got ragged on occasion but should prove a front runner in a Class A chassis in 1985. Others to show well in B included former Formula Atlantic star Richard Morgan, Mike Blanchet, hard trying Steve Bradley who as usual struggled on a half

shoestring budget, his sparring partner Carlton Tingling and Gray Hedley in his ex-Trott Ralt.

Where Volkswagen only got one look-in against the dominant Toyotas last year, the engine tables turned in Germany's favour in 1984, and by the end of the year even hardened Toyota users would grudgingly admit the VW single cammer had a slight advantage. In Europe, the VW served Dumfries and John Nielsen well while the Toyota was again subdued, and Novamotor's Alfa Romeo was its usual successful self, taking Ivan Capelli and Gerhard Berger to top championship slots.

In the chassis stakes it was, of course, Ralt virtually all the way in Britain, but in Europe Enzo Coloni ran Martinis for Capelli with marked success, keeping Mr Tauranac's runners up to par. John Robinson's Magnum 843 led British races in the hands of talented Dutchman Cor Euser, proving more competitive than ever, but when the money ran out the team switched to winning in the

less prestigious Swedish championship. Anson Cars metamorphosed into Anson International midway through the year, but was unable to capture the form that nearly took 1982 Marlboro champion Tommy Byrne to victory in the European opener at Donington in the SA4C.

1985 will see flat bottoms *de rigeur* in F3, which should throw a few variables back into the melting pot. Ralt will have a revised RT3, Magnum has already unveiled its sleek 853, Barron Racing in Holland has tested its boxy F31 and Anson has a new contender on the stocks. But perhaps the most eagerly awaited newcomer is Adrian Reynard's carbon fibre challenger.

On the tyre front Avon, of course, had another successful year as supplier of the Marlboro series' control rubber, while in Europe Michelin and Yokohama slogged it out on pretty much equal terms. Dunlop put in a brief, spectacularly unsuccessful appearance, but hopefully will return

Johnny Dumfries set the Formula 3 standards at home and abroad with his Team BP Ralt-VW.
Photo: Nigel Snowdon

Ross Cheever became a front-runner when Valor Racing bought the American driver a 1984-specification Ralt *(above).*

with better fortune.

If winter promise is fulfilled, Formula 3 in 1985 should be stronger than for some time, with good grids and a variety of competitive machinery. With luck the demise of ground effect should close fields during races and provide better entertainment for the spectators. With the death of the European series it is to be hoped more continental runners are persuaded to race in Britain.

What Formula 3 really must do, though, is get its act finely honed, in terms of organisation and presentation. For example the practice of holding five races on consecutive weekends has to be revised. For the past few years Formula 3 has been in a comfortable position, having usurped the now defunct European Formula 2 championship, but that position could now be in jeopardy. As this is written the signs are that Formula 3000 will succeed where Formula 2 failed recently, because the powers that be *want* it to succeed. It is thus likely to usurp Formula 3's growing role as the Grand Prix nursery. Elsewhere, Formula Turbo Ford is being mooted as a thinly disguised rival to Formula 3 on the domestic front.

For the past few years there has been precious little exposure for Formula 3 outside the specialist press. What is now required is a carefully

coordinated boost from the right quarters if it isn't to be muscled back on to the third rung of the recognised motor racing ladder.

IN MEMORIAM: EUROPEAN F3

The European Formula 3 Championship is dead. Official. That was the news in July, when Formula 3000 was first officially given the green light.

To some, that announcement came almost as a blessed relief, for the series has been dogged with ill-feeling and controversy this year.

Things started well enough, with an enthralling three-way battle at Donington between Johnny Dumfries, Tommy Byrne and erratic American Davy Jones and developed with John Nielsen and Ivan Capelli joining the battle for supremacy along with Austrian Gerhard Berger. Then poor Nielsen was sidelined after an horrific accident at Monaco; one of the better aspects was the success of his recovery, as he won at Nogaro on his return in September.

What wasn't good was the controversy that blew up at Monza in late June, where Capelli won in front of his home crowd in Enzo Coloni's Martini. The speed of his MK42 had raised a few eyebrows

in practice at Silverstone for the previous round, and after the race Capelli's car was protested. Subsequent investigation revealed an elaborate device to bypass the mandatory restrictor in the airbox, boosting engine power. It seemed an open and shut case and that the Italian would be penalised beyond losing his nine points for 'victory' but as the season wore on it became increasingly obvious that nothing was being done. As paddock gossip centred on allegations the matter had been covered up, rumours circulated to the effect that the offending airbox had vanished, with suggestions it found a resting place at the bottom of Lake Como . . .

The effect of the incident was to breed animosity and acrimony which was further inflamed when VW Motorsport protested Capelli's second place car at Nogaro in September only for it to be found to comply fully with the regulations. Sadly, the politics overshadowed the racing and gave Capelli's title victory, cemented when the final round at Croix-en-Ternois was cancelled because of alleged problems with access roads, a hollow ring. Again, it became a matter of What Might Have Been, had Nielsen, who dominated Nogaro, been racing all season in his VW Motorsport Ralt . . .

Ivan Capelli won at Monaco but his victory at Monza was to cloud the final European Championship with controversy *(above left)*.
Russell Spence established himself as a firm runner-up in the championship with the Glenn Waters Ralt-VW *(left)*.
Allen Berg: able, if not startling *(above)*.
Ross Cheever: young, fast, eminently quotable. A good bet for 1985 *(above right)*.

The eighteenth year of the European Formula 2 Championship was one in which one man and one machine reached new peaks but, in total contrast, one in which the Formula as a whole plummeted to a depth from which it is destined never to recover. The man who broke or equalled every record in the book was the new Champion, Mike Thackwell. The car in which he achieved his success was the Ralt-Honda RH6/84. But beyond their achievements which, from 11 races, read 7 wins, 9 fastest laps and 6 pole positions, there was little cheer and by the halfway stage of the season it was apparent that this would necessarily be the final year of Formula 2.

It would be totally wrong to presume that any domination by one driver, car, engine or tyres contributed anything to the Formula's demise. Such performances are to be admired and targeted, as has always happened in the history of any sport. There was nothing wrong with the regulations either. It was, quite simply, a matter of getting stale.

Much of Formula 2's attraction over recent years was that it had somehow remained detached from the real world where commercialism ruled. It became a nomadic circus visiting outposts to satisfy the enthusiasts' idealism. This was the year when reality caught up very quickly. An internal promise of an updated image never saw the light of day. An ill-timed withdrawal by one previously staunch manufacturer started the rot. A commercial take-over was successfully, but badly fought off. In hindsight it would have been better to have lost that battle.

But what has happened cannot be reversed and the future looks bright. Formula 3000 has been conceived over the period of a year and although there are bound to be hiccups on the way it appears to have the makings of a category where the drivers will be the deciding factor between winners and losers but with enough scope for the manufacturers to be keen; above all though it has been designed to be commercially attractive. All the right ingre-

dients are there to make it the Formula for Success. That it will work is almost certain. That it *must* work is imperative.

There was plenty of warning that the season would be a whitewash affair for Ron Tauranac's Ralt-Honda team – they had, after all, won the final six races of the previous season. But although the results had been clear cut, there was an over-riding optimism among the opposition – none of whom were privileged to use the V6 Honda engine – that with some sound engineering application and perhaps a gamble or two there was a good chance that a BMW-powered car could take a seventh champion title in 11 years despite the withdrawal of all factory support.

But in defending his championship title Tauranac was given only one condition to his exclusive deal from Honda: Win. Having learned a considerable amount about honeycomb chassis from his first generation model used in the previous two years, Tauranac built a new monocoque to much the same dimensions but which produced a stiffer and altogether more refined chassis. Honda's Formula 1 relationship with Williams Grand Prix Engineering produced a better engine installation and opened the door to their wind tunnel. In the space of three sessions, a new aerodynamic package was produced for the car and this was the key to what was to be their superiority.

The use of the Williams facilities was barely concealed, the truck carrying a number of wings with the Grand Prix team's sponsors' logos still on them at the early races. Straight out of the box the car was instantly superior, not only to its predecessor, but to the secret weapons which the opposition had developed during the off-season. It was all too easy to point the finger at the Honda engine and state that as the sole reason for the differential in performance. That the engine is, and probably always was, more powerful, wasn't really doubted. But allied to the new chassis and aerodynamic package, the drivers were able to use that extra horsepower in a way that the limitations

of the previous packages had precluded. Such was the advance in the chassis package that it would certainly have been a winner with a BMW engine installed.

But even if there had been no real advantage in the car or engine there is no doubt that the Ralt team's number one driver Mike Thackwell would have wiped the board with whatever he sat in. On the first day of the Silverstone meeting he started the fifth year of his F2 career and reached his 23rd birthday. In fact it was only to be his second full season in the formula, Grand Prix drives, injuries and lack of money having interrupted all the previous attempts. But he came as the team leader and as a personality. As a driver he emerged from the shadows as a perceptive and totally confident performer with the dedicated support of what was undeniably a very strong *team*.

Brazilian Roberto Moreno was a late choice as the team's second driver. Outwardly a more forceful individual than Thackwell, Moreno seized this opportunity to revive his career and, under orders, he was supposed to have won the opening race at Silverstone. But Thackwell made a show of it and Moreno spun at the final corner. At the second race Moreno got his present as the two cars again dominated the race to finish nose to tail.

With the formalities out of the way, Thackwell then took control, winning at Thruxton, Vallelunga, Mugello and Pau without a fight. Nobody, not even Moreno, ever looked like getting anywhere near him. The second Hockenheim saw the Ralts defeated for the first time – but both Moreno and Thackwell were leading when their troubles struck. To make up for it Thackwell won the seventh round of the series at Misano by a whole lap and thereby clinched the Championship in a style which was wholly representative of his season – utter domination. His seventh win came at Enna a week later. His first mistake, if it can be called a mistake, came at Donington when he spun away a solid lead by being the first driver to hit a sumpful

The year of what might have been...

by Ian Phillips, Formula 2 Correspondent, *Autosport*

of BMW oil lying unmarked on the racing line. Inevitably Moreno was there to pick up the spoils for the team.

Ralt won their championship using the wonderfully consistent range of tyres marketed to all who wanted them by Michelin. As if proof were needed to rubber stamp their authority, they switched to the Japanese Bridgestones for the final two races. The winning margin was reduced but the result was the same.

Thackwell gave all the credit to Ralt, Honda, Michelin and his team for his success. But his part should not be understated. The team weaved itself around him in one of those rare, classic motor racing relationships which brings out the best in everyone. And no matter how good a car is it has to be driven well to get the results to match. This was quite literally a combination which embraced the best of all elements. One of the criticisms of Formula 2 is that it never produced a World Champion. Ironically in its final year, it may well have done.

It was unfortunate for Moreno that he should have been teamed with Thackwell reaching this peak, for by any previous standards he had a good first year in the Formula. It has always been regarded as a two-year cycle. For a driver to score

two wins and take two pole positions and three second places in his first season, it would be considered a great performance. In the context of Thackwell and the Ralt-Honda team superiority, however, there was a touch of disappointment about Moreno's results which might well be unjustified. He is certainly one of the smoothest drivers around but on occasions when the car's neck wanted wringing or the circuit needed attacking, that counted against him. But on the whole, to have finished runner-up to his more experienced team-mate in his first go at the Championship was no mean feat.

In the second division, for those using the trusty 4-cylinder BMW engine, there was a battle royale

which took ultimate resolution of third place in the Championship to the final round.

The honour of being the top BMW driver home was all that anybody else had to fight for from the moment practice began at Silverstone. One of the two drivers to win a race in a non-Ralt-Honda was Frenchman Pascal Fabre who was in the right position at the right time in his PMC/BSA March-BMW when the Ralt machine faltered at the second Hockenheim. Having had an undistinguished F2 season with AGS in 1982, Fabre was something of a revelation but, having achieved this ultimate success, he was not seen again due to financial problems.

The driver most deserving of the BMW class honours was Christian Danner. After three years in the works March team, he struggled to find a place before the Bob Sparshott Automotive Cheylesmore team gambled on his experience to aid the drivers they were running for PMC. The new March 842 was an exotic F2 car and by the third race Danner started to show its potential which he continued to do with a new found consistency for the rest of the year. He was the only driver to regularly get a good look at the Ralts in a race. Danner was a much more relaxed driver this year and that appeared to be to his benefit. If there could be any criticism of his otherwise good season, it was that he appeared to lack a killer instinct on occasions.

Michel Ferté is obviously a man with a future. After a couple of exploratory outings for the Marlboro Martini team in 1983, the reigning French F3 Champion was given full Number One status this year. The Martini was not the most sophisticated of cars and Ferté's inexperience sometimes let them down in qualifying. But he was a most aggressive race driver which saw him nearly always in the hunt for BMW class honours.

After being the most consistent challenger to the Ralt drivers in the second half of 1983, much was expected of Philippe Streiff in the Gitanes-sponsored AGS. In the end, his results were disappointing although he suffered more than his fair share of engine failures during a year which robbed him of positions like second at Mugello and third at Silverstone. Initially he erred in his choice

of race tyres in an effort to try and get on terms with the Ralts and, as a ten-tenths driver, his periods of glory, like leading at Thruxton, were necessarily short-lived.

Mike Earle's Onyx outfit was again entrusted with the works March team, the benefit of which this year was reduced to solely an exclusive tyre deal with Bridgestone. Having used a similar arrangement with Michelin in 1982 to their advantage, it was a gamble worth taking now that Michelin were prepared to supply all and sundry. As it happened it took much longer than either party had envisaged to bring the combination to a truly competitive level. This they undoubtedly did by the final quarter of the season although the gain was never going to dissolve the gap to the Ralts. It was interesting, though, that when the Ralts switched to Bridgestone for Donington, Onyx's best driver Emanuele Pirro harried them all the way. Pirro was the youngest man in the series but, after showing a lot of initial promise, he went through a quiet period before coming back strongly in the final races to fulfil his potential. Pierre Petit was the most consistent of the three Onyx drivers and, having finally broken his point scoring duck mid-season, his uncomplicated approach saw him regularly featuring in the top six.

Probably the biggest disappointment of the year was Belgian Thierry Tassin who should have asserted himself as Number One in the team. Finally he had a proper budget and the best team but he tended to let difficulties get on top of him. On the occasions when he forgot everything and just raced as hard as he could, he was as quick as anybody, but that wasn't often enough. Nobody else ever really featured in the championship battle. One man who should have done was Alessandro Nannini, a driver quite capable of winning races but the Italian Minardi cars were dreadfully unreliable and, when they did run cleanly, they were considerably off the pace.

The sheer individual quality of the Thackwell/Ralt-Honda show really overshadowed the Formula's funeral march and, with that as a lasting memory, the future looks bright and healthy as we go into the new era of Formula 3000.

(Above from left to right)
"It's so easy, it's laughable." Mike Thackwell may have been helped by the outstanding qualities of the Ralt-Honda but the New Zealander's driving was such that he could have won the final European Formula 2 Championship in any car.

It was unfortunate that Roberto Moreno's excellent Formula 2 debut should have coincided with Thackwell reaching his peak. The Ralt-Honda team-mates started off the season on an uneasy note at Silverstone when they clashed while disputing the lead going into the final corner.

Philippe Streiff, a constant threat to the Ralts, did not manage his first Formula 2 victory with the AGS-BMW until the final round at Brands Hatch.

Michel Ferte showed style and promise, the Martini driver finishing third in the championship to win the 'BMW division'.

Use of the Williams wind tunnel facility helped Ron Tauranac produce an aerodynamic package to match the performance of the Honda V6.

1984 RESULTS a detailed summary of the season

Formula 2

MARLBORO/DAILY EXPRESS INTERNATIONAL TROPHY, Silverstone Grand Prix Circuit, Great Britain, April 1. European Formula 2 Championship, round 1. 47 laps of the 2·932-mile/4·719-km circuit, 137·80 miles/221·79 km.
1 Mike Thackwell, NZ (Ralt RH6/84-Honda), 1h 01m 04·11s, 135·39 mph/217·89 km/h.
2 Roberto Moreno, BR (Ralt RH6/84-Honda), 1h 01m 38·25s.
3 Michel Ferte, F (Martini 002-BMW), 46 laps.
4 Thierry Tassin, B (March 842-BMW), 46.
5 Pascal Fabre, F (March 842-BMW), 46.
6 Emanuele Pirro, I (March 842-BMW), 46.
7 Christian Danner, D (March 842-BMW), 46; **8** Didier Theys, B (Martini 001-BMW), 46; **9** Allesandro Nannini, I (Minardi M283-BMW), 45; **10** Stefano Livio, I (Merzario M84-BMW), 44; **11** Pierre Petit, F (March 842-BMW), 43.
Fastest lap: Thackwell, 1m 16·00s, 138·88 mph/223·51 km/h (record).
Retired: Guido Dacco, I (March SR832-BMW), 0 laps, accident; Pierre Chauvet, A (Minardi M283-BMW), 0, accident; Aldo Bertuzzi, I (Merzario M84-BMW), 1, accident damage; Lamberto Leoni, I (Minardi M284-BMW), 4, accident; Philippe Streiff, F (AGS JH19C-BMW), 12, engine; Tomas Kaiser, S (March 842-BMW), 18, engine; Beat Jans, CH (March 832H-BMW), 18, engine; Roberto Del Castello, I (Minardi M283-BMW), 29, accident; Jo Gartner, A (Spirit 201-BMW), 29, engine; Rolf Biland, CH (March 832H-BMW), 30, gearbox.
Championship points: 1 Thackwell, 9; **2** Moreno, 6; **3** Ferte, 4; **4** Tassin, 3; **5** Fabre, 2; **6** Pirro, 1.

JIM CLARK RENNEN, Hockenheim-Ring, German Federal Republic, April 8. European Formula 2 Championship, round 2. 30 laps of the 4·223-mile/6·797-km circuit, 126·69 miles/203·91 km.
1 Roberto Moreno, BR (Ralt RH6/84-Honda), 1h 01m 43·63s, 123·17 mph/198·22 km/h.
2 Mike Thackwell, NZ (Ralt RH6/84-Honda), 1h 01m 44·16s.
3 Michel Ferte, F (Martini 002-BMW), 1h 02m 16·49s.
4 Emanuele Pirro, I (March 842-BMW), 1h 02m 23·55s.
5 Philippe Streiff, F (AGS JH19C-BMW), 1h 02m 26·35s.
6 Christian Danner, D (March 842-BMW), 1h 02m 28·37s.
7 Thierry Tassin, B (March 842-BMW), 1h 02m 28·95s; **8** Roberto Del Castello, I (Minardi M283-BMW), 1h 03m 20·64s; **9** Tomas Kaiser, S (March 842-BMW), 1h 03m 46·53s; **10** Guido Dacco, I (March SR832-BMW), 29 laps; **11** Beat Jans, CH (March 832H-BMW), 29; **12** Aldo Bertuzzi, I (Merzario M84-BMW), 28; **13** Stefano Livio, I (Merzario M84-BMW), 27.
Fastest lap: Thackwell, 2m 01·21s, 125·45 mph/201·89 km/h (record).
Retired: Hans-Peter Pandur, D (AGS JH19-BMW), 6 laps, oil pressure; Pierre Chauvet, A (Minardi M283-BMW), 7, engine; Alessandro Nannini, I (Minardi M283-BMW), 11, puncture; Pascal Fabre, F (March 842-BMW), 12, misfire; Lamberto Leoni, I (Minardi M283-BMW), 13, accident; Rolf Biland, CH (March 832H-BMW), 13, accident; Jo Gartner, A (Spirit 201-BMW), 13, engine; Didier Theys, B (Martini 001-BMW), 15, engine; Pierre Petit, F (March 842-BMW), 20, spun.
Did not start: Manfred Anspaan, D (Maurer MM83-BMW), did not qualify; Walter Pedrazza, A (March 812-BMW), did not qualify.
Championship points: 1 Thackwell and Moreno, 15; **3** Ferte, 8; **4** Pirro, 4; **5** Tassin, 3; **6** Fabre and Streiff, 2.

P & O FERRIES/JOCHEN RINDT TROPHY, Thruxton Circuit, Great Britain, April 23. European Formula 2 Championship, round 3. 55 laps of the 2·356-mile/3·792-km circuit, 129·58 miles/208·54 km.
1 Mike Thackwell, NZ (Ralt RH6/84-Honda), 1h 03m 11·78s; 123·02 mph/197·98 km/h.
2 Christian Danner, D (March 842-BMW), 1h 03m 33·05s.
3 Philippe Streiff, F (AGS JH19C-BMW), 1h 04m 22·51s.
4 Emanuele Pirro, I (March 842-BMW), 54 laps.
5 Thierry Tassin, B (March 842-BMW), 54.
6 Didier Theys, B (Martini 002-BMW), 54.
7 Alessandro Nannini, I (Minardi M283-BMW), 53; **8** Guido Dacco, I (March SR832-BMW), 53; **9** Lamberto Leoni, I (Minardi M283-BMW), 53; **10** Roberto Del Castello, I (Minardi M283-BMW), 53; **11** Roland Minder, CH (March 832H-BMW), 51; **12** Stefano Livio, I (Merzario M84-BMW), 49.
Fastest lap: Thackwell, 1m 07·38s, 125·87 mph/202·57 km/h.
Retired: Tomas Kaiser, S (March 842-BMW), 24 laps, engine; Pascal Fabre, F (March 842-BMW), 33, engine; Michel Ferte, F (Martini 002-BMW), 33, transmission; Pierre Petit, F (March 842-BMW), 38, Sparkbox; Roberto Moreno, BR (Ralt RH6/84-Honda), 43, wheel bearing.
Championship points: 1 Thackwell, 24; **2** Moreno, 15; **3** Ferte, 8; **4** Pirro and Danner, 7; **6** Streiff, 6.

34 GRAN PREMIO ROMA, Autodromo di Vallelunga, Italy, May 13. European Formula 2 Championship, round 4. 65 laps of the 1·988-mile/3·200-km circuit, 129·22 miles/208·00 km.
1 Mike Thackwell, NZ (Ralt RH6/84-Honda), 1h 15m 59·41s, 102·05 mph/164·23 km/h.
2 Roberto Moreno, BR (Ralt RH6/84-Honda), 1h 16m 17·87s.
3 Christian Danner, D (March 842-BMW), 1h 16m 37·94s.
4 Michel Ferte, F (Martini 002-BMW), 64 laps.
5 Pascal Fabre, F (March 842-BMW), 64.
6 Didier Theys, B (Martini 002-BMW), 64.
7 Tomas Kaiser, S (March 842-BMW), 64; **8** Roland Minder, CH (March 832H-BMW), 63; **9** Roberto Del Castello, I (Minardi M283-BMW), 62; **10** Thierry Tassin, B (March 842-BMW), 62; **11** Guido Dacco, I (March SR832-BMW), 61.
Fastest lap: Thackwell, 1m 07·38s, 106·24 mph/170·98 km/h (record).
Retired: Stefano Livio, I (Merzario M84-BMW), 7 laps, spun off; Pierre Chauvet, A (Spirit 201-BMW), 16, oil leak; Pierre Petit, F (March 842-BMW), 44, accident; Philippe Streiff, F (AGS JH19C-BMW), 46, engine; Alessandro Nannini, I (Minardi M283-BMW), 53, engine; Emanuele Pirro, I (March 842-BMW), 59, engine.
Championship points: 1 Thackwell, 33; **2** Moreno, 21; **3** Ferte and Danner, 11; **5** Pirro, 7; **6** Streiff, 6.

BANCA TOSCANA TROPHY, Autodromo Internazionale del Mugello, Italy, May 19. European Formula 2 Championship, round 5. 42 laps of the 3·259-mile/5·245-km circuit, 136·88 miles/220·29 km.
1 Mike Thackwell, NZ (Ralt RH6/84-Honda), 1h 13m 38·89s, 111·52 mph/179·47 km/h.
2 Michel Ferte, F (Martini 002-BMW), 1h 14m 58·89s.
3 Christian Danner, D (March 842-BMW), 1h 15m 00·93s.
4 Emanuele Pirro, I (March 842-BMW), 1h 15m 15·35s.
5 Thierry Tassin, B (March 842-BMW), 41 laps.
6 Didier Theys, B (Martini 002-BMW), 41.
7 Pierre Petit, F (March 842-BMW), 41; **8** Guido Dacco, I (March SR832-BMW), 41; **9** Pascal Fabre, F (March 842-BMW), 40; **10** Roland Minder, CH (March 832H-BMW), 40.
Fastest lap: Thackwell, 1m 43·92s, 112·90 mph/181·69 km/h.
Retired: Roberto Moreno, BR (Ralt RH6/84-Honda), 0 laps, accident; Pierre Chauvet, A (Spirit 201-BMW), 2, engine; Tomas Kaiser, S (March 842-BMW), 26, engine; Alessandro Nannini, I (Minardi M283-BMW), 32, accident; Stefano Livio, I (Merzario M84-BMW), 39, still running; Roberto Del Castello, I (Minardi M283-BMW), 39, engine; Philippe Streiff, F (AGS JH19C-BMW), 39, engine.
Championship points: 1 Thackwell, 42; **2** Moreno, 21; **3** Ferte, 17; **4** Danner, 15; **5** Pirro, 10; **6** Tassin, 7.

44 GRAND PRIX DE PAU, Circuit de Pau, France, June 11. European Formula 2 Championship, round 6. 73 laps of the 1·715-mile/2·760-km circuit, 125·20 miles/201·48 km.
1 Mike Thackwell, NZ (Ralt RH6/84-Honda), 1h 29m 39·73s, 83·78 mph/134·83 km/h.
2 Philippe Streiff, F (AGS JH19C-BMW), 1h 30m 20·59s.
3 Roberto Moreno, BR (Ralt RH6/84-Honda), 1h 30m 23·45s.
4 Christian Danner, D (March 842-BMW), 1h 30m 41·70s.
5 Alain Ferte, F (Martini 002-BMW), 1h 30m 48·82s.
6 Pierre Petit, F (March 842-BMW), 72 laps.
7 Pascal Fabre, F (March 842-BMW), 72; **8** Guido Dacco, I (March 832SR-BMW), 70; **9** Marcel Tarres, F (Martini MK43-BMW), 70; **10** Max Busslinger, CH (Merzario M84-BMW), 67.
Fastest lap: Thackwell, 1m 12·65s, 84·98 mph/136·76 km/h.
Retired: Roberto Del Castello, I (Minardi M283-BMW), 8 laps, accident; Michel Ferte, F (Martini 002-BMW), 12, accident; Thierry Tassin, B (March 842-BMW), 15, accident; Beat Jans, CH (March 842-BMW), 16, engine; Alessandro Nannini, I (Minardi M283-BMW), 19, puncture; Stefano Livio, I (Merzario M84-BMW), 25, broken wheel; Emanuele Pirro, I (March 842-BMW), 54, engine; Pierre Chauvet, A (March 842-BMW), 61, spun.
Championship points: 1 Thackwell, 51; **2** Moreno, 25; **3** Danner, 18; **4** Ferte, 17; **5** Streiff, 12; **6** Pirro, 10.

EUROPEAN FORMULA 2 CHAMPIONSHIP RACE, Hockenheim-Ring, German Federal Republic, June 24. European Formula 2 Championship, round 7. 30 laps of the 4·223-mile/6·797-km circuit, 126·69 miles/203·91 km.
1 Pascal Fabre, F (March 842-BMW), 1h 02m 20·22s, 121·94 mph/196·24 km/h.
2 Thierry Tassin, F (March 842-BMW), 1h 02m 27·14s.
3 Michel Ferte, F (Martini 002-BMW), 1h 02m 28·63s.
4 Alessandro Nannini, I (Minardi M283-BMW), 1h 02m 29·28s.
5 Pierre Petit, F (March 842-BMW), 1h 03m 10·93s.
6 Roberto Del Castello, I (Minardi M283-BMW), 1h 03m 11·49s.
7 Pierre Chauvet, A (March 842-BMW), 1h 03m 20·06s; **8** Hans-Peter Pandur, D (Martini 002-BMW), 1h 03m 25·46s; **9** Mike Thackwell, NZ (Ralt RH6/84-Honda), 1h 03m 30·79s; **10** Beat Jans, CH (March 842-BMW), 1h 04m 15·31s; **11** Guido Dacco, I (March 832SR-BMW), 29 laps; **12** Udo Wagenhaüser, D (March 822-BMW), 27.
Fastest lap: Thackwell, 2m 01·73s, 124·89 mph/200·99 km/h.
Retired: Christian Danner, D (March 842-BMW), 4 laps, electrics; Emanuele Pirro, I (March 842-BMW), 8, electrics; Walter Pedrazza, CH (March 812-BMW), 10, engine; Roberto Moreno, BR (Ralt RH6/84-Honda), 13, accident; Gino Bollinger CH (March 802-BMW), 17, engine; Philippe Streiff, F (AGS JH19C-BMW), 17, engine.
Championship points: 1 Thackwell, 51; **2** Moreno, 25; **3** Ferte, 21; **4** Danner, 18; **5** Tassin and Fabre, 13.

EUROPEAN FORMULA 2 CHAMPIONSHIP RACE, Autodromo Santamonica, Misano, Italy, July 22. European Formula 2 Championship, round 8. 58 laps of the 2·167-mile/3·488-km circuit, 125·69 miles/202·30 km.
1 Mike Thackwell, NZ (Ralt RH6/84-Honda), 1h 08m 15·71s, 110·49 mph/177·82 km/h.
2 Philippe Streiff, F (AGS JH19C-BMW), 57 laps.
3 Pierre Petit, F (March 842-BMW), 57.
4 Thierry Tassin, B (March 842-BMW), 57.
5 Guido Dacco, I (March 832SR-BMW), 57.
6 Christian Danner, D (March 842-BMW), 57.
7 Roberto Del Castello, I (Minardi M283-BMW), 57; **8** Tomas Kaiser, S (March 842-BMW), 57; **9** Pierre Chauvet, A (March 842-BMW), 57; **10** Lamberto Leoni, I (Minardi M283-BMW), 56; **11** Stefano Livio, I (AGS JH19-BMW), 55.
Not classified: Roberto Moreno BR (Ralt RH6/84-Honda), 46.
Fastest lap: Moreno, 1m 08·50s, 113·90 mph/183·30 km/h (record).
Retired: Alessandro Nannini, I (Minardi M283-BMW), 11 laps, engine; Emanuele Pirro, I (March 842-BMW), 12, engine; Michel Ferte, F (Martini 002-BMW), 28, engine; Didier Theys, B (March 842-BMW), 50, engine.
Championship points: 1 Thackwell, 60; **2** Moreno, 25; **3** Ferte, 21; **4** Danner, 19; **5** Streiff, 18; **6** Tassin, 16.

22 GRAN PREMIO DEL MEDITERRANEO, Ente Autodromo di Pergusa, Sicily, July 29. European Formula 2 Championship, round 9. 45 laps of the 3·076-mile/4·950-km circuit, 138·42 miles/222·75 km.
1 Mike Thackwell, NZ (Ralt RH6/84-Honda), 1h 08m 55·21s, 120·496 mph/193·919 km/h.
2 Roberto Moreno, BR (Ralt RH6/84-Honda), 1h 08m 57·71s.
3 Alessandro Nannini, I (Minardi M283-BMW), 1h 09m 27·21s.
4 Pierre Petiti, F (March 842-BMW), 1h 08m 27·23s.
5 Michel Ferte, F (Martini 002-BMW), 1h 10m 11·07s.
6 Emanuele Pirro, I (March 842-BMW), 1h 10m 21·32s.
7 Tomas Kaiser, S (March 842-BMW), 44 laps; **8** Guido Dacco, I (March 842-BMW), 44. No other finishers.
Fastest lap: Thackwell, 1m 30·09s, 122·908 mph/197·801 km/h (record).
Retired: Roberto Del Castello, I (Minardi M283-BMW), 1 lap, accident; Beppe Gabbiani, I (March 842-BMW), 2, electrics; Philippe Streiff, F (AGS JH19C-BMW), 5, spun off; Christian Danner, D (March 842-BMW), 37, accident; Lamberto Leoni, I (Minardi M283-BMW), 42, accident.
Championship points: 1 Thackwell, 69; **2** Moreno, 31; **3** Ferte, 23; **4** Danner, 19; **5** Streiff, 18; **6** Tassin, 16.

DERBY EVENING TELEGRAPH RACE, Donington Park Circuit, Great Britain, August 27. European Formula 2 Championship, round 10. 70 laps of the 1·9573-mile/3·1500-km circuit, 137·01 miles/220·50 km.
1 Roberto Moreno, BR (Ralt RH6/84-Honda), 1h 16m 32·37s, 108·40 mph/172·84 km/h.
2 Emanuele Pirro, I (March 842-BMW), 1h 16m 46·50s.
3 Christian Danner, D (March 842-BMW), 1h 16m 47·76s.
4 Mike Thackwell, NZ (Ralt RH6/84-Honda), 1h 16m 51·35s.
5 Thierry Tassin, B (March 842-BMW), 1h 16m 59·21s.
6 Pierre Chauvet, A (March 842-BMW), 69 laps.
7 Philippe Streiff, F (AGS JH19C-BMW), 69; **8** Tomas Kaiser, S (March 842-BMW), 69; **9 Guido Dacco, I (March 842-BMW), 69; 10** Alessandro Nannini, I (Minardi (M283-BMW), 68; **11** Lamberto Leoni, I (Minardi M283-BMW), 68; **12** Roberto Del Castello, I (Minardi (M283-BMW), 68.
Fastest lap: Thackwell, 1m 04·37s, 109·46 mph/176·16 km/h.
Retired: Michel Ferte, F (Martini 002-BMW), 33 laps, accident; Pierre Petiti, F (March 842-BMW), 34, engine; Didier Theys, B (Martini 002-BMW), 58, lost wheel.
Championship points: 1 Thackwell, 72; **2** Moreno, 40; **3** Ferte and Danner, 23; **5** Tassin and Streiff, 18.

DAILY MAIL TROPHY RACE, Brands Hatch Grand Prix Circuit, Great Britain, September 23. European Formula 2 Championship, round 11. 47 laps of the 2·6136-mile/4·2060-km circuit, 122·84 miles/197·68 km. Race run in two parts due to weather.
1 Philippe Streiff, F (AGS JH19C-BMW), 1h 09m 11·39s, 106·52 mph/171·43 km/h.
2 Michel Ferte, F (Martini 002-BMW), 1h 10m 21·48s.
3 Roberto Moreno, BR (Ralt RH6/84-Honda), 1h 10m 32·38s.
4 Tomas Kaiser, S (March 842-BMW), 1h 10m 34·84s.
5 Alessandro Nannini, I (Minardi M283-BMW), 1h 10m 51·63s.
6 Emanuele Pirro, I (March 842-BMW), 46 laps.
7 Thierry Tassin, B (March 842-BMW), 46; **8** Pierre Petit, F (March 842-BMW), 46; **9** Derek Bell, GB (March 842-BMW), 45; **10** Christian Danner, D (March 842-BMW), 45 (DNF, accident); **11** Pierre Chauvet, A (March 842-BMW), 44; **12** Roland Minder, CH (March 842-BMW), 44.
Fastest lap: Moreno, 1m 18·57s, 119·75 mph/192·72 km/h (record).
Retired: Mike Thackwell, NZ (Ralt RH6/84-Honda), 7 laps, engine; Roberto Del Castello, I (Minardi M283-BMW), 28, accident; Guido Dacco, I (March 832SR-BMW), 33, accident.

Final Champiosnhip points:

1	Mike Thackwell, NZ	72
2	Roberto Moreno, BR	44
3	Michel Ferte, F	29
4	Philippe Streiff, F	27
5	Christian Danner, D	23
6=	Thierry Tassin, B	18
6=	Emanuele Pirro, I	18

8 Pascal Fabre, F, 13; **9** Pierre Petiti, F, 10; **10** Alessandro Nannini, I, 9; **11** Didier Theys, B and Tomas Kaiser, S, 3; **13** Alain Ferte, F and Guido Dacco, I, 2; **15** Roberto Del Castello, I and Pierre Chauvet, A, 1.

Formula 3

MARLBORO CHAMPIONSHIP RACE, Silverstone Short Circuit, Great Britain, March 4. Marlboro British Formula 3 Championship, round 1. 20 laps of the 1·608-mile/2·588-km circuit, 32·16 miles/51·76 km.
1 Johnny Dumfries, GB (Ralt RT3/83-VW), 19m 52·80s, 97·06 mph/156·20 km/h.
2 Allen Berg, CDN (Ralt RT3/84-Toyota), 19m 59·46s.
3 Russell Spence, GB (Ralt RT3/84-VW), 19m 59·53s.
4 Andrew Gilbert-Scott, GB (Ralt RT3/84-VW), 20m 02·83s.
5 David Hunt, GB (Ralt RT3/84-Toyota), 20m 06·62s.
6 Cor Euser, NL (Magnum 843-Toyota), 20m 08·40s.
7 Mario Hytten, CH (Ralt RT3/84-VW), 20m 13·58s; **8** Keith Fine, GB (Ralt RT3/83-VW), 20m 14·86s (1st class B); **9** Paul Radisich, NZ (Ralt RT3/84-VW), 20m 20·04s; **10** Mike Blanchet, GB (Ralt RT3/81-Toyota), 20m 20·11s.
Fastest lap: Berg, 58·36s, 99·19 mph/159·63 km/h.
Marlboro Championship points. Class A: 1 Dumfries, 9; **2** Berg, 7; **3** Spence, 4; **4** Gilbert-Scott, 3; **5** Hunt, 2; **6** Euser, 1. **Class B: 1** Fine, 10; **2** Blanchet, 6; **3** Bradley, 4; **4** Olausson, 3; **5** Grant, 2; **6** Horwood, 1.

MARLBORO CHAMPIONSHIP RACE, Thruxton Circuit, Great Britain, March 11. Marlboro British Formula 3 Championship, round 2. 15 lapsl of the 2·356-mile/3·792-km circuit, 35·34 miles/56·88 km.
1 Johnny Dumfries, GB (Ralt RT3/83-VW), 18m 39·60s, 113·63 mph/182·87 km/h.
2 Allen Berg, CDN (Ralt RT3/84-Toyota), 18m 41·05s.
3 Andrew Gilbert-Scott, GB (Ralt RT3/84-VW), 18m 42·37s.
4 Russell Spence, GB (Ralt RT3/84-VW), 18m 53·80s.
5 Keith Fine, GB (Ralt RT3/83-VW), 18m 58·88s (1st class B).
6 Paul Radisich, NZ (Ralt RT3/84-VW), 19m 00·34s.
7 Ross Cheever, USA (Ralt RT3/83-Toyota), 19m 14·91s, **8** Eric Lang, USA (Ralt RT3/84-Toyota), 19m 15·07s; **9** Cor Euser, NL (Magnum 843-Toyota), 19m 23·64s; **10** Thierry Hierman, B (Anson SA4/84-VW), 19m 30·10s.
Fastest lap: Dumfries and Gilbert-Scott, 1m 13·83s, 114·88 mph/184·88 km/h.
Marlboro Championship points. Class A: 1 Dumfries, 19; **2** Berg, 13; **3** Gilbert-Scott, 8; **4** Spence, 7; **5** Hunt and Radisich, 2. **Class B: 1** Fine, 20; **2** Olausson, 7; **3** Blanchet, Bradley and Tingling, 6; **6** Grant, 5.

EUROPEAN FORMULA 3 CHAMPIONSHIP RACE, Donington Park Circuit, Great Britain, March 25. European Formula 3 Championship, round 1. 30 laps of the 1·9573-mile/3·1500-km circuit, 58·72 miles/94·50 km.
1 Johnny Dumfries, GB (Ralt RT3/83-VW), 41m 02·54s, 85·84 mph/138·15 km/h.
2 Tommy Byrne, IRL (Anson SA4B-Alfa Romeo), 41m 11·82s.
3 Claudio Langes, I (Ralt RT3/84-Toyota), 41m 57·73s.
4 Gerhard Berger, A (Ralt RT3/84-Alfa Romeo), 42m 09·93s.
5 David Hunt, GB (Ralt RT3/84-Toyota), 42m 12·08s.
6 John Nielsen, DK (Ralt RT3/84-VW), 42m 12·46s.
7 Cathy Muller, F (Ralt RT3/84-Alfa Romeo), 29 laps; **8** Nils-Kristian Nissen, DK (Ralt RT3/84-Alfa Romeo), 29; **9** Ruggero Melgrati, I (Ralt RT3/84-Alfa Romeo), 29; **10** Tony Trevor, GB (Ralt RT3/81-Toyota), 29.
Fastest lap: Dumfries, 1m 19·94s, 88·14 mph/141·85 km/h.
European Championship points: 1 Dumfries, 9; **2** Byrne, 6; **3** Langes, 4; **4** Berger, 3; **5** Hunt, 2; **6** Nielsen, 1.

MARLBORO CHAMPIONSHIP RACE, Silverstone Grand Prix Circuit, Great Britain, April 1. Marlboro British Formula 3 Championship, round 3. 20 laps of the 2·932-mile/4·719-km circuit, 58·64 miles/94·38 km.
1 Johnny Dumfries, GB (Ralt RT3/83-VW), 29m 33·50s, 119·03 mph/191·56 km/h.
2 Russell Spence, GB (Ralt RT3/84-VW), 29m 35·01s.
3 Carlos Abella, E (Ralt RT3/84-Toyota), 29m 38·18s.
4 Gary Evans, GB (Ralt RT3/84-Toyota), 29m 38·46s.
5 Paul Radisich, NZ (Ralt RT3/84-VW), 29m 40·03s.
6 David Hunt, GB (Ralt RT3/84-Toyota), 29m 42·58s.
7 Calvin Fish, GB (Ralt RT3/84-Toyota), 29m 43·18s; **8** Allen Berg, CDN (Ralt RT3/84-Toyota), 29m 46·78s; **9** Eric Lang, USA (Ralt RT3/84-Toyota), 29m 59·40s; **10** Keith Fine, GB (Ralt RT3/83-VW), 30m 07·19s (1st class B).
Fastest lap: Spence. 1m 25·51s, 123·43 mph/198·64 km/h (record).

Marlboro Championship points. Class A: 1 Dumfries, 28; **2** Spence, 14; **3** Berg, 13; **4** Gilbert-Scott, 8; **5** Radisich and Abella, 4. **Class B: 1** Fine, 30; **2** Bradley, 12; **3** Olausson, 7; **4** Blanchet and Tingling, 6; **6** Grant, 5.

EUROPEAN FORMULA 3 CHAMPIONSHIP RACE, Omloop van Zolder, Belgium, April 15. European Formula 3 Championship, round 2. 22 laps of the 2·648-mile/4·262-km circuit, 58·26 miles/93·76 km.
1 John Nielsen, DK (Ralt RT3/84-VW), 33m 58·40s, 102·89 mph/165·58 km/h.
2 Johnny Dumfries, GB (Ralt RT3/84-VW), 34m 02·3s.
3 Ivan Capelli, I (Martini MK42-Alfa Romeo), 34m 02·8s.
4 Gerhard Berger, A (Ralt RT3/84-Alfa Romeo), 34m 13·2s.
5 Nils-Kristian Nissen, DK (Ralt RT3/84-Alfa Romeo), 34m 20·3s.
6 Cathy Muller, F (Ralt RT3/84-Alfa Romeo), 34m 21·7s.
7 Bernard Santal, F (Martini MK42-Alfa Romeo), 34m 25·6s; **8** Luis Sala, E (Ralt RT3/84-Alfa Romeo), 34m 32·0s; **9** Tommy Byrne, IRL (Anson SA4B-Alfa Romeo), 34m 36·0s; **10** Paul Radisich, NZ (Ralt RT3/84-VW), 34m 54·5s.
Fastest lap: Not given.
European Championship points: 1 Dumfries, 15; **2** Nielsen, 10; **3** Byrne and Berger, 6; **5** Langes and Capelli, 4.

MARLBORO CHAMPIONCHIP RACE, Omloop van Zolder, Belgium, April 15. Marlboro British Formula 3 Championship, round 4. 21 laps of the 2·648-mile/4·262-km circuit, 55·61 miles/89·50 km.
1 Russell Spence, GB (Ralt RT3/84-VW), 32m 45·40s, 101·87 mph/163·94 km/h.
2 Johnny Dumfries, GB (Ralt RT3/83-VW), 32m 47·3s.
3 Allen Berg, CDN (Ralt RT3/84-Toyota), 32m 49·9s.
4 Mario Hytten, CH (Ralt RT3/84-VW), 33m 34·4s.
5 Carlos Abella, E (Ralt RT3/84-Toyota), 34m 42·5s.
6 Gary Evans, GB (Ralt RT3/84-Toyota), 34m 45·5s.
7 Eric Lang, USA (Ralt RT3/84-Toyota), 35m 00·8s; **8** Paul Jackson, GB (Sparton SE420-VW), 20 laps; **9** Marc Simon, B (Ralt RT3/84-VW), 20; **10** Steve Bradley, GB (Ralt RT3/82-Toyota), 20 (1st class B).
Fastest lap: Spence and Dumfries, 1m 32·3s, 103·29 mph/166·23 km/h.
Marlboro Championship points. Class A: 1 Dumfries, 35; **2** Spence, 24; **3** Berg, 17; **4** Gilbert-Scott, 8; **5** Abella, 6; **6** Radisich and Evans, 4. **Class B: 1** Fine, 30; **2** Bradley, 21; **3** Olausson, 7; **4** Blanchet and Tingling, 6; **6** Grant, 5.

MARLBORO CHAMPIONSHIP RACE, Thruxton Circuit, Great Britain, April 23. Marlboro British Formula 3 Championship, round 5. 20 laps of the 2·356-mile/3·792-km circuit, 47·12 miles/55·84 km.
1 Johnny Dumfries, GB (Ralt RT3/83-VW), 24m 57·61s, 113·26 mph/182·27 km/h.
2 Mario Hytten, CH (Ralt RT3/84-VW), 24m 59·90s.
3 Andrew Gilbert-Scott, GB (Ralt RT3/84-VW), 25m 03·38s.
4 Paul Radisich, NZ (Ralt RT3/84-VW), 25m 19·59s.
5 David Hunt, GB (Ralt RT3/84-Toyota), 25m 26·86s.
6 Carlos Abella, E (Ralt RT3/84-Toyota), 25m 32·74s.
7 Gary Evans, GB (Ralt RT3/84-Toyota), 25m 35·10s; **8** Tony Trevor, GB (Ralt RT3/83-VW), 25m 36·59s; **9** Paul Jackson, GB (Sparton SE420-VW), 25m 49·83s; **10** Steve Bradley, GB (Ralt RT3/82-Toyota), 25m 54·26s (1st class B).
Fastest lap: Hytten, 1m 14·17s, 114·35 mph/184·03 km/h.
Marlboro Championship points. Class A: 1 Dumfries, 44; **2** Spence, 24; **3** Berg, 17; **4** Gilbert-Scott, 12; **5** Hytten, 10; **6** Radisich and Abella, 7. **Class B: 1** Fine, 34; **2** Bradley, 30; **3** Tingling, 12; **4** Olausson, 7; **5** Blanchet, 6; **6** Grant and Hedley, 5.

EUROPEAN FORMULA 3 CHAMPIONSHIP RACE, Magny-Cours, France, May 1. European Formula 3 Championship, round 3. 26 laps of the 2·392-mile/3·848-km circuit, 62·19 miles/100·05 km.
1 Ivan Capelli, I (Martini MK42-Alfa Romeo), 36m 23·99s, 103·26 mph/166·18 km/h.
2 John Nielsen, DK (Ralt RT3/84-VW), 36m 25·74s.
3 Tommy Byrne, IRL (Anson SA4B-Alfa Romeo), 36m 30·67s.
4 James Weaver, GB (Ralt RT3/84-Toyota), 36m 45·48s.
5 Nils-Kristian Nissen, DK (Ralt RT3/84-Alfa Romeo), 36m 47·70s.
6 Frédéric Delavallade, F (Martini MK42-Alfa Romeo), 36m 51·59s.
7 Gerhard Berger, A (Ralt RT3/84-Alfa Romeo), 37m 00·63s; **8** Jo Zeller, CH (Ralt RT3/82-Toyota), 37m 01·79s; **9** Ruggero Melgrati, I (Ralt RT3/84-Alfa Romeo), 37m 02·26s; **10** Cathy Muller, F (Ralt RT3/84-Alfa Romeo), 37m 02·67s.
Fastest lap: Nielsen, 1m 23·17s, 103·55 mph/166·65 km/h (record).
European Championship points: 1 Nielsen, 16; **2** Dumfries, 15; **3** Capelli, 13; **4** Byrne, 10; **5** Berger, 6; **6** Langes and Nissen, 4.

MARLBORO CHAMPIONSHIP RACE, Thruxton Circuit, Great Britain, May 7. Marlboro British Formula 3 Championship, round 6. 20 laps of the 2·356-mile/3·792-km circuit, 47·12 miles/55·84 km.
1 Johnny Dumfries, GB (Ralt RT3/83-VW), 24m 44·38s, 114·27 mph/183·90 km/h.
2 Mario Hytten, CH (Ralt RT3/84-VW), 24m 48·90s.
3 Carlos Abella, E (Ralt RT3/84-Toyota), 24m 49·50s.
4 Allen Berg, CDN (Ralt RT3/84-Toyota), 24m 59·96s.
5 Ross Cheever, USA (Ralt RT3/83-Toyota), 25m 06·20s.
6 Russell Spence, GB (Ralt RT3/84-VW), 25m 10·26s.
7 Gary Evans, GB (Ralt RT3/84-Toyota), 25m 15·88s; **8** Tony Trevor, GB (Ralt RT3/83-VW), 25m 16·17s; **9** David Hunt, GB (Ralt RT3/84-Toyota), 25m 19·97s; **10** Eric Lang, USA (Ralt RT3/84-Toyota), 25m 21·19s.
Fastest lap: Dumfries, 1m 13·70s, 115·08 mph/185·20 km/h.
Marlboro Championship points. Class A: 1 Dumfries, 54; **2** Spence, 25; **3** Berg, 20; **4** Hytten, 16; **5** Gilbert-Scott, 12; **6** Abella, 11. **Class B: 1** Fine, 44; **2** Bradley, 34; **3** Tingling, 18; **4** Hedley, 8; **5** Olausson, 7; **6** Blanchet, 6.

EUROPEAN FORMULA 3 CHAMPIONSHIP RACE, La Châtre Circuit, France, May 13. European Formula 3 Championship, round 4. 42 laps of the 1·445-mile/2·325-km circuit, 60·69 miles/97·65 km.
1 Ivan Capelli, I (Martini MK42-Alfa Romeo), 44m 55·10s, 81·05 mph/130·44 km/h.
2 Johnny Dumfries, GB (Ralt RT3/83-VW), 44m 56·24s.
3 Gerhard Berger, A (Ralt RT3/84-Alfa Romeo), 45m 12·83s.
4 Claudio Langes, I (Ralt RT3/84-Toyota), 45m 15·24s.
5 Nils-Kristian Nissen, DK (Ralt RT3/84-Alfa Romeo), 45m 48·03s.
6 Ruggero Melgrati, I (Ralt RT3/84-Alfa Romeo), 45m 59·52s.
7 Tommy Byrne, IRL (Anson SA4B-Alfa Romeo), 41 laps; **8** Hasse Thaung, D (Ralt RT3/84-Alfa Romeo), 40; **9** Christian Estrosi, F (Ralt RT3/84-Toyota), 39. No other finishers.
Fastest lap: Capelli, 1m 03·34s, 82·11 mph/132·14 km/h.
European Championship points: 1 Capelli, 22; **2** Dumfries, 21; **3** Nielsen, 16; **4** Byrne and Berger, 10; **6** Langes, 7.

MARLBORO CHAMPIONSHIP RACE, Donington Park Circuit, Great Britain, May 20. Marlboro British Formula 3 Championship, round 7. 20 laps of the 1·9573-mile/3·1500-km circuit, 39·15 miles/63·00 km.
1 Johnny Dumfries, GB (Ralt RT3/83-VW), 23m 33·36s, 99·70 mph/160·45 km/h.
2 Allen Berg, CDN (Ralt RT3/84-Toyota), 23m 36·57s.
3 Russell Spence, GB (Ralt RT3/84-VW), 23m 40·38s.
4 Tony Trevor, GB (Ralt RT3/83-VW), 23m 57·58s.
5 Ross Cheever, USA (Ralt RT3/83-Toyota), 23m 58·05s.
6 Mario Hytten, CH (Ralt RT3/84-VW), 23m 59·14s.
7 David Hunt, GB (Ralt RT3/84-Toyota), 24m 01·32s; **8** Andrew Gilbert-Scott, GB (Ralt RT3/84-VW), 24m 06·21s; **9** Rob Wilson, NZ (Ralt RT3/84-Toyota), 24m 07·18s; **10** Gary Evans, GB (Ralt RT3/84-Toyota), 24m 07·66s.
Fastest lap: Berg, 1m 09·79s, 100·96 mph/162·48 km/h.
Marlboro Championship points. Class A: 1 Dumfries, 63; **2** Spence, 29; **3** Berg, 27; **4** Hytten, 17; **5** Gilbert-Scott, 12; **6** Abella, 11. **Class B: 1** Fine, 44; **2** Bradley, 34; **3** Tingling, 22; **4** Hedley, 14; **5** Morgan, 10; **6** Olausson, 7.

EUROPEAN FORMULA 3 CHAMPIONSHIP RACE, Osterreichring, Austria, May 27. European Formula 3 Championship, round 5. 16 laps of the 3·6924-mile/5·9424-km circuit, 59·08 miles/95·08 km.
1 Gerhard Berger, A (Ralt RT3/84-Alfa Romeo), 29m 23·93s, 120·56 mph/194·02 km/h.
2 Claudio Langes, I (Ralt RT3/84-Toyota), 29m 29·82s.
3 John Nielsen, DK (Ralt RT3/84-VW), 29m 31·05s.
4 Bernard Santal, F (Martini MK42-Alfa Romeo), 29m 33·77s.
5 Walter Voulaz, F (Ralt RT3/84-Toyota), 29m 39·51s.
6 Nils-Kristian Nissen, DK (Ralt RT3/84-Alfa Romeo), 29m 40·72s.
7 Cathy Muller, F (Ralt RT3/84-Alfa Romeo), 29m 44·83s; **8** Ruggero Melgrati, I (Ralt RT3/84-Alfa Romeo), 29m 45·85s; **9** Adrian Campos, E (Ralt RT3/84-VW), 29m 52·73s; **10** Cosimo Lucchesi, I (Ralt RT3/84-Alfa Romeo), 30m 06·29s.
Fastest lap: Berger, 1m 48·97s, 121·98 mph/196·31 km/h.
European Championship points: 1 Capelli, 22; **2** Dumfries, 21; **3** Nielsen, 20; **4** Berger, 19; **5** Langes, 13; **6** Byrne, 10.

MARLBORO CHAMPIONSHIP RACE, Silverstone Short Circuit, Great Britain, May 28. Marlboro British Formula 3 Championship, round 8. 30 laps of the 1·608-mile/2·588-km circuit, 48·24 miles/77·64 km.
1 Mario Hytten, CH (Ralt RT3/84-VW), 29m 19·21s, 98·71 mph/158·86 km/h.
2 Tony Trevor, GB (Ralt RT3/83-VW), 29m 19·35s.
3 Allen Berg, CDN (Ralt RT3/84-Toyota), 29m 26·88s.
4 Johnny Dumfries, GB (Ralt RT3/83-VW), 29m 31·17s.
5 Eric Lang, USA (Ralt RT3/84-Toyota), 29m 39·44s.
6 Carlos Abella, E (Ralt RT3/84-Toyota), 29m 40·38s.
7 Russell Spence, GB (Ralt RT3/84-VW), 29m 41·09s; **8** Keith Fine, GB (Ralt RT3/83-VW), 29m 41·84s (1st class B); **9** David Hunt, GB (Ralt RT3/84-Toyota), 29m 45·22s; **10** Rob Wilson, NZ (Ralt RT3/84-Toyota), 29m 51·43s.
Fastest lap: Trevor, 56·10s, 103·18 mph/166·05 km/h.
Marlboro Championship points. Class A: 1 Dumfries, 66; **2** Berg, 31; **3** Spence, 29; **4** Hytten, 26; **5** Gilbert-Scott and Abella, 12; **Class B: 1** Fine, 54; **2** Bradley, 40; **3** Tingling, 26; **4** Hedley, 15; **5** Morgan, 10; **6** Olausson, 7.

26 GRAND PRIX DE MONACO FORMULA 3, Monte Carlo, June 2. 24 laps of the 2·058-mile/3·312-km circuit, 49·39 miles/79·49 km.
1 Ivan Capelli, I (Martini MK42-Alfa Romeo), 38m 18·767s, 77·35 mph/124·48 km/h.
2 Gerhard Berger, A (Ralt RT3/84-Alfa Romeo), 38m 32·816s.
3 James Weaver, GB (Ralt RT3/84-Toyota), 38m 35·981s.
4 Tommy Byrne, IRL (Anson SA4B-Alfa Romeo), 38m 44·229s.
5 Allen Berg, CDN (Ralt RT3/84-Toyota), 38m 45·785s.
6 Franco Forini, I (Dallara 384-Alfa Romeo), 38m 59·358s.
7 Ruggero Melgrati, I (Ralt RT3/84-Alfa Romeo), 39m 08·149s; **8** Cathy Muller, F (Ralt RT3/84-Alfa Romeo), 39m 10·896s; **9** Denis Morin, F (Martini MK42-Alfa Romeo), 39m 11·985s; **10** Fabrizio Barbazza, I (Dallara 383-Alfa Romeo), 39m 26·920s.
Fastest lap: Claudio Langes, I (Ralt RT3/84-Toyota), 1m 33·617s, 79·14 mph/127·36 km/h.

ACORN COMPUTER TROPHY, Silverstone Grand Prix Circuit, Great Britain, June 10. European Formula 3 Championship, round 6. 20 laps of the 2·932-mile/4·719-km circuit, 58·64 miles/94·38 km.
1 Johnny Dumfries, GB (Ralt RT3/83-VW), 28m 16·57s, 124·42 mph/200·23 km/h.
2 Russell Spence, GB (Ralt RT3/84-VW), 28m 17·44s.
3 Ivan Capelli, I (Martini MK42-Alfa Romeo), 28m 28·07s.
4 Gerhard Berger, A (Ralt RT3/84-Alfa Romeo), 28m 29·95s.
5 Ruggero Melgrati, I (Ralt RT3/84-Alfa Romeo), 28m 50·12s.
6 Gary Evans, GB (Ralt RT3/84-Toyota), 28m 53·72s.
7 Cathy Muller, F (Ralt RT3/84-Alfa Romeo), 28m 54·72s; **8** Carlos Abella, E (Ralt RT3/84-Toyota), 28m 57·31s; **9** Tommy Byrne, IRL (Anson SA4B-Alfa Romeo), 29m 10·98s; **10** Adrian Campos, E (Ralt RT3/84-VW), 29m 12·55s.
Fastest lap: Spence, 1m 23·79s, 125·97 mph/202·73 km/h (record).
Disqualified: David Hunt, GB (Ralt RT3/84-Toyota), finished 5th in 28m 42·48s but was disqualified due air box infringement.
European Championship points: 1 Dumfries, 30; **2** Capelli, 26; **3** Berger, 22; **4** Nielsen, 20; **5** Langes, 13; **6** Byrne, 10.

EUROPEAN FORMULA 3 CHAMPIONSHIP RACE, Nurburgring, German Federal Republic, June 17. European Formula 3 Championship, round 7. 20 laps of the 2·822-mile/4·542-km circuit, 56·44 miles/90·84 km.
1 Johnny Dumfries, GB (Ralt RT3/83-VW), 32m 39·40s, 103·70 mph/166·89 km/h.
2 Ivan Capelli, I (Martini MK42-Alfa Romeo), 32m 41·14s.
3 Gerhard Berger, A (Ralt RT3/84-Alfa Romeo), 32m 45·54s.
4 Nils-Kristian Nissen, DK (Ralt RT3/84-Alfa Romeo), 32m 51·12s.
5 Adrian Campos, E (Ralt RT3/84-VW), 32m 51·52s.
6 Kurt Thiim, DK (Ralt RT3/84-Alfa Romeo), 32m 56·22s.
7 Davy Jones, USA (Ralt RT3/84-Toyota), 33m 02·92s; **8** Peter Wisskirchen, D (Ralt RT3/84-VW), 33m 17·20s; **9** Luis Villamil, E (Ralt RT3/84-Alfa Romeo), 33m 17·20s; **10** Ruggero Melgrati, I (Ralt RT3/84-Alfa Romeo), 33m 28·66s.
Fastest lap: Capelli, 1m 36·96s, 104·78 mph/168·63 km/h (record).
European Championship points: 1 Dumfries, 39; **2** Capelli, 32; **3** Berger, 26; **4** Nielsen, 20; 5 Langes, 13; **6** Byrne and Nissen, 10.

EUROPEAN FORMULA 3 CHAMPIONSHIP RACE, Autodromo Nazionale di Monza, Italy, June 24. European Formula 3 Championship, round 8. 17 laps of the 3·604-mile/5·800-km circuit, 61·27 miles/98·60 km.
1 Gerhard Berger, A (Ralt RT3/84-Alfa Romeo), 31m 45·92s, 115·73 mph/185·25 km/h.
2 Claudio Langes, I (Ralt RT3/84-Toyota), 31m 46·21s.
3 Franco Forini, I (Dallara 384-Alfa Romeo), 31m 47·46s.
4 Adrian Campos, E (Ralt RT3/84-VW), 31m 51·51s.
5 Fabrizio Barbazza, I (Dallara 384-Alfa Romeo), 31m 59·56s.
6 Cathy Muller, F (Ralt RT3/84-Alfa Romeo), 32m 06·99s.
7 Luis Sala, E (Ralt RT3/84-Alfa Romeo), 32m 15·27s; **8** Darilo Frassoni, I (Ralt RT3/84-VW), 32m 29·44s; **9** Neto Jochamowitz, A (Ralt RT3/84-Alfa Romeo), 32m 32·42s.
Fastest lap: Forini, 1m 50·00s, 117·95 mph/189·82 km/h.
Disqualified: Ivan Capelli, I (Martini MK42-Alfa Romeo) finished 1st in 31m 43·82s but was disqualified due air box infringement.
European Championship points: 1 Dumfries, 39; **2** Berger, 35; **3** Capelli, 32; **4** Nielsen, 20; **5** Langes, 19; **6** Byrne and Nissen, 10.

MARLBORO CHAMPIONSHIP RACE, Snetterton Circuit, Great Britain, July 1. Marlboro British Formula 3 Championship, round 9. 25 laps of the 1·917-mile/3·085-km circuit, 47·93 miles/77·13 km.
1 Johnny Dumfries, GB (Ralt RT3/83-VW), 26m 03·51s, 110·34 mph/177·57 km/h.
2 Carlos Abella, E (Ralt RT3/84-Toyota), 26m 11·36s.
3 Mario Hytten, CH (Ralt RT3/84-VW), 26m 20·57s.
4 Russell Spence, GB (Ralt RT3/84-VW), 26m 31·68s.
5 David Hunt, GB (Ralt RT3/84-Toyota), 26m 36·54s.
6 Andrew Gilbert-Scott, GB (Ralt RT3/84-Toyota), 26m 37·82s.
7 Paul Jackson, GB (Ralt RT3/84-VW), 26m 38·30s; **8** Keith Fine, GB (Ralt RT3/83-VW), 26m 39·43s (1st class B); **9** Gary Evans, GB (Ralt RT3/84-Toyota), 26m 30·81s; **10** Eric Lang, USA (Ralt RT3/84-Toyota), 26m 40·23s.
Fastest lap: Dumfries, 1m 01·98s, 111·34 mph/179·18 km/h (record).
Marlboro Championship points. Class A: 1 Dumfries, 76; **2** Spence, 32; **3** Berg, 31; **4** Hytten, 30; **5** Abella, 18; **6** Gilbert-Scott, 13. **Class B: 1** Fine, 64; **2** Bradley, 40; **3** Tingling, 26; **4** Hedley, 18; **5** Morgan, 14; **6** Olausson, 7.

MARLBORO CHAMPIONSHIP RACE, Donington Park Circuit, Great Britain, July 8. Marlboro British Formula 3 Championship, round 10. 25 laps of the 1·9573-mile/3·1500-km circuit, 48·93 miles/78·75 km.
1 Russell Spence, GB (Ralt RT3/84-VW), 29m 45·17s, 98·67 mph/158·79 km/h.
2 Allen Berg, CDN (Ralt RT3/84-Toyota), 29m 52·51s.
3 Gary Evans, GB (Ralt RT3/84-Toyota), 29m 52·83s.
4 Mario Hytten, CH (Ralt RT3/84-VW), 29m 53·42s.
5 Paul Jackson, GB (Ralt RT3/83-VW), 30m 03·15s.
6 Carlos Abella, E (Ralt RT3/84-Toyota), 30m 09·62s; **8** Tony Trevor, GB (Ralt RT3/83-VW), 30m 24·09s; **9** Johnny Duymfries, GB (Ralt RT3/83-VW), 30m 32·02s; **10** Richard Morgan, GB (Ralt RT3/81-Toyota), 30m 36·24s (1st class B).
Fastest lap: Dumfries, 1m 10·24s, 100·31 mph/161·43 km/hg.
Marlboro Championship points. Class A: 1 Dumfries, 77; **2** Spence, 41; **3** Berg, 37; **4** Hytten, 33; **5** Abella, 19; **6** Gilbert-Scott, 13. **Class B: 1** Fine, 64; **2** Bradley, 40; **3** Tingling, 32; **4** Morgan, 24; **5** Hedley, 21; **6** Olausson, 7.

EUROPEAN FORMULA 3 CHAMPIONSHIP RACE, Ente Autodromo di Pergusa, Enna, Sicily, July 8. European Formula 3 Championship, round 9. 20 laps of the 3·076-mile/4·950-km circuit, 61·52 miles/99·00 km.
1 Ivan Capelli, I (Martini MK42-Alfa Romeo), 32m 45·58s, 112·67 mph/181·32 km/h.
2 Claudio Langes, I (Ralt RT3/84-Toyota), 32m 52·81s.
3 Gerhard Berger, A (Ralt RT3/84-Alfa Romeo), 32m 59·49s.
4 Ruggero Melgrati, I (Ralt RT3/84-Alfa Romeo), 33m 10·52s.
5 Tommy Byrne, IRL (Anson SA4B-VW), 33m 23·09s.
6 Cathy Muller, F (Ralt RT3/84-Alfa Romeo), 33m 23·74s.
7 Luis Sala, E (Ralt RT3/84-Alfa Romeo), 33m 49·18s; **8** Luis Villami, E (Ralt RT3/84-Alfa Romeo), 33m 49·69s. No other finishers.
Fastest lap: Capelli, 1m 37·35s, 113·74 mph/183·05 km/h.
European Championship points: 1 Capelli, 41; **2** Dumfries and Berger, 39; **4** Langes, 25; **5** Nielsen, 20; **6** Byrne, 12.

EUROPEAN FORMULA 3 CHAMPIONSHIP RACE, Autodromo Internazionale del Mugello, Italy, July 15. European Formula 3 Championship round 10. 18 laps of the 3·259-mile/5·245-km circuit, 58·66 miles/94·41 km.
1 Ivan Capelli, I (Martini MK42-Alfa Romeo), 33m 39·56s, 104·57 mph/168·29 km/h.
2 Gerhard Berger, A (Ralt RT3/84-Alfa Romeo), 33m 45·50s.
3 Ruggero Melgrati, I (Ralt RT3/84-Alfa Romeo), 33m 46·32s.
4 Johnny Dumfries, GB (Ralt RT3/83-VW), 33m 55·57s.
5 Claudio Langes, I (Ralt RT3/84-Toyota), 33m 58·07s.
6 Cathy Muller, F (Ralt RT3/84-Alfa Romeo), 33m 58·58s.
7 Gabriele Tarquini, I (Ralt RT3/84-Alfa Romeo), 34m 03·90s; **8** Alessandro Santin, I (Ralt RT3/84-Alfa Romeo), 34m 04·40s; **9** Cosimo Lucchesi, I (Ralt RT3/84-Alfa Romeo), 34m 18·01s; **10** Marco Apicella, I (Ralt RT3/84-Alfa Romeo), 34m 18·50s.
Fastest lap: Capelli, 1m 50·87s, 105·82 mph/170·30 km/h.
European Championship points: 1 Capelli, 50; **2** Berger, 45; **3** Dumfries, 42; **4** Langes, 27; **5** Nielsen, 20; **6** Byrne, 12.

MARLBORO CHAMPIONSHIP RACE, Oulton Park Circuit, Great Britain, August 18. Marlboro British Formula 3 Championship, round 11. 30 laps of the 2·356-mile/3·792-km circuit, 70·68 miles/113·76 km.
1 Russell Spence, GB (Ralt RT3/84-VW), 38m 59·95s, 108·74 mph/175·00 km/h.
2 Dave Scott, GB (Ralt RT3/84-VW), 39m 04·30s.
3 Carlos Abella, E (Ralt RT3/84-Toyota), 39m 04·74s.
4 Eric Lang, USA (Ralt RT3/84-Toyota), 39m 27·01s.
5 David Hunt, GB (Ralt RT3/84-Toyota), 39m 34·94s.
6 Mario Hytten, CH (Ralt RT3/84-VW), 39m 35·37s.
7 Gary Evans, GB (Ralt RT3/84-Toyota), 39m 48·65s; **8** Rob Wilson, NZ (Ralt RT3/84-Toyota), 40m 00·90s; **9** Thierry Heirman, B (Anson SA4/84-VW), 29 laps; **10** Carlton Tingling, JA (Ralt RT3/82-VW), 29 (1st class B).
Fastest lap: Evans, 1m 16·72s, 110·55 mph/177·91 km/h (record).
Marlboro Championship points. Class A: 1 Dumfries, 77; **2** Spence, 50; **3** Berg, 37; **4** Hytten, 34; **5** Abella, 23; **6** Gilbert-Scott, 13. **Class B: 1** Fine, 64; **2** Tingling, 42; **3** Bradley, 40; **4** Morgan, 24; **5** Hedley, 21; **6** Soubriquet, 12.

EUROPEAN FORMULA 3 CHAMPIONSHIP RACE, Ring Knutstorp, Sweden, August 19. European Formula 3 Championship, round 11. 45 laps of the 1·292-mile/2·079-km circuit, 58·14 miles/93·55 km.
1 Claudio Langes, I (Ralt RT3/84-Toyota.), 43m 33·631s, 80·07 mph/860 km/h.
2 Luis Sala, E (Ralt RT3/84-Alfa Romeo), 43m 34·706s.
3 Bernard Santal, F (Ralt RT3/84-VW), 43m 38·453s.
4 Cathy Muller, F (Ralt RT3/84-Alfa Romeo), 43m 48·641s.
5 Leo Andersson, S (Ralt RT3/84-Toyota), 43m 50·971s.

6 Tommy Byrne, IRL (Anson SA4B-VW), 43m 55·324s.
7 Ruggero Melgrati, I (Ralt RT3/84-Alfa Romeo), 44m 03·307s; **8** Hasse Thaung, S (Ralt RT3/84-Alfa Romeo), 44m 14·291s; **9** Steven Andskar, S (Ralt RT3/84-Toyota), 44m 18·968s; **10** Luis Villami, E (Ralt RT3/84-Alfa Romeo), 44m 31·428s.
Fastest lap: Nils-Kristian Nissen, DK (Ralt RT3/84-Alfa Romeo), 57·064s, 81·50 mph/131·16 km/h.
European Championship points: 1 Capelli, 50; **2** Berger, 45; **3** Dumfries, 42; **4** Langes, 36; **5** Nielsen, 20; **6** Byrne, 13.

MARLBORO CHAMPIONSHIP RACE, Silverstone Short Circiut, Great Britain, August 27. Marlboro British Formula 3 Championship, round 12. 30 laps of the 1·608-mile/2·588-km circuit, 48·24 miles/77·64 km.
1 Johnny Dumfries, GB (Ralt RT3/83-VW), 27m 21·84s, 105·77 mph/170·22 km/h.
2 Allen Berg, CDN (Ralt RT3/84-Toyota), 27m 32·10s.
3 Mario Hytten, CH (Ralt RT3/84-VW), 27m 38·49s.
4 Paul Jackson, GB (Ralt RT3/84-VW), 27m 41·95s.
5 Keith Fine, GB (Ralt RT3/83-VW), 27m 42·75s (1st class B).
6 Russell Spence, GB (Ralt RT3/84-VW), 27m 44·69s.
7 Tony Trevor, GB (Ralt RT3/83-VW), 27m 45·96s; **8** Carlos Abella, E (Ralt RT3/84-Toyota), 27m 46·29s; **9** Gary Evans, GB (Ralt RT3/84-Toyota), 27m 47·25s; **10** Rob Wilson, NZ (Ralt RT3/84-Toyota), 27m 50·43s.
Fastest lap: Dumfries, 54·36s, 106·49 mph/171·38 km/h.
Marlboro Championship points. Class A: 1 Dumfries, 87; **2** Spence, 52; **3** Berg, 43; **4** Hytten, 38; **5** Abella, 23; **6** Gilbert-Scott, 13; **Class B: 1** Fine, 74; **2** Bradley and Tingling, 46; **4** Hedley and Morgan, 24; **6** Soubriquet, 12.

MARLBORO CHAMPIONSHIP RACE, Spa-Francorchamps Circuit, Belgium, September 1. Marlboro British Formula 3 Championship, round 13. 15 laps of the 4·3179-mile/6·9490-km circuit, 64·79 miles/104·24 km.
1 Ross Cheever, USA (Ralt RT3/84-VW), 36m 47·54s, 105·66 mph/170·04 km/h.
2 Allen Berg, CDN (Ralt RT3/84-Toyota), 36m 53·37s.
3 Dave Coyne, GB (Ralt RT3/84-VW), 37m 03·99s.
4 Volker Weidler, D (Ralt RT3/874-VW), 37m 06·93s.
5 Gary Evans, GB (Ralt RT3/84-Toyota), 37m 08·14s.
6 Dave Scott, GB (Ralt RT3/84-VW), 37m 10·49s.
7 Johnny Dumfries, GB (Ralt RT3/83-VW), 37m 21·38s; **8** Harald Huysman, B (Ralt RT3/84-Toyota), 37m 44·69s; **9** Alfred Heger, D (Ralt RT3/84-VW), 37m 59·48s0 **10** Russell Spence, GB (Ralt RT3/84-VW), 38m 10·21s.
Fastest lap: Coyne, 2m 26·33s, 106·23 mph/170·96 km/h (record).
Marlboro Championship points. Class A: 1 Dumfries, 87; **2** Spence, 52; **3** Berg, 49; **4** Hytten, 38; **5** Abella, 23; **6** Cheever, 14. **Class B: 1** Fine, 74; **2** Bradley, 56; **3** Tingling, 46; **4** Hedley and Morgan, 24; **6** Hall, 16.

MARLBORO CHAMPIONSHIP RACE, Circuit van Zandvoort, Holland, September 16. Marlboro British Formula 3 Championship, round 14. 20 laps of the 2·642-mile/4·252-km circuit, 52·84 miles/85·04 km.
1 Ross Cheever, USA (Ralt RT3/84-VW), 31m 29·46s, 100·68 mph/162·03 km/h.
2 Russell Spence, GB (Ralt RT3/84-VW), 31m 38·34s.
3 Allen Berg, CDN (Ralt RT3/84-Toyota), 31m 42·56s.
4 Dave Scott, GB (Ralt RT3/84-VW), 31m 43·05s.
5 Carlos Abella, E (Ralt RT3/84-Toyota), 31m 46·42s.
6 Volker Weidler, D (Ralt RT3/83-VW), 31m 51·98s.
7 David Hunt, GB (Ralt RT3/84-Toyota), 32m 08·74s; **8** Eric Lang, USA (Ralt RT3/84-Toyota), 32m 09·12s; **9** Richard Weggelaar, NL (Martini MK42-VW), 32m 54·51s; **10** Carlton Tingling, JA (Ralt RT3/82-VW), 19 laps (1st Class B).
Fastest lap: Cheever, 1m 33·62s, 101·60 mph/163·51 km/h.
Marlboro Championship points. Class A: 1 Dumfries, 87; **2** Spence, 58; **3** Berg, 53; **4** Hytten, 38; **5** Abella, 25; **6** Cheever, 24. **Class B: 1** Fine, 74; **2** Bradley, 57; **3** Tingling, 55; **4** Hedley and Morgan, 24; **6** Sobriquet, 18.

EUROPEAN FORMULA 3 CHAMPIONSHIP RACE, Circuit Automobile Paul Armagnac Nogaro, France, September 16. European Formula 3 Championship, round 12. 30 laps of the 1·939-mile/3·120-km circuit, 58·17 miles/93·60 km.
1 John Nielsen, DK (Ralt RT3/84-VW), 36m 58·16s, 94·39 mph/151·91 km/h.
2 Ivan Capelli, I (Martini MK42-Alfa Romeo), 37m 01·42s.
3 Gerhard Berger, A (Ralt RT3/84-Alfa Romeo), 37m 11·34s.
4 Johnny Dumfries, GB (Ralt RT3/83-VW), 37m 27·15s.
5 Bernard Santal, F (Ralt RT3/84-VW), 37m 31·38s.
6 Tommy Byrne, IRL (Anson SA4B-VW), 37m 37·53s.
7 Cathy Muller, F (Ralt RT3/84-Alfa Romeo), 37m 42·03s; **8** Luis Sala, E (Ralt RT3/84-Alfa Romeo), 37m 43·10s; **9** Claudio Langes, I (Ralt RT3/84-Toyota), 37m 51·19s; **10** Jean-Pierre Hoursourigaray, F (Martini MK42-Alfa Romeo), 37m 52·27s.
Fastest lap: Nielsen, 1m 13·43s, 95·05 mph/152·97 km/h.
European Championship points: 1 Capelli, 56; **2** Berger, 49; **3** Dumfries, 45; **4** Langes, 36; **5** Nielsen, 29; **6** Byrne, 14.

MARLBORO CHAMPIONSHIP RACE, Brands Hatch Grand Prix Circuit, Great Britain, September 23. Marlboro British Formula 3 Championship, round 15. 20 laps of the 2·6136-mile/4·2060-km circuit, 52·27 miles/84·12 km.
1 Ross Cheever, USA (Ralt RT3/84-VW), 28m 33·21s, 109·84 mph/176·77 km/h.
2 Allen Berg, CDN (Ralt RT3/84-Toyota), 28m 33·71s.
3 Dave Scott, GB (Ralt RT3/84-VW), 28m 51·73s.
4 Mario Hytten, CH (Ralt RT3/84-VW), 28m 55·72s.
5 Paul Jackson, GB (Ralt RT3/84-VW), 29m 00·83s.
6 David Hunt, GB (Ralt RT3/84-Toyota), 29m 08·98s.
7 Andrew Gilbert-Scott, GB (Ralt RT3/84-VW), 29m 09·33s; **8** Rob Wilson, NZ (Ralt RT3/84-Toyota), 29m 16·31s; **9** Brett Riley, NZ (Ralt RT3/84-Toyota), 29m 19·06s; **10** Keith Fine, GB (Ralt RT3/83-VW), 29m 44·23s (1st class B).
Fastest lap: Russell Spence, GB (Ralt RT3/84-VW), 1m 24·75s, 111·02 mph/178·67 km/h.
Disqualified: Spence finished 3rd on the road in 28m 49·05s but was disqualified for dangerous driving after incidents with Abella and Dumfries.
Marlboro Championship points. Class A: 1 Dumfries, 87; **2** Berg, 60; **3** Spence, 58; **4** Hytten, 41; **5** Cheever, 33; **6** Abella, 25. **Class B: 1** Fine, 84; **2** Bradley, 61; **3** Tingling, 57; **4** Hedley, 27; **5** Morgan, 24; **6** Soubriquet, 19.

MARLBORO CHAMPIONSHIP RACE, Thruxton Circuit, Great Britain, September 30. Marlboro British Formula 3 Championship, round 16. 20 laps of the 2·356-mile/3·792-km circuit, 47·12 miles/75·84 km.
1 Johnny Dumfries, GB (Ralt RT3/83-VW), 24m 51·01s, 113·76 mph/183·08 km/h.
2 Ross Cheever, USA (Ralt RT3/84-VW), 25m 03·56s.
3 Mario Hytten, CH (Ralt RT3/84-VW), 25m 07·48s.
4 Dave Scott, GB (Ralt RT3/84-VW), 25m 08·95s.
5 Russell Spence, GB (Ralt RT3/84-VW), 25m 10·81s.
6 Allen Berg, CDN (Ralt RT3/84-VW), 25m 12·88s.
7 Carlos Abella, E (Ralt RT3/84-Toyota), 25m 14·11s; **8** David Hunt, GB (Ralt RT3/84-Toyota), 25m 27·61s; **9** Paul Jackson, GB (Ralt RT3/83-VW), 25m 27·95s; **10** Rob Wilson, NZ (Ralt RT3/84-Toyota), 25m 29·20s.
Fastest lap: Dumfries, 1m 13·75s, 115·00 mph/185·07 km/h.
Marlboro Championship points. Class A: 1 Dumfries, 97; **2** Berg, 61; **3** Spence, 60; **4** Hytten, 45; **5** Cheever, 39; **6** Abella, 25. **Class B: 1** Fine, 85; **2** Bradley, 65; **3** Tingling, 63; **4** Hedley, 30; **5** Morgan, 24; **6** Sobriquet, 19.

MARLBORO CHAMPIONSHIP RACE, Silverstone Grand Prix Circuit, Great Britain, October 7. Marlboro British Formula 3 Championship, round 17. 15 laps of the 2·932-mile/4·719-km circuit, 43·98 miles/709·79 km.
1 Johnny Dumfries, GB (Ralt RT3/83-VW), 21m 27·54s, 122·96 mph/197/88 km/h.
2 Allen Berg, CDN (Ralt 83/84-Toyota), 21m 33·56s.
3 Andrew Gilbert-Scott, GB (Ralt RT3/84-VW), 21m 33·88s.
4 Russell Spence, GB (Ralt RT3/84-VW), 21m 34·07s.
5 Dave Scott, GB (Ralt RT3/84-VW), 21m 38·36s.
6 Carlos Abella, E (Ralt RT3/84-Toyota), 21m 40·04s.
7 Gary Evans, GB (Ralt RT3/84-Toyota), 21m 42·65s; **8** Mario Hytten, CH (Ralt RT3/84-VW), 21m 42·76s; **9** Rob Wilson, NZ (Ralt RT3/84-Toyota), 21m 56·38s; **10** Paul Jackson, GB (Ralt RT3/83/84-VW), 21m 56·62s.
Fastest lap: Spence, 1m 25·26s, 123·80 mph/199·24 km/h (record).

Final Marlboro Championship points.
Class A:

1 Johnny Dumfries, GB	106
2 Allen Berg, CDN	67
3 Russell Spence, GB	64
4 Mario Hytten, CH	45
5 Ross Cheever, USA	39
6 Carlos Abella, E	26

7 Dave Scott, GB, 19; **8** Andrew Gilbert-Scott, GB, 17; **9** Gary Evans, GB and Tony Trevor, GB, 11; **11** David Hunt, GB, 10; **12** Paul Radisich, NZ and Paul Jackson, GB, 7; **14** Eric Lang, USA and Dave Coyne, GB, 5; **16** Volker Weidler, D, 4; **17** Cor Euser, NL, 1.
Class B:

1 Keith Fine, GB	95
2 Carlton Tingling, Ja	67
3 Steve Bradley, GB	66
4 Gray Hedley, GB	33
5 Richard Morgan, GB	24
6 Steve Kempton, GB	21

7 Anton Sobirquet, GB, 19; **8** Godfrey Hall, GB, 18; **9** Hakan Olausson, S, 7; **10** Mike Blanchet, GB and Bill Burley, GB, 6.

EUROPEAN FORMULA 3 CHAMPIONSHIP RACE, Circuito Permanente del Jarama, Spain, October 21. European Formula 3 Championship, round 13. 30 laps of the 2·058-mile/3·312-km circuit, 61·74 miles/99·36 km.
1 Johnny Dumfries, GB (Ralt RT3/83-VW), 42m 03·70s, 88·07 mph/141·735 km/h.
2 John Nielsen, DK (Ralt RT3/84-VW), 42m 05·44s.
3 Ivan Capelli, I (Martini MK42-Alfa Romeo), 42m 28·83s.
4 Bernard Santel, F (Ralt RT3/84-VW), 42m 31·61s.
5 Luis Sala, E (Ralt RT3/84-Alfa Romeo), 42m 38·50s.
6 Slim Borgudd, S (Anson SA4B-VW), 42m 40·78s.
7 Ruggero Melgrati, I (Ralt RT3/84-Alfa Romeo), 42m 41·21s; **8** Cathy Muller, F (Ralt RT3/84-Alfa Romeo), 42m 44·26s; **9** Ricardo Galiano, E (Martini MK42-Alfa Romeo), 42m 01·29s; **10** Emilio Zapico, E (Ralt RT3/84-Alfa Romeo), 29 laps.
Fastest lap: Not given.

Final championship points:

1 Ivan Capelli, I	60
2 Johnny Dumfries, GB	54
3 Gerherd Berger, A	49
4 Claudio Langes, I	36
5 John Nielsen, DK	35
6 Tommy Byrne, IRL	14

7 Bernard Santel, F, 12; **8** Nils-Kristian Nissen, DK and Ruggero Melgrati, I, 10; **10** Luis Sala, E, 8; **11** Cathy Muller, F, 7; **12** Russell Spence, GB, 6; **13** Adrian Campos, E, 5; **14** Franco Forini, I, 4; **15** James Weaver, GB, 3; **16** David Hunt, GB, Walter Voulaz, F, Fabrizio Barbazza, I and Leo Andersson, S, 2; **20** Frederic Delavallada, F, Gary Evans, GB, Kurt Thiim, DK and Slim Borgudd, S, 1.

1983 results

The final round of the 1983 World Endurance Championship was run after Autocourse 1983/84 went to press.

CASTROL 1000 KMS, Kyalami Grand Prix Circuit, Johannesburg, South Africa, December 10. World Endurance Championship, round 7. 244 laps of the 2·550-mile/4·104-km circuit, 622·20 miles/1001·38 km.
1 Derek Bell/Stefan Bellof, GB/D (2.6 t/c Porsche 956-83), 5h 44m 06·33s, 108·49 mph/174·60 km/h (1st Group C).
2 Riccardo Patrese/Alessandro Nannini, I/I (2.6 t/c Lancia LC-83), 240 laps.
3 Jacky Ickx/Jochen Mass, B/D (2.6 t/c Porsche 956-83), 236.
4 Dieter Schornstein/"John Winter"/Bob Wollek, D/D/F (2.6 t/c Porsche 956), 228.
5 Jonathan Palmer/Jan Lammers, GB/NL (2.6 t/c Porsche 956), 225.
6 Sarel van der Merwe/Tony Martin/Graham Duxbury, ZA/ZA/ZA (2.6 t/c Porsche 956), 224.
7 Leopold von Bayern/Siggi Brun/Klaus Grogor, D/D/ZA (2.8 t/c Porsche 935C), 217; **8** Jens Winther/Lars-Viggo Jensen, S/S (3.5 BMW M1), 200 (1st Group B); **9** Thomas Wiren/Kenneth Leim, S/S (3.3 t/c Porsche 930), 193; **10** John Cooper/Paul Smith/Gorgio Cavalieri, GB/GB/ZA (3.3 t/c Porsche 930), 193.
Fastest lap: Bellof, 1m 15·59s, 121·44 mph/195·44 km/h.

Final World Endurance Championship points. Drivers:

1 Jacky Ickx, B	97
2 Derek Bell, GB	94
3 Jochen Mass, D	82
4 Stefan Bellof, D	75
5 Bob Wollek, F	64
6 Thierry Boutsen, B	44

7 Jan Lammers, NL, 43; **8** Jurgen Lassig, D and Axel Plankenhorn, D, 42; **10** Vern Schuppan, AUS, 40.

Manufacturers: 1 Porsche, 100(140); **2** Lancia, 32; **3** Nimrod-Aston Martin and March-Nissan, 4; **5** Sauber-BMW, 3; **6** Dome-Toyota, 2; **7** URD-BMW, 1. **FIA Junior Group C Cup: 1** Alba-Giannini, 75; **2** Mazda, Harrier-Maxda and March-Toyota, 20; **FIA Grand Touring Cup (Group B). 1** Porsche, 82; **2** BMW, 80.

1984 results

MONZA 1000 KMS/TROFFO FILIPPO CARACCIOLA, Autodromo Nazionale di Monza, Italy, April 23. World Endurance Championship for Makes, round 1. World Endurance Championship for Drivers, round 1. 173 laps of the 3·604-km mile/5·800-km circuit, 623·49 miles/1003·40 km.
1 Derek Bell/Stefan Bellof, GB/D (2.6 t/c Porsche 956-83), 5h 06m 15·6s, 122·15 mph/196·58 km/h (1st Group C).
2 Jacky Ickx/Jochen Mass B/D (2.6 t/c Porsche 956-83), 5h 06m 39·56s.
3 Hans Stuck/Harald Grohs/Walter Brun, D/D/CH (2.6 t/c Porsche 956), 167 laps.
4 Jonathan Palmer/Jan Lammers, GB/NL (2.6 t/c Porsche 956), 169.
5 Dieter Schornstein/Volkert Merl, D/D (2.6 t/c Porsche 956), 155.
6 Pierre Yver/Bernard de Dryver, F/B (3.3 Rondeau M382-Cosworth DFL), 152.
7 Jim Busby/Rick Knoop, USA/USA (2.6 Lola T616-Mazda), 145 (1st Group C2); **8** Jen Winther/Lars-Viggo Jensen, DK/DK (3.5 BMW M1), 144 (1st Group B); **9** Mike Wilds/Ray Mallock/David Duffield, GB/GB/GB (3.0 Ecosse C284-Cosworth DFV), 141; **10** Carlo Facetti/Martino Finotto, I/I (1.8 t/c Alba 002-Giannini), 140.
Fastest lap: Riccardo Patrese, I (2.6 t/c Lancia LC2-84), 1m 38·0s, 132·39 mph/213·06 km/h (record).
Disqualified: Mauro Baldi/Paolo Barilla, I/I (2.6 t/c Lancia LC2-84) finished 3rd in 168 laps but were disqualified due to weight infringement.
Championship points. Drivers: 1 Bell and Bellof, 20; **3** Ickx and Mass, 15; **5** Stuck, Grohs and Brun, 12.
Manufacturers: 1 Porsche, 20; **2** Rondeau-Ford/Cosworth, 6. **Group C2: 1** Lola-Mazda, 20; **2** Ecosse-Ford/Cosworth, 15; **3** Alba-Giannini, 12; **4** Gebhardt-BMW, 10. **Group B: 1** BMW, 20; **2** Porsche, 15.

GRAND PRIX INTERNATIONAL 1000 KMS, Silverstone Grand Prix Circuit, Great Britain, May 13. World Endurance Championship for Makes, round 2. World Endurance Championship for Drivers, round 2. 212 laps of the 2·932-mile/4·719-km circuit, 621·58 miles/1000·43 km.
1 Jacky Ickx/Jochen Mass, B/D (2.6 t/c Porsche 956-83), 5h 05m 21·20s, 122·13 mph/196·55 km/(1st Group C).
2 Klaus Ludwig/Henri Pescarolo, D/F (2.6 t/c Porsche 956), 210 laps.
3 Rupert Keegan/Guy Edwards, GB/GB (2.6 t/c Porsche 956), 207.
4 Paolo Barilla/Mauro Baldi, I/I (2.6 t/c Lancia LC2-84), 206.
5 Jonathan Palmer/Jan Lammers, GB/NL (2.6 t/c Porsche 956), 203.
6 Franz Konrad/David Sutherland, D/GB (2.6 t/c Porsche 956), 202.
7 Beppe Gabbiani/Pier Luigi Martini, I/I (2.6 t/c Lancia LC2-83), 210; **8** Thierry Boutsen/David Hobbs, B/GB (2.6 t/c Porsche 956), 199; **9** Dieter Schornstein/Volkert Merl/"Johnny Winter", D/D/D (2.6 t/c Porsche 956), 198; **10** Stefan Bellof/Derek Bell, D/GB (2.6 t/c Porsche 956), 195.
Fastest lap: Mass, 1m 16·76s, 137·50 mph/221·28 km/h (record).
Other class winners: Group C2: Almo Copelli/Marco Vanoli/Giorgio Pavia, I/CH/I (1.8 t/c Alba 001-Giannini), 188. **Group B:** Edgar Doren/Walter Mertes, D/D (3.5 BMW M1), 170.
Championship points. Drivers: 1 Ickx and Mass, 35; **3** Bell and Bellof, 21; **5** Palmer and Lammers, 18.
Manufacturers: 1 Porsche, 40; **2** Lancia, 10; **3** Rondeau-Ford/Cosworth, 6. **Group C2: 1** Alba-Giannini, 32; **2** Lola-Mazda, 20; **3** Ecosse-Ford/Cosworth and Alba-Ford/Cosworth, 15; **5** ADA-Ford/Cosworth, 12; **6** Gebhardt-BMW, 10. **Group B: 1** BMW, 40; **2** Porsche, 15.

Le Mans 24 Hours

52 GRAND PRIX D'ENDURANCE, LES 24 HEURES DU MANS, Circuit de la Sarthe, Le Mans, France, June 16/17. World Endurance Championship for Makes, round 3. World Endurance Championship for Drivers, round 3. 359 laps of the 8·467-mile/13·626-km circuit, 3039·65 miles/4891·73 km.
1 Klaus Ludwig/Henri Pescarolo, D/F (2.6 t/c Porsche 956B), 359 laps, 126·88 mph/204·18 km/h (1st Group C).
2 Jean Rondeau/John Paul Jnr/Preston Henn, F/USA/USA (2.6 t/c Porsche 956), 357 laps.
3 David Hobbs/Philippe Streiff/Sarel van der Merwe, GB/F/ZA (2.6 t/c Porsche 956B), 350.
4 Walter Brun/Bob Akin/Leopold von Bayern, CH/USA/D (2.6 t/c Porsche 956B), 339.
5 Volkert Merl/Dieter Schornstein/"Johnny Winter", D/D/D (2.6 t/c Porsche 956), 339.
6 Vern Schuppan/Alan Jones/Jean-Pierre Jarier, AUS/AUS/F (2.6 t/c Porsche 956 B), 336.
7 Oscar Larrauri/Massimo Sigala/Joel Gouthier, RA/I/F (2.6 t/c Porsche 956), 334; **8** Bob Wollek/Alessandro Nannini, F/I (3.0 t/c Lancia LC2-84), 325; **9** Tiff Needel/David Sutherland/Rusty French, GB/GB/AUS (2.6 t/c Porsche 956), 320; **10** John Morton/John O'Steen/Yashima Katayama, USA/USA/J (2.6 Lola T616-Mazda), 319 (1st Group C2); **11** Jean-Paul Liberti/Jean-Philippe Grand/Pascal Witmeur, B/F/B (3.0 Rondeau M379C-Cosworth DFV), 309; **12** Boy Hayje/Jim Busby/Rick Knoop, NL/USA/USA (2.6 Lola T616-Mazda), 294; **13** Jim Mullen/Walt Bohren/Alain Ferte, USA/USA/F (3.3 Rondeau M482-Cosworth DFL), 292; **14** Jean-Francois Yvon/Philippe Dagoreau/Pierre de Thoisy, F/F/F (3.5 BMW M1), 291 (1st Group B); **15** David Kennedy/Jean-Michel Martin/Philippe Martin, IRL/B/B (2.6 Mazda 727C), 290; **16** Claude Haldi/Jean Krucker/Altefried Heger, CH/CH/D (3.3 t/c Porsche 930), 284; **17** Raymond Touroul/Valentin Bertapelle/Thierry Perrier, F/F/F (3.0 Porsche 911), 282; **18** Jean-Marie Almeras/Jacques Almeras/Tom Winlas, F/F/USA (3.3 t/c Porsche 930), 268; **19** Almo Copelli/Guido Dacco/Davide Pavia, I/I/I (1.8 t/c Alba 001-Giannini), 261; **20** Yojiro Terada/Pierre Dieudonne/Tahashi Yorino, J/B/J (2.6 Mazda 727C), 261; **21** Carlo Facetti/Martini Finotto/Marco Vanoli, I/I/I (1.8 t/c Alba 002-Giannini), 257; **22** Raymond Boutinaud/Philippe Renault, F/F (4.7 Porsche 928), 255.
Fastest lap: Wollek, 3m 28·9s, 145·16 mph/234·82 km/h (record).
Retired: Brian Redman/Doc Bundy/Bob Tullius, GB/USA/USA (6.0 Jaguar XJR-5), 291 laps, gearbox; Mauro Baldi/Paolo Barilla/Hans Heyer, I/I/D (3.0 t/c Lancia LC2-84), 275, engine; Alain de Cadanet/Chris Craft/Allan Grice, GB/GB/AUS (2.6 t/c Porsche 956), 274, engine; Michel Ferte/Edgar Doren, F/D (2.6 t/c Porsche 952), 247, ignition; Jonathan Palmer/Jan Lammers, GB/NL (2.6 t/c Porsche 962), 239, fan bearing; John Watson/Claude Ballot-Lena/Tony Adamowicz, GB/F/USA (6.0 Jaguar XJR-5), 212, accident; Stefan Johansson/Jean-Louis Schlesser/Mauricio de Narvaez, S/F/COL (2.6 t/c Porsche 956), 170, accident; Nick Faure/Richard Jones/Mark Galvin, GB/GB/GB (3.3 Dome RC82-Cosworth DFL), 156, oil pressure; Bernard de Dryver/Pierre Yver/Pierre-Francois Rousselot, B/F/F (3.3 Rondeau M382-Cosworth DFL), 155, electrics; Yves Courage/Michel Dubois/John Jellinek, F/F/USA (3.3 Cougar C-02-Cosworth DFL), 153, oil pump; George Fouche/Jurgen Lassig/John Graham, ZA/D/CDN (2.6 t/c Porsche 956), 147, accident; Paul Smith/David Ovey/Maggie Smith-Haas, GB/GB/USA (3.3 t/c Porsche 930), 146, oil leak; Pete Brock/Larry Perkins, AUS/AUS (2.6 t/c Porsche 956), 145, accident; Richard Lloyd/Rene Metge/Nick Mason, GB/F/GB (2.6 t/c Porsche 956-83), 139, disqualified; Roger Dorchy/Alain Couderc/Gerard Patte, F/F/F (2.8 t/c WM P83B-Peugeot), 122, gearbox; Pier Luigi Martini/Beppe Gabbiani/Xavier Lapeyre, I/I/F (2.6 t/c Lancia LC2-84), 117, engine; Jens Winther/David Mercer/Lars-Viggo Jensen, DK/GB/DK (3.5 BMW M1), 96, axle; Ken Madren/M. L. Speer/Wayne Pickering, USA/USA/USA (3.4 t/c March 84G-Buick), 95, engine; Ray Mallock/Drake Olson, GB/USA (5.3 Nimrod C 2B-Aston Martin), 94, accident; Richard Attwood/Mike Salmon/John Sheldon, GB/GB/GB (5.3 Nimrod C 2B-Aston Martin), 92, accident; Marcel Pignard/Jean-Daniel Raulet/Pascal Pettiot, F/F/F (2.8 t/c WM P83B-Peugeot), 74, overheating; Roberto Moreno/Guy Edwards/Rupert Keegan, BR/GB/GB (2.6 t/c Porsche 962), 72, accident; Michel Lateste/"Segolin"/Michel Bienvault, F/F/F (3.3 t/c Porsche 930), 70, engine; Gordon Spice/Neil Crang/Ray Bellm, GB/GB/GB (3.3 Tiga GC84-Cosworth DFL), 69, engine; Mauricio Micangeli/Roberto Marazzi/Daniel Lacaud, I/I/F (4.9 Ferrari 512BB), 65, gearbox; Francois Migault/Steve Kempton/Francois Servanin, F/GB/F (3.3 Lola T610-Cosworth DFL), 52, accident; Christian Bussi/Bruno Lien/Jack Griffin, F/F/USA (3.3 Rondeau

M382-Cosworth DFL), 49, engine; Ian Harrower/Bill Wolff/Glen Smith, GB/USA/USA (3.3 ADA 01-Cosworth DFL), 42, suspension; Hubert Striebig/Jacques Heuclin/Noel del Bello, F/F/F (3.5 Sthemo-BMW), 41, gearbox; Mike Wilds/David Leslie/David Duffield, GB/GB/GB (3.0 Ecosse C284-Cosworth DFV), 36, fuel pump; John Cooper/Dudley Wood/Barry Robinson, GB/GB/GB (2.9 t/c Grid S2-Porsche), 10, electrics.
Championship points. Drivers: 1 Ickx, Mass, Ludwig and Pescarolo, 35; **5** Brun, 22; **6** Bell and Bellof, 21.
Manufacturers: 1 Porsche, 60; **2** Lancia, 13; **3** Rondeau-Ford/Cosworth, 6. **Group C2:** Alba-Giannini and Lola-Mazda, 40; **3** Ecosse-Ford/Cosworth, Rondeau-Ford/Cosworth and Alba-Ford/Cosworth, 15; **6** ADA-Ford/Cosworth, 12. **Group B: 1** BMW, 60; **2** Porsche, 30.

ADAC NURBURGRING 1000 KMS, Nürburgring Circuit, German Federal Republic, July 15. World Endurance Championship for Makes, round 4. World Endurance Championship for Drivers, round 4. 207 laps of the 2·822-mile/4·542-km circuit, 584·15 miles/940·19 km (race shortened to 6 hours).
1 Stefan Bellof/Derek Bell, D/GB (2.6 t/c Porsche 956-83), 6h 00m 43·59s, 97·17 mph/156·38 km/h (1st Group C).
2 Thierry Boutsen/David Hobbs, B/GB (2.6 t/c Porsche 956 B), 6h 00m 59·27s.
3 Sandro Nannini/Paolo Barilla, I/I (3.0 t/c Lancia LC2-84), 206 laps.
4 Jonathan Palmer/Jan Lammers/Christian Danner, GB/NL/D (2.6 t/c Porsche 956), 205.
5 Marc Surer/Manfred Winkelhock, CH/D (2.6 t/c Porsche 956B), 204.
6 Oscar Larrauri/Massimo Sigala, RA/I (2.6 t/c Porsche 956), 203.
7 Jacky Ickx/Jochen Mass, B/D (2.6 t/c Porsche 956-83), 201; **8** Stefan Johansson/Ayrton Senna da Silva/Henri Pescarolo, S/BR/F (2.6 t/c Porsche 956B), 197; **9** Walter Brun/Leopold von Bayern, CH/D (2.6 t/c Porsche 956), 196; **10** Dieter Schornstein/Volkert Merl/"Johnny Winter", D/D/D (2.6 t/c Porsche 956), 194.
Fastest lap: Palmer, 1m 32·75s, 109·55 mph/176·29 km/h (record).
Other class winners: Group C2: Gordon Spice/Neil Crang/Roy Bellm, GB/AUS/GB (3.3 Tiga GC84-Cosworth DFL), 185. **Group B:** Helmut Gall/Kurt Koenig/Altfrid Heger, D/D/D (3.5 BMW M1), 176.
Championship points. Drivers. 1 Bell and Bellof, 41; **3** Ickx and Mass, 39; **5** Pescarolo, 38; **6** Ludwig, 35.
Manufacturers: 1 Porsche, 60; **2** Lancia, 25; **3** Rondeau-Ford/Cosworth, 6. **Group C2: 1** Lola-Mazda, 55; **2** Alba Giannini, 50; **3** Tiga-Ford/Cosworth, 20; **4** Ecosse-Ford/Cosworth, Rondeau-Ford/Cosworth and Alba-Ford/Cosworth, 15. **Group B: 1** BMW, 80; **2** Porsche, 40.

BRITISH AEROSPACE 1000 KMS, Brands Hatch Grand Prix Circuit, Great Britain, July 29. World Endurance Championship for Drivers, round 5. 238 laps of the 2·6136-mile/4·2060-km circuit, 622·04 miles/1001·03 km.
1 Jonathan Palmer/Jan Lammers, GB/NL (2.6 t/c Porsche 956), 5h 41m 46·33s, 109·20 mph/175·74 km/h (1st Group C).
2 Jochen Mass/Henri Pescarolo, D/F (2.6 t/c Porsche 956B), 236 laps.
3 Thierry Boutsen/Ruperb Keegan/Guy Edwards, B/GB/GB (2.6 t/c Porsche 962), 234.
4 David Sutherland/Desire Wilson/George Fouche, GB/ZA/ZA (2.6 t/c Porsche 956), 229.
5 Stefan Bellof/Harald Grohs, D/D (2.6 t/c Porsche 956B), 224.
6 David Hobbs/Guy Edwards/Thierry Boutsen, GB/GB/B (2.6 t/c Porsche 956), 222.
7 Mauro Baldi/Pier Luigi Martini/Bob Wollek, I/I/F (3.0 t/c Lancia LC2-84), 221; **8** Walter Brun/Leopold von Bayern, CH/D (2.6 t/c Porsche 956), 221; **9** Dieter Schornstein/Volkert Merl/"Johnny Winter", D/D/D (2.6 t/c Porsche 956), 217; **10** Neil Crang/Roy Bellm, AUS/GB (3.0 Tiga CG84-Cosworth DFV), 207 (1st Group C2).
Fastest lap: Palmer and Wollek, 1m 21·03s, 116·11 mph/186·66 km/h.
Other class winners. Group B: Jens Winther/David Mercer/Lars-Viggo Jensen, DK/GB/DK (3.5 BMW M1), 191.
Championship points. Drivers: 1 Mass, 54; **2** Pescarolo, 53; **3** Bellof, 49; **4** Palmer and Lammers, 48; **6** Bell, 41.

BUDWEISER GT 1000 KMS, Mosport Park Circuit, Ontario, Canada, August 5. World Endurance Championship for Makes, round 5. World Endurance Championship for Drivers, round 6. 253 laps of the 2·459-mile/3·957-km circuit, 622·13 miles/1001·12 km.
1 Jacky Ickx/Jochen Mass, B/D (2.6 t/c Porsche 956-83), 6h 00m 41·41s, 103·49 mph/166·55 km/h (1st Group C).
2 David Hobbs/Rupert Keegan/Franz Konrad, GB/GB/D (2.6 t/c Porsche 956), 245 laps.
3 Almo Coppelli/Guido Dacco, I/I (1.8 t/c Alba 001-Giannini), 229 (1st Group C2).
4 Stefan Bellof/Derek Bell, D/GB (2.6 t/c Porsche 956-83), 221.
5 Pasquale Barberio/Maurizio Gellini/Gerardo Vettelli, I/I/I (3.0 Alba AR3-Cosworth DFV), 217.
6 Martino Finotto/Carlo Facetti/Alfredo Sebastini, I/I/I (1.8 t/c Alba AR2-Giannini), 204.
7 Jeremy Rossiter/Peter Lockhart/Roy Baker, GB/CDN/GB (1.7 t/c Tiga CG84-Ford), 185. No other finishers.
Fastest lap: Bellof, 1m 13·874s, 119·83 mph/192·85 km/h.
Championship points. Drivers: 1 Mass, 74; **2** Ickx and Bellof, 59; **4** Pescarolo, 53; **5** Bell and Hobbs, 51.
Manufacturers: 1 Porsche, 100; **2** Lancia, 25; **3** Rondeau-Ford/Cosworth, 6. **Group C2: 1** Alba-Giannin, 70; **2** Lola-Mazda, 55; **3** Alba-Ford/Cosworth and Tiga-Ford/Cosworth, 30; **5** Ecosse-Ford/Cosworth and Rondeau-Ford/Cosworth, 15. **Group B: 1** BMW, 80; **2** Porsche, 40.

ROTHMANS SPA 1000 KMS, Spa-Francorchamps Circuit, Belgium, September 2. World Endurance Championship for Makes, round 6. World Endurance Championship for Drivers, round 7. 144 laps of the 4·3179-mile/6·9490-km circuit, 621·78 miles/1000·66 km.
1 Stefan Bellof/Derek Bell, D/GB (2.6 t/c Porsche 956-83), 5h 53m 17·19s, 105·60 mph/169·95 km/h (1st Group C).
2 Jochen Mass/Jacky Ickx, D/B (2.6 t/c Porsche 956-83), 5h 54m 14·90s.
3 Hans Stuck/Harald Grohs/Walter Brun, D/D/CH (2.6 t/c Porsche 956B), 142 laps.
4 Massimo Sigala/Oscar Larrauri, I/RA (2.6 t/c Porsche 956), 141.
5 Jurgen Lässig/Herve Regout/Philippe Martin, D/B/B (2.6 t/c Porsche 956), 141.
6 Vern Schuppan/John Watson, AUS/GB (2.6 t/c Porsche 956-83), 139.
7 George Fouche/Kees Kroesemeijer, ZA/NL (2.6 t/c Porsche 956), 138; **8** Hans Heyer/Dieter Schornstein/"Johnny Winter", D/D/D (2.6 t/c Porsche 956), 137; **9** Gordon Spice/Neil Crang/Ray Bellm, GB/AUS/GB (3.3 Tiga GC84-Cosworth DFL), 128 (1st Group C2); **10** Jean-Philippe Grand/Pascal Witmeur/Jean-Paul Liberti, F/B/B (3.0 Rondeau M379C-Cosworth DFV), 121.
Fastest lap: Bellof, 2m 15·57s, 114·66 mph/184·53 km/h.
Other class winners: Group B: Jens Winther/David Mercer/Lars-Viggo Jensen, DK/GB/DK (3.5 BMW M1), 121.
Championship points. Drivers: 1 Mass, 89; **2** Bellof, 79; **3** Ickx, 74; **4** Bell, 71; **5** Pescarolo, 53; **6** Palmer and Lammers, 48.
Manufacturers: 1 Porsche, 120; **2** Lancia, 25; **3** Rondeau-Ford/Cosworth, 6. **Group C2: 1** Alba-Giannini, 90; **2** Lola-Mazda, 55; **3** Tiga-Ford/Cosworth, 50; **4** Rondeau-Ford/Cosworth and Alba-Ford/Cosworth, 30;) **6** Gebhardt-BMW, 22. **Group B: 1** BMW, 100; **2** Porsche, 52.

1000 KMS di IMOLA, Autodromo Dino Ferrari, Imola, Italy, September 16. World Endurance Championship for drivers, round 8. 199 laps of the 3·132-mile/5·040-km circuit, 623·27 miles/1002·96 km.
1 Stefan Bellof/Hans Stuck, D/D (2.6 t/c Porsche 956B) 5h 54m 56·32s, 105·35 mph/169·54 km/h (1st Group C).
2 Jonathan Palmer/Jan Lammers, GB/NL (2.6 t/c Porsche 956 GTI), 5h 55m 30·53s.
3 Jochen Mass/Henri Pescarolo/Hans Heyer, D/F/D (2.6 t/c Porsche 956B), 197 laps.
4 Walter Brun/George Fouche/Leopold von Bayern, D/ZA/D (2.6 t/c Porsche 956), 195.
5 Oscar Larrauri/Massimo Sigala, RA/I (2.6 t/c Porsche 956), 193.
6 Harald Grohs/Herve Regout/Jurgen Lassig, D/B/D (2.6 t/c Porsche 956), 191.
7 Hans Heyer/"Johnny Winter"/Dieter Schornstein, D/D/D (2.6 t/c Porsche 956), 190; **8** Rupert Keegan/Franz Konrad/David Hobbs, GB/D/GB (2.6 t/c Porsche 956), 190; **9** Mauro Baldi/Pier Luigi Martini, I/I (3.0 t/c Lancia LC2-84), 178; **10** Gordon Spice/Ray Bellm/Neil Crang, GB/GB/AUS (3.3 Tiga GC84-Cosworth DFL), 177 (1st Group C2).
Fastest lap: Martini, 1m 37·84s, 115·24 mph/185·45 km/h (record).
Other class winners: Group B: Rolf Goering/Hans-Jurg Duerig/Claude Haldi, D/D/CH (3.5 BMW M1), 167.
Championship points. Drivers: 1 Mass, 101; **2** Bellof, 99; **3** Ickx, 74; **4** Bell, 71; **5** Pescarolo, 65; **6** Palmer and Lammers, 63.

FUJI 1000 KMS, Fuji International Speedway, Japan, September 30. World Endurance Championship for Makes, round 7. World Endurance Championship for Drivers, round 9. 226 laps of the 2·7404-mile/4·4102-km circuit, 619·33 miles/996·71 km.
1 Stefan Bellof/John Watson, D/GB (2.6 t/c Porsche 956-83), 5h 30m 00·37s, 112·60 mph/181·21 km/h (1st Group C).
2 Jochen Mass/Jacky Ickx, D/B (2.6 t/c Porsche 956-83), 5h 30m 32·67s.
3 Hans Stuck/Vern Schuppan, D/AUS (2.6 t/c Porsche 956), 224 laps.
4 Stefan Johansson/Henri Pescarolo, S/F (2.6 t/c Porsche 956), 222.
5 Manfred Winkelhock/Mike Thackwell, D/NZ (2.6 t/c Porsche 956), 216.
6 Naoki Nagasaka/Keiichi Suzuki, J/J (3.5 Lotec M1C-BMW), 209 (1st Group C2).
7 Eje Elgh/Masanori Sekiya, S/J (2.1 t/c Dome 84C-Toyota), 206; **8** Tohru Shimegi/Kaoru Iida/Norimasa Sakamoto, J/J/J (2.6 March 85SC-Mazda), 205; **9** Jan Lammers/Jonathan Palmer, NL/GB (2.6 t/c Porsche 956 GTi), 204; **10** Chuck Kendall/Jin Cook, USA/USA (5.8 Lola T600-Chevrolet), 201.
Fastest lap: Not available.
Championship points (prior to final rounds in November). Drivers:

1	Stefan Bellof, D	119
2	Jochen Mass, D	116
3	Jacky Ickx, B	89
4	Henri Pescarolo, F	75
5	Derek Bell, GB	71
6=	Jonathan Palmer, GB	63
6=	Jan Lammers, NL	63

8 Hans Stuck, D, 56; **9** David Hobbs, GB, 54; **10** Walter Brun, CH, 49.
Manufacturers:

1	Porsche,	140
2	Lancia,	25
3=	Rondeau-Ford/Cosworth,	6
3=	Dome-Toyota,	6
5	LM-Nissan,	2

Group C2:

1	Alba-Giannini,	90
2	Lola-Mazda,	67
3	Tiga-Ford/Cosworth,	50
4=	Rondeau-Ford/Cosworth,	30
4=	Alba-Ford/Cosworth,	30
6	Gebhardt-BMW,	22

7 Lotec-BMW, 20; **8** Mazda, 16; **9** Ecosse-Ford/Cosworth and March-Mazda, 15.
Group B:

1	BMW,	100
2	Porsche,	52.

Final results will be given in autocourse 1985/86.

European Touring Car Championship

500 KM di MONZA, Autodromo Nazionale di Monza, Italy, April 1. European Touring Car Championship, round 1. 87 laps of the 3·604-mile/5·800-km circuit, 313·55 miles/504·60 km.
1 Tom Walkinshaw/Hans Heyer, GB/D (5.3 Jaguar XJ-S), 3h 25m 31·7s, 91·53 mph/147·30 km/h (1st over 2500 cc class).
2 Helmut Kelleners/Gianfranco Brancatelli, D/I (3.5 BM2 635 CSi), 3h 25m 39·4s.
3 Marc Sourd/Roger Dorchy, F/F (3.5 BMW 635 CSi), 3h 26m 53·4s.
4 Umberto Grano/Sigi Müller Jnr, I/D (3.5 BMW 635 CSi), 86 laps.
5 Alain Cudini/Dirk Vermeersch, F/NL (3.5 BMW 635 CSi), 86.
6 Thomas Lindstrom/Valentin Simons, S/B (2.0 t/c Volvo 240 Turbo), 86.
7 Walter Brun/Harald Grohs, CH/D (3.5 BMW 635 CSi), 86; **8** Willi Bergmeister/Pierre-Alain Thibaut, D/B (3.5 BMW 635 CSi), 85; **9** Marco Vanoli/Rene Hollinger, CH/CH (3.5 BMW 635 CSi), 85; **10** Nils-Kristian Nissen/Peter Elgaard, DK/DK (3.5 BMW 635 CSi), 85.
Fastest lap: Martin Brundle, GB (5.3 Jaguar XJ-S), 2m 15·3s, 95·89 mph/154·32 km/h.
Other class winners. 1601cc-2500cc: Rinaldo Drovandi/Emilio Zapico, I/E (2.5 Alfa Romeo GTV6), 86. **Up to 1600cc:** John Nielsen/Erik Hoyer/Jorgen Poulsen, DK/DK/DK (1.6 Toyota Corolla), 77.
Championship points. Drivers: 1 Walkinshaw and Heyer, 29; **3** Kelleners and Brancatelli, 21; **5** Drovandi, Zapico, Nielsen, Hoyer and Poulsen, 20.
Manufacturers: 1 Jaguar, Alfa Romeo and Toyota, 20; **4** BMW and Ford, 15; **6** Alfa Romeo, 8.

500 KM di VALLELUNGA, Autodromo di Vallelunga, Italy, April 8. European Touring Car Championship, round 2. 157 laps of the 1·988-mile/3·200-km circuit, 312·12 miles/502·40 km.
1 Alain Cudini/Dany Snobeck, F/F (3.5 BMW 635 CSi), 4h 05m 11·96s, 76·39 mph/122·94 km/h (1st over 2500cc class).
2 Hans Stuck/Dieter Quester, D/A (3.5 BMW 635 CSi), 4h 05m 32·13s.
3 Tom Walkinshaw/Hans Heyer, GB/D (5.3 Jaguar XJ-S), 156 laps.
4 Helmut Kelleners/Gianfranco Brancatelli, D/I (3.5 BMW 635 CSi), 155.
5 Maurizio Micangeli/Giancarlo Naddeo, I/I (3.5 BMW 635 CSi), 155.
6 Bretislav Enge/Jacques Isler, CS/CH (3.5 BMW 635 CSi), 154.
7 Umberto Grano/Sigi Muller Jnr, I/D (3.5 BMW 635 CSi), 164; **8** Enzo Calderari/Chuck Nicholson, CH/GB (5.3 Jaguar XJ-S), 154; **9** Stefan Johansson/Zdenek Vojtech, S/CS (3.5 BMW 635 CSi), 153; **10** Pierre DieudonneMichel Delcourt, B/B (2.0 t/c Volvo 240 Turbo), 153.
Fastest lap: Kelleners/Brancatelli, 1m 25·66s, 83·57 mph/134·49 km/h.
Other class winners. 1601cc-2500cc: Marcello Cipriani/Daniele Toffoli, I/I (2.5 Alfa Romeo GTV6), 150. **Up to 1600cc:** Pierre Fermine/Simon de Liedekerke, B/B (1.6 VW Golf GTi), 139.
Championship points. Drivers: 1 Walkinshaw and Heyer, 45; **3** Cudini, 39; **4** Nielsen and Hoyer, 35; **6** Kelleners and Brancatelli, 34.
Manufacturers: 1 Alfa Romeo, 40; **2** BMW and Toyota, 35; **4** Jaguar, 32; **5** VW, 20; **6** Ford, 15.

DONINGTON 500, Donington Park Circuit, Great Britain, April 29. European Touring Car Championship, round 3. 160 laps of the 1·9573-mile/3·1500-km circuit, 313·17 miles/504·00 km.
1 Win Percy/Chuck Nicholson, GB/GB (5.3 Jaguar XJ-S), 3h 42m 42·55s, 84·37 mph/135·78 km/h (1st over 2500 cc class).
2 James Weaver/Vince Woodman, GB/GB (3.5 BMW 635 CSi), 3h 43m 11·33s.
3 Dieter Quester/Hans Stuck, A/D (3.5 BMW 635 CSi), 159 laps.
4 Umberto Grano/Sigi Müller Jnr, I/D (3.5 BMW 635 CSi), 159.
5 Jean-Louis Schlesser/Enzo Calderari, F/Ch (5.3 Jaguar XJ-S), 159.
6 Alain Cudini/Dany Snobeck, F/F (3.5 BMW 635 CSi), 159.
7 Frank Sytner/Barrie Williams, GB/GB (3.5 BMW 635 CSi), 158; **8** Ulf Granberg/Gregor Petersson, S/S (2.0 t/c Tolvo 242 Turbo), 159; **9** Tom Walkinshaw/Hans Heyer, GB/D (5.3 Jaguar XJ-S), 158; **10** Armin Hahne/Marc Duez, D/B (3.5 Rover Vitesse), 156.
Fastest lap: Walkinshaw, 1m 19·33s, 88·82 mph/142·94 km/h (record).
Other class winners. Combined up to 1600cc and 1601cc-2500cc: Georges Cremer/Dany Swyssen, B/B (2.5 Alfa Romeo GTV6), 152.
Championship points. Drivers: 1 Walkinshaw and Heyer, 47; **3** Cudini, 46; **4** Hoyer and Poulsen, 45; **6** Cipriani and Toffoli, 38.
Manufacturers: 1 Alfa Romeo, 60; **2** Jaguar, 52; **3** BMW, 50; **4** Toyota, 35; **5** Ford, 27; **6** VW, 20.

ENNA-PERGUSA 500 KMS, Ente Autodromo di Pergusa, Enna, Sicily, May 13. European Touring Car Championship, round 4. 102 laps of the 3·076-mile/4·950-km circuit, 313·75 miles/504·90 km.
1 Martin Brundle/Enzo Calderari, GB/CH (5.3 Jaguar XJ-S), 3h 12m 23·52s, 97·84 mph/157·46 km/h (1st over 2500cc class).
2 Tom Walkinshaw/Hans Heyer, GB/D (5.3 Jaguar XJ-S), 3h 12m 45·01s.
3 Win Percy/Chuck Nicholson, GB/GB (5.3 Jaguar XJ-S), 3h 12m 50·10s.
4 Helmut Kelleners/Gianfranco Brancatelli, D/I (3.5 BMW 635 CSi), 101 laps.
5 Dieter Quester/Hans Stuck, A/D (3.5 BMW 635 CSi), 101.
6 Anders Olofsson/Thomas Lindstrom, S/S (2.0 t/c Volvo 242 Turbo), 100.
7 Marco Micangeli/Maurizio Micangeli, I/I (3.5 BMW 635 CSi), 100; **8** Ulf Granberg/Gregor Petersson, S/S (2.0 t/c Volvo 242 Turbo), 100; **9** Axel Felder/Jurgen Hamelmann, D/D (3.5 BMW 635 CSi), 99; **10** Rinaldo Drovandi/Emilio Zapico, I/E (2.5 Alfa Romeo GTV6), 98 (1st 1601cc-2500cc class.
Fastest lap: Brundle, 1m 50·20s, 100·48 mph/161·71 km/h.
Other class winners. Up to 1600cc: John Nielsen/Eric Joyer/Jorgen Poulsen, DK/DK/DK (1.6 Toyota Corolla).
Championship points. Drivers: 1 Walkinshaw and Heyer, 68; **3** Hoyer and Poulsen, 65; **5** Nielsen, 55; **6** Drovandi, Zapico, Cipriani and Toffoli, 50.
Manufacturers: 1 Alfa Romeo, 80; **2** Jaguar, 72; **3** BMW, 60; **4** Toyota, 35; **5** Ford, 39; **6** VW, 35.

EUROPEAN TOURING CAR CHAMPIONSHIP RACE, Brno, Czechoslovakia, June 10. European Touring Car Championship, round 5. 57 laps of the 6·788-mile/10·925-km circuit, 386·92 miles/622·73 km.
1 Tom Walkinshaw/Hans Heyer, GB/D (5.3 Jaguar XJ-S), 3h 32m 20·50s, 109·28 mph/175·87 km/h (1st over 2500cc class).
2 Win Percy/Chuck Nicholson, GB/GB (5.3 Jaguar XJ-S), 3h 33m 02·62s.
3 Enzo Calderari/David Sears, CH/GB (5.3 Jaguar XJ-S), 56 laps.
4 Eje Elgh/Ulf Granberg, S/S (2.0 t/c Volvo 240 Turbo), 56.
5 Helmut Kelleners/Gianfranco Brancatelli, D/I (3.5 BMW 635 CSi), 56.
6 Hans Stuck/Dieter Quester, D/A (3.5 BMW 635 CSi), 56.
7 Jeff Allam/Marc Duez, GB/B (3.5 Rover Vitesse), 56; **8** Sigi Muller Jnr/Umberto Grano, D/I (3.5 BMW 635 CSi), 55; **9** Bretislav Enge/Eddy Joosen, CS/B (3.5 BMW 635 CSi), 55; **10** Marco Micangeli/Maurizio Micangeli, I/I (3.5 BMW 635 CSi), 55.
Fastest lap: Not given
Other class winners. 1601cc-2500cc: Lella Lombardi/Giorgio Francia, I/I (2.5 Alfa Romeo GTV6), 54. **Up to 1600cc:** Hagen Arit/Elmar Holscher, D/D (1.6 Audi 80 GLE), 49.
Championship points. Drivers: 1 Walkinshaw and Heyer, 97; **3** Hoyer and Poulsen, 73; **5** Percy, 66; **6** Drovandi, 62.
Manufacturers: 1 Alfa Romeo, 100; **2** Jaguar, 92; **3** BMW, 68; **4** Toyota, 63; **5** VW, 50; **6** Ford, 49.

EUROPEAN TOURING CAR CHAMPIONSHIP RACE, Österreichring, Austria, June 17. European Touring Car Championship, round 6. 99 laps of the 3·692-mile/5·942-km circuit, 365·51 miles/588·26 km.
1 Tom Walkinshaw/Hans Heyer, GB/D (5.3 Jaguar XJ-S), 3h 31m 10·19s, 104·48 mph/168·14 km/h (1st over 2500cc class).
2 Wins Percy/Chuck Nicholson, GB/GB (5.3 Jaguar XJ-S), 3h 31m 42·18s.
3 Umberto Grano/Sigi Muller Jnr, I/D (3.5 BMW 635 CSi), 98 laps.
4 Thomas Lindstrom/Anders Olofsson, S/S (2.0 t/c Volvo 240 Turbo), 98.
5 Dieter Quester/Hans Stuck, A/D (3.5 BMW 635 CSi), 97.
6 Helmut Kelleners/Gianfranco Brancatelli, D/I (3.5 BMW 635 CSi), 97.
7 Marc Duez/Jeff Allam, B/GB (3.5 Rover Vitesse), 97; **8** Patrick Neve/Jean-Marie Pirnay, B/B (2.0 t/c Volvo 242 Turbo), 97; **9** Bretislav Enge/Manfred Wergeniz, CS/A (3.5 BMW 635 CSi), 96; **10** Roberto Sigala/Marco Micangeli, I/I (3.5 BMW 635 CSi), 96.
Fastest lap: Walkinshaw, 2m 04·44s, 107·45 mph/172·92 km/h.
Other class winners, 1601cc-2500cc: Rinaldo Drovandi/Dagmar Suster, I/CH (2.5 Alfa Romeo GTV6), 95. **Up to 1600cc:** Pierre Fermine/Simon de Liedekerke, B/B (1.6 VW Golf GTi), 88.
Championship points. Drivers: 1 Walkinshaw and Heyer, 126; **3** Percy, 87; **4** Drovandi, 82; **5** Hoyer and Poulsen, 73.
Manufacturers: 1 Alfa Romeo, 120; **2** Jaguar, 112; **3** BMW, 40; **4** Toyota, 73; **5** VW, 70; **6** Ford, 49.

EUROPEAN TOURING CAR CHAMPIONSHIP RACE, Salzburgring, Austria, July 1. European Touring Car Championship, round 7. 141 laps of the 2·635-mile/4·241-ikm circuit, 371·54 miles/597·98 km.
1 Win Percy/Chuck Nicholson, GB/GB (5.3 Jaguar XJ-S), 3h 31m 27·16s, 105·82 mph/170·30 km/h (1st over 2500cc class).
2 Enzo Calderari/David Sears, CH/GB (5.3 Jaguar XJ-S), 3h 32m 32s.
3 Helmut Kelleners/Gianfranco Brancatelli, D/I (3.5 BMW 635 CSi), 140 laps.
4 Ulf Granberg/Eje Elgh, S/S (2.0 t/c Volvo 240 Turbo), 140.
5 Steve Soper/Armin Hahne, GB/D (3.5 Rover Vitesse), 139.
6 Umberto Grano/Sigi Muller Jnr, I/D (3.5 BMW 635 CSi), 139.
7 Jeff Allam/Eddy Joosen, GB/B (3.5 Rover Vitesse), 139; **8** Gerhard Berger/Roberto Ravaglia, A/I (3.5 BMW 635 CSi), 138; **9** Pierre Dieudonne/Michel Delcourt, B/B (3.5 Rover Vitesse), 134; **10** Dieter Quester/Hans Stuck, A/D (3.5 BMW 635 CSi), 134.
Fastest lap: Percy, 1m 26·93s, 109·09 mph/175·56 km/h.
Other class winners: 1601cc-2500cc: Lella Lombardi/Giorgio Francia, I/I (2.5 Alfa Romeo GTV6), 133. **Up to 1600cc:** John Nielsen/Eric Hoyer, DK/DK (1.6 Toyota Corolla), 124.
Championship points. Drivers: 1 Walkinshaw and Heyer, 126; **3** Percy, 116; **4** Hoyer and Poulsen, 93; **6** Lombardi and Francia, 85.
Manufacturers: 1 Alfa Romeo, 140; **2** Jaguar, 132; **3** BMW, 92; **4** Toyota, 93; **5** VW, 85; **6** Ford, 49.

GROSSER PREIS der TOURENWAGEN, Nürburgring, German Federal Republic, July 8.

European Touring Car Championship, round 8. 111 laps of the 2·822-mile/4·542-km circuit, 313·24 miles/504·16 km.
1 Helmut Kelleners/Gianfranco Brancatelli, D/I (3.5 BMW 635 CSi), 3h 37m 38·91s, 86·35 mph/138·97 km/h (1st over 2500cc class).
2 Jeff Allam/Marc Duez, GB/B (3.5 Rover Vitesse), 3h 38m 09·11s.
3 Jo Gartner/Alain Cudini, A/F (3.5 BMW 635 CSi), 3h 38m 10·49s.
4 Rene Hollinger/Fabien Giroix, CH/F (3.5 BMW CSi), 3h 38m 55·16s.
5 Win Percy/Hans Heyer/Tom Walkinshaw, GB/D/GB (5.3 Jaguar XJ-S), 110 laps.
6 Thomas Lindstrom/Anders Olofson, S/S (2.0 t/c Volvo 240 Turbo), 110.
7 Sigi Muller Jnr/Umberto Grano, D/I (3.5 BMW 635 CSi), 110; **8** Roberto Ravaglia/Christian Danner, I/D (3.5 BMW 635 CSi), 110; **9** Per Stureson/Ingmar Persson, S/S (2.0 t/c Volvo 240 Turbo), 109; **10** Jean-Marie Pirnay/Patrick Neve, B/B (2.0 t/c Volvo 242 Turbo), 108.
Fastest lap: Percy, 1m 53·58s, 89·45 mph/143·96 km/h (record).
Other class winners: 1601cc-2500cc: Georges Kremer/Rinaldo Drovandi, B/I (2.5 Alfa Romeo GTV6), 106. **Up to 1600cc:** Heinz Pütz/Wolfgang Kudrass/Bodo Eichner, D/D/D (1.6 VW Golf GTi), 100.
Championship points. Drivers: 1 Walkinshaw, 136; **2** Heyer, 126; **3** Percy, 116; **4** Kelleners and Brancatelli, 109; **6** Hoyer and Poulsen, 105.
Manufacturers: 1 Alfa Romeo, 160; **2** Jaguar, 140; **3** BMW, 112; **4** Toyota and VW, 105; **6** Volvo, 52.

SPA 24 HOURS, Spa-Francorchamps, Belgium, July 28/29. European Touring Car Championship, round 9. 453 laps of the 4·3179-mile/6·9490-km circuit, 1956·01 miles/3147·90 km.
1 Tom Walkinshaw/Hans Heyer/Win Percy, GB/D/GB (5.3 Jaguar XJ-S), 2h 00m 47·06s, 81·46 mph/131·10 km/h (1st over 2500cc class).
2 Alain Cudini/Dany Snobeck/Thierry Tassin, F/F/B (3.5 BMW 635 CSi), 450 laps.
3 Hans Stuck/Dieter Quester/James Weaver, D/A/GB (3.5 BMW 635 CSi), 449.
4 Pierre-Alain Thaibaut/Jo Gartner/Lucien Guitteny, B/A/F (3.5 BMW 635 CSi), 449.
5 Gordon Spice/Jean-Michel Martin/Philippe Martin, GB/B/B (2.8 Toyota Celica Supra), 443.
6 Umberto Grano/Sigi Muller Jnr/Bruno Giacomelli, I/D/I (3.5 BMW 635 CSi), 442.
7 Fabien Giroix/Jean Krucker/Rene Hollinger, F/CH/CH (3.5 BMW 635 CSi), 440; **8** Peter Lovett/Marc Duez/Jean-Louis Schlesser, GB/B/F (3.5 Rover Vitesse), 437; **9** Frank Sytner/Valentin Simons/Paul Simons, GB/B/B (3.5 BMW 635 CSi), 436; **10** Bernard de Dryver/Alain Semoulin/Herve Regout, B/B/B (3.0 Ford Capri), 436.
Fastest lap: Walkinshaw/Heyer/Percy, 2m 48·77s, 92·10 mph/148·22 km/h.
Other class winners: 1601cc-2500cc; Giorgio Francia/Lella Lombardi, I/I (2.5 Alfa Romeo GTV6), 420. **Up to 1600cc:** Jose Close/Ande Hardy/Manu Remion, B/B/B (1.6 Toyota Corolla), 405.
Championship points. Drivers: 1 Walkinshaw, 165; **2** Heyer, 155; **3** Percy, 145; **4** Hoyer and Poulsen, 117; **6** Kelleners, Brancatelli and Nielsen, 109.
Manufacturers: 1 Alfa Romeo, 180; **2** Jaguar, 160; **3** BMW, 127; **4** Toyota, 125; **5** VW, 105; **6** Volvo, 52.

ISTEL TOURIST TROPHY, Silverstone Grand Prix Circuit, Great Britain, September 2. European Touring Car Championship, round 10. 107 laps of the 2·932-mile4·719-km circuit, 313·72 miles/504·93 km.
1 Helmut Kellenrs/Gianfranco Bracatelli, D/I (3.5 BMW 635 CSi), 3h 22m 26·77s, 92·97 mph/149·62 km/h (1st over 2500cc class).
2 Enzo Calderari/David Sears, CH/GB (5.3 Jaguar XJ-S), 3h 23m 01·65s.
3 Hans Stuck/Dieter Quester, D/A (3.5 BMW 635 CSi), 3h 23m 14·55s.
4 James Weaver/Mike Thackwell, GB/NZ (3.5 BMW 635 CSi), 3h 24m 06·09s.
5 Michel Delcourt/Pierre Dieudonne, B/B (2.0 t/c Volvo 240 Turbo), 106 laps.
6 Thomas Lindstrom/Anders Olofsson, S/S (2.0 t/c Volvo 240 Turbo), 106.
7 Ulf Granberg/Eje Elgh, S/S (2.0 t/c Volvo 240 Turbo), 106; **8** Georges Bosshard/Philippe Haezebrouck, D/B (3.5 BMW 635 CSi), 105; **9** Bretislav Enge/Herbert Werginz, CS/A (3.5 BMW 635 CSi), 104; **10** Lella Lombardi/Giorgio Francia, I/I (2.5 Alfa Romeo GTV6), 103 (1st 1601cc-2500cc class).
Fastest lap: Tom Walkinshaw, GB (5.3 Jaguar XJ-S), 1m 38·77s, 106·86 mph/161·97 km/h (record).
Other class winners: Up to 1600cc: Richard Longman/Alan Curnow, GB/GB (1.6 Ford Escort RS1600i), 98.
Championship points. Drivers: 1 Walkinshaw, 165; **2** Heyer, 155; **3** Percy, 145; **4** Brancatelli and Kelleners, 138; **6** Lombardi and Francia, 125.
Manufacturers: 1 Alfa Romeo, 180(200); **2** Jaguar, 167(175); **3** BMW, 139(147); **4** Toyota, 125; **5** VW, 120; **6** Ford, 69.

EUROPEAN TOURING CAR CHAMPIONSHIP RACE, Omloop van Zolder, Belgium, September 23. European Touring Car Championship, round 11. 107 laps of the 2·648-mile/4·262-km circuit, 283·34 miles/45·03 km.
1 Ulf Granberg/Robert Kvist, S/S (2.0 t/c Volvo 240 Turbo), 3h 30m 32·72s, 80·75 mph/129·95 km/h (1st over 250cc class).
2 Hans Stuck/Dieter Quester, D/A (3.5 BMW 635 CSi), 3h 30m 41·32s.
3 Tom Walkinshaw/Hans Heyer, GB/D (5.3 Jaguar XJ-S), 3h 31m 20·85s.
4 Enzo Calderari/Win Percy, CH/GB (5.3 Jaguar XJ-S), 106 laps.
5 Thomas Lindstrom/Anders Olofsson, S/S (2.0 t/c Volvo 240 Turbo), 106.
6 Bernard de Dryver/Michel Delcourt, B/B (2.0 t/c Volvo 242 Turbo), 105.
7 Marc Duez/Armin Hahne, B/D (3.5 Rover Vitesse), 105; **8** Eddy Joosen/Tony Pond, B/GB (3.5 Rover Vitesse), 104; **9** Tony Palma/Giancarlo Naddao, I/U (3.5 BMW 635 CSi), 104; **10** Patrick Neve/Jean-Marie Pirnay, B/B (2.0 t/c Volvo 242 Turbo), 104.
Fastest lap: Granberg, 1m 46·60s, 89·43 mph/143·92 km/h.
Other class winners: 1601cc-2500cc; Georges Cremer/Rinaldo Drovandi, B/I (2.5 Alfa Romeo GTV6), 106; **Up to 1600cc:** Gunther Schmidt/Claus Kathner-Diercks, D/D (1.6 VW Golf GTi), 96.
Championship points. Drivers: 1 Walkinshaw, 181; **2** Heyer, 171; **3** Percy, 145; **4** Brancatelli and Kelleners, 138; **6** Drovandi, Lombardi and Francia, 137.
Manufacturers: 1 Alfa Romeo, 180(220); **2** Jaguar, 167(187); **3** BMW, 144(162); **4** VW and Toyota, 140; **6** Volvo, 79(80).

MUGELLO 500 KMS, Autodromo Internazionale del Mugello, Italy, October 21. European Touring Car Championship, round 12. 96 laps of the 3·259-mile/5·245-km circuit, 312·86 miles/502·52 km.
1 Roberto Ravaglia/Hans Stuck, I/D (3·5 BMW 635 CSi) (1st over 2500 cc class).
2 Ulf Granberg/Eje Elgh, S/S (2·0 t/c Volvo 240 Turbo).
3 Thomas Lindstrom/Anders Olofsson, S/S (2·0 t/c Volvo 240 Turbo).
4 Helmut Kelleners/Gianfranco Brancatelli, D/I (3·5 BMW 635 CSi).
5 Enzo Calderari/Martin Brundle/Win Percy, CH/GB/GB (5·3 Jaguar XJ-S).
6 Sigi Muller Jnr/Umberto Grano, D/I (3·5 BMW 635 CSi).
7 Jurgen Hamelmann/Axel Felder, D/D (3·5 BMW 635 CSi); **8** Maurizio Macangeli/Roberto Sigala/Herbert Werginz, I/I/A (3·5 BMW 635 CSi); **9** Patrick Neve/Jean-Marie Pirney, B/B (2·0 t/c Volvo 242 Turbo); **10** Rinaldo Drovandi/Georges Cremer, I/B (2·5 Alfa Romeo GTV6) (1st 1601 cc – 2500 cc class).
Other class winners. Up to 1600 cc: John Nielsen/Eric Hoyer/Jorgen Poulsen, DK/DK/DK (1·6 Toyota Corolla).
Full results not available when Autocourse 1984/85 went to press.

Final Championship points.
Drivers:

1	Tom Walkinshaw, GB	181
2	Hans Heyer, D	171
3	Rinaldo Drovandi, I	157
4	Helmut Kelleners, D	151
	Gianfranco Brancatelli, I	151
6	Hans Stuck, D	147

Manufacturers:

1	Alfa Romeo	180 (240)
2	Jaguar	167 (195)
3	VW	155
4	BMW	152 (182)
	Toyota	152 (160)
6	Volvo	91 (95)

Robert Bosch/VW Super Vee

ROBERT BOSCH/VW SUPER VEE RACE, Long Beach Circuit, Long Beach, California, United States of America, April 1. Robert Bosch/VW Super Vee Championship, round 1. 37 laps of the 1·67-mile/2·69-km circuit, 61·79 miles/99·53 km.
1 Chip Robinson, USA (Ralt RT5-VW), 48m 47·00s, 75·985 mph/122·286 km/h.
2 Arie Luyendyk, NL (Ralt RT5-VW), 48m 59·08s.
3 Steve Millen, NZ (Ralt RT5-VW), 37 laps.
4 John David Briggs, USA (Ralt RT5-VW), 37.
5 Ted Prappas, USA (Ralt RT5-VW), 37.
6 Jeff MacPherson, USA (Ralt RT5-VW), 37.
7 Lugwig Heimrath Jnr, CDN (Ralt RT5-VW), 37; **8** Mike Hooper, USA (Ralt RT5-VW), 37; **9** Mike Rosen, USA (Ralt RT5-VW), 37; **10** Ken Johnson, USA (Ralt RT5-VW), 37.
Fastest lap: Tommy Byrne, IRL (Anson SA4-VW), 1m 12·600s, 82·810 mph/133·269 km/h.
Championship points: 1 Robinson, 20; **2** Luyendyk, 16; **3** Millen, 14; **4** Briggs, 12; **5** Prappas, 11; **6** MacPherson, 10.

ROBERT BOSCH/VW SUPER VEE RACE, Phoenix International Raceway, Arizona, United States of America, April 15. Robert Bosch/VW Super Vee Championship, round 2. 60 laps of the 1·000-mile/1·609-km circuit, 60·00 miles/96·54 km.
1 Ludwig Heimrath Jnr, CDN (Ralt RT5-VW), 33m 00·786, 109·048 mph/175·495 km/h.
2 Roger Penske Jnr, USA (Ralt RT5-VW), 33m 02·326s.
3 Ted Prappas, USA (Ralt RT5-VW), 60 laps.
4 Rich Vogler, USA (Ralt RT5-VW), 60.
5 Ben Gustafson, USA (Ralt RT5-VW), 60.
6 Jeff MacPherson, USA (Ralt RT5-VW), 60.
7 Peter Moodie, JA (Ralt RT5-VW), 59; **8** Mike Hooper, USA (Ralt RT5-VW), 59; **9** Craig Dummit, USA (Ralt RT5-VW), 59; **10** Chip Robinson, USA (Ralt RT5-VW), 59.
Fastest lap: Not available.
Championship points: 1 Heimrath Jnr, 29; **2** Robinson, 26; **3** Prappas, 25; **4** MacPherson, 20; **5** Luyendyk, Penske Jnr and Hooper, 16.

ROBERT BOSCH/VW SUPER VEE RACE, Wisconsin State Fair Park Speedway, Milwaukee, United States of America, June 3. Robert Bosch/VW Super Vee Championship, round 3. 62 laps of the 1·000-mile/1·609-km circuit, 62·00 miles/99·76 km.
1 Arie Luyendyk, NL (Ralt RT5-VW), 36m 28s, 102·011 mph/164·170 km/h.
2 Chip Robinson, USA (Ralt RT5-VW), 36m 28·5s.
3 Ken Johnson, USA (Ralt RT5-VW), 62 laps.
4 Jerrill Rice, USA (Anson SA4-VW), 62.
5 Ben Gustafson, USA (Ralt RT5-VW), 62.
6 Jeff MacPherson, USA (Ralt RT5-VW), 62.
7 Ted Prappas, USA (Ralt RT5-VW), 62; **8** Mark Dismore, USA (Ralt RT5-VW), 61; **9** Bobby Fix, USA (Ralt RT5-VW), 61; **10** Justin Revene, USA (Ralt RT5-VW), 61.
Fastest lap: Not available.
Championship points: 1 Robinson, 42; **2** Luyendyk, 36; **3** Prappas, 34; **4** MacPherson, 30; **5** Heimrath Jnr, 29; **6** Gustafson, 23.

ROBERT BOSCH/VW SUPER VEE RACE, Portland International Raceway, Oregon, United States of America, June 17. Robert Bosch/VW Super Vee Championship, round 4. 32 laps of the 1·918-mile/3·087-km circuit, 61·38 miles/98·78 km.
1 Ludwig Heimrath Jnr, CDN (Ralt RT5-VW), 39m 27·100s, 93·340 mph/150·216 km/h.
2 Peter Moodie, JA (Ralt RT5-VW), 39m 36·290s.
3 Arie Luyendyk, NL (Ralt RT5-VW), 32 laps.
4 Dominic Dobson, USA (Ralt RT5-VW), 32 laps.
5 Steve Millen, NZ (Ralt RT5-VW), 32.
6 Mike Hooper, USA (Ralt RT6-VW), 32.
7 Craig Dummit, USA (Ralt RT5-VW), 32; **8** Bobby Fix, USA (Ralt RT5-VW), 31; **9** Chip Robinson, USA (Ralt RT5-VW), 31; **10** Rick Jackson, USA (March 81V-VW), 31.
Fastest lap: Heimrath Jnr, 1m 06·370s, 104·034 mph/167·426 km/g (record).
Championship points: 1 Luyendyk, 50; **2** Heimrath Jnr and Robinson, 49; **4** Prappas, 36; **5** MacPherson, 34; **6** Hooper, 26.

ROBERT BOSCH/VW SUPER VEE RACE, Meadowlands Grand Prix Circuit, New York, United States of America, July 1. Robert Bosch/VW Super Vee Championship, round 5. 33 laps of the 1·682-mile/2·707-km circuit, 55·51 miles/89·33 km.
1 Chip Robinson, USA (Ralt RT5-VW), 46m 40·454s, 71·35 mph/114·83 km/h.
2 Dominic Dobson, USA (Ralt RT5-VW), 46m 49·134s.
3 Arie Luyendyk, NL (Ralt RT5-VW), 33 laps.
4 Peter Moodie, JA (Ralt RT5-VW), 33.
5 Roger Penske, Jnr, USA (Ralt RT5-VW), 33.
6 John Fergus, USA (Ralt RT5-VW), 33.
7 Mike Hooper, USA (Ralt RT5-VW), 33; **8** Hank Chapman, USA (Ralt RT5-VW), 32; **9** John Gimble, USA (Ralt RT5-VW), 32; **10** Justin Revene, USA (Ralt RT5-VW), 31.
Fastest lap: Robinson, 1m 20·687s, 75·04 mph/120·76 km/h (record).
Championship points: 1 Robinson, 69; **2** Luyendyk, 64; **3** Heimrath Jnr, 49; **4** Moodie, 37; **5** Prappas, 36; **6** Hooper, 35.

ROBERT BOSCH/VW SUPER VEE RACE, Burke Lakefront Airport Circuit, Cleveland, United States of America, July 8. Robert Bosch/VW Super Vee Championship, round 6. 25 laps of the 2·485-mile/3·999-km circuit, 62·13 mniles/99·98 km.
1 Arie Luyendyk, NL (Ralt RT5-VW), 31m 40·32s, 117·46 mph/189·03 km/h.
2 Chip Robinson, USA (Ralt RT5-VW), 31m 47·05s.
3 Peter Moodie, JA (Ralt RT5-VW), 25 laps.
4 Roger Penske Jnr, USA (Ralt RT5-VW), 25.
5 Dominic Dobson, USA (Ralt RT5-VW), 25.
6 Jeff MacPherson, USA (Ralt RT5-VW), 25.
7 Craig Dummit, USA (Ralt RT5-VW), 25; **8** John Fergus, USA (Ralt RT5-VW), 24; **9** Marc Dismore, USA (Ralt RT5-VW), 24; **10** John Richards, USA (Ralt RT5-VW), 24.
Fastest lap: Luyendyk, 1m 14·784s, 119·78 mph/192·77 km/h (record).
Championship points: 1 Robinson, 85; **2** Luyendyk, 84; **3** Moodie, 51; **4** Heimrath Jnr, 49; **5** MacPherson, 44; **6** Penske Jnr, 43.

ROBERT BOSCH/VW SUPER VEE RACE, Road America, Elkhart Lake, Wisconsin, United States of America, August 5. Robert Bosch/VW Super Vee Championship, round 7. 15 laps of the 4·000-mile/6·437-km circuit, 60·00 miles/96·56 km.
1 Chip Robinson, USA (Ralt RT5-VW), 37m 57·44s, 98·843 mph/159·072 km/h.
2 Arie Luyendyk, NL (Ralt RT5-VW), 38m 02·02s.
3 Ludwig Heimrath Jnr, CDN (Ralt RT5-VW), 15 laps.
4 John David Briggs, USA (Ralt RT5-VW), 15.
5 Jeff MacPherson, USA (Ralt RT5-VW), 15.
6 Ted Prappas, USA (Ralt RT5-VW), 15.
7 John Richards, USA (Ralt RT5-VW), 15; **8** Justin Revene, USA (Ralt RT5-VW), 15; **9** Gary Bren, USA (Ralt RT5-VW), 15; **10** Tommy Grunnah, USA (Venture GR003-VW), 15.
Fastest lap: Lurendyk, 2m 09·454s, 111·236 mph/179·017 km/h (record).
Championship points: 1 Robinson, 105; **2** Luyendyk, 100; **3** Heimrath Jnr, 63; **4** MacPherson, 55; **5** Moodie, 51; **6** Prappas, 46.

ROBERT BOSCH/VW SUPER VEE RACE, Watkins Glen Grand Prix Circuit, New York, United States of America, August 19. Robert Bosch/VW Super Vee Championship, round 8. 18 laps of the 3·377-mile/5·435-km circuit, 60·79 miles/97·83 km.
1 Arie Luyendyk, NL (Ralt RT5-VW), 35m 33·384s, 102·58 mph/165·09 km/h.
2 Chip Robinson, USA (Ralt RT5-VW), 35m 34·459s.
3 Roger Penske Jnr, USA (Ralt RT5-VW), 18 laps.
4 John Richards, USA (Ralt RT5-VW), 18.
5 Gary Bren, USA (Ralt RT5-VW), 18.
6 John Fergus, USA (Ralt RT5-VW), 18.
7 John Gimbel, USA (Ralt RT5-VW), 18; **8** Craig Dummit, USA (Ralt RT5-VW), 18; **9** Jeff MacPherson, USA (Ralt RT5-VW), 18; **10** Ludwig Heimrath Jnr, CDN (Ralt RT5-VW), 18.
Fastest lap: Heimrath Jnr, 1m 47·863s, 112·711 mph/181·390 km/h (record).
Championship points: 1 Robinson, 121; **2** Luyendyk, 120; **3** Heimrath, Jnr, 69; **4** MacPherson, 62; **6** Penske Jnr, 57; **6** Moodie, 51.

ROBERT BOSCH/VW SUPER VEE RACE, Trois-Rivieres, Quebec, Canada, September 2. Robert Bosch/VW Super Vee Championship, round 9. 30 laps of the 2·100-mile/3·380-km circuit, 63·00 miles/101·40 km.
1 Arie Luyendyk, NL (Ralt RT5-VW), 45m 43·548s, 82·667 mph/133·039 km/h.
2 Tommy Byrne, IRL (Ralt RT5-VW), 45m 44·197s.
3 Peter Moodie, JA (Ralt RT5-VW), 30 laps.
4 Roger Penske Jnr, USA (Ralt RT5-VW), 30.
5 Ludwig Heimrath Jnr, CDN (Ralt RT5-VW), 30.
6 Jeff MacPherson, USA (Ralt RT5-VW), 30.
7 Craig Horning, USA (Ralt RT5-VW), 29; **8** Ken Murrey, USA (Ralt RT5-VW), 29; **9** Chip Robinson, USA (Ralt RT5-VW), 24; **10** Mike Hooper, USA (Ralt RT5-VW), 10.
Fastest lap: Luyendyk, 1m 27·478s, 86·422 mph/139·082 km/h (record).
Championship points: 1 Luyendyk, 140; **2** Robinson, 127; **3** Heimrath Jnr, 79; **4** MacPherson, 71; **5** Penske Jnr, 69; **6** Moodie, 65.

ROBERT BOSCH/VW SUPER VEE RACE, Michigan International Raceway, Brooklyn, Michigan, United States of America, September 24. Robert Bosch/VW Super Vee Championship, round 10. 30 laps of the 2·000-mile/3·219-km circuit, 60·00 miles/96·57 km.
1 Jeff MacPherson, USA (Ralt RT5-VW), 26m 34·98s, 135·45 mph/217·99 km/h.
2 Arie Luyendyk, NL (Ralt RT5-VW), 26m 34·981s.
3 Mike Hooper, USA (Ralt RT5-VW), 30 laps.
4 Chip Robinson, USA (Ralt RT5-VW), 30.
5 Ludwig Heimrath Jnr, CDN (Ralt RT5-VW), 30.
6 Peter Moodie, JA (Ralt RT5-VW), 30.
7 John Gimbel, USA (Ralt RT5-VW), 30; **8** Steve Thompson, USA (Argo JM12-VW), 30; **9** Bobby Reen, USA (Ralt RT5-VW), 30; **10** Rob Stevens, USA (Ralt RT5-VW), 30.
Fastest lap: Luyendyk, 44·58s, 161·51 mph/259·92 km/h.
Championship points: 1 Luyendyk, 156; **2** Robinson, 139; **3** MacPherson, 91; **4** Heimrath Jnr, 90; **5** Moodie, 75; **6** Penske Jnr, 74.

ROBERT BOSCH/VW SUPER VEE RACE, Laguna Seca Raceway, California, United States of America, October 21. Robert Bosch/VW Super Vee Championship, round 11. 32 laps of the 1·900-mile/3·056-km circuit, 60·80 miles/97·79 km.
1 Ted Prappas, USA (Ralt RT5-VW), 33m 25·300s, 109·151 mph/175·661 km/h.
2 Roger Penske Jnr, USA (Ralt RT5-VW), 33m 44·160s.
3 Jeff MacPherson, USA (Ralt RT5-VW), 32 laps.
4 Mike Hooper, USA (Ralt RT5-VW), 32.
5 Peter Moodie, JA (Ralt RT5-VW), 32.
6 John Richards, USA (Ralt RT5-VW), 32.
7 Dominic Dobson, USA (Ralt RT5-VW), 32; **8** Davey Jones, USA (Ralt RT5-VW), 32; **9** Craig Dummit, USA (Ralt RT5-VW), 32; **10** Ron Nelson, USA (Ralt RT5-VW), 32.
Fastest lap: Ludwig Heimrath Jnr, CDN (Ralt RT5-VW), 1m 01·120s, 111·910 mph/180·101 km/h (record).

Championship points (Prior to final round at Caesars Palace on November 11).

1	Arie Luyendyk, NL	156
2	Chip Robinson, USA	144
3	Jeff MacPherson, USA	106
4	Ludwig Heimrath Jnr, CDN	91
5	Roger Penske Jnr, USA	90
6	Peter Moodie, JA	86

7 Mike Hooper, USA, 76; **8** Ted Prappas, USA, 66; **9** Craig Dummit, USA, 49; **10** Dominic Dobson, USA, 48; **11** John Richards, USA, 44; **12** Ben Gustavson, USA, 28; **13** John Fergus, USA, 28; **14** Gary Bren, USA, 26; **15** Steve Millen, NZ, John Gimbel, USA and Justin Revene, USA, 25.
Final results will be given in Autocourse 1985/86.

Indianapolis 500

INDIANAPOLIS 500, Indianapolis Motor Speedway, Indiana, United States of America, May 27. CART PPG Indy Car World Series, round 3. 200 laps of the 2·500-mile/4·023-km circuit, 500·00 miles/804·57 km.
1 Rick Mears, USA (March 84C-Cosworth DFX), 3h 03m 21·66s, 163·612 mph/263·307 km/h.
2 Roberto Guerrero, COL (March 84C-Cosworth DFX), 198 laps.
3 Al Unser, USA (March 84C-Cosworth DFX), 198.
4 Al Holbert, USA (March 84C-Cosworth DFX), 198.
5 Mike Andretti, USA (March 84C-Cosworth DFX), 198.
6 A. J. Foyt, USA (March 84C-Cosworth DFX), 197.
7 Bobby Rahal, USA (March 84C-Cosworth DFX), 197; **8** Herm Johnson, USA (March 84C-Cosworth DFX), 194; **9** Danny Ongais, USA (March 84C-Cosworth DFX), 193; **10** Josele Garza, MEX (March 84C-Cosworth DFX), 193; **11** George Snider, USA (March 84C-Cosworth DFX), 193; **12** Dennis Firestone, USA (March 82/83C-Cosworth DFX), 186; **13** Howdy Holmes, USA (March 84C-Cosworth DFX), 185; **14** Tom Gloy, USA (March 84C-Cosworth DFX), 179; **15** Chris Kneifel, USA (Primus 84-Cosworth DFX), 175 (DNF, halfshaft); **16** Tom Sneva, USA (March 84C-Cosworth DFX), 168 (DNF, cv joint); **17** Mario Andretti, USA (Lola T800-Cosworth DFX), 153 (DNF, accident); **18** Scott Brayton, USA (March 84C-Buick), 150 (DNF, engine); **19** Pancho Carter, USA (March 84C-Cosworth DFX), 141 (DNF, engine); **20** Kevin Cogan, USA (Eagle 84-Pontiac), 137 (DNF, jammed wheel); **21** Al Unser Jnr, USA (March 84C-Cosworth DFX), 131 (DNF, water pipe); **22** Johnny Rutherford, USA (March 84C-Cosworth DFX), 116 (DNF, engine); **23** Dick Simon, USA (March 84C-Cosworth DFX), 112 (DNF, driveshaft); **24** Teo Fabi, I (March 84C-Cosworth DFX), 112 (DNF, fuel pump drive); **25** Gordon Johncock, USA (March 84C-Cosworth DFX), 104 (DNF, accident); **26** Tony Bettenhausen, USA (March 84C-Cosworth DFX), 86 (DNF, piston); **27** Derek Daly, IRL (March 84C-Cosworth DFX), 76 (DNF, handling); **28** Chip Ganassi, USA (March 84C-Cosworth DFX), 61 (DNF, fuel pump); **29** Danny Sullivan, USA (Lola

T800-Cosworth DFX), 57 (DNF, accident); **30** Pat Bedard, USA (March 84C-Buick), 55 (DNF, accident); **31** Spike Gehlhausen, USA (March 83C-Cosworth DFX), 45 (DNF, tyre); **32** Emerson Fittipaldi, BR (March 84C-Cosworth DFX), 37 (DNF, engine); **33** Geoff Brabham, AUS (March 84C-Cosworth DFX), 1 (DNF, fire).
Fastest Qualifier: Sneva, 2m 51·405s, 210·029 mph/338·008 km/h (4 laps).
Fastest lap: Not available.
Championship points: **1** Sneva, 37; **2** Andretti (Mike), 27; **3** Andretti (Mario), 22; **4** Mears, 21; **5** Brabham, Holmes and Guerrero, 16.

CRC Chemicals Can-Am Championship

CRC CHEMICALS CAN-AM CHAMPIONSHIP RACE, Mosport Park Circuit, Ontario, Canada, June 10. CRC Chemicals Can-Am Championship, round 1. 60 laps of the 2·459-mile/3·957-km circuit, 147·54 miles/237·42 km.
1 Michael Roe, IRL (5.0 VDS 002-Chevrolet), 1h 32m 27·592s, 95·74 mph/154·08 km/h.
2 Jim Crawford, GB (5.0 March 847-Chevrolet), 1h 33m 07·262s.
3 Charles Monk, CDN (5.0 Lola T333-Chevrolet), 60 laps.
4 Horse Kroll, CDN (5.0 Frissbee KR3-Chevrolet), 59.
5 Jim Cooke, CDN (5.0 Lola T333CS-Chevrolet), 57.
6 Jeremy Hill, CDN (2.0 Photon JH2-Hart), 57.
7 Bertil Roos, S (2.0 Marguey CA 82-Hart), 57; **8** Sylvia Perigny, CDN (2.0 Ralt RT1-Mazda), 55; **9** John Macaluso, USA (5.0 Lola T333-Chevrolet), 54; **10** Bill Alsup, USA (2.0 Toleman TG280-Hart), 47.
Fastest lap: Roe, 1m 13·420s, 120·57 mph/194·04 km/h.
Championship points: **1** Roe, 20; **2** Crawford, 16; **3** Monk, 14; **4** Kroll, 12; **5** Cooke, 11; **6** Hill, 10.

CRC CHEMICALS CAN-AM CHAMPIONSHIP RACE, Dallas Grand Prix Circuit, Dallas, Texas, United States of America, July 7. CRC Chemicals Can-Am Championship, round 2. 50 laps of the 2·424-mile/3·901-km circuit, 121·20 miles/195·05 km.
1 Michael Roe, IRL (5.0 VDS 002-Chevrolet), 1h 46m 58·143s, 67·982 mph/109·406 km/h.
2 Jim Crawford, GB (5.0 March 847-Chevrolet), 1h 47m 06·439s.
3 Juan Manuel Fangio, RA (2.0 Ralt RT2-Hart), 49 laps.
4 Charles Monk, CDN (5.0 Lola T333-Chevrolet), 49.
5 Kim Campbell, USA (2.0 March 832-BMW), 48.
6 Phil Compton, USA (5.0 Frissbee-Chevrolet), 48; **7** Enrique Mansilla, RA (2.0 March 822-BMW), 48; **8** Horst Kroll, CDN (5.0 Frissbee KR3-Chevrolet), 46; **9** Clive Bush, NZ (5.0 Conquest B2-Chevrolet), 46; **10** Ron Canizares, USA (2.0 March 812-Hart), 46.
Fastest lap: Roe, 1m 45·165s, 82·978 mph/133·540 km/h (record).
Championship points: **1** Roe, 40; **2** Crawford, 32; **3** Monk, 26; **4** Kroll, 20; **5** Fangio, 14; **6** Cooke and Campbell, 11.

CRC CHEMICALS CAN-AM CHAMPIONSHIP RACE, Brainerd International Raceway, Minnesota, United States of America, July 22. CRC Chemicals Can-Am Championship, round 3. 40 laps of the 3·000-mile/4·828-km circuit, 120·00 miles/193·12 km.
1 Michael Roe, IRL (5.0 VDS 002-Chevrolet), 1h 00m 54·53s, 118·208 mph/190·237 km/h.
2 Horst Kroll, CDN (5.0 Frissbee KR3-Chevrolet), 39 laps.
3 Kim Campbell, USA (2.0 March 832-BMW), 38.
4 Eddie Wachs, USA (2.0 Toleman TG280-Hart), 38.
5 Jerry Hansen, USA (5.0 VDS 001-Chevrolet), 36.
6 Ron Canizares, USA (2.0 March 812-Hart), 36.
7 Drake Olson, USA (5.0 Frissbee-Chevrolet), 35; **8** Armando Trentini, USA (2.0 Osella PA9-BMW), 34; **9** John Gunn, USA (5.0 Phoenix 84-Chevrolet), 34; **10** Randy Zimmer, USA (2.0 Roundel-Mazda), 29.
Fastest lap: Roe, 1m 27·09s, 124·009 mph/199·573 km/h.
Championship points: **1** Roe, 60; **2** Kroll, 36; **3** Crawford, 32; **4** Monk, 26; **5** Campbell, 25; **6** Wachs, 17.

CRC CHEMICALS CAN-AM CHAMPIONSHIP RACE, Lime Rock Park, Connecticut, United States of America, August 4. CRC Chemicals Can-Am Championship, round 4. 80 laps of the 1·53-mile/2·46-km circuit, 122·40 miles/196·80 km.
1 Michael Roe, IRL (5.0 VDS 002-Chevrolet), 1h 08m 08·106s, 107·79 mph/173·471 km/h.
2 Jim Crawford, GB (5.0 March 847-Chevrolet), 1h 08m 49·552s.
3 Walter Lechner, A (3.0 Williams FW07-Cosworth DFV), 79 laps.
4 Kim Campbell, USA (2.0 March 832-BMW), 79.
5 Horst Kroll, CDN (5.0 Frissbee KR3-Chevrolet), 78.
6 Eddie Wachs, USA (2.0 Toleman TG280-Hart), 77.
7 Bill Alsup, USA (2.0 Toleman TG280-Hart), 74; **8** Sylvain Perigny, CDN (2.0 Ralt RT1-Hart), 73; **9** John Macaluso, USA (5.0 Lola T333-Chevrolet), 71; **10** Armando Trentini, USA (2.0 Osella PA9-BMW), 70.
Fastest lap: Roe, 46·984s, 117·23 mph/188·66 km/h.
Championship points: **1** Roe, 80; **2** Crawford, 48; **3** Kroll, 47; **4** Campbell, 37; **5** Wachs, 27; **6** Monk, 26.

CRC CHEMICALS CAN-AM CHAMPIONSHIP RACE, Road Atlanta, Georgia, United States of America, August 19. CRC Chemicals Can-Am Championship, round 5. 50 laps of the 2·520-mile/4·055-km circuit, 126·00 miles/202·75 km.
1 Jim Crawford, GB (5.0 March 847-Chevrolet), 1h 09m 08·085s, 109·352 mph/174·375 km/h.
2 Horst Kroll, CDN (5.0 Frissbee KR3-Chevrolet), 49 laps.
3 John Gunn, USA (5.0 Phoenix 84-Chevrolet), 48.
4 Ron Canizares, USA (2.0 March 812-Hart), 48.
5 Rod Cusumano, USA (2.0 March 822-BMW), 45.
6 Peter Greenfield, USA (2.0 Ralt RT4-Hart), 45.
7 Jim Cooke, CDN (5.0 Lola T333-Chevrolet), 44; **8** Armando Trentini, USA (2.0 Osella PA9-BMW), 44; **9** Tod Tuttle, USA (5.0 Chevron B51-Chevrolet), 41; **10** Bill Tempero, USA (5.0 Theodore TY01-Chevrolet), 34.
Fastest lap: Roe, 1m 14·95s, 121·040 mph/194·795 km/h.
Championship points: **1** Roe, 84; **2** Crawford, 68; **3** Kroll, 61; **4** Campbell, 40; **5** Trentini and Canizares, 29.

CRC CHEMICALS CAN-AM CHAMPIONSHIP RACE, Trois-Rivieres, Quebec, Canada, September 2. CRC Chemicals Can-Am Championship, round 6. 60 laps of the 2·100-mile/3·380-km circuit, 126·00 miles/202·80 km.
1 Jim Crawford, GB (5.0 March 847-Chevrolet), 1h 28m 04·8s, 85·831 mph/138·131 km/h.
2 Marzio Romano, CH (2.0 Ralt RT2-Hart), 59 laps.
3 Kim Campbell, USA (2.0 March 832-BMW), 59.
4 Horst Kroll, CDN (5.0 Frissbee KR3-Chevrolet), 59.
5 Michael Roe, IRL (5.0 VDS 003-Chevrolet), 58.
6 Enrique Mansilla, RA (2.0 Toleman TG280-Hart), 57.
7 Wally Dallenbach Jnr, USA (2.0 Toleman TG280-Hart), 56; **8** Roman Pechman, CDN (2.0 Lola T290-Ford), 53; **9** Sylvain Perigny, CDN (2.0 Ralt RT1-Mazda), 51; **10** Armando Trentini, USA (2.0 Osella PA9-BMW), 49.
Fastest lap: Roe, 1m 25·667s, 88·249 mph/142·023 km/h.
Championship points: **1** Roe, 95; **2** Crawford, 88; **3** Kroll, 75; **4** Campbell, 54; **5** Trentini, 35; **6** Canizares, 29.

CRC CHEMICALS CAN-AM CHAMPIONSHIP RACE, Mosport Park Circuit, Ontario, Canada, September 9. CRC Chemicals Can-Am Championship, round 7. 60 laps of the 2·459-mile/3·957-km circuit, 147·54 miles/237·42 km.
1 Michael Roe, IRL (5.0 VDS 002-Chevrolet), 1h 16m 31·774s, 113·75 mph/183·06 km/h.
2 Jim Crawford, GB (5.0 March 847-Chevrolet), 1h 17m 49·028s.
3 Horso Kroll, CDN (5.0 Frissbee KR3-Chevrolet), 58 laps.
4 Charles Monk, CDN (5.0 Lola T333-Chevrolet), 57.
5 Kim Campbell, USA (2.0 March 832-BMW), 57.
6 Jeremy Hill, CDN (2.0 Photon JH2-Hart), 57.
7 Peter Greenfield, USA (2.0 Ralt RT4-Hart), 57; **8** Jerry Molner, USA (2.0 Invader-BMW), 56; **9** Walter Lechner, A (3.0 Williams FW07-Cosworth DFV), 54; **10** John Macaluso, USA (5.0 Lola T333-Chevrolet), 54.
Fastest lap: Roe, 1m 13·741s, 120·05 mph/193·20 km/h.
Championship points: **1** Roe, 115; **2** Crawford, 104; **3** Kroll, 89; **4** Campbell, 65; **5** Monk, 38; **6** Trentini, 36.

CRC CHEMICALS CAN-AM CHAMPIONSHIP RACE, Sears Point International Raceway, Sonoma, California, United States of America, September 30. CRC Chemicals Can-Am Championship, round 8. 50 laps of the 2·523-mile/4·060-km circuit, 126·15 miles/203·00 km.
1 Michael Roe, IRL (5.0 VDS 002-Chevrolet), 1h 16m 02·39s, 99·54 mph/160·19 km/h.
2 Jim Crawford, GB (5.0 March 847-Chevrolet), 1h 16m 45·10s.
3 Kim Campbell, USA (2.0 March 832-BMW), 48 laps.
4 Rod Cusumano, USA (2.0 March 822-Hart), 48.
5 Richard Guider, USA (2.0 Marguey-Hart), 47.
6 Robert Meyer, USA (5.0 Frissbee-Chevrolet), 46.
7 Armando Trentini, USA (2.0 Osella PA9-BMW), 46; **8** Horst Kroll, CDN (5.0 Frissbee KR3-Chevrolet), 44; **9** Bill Tempero, USA (3.0 Theodore TY02-Cosworth DFV), 41; **10** Merle Brennen, USA (5.0 Lola T333-Chevrolet), 38.
Fastest lap: Roe, 1m 23·443s, 99·540 mph/160·194 km/h.
Championship points: **1** Roe, 135; **2** Crawford, 120; **3** Kroll, 97; **4** Campbell, 79; **5** Trentini, 45; **6** Monk, 38.

CRC CHEMICALS CAN-AM CHAMPIONSHIP RACE, Riverside International Raceway, California, United States of America, October 7. CRC Chemicals Can-Am Championship, round 9. 50 laps of the 2·547-mile/4·099-km circuit, 127·35 miles/204·95 km.
1 Michael Roe, IRL (5.0 VDS 002-Chevrolet), 1h 03m 50·486s, 119·687 mph/192·617 km/h.
2 Jim Crawford, GB (5.0 March 847-Chevrolet), 1h 04m 59·113s.
3 Horst Kroll, CDN (5.0 Frissbee KR3-Chevrolet), 48 laps.
4 Rod Cusumano, USA (2.0 March 822-Hart), 47.
5 Walter Lechner, A (3.0 Cobra March-Cosworth DFV), 47.
6 Richard Guider, USA (2.0 Marguey-Hart), 46.
7 Garth Pollard, USA (2.0 Toleman TG280-Hart), 45; **8** Bill Hill, USA (2.0 Mazda), 39; **9** Armando Trentini, USA (2.0 Osella PA9-BMW), 31; **10** Frank Joyce, USA (5.0 Lola T333-Chevrolet), 29.
Fastest lap: Roe, 1m 10·127s, 130·751 mph/210·423 km/h.

Championship points (prior to final round at Green Valley on October 28).

1 Michael Roe, IRL	155
2 Jim Crawford, GB	136
3 Horst Kroll, CDN	111
4 Kim Campbell, USA	84
5 Armando Trentini, USA	52
6 Rod Cusumano, USA	43

7 Charles Monk, CDN, 38; **8** Walter Lechner, A, 37; **9** Ron Canizares, USA, 29; **10** Eddie Wachs, USA, 27; **11** Jeremy Hill, CDN, 26; **12** John Gunn, USA, 25; **13** Jim Cooke, CDN and Peter Greenfield, USA, 24; **15** Sylvain Periguy, CDN and John Macaluso, USA, 23.
Final results will be given in Autocourse 1985/86.

SCCA Budweiser Trans-Am Championship

SCCA BUDWEISER TRANS-AM CHAMPIONSHIP RACE, Road Atlanta, Georgia, United States of America, May 6. SCCA Budweiser Trans-Am Championship, round 1. 40 laps of the 2·520-mile/4·055-km circuit, 100·80 miles/162·20 km.
1 Darin Brassfield, USA (Chevrolet Corvette), 1h 02m 50·847s, 96·233 mph/154·872 km/h.
2 Bob Lobenberg, USA (Pontiac Trans-Am), 1h 03m 34·106s.
3 David Hobbs, GB (Chevrolet Corvette), 40 laps.
4 Wally Dallenbach Jnr, USA (Chevrolet Camaro), 40.
5 Eppie Wietzes, CDN (Pontiac Firebird), 40.
6 Paul Miller, USA (Porsche Carrera Turbo), 40.
7 John Brandt, USA (Chevrolet Corvette), 40; **8** Phil Currin, USA (Chevrolet Corvette), 39; **9** Steve Hagerman, USA (Chevrolet Camaro), 39; **10** Dave Watson, USA (Pontiac Firebird), 39.
Fastest Qualifier: Lobenberg, 1m 24·095s, 107·878 mph/173·612 km/h (record).
Fastest lap: Brassfield, 1m 26·200s, 105·243 mph/169·372 km/h (record).
Championship points. Drivers: **1** Brassfield, 21; **2** Lobenberg, 17; **3** Hobbs, 14; **4** Dallenbach Jnr, 12; **5** Wietzes, 11; **6** Miller, 10.
Manufacturers: **1** Chevrolet, 9; **2** Pontiac, 6; **3** Porsche, 1.

SCCA BUDWEISER TRANS-AM CHAMPIONSHIP RACE, Summit Point International Raceway, West Virginia, United States of America, May 20. SCCA Budweiser Trans-Am Championship, round 2. 50 laps of the 2·00-mile/3·22-km circuit, 100·00 miles/161·00 km.
1 Bob Lobenberg, USA (Pontiac Trans-Am), 1h 07m 20·36s, 80·81 mph/130·05 km/h.
2 David Hobbs, GB (Chevrolet Corvette), 1h 07m 30·60s.
3 Tom Gloy, USA (Mercury Capri), 50 laps.
4 Eppie Wietzes, CDN (Pontiac Trans-Am), 50.
5 Greg Pickett, USA (Mercury Capri), 49.
6 Paul Miller, USA (Porsche Carrera Turbo), 49.
7 Chris Gleason, USA (Pontiac Trans-Am), 49; **8** Jim Derhaag, USA (Pontiac Trans-Am), 49; **9** Bill Scott, USA (Chevrolet Corvette), 48; **10** John Brandt, USA (Chevrolet Corvette), 48.
Fastest Qualifier: Hobbs, 1m 14·259s, 96·908 mph/155·958 km/h (record).
Fastest lap: Lobenberg, 1m 15·94s, 94·811 mph/152·583 km/h.
Championship points. Drivers: **1** Lobenberg, 37; **2** Hobbs, 31; **3** Brassfield, 24; **4** Wietzes, 23; **5** Miller, 20; **6** Brandt, 15.
Manufacturers: **1** Chevrolet and Pontiac, 15; **3** Mercury, 4; **4** Porsche, 1.

SCCA BUDWEISER TRANS-AM CHAMPIONSHIP RACE, Sears Point International Raceway, Sonoma, California, United States of America, June 3. SCCA Budweiser Trans-Am Championship, round 3. 40 laps of the 2·523-mile/4·060-km circuit, 100·92 miles/162·40 km.
1 Greg Pickett, USA (Mercury Capri), 1h 13m 27·490s, 82·431 mph/132·660 km/h.
2 Tom Gloy, USA (Mercury Capri), 1h 13m 33·020s.
3 Darin Brassfield, USA (Chevrolet Corvette), 40 laps.
4 Wally Dallenbach Jnr, USA (Chevrolet Camaro), 40.
5 Paul Newman, USA (Nissan 300ZX Turbo), 40.
6 Jim Derhaag, USA (Pontiac Trans-Am), 40.
7 Bob Lobenberg, USA (Pontiac Trans-Am), 40; **8** Jim Miller, USA (Pontiac Trans-Am), 40; **9** Rob McFarlin, USA (Pontiac Firebird), 49; **10** David Hobbs, GB (Chevrolet Corvette), 40.
Fastest qualifier: Gloy, 1m 38·659s, 92·063 mph/148·161 km/h.
Fastest lap: Gloy, 1m 41·440s, 89·539 mph/144·099 km/h.
Championship points. Drivers: **1** Lobenberg, 46; **2** Brassfield, 38; **3** Hobbs, 37; **4** Gloy and Pickett, 32; **6** Dallenbach Jnr, 24.
Manufacturers: **1** Chevrolet, 19; **2** Pontiac, 16; **3** Mercury, 13; **4** Porsche and Nissan, 2.

SCCA BUDWEISER TRANS-AM CHAMPIONSHIP RACE, Portland International Raceway, Oregon, United States of America, June 16. SCCA Budweiser Trans-Am Championship, round 4. 53 laps of the 1·915-mile/3·082-km circuit, 101·45 miles/163·65 km.
1 Greg Pickett, USA (Mercury Capri), 1h 05m 06·510s, 93·678 mph/150·760 km/h.
2 Tom Gloy, USA (Mercury Capri), 1h 05m 52·520s.
3 Darin Brassfield, USA (Chevrolet Corvette), 53 laps.
4 Paul Newman, USA (Nissan 300ZX Turbo), 52.
5 Jim Miller, USA (Pontiac Trans-Am), 52.
6 Wally Dallenbach Jnr, USA (Chevrolet Camaro), 52.
7 Gene Felton, USA (Pontiac Firebird), 52; **8** Andy Porterfield, USA (Chevrolet Camaro), 51; **9** Jim Derhaag, USA (Pontiac Trans-Am), 51; **10** Richard Wall, USA (Chevrolet Camaro), 50.
Fastest Qualifier: Pickett, 1m 11·211s, 96·962 mph/156·045 km/h.
Fastest lap: Pickett, 1m 11·090s, 97·127 mph/156·310 km/h.
Championship points. Drivers: **1** Pickett, 54; **2** Brassfield, 52; **3** Lobenberg and Gloy, 48; **5** Hobbs, 37; **6** Dallenbach Jnr, 34.
Manufacturers: **1** Chevrolet, 23; **2** Mercury, 22; **3** Pontiac, 18; **4** Nissan, 5; **5** Porsche, 2.

SCCA BUDWEISER TRANS-AM CHAMPIONSHIP RACE, Detroit Grand Prix Circuit, Michigan, United States of America, June 23. SCCA Budweiser Trans-Am Championship, round 5. 40 laps of the 2·500-mile/4·023-km circuit, 100·00 miles/160·92 km.
1 Tom Gloy, USA (Mercury Capri), 1h 31m 41·242s, 65·440 mph/105·315 km/h.
2 Willy T. Ribbs, USA (Mercury Capri), 1h 31m 46·317s.
3 Greg Pickett, USA (Mercury Capri), 40 laps.
4 Wally Dallenbach Jnr, USA (Chevrolet Camaro), 40.
5 Dave Watson, USA (Pontiac Firebird), 40.
6 Tim Evans, USA (Pontiac Trans-Am), 40.
7 David Hobbs, GB (Chevrolet Corvette), 40; **8** John Brandt, USA (Chevrolet Corvette), 39; **9** Murray Edwards, CDN (Chevrolet Corvette) 38; **10** John Jones, CDN (Pontiac Trans-Am), 38.
Fastest Qualifier: Bob Lobenberg, USA (Pontiac Trans-Am), 2m 04·388s, 72·354 mph/116·442 km/h (record).
Fastest lap: Gloy, 2m 05·451s, 71·741 mph/115·456 km/h (record).
Championship points. Drivers: **1** Gloy and Pickett, 68; **3** Brassfield, 52; **4** Lobenberg, 49; **5** Hobbs, 47; **6** Dallenbach Jnr, 46.
Manufacturers: **1** Mercury, 31; **2** Chevrolet, 26; **3** Pontiac, 20; **4** Nissan, 5; **5** Porsche, 2.

SCCA BUDWEISER TRANS-AM CHAMPIONSHIP RACE, Daytona International Speedway, Florida, United States of America, July 3. SCCA Budweiser Trans-Am Championship, round 6. Aggregate of two 22 lap heats of the 3·56-mile/5·73-km circuit, 44 laps, 156·64 miles/252·12 km.
1 Willy T. Ribbs, USA (Mercury Capri), 4 pts.
2 Tom Gloy, USA (Mercury Capri), 4.
3 Bob Lobenberg, USA (Pontiac Trans-Am), 9.
4 Jim Miller, USA (Pontiac Trans-Am), 11.
5 Dave Watson, USA (Pontiac Firebird), 13.
6 Darin Brassfield, USA (Chevrolet Corvette), 17.
7 Rob McFarlin, USA (Pontiac Trans-Am), 17; **8** Del Taylor, USA (Pontiac Trans-Am), 19; **9** Jim Derhaag, USA (Pontiac Trans-Am), 22; **10** Clay Young, USA (Pontiac Trans-Am), 22.
Fastest Qualifier: Gloy, 1m 54·721s, 111·725 mph/179·787 km/h.
Fastest lap: David Hobbs, GB (Chevrolet Corvette), 1m 59·229s, 107·492 mph/172·991 km/h.
Championship points. drivers: **1** Gloy, 85; **2** Pickett, 73; **3** Lobenberg, 63; **4** Brassfield, 62; **5** Dallenbach Jnr, 49; **6** Hobbs, 47.
Manufacturers: **1** Mercury, 40; **2** Chevrolet, 27; **3** Pontiac, 24; **4** Nissan, 5; **5** Porsche, 2.

SCCA BUDWEISER TRANS-AM CHAMPIONSHIP RACE, Brainerd International Raceway, Minnesota, United States of America, July 22. SCCA Budweiser Trans-Am Championship, round 7. 33 laps of the 3·000-mile/4·828-km circuit, 99·00 miles/159·32 km.
1 Willy T. Ribbs, USA (Mercury Capri), 56m 02·31s, 105·99 mph/170·57 km/h.
2 Bob Lobenberg, USA (Pontiac Trans-Am), 56m 05·44s.
3 Tom Gloy, USA (Mercury Trans-Am), 33 laps.
4 Greg Pickett, USA (Mercury Capri), 33.
5 Jim Miller, USA (Pontiac Trans-Am), 33.
6 Wally Dallenbach Jnr, USA (Chevrolet Camaro), 33.
7 Darin Brassfield, USA (Chevrolet Corvette), 33; **8** David Hobbs, GB (Chevrolet Corvette), 32; **9** Tim Evans, USA (Pontiac Trans-Am), 32; **10** Rob McFarlin, USA (Pontiac Trans-Am), 31.
Fastest Qualifier: Lobenberg, 1m 36·99s, 111·35 mph/179·20 km/h.
Fastest lap: Ribbs, 1m 39·965s, 108·04 mph/173·87 km/h.
Championship points. Drivers: **1** Gloy, 99; **2** Pickett, 85; **3** Lobenberg, 80; **4** Brassfield, 71; **5** Dallenbach Jnr, 59; **6** Ribbs, 58.
Manufacturers: **1** Mercury, 49; **2** Pontiac, 30; **3** Chevrolet, 28; **4** Nissan, 5; **5** Porsche, 2.

SCCA BUDWEISER TRANS-AM CHAMPIONSHIP RACE, Road America, Elkhart Lake, Wisconsin, United States of America, August 5. SCCA Budweiser Trans-Am Championship, round 8. 25 laps of the 4·000-mile/6·437-km circuit, 100·00 miles/160·93 km.
1 Richard Spenard, CDN (Chevrolet Corvette), 58m 59·64s, 101·705 mph/163·678 km/h.
2 Tom Gloy, USA (Mercury Capri), 59m 07·14s.
3 Jim Miller, USA (Pontiac Trans-Am), 25 laps.
4 Paul Newman, USA (Nissan 300ZX Turbo), 25.
5 Wally Dallenbach Jnr, USA (Chevrolet Camaro), 25.
6 Darin Brassfield, USA (Chevrolet Corvette), 25.
7 Greg Pickett, USA (Mercury Capri), 25; **8** Bob Lobenberg, USA (Pontiac Trans-Am), 24; **9** Rob McFarlin, USA (Pontiac Trans-Am), 24; **10** Duane Smith, USA (Pontiac Firebird), 24.
Fastest Qualifier: Lobenberg, 2m 16·340s, 105·618 mph/169·975 km/h (record).
Fastest lap: Gloy, 2m 18·980s, 104·931 mph/168·870 km/h (record).
Championship points. Drivers: **1** Gloy, 115; **2** Pickett, 94; **3** Lobenberg, 90; **4** Brassfield, 81; **5** Dallenbach Jnr, 70; **6** Ribbs, 58.
Manufacturers: **1** Mercury, 55; **2** Chevrolet, 37; **3** Pontiac, 34; **4** Nissan, 8; **5** Porsche, 2.

SCCA BUDWEISER TRANS-AM CHAMPIONSHIP RACE, Watkins Glen Grand Prix Circuit, New York, United States of America, August 19. SCCA Budweiser Trans-Am Championship, round 9. 30 laps of the 3·377-mile/5·435-km circuit, 101·31 miles/163·05 km.
1 Willy T. Ribbs, USA (Mercury Capri), 1h 04m 30·976s, 94·22 mph/151·63 km/h.
2 Tom Gloy, USA (Mercury Capri), 1h 04m 38·886s.
3 David Hobbs, GB (Chevrolet Corvette), 30 laps.
4 Wally Dallenbach Jnr, USA (Chevrolet Camaro), 30.
5 Eppie Wietzes, CDN (Pontiac Firebird), 30.
6 Jim Miller, USA (Pontiac Trans-Am), 30.
7 Jim Fitzgerald, USA (Datsun 280ZX Turbo), 30; **8** Peter Dus, USA (Chevrolet Corvette), 29; **9** Russ Theus, USA (Lincoln Mark VII), 29; **10** Jim San-

born, USA (Pontiac Trans-Am), 29.
Fastest Qualifier: Bob Lobenberg, USA (Pontiac Trans-Am), 1h 52·647s, 107·923 mph/173·685 km/h (record).
Fastest lap: Dallenbach Jnr, 1m 54·402s, 106·267 mph/171·020 km/h (record).
Championship points. Drivers: 1 Gloy, 131; **2** Pickett, 94; **3** Lobenberg, 91; **4** Dallenbach Jnr, 82; **5** Brassfield, 81; **6** Ribbs, 79.
Manufacturers: 1 Mercury, 64; **2** Chevrolet, 41; **3** Pontiac, 36; **4** Nissan, 8; **5** Porsche, 2.

SCCA BUDWEISER TRANS-AM CHAMPIONSHIP RACE, Trois-Rivieres, Quebec, Canada, September 2. SCCA Budweiser Trans-Am Championship round 10. 35 laps of the 2·100-mile/3·380-km circuit, 73·50 miles/118·30 km.
1 Tom Gloy, USA (Mercury Capri), 59m 29·490s, 74·128 mph/119·297 km/h.
2 Greg Pickett, USA (Mercury Capri), 59m 32·380s.
3 Eppie Wietzes, CDN (Pontiac Firebird), 35 laps.
4 Richard Spenard, CDN (Chevrolet Corvette), 35.
5 Paul Miller, USA (Porsche 924 Turbo), 35.
6 Jim Miller, USA (Pontiac Trans-Am), 35.
7 John Jones, CDN (Mercury Capri), 35; **8** Willy T. Ribbs, USA (Mercury Capri), 35; **9** Wally Dallenbach Jnr, USA (Chevrolet Camaro), 35; **10** Peter Deman, CDN (Chevrolet Corvette), 34.
Fastest Qualifier: Philippe Alliot, F (Pontiac Trans Am), 1m 34·1412s, 80·305 mph/129·238 km/h (record).
Fastest lap: Ribbs, 1m 33·974s, 80·477 mph/129·467 km/h (record).
Championship points. Drivers: 1 Gloy, 152; **2** Pickett, 110; **3** Lobenberg, 91; **4** Dallenbach Jnr, 89; **5** Ribbs, 87; **6** Brassfield, 81.
Manufacturers: 1 Mercury, 73; **2** Chevrolet, 48; **3** Pontiac, 40; **4** Nissan, 8; **5** Porsche, 4.

SCCA BUDWEISER TRANS-AM CHAMPIONSHIP RACE, Mosport Park Circuit, Ontario, Canada, September 9. SCCA Budweiser Trans-Am Championship, round 11. 40 laps of the 2·459-mile/3·957-km circuit, 98·36 miles/158·28 km.
1 Paul Miller, USA (Porsche 924 Turbo), 59m 28·558s, 99·22 mph/159·68 km/h.
2 Greg Pickett, USA (Mercury Capri), 59m 32·517s.
3 Willy T. Ribbs, USA (Mercury Capri), 40 laps.
4 Tom Gloy, USA (Mercury Capri), 40.
5 Bob Lobenberg, USA (Pontiac Trans-Am), 40.
6 Wally Dallenbach, Jnr, USA (Chevrolet Camaro), 40.
7 Darin Brassfield, USA (Chevrolet Corvette), 40; **8** Eppie Wietzes, CDN (Pontiac Firebird), 39; **9** David Hobbs, GB (Chevrolet Corvette), 39; **10** Jim Miller, USA (Pontiac Trans-Am), 39.
Fastest Qualifier: Ribbs, 1m 23·282s, 106·29 mph/171·06 km/h (record).
Fastest lap: P. Miller, 1m 24·897s, 104·27 mph/167·81 km/h (record).
Championship points. Drivers: 1 Gloy, 164; **2** Pickett, 126; **3** Ribbs, 103; **4** Lobenberg, 102; **5** Dallenbach Jnr, 99; **6** Brassfield, 90.
Manufacturers: 1 Mercury, 79; **2** Chevreolet, 45; **3** Pontiac, 42; **4** Porsche, 13; **5** Nissan, 8.

SCCA BUDWEISER TRANS-AM CHAMPIONSHIP RACE, Seattle International Raceway, Washington, United States of America, September 23. SCCA Budweiser Trans-Am Championship, round 12. 44 laps of the 2·250-mile/3·621-km circuit, 99·00 miles/159·32 km.
1 Greg Pickett, USA (Mercury Capri), 1h 02m 38·17s, 94·833 mph/152·619 km/h.
2 Tom Gloy, USA (Mercury Capri), 1h 03m 55·77s.
3 Jim Miller, USA (Pontiac Trans-Am), 44 laps.
4 David Hobbs, GB (Chevrolet Corvette), 43.
5 Wally Dallenbach Jnr, USA (Chevrolet Camaro), 43.
6 Richard Wall, USA (Chevrolet Camaro), 43.
7 Jim Derhaag, USA (Pontiac Trans-Am), 43; **8** David Schroeder, USA (Chevrolet Corvette), 43; **9** Dennis Krueger, USA (Pontiac Firebird), 42; **10** Les Lindley, USA (Chevrolet Camaro), 42.
Fastest Qualifier: Bob Lobenberg, USA (Pontiac Trans-Am), 1m 21·870s, 98·940 mph/159·228 km/h (record).
Fastest lap: Not available.
Championship points. Drivers: 1 Gloy, 180; **2** Pickett, 147; **3** Dallenbach Jnr, 110; **4** Lobenberg and Ribbs, 103; **6** Miller, 96.
Manufacturers: 1 Mercury, 88; **2** Chevrolet, 48; **3** Pontiac, 46; **4** Porsche, 13; **5** Nissan, 8.

SCCA BUDWEISER TRANS-AM CHAMPIONSHIP RACE, Sears Point International Raceway, Sonoma, California, United States of America, September 30. SCCA Budweiser Trans-Am Championship, round 13. 40 laps of the 2·523-mile/4·060-km circuit, 100·92 miles/162·40 km.
1 Greg Pickett, USA (Mercury Capri), 1h 13m 28·170s, 82·419 mph/132·640 km/h.
2 Willy T. Ribbs, USA (Mercury Capri), 1h 13m 32·960s.
3 Bob Lobenberg, USA (Pontiac Trans-Am), 40 laps.
4 Paul Miller, UsA (Porsche Carrera Turbo), 40.
5 Tom Gloy, USA (Mercury Capri), 40.
6 Richard Wall, USA (Chevrolet Camaro), 40.
7 Darin Brassfield, USA (Chevrolet Camaro), 40; **8** Jim Derhaag, USA (Pontiac Trans-Am), 40; **9** George Follmer, USA (Chevrolet Corvette), 40; **10** Bill Doyle, USA (Pontiac Trans-Am), 40.
Fastest Qualifier: Gloy, 1m 38·432s, 92·275 mph/148·502 km/h (record).
Fastest lap: Lobenberg, 1m 40·170s, 90·566 mph/145·741 km/h (record).
Championship points. Drivers: 1 Gloy, 192; **2** Pickett, 167; **3** Ribbs, 119; **4** Lobenberg, 118; **5** Dallenbach Jnr, 110; **6** Brassfield, 99.
Manufacturers: 1 Mercury, 97; **2** Pontiac, 50; **3** Chevrolet, 49; **4** Porsche, 16; **5** Nissan, 8.

SCCA BUDWEISER TRANS-AM CHAMPIONSHIP RACE, Riverside International Raceway, California, United States of America, October 7. SCCA Budweiser Trans-Am Championship, round 14. 40 laps of the 2·547-mile/4·099-km circuit, 101·88 miles/163·69 km.
1 Darin Brassfield, USA (Chevrolet Corvette), 58m 00·485s, 105·378 mph/169·589 km/h.
2 Wally Dallenbach Jnr, USA (Chevrolet Camaro), 58m 36·375s.
3 Willy T. Ribbs, USA (Mercury Capri), 40 laps.
4 Tom Gloy, USA (Mercury Capri), 40.
5 Paul Miller, USA (Porsche 924 Turbo), 40.
6 Greg Pickett, USA (Mercury Capri), 40.
7 Bob Lobenberg, USA (Pontiac Trans-Am), 40; **8** Wayne Harper, USA (Mercury Capri), 39; **9** Dave Watson, USA (Chevrolet Corvette), 39; **10** Larry Park, USA (Chevrolet Corvette).
Fastest Qualifier: Lobenberg, 1m 21·834s, 113·152 mph/182·100 km/h (record).
Fastest lap: Brassfield, 1m 22·393s, 107·921 mph/173·682 km/h (record).

Championship points (prior to final two rounds on October 28 and November 11).
Drivers:

1 Tom Gloy, USA	204
2 Greg Pickett, USA	177
3 Willy T. Ribbs, USA	133
4 Bob Lobenberg, USA	128
5 Wally Dallenbach, Jnr, USA	126
6 Darin Brassfield, USA	120

7 Jim Miller, USA, 96; **8** Davids Hobbs, GB, 92; **9** Paul Miller, USA, 74; **10** Jim Derhagg, USA, 59; **11** Eppie Wietzes, CDN, 56; **12** Paul Newman, USA, 39; **13** Dave Watson, USA, 35; **14** Richard Spenard, CDN, 32; **15** Richard Wall, USA, 31.

Manufacturers:

1 Mercury	101
2 Chevrolet	59
3 Pontiac	50
4 Porsche	18
5 Nissan	8

Final results will be given in Autocourse 1985/86.

CART/PPG Indy Car World Series

TOYOTA GRAND PRIX OF LONG BEACH, Long Beach Circuit, Long Beach, California, United States of America, April 1. CART PPG Indy Car World Series, round 1. 112 laps of the 1·67-mile/2·69-km circuit, 187·94 miles/301·28 km.
1 Mario Andretti, USA (Lola T800-Cosworth DFX), 2h 15m 23s, 82·898 mph/133·411 km/h.
2 Geoff Brabham, AUS (March 84C-Cosworth DFX), 2h 16m 26s.
3 Tom Sneva, USA (March 84C-Cosworth DFX), 111 laps.
4 Jim Crawford, GB (Theodore 83-Cosworth DFX), 111.
5 Emerson Fittipaldi, BR (March 83C-Cosworth DFX), 110.
6 Jacques Villeneuve, CDN (March 83C-Cosworth DFX), 109.
7 Derek Daly, IRL (March 84C-Cosworth DFX), 109; **8** Pete Halsmer, USA (Penske PC10B-Cosworth DFX), 107; **9** John Morton, USA (Eagle 83-Chevrolet), 106; **10** Mike Andretti, USA (March 84C-Cosworth DFX), 105; **11** Gordon Johncock, USA (Wildcat MK10-Cosworth DFX), 104; **12** Ed Pimm, USA (March 83C-Chevrolet), 80 (DNF, half shaft).
Fastest Qualifier: Andretti, 1m 06·263s, 90·729 mph/146·014 km/h.
Championship points: 1 Andretti, 22; **2** Brabham, 16; **3** Sneva, 14; **4** Crawford, 12; **5** Fittipaldi, 10; **6** Villeneuve, 8.

DANA-JIMMY BRYAN 150, Phoenix International Raceway, Arizona, United States of America, April 15. CART PPG Indy Car World Series, round 2. 150 laps of the 1·000-mile/1·609-km circuit, 150·00 miles/241·40 km.
1 Tom Sneva, USA (March 84C-Cosworth DFX), 1h 14m 39·420s, 120·555 mph/194·014 km/h.
2 Howdy Holmes, USA (March 84C-Cosworth DFX), 1h 15m 04·220s.
3 Mike Andretti, USA (March 84C-Cosworth DFX), 149 laps.
4 Dick Simon, USA (March 84C-Cosworth DFX), 148.
5 Danny Ongais, USA (March 84C-Cosworth DFX), 148.
6 Danny Sullivan, USA (Shierson DSR1-Cosworth DFX), 156.
7 Bobby Rahal, USA (March 84C-Cosworth DFX), 146; **8** Kevin Cogan, USA (Eagle 84-Pontiac), 145; **9** Chris Kneifel, USA (Primus 84-Cosworth DFX), 145; **10** Gordon Johncock, USA (March 84C-Cosworth DFX), 145; **11** Chip Ganassi, USA (Wildcat Mk4B-Cosworth DFX), 144; **12** Emerson Fittipaldi, BR (March 83C-Cosworth DFX), 143.
Fastest Qualifier: Sneva, 24·070s, 149·564 mph/240·699 km/h.
Championship points: 1 Sneva, 36; **2** Andretti (Mario), 22; **3** Andretti (Mike), 17; **4** Holmes and Brabham, 16; **6** Crawford and Simon, 12.

DANA-REX MAYS CLASSIC 200, Wisconsin State Fair Park Speedway, Milwaukee, Wisconsin, United States of America, June 3. CART PPG Indy Car World Series, round 4. 200 laps of the 1·000-mile/1·609-km circuit, 200·00 miles/321·80 km.
1 Tom Sneva, USA (March 84C-Cosworth DFX), 1h 41m 40·128s, 118·030 mph/189·950 km/h.
2 Rick Mears, USA (March 84C-Cosworth DFX), 1h 41m 44·000s.
3 Al Unser Jnr, USA (March 84C-Cosworth DFX), 200 laps.
4 Mike Andretti, USA (March 84C-Cosworth DFX), 199.
5 Al Unser, USA (March 84C-Cosworth DFX), 199.
6 Gordon Johncock, USA (March 84C-Cosworth DFX), 197.
7 Howdy Holmes, USA (March 84C-Cosworth DFX), 196; **8** Mario Andretti, USA (Lola T800-Cosworth DFX), 196; **9** Kevin Cogan, USA (Eagle 84-Pontiac), 195; **10** Danny Ongais, USA (March 84C-Cosworth DFX), 195; **11** Chip Ganassi, USA (Wildcat Mk9B-Cosworth DFX) 195; **12** Teo Fabi, I (March 84C-Cosworth DFX), 194.
Fastest Qualifier: Mears, 25·173s, 143·010 mph/230·152 km/h.
Championship points: 1 Sneva, 58; **2** Andretti (Mike), 39; **3** Mears, 38; **4** Andretti (Mario), 27; **5** Unser, 24; **6** Holmes, 22.

STROH'S/G. I. JOE'S 200, Portland International Raceway, Oregon, United States of America, June 17. CART PPG Indy Car World Series, round 5. 104 laps of the 1·915-mile/3·082-km circuit, 199·16 miles/320·53 km.
1 Al Unser Jnr, USA (March 84C-Cosworth DFX), 1h 53m 17·39s, 105·484 mph/169·758 km/h.
2 Geoff Brabham, AUS (March 84C-Cosworth DFX), 1h 53m 57·30s.
3 Teo Fabi, I (March 84C-Cosworth DFX), 104 laps.
4 Derek Daly, IRL (March 84C-Cosworth DFX), 103.
5 Tom Sneva, USA (March 84C-Cosworth DFX), 102.
6 Jacques Villeneuve, CDN (March 83C-Cosworth DFX), 100.
7 Josele Garza, MEX (March 84C-Cosworth DFX), 99; **8** Chris Kneifel, USA (Primus 84-Cosworth DFX), 99; **9** Gordon Johncock, USA (March 84C-Cosworth DFX), 99; **10** Rick Mears, USA (March 84C-Cosworth DFX), 99; **11** Danny Ongais, USA (March 84C-Cosworth DFX), 97 (DNF, out of fuel); **12** Mike Andretti, USA (March 84C-Cosworth DFX), 96.
Fastest Qualifier: Mario Andretti, USA (Lola T800-Cosworth DFX), 59·437s, 115·988 mph/186·664 km/h.
Championship points: 1 Sneva, 68; **2** Mears, 41; **3** Andretti (Mike), 40; **4** Unser Jnr, 35; **5** Brabham, 32; **6** Andretti (Mario), 28.

MEADOWLANDS GRAND PRIX, Meadowlands Circuit, New York, United States of America, July 1. CART PPG Indy Car World Series, round 6. 100 laps of the 1·682-mile/2·707-km circuit, 168·20 miles/270·70 km.
1 Mario Andretti, USA (Lola T800-Cosworth DFX), 2h 04m 59·4s, 80·742 mph/129·94 km/h.
2 Danny Sullivan, USA (Lola T800-Cosworth DFX), 2h 05m 51·1s.
3 Geoff Brabham, AUS (March 84C-Cosworth DFX), 99 laps.
4 Al Unser Jnr, USA (March 84C-Cosworth DFX), 99.
5 Al Holbert, USA (March 84C-Cosworth DFX), 98.
6 Tom Sneva, USA (March 84C-Cosworth DFX), 98.
7 Emerson Fittipaldi, BR (March 84C-Cosworth DFX), 98; **8** Al Unser, USA (March 84C-Cosworth DFX), 97; **9** Chip Ganassi, USA (March 84C-Cosworth DFX), 97; **10** Rick Mears, USA (March 84C-Cosworth DFX) 96; **11** Bobby Rahal, USA (March 84C-Cosworth DFX), 96; **12** Gordon Johncock, USA (March 84C-Cosworth DFX), 96.
Fastest Qualifier: Andretti (Mario), 1m 03·067s, 96·012 mph/154·52 km/h (record).
Championship points: 1 Sneva, 76; **2** Andretti (Mario), 50; **3** Unser Jnr, 47; **4** Brabham, 46; **5** Mears, 44; **6** Andretti (Mike), 40.

BUDWEISER CLEVELAND GRAND PRIX, Burke Lakefront Airport Circuit, Cleveland, Ohio, United States of America, July 8. CART PPG Indy Car World Series, round 7. 88 laps of the 2.485-mile/3.999-km circuit, 218.68 miles/351·91 km.
1 Danny Sullivan, USA (Lola T800-Cosworth DFX), 1h 50m 17s, 118·734 mph/191·083 km/h.
2 Chip Ganassi, USA (March 84C-Cosworth DFX), 86 laps.
3 Mike Andretti, USA (March 84C-Cosworth DFX), 86.
4 Rick Mears, USA (March 84C-Cosworth DFX), 86.
5 Roberto Guerrero, COL (March 84C-Cosworth DFX), 86.
6 Derek Daly, IRL (March 84C-Cosworth DFX), 85.
7 Al Holbert, USA (March 84C-Cosworth DFX), 85; **8** Geoff Brabham, AUS (March 84C-Cosworth DFX) 85; **9** Jacques Villeneuve, CDN (March 84C-Cosworth DFX), 85; **10** Al Unser, USA (March 84C-Cosworth DFX), 85; **11** Scott Brayton, USA (March 84C-Cosworth DFX), 85; **12** Howdy Holmes, USA (March 84C-Cosworth DFX), 83.
Fastest Qualifier: Mario Andretti, USA (Lola T800-Cosworth DFX), 1m 10·637, 126·393 mph/203·409 km/h (record).
Championship points: 1 Sneva, 76; **2** Mears, 56; **3** Andretti (Mike)l 54; **4** Brabham and Andretti (Mario), 51; **6** Unser Jnr, 47.

NORTON MICHIGAN 500, Michigan International Speedway, Brooklyn, United States of America, July 15. CART PPG Indy Car World Series, round 8. 250 laps of the 2·000-mile/3·219-km circuit, 500·00 miles/804·75 km.
1 Mario Andretti, USA (Lola T800-Cosworth DFX), 3h 44m 45·00s, 133·482 mph/214·818 km/h.
2 Tom Sneva, USA (March 84C-Cosworth DFX), 3h 44m 45·14s.
3 Rick Mears, USA (March 84C-Cosworth DFX), 250 laps.
4 Gordon Johncock, USA (March 84C-Cosworth DFX), 250.
5 Roberto Guerrero, COL (March 84C-Cosworth DFX), 250.
6 Pancho Carter, USA (March 84C-Cosworth DFX), 249 (DNF, accident).
7 Johnny Rutherford, USA (March 84C-Cosworth DFX), 249; **8** Kevin Cogan, USA (March 84C-Cosworth DFX), 249; **9** Geoff Brabham, AUS (March 84C-Cosworth DFX), 248; **10** Danny Sullivan, USA (Lola T800-Cosworth DFX), 248; **11** Josele Garza, MEX (March 84C-Cosworth DFX), 244; **12** Dick Simon, USA (March 84C-Cosworth DFX), 241.
Fastest Qualifier: Andretti, 34·109s, 211·088 mph/339·712 km/h.
Championship points: 1 Sneva, 93; **2** Andretti (Mario), 72; **3** Mears, 70; **4** Brabham, 55; **5** Andretti (Mike), 54; **6** Sullivan and Unser Jnr, 47.

PROVIMI VEAL 200, Road America, Elkhart Lake, Wisconsin, United States of America, August 5. CART PPG Indy Car World Series, round 9. 50 laps of the 4·000-mile/6·437-km circuit, 200·00 miles/257·48 km.
1 Mario Andretti, USA (Lola T800-Cosworth DFX), 1h 43m 08·409s, 116·347 mph/187·242 km/h.
2 Bobby Rahal, USA (March 84C-Cosworth DFX), 1h 44m 23·24s.
3 Al Unser, USA (March 84C-Cosworth DFX), 49 laps.
4 Rick Mears, USA (March 84C-Cosworth DFX), 49.
5 Geoff Brabham, AUS (March 84C-Cosworth DFX), 49.
6 John Paul Jnr, USA (March 84C-Cosworth DFX), 49.
7 Josele Garza, MEX (March 84C-Cosworth DFX), 49; **8** Arie Luyendyk, NL (March 84C-Cosworth DFX), 48; **9** Gordon Johncock, USA (March 84C-Cosworth DFX), 48; **10** Kevin Cogan, USA (March 84C-Cosworth DFX), 48; **11** Roberto Guerrero, COL (March 84C-Cosworth DFX), 48; **12** Scott Brayton, USA (March 84C-Cosworth DFX), 47.
Fastest Qualifier: Andretti, 1m 55·187s, 125·014 mph/201·190 km/h.
Championship points: 1 Andretti (Mario), 94; **2** Sneva, 93; **3** Mears, 82; **4** Brabham, 65; **5** Andretti (Mike), 54; **6** Sullivan and Unser Jnr, 47.

DOMINO'S PIZZA POCONO 500, Pocono International Raceway, Pennsylvania, United States of America, August 19. CART PPG Indy Car World Series, round 10. 200 laps of the 2·500-mile/4·023-km circuit, 500·00 miles/804·60 km.
1 Danny Sullivan, USA (Lola T800-Cosworth DFX), 3h 38m 29·69s, 137·303 mph/220·967 km/h.
2 Rick Mears, USA (March 84C-Cosworth DFX), 3h 38m 29·96s.
3 Bobby Rahal, USA (March 84C-Cosworth DFX), 200 laps.
4 Tom Sneva, USA (March 84C-Cosworth DFX), 200.
5 Danny Ongais, USA (March 84C-Cosworth DFX), 199.
6 Scott Brayton, USA (March 84C-Cosworth DFX), 199.
7 Pancho Carter, USA (March 84C-Cosworth DFX), 199; **8** Al Unser, USA (March 84C-Cosworth DFX), 199; **9** Howdy Holmes, USA (March 84C-Cosworth DFX), 194; **10** Gary Bettenhausen, USA (March 84C-Cosworth DFX), 192; **11** Gordon Johncock, USA (March 84C-Cosworth DFX), 192; **12** Dick Simon, USA (March 84C-Cosworth DFX), 191.
Fastest Qualifier: Mears, 44·363s, 202·872 mph/326·490 km/h.
Championship points: 1 Sneva, 105; **2** Mears, 100; **3** Andretti (Mario), 94; **4** Sullivan, 67; **5** Brabham, 65; **6** Andretti (Mike), 54.

ESCORT RADAR WARNING 200, Mid-Ohio Sports Car Course, Lexington, Ohio, United States of America, September 2. CART PPG Indy Car World Series, round 11. 84 laps of the 2·400-mile/3·863-km circuit, 201·60 miles/324·41 km.
1 Mario Andretti, USA (Lola T800-Cosworth DFX), 1h 59m 50·11s, 100·368 mph/161·526 km/h.
2 Bobby Rahal, USA (March 84C-Cosworth DFX), 2h 00m 28·01s.
3 Danny Sullivan, USA (Lola T800-Cosworth DFX), 83 laps.
4 Emerson Fittipaldi, BR (March 84C-Cosworth DFX), 82.
5 Rick Mears, USA (March 84C-Cosworth DFX), 82.
6 Howdy Holmes, USA (March 84C-Cosworth DFX), 82.
7 Tom Sneva, USA (March 84C-Cosworth DFX), 82; **8** Al Unser, USA (March 84C-Cosworth DFX), 81; **9** John Paul Jnr, USA (March 84C-Cosworth DFX), 81; **10** Gordon Johncock, USA (March 84C-Cosworth DFX), 80; **11** Josele Garza, MEX (March 84C-Cosworth DFX), 77; **12** Scott Brayton, USA (March 84C-Cosworth DFX), 76.
Fastest Qualifier: Andretti, 1m 22·215s, 105·090 mph/169·126 km/h.
Championship points: 1 Andretti (Mario), 116; **2** Sneva, 111; **3** Mears, 110; **4** Sullivan, 81; **5** Brabham, 65; **6** Rahal, 61.

MOLSON BREWERIES 200, Sanair Superspeedway, Quebec, Canada, September 9. CART PPG Indy Car World Series, round 12. 225 laps of the 0·826-mile/1·329-km circuit, 185·85 miles/229·03 km.
1 Danny Sullivan, USA (Lola T800-Cosworth DFX), 1h 39m 49·43s, 111·707 mph/179·775 km/h.
2 Bobby Rahal, USA (March 84C-Cosworth DFX), 1h 39m 59·77s.
3 Mike Andretti, USA (March 84C-Cosworth DFX), 225 laps.
4 Josele Garza, MEX (March 84C-Cosworth DFX), 224.
5 Johnny Rutherford, USA (March 84C-Cosworth DFX), 224.
6 Al Unser Jnr, USA (March 84C-Cosworth DFX), 224.
7 Mario Andretti, USA (Lola T800-Cosworth DFX), 222; **8** Jacques Villeneuve, CDN(March 84C-Cosworth DFX), 218; **9** Howdy Holmes, USA (March 84C-Cosworth DFX), 216; **10** Corrado Fabi, I (Lola T800-Cosworth DFX), 213; **11** Scott Brayton, USA (March 84C-Cosworth DFX), 213; **12** Dick Simon, USA (March 84C-Cosworth DFX), 211.
Fastest Qualifier: Rahal, 20·718s, 143·527 mph/230·984 km/h (record).
Championship points: 1 Andretti (Mario), 122; **2** Sneva, 111; **3** Mears, 110; **4** Sullivan, 101; **5** Rahal, 79; **6** Andretti (Mike), 68.

DETROIT NEWS GRAND PRIX 200, Michigan International Speedway, Brooklyn, Michigan, United States of America, September 22/23. CART PPG Indy Car World Series, round 13. 100 laps of the 2·000-mile/3·219-km circuit, 200·00 miles/321·90 km (race run in two parts due to rain).

1 Mario Andretti, USA (Lola T800-Cosworth DFX), 1h 11m 12·42s, 168·523 mph/271·211 km/h.
2 Tom Sneva, USA (March 84C-Cosworth DFX), 1h 11m 13·60s.
3 Danny Ongais, USA (March 84C-Cosworth DFX), 100 laps.
4 Al Unser, USA (March 84C-Cosworth DFX), 100.
5 Bobby Rahal, USA (March 84C-Cosworth DFX), 100.
6 Al Unser Jnr, USA (March 84C-Cosworth DFX), 100.
7 Mike Andretti, USA (March 84C-Cosworth DFX), 100; **8** Howdy Holmes, USA (March 84C-Cosworth DFX), 98; **9** Danny Sullivan, USA (Lola T800-Cosworth DFX), 98; **10** Josele Garza, MEX (March 84C-Cosworth DFX), 97; **11** Geoff Brabham, AUS (March 84C-Cosworth DFX), 97; **12** Emerson Fittipaldi, BR (March 84C-Cosworth DFX), 96.
Fastest Qualifier: Johnny Rutherford, USA (March 84C-Cosworth DFX), 33·458s, 215·189 mph/346·312 km/h (record).
Championship points: 1 Andretti (Mario), 143; **2** Sneva, 127; **3** Mears, 110; **4** Sullivan, 105; **5** Rahal, 89; **6** Andretti (Mike), 74.

BOBBY BALL 150, Phoenix International Raceway, Arizona, United States of America, October 14. CART PPG Indy Car World Series, round 14. 150 laps of the 1·000-mile/1·609-km circuit, 150·00 miles/241·40 km.
1 Bobby Rahal, USA (March 84C-Cosworth DFX), 1h 31m 47·49s, 98·048 mph/157·793 km/h.
2 Al Unser Jnr, USA (March 84C-Cosworth DFX), 1h 31m 48·31s.
3 Mike Andretti, USA (March 84C-Cosworth DFX), 150 laps.
4 Tom Sneva, USA (March 84C-Cosworth DFX), 150.
5 Danny Ongais, USA (March 84C-Cosworth DFX), 150.
6 Corrado Fabi, I (Lola T800-Cosworth DFX), 149.
7 Pancho Carter, USA (March 84C-Cosworth DFX), 149; **8** Josele Garza, MEX (March 84C-Cosworth DFX), 149; **9** Jacques Villeneuve, CDN (March 84C-Cosworth DFX), 146; **10** Ed Pimm, USA (Eagle 84-Pontiac), 146; **11** Johnny Rutherford, USA (March 84C-Cosworth DFX), 146; **12** Mario Andretti, USA (Lola T800-Cosworth DFX), 144.
Fastest Qualifier: Villeneuve, 23·155s, 155·474 mph/250·211 km/h.
Championship points: 1 Andretti (Mario), 144; **2** Sneva, 139; **3** Rahal and Mears, 110; **5** Sullivan, 105; **6** Andretti (Mike), 88.

CRIBARI WINES 300 KMS, Laguna Seca Raceway, California, United States of America, October 21. CART PPG Indy Car World Series, round 15. 98 laps of the 1·900-mile/3·056-km circuit, 186·20 miles/299·49 km.
1 Bobby Rahal, USA (March 84C-Cosworth DFX), 1h 33m 47·97s, 116·619 mph/187·680 km/h.
2 Mario Andretti, USA (Lola T800-Cosworth DFX), 1h 34m 01·04s.
3 Mike Andretti, USA (March 84C-Cosworth DFX), 98 laps.
4 Al Unser Jnr, USA (March 84C-Cosworth DFX), 98.
5 Geoff Brabham, AUS (March 84C-Cosworth DFX), 97.
6 Al Unser, USA (March 84C-Cosworth DFX), 97.
7 Roberto Guerrero, COL (March 84C-Cosworth DFX), 97; **8** Bruno Giacomelli, I (March 84C-Cosworth DFX), 96; **9** Danny Sullivan, USA (Lola T800-Cosworth DFX), 96; **10** Tom Sneva, USA (March 84C-Cosworth DFX), 96; **11** John Paul Jnr, USA (March 84C-Cosworth DFX), 95; **12** Ed Pimm, USA (Eagle 84-Pontiac), 93.
Fastest Qualifier: Mario Andretti, 54·030s, 126·596 mph/203·736 km/h.

Championship points (prior to final round at Las Vegas on November 11).

1 Mario Andretti, USA	160
2 Tom Sneva, USA	142
3 Bobby Rahal, USA	131
4 Rick Mears, USA	110
5 Danny Sullivan, USA	109
6 Mike Andretti, USA	102

7 Al Unser Jnr, USA, 91; **8** Al Unser, USA, 76; **9** Danny Ongais, USA, 53; **10** Howdy Holmes, USA and Roberto Guerrero, COL, 44; **12** Gordon Johncock, USA and Josele Garza, MEX, 39; **14** Emerson Fittipaldi, BR and Jacques Villeneuve, CDN, 30.
Final results will be given in Autocourse 1985/86.

NASCAR Winston Cup Grand Nationals 1983 results

The final rounds of the 1983 NASCAR Winston Cup Grand National series were run after Autocourse 1983/84 went to press.

WARNER W HODGDON AMERICAN 500, North Carolina Motor Speedway, Rockingham, North Carolina, United States of America, October 30. NASCAR Winston Cup Grand National, round 28. 492 laps of the 1·017-mile/1·637-km circuit, 500·36 miles/805·26 km.
1 Terry Labonte, USA (Chevrolet), 4h 11m 36s, 119·324 mph/192·033 km/h.
2 Tim Richmond, USA (Pontiac), 4h 11m 37s.
3 Ricky Rudd, USA (Chevrolet), 491 laps.
4 Neil Bonnet, USA (Chevrolet), 490.
5 Darrell Waltrip, USA (Chevrolet), 489.
6 Ron Bouchard, USA (Buick), 486.
7 Dave Marcis, USA (Chevrolet), 486; **8** Lennie Pond, USA (Buick), 476; **9** Jimmy Means, USA (Chevrolet), 475; **10** Tommy Gale, USA (Ford), 471.
Fastest Qualifier: Bonnett, 25·447s, 143·876 mph/231·545 km/h (record).
Championship points. Drivers: 1 Allison, 4349; **2** Waltrip, 4322; **3** Elliott, 3949; **4** Petty, 3743; **5** Labonte, 3693; **6** Gant, 3668.
Manufacturers: 1 Chevrolet, 196; **2** Buick, 135; **3** Pontiac, 99; **4** Ford, 97.

ATLANTA JOURNAL 500, Atlanta International Raceway, Hampton, Georgia, United States of America, November 6. NASCAR Winston Cup Grand National, round 29. 328 laps of the 1·522-mile/2·449-km circuit, 499·22 miles/803·41 km.
1 Neil Bonnett, USA (Chevrolet), 3h 37m 37s, 137·643 mph/221·514 km/h.
2 Buddy Baker, USA (Ford), 3h 37m 37·5s.
3 Bobby Allison, USA (Buick), 328 laps.
4 Terry Labonte, USA (Chevrolet), 327.
5 Richard Petty, USA (Pontiac), 326.
6 Bill Elliott, USA (Ford), 326.
7 Morgan Shepherd, USA (Buick), 325; **8** Dean Combs, USA (Oldsmobile), 324; **9** Darrell Waltrip, USA (Chevrolet), 323; **10** Jody Ridley, USA (Chevrolet), 323.
Fastest Qualifier: Tim Richmond, USA (Pontiac), 32·585s, 168·151 mph/270·612 km/h.
Championship points. Drivers: 1 Allison, 4524; **2** Waltrip, 4460; **3** Elliott, 4099; **4** Petty, 3903; **5** Labonte, 3858; **6** Gant, 3720.
Manufacturers: 1 Chevrolet, 205; **2** Buick, 139; **3** Ford, 103; **4** Pontiac, 101.

WINSTON WESTERN 500, Riverside International Raceway, Riverside, California, United States of America, November 20. NASCAR Winston Cup Grand National, round 30. 119 laps of the 2·620-mile/4·216-km circuit, 311·78 miles/501·76 km.
1 Bill Elliott, USA (Ford), 3h 15m 09s, 95·859 mph/154·270 km/h.
2 Benny Parsons, USA (Chevrolet), 3h 15m 12s.
3 Neil Bonnett, USA (Chevrolet), 119 laps.
4 Dale Earnhardt, USA (Ford), 119.
5 Tim Richmond, USA (Pontiac), 119.
6 Darrell Waltrip, USA (Chevrolet), 119.
7 Terry Labonte, USA (Chevrolet), 119; **8** Herschel McGriff, USA (Buick), 119; **9** Bobby Allison, USA (Buick), 119; **10** Richard Petty, USA (Pontiac), 118.
Fastest Qualifier: Waltrip, 1m 20·766s, 116·782 mph/187·942 km/h (record).

Final Championship points. Drivers:

1 Bobby Allison, USA	4667
2 Darrell Waltrip, USA	4620
3 Bill Elliott, USA	4279
4 Richard Petty, USA	4042
5 Terry Labonte, USA	4004
6 Neil Bonnet, USA	3842

7 Harry Gant, USA, 3790; **8** Dale Earnhardt, USA, 3732; **9** Ricky Rudd, USA, 3693; **10** Tim Richmond, USA, 3612; **11** Dave Marcis, USA, 3361; **12** Joe Ruttman, USA, 3342; **13** Kyle Petty, USA, 3261; **14** Dick Brooks, USA, 3230; **15** Buddy Arrington, USA, 3158; **16** Ron Bouchard, USA, 3113; **17** Geoff Bodine, USA, 3019; **18** Jimmy Means, USA, 2983; **19** Sterling Marlin, USA, 2980; **20** Morgan Shepherd, USA, 2733.
Manufacturers:

1 Chevrolet	211
2 Buick	139
3 Ford	112
4 Pontiac	103

1984 results

DAYTONA 500, Daytona International Speedway, Florida, United States of America, February 19. NASCAR Winston Cup Grand National, round 1. 200 laps of the 2·500-mile/4·023-km circuit, 500·00 miles/804·67 km.
1 Cale Yarborough, USA (Chevrolet), 3h 18m 41s, 150·994 mph/243·001 km/h.
2 Dale Earnhardt, USA (Chevrolet), 3h 18m 41s (Yarborough won by 8 car lengths).
3 Darrell Waltrip, USA (Chevrolet), 200 laps.
4 Neil Bonnett, USA (Chevrolet), 200.
5 Bill Elliott, USA (Ford), 200.
6 Harry Gant, USA (Chevrolet), 200.
7 Ricky Rudd, USA (Ford), 199; **8** Geoff Bodine, USA (Chevrolet), 199; **9** David Pearson, USA (Chevrolet), 198; **10** Jody Ridley, USA (Chevrolet), 198.
Fastest Qualifier: Yarborough, 44·588s, 201·848 mph/324·842 km/h (record).
Championship points. Drivers: 1 Yarborough, 185; **2** Earnhardt, 175; **3** Waltrip, 170; **4** Bonnett, 165; **5** Elliott, 160; **6** Gant, 155.
Manufacturers: 1 Chevrolet, 9; **2** Ford, 2.

MILLER HIGH LIFE 400, Richmond Fairgrounds Raceway, Virginia, United States of America, February 26. NASCAR Winston Cup Grand National, round 2. 400 laps of the 0·542-mile/0·872-km circuit, 216·80 miles/348·80 km.
1 Ricky Rudd, USA (Ford), 2h 09m 31s, 76·736 mph/126·713 km/h.
2 Darrell Waltrip, USA (Chevrolet), 2h 09m 32s.
3 Terry Labonte, USA (Chevrolet), 400 laps.
4 Bill Elliott, USA (Ford), 399.
5 Neil Bonnett, USA (Chevrolet), 399.
6 Dale Earnhardt, USA (Chevrolet), 399.
7 Tim Richmond, USA (Pontiac), 399; **8** Harry Gant, USA (Chevrolet), 399; **9** Geoff Bodine, USA (Chevrolet), 399; **10** Joe Ruttman, USA (Chevrolet), 399.
Fastest Qualifier: Waltrip, 20·798s, 93·817 mph/150·983 km/g (record).
Championship points. Drivers: 1 Waltrip, 350; **2** Rudd, 326; **3** Bonnett, 325; **4** Earnhardt, 325; **5** Elliott, 320; **6** Yarborough, 306.
Manufacturers: 1 Chevrolet, 15; **2** Ford, 11.

WARNER W HODGDON CAROLINE 500, North Carolina Motor Speedway, North Carolina, United States of America, March 4. NASCAR Winston Cup Grand National, round 3. 492 laps of the 1·017-mile/1·637-km circuit, 500·36 miles/805·26 km.
1 Bobby Allison, USA (Buick), 4h 03m 55s, 122·931 mph/197·838 km/h.
2 Terry Labonte, USA (Chevrolet), 4h 03m 59s.
3 Lake Speed, USA (Chevrolet), 492 laps.
4 Richard Petty, USA (Pontiac), 491.
5 Buddy Baker, USA (Ford), 488.
6 Geoff Bodine, USA (Chevrolet), 488.
7 Ricky Rudd, USA (Ford), 488; **8** Bill Elliott, USA (Ford), 488; **9** Dave Marcis, USA (Pontiac), 487; **10** Darrell Waltrip, USA (Chevrolet), 478.
Fastest Qualifier: Harry Gant, USA (Chevrolet), 25·235s, 145·084 mph/233·490 km/h (record).
Championship points. Drivers: 1 Waltrip, 484; **2** Labonte, 477; **3** Rudd, 472; **4** Elliott, 462; **5** Earnhardt, 446; **6** Bodine, 430.
Manufacturers: 1 Chevrolet, 21; **2** Ford, 13; **3** Buick, 9; **4** Pontiac, 3.

COCA-COLA 500, Atlanta International Raceway, Georgia, United States of America, March 18. NASCAR Winston Cup Grand National, round 4. 328 laps of the 1·522-mile/2·449-km circuit, 499·22 miles/803·27 km.
1 Benny Parsons, USA (Chevrolet), 3h 26m 39s, 144·945 mph/233·266 km/h.
2 Dale Earnhardt, USA (Chevrolet), 3h 26m 39·5s.
3 Cale Yarborough, USA (Chevrolet), 328 laps.
4 Richard Petty, USA (Pontiac), 327.
5 Bobby Allison, USA (Buick), 326.
6 Harry Gant, USA (Chevrolet), 326.
7 Terry Labonte, USA (Chevrolet), 326; **8** Ricky Rudd, USA (Ford), 326; **9** Lake Speed, USA (Chevrolet) 326; **10** Darrell Waltrip, USA (Chevrolet), 326.
Fastest Qualifier: Buddy Baker, USA (Ford), 32·880s, 166·642 mph/268·184 km/h (record).
Championship points. Drivers: 1 Labonte, 623; **2** Earnhardt, 621; **3** Waltrip, 618; **4** Rudd, 614; **5** Elliott, 592; **6** Bodine, 554.
Manufacturers: 1 Chevrolet, 30; **2** Ford, 13; **3** Buick, 11; **4** Pontiac, 7.

VALLEYDALE 500, Bristol International Raceway, Tennessee, United States of America, April 1. NASCAR Winston Cup Grand National, round 5. 500 laps of the 0·533-mile/0·858-km circuit, 266·50 miles/428·89 km.
1 Darrell Waltrip, USA (Chevrolet), 2h 50m 10s, 93·967 mph/151·225 km/h.
2 Terry Labonte, USA (Chevrolet), 2h 50m 12s.
3 Ron Bouchard, USA (Buick), 500 laps.
4 Dave Marcis, USA (Pontiac), 499.
5 Tim Richmond, USA (Pontiac), 499.
6 Ricky Rudd, USA (Ford), 498.
7 Dale Earnhardt, USA (Chevrolet), 498; **8** Richard Petty, USA (Pontiac), 498; **9** Bill Elliott, USA (Ford), 497; **10** Joe Ruttman, USA (Chevrolet), 496.
Fastest Qualifier: Rudd, 17·226s, 111·390 mph/179·264 km/h.
Championship points. Drivers: 1 Waltrip, 803; **2** Labonte, 798; **3** Earnhardt, 772; **4** Rudd, 764; **5** Elliott, 735; **6** Petty, 655.
Manufacturers: 1 Chevrolet, 39; **2** Buick, 15; **3** Ford, 14; **4** Pontiac, 9.

NORTHWESTERN BANK 400, North Wilkesboro Speedway, North Carolina, United States of America, April 8. NASCAR Winston Cup Grand National, round 6. 400 laps of the 0·625-mile/1·006-km circuit, 250·00 miles/402·34 km.
1 Tim Richmond, USA (Pontiac), 2h 33m 19s, 97·830 mph/157·442 km/h.
2 Harry Gant, USA (Chevrolet), 2h 33m 19·5s.
3 Ricky Rudd, USA (Ford), 400 laps.
4 Terry Labonte, USA (Chevrolet), 400.
5 Kyle Petty, USA (Ford), 400.
6 Darrell Waltrip, USA (Chevrolet), 399.
7 Ron Bouchard, USA (Buick), 399; **8** Dale Earnhardt, USA (Chevrolet), 399; **9** Neil Bonnett, USA (Chevrolet), 399; **10** Bill Elliott, USA (Ford), 399.
Fastest Qualifier: Rudd, 39·652s, 113·487 mph/182·638 km/h.
Championship points. Drivers: 1 Labonte, 963; **2** Waltrip, 953; **3** Rudd, 939; **4** Earnhardt, 914; **5** Elliott, 869; **6** Gant, 817.
Manufacturers: 1 Chevrolet, 45; **2** Ford, 18; **3** Pontiac, 18; **4** Buick, 15.

TRANSOUTH 500, Darlington International Raceway, South Carolina, United States of America, April 15. NASCAR Winston Cup Grand National, round 7. 367 laps of the 1·366-mile/2·198-km circuit, 501·32 miles/806·67 km.
1 Darrell Waltrip, USA (Chevrolet), 4h 18m 16s, 119·925 mph/193·000 km/h.
2 Terry Labonte, USA (Chevrolet), 4h 18m 18s.
3 Bill Elliott, USA (Ford), 366 laps.
4 Cale Yarborough, USA (Chevrolet), 366.
5 Dale Earnhardt, USA (Chevrolet), 366.
6 Harry Gant, USA (Chevrolet), 366.
7 Richard Petty, USA (Pontiac), 364; **8** Phil Parsons, USA (Chevrolet), 358; **9** Ricky Rudd, USA (Ford), 358; **10** Neil Bonnett, USA (Chevrolet), 354.
Fastest Qualifier: Benny Parsons, USA (Chevrolet), 31·157s, 156·328 mph/251·585 km/h.
Championship points. Drivers: 1 Waltrip and Labonte, 1138; **3** Rudd, 1082; **4** Earnhardt, 1074; **5** Elliott, 1039; **6** Gant, 967.
Manufacturers: 1 Chevrolet, 54; **2** Ford, 22; **3** Pontiac, 18; **4** Buick, 15.

SOVRAN BANK 500, Martinsville Speedway, Virginia, United States of America, April 29. NASCAR Winston Cup Grand National, round 8. 500 laps of the 0·525-mile/0·845-km circuit, 262·50 miles/422·45 km.
1 Geoff Bodine, USA (Chevrolet), 3h 35m 23s, 73·264 mph/117·906 km/h.
2 Ron Bouchard, USA (Buick), 3h 35m 29s.
3 Darrell Waltrip, USA (Chevrolet), 500 laps.
4 Bobby Allison, USA (Buick), 500.
5 Neil Bonnett, USA (Chevrolet), 499.
6 Joe Ruttman, USA (Chevrolet), 499.
7 Bill Elliott, USA (Ford), 499; **8** Kyle Petty, USA (Ford), 498; **9** Dale Earnhardt, USA (Chevrolet), 497; **10** Buddy Baker, USA (Ford), 495.
Fastest Qualifier: Ruttman, 21·175s, 89·426 mph/143·917 km/h.
Championship points. Drivers: 1 Waltrip, 1308; **2** Labonte, 1234; **3** Earnhardt, 1212; **4** Rudd, 1196; **5** Elliott, 1185; **6** Gant, 1091.
Manufacturers: 1 Chevrolet, 63; **2** Ford, 22; **3** Buick, 21; **4** Pontiac, 18.

WINSTON 500, Alabama International Motor Speedway, Talladega, Alabama, United States of America, May 6. NASCAR Winston Cup Grand National, round 9. 188 laps of the 2·660-mile/4·281-km circuit, 500·08 miles/804·80 km.
1 Cale Yarborough, USA (Chevrolet), 2h 53m 27s, 172·988 mph/278·397 km/h.
2 Harry Gant, USA (Chevrolet), 2h 53m 27s (Yarborough won by 1 car length).
3 Buddy Baker, USA (Ford), 188 laps.
4 Bobby Allison, USA (Buick), 188.
5 Benny Parsons, USA (Chevrolet), 188.
6 Richard Petty, USA (Pontiac), 187.
7 Phil Parsons, USA (Chevrolet), 187; **8** Dave Marcis, USA (Pontiac), 187; **9** Bill Elliott, USA (Ford), 187; **10** Ron Bouchard, USA (Buick), 186.
Fastest Qualifier: Yarborough, 47·244s, 202·692 mph/326·200 km/h (record).
Championship points. Drivers: 1 Waltrip, 1357; **2** Elliott, 1328; **3** Labonte, 1327; **4** Earnhardt, 1299; **5** Rudd, 1293; **6** Gant, 1266.
Manufacturers: 1 Chevrolet, 72; **2** Ford, 26; **3** Buick, 24; **4** Pontiac, 19.

COORS 420, Nashville International Raceway, Tennessee, United States of America, May 12. NASCAR Winston Cup Grand National, round 10. 420 laps of the 0·592-mile/0·959-km circuit, 250·32 miles/402·78 km.
1 Darrell Waltrip, USA (Chevrolet), 2h 55m 15s, 85·702 mph/137·924 km/h.
2 Neil Bonnett, USA (Chevrolet), 2h 55m 15s (Waltrip won by one car length).
3 Geoff Bodine, USA (Chevrolet), 420 laps.
4 Ricky Rudd, USA (Ford), 420.
5 Ron Bouchard, USA (Buick), 420.
6 Rusty Wallace, USA (Pontiac), 420.
7 Richard Petty, USA (Pontiac), 420; **8** Terry Labonte, USA (Chevrolet), 419; **9** Dick Brooks, USA (Ford), 419; **10** Dave Marcis, USA (Pontiac), 418.
Fastest Qualifier: Waltrip, 20·544s, 104·439 mph/168·078 km/h.
Championship points. Drivers: 1 Waltrip, 1537; **2** Labonte, 1469; **3** Rudd, 1453; **4** Elliott, 1431; **5** Earnhardt, 1405; **6** Gant, 1381.
Manufacturers: 1 Chevrolet, 81; **2** Ford, 29; **3** Buick, 26; **4** Pontiac, 20.

BUDWEISER 500, Dover Downs International Speedway, Delaware, United States of America, May 20. NASCAR Winston Cup Grand National, round 11. 500 laps of the 1·000-mile/1·609-km circuit, 500·00 miles/804·67 km.
1 Richard Petty, USA (Pontiac), 4h 12m 42s, 118·717 mph/191·056 km/h.
2 Tim Richmond, USA (Pontiac), 4h 12m 46s.
3 Terry Labonte, USA (Chevrolet), 500 laps.
4 Bill Elliott, USA (Ford), 500.
5 Dale Earnhardt, USA (Chevrolet), 499.
6 Darrell Waltrip, USA (Chevrolet), 499.
7 Buddy Baker, USA (Ford), 497; **8** Ricky Rudd, USA (Ford), 497; **9** Ron Bouchard, USA (Buick), 497; **10** Geoff Bodine, USA (Chevrolet), 497.
Fastest Qualifier: Rudd, 25·567s, 140·807 mph/226·606 km/h (record).
Championship points. Drivers: 1 Waltrip, 1687; **2** Labonte, 1634; **3** Rudd, 1600; **4** Elliott, 1596; **5** Earnhardt, 1560; **6** Petty, 1546.
Manufacturers: 1 Chevrolet, 85; **2** Ford, 32; **3** Pontiac, 29; **4** Buick, 26.

WORLD 600, Charlotte Motor Speedway, North Carolina, United States of America, May 27. NASCAR Winston Cup Grand National, round 12. 400 laps of the 1·500-mile/2·414-km circuit, 600·00 miles/965·80 km.
1 Bobby Allison, USA (Buick), 4h 38m 34s, 129·233 mph/207·980 km/h.
2 Dale Earnhardt, USA (Chevrolet), 4h 38m 51s.
3 Ron Bouchard, USA (Buick), 399 laps.
4 Harry Gant, USA (Chevrolet) 399.
5 Geoff Bodine, USA (Chevrolet), 399.
6 Lake Speed, USA (Chevrolet), 398.
7 Buddy Baker, USA (Ford), 398; **8** Jody Ridley, USA (Chevrolet), 398; **9** David Pearson, USA (Chevrolet), 397; **10** Tim Richmond, USA (Pontiac), 396.
Fastest Qualifier: Gant, 2m 12·926s, 162·496 mph/261·511 km/h (4 laps).
Championship points. Drivers: 1 Waltrip, 1777; **2** Earnhardt, 1735; **3** Rudd, 1730; **4** Labonte, 1712; **5** Elliott, 1675; **6** Gant, 1638.
Manufacturers: 1 Chevrolet, 91; **2** Buick, 35; **3** Ford, 32; **4** Pontiac, 29.

BUDWEISER 400, Riverside International Raceway, California, United States of America, June 3. NASCAR Winston Cup Grand National, round 13. 95 laps of the 2·620-mile/4·216-km circuit, 248·90 miles/400·56 km.
1 Terry Labonte, USA (Chevrolet), 2h 25m 07s, 102·910 mph/165·617 km/h.
2 Neil Bonnett, USA (Chevrolet), 2h 25m 16s.
3 Bobby Allison, USA (Buick), 95 laps.
4 Geoff Bodine, USA (Chevrolet), 95.
5 Dale Earnhardt, USA (Chevrolet), 95.
6 Tim Richmond, USA (Pontiac), 95.
7 Joe Ruttman, USA (Chevrolet), 95; **8** Kyle Petty, USA (Ford), 95; **9** Ricky Rudd, USA (Ford), 94; **10** Bill Elliott, USA (Ford), 94.
Fastest Qualifier: Labonte, 1m 21·366s, 115·921 mph/186·556 km/h.
Championship points. Drivers: 1 Waltrip, 1912; **2** Labonte, 1897; **3** Earnhardt, 1890; **4** Rudd, 1868; **5** Elliott, 1809; **6** Allison, 1739.
Manufacturers: 1 Chevrolet, 100; **2** Buick, 41; **3** Ford, 32; **4** Pontiac, 30.

VAN SCOY DIAMOND MINES 500, Pocono International Raceway, Pennsylvania, United States of America, June 10. NASCAR Winston Cup Grand National, round 14. 200 laps of the 2·500-mile/4·023-km circuit, 500·00 miles/804·57 km.
1 Cale Yarborough, USA (Chevrolet), 3h 37m 08s, 138·164 mph/222·353 km/h.
2 Harry Gant, USA (Chevrolet), 3h 37m 12s.
3 Terry Labonte, USA (Chevrolet), 200 laps.

4 Bill Elliott, USA (Ford), 200.
5 Tim Richmond, USA (Pontiac), 200.
6 Darrell Waltrip, USA (Chevrolet), 200.
7 Bobby Allison, USA (Buick), 199; **8** Dale Earnhardt, USA (Chevrolet), 199; **9** Benny Parsons, USA (Chevrolet), 199; **10** Lake Speed, USA (Chevrolet), 199.
Fastest Qualifier: David Pearson, USA (Chevrolet), 59·634s, 150·921 mph/242·883 km/h.
Championship points. Drivers: 1 Waltrip and Labonte, 2067; **3** Earnhardt, 2037; **4** Rudd, 1977; **5** Elliott, 1974; **6** Allison, 1890.
Manufacturers: 1 Chevrolet, 109; **2** Buick, 41; **3** Ford, 35; **4** Pontiac, 32.

MILLER HIGH LIFE 400, Michigan International Speedway, Brooklyn, Michigan, United States of America, June 17. NASCAR Winston Cup Grand National, round 15. 200 laps of the 2·000-mile/3·219-km circuit, 400·00 miles/643·80 km.
1 Bill Elliott, USA (Ford), 2h 58m 10s, 134·705 mph/216·786 km/h.
2 Dale Earnhardt, USA (Chevrolet), 2h 58m 12s.
3 Darrell Waltrip, USA (Chevrolet), 200 laps.
4 Harry Gant, USA (Chevrolet), 200.
5 Lake Speed, USA (Chevrolet), 200.
6 Bobby Allison, USA (Buick), 200.
7 Geoff Bodine, USA (Chevrolet), 200; **8** Joe Ruttman, USA (Chevrolet), 200; **9** David Pearson, USA (Chevrolet), 200; **10** Buddy Baker, USA (Ford), 199.
Fastest Qualifier: Elliott, 43·812s, 164·339 mph/264·477 km/h.
Championship points. Drivers: 1 Waltrip, 2237; **2** Earnhardt, 2207; **3** Elliott, 2154; **4** Labonte, 2142; **5** Gant, 2054; **6** Allison, 2045.
Manufacturers: 1 Chevrolet, 115; **2** Ford, 44; **3** Buick, 42; **4** Pontiac, 32.

PEPSI FIRECRACKER 400, Daytona International Speedway, Florida, United States of America, July 4. NASCAR Winston Cup Grand National, round 16. 160 laps of the 2·500-mile/4·023-km circuit, 400·00 miles/643·68 km.
1 Richard Petty, USA (Pontiac), 2h 19m 59s, 171·204 mph/275·525 km/h.
2 Harry Gant, USA (Chevrolet), 160 laps.
3 Cale Yarborough, USA (Chevrolet), 160.
4 Bobby Allison, USA (Buick), 160.
5 Benny Parsons, USA (Chevrolet), 160.
6 Bill Elliott, USA (Ford), 160.
7 Terry Labonte, USA (Chevrolet), 159; **8** Dale Earnhardt, USA (Chevrolet), 159; **9** Neil Bonnet, USA (Chevrolet), 159; **10** Joe Ruttman, USA (Chevrolet), 157.
Fastest Qualifier: Yarborough, 45·058s, 199·743 mph/321·454 km/h.
Championship points. Drivers: 1 Earnhardt, 2354; **2** Waltrip, 2307; **3** Elliott, 2304; **4** Labonte, 2293; **5** Gant, 2229; **6** Allison, 2210.
Manufacturers: 1 Chevrolet, 121; **2** Ford, 45; **3** Buick, 45; **4** Pontiac, 41.

PEPSI 420, Nashville International Raceway, Tennessee, United States of America, July 14. NASCAR Winston Cup Grand National, round 17. 420 laps of the 0·596-mile/0·959-km circuit, 250·32 miles/402·78 km.
1 Geoff Bodine, USA (Chevrolet), 3h 05m 38s, 80·908 mph/130·208 km/h.
2 Darrell Waltrip, USA (Chevrolet), 3h 05m 38s (Bodine won by 1 car length).
3 Dale Earnhardt, USA (Chevrolet), 419 laps.
4 Ron Bouchard, USA (Buick), 419.
5 Bobby Allison, USA (Buick), 419.
6 Terry Labonte, USA (Chevrolet), 419.
7 Bill Elliott, USA (Ford), 419; **8** Joe Ruttman, USA (Chevrolet), 417; **9** Harry Gant, USA (Chevrolet), 417; **10** Neil Bonnett, USA (Chevrolet), 416.
Fastest Qualifier: Ricky Rudd, USA (Ford), 20·607s, 104·120 mph/167·564 km/h.
Championship points. Drivers: 1 Earnhardt, 2524; **2** Waltrip, 2482; **3** Elliott, 2455; **4** Labonte, 2443; **5** Allison, 2370; **6** Gant, 2367.
Manufacturers: 1 Chevrolet, 130; **2** Buick, 48; **3** Buick, 48; **3** Ford, 45; **4** Pontiac, 41.

LIKE COLA 500, Pocono International Raceway, Pennsylvania, United States of America, July 27. NASCAR Winston Cup Grand National, round 18. 200 laps of the 2·500-mile/4·023-km circuit, 500·00 miles/804·60 km.
1 Harry Gant, USA (Chevrolet), 4h 07s 21s, 121·351 mph/195·295 km/h.
2 Cale Yarborough, USA (Chevrolet), 4h 07s 21s (Gant won by 2 car lengths).
3 Bill Elliott, USA (Ford), 200 laps.
4 Terry Labonte, USA (Chevrolet), 200.
5 Benny Parsons, USA (Chevrolet), 200.
6 Rusty Wallace, USA (Pontiac), 200.
7 Ron Bouchard, USA (Buick), 199; **8** Kyle Petty, USA (Ford), 199; **9** Tim Richmond, USA (Pontiac), 199; **10** Dale Earnhardt, USA (Chevrolet), 198.
Fastest Qualifier: Elliott, 59·139s, 152·184 mph/244·916 km/h.
Championship points. Drivers: 1 Earnhardt, 2663; **2** Elliott, 2625; **3** Labonte, 2608; **4** Waltrip, 2579; **5** Gant, 2552; **6** Allison, 2454.
Manufacturers: 1 Chevrolet, 139; **2** Ford, 49; **3** Buick, 48; **4** Pontiac, 42.

TALLADEGA 500, Alabama International Motor Speedway, Talladega, Alabama, United States of America, July 29. NASCAR Winston Cup Grand National, round 20. 188 laps of the 2·660-mile/4·281-km circuit, 500·08 miles/804·83 km.
1 Dale Earnhardt, USA (Chevrolet), 3h 12m 04s, 155·485 mph/250·228 km/h.
2 Buddy Baker, USA (Ford), 3h 12m 05·66s.
3 Terry Labonte, USA (Chevrolet), 188 laps.
4 Bobby Allison, USA (Buick), 188.
5 Cale Yarborough, USA (Chevrolet), 188.
6 Darrell Waltrip, USA (Chevrolet), 188.
7 Harry Gant, USA (Chevrolet), 188; **8** Lake Speed, USA (Chevrolet), 188; **9** Tommy Ellis, USA (Chevrolet), 188; **10** Bill Elliott, USA (Ford), 188.
Fastest Qualifier: Yarborough, 47·295s, 202·474 mph/325·850 km/h.
Championship points. Drivers: 1 Earnhardt, 2843; **2** Labonte, 2778; **3** Elliott, 2764; **4** Waltrip, 2734; **5** Gant, 2703; **6** Allison, 2619.
Manufacturers: 1 Chevrolet, 148; **2** Ford, 55; **3** Buick, 51; **4** Pontiac, 42.

CHAMPION SPARK PLUG 400, Michigan International Speedway, Brooklyn, Michigan, United States of America, August 12. NASCAR Winston Cup Grand National, round 20. 200 laps of the 2·000-mile/3·219-km circuit, 400·00 miles/643·80 km.
1 Darrell Waltrip, USA (Chevrolet), 2h 35m 59s, 153·863 mph/247·618 km/h.
2 Terry Labonte, USA (Chevrolet), 2h 36m 00.s
3 Bill Elliott, USA (Ford), 200 laps.
4 Harry Gant, USA (Chevrolet), 200.
5 Cale Yarborough, USA (Chevrolet), 199.
7 Dale Earnhardt, USA (Chevrolet), 199; **8** Buddy Baker, USA (Ford), 199; **9** Richard Petty, USA (Pontiac), 199; **10** Ron Bouchard, USA (Buick), 198.
Fastest Qualifier: Elliott, 43·579s, 165·217 mph/265·890 km/h (record).
Championship points. Drivers: 1 Earnhardt, 2989; **2** Labonte, 2958; **3** Elliott, 2934; **4** Waltrip, 2914; **5** Gant, 2868; **6** Allison, 2754.
Manufacturers: 1 Chevrolet, 157; **2** Ford, 59; **3** Buick, 51; **4** Pontiac, 42.

BUSCH 500, Bristol International Raceway, Tennessee, United States of America, August 25. NASCAR Winston Cup Grand National, round 21. 500 laps of the 0·533-mile/0·858-km circuit, 266·50 miles/429·00 km.
1 Terry Labonte, USA (Chevrolet), 3h 07m 19s, 85·365 mph/137·381 km/h.
2 Bobby Allison, USA (Buick), 3h 07m 20·44s.
3 Dick Brookes, USA (Ford), 498 laps.
4 Dave Marcis, USA (Pontiac), 494.
5 Harry Gant, USA (Chevrolet), 494.
6 Bill Elliott, USA (Ford), 491.
7 Mike Alexander, USA (Oldsmobile), 485; **8** Sterling Marlin, USA (Oldsmobile), 484; **9** Greg Sacks, USA (Chevrolet), 480; **10** Dale Earnhardt, USA (Chevrolet), 478.
Fastest Qualifier: Geoff Bodine, USA (Chevrolet), 17·123s, 111·734 mph/179·818 km/h.
Championship points. Drivers: 1 Labonte, 3143; **2** Earnhardt, 3128; **3** Elliott, 3084; **4** Waltrip, 3024; **5** Gant, 3023; **6** Allison, 2933.
Manufacturers: 1 Chevrolet, 166; **2** Ford, 63; **3** Buick, 55; **4** Pontiac, 45.

SOUTHERN 500, Darlington International Raceway, South Carolina, United States of America, September 2. NASCAR Winston Cup Grand National, round 22. 367 laps of the 1·366-mile/2·198-km circuit, 501·32 miles/806·67 km.
1 Harry Gant, USA (Chevrolet), 3h 54m 02s, 128·270 mph/206·430 km/h.
2 Tim Richmond, USA (Pontiac), 3h 54m 04s.
3 Buddy Baker, USA (Ford), 367 laps.
4 Rusty Wallace, USA (Pontiac), 365.
5 Ricky Rudd, USA (Ford), 364.
6 Dick Brooks, USA (Ford), 364.
7 Phil Parsons, USA (Chevrolet), 362; **8** Terry Labonte, USA (Chevrolet), 359; **9** Benny Parsons, USA (Chevrolet), 359; **10** Bobby Allison, USA (Buick), 358.
Fastest Qualifier: Gant, 31·624s, 155·502 mph/250·256 km/h.
Championship points. Drivers: 1 Labonte, 3290; **2** Gant, 3208; **3** Elliott, 3207; **4** Earnhardt, 3177; **5** Allison, 3072; **6** Waltrip, 3067.
Manufacturers: 1 Chevrolet, 175; **2** Ford, 67; **3** Buick, 55; **4** Pontiac, 51.

Wrangler SanForest 400, Richmond Fairgrounds Raceway, Virginia, United States of America, September 9. NASCAR Winston Cup Grand National, round 23. 400 laps of the 0·542-mile/0·972-km circuit, 216·80 miles/348·90 km.
1 Darrell Waltrip, USA (Chevrolet), 2h 53m 57s, 74·780 mph/120·346 km/h.
2 Ricky Rudd, USA (Ford), 2h 54m 00s.
3 Dale Earnhardt, USA (Chevrolet), 400 laps.
4 Geoff Bodine, USA (Chevrolet), 399.
5 Richard Petty, USA (Pontiac), 399.
6 Kyle Petty, USA (Ford), 398.
7 Neil Bonnett, USA (Chevrolet) 398; **8** Terry Labonte, USA (Chevrolet), 398; **9** Harry Gant, USA (Chevrolet) 398; **10** Dick Brooks, USA (Ford), 398.
Fastest Qualifier: Waltrip, 21·090s, 92·518 mph/148·893 km/h.
Championship points. Drivers: 1 Labonte, 3437; **2** Earnhardt, 3347; **3** Gant, 3346; **4** Elliott, 3303; **5** Waltrip, 3252; **6** Allison, 3160.
Manufacturers: 1 Chevrolet, 184; **2** Ford, 73; **3** Buick, 55; **4** Pontiac, 53.

DELAWARE 500, Dover Downs International Speedway, Delaware, United States of America, September 16. NASCAR Winston Cup Grand National, round 24. 500 laps of the 1·000-mile/1·609-km circuit, 500·00 miles/804·50 km.
1 Harry Gant, USA (Chevrolet), 4h 28m 12s, 111·856 mph/180·014 km/h.
2 Terry Labonte, USA (Chevrolet), 500 laps.
3 Ricky Rudd, USA (Ford), 498.
4 Dave Marcis, USA (Pontiac), 497.
5 Dale Earnhardt, USA (Chevrolet), 497.
6 Neil Bonnett, USA (Chevrolet), 497.
7 Dick Brooks, USA (Ford), 497; **8** Ron Bouchard, USA (Buick), 495; **9** Geoff Bodine, USA (Chevrolet), 492; **10** Trevor Boys, USA (Chevrolet), 491.
Fastest Qualifier: Not given.
Championship points. Drivers: 1 Labonte, 3612; **2** Gant, 3531; **3** Earnhardt, 3597; **4** Waltrip, 3387; **5** Elliott, 3370; **6** Allison, 3220.
Manufacturers: 1 Chevrolet, 193; **2** Ford, 73; **3** Pontiac, 56; **4** Buick, 55.

GOODY'S 500, Martinsville Speedway, Virginia, United States of America, September 23. NASCAR Winston Cup Grand National, round 25. 500 laps of the 0·525-mile/0·845-km circuit, 262·50 miles/422·25 km.
1 Darrell Waltrip, USA (Chevrolet), 3h 28m 55s, 75·532 mph/121·557 km/h.
2 Terry Labonte, USA (Chevrolet), 499 laps.
3 Bill Elliott, USA (Ford), 499.
4 Harry Gant, USA (Chevrolet), 498.
5 Neil Bonnett, USA (Chevrolet), 498.
6 Buddy Baker, USA (Ford), 498.
7 Dave Marcis, USA (Pontiac), 496; **8** Richard Petty, USA (Pontiac), 494; **9** Lennie Pond, USA (Chevrolet), 491; **10** Kyle Petty, USA (Ford), 489.
Fastest Qualifier: Geoff Bodine, USA (Chevrolet), 21·152s, 89·523 mph/144·073 km/h.
Championship points. Drivers: 1 Labonte, 3787; **2** Gant, 3696; **3** Earnhardt, 3634; **4** Waltrip, 3572; **5** Elliott, 3540; **6** Allison, 3314.
Manufacturers: 1 Chevrolet, 202; **2** Ford, 79; **3** Pontiac, 56; **4** Buick, 55.

MILLER HIGH LIFE 500, Charlotte Motor Speedway, North Carolina, United States of America, October 7. NASCAR Winston Cup Grand National, round 26. 334 laps of the 1·500-mile/2·414-km circuit, 501·00 miles/806·28 km.
1 Bill Elliott, USA (Ford), 3h 24m 41s, 146·861 mph/236·349 km/h.
2 Benny Parsons, USA (Chevrolet), 3h 24m 55s.
3 Cale Yarborough, USA (Chevrolet), 334 laps.
4 Harry Gant, USA (Chevrolet), 334.
5 Terry Labonte, USA (Chevrolet), 333.
6 Geoff Bodine, USA (Chevrolet), 333.
7 Jody Ridley, USA (Chevrolet), 332; **8** Ricky Rudd, USA (Ford), 332; **9** Richard Petty USA (Pontiac), 332; **10** Bobby Allison, USA (Buick), 332.
Fastest Qualifier: Parsons, 2m 10·451s, 165·579 mph/266·473 km/h (4 lap average).
Championship points. Drivers: 1 Labonte, 3947; **2** Gant, 3861; **3** Elliott, 3720; **4** Earnhardt, 3680; **5** Waltrip, 3659; **6** Allison, 3448.
Manufacturers: 1 Chevrolet, 208; **2** Ford, 88; **3** Pontiac, 56; **4** Buick, 55.

HOLLY FARMS 400, North Wilkesboro Speedway, North Carolina, United States of America, October 14. NASCAR Winston Cup Grand National, round 27. 400 laps of the 0·265-mile/1·006-km circuit, 250·00 miles/402·34 km.
1 Darrell Waltrip, USA (Chevrolet), 2h 45m 42s, 90·525 mph/145·686 km/h.
2 Harry Gant, USA (Chevrolet), 2h 45m 42·5s.
3 Bobby Allison, USA (Buick), 400 laps.
4 Neil Bonnett, USA (Chevrolet), 400.
5 Rusty Wallace, USA (Pontiac), 400.
6 Ricky Rudd, USA (Ford), 400.
7 Dale Earnhardt, USA (Chevrolet), 400; **8** Bill Elliott, USA (Ford), 399; **9** Terry Labonte, USA (Chevrolet), 399; **10** Buddy Baker, USA (Ford), 398.
Fastest Qualifier: Waltrip, 113·304 mph/182·345 km/h.
Championship points. Drivers: 1 Labonte, 4090; **2** Gant, 4031; **3** Elliott, 3862; **4** Waltrip, 3844; **5** Earnhardt, 3826; **6** Allison, 3618.
Manufacturers: 1 Chevrolet, 217; **2** Ford, 89; **3** Buick, 59; **4** Pontiac, 58.

WARNER W. HODGDON AMERICAN 500, North Carolina Motor Speedway, Rockingham, North Carolina, United States of America, October 21. NASCAR Winston Cup Grand National, round 28. 492 laps of the 1·017-mile/1·637-km circuit, 500·36 miles/805·26 km.
1 Bill Elliott, USA (Ford), 4h 26m 35s, 112·617 mph/181·239 km/h.
2 Harry Gant, USA (Chevrolet), 4h 26m 35s (Elliott won by 1 foot).
3 Terry Labonte, USA (Chevrolet), 492 laps.
4 Darrell Waltrip, USA (Chevrolet), 492.
5 Bobby Allison, USA (Buick), 491.
6 Morgan Shepherd, USA (Chevrolet), 490.
7 Buddy Baker, USA (Ford), 488; **8** Tim Richmond, USA (Pontiac), 487; **9** Dave Marcis, USA (Pontiac), 484; **10** Lennie Pond, USA (Oldsmobile), 480.
Fastest Qualifier: Geoff Bodine, USA (Chevrolet), 25·352s, 144·415 mph/232·413 km/h.

Championship points (prior to final two races at Atlanta on November 4 and Riverside on November 18.
Drivers:

1 Terry Labonte, USA	4260
2 Harry Gant, USA	4211
3 Bill Elliott, USA	4042
4 Darrell Waltrip, USA	4009
5 Dale Earnhardt, USA	3955
6 Bobby Allison, USA	3778

Manufacturers:

1 Chevrolet	223
2 Ford	98
3 Buick	61
4 Pontiac	58

Final results will be given in Autocourse 1985/86.

IMSA Camel GT Championship 1983 results

The final round of the 1983 IMSA Camel GT Championship was run after Autocourse 1983/84 went to press.

EASTERN AIRLINES 3 HOUR CAMEL GT, Daytona International Speedway, Florida, United State of America, November 27. IMSA CAMEL GT Championship, round 17. 91 laps of the 3·840-mile/6·180-km circuit, 349·44 miles/562·38 km.
1 Al Holbert/Jim Trueman, USA/USA (3·0 t/c March 83G-Porsche), 3h 01m 25·840s, 115·562 mph/185·979 km/h.
2 Bob Akin/John O'Steen, USA/USA (3·2 t/c Porsche 935), 3h 03m 15·810s.
3 John Kalagian/John Lloyd, USA/USA (5·8 Lola T600-Chevrolet), 90 laps.
4 David Cowart/Kenper Miller, USA/USA (5·7 March 85G-Chevrolet), 89.
5 Tico Almeida/Miguel Morejon, USA/USA (3·2 t/c Porsche 935), 87.
6 M. L. Speer/Ken Madren, USA/USA (3·5 t/c March 84G-Buick), 87.
7 Gianpiero Moretti/Sarel van der Merwe, I/ZA (3·2 t/c Porsche 935), 87; **8** Jack Miller/Carlos Ramirez, USA/USA (5·3 Nimrod-Aston Martin), 84; **9** "Fomfor", ES (3·5 BMW M1), 84 (1st over 2500 cc GT class); **10** Robert Overby, USA (5·8 Buick Regal), 83.
1st up to 2500cc GT class: John Schneider/Bruce Leven, USA/USA (2·0 Porsche 944), 82.
Fastest Qualifier: Holbert, 1m 42·768s, 134·517 mph/216·484 km/h.
Fastest lap: Klaus Ludwig, D (1·7 t/c Ford Mustang GTP), 1m 48·360s, 127·575 mph/205·312 km/h.

Final Championship points. Overall:

1 Al Holbert, USA	204
2 Bob Tullius, USA	121
3 Jim Trueman, USA	113
4 Bob Akin, USA	113
5 John O'Steen, USA	95
6 Bill Adam, CDN	78

7 Kenper Miller, USA, 73; **8** David Cowart, USA, 73; **9** Hurley Haywood, USA, 71; **10** M. L. Speer, USA, 59.

Over 2500cc GT class:

1 Wayne Baker, USA	174
2 Jim Mullen, USA	154
3 Gene Felton, USA	145
4 Billy Hagen, USA	137
5 "Fomfor", ES	118
6 Don Devendorf, USA	115

Up to 2500cc GT class:

1 Roger Mandeville, USA	216
2 Jim Downing, USA	184
3 Amos Johnson, USA	166
4 John Maffucci, USA	158
5 Joe Varde, USA	124
6 Jack Baldwin, USA	102

1984 results

23 SUNBANK DAYTONA 24 HOURS, Daytona International Speedway, Florida, United States of America, February 4/5. IMSA CAMEL GT Championship, round 1. 640 laps of the 3·870-mile/6·228-km circuit, 2476·80 miles/3985·02 km.
1 Sarel van der Merwe/Tony Martin/Graham Duxbury, ZA/ZA/ZA (3·1 t/c March 83G-Porsche), 24h 01m 07·530s, 103·119 mph/174·000 km/h.
2 Bob Wollek/Derek Bell/A. J. Foyt, F/GB/USA (3·2 t/c Porsche 935), 631 laps.
3 Bob Tullius/David Hobbs/Doc Bundy, USA/GB/USA (5·3 Jaguar XJR-5), 612.
4 Bruce Leven/Hurley Haywood/Al Holbert/Claude Ballot-Lena, USA/USA/USA/F (3·2 t/c Porsche 935), 604.
5 Wayne Baker/Jim Mullen/Tom Blackaller, USA/USA/USA (3·2 t/c Porsche 934/935), 602.
6 Billy Hagen/Terry Labonte/Gene Felton, USA/USA/USA (5·8 Chevrolet Camaro), 588 (1st over 2500 cc GT class).
7 John Cooper/Bob Evans/Paul Smith, GB/GB/GB (5·3 Nimrod-Aston-Martin), 587; **8** Al Leon/Art Leon/Terry Wolters, USA/USA/USA (5·8 March 84G-Chevrolet), 586; **9** Jim Downing/John Maffucci/Witney Ganz, USA/USA/USA (2·6 Argo JM16-Mazda), 579; **10** Lance Van Every/Ash Tisdelle, USA/USA (3·0 Porsche Carrera), 579.
1st up to 2500 cc GT class: Jack Baldwin/Ira Young/Robert Reed/Jim Cook, USA/USA/USA/USA (2·3 Mazda RX-7), 574.
Fastest Qualifier: Mario Andretti, USA (2·8 t/c Porsche 962), 1m 50·969s, 125·549 mph/202·051 km/h (record).
Fastest lap: Brian Redman, GB (5·3 Jaguar XJR-5), 1m 57·364s, 118·708 mph/191·042 km/h (record).
Championship points. Overall: 1 Martin, Duxbury and van der Merwe, 20; **4** Wollek, Foyt and Bell, 15. **GT over 2500 cc: 1** Felton, Labonté and Hagan, 20. **GT up to 2500cc: 1** Baldwin, Young and Reed, 20.

BUDWEISER GRAND PRIX OF MIAMI CAMEL GT, Miami, Florida, United States of America, February 26. IMSA CAMEL GT Championship, round 2. 118 laps of the 1·85-mile/2·98-km circuit, 2189·30 miles/351·64 km.
1 Brian Redman/Doc Bundy, GB/USA (5·3 Jaguar XJR-5), 3h 00m 21·340s, 72·623 mph/116·875 km/h.
2 Bob Tullius/Pat Bedard, USA/USA (5·3 Jaguar XJR-5), 3h 01m 42·630s.
3 John Morton/Bob Lobenberg, USA/USA (5·8 Lola T600-Chevrolet), 117 laps.
4 Bob Wollek/A. J. Foyt, F/USA (3·2 t/c Porsche 935), 115.
5 Pete Halsmer/Boy Hayje, USA/NL (2·6 Lola T616-Mazda), 114.
6 Jim Busby/Rick Knoop, USA/USA (2·6 Lola T616-Mazda), 114.
7 John Kalagian/John Lloyd, USA/USA (5·8 Lola T600-Chevrolet), 113; **8** Sarel van der Merwe/Tony Martin, ZA/ZA (3·1 t/c March 83G-Porsche), 112; **9** David Cowart/Kenper Miller, USA/USA (5·8 March 83G-Chevrolet), 112; **10** Albert Naon/"Fomfor"/Willy Valiente, USA/ES/ES (3·5 Sauber C7-BMW), 111.
Fastest Qualifier: Emerson Fittipaldi, BR (5·8 March 83G-Chevrolet), 1m 24·84s, 78·501 mph/126·335 km/h.
Fastest lap: Tullius, 1m 24·203s, 79·095 mph/127·291 km/h (record).

BUDWEISER GRAND PRIX OF MIAMI CAMEL GTO, Miami, Florida, United States of America, February 26. 27 laps of the 1·85-mile/2·98-km circuit, 49·95 miles/80·46 km.
1 Walt Bohren, USA (5·8 Chevrolet Corvette), 46m 29·440s, 64·465 mph/103·746 km/h.
2 Tommy Riggins, USA (5·8 Chevrolet Camaro), 46m 43·550s.
3 Luis Mendez, DOM (3·0 Porsche Carrera), 27 laps.
4 Roger Mandeville, USA (2·6 Mazda RX-7), 27.
5 John Carusso, USA (5·8 Chevrolet Corvette), 26.

6 Gene Felton, USA (5·8 Chevrolet Corvette), 26. **7** "Fomfor", ES (3·5 BMW M1), 25; **8** Al Levenson, USA (5·8 Chevrolet Corvette), 25; **9** Jack Griffin, USA (3·0 Porsche Carrera), 25; **10** Carlos Munoz, USA (3·0 Porsche Carrera), 25.
Fastest lap: Felton, 1m 30·535s, 73·563 mph/118·388 km/h (record).
2500cc race winner: Chris Cord, USA (2·0 Toyota Celica), 26 laps, 48·10 miles/77·48 km in 45m 35·590s, 63·299 mph/101·870 km/h (record).
Championship points. Overall: 1 Bundy, 32; **2** Tullius, 27; **3** Wollek, 25; **4** van der Merwe and Martin, 23; **6** Duxbury and Redman, 20. **GT over 2500cc: 1** Felton, 26; **2** Mandeville, 22; **3** Hagan, Labonte and Bohren, 20. **GT up to 2500cc: 1** Baldwin, 28; **2** Mueller, 25; **3** Dunham, 22.

COCA COLA 12 HOURS OF SEBRING CAMEL GT, Sebring International Raceway, Florida, United States of America, March 24. IMSA CAMEL GT Championship, round 3. 263 laps of the 4·86-mile/7·82-km circuit, 1278·18 miles/2056·66 km.
1 Mauricio DeNarvaez/Hans Heyer/Stefan Johansson, COL/D/S (3·2 t/c Porsche 935), 12h 01m 01·415s, 106·364 mph/171·176 km/h.
2 Randy Lanier/Bill Whittington/Marty Hinze, USA/USA/USA (5·9 March 83G-Chevrolet), 261 laps.
3 Bob Wollek/A.J. Foyt/Derek Bell, F/USA/GB (3·2 t/c Porsche 935), 258.
4 Wayne Baker/Jim Mullen/Tom Blackaller, USA/USA/USA (3·2 t/c Porsche 935), 258.
5 Bob Akin/John O'Steen/Hans Stuck, USA/USA/D (3·2 t/c Porsche 935), 256.
6 John Graham/Hugo Gralia/Preston Henn/Bob Wollek/Al Holbert, USA/USA/USA/F/USA (3·2 t/c Porsche 935), 246.
7 John Morton/Tony Garcia/Tony Adamowicz, USA/USA/USA (5·9 Lola T600-Chevrolet), 244; **8** Billy Hagen/Gene Felton/Terry Labonte, USA/USA/USA (5·8 Chevrolet Camaro), 243 (1st over 2500cc GT class); **9** Jack Baldwin/Ira Young/Robert Reed USA/USA/USA (2·3 Mazda RX-7), 238 (1st up to 2500cc GT class); **10** George Alderman/Carson Baird/Lew Price, USA/USA/USA (2·5 Datsun ZX), 234.
Fastest Qualifier: Brian Redman, GB (5·3 Jaguar XJR-5), 2m 18·965s, 125·902 mph/202·619 km/h (record).
Fastest lap: Redman, 2m 22·751s, 122·563 mph/197/246 km/h (record).
Championship points. Overall: 1 Bundy, 32; **2** Tullius and Bell, 27; **4** Wollek, 25; **5** van der Merwe, Martin and Redman, 23. **GT over 2500cc: 1** Felton, 46; **2** Hagen and Labonte, 40. **GT up to 2500cc: 1** Baldwin, 48; **2** Reed, 40; **3** Bond, Pridgen and Tilton, 27.

ROAD ATLANTA 500 KM CAMEL GT, Road Atlanta, Georgia, United States of America, April 8. IMSA CAMEL GT Championship, round 4. 124 laps of the 2·520-mile/4·055-km circuit, 312·48 miles/502·82 km.
1 Don Whittington, USA (5·8 March 84G-Chevrolet), 3h 07m 30·467s, 99·989 mph/160·916 km/h.
2 Bill Whittington, USA (5·8 March 84G-Chevrolet), 3h 07m 45·418s.
3 Brian Redman/Pat Bedard, GB/USA (5·3 Jaguar XJR-5), 123 laps.
4 David Cowart/Kenper Miller, USA/USA (5·8 March 83G-Chevrolet), 122.
5 Al Leon/Art Leon/Hurley Haywood, USA/USA/USA (5·8 March 84G-Chevrolet), 121.
6 Bob Akin/John O'Steen, USA/USA (3·2 t/c Porsche 935), 121.
7 "Fomfor"/Willy Valiente, ES/ES (3·5 Sauber C7-BMW), 116; **8** Billy Hagen/Gene Felton, USA/USA (5·9 Chevrolet Camaro), 116 (1st over 2500cc GT class); **9** Jim Downing/John Maffucci, USA/USA (2·6 Argo JM16-Mazda), 115; **10** Don Courtney/Brent O'Neill, USA/USA (3·0 Argo JM16-Cosworth DFV), 115.
1st up to 2500cc GT class: Jack Baldwin/Robert Reed, USA/USA (2·3 Mazda RX-7), 111.
Fastest Qualifier: Klaus Ludwig, D (2·1 t/c Ford Mustang GTP), 1m 15·964s, 119·425 mph/192·195 km/h (record).
Fastest lap: Doc Bundy, USA (5·3 Jaguar XJR-5), 1m 18·830s, 115·083 mph/185·208 km/h (record).
Championship points. Overall: 1 Redman, 35; **2** Bundy, 32; **3** Bedard and B. Whittington, 30; **5** Tullius and Bell, 27. **GT over 2500cc: 1** Felton, 66; **2** Hagen, 60; **3** Mandeville, 52. **GT up to 2500cc: 1** Baldwin, 68; **2** Reed, 60; **3** Dunham, 37.

LOS ANGELES TIMES/NISSAN GRAND PRIX OF ENDURANCE, Riverside International Raceway, California, United States of America, April 29. IMSA CAMEL GT Championship, round 5. 204 laps of the 3·25-mile/5·23-km circuit, 663·00 miles/1066·92 km.
1 Randy Lanier/Bill Whittington, USA/USA (5·8 March 84G-Chevrolet), 6h 00m 09·675s, 110·451 mph/177·753 km/h.
2 Al Holbert/Derek Bell, USA/GB (2·6 t/c Porsche 962), 6h 00m 14·616s.
3 Kenper Miller/Mauricio DeNarvaez, USA/COL (5·8 March 84G-Chevrolet), 199 laps.
4 John Morton/Tony Adamowicz, USA/USA (5·8 Lola T600-Chevrolet), 197.
5 Chuck Kendall/Jim Cook, USA/USA (5·8 Lola T600-Chevrolet), 196.
6 Sarel van der Merwe/Tony Martin, ZA/ZA (3·1 t/c March 84G-Porsche), 190.
7 Gianpiero Moretti/Fulvio Ballabio, I/I (3·3 Momo AR3-Cosworth DFL), 187; **8** Bob Akin/John O'Steen, USA/USA (3·2 t/c Porsche 935/84), 184; **9** John Schneider/Elliott Forbes-Robinson, USA/USA (2·0 t/c Porsche 924 Carrera), 182 (1st up to 2500cc GT class); **10** Jim Downing/John Maffucci, USA/USA (2·6 Argo JM16-Mazda), 181.
1st over 2500cc GT class: Roger Mandeville/Amos Johnson, USA/USA (2·6 Mazda RX-7), 180.
Fastest Qualifier: Klaus Ludwig, D (2·1 t/c Ford Mustang GTP), 1m 34·061s, 124·387 mph/200·181 km/h (record).
Fastest lap: Bell, 1m 36·540s, 121·193 mph/195·041 km/h (record).
Championship points. Overall: 1 Whittington, 50; **2** Bell, 42; **3** Redman and Lanier, 35; **5** Bundy and DeNarvaez, 32. **GT over 2500cc: 1** Mandeville, 70; **2** Felton, 69; **3** Hagen, 63. **GT up to 2500cc: 1** Baldwin, 76; **2** Reed, 68; **3** Dunham, 52.

RED LOBSTER MONTEREY TRIPLE CROWN CAMEL GT, Laguna Seca Raceway, California, United States of America, May 6. IMSA CAMEL GT Championship, round 6. 53 laps of the 1·900-mile/3·058-km circuit, 100·70 miles/162·07 km.
1 Randy Lanier, USA (5·8 March 84G-Chevrolet), 54m 58·590s, 109·902 mph/176·870 km/h.
2 Kenper Miller, USA, (5·8 March 84G-Chevrolet), 55m 02·200s.
3 Sarel van der Merwe, ZA (3·2 t/c March 84G-Porsche), 53 laps.
4 John Gunn, USA (5·0 Phoenix JG1-Chevrolet), 53.
5 John Morton, USA (5·8 Lola T600-Chevrolet), 53.
6 John Kalagian, USA (5·8 Lola T600-Chevrolet), 53.
7 Gianpiero Moretti, I (3·0 Momo AR3-Cosworth DFV), 52; **8** Derek Bell, GB (2·6 t/c Porsche 962), 52; **9** Chuck Kendall, USA (5·8 Lola T600-Chevrolet), 52; **10** Lynn St. James, USA (3·0 Argo JM16-Cosworth DFV), 50.
Fastest Qualifier: Bill Whittington, USA (5·8 March 84G-Chevrolet), 58·990s, 115·952 mph/186·606 km/h (record).
Fastest lap: Whittington, 1m 01·250s, 111·673 mph/179·720 km/h (record).

MONTEREY TRIPLE CROWN CAMEL GTO/GTU, Laguna Seca Raceway, California, United States of America, May 6. 39 laps of the 1·900-mile/3·058-km circuit, 74·10 miles/119·26 km.
1 John Bauer, USA (5·9 Ford Thunderbird), 45m 14·450s, 98·274 mph/158·156 km/h.
2 Gene Felton, USA (5·9 Pontiac Firebird), 46m 02·450s.
3 George Follmer, USA (5·9 Chevrolet Corvette), 39 laps.
4 "Fomfor", ES (3·5 BMW M1), 39.
5 Les Lindley, USA (5·9 Chevrolet Camaro), 38.
6 Jim Adams, USA (2·0 Toyota Celica), 38 (1st up to 2500cc GT class).
7 Roger Mandeville, USA (2·6 Mazda RX-7), 38; **8** Jack Baldwin, USA (2·3 Mazda RX-7), 38; **9** Logan Blackburn, USA (2·5 Datsun ZX), 38; **10** Billy Hagen, USA (5·9 Chevrolet Camaro), 38.
Fastest lap: Bauer, 1m 06·660s, 102·610 mph/165·134 km/h (record).
Championship points. Overall: 1 Lanier, 55; **2** B. Whittington, 50; **3** Bell, 45; **4** van der Merwe, 41; **5** Miller, 39; **6** Morton, 36. **GT over 2500cc: 1** Felton, 84; **2** Mandeville, 78; **3** Hagen, 67. **GT up to 2500cc: 1** Baldwin, 91; **2** Reed, 68; **3** Dunham, 56.

CHARLOTTE CAMEL GT 500, Charlotte Motor Speedway, North Carolina, United States of America, May 20. IMSA CAMEL GT Championship, round 7. 138 laps of the 2·250-mile/3·621-km circuit, 310·50 miles/499·70 km.
1 Randy Lanier/Bill Whittington, USA/USA (5·8 March 84G-Chevrolet), 2h 59m 35·930s, 103·731 mph/166·938 km/h.
2 Bob Tullius/Doc Bundy, USA/USA (6·0 Jaguar XJR-5), 135 laps.
3 Brian Redman/Pat Bedard, GB/USA (6·0 Jaguar XJR-5), 134.
4 John Morton/Tony Adamowicz, USA/USA (5·8 March 84G-Chevrolet), 132.
5 Billy Hagen/Gene Felton, USA/USA (5·9 Chevrolet Camaro), 129 (1st over 2500cc GT class).
6 Walt Bohren, USA (5·9 Chevrolet Corvette), 128.
7 Chester Vincentz/Dave White, USA/USA (3·0 Porsche 934), 127; **8** Jim Downing/John Maffucci, USA/USA (2·6 Argo JM16-Mazda), 127; **9** Al Leon/Art Leon, USA/USA (5·8 March 84G-Chevrolet), 127; **10** Charles Morgan/Whitney Ganz, USA/USA (3·5 Argo JM16-Buick), 125.
1st up to 2500cc GT class: Chris Cord/Jim Adams, USA/USA (2·0 Toyota Celica), 124.
Fastest Qualifier: Whittington, 1m 06·525s, 121·759 mph/195·952 km/h (record).
Fastest lap: Bob Wollek, F (2·1 t/c Ford Mustang GTP), 1m 08·170s, 118·821 mph/191·234 km/h (record).
Championship points. Overall: 1 Lanier, 75; **2** Whittington, 70; **3** Bell, 48; **4** Redman and Bundy, 47; **6** Morton, 46. **GT over 2500cc: 1** Felton, 104; **2** Hagen, 87; **3** Mandeville, 80;. **GT up to 2500cc: 1** Baldwin, 101; **2** Reed, 68; **3** Dunham, 59.

COCA COLA 500 1 HOUR CAMEL GT, Lime Rock Park, Connecticut, United States of America, May 28. IMSA CAMEL GT Championship, round 8. 56 laps of the 1·53-mile/2·46-km circuit, 85·68 miles/137·76 km.
1 Sarel van der Merwe, ZA (3·1 t/c March 84G-Porsche), 1h 01m 01·103s, 84·250 mph/135·59 km/h.
2 Randy Lanier, USA (5·8 March 84G-Chevrolet), 1h 02m 04·968s.
3 Al Holbert, USA (2·6 t/c Porsche 962), 55 laps.
4 Gianpiero Moretti, I (3·0 Momo AR3-Cosworth DFV), 55.
5 Whitney Ganz, USA (3·5 Argo JM16-Buick), 55.
6 Kenper Miller, USA (5·8 March 84G-Chevrolet), 54.
7 John O'Steen, USA (3·2 t/c Porsche 935), 54; **8** Bill Whittington, USA (5·8 March 84G-Chevrolet), 52; **9** Pierre Honegger, USA (2·6 Mazda GTP), 51; **10** Brent O'Neill, USA (3·0 Argo JM16-Cosworth DFV), 51.
Fastest Qualifier: Whittingotn, 47·602s, 115·709 mph/186·215 km/h (record).
Fastest lap: Lanier, 1m 01·970s, 88·882 mph/143·041 km/h.

COCA COLA 500 45 MINUTE CAMEL GTO, Lime Rock Park, Connecticut, United States of America, May 28. 36 laps of the 1·53-mile/2·46-km circuit, 55·08 miles/88·56 km.
1 Roger Mandeville, USA (2·6 Mazda RX-7), 45m 38·795s, 72·400 mph/116·516 km/h.
2 Carson Baird, USA (2·8 Datsun ZX), 45m 40·591s.
3 Billy Hagen, USA (5·9 Chevrolet Camaro), 34 laps.
4 Walt Bohren, USA (5·9 Chevrolet Corvette), 34.
5 Andras Petery, USA (5·9 Chevrolet Camaro), 34.
6 Paul Pettey, USA (5·3 Jaguar XJS), 30.
7 Diego Montoya, USA (3·5 BMW M1), 29. No other finishers.
Fastest lap: Bohren, 1m 09·630s, 79·104 mph/127·305 km/h.
2500cc race winner: Jack Baldwin, USA (2·3 Mazda RX-7), 39 laps, 59·67-miles/95·94 km in 45m 50·761s, 78·092 mph/125·677 km/h.
Championship points. Overall: 1 Lanier, 90; **2** Whittington, 73; **3** van der Merwe, 61; **4** Bell, 48; **5** Redman, Bundy and Miller, 47. **GT over 2500cc: 1** Felton, 104; **2** Mandeville, 100; **3** Hagen, 99. **GT up to 2500cc: 1** Baldwin, 121; **2** Dunham, 69; **3** Reed, 68.

LUMBERMENS 500 CAMEL GT, Mid-Ohio Sports Car Course, Ohio, United States of America, June 10. IMSA CAMEL GT Championship, round 9. 129 laps of the 2·400-mile/3·862-km circuit, 309·60 miles/498·20 km.
1 Al Holbert/Derek Bell, GB/USA (2·6 t/c Porsche 962), 3h 25m 18·745s, 90·477 mph/145·608 km/h.
2 Randy Lanier/Bill Whittington, USA/USA (5·8 March 84G-Chevrolet), 3h 25m 22·734s.
3 Hurley Haywood/Bobby Rahal, USA/USA (2·6 t/c Porsche 962), 129 laps.
4 John Morton/Richard Spenard, USA/USA (5·8 March 84G-Chevrolet), 129.
5 Sarel van der Merwe/Tony Martin, ZA/ZA (3·1 t/c March 84G-Porsche), 128.
6 Gianpiero Moretti/Fulvio Ballabio, I/I (3·0 Momo AR3-Cosworth DFV), 121.
7 Jim Downing/John Maffucci, USA/USA (2·6 Argo JM16-Mazda), 119; **8** Jim Busby/Pete Halsmer, USA/USA (2·6 Lola T616-Mazda), 119; **9** Chester Vincentz/Dave White, USA/USA (3·0 Porsche 934), 119 (1st over 2500cc GT class); **10** Roger Mandeville/Amos Johnson, USA/USA (2·6 Mazda RX-7), 117.
1st up to 2500cc GT class: Jack Dunham/Jeff Kline, USA/USA (2·3 Mazda RX-7), 115.
Fastest Qualifier: Whittington, 1m 23·621s, 103·323 mph/166·282 km/h (record).
Fastest lap: Whittington, 1m 28·760s, 97·341 mph/156·655 km/h.
Championship points. Overall: 1 Lanier, 105; **2** Whittington, 88; **3** van der Merwe, 69; **4** Bell, 68; **5** Holbert, 60; **6** Morton, 56. **GT over 2500cc: 1** Mandeville, 115; **2** Felton, 104; **3** Hagen, 99. **GT up to 2500cc: 1** Baldwin, 131; **2** Dunham, 89; **3** Reed, 78.

CAMEL CONTINENTAL DOUBLE THREE HOUR CAMEL GT, Watkins Glen Grand Prix Circuit, New York, United States of America, July 8. IMSA CAMEL GT Championship, round 10. Aggregate of two three hour heats of the 3·377-mile/5·435-km circuit, 194 laps, 655·138 miles/1054·39 km.
1 Al Holbert/Derek Bell/Jim Adams, USA/GB/USA (2.6 t/c Porsche 962), 6h 02m 20·735s, 108·483 mph/174·586 km/h.
2 Bruce Leven/John Paul Jnr, USA/USA (2.6 t/c Porsche 962), 191 laps.
3 Brian Redman/Hurley Haywood, GB/USA (6.0 Jaguar XJR-5), 186.
4 Jim Downing/John Maffucci, USA/USA (2.6 Argo JM16-Mazda), 181.
5 Jim Busby/Rick Knoop, USA/USA (2.6 Lola T616-Mazda), 181.
6 Chet Vincentz/Jim Mullen, USA/USA (3.0 Porsche 934), 176 (1st over 2500cc GT class).
7 John Schneider/Elliott Forbes-Robinson, USA/USA (2.0 Porsche 924 Carrera), 172 (1st up to 2500cc GT class); **8** Lyn St. James/Herm Johnson, USA/USA (3.0 Argo JM16-Cosworth DFV), 171; **9** Gianpiero Moretti/Fulvio Ballabio, I/I (3.0 Momo AR3-Cosworth DFV), 171; **10** David Loring/Frank Jellinek, USA/USA (2.6 Mazda GTP), 171.
Fastest Qualifier: Bell, 1m 41·966s, 119·228 mph/191·878 km/h (record).
Fastest lap: Bell, 1m 44·710s, 116·104 mph/186·851 km/h (record).
Championship points. Overall: 1 Lanier, 105; **2** Whittington and Bell, 88; **4** van der Merwe, 69; **5** Holbert, 60; **6** Redman, 59. **GT over 2500cc: 1** Mandeville, 130; **2** Felton, 104; **3** Hagen, 99. **GT up to 2500cc: 1** Baldwin, 135; **2** Dunham, 104; **3** Kline, 88.

G. I. JOE'S GRAN PRIX 3 HOUR CAMEL GT, Portland International Raceway, Portland, Oregon, United States of America, July 29. IMSA CAMEL GT Championship, round 11. 145 laps of the 1·915-mile/3·082-km circuit, 277·68 miles/446·89 km.
1 Randy Lanier/Bill Whittington, USA/USA (5.8 March 84G-Chevrolet), 3h 00m 46·080s, 92·165 mph/148·32 km/h.
2 Bob Tullius/Doc Bundy, USA/USA (6.0 Jaguar XJR-5), 3h 00m 52·400s.
3 Al Holbert/Derek Bell, USA/GB (2.6 t/c Porsche 962), 145 laps.
4 Bruce Leven/Jim Adams, USA/USA (2.6 t/c Porsche 962), 143.
5 Gianpiero Moretti/Dennis Aase, I/USA (3.0 Momo AR3-Cosworth DFV), 143.
6 Bill Whittington/Dale Whittington, USA/USA (5.8 March 84G-Chevrolet), 143.
7 John Kalagian/John Lloyd, USA/USA (5.8 March 84G-Chevrolet), 142; **8** Brian Redman/Hurley Haywood, GB/USA (6.0 Jaguar XJR-5), 141; **9** Wayne Baker/Jack Newsum, USA/USA (5.8 March 84G-Chevrolet), 139; **10** Al Leon/Art Leon/Skeeter McKitterick, USA/USA/USA (5.8 March 84G-Chevrolet), 139.
1st over 2500cc GT class: David Schroeder/Tom Hendrickson, USA/USA (5.8 Chevrolet Corvette), 132.
Fastest Qualifier: Sarel van der Merwe, ZA (3.1 t/c March 84G-Porsche), 1m 01·396s, 112·287 mph/180·708 km/h (record).
Fastest lap: Redman, 1m 03·100s, 109·255 mph/174·219 km/h (record).
2500cc race winner: Jack Baldwin, USA (2.3 Mazda RX-7), 25 laps, 47·875 miles/77·050 km in 30m 43·890s, 93·471 mph/150·427 km/h.
Championship points. Overall: 1 Lanier, 125; **2** Whittington, 108; **3** Bell, 100; **4** Holbert, 72; **5** van der Merwe, 69; **6** Bundy and Redman, 62. **GT over 2500cc: 1** Mandeville, 145; **2** Felton, 116; **3** Hagen, 111. **GT up to 2500cc: 1** Baldwin, 155; **2** Dunham, 108; **3** Kline, 94.

FORD CALIFORNIA CAMEL GT, Sears Point International Raceway, Sonoma, California, United States of America, August 5. IMSA CAMEL GT Championship, round 12. 40 laps of the 2·523-mile/4·060-km circuit, 100·92 miles/162·40 km.
1 Bill Whittington, USA (5.8 March 84G-Chevrolet), 1h 02m 21·556s, 96·217 mph/154·846 km/h.
2 Doc Bundy, USA (6.0 Jaguar XJR-5), 1h 02m 34·379s.
3 Brian Redman, GB (5.0 Jaguar XJR-5), 40 laps.
4 Sarel van der Merwe, ZA (2.6 t/c Porsche 962), 40.
5 Klaus Ludwig, D (2.1 t/c Ford Mustang GTP), 40.
6 Kenper Miller, USA (5.8 March 84G-Chevrolet), 39.
7 Randy Lanier, USA (5.8 March 84G-Chevrolet), 39; **8** Gianpiero Moretti, I (3.0 Momo AR3-Cosworth DFV), 39; **9** Al Leon, USA (5.8 March 84G-Chevrolet), 39; **10** Lynn St. James, USA (3.0 Argo JM16-Cosworth DFV), 38.
Fastest Qualifier: Whittington, 1m 27·783s, 102·526 mph/164·999 km/h (record).
Fastest lap: Whittington, 1m 32·084s, 97·737 mph/157·292 km/h (record).

FORD CALIFORNIA CAMEL GTO/GTU, Sears Point International Raceway, Sonoma, California, United States of America, August 5. 30 laps of the 2·523-mile/4·060-km circuit, 75·69 miles/121·80 km.
1 John Bauer, USA (5.9 Ford Thunderbird), 51m 50·628s, 86·799 mph/139·689 km/h.
2 Dennis Aase, USA (2.0 Toyota Celica), 52m 26·010s, (1st up to 2500cc GT class).
3 Chris Cord, USA (2.0 Toyota Celica), 30 laps.
4 Jack Baldwin, USA (2.3 Mazda RX-7), 30.
5 Clay Young, USA (5.9 Pontiac Fiero), 30.
6 Gene Felton, USA (5.9 Pontiac Firebird), 30.
7 Roger Mandeville, USA (2.6 Mazda RX-7); 30; **8** Bob Bergstrom, USA (2.0 Porsche 924), 30; **9** Scott Pruett, USA (2.3 Mazda RX-7), 30; **10** Harry Kauffman, USA (5.9 Pontiac Firebird), 29.
Fastest lap: Bauer, 1m 39·856s, 90·130 mph/145·050 km/h (record).
Championship points. Overall: 1 Lanier, 129; **2** Whittington, 128; **3** Bell, 100; **4** van der Merwe, 79; **5** Bundy, 77; **6** Redman, 77. **GT over 2500cc: 1** Mandeville, 157; **2** Felton, 131; **3** Hagen, 119. **GT up to 2500cc: 1** Baldwin, 167; **2** Dunham, 112; **3** Kline, 94.

BUDWEISER 500 CAMEL GT, Road America, Elkhart Lake, Wisconsin, United States of America, August 26. IMSA CAMEL GT Championship, round 13. 125 laps of the 4·000-mile/6·437-km circuit, 500·00 miles/804·63 km.
1 Al Holbert/Derek Bell, USA/GB (2.6 t/c Porsche 962), 4h 42m 02·110s, 106·370 mph/171·185 km/h.
2 Bruce Leven/David Hobbs, USA/GB (2.6 t/c Porsche 962), 122 laps.
3 Randy Lanier/Bill Whittington, USA/USA (5.8 March 84G-Chevrolet), 120.
4 Sarel van der Merwe/Ian Scheckter, ZA/ZA (3.1 t/c March 84G-Porsche), 117.
5 Brian Redman/Hurley Haywood, GB/USA (6.0 Jaguar XJR-5), 115.
6 Bob Akin/John O'Steen, USA/USA (2.6 t/c Porsche 962), 115.
7 Bard Boand/Rich Anderson, USA/USA (5.8 Lola T600-Chevrolet), 114; **8** John Paul Jnr/John Morton, USA/USA (5.8 March 84G-Chevrolet), 113; **9** Jim Downing/John Maffucci, USA/USA (2.6 Argo JM16-Mazda), 113; **10** Chet Vincentz/Jim Mullen/Kees Nierop, USA/USA/CDN (3.0 t/c Porsche 934), 113 (1st over 2500cc GT class).
1st up to 2500cc GT class: Jack Dunham/Jeff Kline, USA/USA (2.3 Mazda RX-7), 107.
Fastest Qualifier: Holbert, 2m 02·377s, 117·669 mph/189·369 km/h (record).
Fastest lap: Holbert, 2m 06·260s, 114·050 mph/183·545 km/h (record).
Championship points. Overall: 1 Lanier, 141; **2** Whittington, 140; **3** Bell, 120; **4** Holbert, 92; **5** van der Merwe, 89; **6** Redman, 82. **GT over 2500cc: 1** Mandeville, 165; **2** Felton, 143; **3** Hagen, 131. **GT up to 2500cc: 1** Baldwin, 175; **2** Dunham, 132; **3** Kline, 114.

POCONO 500 KM CAMEL GT, Pocono International Raceway, Pennsylvania, United States of America, September 9. IMSA CAMEL GT Championship, round 14. 111 laps of the 2·800-mile/4·506-km circuit, 310·80 miles/500·17 km.
1 Al Holbert/Derek Bell, USA/GB (2.6 t/c Porsche 962), 2h 42m 14·801s, 114·936 mph/184·971 km/h.
2 Bob Tullius/Doc Bundy, USA/USA (6.0 Jaguar XJR-5), 110 laps.
3 Don Whittington/Dale Whittington, USA/USA (5.8 March 84G-Chevrolet), 110.
4 Sarel van der Merwe/Tony Martin, ZA/ZA (3.1 t/c March 84G-Porsche), 110.
5 Randy Lanier/Bill Whittington, USA/USA (5.8 March 84G-Chevrolet), 107.
6 Bob Akin/John O'Steen, USA/USA (2.6 t/c Porsche 962), 107.
7 Andy Blank/John Andretti, USA/USA (3.0 Argo JM16-Cosworth DFV), 106; **8** Jim Downing/John Maffucci, USA/USA (2.6 Argo JM16-Mazda), 101; **9** Don Bell/Robert Overby, USA/USA (3.5 Argo JM16-Buick), 99; **10** Gene Felton, USA (5.9 Chevrolet Camaro), 99 (1st over 2500cc GT class).
1st up to 2500cc GT class: John Schneider/Elliott Forbes-Robinson, USA/USA (2.0 Porsche 924 Carrera), 97.
Fastest Qualifier: B. Whittington, 1m 21·478s, 123·714 mph/199·098 km/h (record).
Fastest lap: van der Merwe, 1m 23·280s, 121·037 mph/194·790 km/h (record).
Championship points. Overall: 1 Lanier, 149; **2** B. Whittington, 148; **3** Bell, 140; **4** Holbert, 112; **5** van der Merwe, 99; **6** Bundy, 92. **GT over 2500cc: 1** Mandeville, 175; **2** Felton, 163; **3** Hagan, 131. **GT up to 2500cc: 1** Baldwin, 190; **2** Dunham, 144; **3** Kline, 126.

MICHIGAN 500 KM CAMEL GTP/GTO, Michigan International Speedway, Brooklyn, Michigan, United States of America, September 16. IMSA CAMEL GT Championship, round 15. 163 laps of the 1·900-mile/3·058-km circuit, 309·70 miles/498·45 km.

1 Randy Lanier/Bill Whittington, USA/USA (5.8 March 84G-Chevrolet), 3h 17m 38·952s, 94·094 mph/151·429 km/h.
2 David Cowart/Kenper Miller, USA/USA (5.8 March 84G-Chevrolet), 161 laps.
3 Bruce Leven/Bill Adam, USA/USA (2.6 t/c Porsche 962), 161.
4 John Kalagian/John Lloyd, USA (5.8 March 84G-Chevrolet), 157.
5 Chester Vincentz/Jim Mullen, USA/USA (3.0 t/c Porsche 934), 152 (1st over 2500cc GT class).
6 Ray McIntyre/Mike Brockman, USA/USA (5.8 Lola T600-Chevrolet), 151.
7 Charles Morgan/Whitnay Ganz, USA/USA (3.5 t/c Argo JM16-Buick), 151; **8** John Bauer/Bruce Jenner, USA/USA (5.9 Ford Thunderbird), 150; **9** Al Holbert/Derek Bell, USA/GB (2.6 t/c Porsche 962), 150; **10** Gianpiero Moretti/Dennis Aase, I/USA (3.0 Momo AR3-Cosworth DFV), 148.
Fastest Qualifier: Klaus Ludwig, D (2.1 t/c Ford Mustang GTP), 1m 05·016s, 105·205 mph/169·311 km/h (record).
Fastest lap: Whittington, 1m 06·060s, 103·542 mph/166·634 km/h (record).
2500cc race winner, September 15: Clay Young, USA (2.3 Pontiac Fiero), 33 laps, 119·13 miles/100·91 km in 41m 27·026s, 90·759 mph/146·062 km/h.
Championship points. Overall: 1 Lanier, 169; **2** Whittington, 168; **3** Bell, 144; **4** Holbert, 116; **5** van der Merwe, 99; **6** Bundy, 94. **GT over 2500cc: 1** Mandeville, 185; **2** Felton, 163; **3** Johnson, 137. **GT up to 2500cc: 1** Baldwin, 202; **2** Dunham, 154; **3** Kline, 126.

NEW YORK 500 STEUVEN CUP, Watkins Glen Grand Prix Circuit, New York, United States of America, September 30. IMSA CAMEL GT Championship, round 16. 92 laps of the 3·377-mile/5·435-km circuit, 310·684 miles/500·02 km.

1 Dale Whittington/Randy Lanier, USA/USA (5.8 March 84G-Chevrolet), 3h 09m 02·682s, 98·607 mph/158·692 km/H.
/ John Kalagian/John Lloyd, USA/USA (5.8 March 84G-Chevrolet), 3h 10m 36·150s.
3 Lyn St. James/Howdy Holmes, USA/USA (3.0 Argo JM16-Cosworth DFV), 92 laps.
4 Charles Morgan/Whitney Ganz, USA/USA (3.5 t/c Argo JM16-Buick), 90.
5 Jim Downing/John Maffucci, USA/USA (2.6 Argo JM16-Mazda), 89.
6 Werner Frank/Dave White, USA/USA (3.1 t/c Porsche 935), 88.
7 Clay Young, USA (2.3 Pontiac Fiero), 86 (1st up to 2500cc GT class); **8** Chet Vincentz/Jim Mullen, USA/USA (3.0 t/c Porsche 934), 86 (1st over 2500cc GT class); **9** John Jellinek/Alain de Cadenet/Yves Courage, USA/GB/F (3.0 Cougar-Cosworth DFV), 85; **10** Ray McIntyre, USA (5.8 Lola T600-Chevrolet), 85.
Fastest Qualifier: Bill Whittington, USA (5.8 March 84G-Chevrolet), 1m 39·090s, 122·688 mph/197·447 km/h (record).
Fastest lap: Al Holbert, USA (2.6 t/c Porsche 962), 1m 42·100s, 119·0781 mph/191·626 km/h (record).

Championship points (prior to final round at Daytona on November 25).
Overall:

1	Randy Lanier, USA (Champion)	189
2	Bill Whittington, USA	168
3	Derek Bell, GB	144
4	Al Holbert, USA	116
5	Sarel van der Merwe, ZA	99
6	Doc Bundy, USA	94

7 Brian Redman, GB, 82; **8** Bob Tullius, 74; **9** Kenper Miller, USA, 70; **10** John Morton, USA, 59. **GT over 2500cc: 1** Roger Mandeville, USA, 200 (Champion); **2** Gene Felton, USA, 163; **3** Amos Johnson, USA, 152; **4** Chet Vincentz, USA, 139; **5** Billy Hagen, USA, 131; **6** Jim Mullen, USA, 75. **GT up to 2500cc: 1** Jack Baldwin, USA, 210 (Champion); **2** Jack Dunham, USA, 154; **3** Jeff Kline, USA, 126; **4** John Schneider, USA, 104; **5** Chris Cord, USA, 94; **6** Clay Young, USA, 92.
Final results will be given in Autocourse 1985/86.